# STRUGGLES IN THE STATE

# STRUGGLES IN THE STATE:
## Sources and Patterns of
## World Revolution

-》》-》》-》》-》》-》》-》》-》》-》》-》》-》》-》》-》》-》》-》》-》》-》》-》》-》》-》》-》》-》》-》》-》》-》》-》》

*Edited by*
**George A. Kelly**
Brandeis University

**Clifford W. Brown, Jr.**
State University of
New York, Albany

*John Wiley & Sons, Inc., New York · London · Sydney · Toronto*

Library of Congress Catalogue Card Number: 70-121908

ISBN 0-471-46808-8

Printed in the United States of America

10  9  8  7  6  5  4  3  2  1

# Preface

The wars that "made" nations and the wars waged between nations have been the traditional province of the historian. But it has been the bias of the Western tradition of political research to assume that once nations were "made," internal violence was a disagreeable and aberrational activity destructive to political life, rather than a revelation of some of its deepest sources. Today the analyst views a world of developmentally staggered political systems and mixed processes of interaction. Some states are enduring the crude "nation-making" type of internal incoherence; others are buffeted by the play of international forces stronger than their own capacities of restraint; and yet other "made" nations experience organized violence because there is still social strife over principles of political organization, distribution of the national wealth, or the assimilation of regional residues. Simply stated: internal war is not a mere measles and mumps of politics. Instead, it is one of the striking aspects of political change in our times and—at least, for the forseeable future—a major compartment of politics in general. Thus, in focusing on the phenomenon of internal war, this book is not a collection of rare and esoteric cases; it, too, is about politics in general.

The chief stimulus for this collection arose from a practical difficulty. One of us (G. A. K.), in attempting, on two occasions (at Harvard and at Brandeis), to teach a wide-ranging course in the historical sociology of internal war, found himself handicapped by the extreme scattering of the most useful materials. Despite modern library resources, teachers get uneasy when they have to send students racing from journal to journal and book to book to seek out the guts of a subject. Thus the natural idea arose of consolidating a body of theoretical and analytical writing on internal war as effectively as possible. A sympathetic collaboration was formed (G. A. K. and C. W. B., Jr.), and we attempted, here, to assemble the essays and chapters that have proved valuable in the classroom, enhanced by some new additions. Conversations and exchanges with other social scientists confirmed our

view that what we envisaged would not be "just another anthology"
but a genuinely effective intellectual tool for work in an understudied
area.

Although the body of writing on internal war and revolution is
relatively meager, there were still choices to make:

1. With a few exceptions that seemed to us indispensable, we ruled
out texts that were very familiar, widely available, or not easily subject
to segmentation (the writings of Marx and Engels, of Frantz Fanon,
Crane Brinton's *The Anatomy of Revolution*, and E. J. Hobsbawm's
*Primitive Rebels* are examples).

2. We dismissed, for our purposes, psychological, neurological,
and biological interpretations of violence centering around such concepts as frustration, aggression, the "territorial instinct," and the like.
As political scientists, we felt that studies of this kind were peripheral
to the type of work we are engaged in. We did not feel fully confident
in evaluating them, and we were aware that many of these texts were
easily obtainable by the student.

3. We omitted essays bearing on the United States; for a generous
selection of them, the reader may consult the Report to the National
Commission on the Causes and Prevention of Violence.*

4. We included (and possibly this reflects our own research bias)
a fairly high proportion of articles dealing with the international dimensions of internal strife—a promising and relatively untapped area of
scholarship.

5. We refused to be swept away by policy-interested questions,
notably the "guerrilla" or "unconventional" war mania of the last
decade. There are a number of interesting government-stimulated
papers on internal war, but they are not included here.

6. We attempted to make our collection politically eclectic: its
unifying theme is its subject matter treated in a variety of ways, not
our own disposition toward the phenomena studied.

7. Realizing full well, despite the alleged primacy of social science
in America, that not all wisdom on this subject is indigenous, we looked
abroad for many of our selections. Of these, the Dorso and Duverger
essays are original translations.

There has been a method in our order of presentation. We move
from the general toward the particular by natural procedures. Thus we
begin with a philosophical investigation of revolution and continue with
a set of essays that attempt to apply some form of general social theory

---

* H. D. Graham and T. R. Gurr, eds., *Violence in America*, New York, 1969.

to political violence (Dahrendorf, Coser, Dorso, and Johnson). More-particularized theoretical studies follow, and the treatment of the international repercussions of civil violence is reserved for the end of the sequence. Then we consider a series of case studies, each of which is either (in its way) a cardinal document of the event or an attempt to theorize inductively from the event. In this plan the discrimination between theorizing and empirical analysis is scarcely absolute; and there is an intentional connection between the two kinds of essay.

We do not expect that our selections will appeal to all readers. In most books of this sort, there is a tendency to include contributions from all corners of the world—at least, from every presently acknowledged "subsystem" of international politics. But we have not done this. For example, we have not included any writings of direct concern to African or Middle Eastern specialists, or attempted to account for numerous contemporary cases of internal violence. There are limits to an intended focus. Also there are space limitations. We could not adopt an encyclopedic or globe-girdling approach without sacrificing a concentration that is easily defensible, in view of the historical genesis of the forms and scope of internal warfare. We feel, nevertheless, that area specialists can benefit from the broader theoretical arguments presented here.

We shall not make any prefatory comment on the writings that we have chosen, since explanatory introductions discussing methodological issues and the discrimination of schools of thought precede each selection. Some of the essays are abridged; all excisions have been indicated. Our objective has been to unite a great many of the most provocative writings in the field for the benefit of student and scholar alike, to energize creative debate, and to promote a more effective understanding of the politics of internal war seen through the clarifying discipline of historical sociology.

*George A. Kelly*
*Clifford W. Brown, Jr.*

# Contents

# STRUGGLES IN THE STATE

# 1

# Aristotle and Hobbes: The Speculative Antagonism of Civil Disorder

*Clifford W. Brown, Jr.*

※←※←※←※←※←※←※←※←※←※←※←※←※←※←※←※←※←※←※←※←※←※←※←※←※←※←※←※←

## EDITORS' COMMENT

The essay which follows was written specifically to provide an introduction to some of the concepts discussed in the remainder of the book.
It presents some of the problems of civil disorder in long-range terms
and examines some of the philosophical questions which writers on
internal war must confront. This essay is not an attempt to present
the definitive views of Aristotle and Hobbes on civil violence, but it
investigates some of the problems they raised and some of the answers
they gave which are of interest to the contemporary student of internal
war. Nor is this essay a discussion of consent, obligation, and the
"right" to revolution but, instead, it is a description of the causes—
"etiology"—which Aristotle and Hobbes found to be crucial in explaining why a state fell into "sedition." A number of topics are discussed
by these writers which can be compared to the ones of other theorists
in this text.

First, it is not surprising that Aristotle's analysis of the interaction

1

between domestic and international events provides links with Gould-ner's description of the same historical phenomena. However, Aris-totle's analysis of the origins of civil disturbance—in the nature of how men think of themselves and others—moves the discussion from one of a strictly economic nature to a conceptual level which has much wider implications.

Second, it could be argued that Aristotle is an ancestor of the equilibrium and structural–functional schools of analysis. In this respect a comparison could be made of his assumptions with those of Chalmers Johnson—especially the ones found in *Revolutionary Change*. There is a very close relationship between the Aristotelian and Johnsonian teleologies. The concept of "purpose" and the concept of "function" are almost identical in the two analyses, and the division between contribution and receipt exists for both, although much more markedly in Aristotle. Methodological and metaphysical *a prioris* are not so easy to distinguish. We might ask whether there is any notion of "dysfunc-tion" in Aristotle—and what might be a substitute for it. Is it de-ficiency, evil, or what?

Third, it is argued in this essay that, to Aristotle, civil violence results in part from two competing views of justice—one originating from a presumption of *economic inequality*, the other from a presump-tion of *political equality*. It is desirable to examine just what the rela-tionship is between a structural-functional approach and the need to presume inequality in a society. Are they necessarily related? Does Chalmers Johnson presume inequality? If there is a presumption of inequality in one area (economics), how would the presumption of equality in the political area affect the society? Is it really possible for a modern theorist of this school to separate the two? These questions have no simple answer, but a reading of Aristotle may shed light on the strengths and weaknesses of an equilibrium approach.

Fourth, it is interesting to compare the arguments of Hobbes with those of Ralf Dahrendorf, a contemporary critic of equilibrium theo-rists. Dahrendorf argues with Hobbes that relations between men are defined in terms of power—and that power, not function, is the best analytic tool for describing human behavior. The arguments by Dahrendorf with respect to David Easton parallel, to some extent, the arguments of Hobbes with respect to Aristotle. These questions must arise in any discussion of power: What role do rationality and interest play in the ordering of society? What is the difference between interest, defined in terms of power, and self-preservation and interest, defined in terms of receipt and contribution; what are their differing implica-tions for social cohesion?

Fifth, both Hobbes and Aristotle are interested in the role of ideas and of subjective attitudes in promoting "sedition." Aristotle's suggestion that revolutions result from competing notions of justice and Hobbes' suggestion that "pretense of right" is necessary for a successful rebellion should be compared with Eckstein's analysis of behavioralism—or with Sorokin's views of the "major premise" in a society. What, precisely, is the role of ideology in civil conflict? Why, from the standpoint of the government, are ideas so difficult to deal with?

Sixth, both Aristotle and Hobbes have a view of the possibility of the conscious manipulation of a society to preserve the social order—to them, the role of the incumbent is extremely important—as, indeed, it is to Locke (also discussed in the essay). Their arguments, again, could be compared to those of Eckstein. What are the limits to the incumbent's ability to control a revolutionary situation? Is the incumbent doomed by his inadequate ideological view of the situation?

Seventh, both Aristotle and Hobbes are "nondirectional" theorists, who view man as unchanging, and who find no sense of progress or regress in history. Their assumptions that there are basic human problems persisting in any type of society can be compared with the ones of the progressive theorists (for example, the Marxists), who transcend the ancient problems which Hobbes and Aristotle assert to be eternal.

Finally, the following essay maintains that both Aristotle and Hobbes find that a form of depersonalization may be the solution to civil violence, although their definitions of this concept differ. The role of personality, ambition, and simple human drives in the creation of civil violence has been somewhat neglected because of the extreme difficulty in conceptualizing or in theorizing these factors. As Eckstein points out, there is a great tension between unique events and processes. The role of the unique in history is clearly recognized by Aristotle, and, more ambiguously, by Hobbes. What is its relevance to the sociology of internal war?

# ARISTOTLE AND HOBBES: THE SPECULATIVE ANTAGONISM OF CIVIL DISORDER

CLIFFORD W. BROWN, JR.

> The babbling philosophy of Aristotle . . . serves only to breed disaffection, dissention, and finally sedition and civil war.
>
> BEHEMOTH (*E.W.* VI-282–83)

> And I believe that scarce anything can be more absurdly said in natural philosophy, than that which is now called *Aristotle's Metaphysics;* nor more repugnant to government, than much of that he hath said in his *Politics;* nor more ignorantly, than a great part of his *Ethics.*
>
> LEVIATHAN (*L.* 439)

It would be difficult to find two philosophers whose views of man and society are more distinct, for virtually every assumption by Aristotle finds its refutation in Hobbes: some men are by nature superior to others—men by nature have equal capacities; men are social animals—men are lethally asocial; the state is natural—the state is an artifice; the aim of society is the highest good—there is no highest good. The list could go on forever. Perhaps their only similarity is a shared concern for many of the problems which man has managed to create for himself—and which easily span the millenia which separate the two men.

Internal war is one of these problems. Given their widely divergent assumptions, and the vastly different societies with which they were personally familiar, it is not surprising that their views of civil violence are correspondingly discrete. Aristotle starts with the presumption that civil society is a natural phenomenon—that the polis is a self-sufficient organism unified by basic social interests and natural instinct. Hence, revolution and civil violence are aberrations or diseases in the body politic. Hobbes starts with the presumption that the natural condition is one of war, conflict, and violence—that the state is an artifice created to avert these misfortunes, unified by the threat of force. Revolution and civil violence, therefore, are not aberrations or

4

diseases in the Aristotelian sense but potential conditions ever present beneath the surface of any state at any time.

The problem of whether internal war is an artificial or natural phenomenon is closely related to a theorist's basic assumptions about the nature of civil cohesion. For Aristotle, men are related to each other in society by an interaction of purpose and interest, which constitutes the meaning of teleology. For Hobbes, society is held together by an interaction of power and interest. These assumptions, in turn, are closely related to Aristotle's belief in the inequality of men and to Hobbes' belief in the equality of men.

The purpose of this essay is to examine briefly the effects that such assumptions have on an analysis of internal war, since both Aristotle and Hobbes have their intellectual descendants today—the theorists of functionalism and equilibrium in one case, and the theorists of power in the other. Hopefully, an understanding of Aristotle and Hobbes will shed light on these two approaches, since an examination of philosophic underpinnings often clarifies a dispute and enables men to talk to each other, not past each other. We shall start with Aristotle and, because he begins with the presumption of unity and regards disunity as an aberration, we must examine the factors that hold a state together and then must proceed to the question of what destroys the polis.

## I

What we would call unity in the polis is the central problem of Aristotle's *Politics* for although the state is a "natural" organism[1] and man is a "political animal,"[2] the highest good in the polis is a form of activity—the performance of "good" or "noble" *political* acts of a voluntary nature. Any form of political activity, however, is potentially disruptive, and the difficulty becomes one of how to provide

[1] For the best expression of this assumption, see Book I, Chapter 2 of *Politics* (1252a–1253a). All references to Aristotle will use the standard numbering system, and all quotations, unless otherwise designated are from the Ernest Barker translation of *Politics* and the W. D. Ross translation of *Ethics*. All references to Hobbes from the *Leviathan* will be from the Oakeshott edition (Oxford, 1960), designated by "*L*" followed by the page. References to Hobbes other than from the *Leviathan* are from *The English Works*, reprint of the edition of 1840, collected and edited by Sir William Molesworth, designated by "E. W." followed by the volume in Roman and page in Arabic. References to Locke are from the Laslett edition, *Two Treatises on Government*, Mentor Paperback (New York and Toronto: New American Library, 1965; designated by "Locke" followed by the page).

[2] Jowett Translation. Barker renders it: "Man is by nature an animal intended to live in a polis" (1253a).

a framework where men can be politically active, yet not destroy the state.

This underlying tension between unity and activity is clearly illustrated by Aristotle's discussion of the merits of politically active and politically contemplative lives in both *Ethics* and *Politics*. The problem is that a politically active life is somewhat analogous to a militarily active life (1324a–1325a), and success in either is equivalent to aggrandizement at the expense of others. For instance, in Sparta, "noble" acts either by the individual or by the state necessitate an imperial policy by the polis, since such acts are equated with military valor and require warfare. However, by analogy, such an emphasis on aggrandizement and military success has grave domestic implications since, obviously, it implies that the objective of any citizen who can do so should be to capture the government of his own state (1333b). Although Aristotle rejects the Spartan image of a noble act, he cannot escape the resemblance between it and all forms of political activity.[3] Making a clear analogy between the political activity of the state and of the individual, Aristotle suggests that the solution to this problem is to turn the activity inward: the state ideally should be in isolation and should be concerned actively with its own domestic affairs (1325a to b) and the individual should turn inward in a life of active political contemplation (1177a–1178b). Later we shall examine the obvious paradoxes involved here, but the point is that at the heart of man's highest aim is a very serious tension: the highest good is active political participation, yet too much of this can destroy the polis. This tension, of course, is a reflection of his great philosophical concern for finding a middle point between extremes—active contemplation lying between inaction and intense political activity.

But the problem of unity is far more complex for a number of reasons. The solution provided by active contemplation is only possible among the "virtuous" peers at the apex of the society—it cannot apply to the much larger and differentiated mass of men below nor to the "nonvirtuous" at any level. Furthermore, the above mean is only to be achieved as the result of a very special education and, perhaps, can be found only in a state which exists in isolation (although the latter is not clear).[4] Where, then, is unity to be found?

First, unity is *not* achieved as the result of a polis being composed of equal or similar elements: "a real unity, such as a polis, must be made up of elements which differ in kind" (1261a). Before examining

---

[3] See the analogy between aggrandizement or rule and mastery over others (1324b), and the discussion of the Spartan image, (1333b–1334a).

[4] This is the implication of *Politics* (1325b), but it is not so stated in *Ethics*.

why differentiation *is* necessary for unity, let us examine Aristotle's reasons why equality *is not* a source of unity. These arguments operate on three levels.

On the first level, there is the strong implication that the highest form of association which can be achieved by a large number of equals is in the nature of a contractual agreement for a specific purpose—for example, a military alliance (1261a) between states, a social compact for mutual defence, or an economic agreement.[5] Because associations of this sort are formed for a specific purpose, they are temporary in nature and, consequently, are not the bases of the type of unity with which we are concerned.

On the second level, such arrangements depend for their cohesiveness on an external binding force. Within a state, for instance, the democratic and oligarchic classes act cohesively only in opposition to each other.[6] The wealthy are generally strong enough in any state to stimulate a cohesive democratic element,[7] but the wealthy only act as one when the democratic element (usually led by demagogues) threaten either the entire wealthy class—or a sufficient number of the rich, for all to be afraid.[8]

This phenomenon also operates between states, as the unity between either Athens or Sparta and one of its clients is often the product of diversity within the client, as the democratic or oligarchic elements align with Athens and Sparta, respectively.[9]

But to Aristotle there is yet another level of analysis—a far more fundamental reason why similarity and equality cannot be the basis for unity among men without the existence of an external force. This argument is developed as follows.

First, Aristotle argues that when one is talking about "my" brother, "my" friend, or "my" property—in the sense that I, as an individual have a brother, a friend, or some property—the meaning of the word "my" is quite distinct from the meaning of the word "my" when used to signify that I, as part of a group, have a brother, a friend, and so on. "My" totally is distinct from "my" fractionally.[10]

Second, the concepts brother, friend, or property imply a unique relationship—the very meaning of the words implies a singular, not

---

[5] The latter, implied in Book I of *Politics* are made explicit in Book III (1280a).

[6] Notice the similarity of this argument to the one used by Sorel.

[7] This is implied by a passage (1302a) but not explicitly stated. It seems inherent in the logic of his argument.

[8] This is explicitly argued (1304b–1305a).

[9] See (1296a); also, the Gouldner essay in this volume.

[10] See arguments developed in Book II, Chapter 2 and 3, especially (1262a–1262b).

collective relationship.[11] For instance, "One cannot be a friend to many people in the sense of having friendship of the perfect type with them, just as one cannot be in love with many people at once (for love is a sort of excess of feeling, and it is the nature of such only to be felt toward one person)" (1158a). The same fact of uniqueness is applied to family relations—brother, cousin, relative, and so on (1262a).

Aristotle, then, is arguing that the "unity" resulting from the relationship between a man and his brother or his friend is the product of the uniqueness of the relationship—the uniqueness of the linkage of my and the object of that linkage—friend. At this stage of the argument he is simply suggesting that these relationships become watered down (1262b) as they spread: that their unifying force is somehow in inverse proportion to the degree of their extent.[12]

There is, however, a fourth stage to the argument—one not stated expressly by Aristotle but which is implicit in the logic of the situation and crucial to an understanding of the source of his three points mentioned above. If the unity of the relationship is the product of its uniqueness, this is simply another way of saying that unity of this kind is the product of a wider diversity. To move to the conceptual realm, one perceives similarities between objects by perceiving distinctions between these objects and other objects, or synthesis presumes analysis.[13]

We have, then, a clear picture of the reasons why equality and similarity alone cannot produce unity apart from an external force. A state cannot be based on "brotherhood," because when universally applied it is a verbal deception. For the same reasons, community of wives or property is not a source of unity[14]—the very binding nature of the relationship of man to wife or man to his property is a product of the uniqueness of the relationship—and depends upon a wider diversity.

That this phenomenon exists on the conceptual level as well as simply on the level of interest (which forces the oligarchs to unite) is difficult to document but, nonetheless, is present in Aristotle. There is a clear sense in Aristotle that the meaning of "Athenian" or "Spartan" is derived by distinguishing the two; there is a clearer sense that "Greek" is defined by contrast to "barbarian."[15]

---

[11] "Friendship" in the next few paragraphs refers to the first of the three types described below. See note 19.

[12] Presumably this also applies to friendship.

[13] To use the terminology of Kant who, however, could not hold such a view.

[14] See the whole argument, Book II, Chapters 3 and 4 of *Politics*.

[15] For example, see his discussion of Greeks and Slavery (1255a) or, more especially, his discussion of natural distinctions (1327b).

It is interesting to notice that this phenomenon is present in Marx on the same two levels. With respect to the events of 1848, he suggested that "revolutionary advance made headway not by its immediate tragi-comic achievements, but on the contrary by the creation of a power-ful, united counter-revolution, by the creation of an opponent [against] whom the party of revolt first ripened into a revolutionary party."[16] On the other level, class consciousness develops as the result of the con-flict, the antagonisms, and the divisions within the society.[17]

On both levels of analysis we have here a dilemma which must rank with Hobbes' famous security dilemma[18] as one of the most dis-quieting aspects of human relationships. The stressing of similar "prop-erties" or shared characteristics or even values between a group of people—no matter how large or how small—can only be done by ex-pressing or by implying the dissimilar characteristics between that group and the rest of the human race. To the extent that "communi-ties" are the result of similarities, they do not provide a solution to human conflict. They merely translate the divisions to a higher level, either within or between states. Conflict arises not only when Rous-seau's savage compares himself to another and discovers that he is dis-tinct—but also when that savage compares himself to another and discovers that, in some respect, he is similar.

Is external force the only answer? Clearly not to Aristotle. What, then, is the source of unity in the state?

The first answer is friendship, which "seems to hold states to-gether" (1155a). But there are several kinds of friendship. First, there is friendship based upon virtue,[19] the kind of excellent and unique rela-tionship referred to previously. Although there are elements of self-inter-est in this concept of friendship,[20] it comes close to our notions of

---

[16] *Class Struggles in France 1848–1850* (New York: International Publishers, 1964), p. 33.

[17] Most of the arguments about Marx and Engels in this paper come from the *German Ideology* (New York: International Publishers, New World Paperback, 1965). In this particular work, the arguments about class consciousness are developed, pp. 27–43, and 76–78. However, this entire problem is a very complex one and much more could be said on the subject.

[18] Students of international relations make the comparison between the Hobbesian state of nature and the international competition. The security dilemma is often posed thus: "The absolute security of one state necessitates the absolute insecurity of all other states."

[19] It could be argued that this is the only real form of friendship, the other two being perverted forms, but the weight of evidence is on the above assertion, as documented below (footnote 23).

[20] For instance, see (1157a–1158b), but this is more clearly illustrated (1168a–1169b).

altruism, is permanent, and forms the bond between virtuous men, presumably, limiting to a degree the centrifugal forces of "active political life" described above. But this kind of friendship can only be attained by those at the apex of the social order (liberality, for instance, is an integral part of such friendship) and, certainly, in any given state not all of those at the apex enjoy this kind of friendship. Virtue is not a test for citizenship.[21]

Therefore, we must consider the other two forms of friendship to determine what holds men together on all levels of society—and among all levels. These concepts are based on "pleasure" and "utility"—but Aristotle makes it apparent that both depend on *interest*.[22] Incidentally, clearly present is the notion that these three are related to each other by analogy and, hence, the latter two are distinct from the concept of interest itself.[23]

How does friendship based on interest unify the state? Obviously, there is unity when there is an identity of interests among the citizens. Unanimity "seems to be a friendly relation. For this reason it is not identity of opinion [such as agreement on a scientific fact] . . . but we do say that a city is unanimous when men have the same opinion about what is to their interest, and choose the same actions, and do what they have resolved in common" (1267a). Unanimity, however, is virtually impossible, because it also requires that men be "good" since, if they are not, factions will always arise.[24]

Aristotle also suggests that friendship based on interest unifies the state in a fashion analogous to the way it unifies the family. This is only an analogy, since Aristotle clearly indicates that statesmanship is quite distinct from the management of a household. The friendship that a father has for a son, which is quite distinct from the friendship a son has for his father, is based on a form of interest (1158b, 1161a). There is the self-interest of pleasure, but Aristotle makes it apparent that the "rule" of the father over the son is in the interest of the son (1161a). The analogy to kingly rule is clear. "The friendship be-

[21] See the discussion of qualifications for citizenship and the relationship between the "good man" and the "good citizen," *Politics*, Book III, Chapters 4 and 5 (1276b–1278b).

[22] (1155b–1156b). Friendship is based on love, but love in these two instances is selfish love—hence, the basis of interest.

[23] See (1157a). There *is* a difference between friendship based on utility and interest—for Aristotle is making the point that this form of relationship is a social relationship which makes the economc relationship possible.

[24] This is not a tautology. See (1167a–1167b). The "bad" "aim at getting more than their share of advantages" and this leads to faction, compulsion, and the destruction of the unanimity.

tween a king and his subjects depends on an excess of benefits conferred. . . . Such too is the friendship of a father, though this exceeds the other in the greatness of the benefits conferred. . ." (1161a). The analogy is repeated for an aristocracy (husband-wife) and a polity (brother-brother) (1160b–1161a). When the rule, however, is in the interest of the ruler, then it becomes the analogy of master-slave—and in such states there is no friendship (1161a–1161b). What we have here is a friendship between unequal parties, based on mutual interest and, hence, resulting in a form of exchange. The relationship between these arrangements and Aristotle's ideas of distributive justice are obvious and are explicitly noted by him: "each of the constitutions may be seen to involve friendship just in so far as it involves justice."[25] Aristotle admits that, in an objective sense, it is difficult to calculate in a friendship of this sort the "gains" and "losses" to both sides, but he believes that it is subjectively possible—and uses the rule of proportionality developed in *Ethics* with respect to justice.[26]

Friendship based on interest unifies the state in a third way, since friendship extends to the economic sphere and makes commercial relations possible which, in turn, provide a form of unity (1157b–1162b). But, when one moves to the economic sphere, *interest* is the important concept, and friendship is simply an amenity to facilitate the pursuit of interest. But how does interest unify? Hobbes wrestled with this problem and concluded that the pursuit of self-interest emphatically divides men. To him interest can only be a source of unity when an external force "harmonizes" these interests. But Hobbes starts with the premise of equality among men. Aristotle starts with the premise of inequality and, given this premise, finds that interest can be a unifying element without the threat of external force—although, for a number of reasons, it is not alone sufficient to provide unity. One must make a clear distinction here between the economic and the political realms. We shall first examine the economic realm.

In the economic sphere it is evident that interest acts with inequality to produce a sort of unity; this is the meaning of the division of labor:

> There must necessarily be a union of the naturally ruling element
> with the naturally ruled, for the preservation of both. The element
> which is able, by virtue of its intelligence to exercise forethought.

---

[25] (1161a). One must be very careful not to take this analogy based on friendship to indicate that the governance of the family is the same as the governance of polis—a point Aristotle makes time and time again.

[26] See (1162a–1163b). The distinction between contribution and receipt is also indicated here.

is naturally a ruling and master element; the element which is able, by virtue of its bodily power to do what the other element plans, is a ruled element, which is naturally in a state of slavery; and master and slave have accordingly [as they thus complete one another] a common interest. . . . (1252a).

Implied in this passage is not only a "common interest" but also a very strong binding force: "the preservation of both." By extrapolation this argument is carried to a larger division of labor which embraces not only slaves but artisans, mechanics, specialists (such as navigators), and physicians (e.g. 1276b). Theoretically this division is widespread for nature "makes each separate thing for a separate end; and she does so because each instrument has the finest finish when it serves a single purpose and not a variety of purposes" (1252b). Interest then, provides some unity in the polis precisely because of the premise of inequality. As an economist would put it, trade is the result of comparative advantage. (Now we can understand why a polis is not analogous to a military alliance or a simple union among families for the common defense.[27] These arrangements lack interdependence, and unity in them exists as the result of an external force.)

Interest combined with the premise of inequality is not a perfect solution to the problem of unity, since there are a number of imperfections present in any real situation. They arise chiefly from the distinction between "purpose" and "interest": that is, between what is given and what is received.[28] Aristotle does not systematically develop his economic theory, but there are distinct economic implications in his discussion of exchange with respect to friendship.[29] There is the obvious problem: "friendship of utility [which incidentally encompasses economic transactions] is full of complaints; for as they use each other for their own interests they always want to get the better of the bargain, and think they have got less than they should. . . ." (1162b). But Aristotle also raises problems about the distinct differences in value to the giver and receiver of any gift and the difficult implications of these distinctions to reciprocity (1162b–1163a). The point is that he recognizes these difficulties but assumes that they can be solved by "proportional

[27] "There is a point at which a polis, by advancing in unity, will cease to be a polis. . . . It is as if you were to turn harmony into mere unison. . . ." (1263b). Diversity is mandatory.

[28] Again, see (1162b–1163b). This should be compared to his arguments about distributive justice in Book V of *Ethics*.

[29] Both with respect to friendship based on utility and on pleasure. For the former, see (1162b) where the analogy to debt is made. For the latter, see (1163b) where the analogy to the political friendship is made, again using the concept of a commercial debt.

equality"—which is a means of unequal distribution to parallel unequal contribution.[30] Thus, in the economic realm, inequality interacting with interest in a sense produces a form of unity.

It would be interesting to compare Aristotle's views on the subject with those of Marx and Engels, expressed in the *Manifesto* and the *German Ideology*. We might ask this question: Does the division of labor (with its rational expression, the "cash nexus") unite or divide men? Clearly, Marx and Engels give two answers. In one sense, the division of labor and the cash nexus are forces which unite all men—creating a world market, providing the rationale for the relations between men, cities, and nations, making every producer and consumer dependent on every other, binding all together by strong economic forces.[31] Yet, in another sense, it is certainly maintained that the division of labor does, indeed, divide—it divides worker from artisan, town from country, class from class, producer from consumer, and individual from communal interest.[32]

But this is really not a paradox at all. For when Marx and Engels refer to the unifying aspects of the division of labor, they are referring to it as unifying unequals—artificially created unequals—and when they refer to it as dividing men, there is the presumption of a natural equality among the men who are being divided. The presumption of equality on the part of Marx and Engels makes the division of labor the root of injustice whereas, to Aristotle, with the presumption of inequality, it is the root of justice and social accommodation. For all three, the common interest is the mutual interdependence of men, yet Marx and Engels believe that this common interest is artificial, since men must be presumed to be equal and mutual interdependence forces each to specialize, creating an artificial inequality.

This inequality is given more concrete expressions by the divisions between production and consumption. The whole theory of surplus value, when grafted onto the above sets of division, is the source of complete injustice to Marx. Aristotle also is aware of the distinction between production and consumption. The notion of proportional distribution is to rectify the problem by giving each his due—in line with his (unequal) contribution. Aristotle believes that the artificialities of the economic system (for example, usury) can be controlled

[30] See the opening passages of Ethics, Book IX, for example and, again, the example of money.

[31] "Manifesto" (*Marx & Engels: Basic Writings on Politics and Philosophy*), Lewis S. Feuer (ed.) (Garden City, New York: Anchor Books, Doubleday and Company, Inc.), pp. 8–12.

[32] *German Ideology, op. cit.* pp. 43 ff.

and that proportional distribution can be achieved—and, indeed, money, as Marx indicates above, given the inequalities of men, becomes a means of commensurating needs and contributions.[33] Marx, however, eventually separates contribution and production. The statement, "from each according to his abilities, to each according to his needs," if it has any meaning at all, does *not* imply distributive justice. We must observe that Marx and Engels do not develop a systematic theory of equality and inequality, but it seems evident, from the thrust of their arguments, that the distinctions we have extrapolated here lie at the basis of their reasoning.[34]

One would expect Aristotle to translate the arguments from the economic to the political sphere and, like Plato, to institute a hierarchy of political virtues and thus, with inequality and interest, to unify the polis in this realm as well. But, when we look at this side of the coin, we find only a series of hesitations. Clearly present in Aristotle's thought is a desire that the "best" man or men should rule. Indeed, "Those who are preeminent in merit would be the most justified in attempting sedition (though they are the last to make the attempt), for they—and they only—can reasonably be regarded as enjoying an absolute superiority" (1301a–1301b). And in the distribution of the social benefits, that is, offices, money, and so on:

> Those who contribute most to an association of this character [i.e. who contribute most to good action] have a greater share in the polis [and should therefore, in justice, receive a larger recognition from it] than those who are equal to them (or even greater) in free birth and descent, but unequal in civic excellence, or than those who surpass them in wealth but are surpassed by them in excellence (1281a).

Here, Aristotle illustrates his famous doctrine of "proportional equality" and its legal expression—distributive justice.[35]

But Aristotle is enough of a realist to recognize the impossibility of always finding virtuous rulers—kings or nobles. There are two alternatives: good laws or "democracy." His preference is for good laws: "rightly constituted laws should be the final soverign; and personal rule, whether it be exercised by a single person or a body of persons, should be sovereign only in those matters on which law is un-

---

[33] See (1133a–1134a) and (1164a–1164b).

[34] This assertion cannot be documented or proved deductively, but if it were *not* true, the moral invective of his work would be meaningless, and a theory of exploitation could not really be developed.

[35] Compare this quotation with his discussion of distributive justice in *Ethics* (1131a–1131b).

able . . . to make an exact pronouncment" (1282b). However, he continues, "what rightly constituted laws ought to be is a matter that is not yet clear" (1282b).

This desire to place law above men, to depersonalize politics, is one of Aristotle's most fundamental yearnings, since he believes that only through such an arrangement can civil peace be assured. We shall return to this problem later.

Thus, Aristotle is driven by default to state, "That the people at large should be sovereign rather than the few best—would appear to be defensible, and while it presents some difficulty it perhaps also contains some truth" (1281a). Although he bases his reasoning on a notion of expertise to be found among "all," he admits that in the political realm, natural superiority and station are impracticable—that there may be some justification for the doctrine of numerical equality (1281b–1282b).

Hence, in the political realm, interest and inequality cannot interact to provide a unifying force, simply, because the "natural" inequalities are much less distinct—if discernible at all. However, when the political and economic realms are brought together in the real world, the result is a very explosive mixture.

To Aristotle, the distinction between wealthy and poor, as we have indicated, is natural and is justified by a doctrine of natural superiority—in this realm. Yet, in the political realm, the doctrine of equality is sufficiently justifiable for large numbers of citizens to believe it. The interaction between the two creates political faction as citizens mix the two doctrines.

> Democracy arose in the strength of an opinion that those who were equal in any one respect were equal absolutely, and in all respects (men are prone to think that the fact of their all being equally free-born means that they are all absolutely equal). Oligarchy similarly arose from an opinion that those who were unequal in some one respect were altogether unequal. . . . (1301a).

To put it simply, the democrats, believing in equality, want to equalize the wealth: they want the rich's money. The oligarchs believe that, because they have the money, they should have the power to go with it.

"Sedition" then arises from some whose "minds are filled with a passion for equality," and from others whose "minds are filled with a passion for inequality" (1302a). Thus "inferiors become revolutionaries in order to be equals, and equals in order to be superiors" (1302a) and the unity of the polis is exploded. The objects for which men revolt are profit and honor, corresponding directly to the economic and political realms (1302a).

Ideas may inspire revolutions, but they do not carry them out. We must now consider the dynamics of civil violence in the polis.

Aristotle, in one sense, is an "equilibrium" theorist—methodologically he starts with the presumption of stability and describes the various ways any government can shift—as defects in that type of government. Of course, he has no illusions about the possibility of permanent stability in any form of government, although a clear case can be made that he regards stability as very desirable). In discussing "revolution," he is concerned with change of any kind. For instance, he does not distinguish violent from nonviolent change. It is the aim of the revolution, not the method of its execution which distinguishes its type. Hence, we must group violent and nonviolent change together.

There are two major categories of governmental change. The first is directed against the constitution itself—it changes one of the major types of government (kingship, aristocracy, polity, tyranny, oligarchy, or democracy) into another of these types (1301b). The second aims at altering the constitution while preserving its basic (oligarchic, democratic, etc.) character. The latter would include personnel changes, the alteration or abolition of a particular magistracy, or making the basic type more or less pronounced: "to make a democracy more or less democratic" (1301b).

Although Aristotle recognizes the possibility of what we would call a personal *coup d'état*,[36] the basis of most constitutional change is the existence of faction, as indicated by his use of *stasis* (sedition) for revolutionary activity.[37] Even *coups* depend on faction for their success (1303b–1304a). The democratic and oligarchic elements which exist in every state constitute the factions most responsible for sedition (1301a–1302a). But also there may be factions within an oligarchy that are based on personal jealousies (1306a–1306b), restricted suffrage (1306a), and on the heterogeneity of territory or population (for example, when the population of two cities are artificially joined) (1303a–1303b).

How do these forces fall into sedition? The answer is a mixture of personal artifice and of "natural" change (usually economic or accidental), which shifts the balance of power relationships between the factions. In the latter category are found such phenomena as (1) a shift in the relative sizes of two factions—resulting from *de facto* shifts

---

[36] See, for example, his description of the coup of Pisistratus in the *Constitution of Athens* (New York: Hafner Library of Classics, 1964), Chapter 15.

[37] See note 1, p. 204 of Ernest Barker's translation: *Politics of Aristotle* (London, Oxford, New York: Oxford University Press, 1968).

in the economic test for citizenship, for instance (1306b)—or in the battle deaths of the nobility (1303a), (2) a shift in the relative economic power of two factions (1306b), or (3) a shift in the relative prestige of factions—as when the democratic faction is discredited or the nobility's reputation enhanced for their conduct of a war (1304a). When a faction denied political power finds that it is stronger than those in power, or when two contending factions are equally balanced, the state falls into sedition (1304a–1304b).

Personal artifice generally plays a major role in seditions. Demagogues are chiefly responsible for stirring up the democratic element against the nobility (1304b, 1305b). Generals seize power (1305a, 1307b), and men stung by insult often conspire to overthrow the state (1303b, 1304a, 1311a).

Let us not forget, however, that the objects of revolution are hope for profit, hope for honor, fear of loss, and fear of dishonor. Revolutions are not caused by natural forces; they simply may be made possible by natural forces. Among the steps rulers can take to thwart revolutions are the following:

1. They can make shifts in voting qualifications to compensate for economic changes (1308a–1308b).

2. They can ostracize any outstanding figure who threatens to overthrow the state (1308b).

3. They can make certain that the quarrels among nobles do not get out of hand (1303a).

4. They can behave personally so that they do not incite jealousy or fear on the part of any major faction (1308b).

5. They can foster fear of an outside threat to the constitution (1308a).

6. They can take precautions against small inroads on the structure of the constitution (1307b).

In a number of ways they can make specific policies which will either reduce the fears (or the hopes) of factions and will outmaneuver the ambitious and the demagogues.

The use of artifice to control faction is illustrated by Aristotle's description of the two methods of preserving tyranny: either one should manipulate the factions, divide the population, weaken it, and rule through force, or should play the king, serve the people, and induce both major factions "to think that it is the tyrant's power which serves them in their position."[38]

[38] See Chapter XI of Book V for the most interesting contrast between the use of power and the use of consent to maintain a government.

But the prudence of the rulers is no certain answer to the problems of constitutional change, since there is no guarantee that the ruler will be any shrewder than the demagogues. Can one resolve the basic contradiction between economic inequality and political equality which destroys the unity of the polis? Aristotle is able to provide only a series of respites, not solutions, to this problem.

The first respite is provided implicity in *Ethics* where he discusses the differences which arise in friendships based on superiority.[39] In such a friendship the superior feels he should receive more in virtue of his greater contribution to the friendship; the inferior feels he should receive more because of his greater need. The difficulty is resolved by the superior receiving more in *honor* and the inferior more in *wealth*. By asserting a commensurability between honor and wealth, he is able to bridge the inequality and the distinction between contribution and receipt, which we discussed previously. In a society, the implication is that the rich should contribute part of their wealth to the poor in exchange for honor from the poor. This suggestion is related to his admonition never to hurt the nobles in a matter of honor or to harm the people in a matter of money. Under the assumption that the nobles revolt for honor and the people for money, this exchange seems profitable from the standpoint of stability.

The second respite is to mix the democratic and oligarchic rulers for the selection of magistrates, so that it is impossible to ascertain whether the state is democratic or oligarchic. This creates a polity or mixed constitution. If this well-tempered balance can be achieved, the strength of the state arises from the fact "not that a majority are in favor of its continuance . . . but rather that there is no single section in all the state which would favor a change to a different constitution" (1294b).

The third respite is to attempt a compromise in a way that meets the basic grievances of both but does not threaten the security of either. This is the method of Solon in *The Constitution of Athens,* but the difficulties of actually achieving this are often insurmountable.[40]

The fourth respite, difficult to achieve in practice, but the most lasting solution when achieved, is to create a large middle class. This class serves three functions. First, the unifying forces of economic interdependence are more clearly realized when there is such a class mediating between rich and poor. We observed above that, in theory, the master-slave relationship existed for the mutual benefit of both. But,

---

[39] See (1163a–1163b). This argument is somewhat inconsistent with his views of commensurability measured by money.

[40] *Constitution of Athens,* Chapters 7 to 12.

in practice, Aristotle suggests a series of qualifications. In one passage he indicates that the master-slave relationship is primarily in the interest of the master and only *incidentally* in the interest of the slave (1278b). In another passage he suggests that the promise of emancipation is the most effective incentive to make slaves work[41]—which to some degree undermines the notion of interest-based natural inferiors. Consequently, there are distinct limits in his mind to this form of mutual benefit. In the social analogy, where there is no middle class, rich and poor are driven more and more into a master-slave relationship with the severe curtailment of the unifying effects of interdependence. A middle class mixes things up sufficiently to provide either real interdependence or, at least, the appearance of it.

Second, the middle class, in the political realm, comes closest to the achievement of the ideal of equality: "A state aims at being, as far as it can be, a society composed of equals and peers [who, as such, can be friends and associates]; and the middle class, more than any other, has this sort of composition" (1295b). The middle class provides a sort of bridge between the two notions of justice.

Finally, a reliance on the middle classes is a clear extrapolation from the assertion that the people are basically a source of stability in society—and that most trouble, after all, arises from personal conflicts among the oligarchies. Here, we observe the middle class employed as a vehicle of depersonalization: stability will result from the removal of political questions from the rivalry of the few.

There are also a number of practical reasons why a large middle class provides stability: its members do not have excessive envy for the rich; the poor do not have excessive envy for it (1295b). Very little likelihood exists that rich and poor will combine against it and, if it is sufficiently large, it can combine with either to thwart the ambitions of the other (1296b–1297a). Finally, to some degree, its interests are closer to the common interest than the ones of the rich or the poor (1297a).

But all of these recommendations are only respites. As long as two competing views of justice persist—the one solidly based in the logic of economics, the other solidly based in the logic of politics, the one justifying natural inequality, the other indicating the probable justice of equality—the state must remain in a condition of potential sedition. But could the problem be solved if either of these doctrines could be carried into the other realm, or if the effects of either could be eliminated?

[41] See *Politics* (1330a); *Economics* (1344b), although the latter may not be Aristotles own work.

With respect to inequality, the answer is *perhaps*—itself an indication of Aristotle's preference. If a political analogy to "purpose" and "interest" (contribution and receipt) could be established—if distributive justice could be made to operate—then, perhaps, a natural order of things based on the premise of a static society could be established.

But, with respect to equality, the answer is *no*—not only because there never can be equality in the economic realm—but because equality is the source of disunity and dissention in the absence of an external force. No matter how much education in the virtues of temperance one receives, the paradox of activity and unity persists. Contemplation for an individual or isolation for the state can only be partial answers which the physical dimensions of the real world rule out.

Finally, what about depersonalization? Can this be the solution to the problem? We have noticed a number of hints by Aristotle to this effect—that friendship could be rationalized, that the division of labor and money, working together, could rationally solve the problems of contribution and receipt, that the middle class, by virtue of its size, could bury the conflicts arising from personality, and that law might replace men as the governor of society, and that, perhaps, a Solon *could* institute a system of laws and rightfully retire to Egypt for a decade and let the laws rule without the need for his personal interpretation.[42]

This hope, however, has given rise to three major criticisms. First, there is the criticism by Marx and Engels, indicated previously, which suggests that the forms of depersonalization envisioned by Aristotle would perhaps lead to a tyranny far worse than personal tyrannies or than civil dislocation. Compare the following passage from *The German Ideology* with Aristotle's comments on the division of labor:

> Further the division of labor implies the contradiction between the interest of the separate individual or the individual family and the commual interest of all individuals who have intercourse with one another. And indeed this communal interest does not exist merely in the imagination, as "the general good," but first of all in reality, as the mutual interdependence of the individuals among whom the labor is divided. . . . as long as a cleavage exists between the particular and the common interest . . . man's own deed becomes an alien power opposed to him. . . .
>
> This crystallization of social activity, this consolidation of what we ourselves produce into an objective power above us, growing out of our control, thwarting our expectations . . . is one of the chief factors in historical development up till now.[43]

[42] *Constitution of Athens*, Chapter 11.

[43] *Op. cit.*, pp. 22–23.

Second, there is the criticism by Locke (discussed below) that the existence of a discernable higher law or the rule of law itself (given human frailties) can and, sometimes, should lead to revolution.

Finally, there is the criticism by Hobbes which asserts that rule by law is a logical absurdity:

> . . . And therefore this is another error of Aristotle's politics, that in a well ordered commonwealth, not men should govern, but the laws. What man that has his natural senses, though he can neither write nor read, does not find himself governed by them he fears, and believes can kill or hurt him when he obeyeth not? Or that believes the law can hurt him; that is words and paper, without the hands and swords of men? (*L.* 448).

But what are the alternatives? Let us turn to Hobbes and begin by examining the doctrine of equality.

## II

We have suggested that Aristotle believed that unity among equals could only be achieved by virtue of an external agent. The agent could either be an opposing group or state which threatened the interests of this collection of equals or else a group or state whose existence apart from the collection of equals enabled them to "distinguish" themselves from the agent—and, hence, to perceive similarities between themselves. This external agent, in a sense, is incidental; its purpose or conscious aim is, presumably, not to unify the equals it exists in opposition to. But Hobbes examines the situation whereby an agent is instituted—again, externally—with the express purpose of bringing a form of unity to the contending equals. (The fact that this agent is external is clear. The sovereign in a state, by the very nature of the social contract, is created distinct from the citizens with no binding relation to the citizens. The fact that he is apart is fundamental to the whole scheme.) This question naturally comes to mind: Does not such an arrangement really preserve the basic disunity of the state— and create division (a potential state of war) between sovereigns and citizens? Let us first examine how the state is unified and then return to this problem later with a brief discussion of Locke.

In Aristotle, equality and inequality are both conditions and doctrines; the polis is rent by the inconsistencies between them. In Hobbes, the state is also rent by inconsistencies between conditions and doctrines, but their origins and nature are quite different from those in Aristotle, since it is the reasoning process itself (and its limitations) which causes civil violence. It is therefore essential to examine briefly this reasoning process to understand these distinctions.

Hobbes asserts that human knowledge is divided into two parts:

one is called "knowledge of fact" and the other is called "knowledge of the consequences of one affirmation to another." The first produces history, the second science (or philosophy) (*L.* 53). The source of the first is experience (*L.* 45). The source of the second is what we would call ratiocination and consists of a system of elements (words) and the logic which relates these elements by a system of reckoning, based on a mathematical analogy (*L.* 29, 40, 53). The object of the first in the civil realm is to determine good and evil (what is beneficial and nonbeneficial) (*L.* 31–33). The object of the second is to determine what is just and unjust (right and wrong).[44] Possession of the first is called prudence; of the second, sapience (*L.* 30). Excellence in the first is natural wit; in the second, acquired wit (*L.* 43, 46). Because of the importance which Hobbes attaches to terminology in both realms of knowledge it is easy to confuse the two.[45] But the division is absolutely fundamental to Hobbes, and his political writings (especially the ones on "sedition") cannot be understood without keeping this distinction clearly in mind.

It is not within the scope of this essay to examine the philosophical implications of this distinction, but it is necessary to realize that the will—the source of all political activity—emanates exclusively from the first area of mental activity (which we shall refer to as the realm of prudence), never from the second (the realm of sapience) (*L.* 37–38). It is also necessary to recall that in human beings the will is not an arbitrary force but is defined as the result of what we would describe as a rational process (*L.* 37–38). The will is the last act of deliberation, which is simply a process of assessing whether one has an appetite or an aversion to a future state over which one has control (*L.* 38). This assessment is based on "the trial of . . . effects upon themselves or other men" (*L.* 32), that is to say, experience.

However, the realm of prudence has two major internal logical limitations. First, all experience which man can have is necessarily incomplete (*L.* 16). Second, experience, however complete, is never certain: "for though a man have always seen the day and night to follow one another hitherto; yet can he thence conclude they shall do so, or that they have done so eternally: *experience concludeth nothing universally* (*E.W.* IV. 18), observes Hobbes nearly a century before Hume.

---

[44] See Chapter IX for a description of the parallelism of the two types of knowledge and, especially, the chart of *Science* (*L.* 54–55).

[45] In the *Leviathan*, Chapters 4 and 5 are devoted to a discussion of the realm of sapience (not 5 and 6 as Hobbes himself states on *L.* 46), Chapter 6 to the realm of prudence, Chapter 7 to sapience, Chapter 8 to both, etc.

The realm of prudence also has two major limitations based on the specifics of the human situation. First, humans differ in their physical constitutions and specific personal experience, so that it is impossible for one human to assess what another regards as "good" or "prudent" (*L.* 32–33). Second, this limitation leads to several restrictions on one's ability to assess the motives and, hence, future actions of others, since the only way to assess motives is to compare them with our own, and to distinguish "all circumstances, by which the case may come to be altered" (*L.* 6).

Despite these limitations, prudence is one source of equality: Hobbes asserts, "I find yet a greater equality amongst men than that of strength. For prudence is but experience, which equal time equally bestows on all men, in those things they equally apply themselves to" (*L.* 80). Shrewdness based on prudence also enables men to overcome physical differences (*L.* 80).

This equality of capacity combined with the limitations on prudence, described above, leads to Hobbes' special state of war. Competition may have been the first cause of the state of war (*L.* 81), but the necessity for anticipation is what turns an inconvenience (as in Locke) into a nightmare. The famous "security dilemma"[46] of the Hobbesian state of nature derives from an equality of capacity combined with an inability to assess accurately the motives of others—or the results of one's actions. Because one cannot predict, one must leave as little to chance as possible and, hence, one must anticipate.

To solve this problem, a sovereign power is instituted, apart from the citizens, not to impose order through the exercise of an arbitrary will, but to impose a system which introduces predictability into human affairs. One can predict with reasonable certainty that one will be hanged if one kills one's neighbor. More important, one can predict what will happen to one's neighbor if he kills you and, given the rough equivalence of human prudence and a universal fear of death (the gallows), one can predict that one's neighbor will not commit murder. The state of competition—to some degree, of war—still persists (one still locks one's doors and chests), but the nightmare of anticipation is eliminated.[47]

The purpose of the state, then, is to provide clearly forseeable dire consequences for certain actions it regards as nonbeneficial to its citizens and, thereby, to introduce an element of rational certainty

[46] See footnote 18.

[47] By the need for anticipation, I mean not only the need to kill before being killed, but also the need to foresee without criteria for prediction. One may well speculate on which is the worse dilemma.

into human calculations. Order in the state is based, not on force, but the threat of force, and its penal system is based on deterrence, not retribution.[48] The relationship between law, thought, prudence and, hence, evil is clearly illustrated by the following:

> Sometimes a man desires to know the event of an action; and then he thinketh of some like action past, and the events thereof one after another; supposing like events will follow like actions. As he that foresees what will become of a criminal, reckons what he has seen follow on the like crime before; having this order of thoughts, the crime, the officer, the prison, the judge, and the gallows. Which kind of thoughts is called *foresight* and *prudence* (*L.* pp. 15–16).

How effective is the interaction between force and rational calculation in preserving order in the state? Before examining the theoretical problems which arise, let us consider the causes of actual sedition in the state.

Sedition is caused by the simultaneous concurrence of four necessary conditions. First is widespread *discontent:* "For as long as a man thinketh himself well, and that the present government standeth not in his way to hinder his proceeding from well to better, it is impossible for him to desire the change thereof" (*E.W.* IV-200). Second is the *pretense of right:* "For though a man be discontent, yet if in his own opinion there be no just cause of stirring against, or resisting the government established, nor any pretense to justify his resistance, and to procure aid, he will never show it [discontent]" (*E.W.* IV. 200–201). Third is *hope of success:* "For it were madness to attempt without hope, when to fail, is to die the death of a traitor" (*E.W.* IV. 201). Finally, if these conditions exist, "There wanteth nothing thereto but a man of credit to set up the standard and to blow the trumpet" (*E.W.* IV. 201). Let us examine each of these categories in turn.

Discontent arises from two sources: fear (or hope) of economic or physical harm (or gain) and a desire for preeminence. In this first category, Hobbes lists: (1) fear of want (*E.W.* IV. 201), hence, (2) excessive taxation: "great exactions, though the right [to Hobbes] thereof be acknowledged, have caused great seditions" (*E.W.* IV. 201); (3) that occasion "when a multitude . . . have concurred in a crime worthy of death, they join together, and take arms to defend themselves for fear thereof" (*E.W.* IV. 201). (4) when the poor hope to profit: "These [in Stuart England] longed for war, and hoped to maintain themselves

---

[48] One of Hobbes' alleged inconsistencies is that the citizen is permitted to flee when the authorities arrive to arrest him for a capital or other infamous crime. But this doctrine is totally consistent with a deterrence system of punishment—in which the commission of a crime is an indication of the breakdown of the system.

hereafter by the lucky choosing of a party to side with. . ." (*E.W.* VI-168), and (5) when the rich hoped to profit: "the city of London and other great towns of trade, having in admiration the prosperity of the Low Countries after they had revolted from their monarch, the King of Spain, were inclined to think that the like change of government here, would to them produce the like prosperity" (*E.W.* VI. 168).

In the second place, discontent is caused by ambition which, in turn, arises from comparison. Ambition exists at the highest levels where "such men must needs take it ill, and be grieved with the state as find themselves postposed to those in honor, whom they think they excel in virtue and ability to govern" (*E.W.* IV-202). Ambition exists also on lower levels when the normal competition in pursuit of felicity turns men to political goals—like the ones that the Presbyterian clergy described in *Behemoth* were disposed to pursue.[49]

Whereas *discontent* arises as the faculty of *prudence* defines appetite and aversion, *pretense of right* arises as the faculty of sapience defines justice and injustice. Scattered throughout Hobbes' works are definitions of ten distinct categories of "seditious doctrines":[50]

1. The generic doctrine that the "knowledge of good and evil" should belong to each man in a political society.

2. The generic doctrine that the knowledge of just and unjust should belong to each man in a political society. This is what we would call the existence of conscience.

3. The general category of instruction in Aristotelianism (Scholasticism).

4. The doctrine of divided sovereignty—which includes the separation of church from state.

---

[49] At both levels, the university is often at the root of it all: "And as the Presbyterians brought with them into their churches their divinity from the universities, so did many of the gentlemen bring their politics thence into the Parliament . . . . the chief leaders were the ambitious ministers and ambitious gentlemen; the ministers envying the authority of bishops whom they thought less learned; and the gentlemen envying the privy council, whom they thought less wise than themselves. For it is a hard matter for men, who all think highly of their own wits, when they have also acquired the learning of the university, to be persuaded that they want any ability requisite for the government of a commonwealth" (*E.W.* VI 192–193).

[50] Hobbes lists "seditious doctrines" in *Leviathan, De Cive,* and *De Corpore Politico,* but no list corresponds entirely to another. The four common to all lists (numbers 2, 4, 5, and 6 above) are fundamental tenets of John Locke's philosophy. Seditious doctrines are discussed: (*E.W.* II 149–158; IV 203–208; VI 191–197; and *L.* 210–216).

5. The doctrine that the sovereign is subject to fundamental or promulgated law.

6. The doctrine that property is prior to the state and, hence, cannot be taken without consent.

7. The doctrine that a "multitude" is equivalent to a "people" (which is closely analogous to what we would call majority rights—or even majority rule).

8. The doctrine that faith comes from inspired sources, not reason.

9. The doctrine that tyrannicide is justifiable.

10. The general category of the virtues of emulating other societies, especially ancient.

The necessary ingredients for *hope of success* are that the discontented have "mutual intelligence," are large in number, well-armed. and have an energetic and competent *leader*. (There are the implied reciprocal deficiencies in the sovereign authority.)

Although all four conditions are to some degree necessary for a successful sedition, the most interesting one for our purposes is the pretense of right: That is, how are seditious doctrines generated, and how do they take concrete political effect?

The origin of seditious doctrines is not a simple question to Hobbes, and his hesitations, possible contradictions, and eventual answers provide some very interesting insights for the student of civil violence. The faculty of science is supposed to define just and unjust—that is to say, what is right. Seditious doctrines (the "pretense of right") clearly deal with the same subject matter, so one would expect them to be the result of what Hobbes calls "error" or "absurdity"—arising from faulty logic or definitions, but within the faculty of science. Some passages in *Leviathan* can be cited in support of this contention,[51] but Hobbes perceived a great difficulty for his position. Recognizing the possibility for error in science and, consequently, the need for a judge, he had gone far toward establishing a relativistic view on the question of right. Obviously, this was in conflict with his views that there was, after all, a right reason which all could know if the proper logical paths were followed. To avoid this difficulty, Hobbes argued that seditious doctrines occurred when passions (from the realm of prudence) infected the reasoning process by affecting the definition of terms. This process is clear from a reading of the *De Corpore Politico* where, in a complex passage, Hobbes introduces the distinction between the faculties, reiterates the importance of names to the faculty of sci-

---

[51] See, for example, the passage on "science" (*L.* 29–30), especially the last paragraph.

ence, and then indicates the intrusion of the passions: "It remaineth therefore, that they be such, as name things, not according to their true and generally agreed upon names, but call right and wrong, good and bad, according to their passions, or according to the authorities or such as they admire. . ." (*E.W.* IV. 211). Remembering, however, that the passions are defined in terms of *interest*, we detect the introduction of interest into the definition of right and wrong.

Is this a conscious process, or is it simply error? Are the authors of seditious doctrines aware that they are erroneous? "For they could not poison the people with those absurd opinions contrary to peace and civil society, unless they held them themselves; which sure is ignorance greater than can well befall any wise man" (*E.W.* II. 162). In *Behemoth*, a later work, Hobbes plainly states that seditious doctrines, while erroneous [to Hobbes], were being used as conscious political weapons:

> [The Presbyterian] clergy so framed their countenance and gesture at their entrance into the pulpit, and their pronunciation both in prayer and sermon, and used the scripture phrase (whether understood by the people or not), as that no tragedian in the world could have acted the part of a right godly man better than these did; insomuch that a man unacquainted with such art, could never suspect any ambitious plot in them to raise sedition against the state, as they then designed . . . (*E.W.* VI. 193).

Hobbes has now added the secularization of religious doctrines in *Behemoth* to the secularization of natural law in *Leviathan*. To understand the process by which this occurred, we must return to the distinction between prudence and sapience. Political actions must take place as the result of prudence: that is, as the result of the exercise of human will in the pursuit of felicity. But success in pursuing felicity is based on an accurate reading of history—that is, experience. Hence, the rules of experience, not the rules of justice, must govern concrete human political activity. Men begin to tailor their notions of justice to fit concrete tactical considerations, and doctrine becomes the product of interest and tactics. As doctrines become weapons, they become governed by the laws of war, as it were. Religious and doctrinaire conflicts, based on notions of right become, for Hobbes, simply different manifestations of political conflict. To Hobbes, religion is nothing more than a *political* disease. One institutes an established church, not to prop up the regime and lend support to it, but to provide a sort of vaccine—to infect the population in a controlled way to prevent the Jesuits and Presbyterians from infecting it in a fatal way.

The relationship between doctrines and interest is clearly illustrated by the answer to the second question above: How do doctrines take concrete political effects?

The answer is through the vehicle of eloquence. Eloquence has some interesting philosophical attributes: it is the mediator between the realms of prudence and sapience, and it has two component parts— logic and rhetoric. But the dictates of political goals (especially ambition) drives it in the latter direction. In this respect,

> Eloquence is nothing else but the power of winning belief of what we say. And to that end we must have aid from the passions of the hearer. Now to demonstration and teaching of the truth, there are required long deductions, and great attention, which is unpleasant to the hearer. Therefore they which seek not truth, but belief, must take another way, and not only derive what they would have believed, from somewhat believed already, but also, by aggravations and extenuations, made good and bad, right and wrong, appear great or less, according as shall serve their turns. And such is the power of eloquence, for many times a man is made to believe thereby, that he sensibly feeleth smart and damage, when he feeleth none, and to enter into rage and indignation without any other cause, than what is in the words and passion of the speaker (*E.W.* IV. 211–12).

But eloquence cannot have political effect without organization and, consequently, the need for "factions" arises. Factions are created by adventurers to serve their own interests by making themselves "the realtors and interpreters of the counsels and actions of single men," and by nominating "the persons and places to assemble and deliberate of such things whereby the present government may be reformed." The ambitious rule factions by creating a small faction within the faction. Hobbes clearly has in mind an assemblage, such as a legislative body, since the smaller faction meets in secret, "where they may order what shall afterward be propounded in a general meeting, and by whom. and on what subject, and in what order each of them shall speak. and how they may draw the powerfullest and most popular men of the faction to their side" (*E.W.* II-163).

Civil violence occurs when "they have got a faction big enough in which they may rule by their eloquence, [and] they move to take it upon the managing of affairs" (*E.W.* II. 163–164).

How does the sovereign authority deal with the problem of sedition? A prudent ruler can stifle "hope of success" by maintaining a sufficiently large standing army—if he keeps his finances in order. To combat discontent, Hobbes recommends that the ruler improve the economy, establish an equitable system of taxation (which, to Hobbes, was a form of sales tax), leave as much liberty to subjects as possible— especially in the economic sphere, institute a system of impartial justice, and buy off the ambitious by giving them high posts of honor that would also keep them well occupied.

But what about the problem of doctrines? Here, there is a development and a growing sense of frustration in his writings. In *De Cive*, Hobbes argues that education can cure the problem: "It is therefore the duty of those who have the chief authority, to root those [doctrines] out of the mind of men, not by commanding, but by teaching; not by the tenor of penalties, but by the perspicuity of reasons" (*E.W.* II. 171–72). Hobbes' liberal assumptions about the force of logic led him to assert that men, if once instructed in the truth, would disseminate it with much more vigor than they disseminate falsehood. All one had to do was clean out the universities, which "have been to this nation, as the wooden horse was to the Trojans" (*E.W.* VI. 213) and to impose religious orthodoxy through an established church. And, in *De Corpore Politico*, he suggests that "opinions which are gotten by education, and in the length of time, are made habitual, cannot be taken away by force, and upon the sudden; they must therefore be taken away also by time and education" (*E.W.* IV. 219). But by the time that he wrote *Behemoth* his patience with rationality was wearing thin, and he was suggesting—perhaps, half-seriously—that the only way to deal with sedition was to hang the Presbyterian clergy (*E.W.* VI. 282).

Hobbes, then, is not very reassuring to the upholders of civil order. He has moments of optimism about the potentialities of reason and the possibilities of prudently ordering the state, but there is a haunting fear at all times that seditious doctrines can arise in any situation and arm ambitious men to overthrow the state. There is a sort of sanctuary provided by human mental activities which the threat of force cannot touch. Even right reason itself has a serious flaw: right reason, in order to establish that it is right reason, needs an arbiter. But the sovereign's right to be the arbiter is itself established by right reason, and so forth.

In the realm of prudence and in the realm of sapience, then, the source of civil misery is human stupidity and error.[52] The role of the sovereign is to eliminate that error—to provide a rationalizing element in both realms—that is, the creation of a deterrence scheme

---

[52] And the perpetrators fare little better than their victims: "For of them that are the first movers in the disturbance of commonwealth, which can never happen without a civil war, very few are left alive long enough, to see their new designs established: so that the benefit of their crimes redoundeth to posterity, and such as would have least have wished it: which argues that they were not so wise, as they thought they were" (*L.* 194).

of law for prudence and the erection of right reason to preside over the realm of science. In this sense Hobbes, too, is engaged in a process of depersonalizing politics, and it is interesting to compare his efforts with those of Aristotle. Together with the rationalizing aspects of the division of labor, interdependence, and proportional equality, and the prudential aspects of letting the people provide a source of stability, Aristotle, also, relies on the concept of law to provide civil order, as we previously observed. Throughout his works, this question is ever present: "Is it more expedient to be ruled by the one best man, or by the best laws?" (1286a). Although one passage can be cited in support of the best man (1288a), this argument really runs counter to the whole tenor of philosophy. Such a man would almost be a God— and, hence, apart from the society anyway. Aristotle concludes:

> He who commands that law should rule may thus be regarded as commanding that God and reason alone should rule; he who commands that a man should rule adds the character of the beast. Appetite has that character; and high spirit, too, perverts the holders of office, even when they are the best of men. Law . . . may thus be defined as "reason free from all passion" (1287a).

Although striking similarities between Hobbes and Aristotle can be observed in this passage, it is necessary to emphasize that, in Hobbes, although right reason exists, the will of the sovereign (presumably, also subject to passion) is still the source of law. What Hobbes assumes, and Aristotle does not assume, is that the locus of power itself provides the rationalizing element. And what Hobbes insists is that human will—the will of the sovereign—must remain in some form so that the power relationship can persist. To depersonalize law completely is to destroy law.

We must now return to a question raised earlier—does not the creation of this external force in the state create yet another division— between the ruler and the ruled—a division as fundamental as the one between the various equal elements in the state before the erection of the sovereign? Hobbes would answer *no* for two reasons. First, no matter how rapacious the sovereign, the situation could never be worse than in a state of anticipation and war. But second, and far more important, Hobbes would argue that the sovereign, after all, was simply the vehicle of imposing rationality on human affairs. The link between sovereign and subject was law and right reason—the function of centralized power by its very nature was not an arbitrary force in society but a rationalizing force.

But what if the concept of justice should find its authority outside the concept of the sovereign? What if Hobbes' proviso that science as well as prudence requires a supreme judge is removed? What if this final step of "depersonalization" is taken? Let us examine the work of John Locke for an elucidation of these points.

### III

There are a number of areas of agreement between Hobbes and Locke on the causes of civil dislocation. Locke admits both that the "pride, ambition, and turbulency of private men have caused great disorders in commonwealths," and that "factions have been fatal to States and Kingdoms." Moreover, the author of the *Second Treatise* could not have been totally unaware of the role that "seditious doctrines" played in revolutions. But their views are developed along widely divergent paths. The reason for this is a set of basically different assumptions which, at the risk of covering familiar territory, we must review.

First, Locke's state of nature is a less terrifying condition than the one described in *Leviathan*. To Hobbes the state of nature has to be a state of war, because prudence dictates anticipation. Locke believes that the state of nature (the lack of a legitimate legal and judicial authority) does not necessarily imply a state of war (the existence of the threat of force to deny freedom and, hence, everything). But even if a state of war exists, with some men threatening such force, the situation does not become critical. Anyone can develop an understanding of the law of nature; the law of nature confers certain rights and duties; men, discerning these rights and duties, presumably respond to them. When someone breaks the law of nature, all have a right to punish him—since he has committed a "trespass against the whole species" (Locke, 312). In such a situation where everyone has a right (and knows it) to punish an offender, there is implied a sort of collective security arrangement—far different from the doctrine of total self-help, leading to anticipation, stated by Hobbes.

Second, Locke makes a clear distinction between a government and a society (or a people). Once the state of nature is left behind, the social compact sets up a society which, in turn, institutes a legislative and, hence, the rest of the government: "The constitution of the legislative is the first and fundamental act of society, whereby provision is made for the continuation [note] of their union . . . " (Locke, 455–6). There is room for debate on this point, but Locke places so much emphasis on this distinction in his writings on revolution that his views on revolution must be interpreted in light of this distinction. To Hobbes, of course, such a distinction is absurd. It could be argued that, to Hobbes, there is a difference between government and society in the sense that there are areas of human activity which invariably are not limited by law—even here one is on shaky ground. But that there could be a legitimate aggregation existing apart from the government, to him, would be unthinkable.

Third, it is almost impossible to destroy a society. The only way to do so (which Locke mentions) is by foreign invasion (Locke, 454.). He, therefore, can view revolution in a calmer light. One can alter governments without rending the fabric of society, and even if that fabric should be destroyed, the result would not be so horrible that it might not be preferable to existing conditions.

We may well ask what Locke meant by Revolution. He is mostly interested in "dissolution of government"—a category which includes many forms of peaceful—although not legal—change. However, as with Aristotle, it would ruin the unity of his arguments to distinguish his categories by the criterion of violence—since he regards the use of artifice by a prince in subverting a legislature and the use of force by a people to restore the legislature simply as two types of tactics. There is a sort of reciprocity at work. The prince has many weapons at his disposal; the people have only one. The subversion of a legislature must be regarded by the people as the first step toward total forceful oppression of the society—Locke, too, has a doctrine of anticipation—hence, there is a reciprocity of force implied by Locke to justify the use of force by the people (Locke, 458–460).

Although Locke does not have a developed theory of the dynamics of a violent revolution, he does have some interesting points about when these revolutions might be expected to occur.

First, although he acknowledges, as noted above, that revolutions can take place as a result of ambition, factions, and so on, he strongly suggests that the responsibility for a revolutionary situation almost always rests on the government in power. He implies in an ironic passage that "The Rulers Insolence," and not "Peoples wantonness" is chiefly to blame (Locke, 467).

Second, people revolt, not because rulers make mistakes (although mistakes may make a revolution successful), but because rulers break faith.

Third, this breach of trust will not cause revolution if it is only with a few individuals—it must be with the people as a whole—which means that the act must be a constitutional, not a personal transgression. Such a breach occurs in two forms: (1) the alteration of the governmental structure by "changing the legislature" or (2), without so altering it, the making of laws that are contrary to the purposes for which the society was formed (Locke, 460–461). In the first category are an interference with elections to the legislature, an interference with the deliberations of the legislature, passing laws over the head of the legislature, and selling the country to a foreign prince. In the second category is the seizure of property without consent.

Finally, Locke emphasizes, like Aristotle, that the people are most reluctant to revolt. Habit is a strong force in society: "They are hardly to be prevailed with to amend the acknowledged faults, in the frame they have been accustomed to" (Locke, 462). Slow change also seldom makes people revolt. It is only when "a long train of abuses, prevarications, and artifices, all tending the same way, make the design visible to the people . . . [and they can] feel, what they lie under and see, whither they are going" (Locke, 463). The important point is to notice the orientation to the future. It will be recalled that the Glorious Revolution occurred after the birth of a male heir which promised an indefinite continuation of the religious problem. This discontent must be very widespread.

These conditions prevailing, "the people generally ill treated . . . will be ready upon any occasion to ease themselves of a burden that sits heavy upon them. They will wish and seek for the opportunity, which, in the change, weakness, and accidents of human affairs, seldom delays long to offer itself" (Locke, 463).

Locke is simply raising once more the question of division in society—here between sovereign and subject—but articulated, ironically, in terms of that same type of natural law that Hobbes had instituted to remove the division. Here, however, Locke is employing what to Hobbes would be faulty science to justify a set of "seditious doctrines" almost identical to the ones that Hobbes had enumerated a generation before. And, indeed, Parliament, using such a set of "seditious doctrines," fittingly celebrated the 100th anniversary of Hobbes' birth by tossing out the sovereign. Thus Locke showed that the same natural law which Hobbes had so carefully erected on grounds of right reason in order to show man the folly of insurrection could itself become the source of revolution. When Hobbes' important qualification (that the sovereign be judge in matters of right reason) is removed—law is truly depersonalized and can become the source of disruption as easily as it was previously assumed to be the source of constraint.

Thus we come to the final paradox. Not only do Marx and Engels raise serious doubts about the Aristotelian assertion that "while people hate *men* who oppose their impulses, even if they oppose them rightly, the law in its ordaining of what is good is not burdensome" (1180a), but the doctrines of Locke raise serious doubts about whether depersonalization itself can provide order. Perhaps, there is something to Hobbes' assertion that somehow, somewhere men must be tied to the law or to the system. Man, may be, as Kant asserts, an animal that needs a master. But man does not want a master.

*2*

# In Praise of Thrasymachus

*Ralf Dahrendorf*

〈〈〈〈〈〈〈〈〈〈〈〈〈〈〈〈〈〈〈〈〈〈〈〈〈〈〈〈〈〈〈〈〈〈〈〈〈〈〈〈〈〈〈〈〈〈〈〈〈〈

## EDITORS' COMMENT

As the reader will shortly discover, Ralf Dahrendorf "praises" Thrasy-machus not because of the nobility of his sentiments but because he is the distant parent of a kind of social theory. It is not the "right of the stronger" that we are concerned with here but the alleged *fact* that structural inequalities—relations of "coerciveness" or "constraint"—are primary phenomena in the social order and are clues to answering Simmel's famous question: "How is society possible?" Or, as Dahrendorf has written elsewhere (*Class and Class Conflict in Industrial Society*, Stanford: Stanford University Press, 1959, p. 64):

> Some authors have visualized a state in which there are no classes and no class conflicts, because there is simply nothing to quarrel about. I do not think that such a state is ever likely to occur. . . . I shall

SOURCE. Ralf Dahrendorf, "In Praise of Thrasymachus," from *Essays in the Theory of Society* (Stanford: Stanford University Press, 1968), pp. 129–150, excerpted. Reprinted with the permission of the publishers. Copyright 1968 by the Board of Trustees of the Leland Stanford Junior University.

suggest . . . that the fundamental inequality of social structure, and the lasting determinant of social conflict, is the inequality of power and authority which inevitably accompanies social organization.

Dahrendorf has been a meteor on both the academic and political scenes in the last decade. His sociological writings, largely concerned with "grand theory," have been acclaimed not only for their brilliance and coherence but also for the trenchancy of the debates that they provoke and for their sweep and urbane literacy. Dahrendorf has also been deeply involved in practical matters relating to West German politics and society. A few years ago he left the Socialist Party and joined the FDP (Liberals) together with a few other progressive intellectuals. In addition to holding a chair of Sociology at the University of Constanz, he currently sits in the Federal Bundestag as an FDP member.

The political position of a "rejuvenated liberalism" and the implications of Dahrendorf's "constraint theory" would seem to go hand in hand, at least for purposes of our present "realistic" age. Although it is widely believed that liberal doctrine entails notions such as enlightened and rational consent as the basis for society and the goodness and perfectibility of human nature, there has always been a more tough-minded strain that sought its point of departure not from nature but from society and the antecedent fact of authority relations based on the power to coerce. Hobbes is the father of this school of thought, and it is not very far beneath the surface in the political writings of Immanuel Kant, the author of the aphorism, "Man is an animal that needs a master."

The essay reprinted here is one of the most recent and succinct statements of Dahrendorf's position. Its content is much enhanced by his verve of style. His adversaries are a long line of "equilibrium theorists," beginning with Plato and ending with Talcott Parsons and David Easton, men whose doctrines, Dahrendorf believes, lead straight to the boredom or tyranny of the "closed society." But beneath the polemic that springs so easily from his pen some of the most difficult questions of social theory are analyzed. Can social change be meaningfully interpreted as occurring "homeostatically" within existing structures, as the "integrationists" imply? Can a hypothetical social system based on value-sharing allow for structurally generated conflicts? What kind of theoretical model of society can best explain the range of events and phenomena, including civil conflict and revolution, to which real societies are subject? Does "constraint theory" supply useful generalizations about the real world?

Obviously Dahrendorf's argument is not directly focused on the specific problem of internal war. Some would even deny that social theorizing at such a broad level can aid us much in understanding specific movements of organized civil violence. However, if these applications prove empirically fruitful, it is likely that a mode of explanation that reasons from the universality of coercion to the various *explicanda* of social stability, social breakdown, and social change will have greater interest for students of revolution than the theories that begin with the premise of a "moral community" of value-sharing compatriots. A hint of why this is so can be obtained from the passages on Nazism in the present essay.

# IN PRAISE OF THRASYMACHUS

RALF DAHRENDORF

Tradition has been rather less than fair to Thrasymachus of Chalcedon, who, even if he has no other claim to fame, deserves to be remembered for the remarkable achievement of holding his own in an encounter with that champion dialectician, Socrates. Despite the impressions of some of the bystanders and, perhaps, of Socrates himself, Thrasymachus emerged unconvinced by Socrates' arguments, and with his heavy irony intact, from the vicious debate about justice that distinguishes the first book of the *Republic* from so many of Plato's other dialogues. "Well," he said in response to his opponent's final thrust, "this is a feast day, and you may take all this as your share of the entertainment."[1]

Our reasons for recalling the rude visitor from Chalcedon are by no means merely rhetorical. Indeed, the first book of the *Republic* deserves much more attention from those who have lightly dismissed it as an early and playful prologue to the serious discussions of the nine remaining books. It was in this initial dialogue, or perhaps more

[1] Plato. *The Republic*. Trans. F. M. Cornford. New York: Oxford University Press (1945), 32nd ed., 1966, p. 39.

appropriately debate, that two incompatible views of society were stated for the first time in the history of social and political thought. The conflict between these two views has since proved to be the single most persistent conflict in the ranks of those who seek to understand the workings of human society, and among today's scholars it rages still. This conflict has assumed many forms since the admittedly rather crude statement of the two views in the first book of the *Republic*, and we shall here be considering some of these forms right down to contemporary sociological and political theory; but its basic terms were set in that apparently accidental encounter between Thrasymachus and Socrates.

What is more, it seems to me that despite his rather formidable temper and abusive language, Thrasymachus had the better arguments on his side. We have to assist him a little, to be sure, to make his case fully convincing; we shall have to interpolate or even extrapolate his arguments rather than simply interpret them; but with the ideas of Thrasymachus as a starting point, we can develop an image of society that helps us to understand both some basic problems of political theory and the patterns of the good society in our time. This is what I shall try to do here.

Let us return for a moment to the home of Cephalus and Polemarchus in Piraeus, the port of Athens. Socrates, on his way home from the festivities in honor of Bendis, is almost literally dragged into the house, where he is greeted with varying degrees of delight and soon finds himself engaged in his favorite sport, talking. After a polite exchange with the aging master of the house about wisdom and old age, he engages Polemarchus, the son of Cephalus, in one of those supposedly educational circular debates in which the dialogues of Plato abound. The subject is justice, and the conclusion is an open question: "Now what, after all that, might justice be?"

Thrasymachus, understandably impatient, forgets his manners ("gathering himself up like a wild beast," says Socrates, "he sprang at us as if he would tear us in pieces") and begins: "What is the matter with you two, Socrates? Why do you go on in this imbecile way, politely deferring to each other's nonsense? . . . I want a clear and precise statement: I won't put up with that sort of verbiage."[2]

After some further interchanges, Thrasymachus proceeds to make himself quite clear in a few stark statements interrupted by Socratic doubts:

> "Listen then," Thrasymachus began. "What I say is that 'just' or 'right' means nothing but what is to the interest of the stronger party.

[2] *Ibid.*, pp. 15–16.

Well, where is your praise? You don't mean to give it me."

"I will, as soon as I understand," I said. "I don't see yet what you mean by right being the interest of the stronger party. For instance, Polydamas, the athlete, is stronger than we are, and it is to his interest to eat beef for the sake of his muscles; but surely you don't mean that the same diet would be good for weaker men and therefore be right for us?"

"You are trying to be funny, Socrates. It's a low trick to take my words in the sense you think will be most damaging."

"No, no," I protested: "but you must explain."

"Don't you know, then, that a state may be ruled by a despot, or a democracy, or an aristocracy?"

"Of course."

"And that the ruling element is always the strongest?"

"Yes."

"Well then, in every case the laws are made by the ruling party in its own interest; a democracy makes democratic laws, a despot autocratic ones, and so on. By making these laws they define as 'right' for their subjects whatever is for their own interest, and they call anyone who breaks them a 'wrongdoer' and punish him accordingly. That is what I mean: in all states alike 'right' has the same meaning, namely what is for the interest of the party established in power, and that is the strongest. So the sound conclusion is that what is 'right' is the same everywhere: the interest of the stronger party."[3]

The scene is set, and Socrates is quick to respond. He tries to entangle Thrasymachus in contradictions, making him admit that the powerful may be in error about what is useful to them. Thrasymachus parries rather well by pointing out the difference between positions of power ("the rulers insofar as they are acting as rulers") and their incumbents.

Soon Socrates approaches the central issue of the controversy. He argues that all human activity must be directed toward some goal, and that the value of any such activity must therefore be found in its goal, not in the activity itself.

And so with government of any kind: no ruler, insofar as he is acting as ruler, will study or enjoin what is for his own interest. All that he says and does will be said and done with a view to what is good and proper for the subject for whom he practices his art.[4]

In response to this apparent reversal of his own original statement, Thrasymachus bursts into a long argument to the effect that whatever those in power do is bound to be harmful to their subjects. And now that he has lost his temper, Thrasymachus adds somewhat inconsis-

---

[3] *Ibid.*, p. 18.

[4] *Ibid.*, p. 24.

tently that for this reason injustice pays and a belief in justice is naïve.

This remark provides Socrates with an easy opening for a whole shower of counterarguments, in the course of which, contrary to his rhetorical principles, he states a case of his own. He clearly has no other choice, since no amount of Socratic irony can force his adversary to state the Socratic case. It had been agreed, Socrates claims (of course he is wrong), "that any kind of authority, in the state or in private life, must, in its character of authority, consider solely what is best for those under its care."[5]

Repeatedly Socrates insists on the essentially harmonious relationship between rulers and ruled. Indeed, he uses an argument against Thrasymachus that his opponent, had he not by this time been blind with fury, might well have turned into one for his own case: namely that if Thrasymachus's notion of justice were correct, people would be divided, hate one another, and engage in conflict. And wherever this sort of justice occurs—"in a state or a family or an army or anywhere else"—the effect is "to make united action impossible because of factions and quarrels, and moreover to set whatever it resides in at enmity with itself as well as with any opponent and with all who are just."[6]

"Enjoy your triumph," is all that Thrasymachus can reply. "You need not fear my contradicting you. I have no wish to give offense to the company."[7] The answer is in accord with his theory, if one assumes that those present were stronger, but the arsenal of Thrasymachus was still full. It would be fun to try out the weapons it contained in defense of the proud and angry Sophist from Chalcedon. [. . .]

## II

Thrasymachus was the first to state his case. In all human societies, there are positions that enable their bearers to exercise power. These positions are endowed with sovereignty—the men who hold them lay down the law for their subjects. Obedience is enforced, for the most important single aspect of power is the control of sanctions. (Sanctions do not always have to be applied: mere anticipation of their effect may suffice to guarantee compliance with the law.) It follows from this notion of power and sanctions that there is always resistance to the exercise of power, and that both the effectiveness and the legiti-

[5] *Ibid.*, p. 27.
[6] *Ibid.*, p. 35.
[7] *Ibid.*, p. 36.

macy of power—if there is any difference between these two concepts—are precarious. Normally those in power manage to stay in
power. Theirs is the stronger group, and society is held together by
the exercise of their strength, that is, by constraint.

Now for Socrates' position. It is true, he says, that power is exercised in human societies, but it is exercised on behalf of societies rather
than against them. Positions of power are created to give active expression to a general will that represents the consensus of the society's
members. What appears to be obedience is in many ways but an expression of this consensus. The exercise of power is dependent on the support of those who are apparently subject to it. Subjection never involves
a renunciation of sovereignty; rather, sovereignty remains with the
total body politic, with all the citizens of a society. Any differences
and divisions in a society are due to outside interference with a basically legitimate system; such divisive influences are in any case destructive of society. Normally, society is held together by the agreement
of all citizens on certain fundamental tenets, to which they then adhere
voluntarily as a way of protecting their own interests.

This language, of course, is no longer that of Thrasymachus and
Socrates, but that of a much later pair of political thinkers, Thomas
Hobbes and Jean-Jacques Rousseau. Though separated by more than
a century, Hobbes and Rousseau are properly discussed together, as
the brilliant article on Hobbes in the *Encyclopédie* was the first to
point out.[8] It was they who wrote the next act in our drama.

In the extended debate over the social contract (yet another translation of Plato's "justice") two conflicting notions were repeatedly advanced.[9] One was the notion of the social contract of association (*pacte
d'association*), according to which society was originally formed by
a free agreement to join in a common enterprise involving no abdication of any participant's rights. An odd contract this, or so one might
think, but then there are other weaknesses of the Socratic—or Rousseauist—position. The other notion, that of the contract of government
(*pacte de gouvernment*), postulated an original agreement setting
up an agency responsible for holding society together, an agency to
which every party to the agreement must be to some extent subject.
This agency is, of course, government, and in this form the social
contract becomes a real contract with all the attendant problems.

---

[8] *Encyclopédie, ou Dictionnaire raisonné etc.* New ed., Lausanne, 1786, p. 589.
[9] For a historical account of the social contract debate that is informed by a
sense of its sociological relevance, see the study by J. W. Gough: *The Social Contract: A Critical Study of its Development.* Oxford: Clarendon Press, 2nd ed., 1957.

The consequences of this conflict between notions of the social contract were many, although there is little agreement even today on exactly what they were. Hobbes has been called the father of authoritarianism; he has even been used by German sociologists to clothe Nazi rule in an ancient ideology; but the same Hobbes has also been regarded as a forefather of modern liberal theory. Rousseau was long considered the great theorist of democracy; only recently have some political historians discovered that this notion of democracy is distinctly ambiguous, and that perhaps Rousseau bears as much responsibility for totalitarian democracy as for its liberal counterpart.

In the social contract debate, the ancient dispute about the basis of justice was resumed on a more sophisticated level, but with inconclusive results. Its nineteenth-century version, the many-sided conflict between a Socratic *Gemeinschaft* and a Thrasymachean *Gesellschaft*, was equally inconclusive. To find definitive answers, we shall have to take the final step to the present-day version of this debate.

When we do, the first discovery we make is a telling reversal of order. Today, it is the party of Socrates that has stated its case first, and the party of Thrasymachus that has so far confined itself to putting its opposition on record in the most general terms. The surnames of Socrates in our time are many; indeed one can hardly speak of a "party" here, so varied are the approaches of Socratic theorists today. This group includes economists like Kenneth Arrow and Anthony Downs, political scientists like Karl Deutsch and David Easton, sociologists like Talcott Parsons and Neil Smelser, and many others whose analysis rests on an equilibrium model of social life.

Equilibrium theories differ greatly in the degree to which their basic concepts are reified. Not all of them, for example, assume explicitly that there is a general consensus on values among the members of a society. In one way or another, however, they all regard the exercise of power as an exchange in which all citizens participate, and which in theory makes it possible to think of society as a system held in equilibrium so far as its constituent parts are concerned. Disturbances of the system are either ruled out as beyond the boundaries of this type of analysis (i.e., regarded as unfortunate intrusions of the complicated world of uncertainty) or classified as unexplained accidents. Although such disturbances may produce stress or failure of communication within the system, they are generated outside it. The system is regarded as persisting through time by virtue of the equilibrium created either by its internal cycles of power and support, or by the flow of communications, or by the interchange between subsystems as mediated by the currency of power.

What resistance there has been to this approach has been much less subtle than the various versions of the equilibrium theory itself. In this respect, at least, the school of Thrasymachus has remained true to its founder. There have been noisy and ambitious proclamations of a new sociology or a true science of politics, but these have so far resulted in little more than some rather old-fashioned protestations to the effect that power is important, conflict and change omnipresent, and the political process incalculable. There has not yet been any considered statement of how else one might look at society, or explain the political process, or argue for the good society, without abandoning the indubitable technical advances of modern social science.[10] Not infrequently, laudable sentiments have taken the place of necessary arguments. This is as true, it seems to me, of C. Wright Mills and his numerous followers today as it is of Raymond Aron. (The pairing of these two names may perhaps suggest the profound ambiguity in any Thrasymachean position!)

There is no intrinsic objection to an analysis of society in which power figures as an agent of constraint. To be sure, we see in modern economics a remarkable contrast between the technical refinement of equilibrium theories and the nineteenth-century crudeness of theories of development; and our concern here is with a similar contrast between an emphasis on continuity and an emphasis on change. But refinement is not necessarily a sign of truth; and it might be suggested that if Thrasymachean theories seem crude, it is only because the imagination that has gone into formulating them has so far not been accompanied by a corresponding precision of craftsmanship.

In a Thrasymachean theory, power is a central notion. It is seen as unequally divided, and therefore as a lasting source of friction; legitimacy amounts at best to a precarious preponderance of power over the resistance it engenders. Of all states, equilibrium is the least likely, a freakish accident rather than the rule; and there is little to be gained by making it a basic assumption. The dialectic of power and resistance determines the rate and direction of change.

## III

At the point we have now reached, general statements are no longer very helpful. Let me turn, therefore, to three sets of questions and apply our two approaches to them in some detail.

---

[10] Once again, distinctions are necessary in the interests of fairness. The statement above is truer of C. Wright Mills than of Wilbert E. Moore; truer of Irving L. Horowitz than of Dennis Wrong; and only after considerable qualification would it apply to Raymond Aron. As for the "leftist" opposition to orthodox social science, *The New Sociology*, edited by Horowitz, New York: Oxford University Press, 1965, affords a clear view of the opportunities and limits of a modern Thrasymachus.

How is society possible? This is, of course, what Talcott Parsons called the Hobbesian problem of order, even though he proposed a very Rousseauist solution to it. According to Parsons, society is possible by virtue of some assumed general agreement on a set of values that define the boundaries and coordinates of the social order and of individual identity in social groups. Societies vary—and change—in their degree of internal differentiation, but at any given time social roles and institutions are integrated by the functional contribution of every one of them to the maintenance of the whole as a going concern. The concern is a going one in the sense that it can adapt to changing environmental conditions, to internal processes of differentiation and functional reallocation, and perhaps even to stresses caused by internal factors (of mysterious origin). Its adaptations are made possible in part by the processes of interchange variously described as feedback processes, as input-output relations, or as manifestations of the flow of power in a system of support and initative.

By pointing to concrete historical experiences such as revolutions, or to the constraints involved in the actual exercise of power, it is relatively easy to make Parsons's modern equilibrium approach appear hopelessly abstract and formal—even absurd. But the approach was not primarily intended to be descriptive, and as an explanation of the continuity of society it is less easily dismissed.

There is, however, another approach, closer to the experience of the historian and the politician, to problems that do not yield to the equilibrium approach. Continuity is without doubt one of the fundamental puzzles of social life; but continuity may be regarded as a result not of equilibrium but of constraint, if not force. Whereas in the equilibrium approach the notion of power has but a marginal place—"Power," says Deutsch in summarizing Parsons, "is thus neither the center nor the essence of politics,"[11] to say nothing of society—it is a fundamental category of the constraint approach to social analysis. Societies are moral entities, i.e., definable by normative structures; to this extent the two approaches agree. But according to the constraint approach norms are established and maintained only by power, and their substance may well be explained in terms of the interests of the powerful.

If one states the case this way, a third concept is necessary: sanctions. Norms differ from values—"mere" values—in being associated with sanctions and thus having a binding force. But the translation of values into norms, the application of sanctions, and the maintenance of stability all refer back to power as a constraining force rather than

[11] K. Deutsch. *The Nerves of Government.* New York: Free Press, 1963, p. 124.

a currency of exchange or an expression of social integration. Political power, then, to summarize this view in John Locke's words, is seen as "a right of making laws with penalties of death and, consequently, all less penalties."[12]

The ramifications of these different approaches to the Hobbesian problem of order are numerous and fascinating. In the sociology of law, for example, the equilibrium approach is likely to be associated with the old—and demonstrably unsatisfactory, if not wrong—theory that laws grow "organically" out of people's values and habits, whereas the constraint approach would lead to a more adequate, if apparently more Machiavellian, view of the genesis of laws. To the equilibrium theorist, conflict must forever remain a *diabolus ex machina*, the product of an abstract enemy without or an inexplicable dysfunction within, whereas to the constraint theorist it comes of necessity from the resistance provoked by the exercise of power. Social stratification in the equilibrium approach expresses an objective consensus on the "functional importance" of social positions; in the constraint approach it comes from the selective application of sanctions and thus expresses the relationship between social positions and the ruling values. . . .

## IV

Let us move on, therefore, to the second kind of question raised by the ancient problem of justice, namely the analysis of the political process, or of more specific events involving total societies. How do Socratic and Thrasymachean views of justice fare if we apply them to specific problems whose theoretical solutions we are in a position to test empirically?

Clearly, there is no answering this question in the abstract. I have therefore selected a problem that to my mind critically tests any total social analysis purporting to explain the political process: the rise and success of National Socialism in Germany. Here we encounter a dramatic sequence of political events with obvious social undercurrents and ramifications. If our theories of the political process are worth anything at all, they should enable us to explain why what happened had to happen. Since ample documentation of the events that took place in Germany both before and after 1933 is available today, it would seem possible to test almost any theory put forward.

The difficulty of accounting for the rise and persistence of Nazism by traditional social theories makes this problem even better for our purposes. A Marxian theory of class conflict does little to explain why

[12] J. Locke. *Second Treatise of Government.* New ed., New York: Liberal Arts Press, 1952, p. 4.

the working class was as hopelessly divided as the entrepreneurial class. Some of the historians who have described the events of the 1920's and 1930's in Germany in great detail have pronounced them inevitable, i.e., have claimed that by some mysterious transformation the chronological sequence of events is a causal sequence as well; but they have scarcely succeeded in convincing even their colleagues. Inveterate metaphysicians continue to speak, following Tacitus, of some strange infection in the German soul that pervades Germany's body politic and causes occasional outbreaks of fever; but they pay little heed to the extraordinary changeability of social structures and indeed of human nature, which exceeds even the imagination of social scientists. Champions of comparative research have brought out certain features of German society that may well have a bearing on the rise of National Socialism, but that unfortunately were also present in countries whose political history took a very different course from Germany's for reasons that usually go unexplained. There are other explanations, but to this day none that can be called fully satisfactory, so that the attempt to apply our competing orientations to this problem is more than a pedagogical exercise.

In his *Framework for Political Analysis*, David Easton mentions National Socialism twice; and though he would obviously have much more to say on the subject if he dealt with it systematically, these two remarks so clearly reveal the deficiencies of the equilibrium approach that I should like to take them as a point of departure for my argument against it. First, Easton observes that despite various profound changes "a political system has managed to persist in the United States over the years." This is a rather cautious remark, but it is followed by a surprisingly incautious one: "Similarly in Germany, although the Imperial order fell to the Weimar Republic which in turn yielded to the Nazi regime to be succeeded by a third order after World War II, some form of political system persisted. Change does not seem to be incompatible with continuity."[13] This may well be true—but what a miserable, indeed almost inhuman, way to describe the most dramatic changes in the composition and substance of Germany's political order!

Even in its own context, Easton's formulation is rather extreme; but it serves to show that an equilibrium approach cannot come to terms with certain substantive problems of change. Equilibrium theorists are interested above all in the continuity of the system, and

[13]D. Easton. *A Framework for Political Analysis*. Englewood Cliffs, N.J.: Prentice-Hall, 1965, p. 84.

in this respect the Nazis did them the special favor of establishing their rule within the existing order, which was then changed—adapted perhaps?—in a series of steps, in other words gradually, after 1933. What analysis of change there is in studies based on the equilibrium model never penetrates to such substantive questions as whether a regime is liberal or totalitarian, or whether the determining elements of a society are military, economic, or narrowly political. The equilibrium theorist may claim, of course, that he never wanted to tackle this type of question in the first place, and there is some justice to this claim. But the fact remains that even if he wanted to, he could not do so with the theoretical resources at his disposal, and that a good deal can be said for wanting to look at the substance of change. Equilibrium theories lend themselves to explaining continuity alone, and even this only with respect to the most formal aspects of the political system.

It is only to be expected, then, that when equilibrium theorists come to explaining the changes they like to describe as adaptations. they generally have recourse to random factors, which they often introduce very crudely. Later in the same book Easton says, "Although the German political system shifted [*shifted!*] from the Weimar Republic to a totalitarian regime and in this way adapted to the stresses attendant upon defeat in World War I and its ensuing economic inflation, a considerable range of alternatives was possible."[14] We learn that Germany's political regime "shifted," and that it did so by a process of "adaptation," which was a response to "stresses." But where did the "stresses" come from? Here Easton seriously offers us the half-baked explanation of the Nazis' seizure of power that has been offered so often in the past, notably by the Nazis themselves. The stresses came from defeat in World War I, that is, from the Treaty of Versailles. Did the treaty make a National Socialist response inevitable? And if so, by what strange law of human nature or society? The inflation, of course, was not "ensuing" in any sense, but by impoverishing the self-employed middle classes it was bound to have some effect on Germany's politics; yet it would seem that the German political system adapted very well to this stress, since the five years following the inflation were the only stable years of the Weimar Republic!

Finally, and most important, how does Easton set about identifying his "stresses"? Does their identification follow in any way from his general approach? Seemingly not; in fact, the "stresses" are introduced at random. To be sure, Easton has done rather badly even for

[14] *Ibid.*, p. 89.

an equilibrium theorist; Parsons, for example, did much better in "Democracy and Social Structure in Pre-Nazi Germany." But the methodological basis is the same in both cases, and its weakness shows that the equilibrium theory is ill-adapted to identifying the rate, depth, and direction of social change in pre-Nazi and Nazi Germany.

However, we must now ask how Thrasymachus would acquit himself if he were faced with the problem of explaining National Socialism. Would he really do much better? Probably not well enough to satisfy our rigorous methodological standards; still, some of the broad advantages of his approach are readily demonstrated. To begin with, a constraint approach leads us to recognize the Nazi seizure of power as an important problem for analysis. Second, it enables us to focus on the internal processes in German society that may account for the events of 1933. Third, a developed Thrasymachean approach would systematically guide us to some of the factors that determine the rate, depth, and direction of change. Where we would fail, or at least temporarily fall short of our expectations, would be in the technical refinement of identifying empirically some of the conditions that we can describe in general theoretical terms.

Any given political situation—such as that of January 29, 1933, in Germany—may be described in terms of the antagonism between power and resistance. As long as power is exercised within certain boundaries set by social structures, and is therefore stronger than the resistance inevitably offered to it—or, in less abstract terms, so long as the ruling groups are effectively superior to the ruled—we can analyze the course a society takes in terms of the interests, goals, and social personalities of those in power. From 1929 on, the interplay of power and resistance in Germany found the powerful increasingly weak, and their opponents correspondingly strong. In the end, it became virtually impossible to exercise power effectively, and completely impossible to control those in opposition. As the status of those in power became more and more precarious, their opponents prepared to take over and translate their interests into norms.

So far, this description seems no less formal than the equilibrium theorist's. But then, a description is merely the beginning of analysis, and the crucial step is the next one. Both power and resistance are structured socially. Those in power pursue certain interests by virtue of their position; and by these interests certain groups in society are tied to them. Similarly, opposition is based on interests, and social groups with these interests adhere to the opposition cause. As the history of the Weimar Republic took its course, there were fewer and fewer groups whose interests could best be satisfied within the existing constitutional order, and, conversely, more and more groups who impatiently demanded a new political system. In the end, even those in positions of power began to doubt their seemingly vested interest in the status quo, and at least three in many respects incompatible groups—the National Socialists, the Communists, and the traditionalist German Nationalists—united for a short time, a very short time, to dislodge those in power and replace them with a new set of leaders.

The next step in our analysis would take us to the conditions under which such alliances, doubts, and ambitions come into being. Note, however, that the direction of the changes of the early 1930's can already be inferred to a considerable extent from the analysis to this point. Given the broad range of the opposition and the weakness of those in power in the final stages of the Weimar Republic, it was predictable that even sweeping changes would meet with little effective resistance for a while. It was clear, moreover, from the interests of those who tried to destroy the Weimar Republic that the new regime would not be democratic; and equally clear from the relative strengths of the interest groups involved that it would not be Communist either.

In this brief outline, we have passed over literally dozens of questions to which this approach gives rise. For example, who were the elites and what were their politics? At what point and why did middle-class groups reject the existing order and go over to resistance? To what extent can an analysis of this sort predict which points in the National Socialist program would be realized and which dropped? How are we to explain the temporary union between traditionalists and totalitarian modernists?

As we go on asking these questions, two things at least become obvious. One is that we are still a long way from a satisfactory explanation of the Nazis' rise to power; the other is that in any such explanation we shall have to supplant formal theories with historical description and apt interpretation. It follows that the framework of a Thrasymachean analysis of change is also quite unfinished, and to this extent praising Thrasymachus is praising a mere program after all. But there is more to be said: namely, that by taking the approach I am urging here, we can escape the melancholy emptiness of formal analysis. To be sure, an equilibrium theorist can pride himself on being at least scientific, even if he does not have much to tell us about his subject; but a constraint theorist can afford to remain much closer to the richness and color of events.

There is no conflict, no basic methodological incompatibility, between the study of history and a Thrasymachean approach to the study of society, much as the epistemological goals of historiography and sociology may differ. The historian's insistence on the uniqueness of events (as opposed to the search for empty generalities) and his preference for interpretative analysis may be unsatisfactory in strict theoretical terms, but they are essential, both as a stimulus and as a component, to the approach I am advocating here. In this sense, our approach may combine the vitality of an account of real events with the excitement of theoretical explanation.[15]

There are events more obviously suited to this approach that the National Socialist seizure of power in Germany. Traditional revolutions, for example (the French, the Russian, perhaps the Cuban and the Hungarian), defy all but the most vacuous analysis in equilibrium terms; for when we say that in all cases internal stresses became so severe as to disrupt temporarily the very continuity of the system, we are saying almost nothing. In the theory of revolution, which has been one of the more distinguished branches of social analysis since Tocqueville and Marx, power has never figured as a mere medium of exchange or an almost randomly chosen point in a feedback process. Of course revolutions are exceptional events—but are they more exceptional than the perfect equilibrium of stagnation? And if not, might we not find a better clue to the more ordinary types of change in the special case of revolutions than in the special case of stagnation?

## V

Though I have made my own opinion clear, I realize that so far I have offered no dramatic proof for the superiority of the Thrasymachean approach over the Socratic. Given the present technical refinement of social science, it may well be impossible today to offer such proof with respect to the area we have just discussed, that of social analysis. But when it comes to our third and final area of discussion, political theory, the picture is considerably clearer; indeed, it is with regard to the problem of constructing the good society that our two approaches have their most dramatically contrary implications. And at all times, or so it seems to me, the arguments have overwhelmingly favored a Hobbesian solution to the Hobbesian problem of order.

One may imagine a delightful country in which power is exercised on behalf of the whole society and with its support. Political decisions

---

[15] It is desirable to discriminate here between the two very different forms taken by analysis of change. One is structural, based on the analysis of roles and role interests, and is thus largely formal. The other is historical, a matter of actual groups and their actual goals, and is accordingly substantive. Although the two may be related, they are by no means identical. For example, whereas the work of C. Wright Mills might be put in the historical class, my *Class and Class Conflict*, Stanford, Calif.: Stanford University Press (1959), 4th ed., is closer to the structural.

are essentially the expression of a common or general will. Power is not a zero-sum concept, but a currency of which every citizen has his share. A universal system of participation, an undisturbed flow of communications, characterizes the political process and its inherent "justice."

But, as so often, it is worth taking a second look at this pleasing picture. What happens, for example, if somebody does not agree with the alleged general will? This should not happen, of course, but what if it does? If the theory of the general will is made a dogma, the deviant will have to be persecuted, and if necessary exiled; if he is not, the theory is refuted. What happens if someone gets an idea about how to do things better and gathers support for it? And above all, what if those in power forget about the feedback processes and begin to hoard the cherished currency of power?

The answer is the same in every case. Either the general will is upheld by the use of force (it is for urging the use of force in this circumstance that Rousseau is sometimes called the father of totalitarian democracy), or force is not used and the general will is discredited. In terms of political theory, the assumption of certainty implicit in all equilibrium theories, or at least in their ideal-type extremes, turns out to be a deadly weapon against individual freedom in a living, changing society.

By contrast, the society envisioned by Hobbes, or Thrasymachus, is not very appealing at first sight. Its virtues become clear only when we consider that institutions exist to protect men from the badness of their fellowmen rather than as monuments of consensus.[16] The underlying assumption of all constraint theories of politics is that man lives in a world of uncertainty. Since nobody is capable of giving only right answers, we have to protect ourselves from the tyranny of wrong answers, and that includes the tyranny of a stagnant status quo. Institutions have to be set up in such a way as to accommodate change, conflict, and the interplay of power and resistance. There is no foolproof recipe for creating such institutions, and someday we may well conclude that parliaments, elections, and the other traditional democratic political machinery are only one of many arrangements of roughly equal effectiveness. In any case, such institutions should allow for conflict; they should be designed to control power rather than to camouflage it behind an ideology of consensus, and they should permit change even in the unwieldy structure of a complex modern society.

[16] This somewhat cynical definition of institutions I owe to my former colleague, the Tübingen political scientist, Theodor Eschenburg.

These conflicting principles of political theory—totalitarianism and liberalism—are what Karl Popper and others would call the pragmatic implications of the two views I have discussed in this essay. Human beings need not be consistent to survive, and it may well be fortunate that they are often very inconsistent indeed. One may hold a view but be horrified by its implications; and I suspect that few of the equilibrium theorists, certainly none of those I mentioned, deserve to be identified with totalitarian political theory. But the fact that inconsistency is psychologically viable does not lessen the logical force, and above all the moral force, of consistency. A liberal theory of politics is plausible in part because it shares certain assumptions with scientific analysis and para-theory. One is the assumption of uncertainty. Another is the relation between power, conflict, and change. In view of the apparent persistence of change, this assumption seems likely to play a part in any effort to formulate a general explanatory theory.

The pragmatic implications of our two approaches for the shape of the good society may thus be turned around, so that the theoretical and para-theoretical approaches appear as implications of a pragmatic, normative notion of justice. It is this relationship that seems to me to tip the scales finally in favor of Thrasymachus. I make this statement without qualification; that is to say, I no longer take the tolerant view that the two approaches discussed are essentially equivalent ways of understanding a given problem or of understanding two different sets of problems.[17]

It can be argued, I think—and I have at least tried to argue—that the constraint approach is superior to the equilibrium approach. There is no problem that can be described in equilibrium terms that cannot be described at least as well in constraint terms, and there are many problems that Thrasymachus can tackle but Socrates cannot. The constraint approach, being more general, more plausible, and generally more informative about the problems of social and political life, should for these reasons replace the approach now so surprisingly in vogue in social science. . . .

---

[17] I tentatively espoused the more tolerant view in "Out of Utopia" as well as in *Class and Class Conflict*. Another repudiation of it appears in "On the Origin of Inequality among Men" [Both essays contained in *Essays in the Theory of Society*, Stanford, 1968].

*3*

# Social Conflict and the
# Theory of Social Change

*Lewis A. Coser*

≪≪-≪≪-≪≪-≪≪-≪≪-≪≪-≪≪-≪≪-≪≪-≪≪-≪≪-≪≪-≪≪-≪≪-≪≪-≪≪-≪≪-≪≪-≪≪-≪≪-≪≪-≪≪-≪≪-≪≪-≪≪-≪≪-≪≪

## EDITORS' COMMENT

*Conflict* is somewhat of a weasel word. Years ago, United States Army information and education lectures made studious reference to the "Korean conflict." Thus, one says "conflict" when he wants to avoid saying "war." Modern sociology tends to reserve conflict for situations of group antagonism where the issues are persistently defined and not casual, and where organized physical violence is not necessarily the distinguishing feature. Conflict involves endemic discontent relative to the distribution of the goods of society, but it is not combat pure and simple. However, if society lacks the sufficient means of adjusting its conflicts, there may be escalation through progressively premeditated forms of group violence to literal conditions of warfare. Conse-

SOURCE. Lewis A. Coser, "Social Conflict and the Theory of Social Change," from *Continuities in the Study of Social Conflict* (New York: The Free Press, 1968), pp. 19–35. Reprinted with permission of the publishers. Copyright 1968 by the Macmillan Co.

quently, although, as Lewis Coser insists, it would be a serious error to confuse the functions of conflict with the functions of war, it may be fruitful to approach the study of internal war by way of the theory of conflict.

As opposed to Dahrendorf's general theory of society (see the previous selection), Coser's analysis commences with a modified acceptance of the structural-functional thesis. He does not insist on constraint as the primary feature of social life. On the other hand, he acknowledges the wide mission of conflict in society, and his point of departure is the discrimination of the roles and types of conflict. An earlier and highly regarded work, *The Functions of Social Conflict* (New York: The Free Press, 1956) reexplores the contention of the German sociologist Georg Simmel that "conflict is a form of socialization" and seeks to set forth the conditions where this is the case. If "a certain degree of conflict is an essential element in group formation and the persistence of group life" (*Functions*, p. 31), then it is misleading to treat conflict merely as an endemic "disease," and the task becomes one of identifying the kinds of societies that contain and channel conflicts successfully while capitalizing on their "functional" features. The general argument that Coser deploys, if recast in a political vocabulary, bears a more than casual resemblance to what Guido Dorso says about "political struggle" (Selection 4), although the treatment of elites clearly sets them apart.

According to Coser, a main challenge that society faces is "the institutionalization and tolerance of conflict" (*Functions*, p. 152). Like Eckstein (see Selection 9 in this volume), he finds that revolutionary or structural change is heavily implicated with the values and the policies of the incumbent, and he accuses "the rigidity . . . which permits hostilities to accumulate and to be channeled along one major line of cleavage once they break out in conflict" (*Functions*, p. 157). The saving devices are, broadly speaking, the ways of distributing conflict (inasmuch as their multiplicity varies inversely with their intensity); and "safety-valve institutions" that relieve repressed social frustration and allow conflict to be directed into productive forms. Coser also points out that personal or "realistic" conflict is safer than the ideologized and idealized group conflict, often stimulated by intellectuals, which tends to take a "radical and merciless" turn (*Functions*, p. 118).

In the following essay Coser supports, by implication, the same normative notions of what a conflict-regulating society should be. He also calls attention to the analytical problem of treating conflict as a means of inducing change *within* a social system and change *between* social systems. In the former case, he takes his cue from Sorel's notion that the absence of conflict promotes decadence. In the latter, he expands on Marx's observation that the dysfunctions (or "negative moment") of one social system may contain in germ the functional prerequisites for its successor.

All of this is highly relevant to the analysis of internal war movements and patterns if the scholar takes special care (and care is needed) not to read back upon his field of inquiry utopian feelings or teleological projections of the good society. Aside from Coser's creative insights into the problem of social change by way of the concepts of "functional" and "dysfunctional" conflict, he also opts normatively for a criterion of "flexibility." And it is not always easy to see what that flexibility consists of.

# SOCIAL CONFLICT AND THE THEORY OF SOCIAL CHANGE

Lewis A. Coser

This [essay] attempts to examine some of the functions of social conflict in the process of social change. I shall first deal with some functions of conflict *within* social systems, more specifically with its relation to institutional rigidities, technical progress, and productivity, and will then concern myself with the relation between social conflict and the changes *of* social systems.

A central observation of George Sorel in his *Reflections on Violence* which has not as yet been accorded sufficient attention by sociologists may serve as a convenient springboard. Sorel wrote:

> We are today faced with a new and unforeseen fact—a middle class which seeks to weaken its own strength. The race of bold captains who made the greatness of modern industry disappears to make way for an ultracivilized aristocracy which asks to be allowed to live in peace.
>
> The threatening decadence may be avoided if the proletariat hold on with obstinacy to revolutionary ideas. *The antagonistic classes influence each other in a partly indirect but decisive manner.* Everything

may be saved if the proletariat, by their use of violence, restore to the middle class something of its former energy.[1]

Sorel's specific doctrine of class struggle is not of immediate concern here. What is important for us is the idea that conflict (which Sorel calls violence, using the word in a very special sense) prevents the ossification of the social system by exerting pressure for innovation and creativity. Though Sorel's call to action was addressed to the working class and its interests, he conceived it to be of general importance for the total social system; to his mind the gradual disappearance of class conflict might well lead to the decadence of European culture. A social system, he felt, was in need of conflict if only to renew its energies and revitalize its creative forces.

This conception seems to be more generally applicable than to class struggle alone. Conflict within and between groups in a society can prevent accommodations and habitual relations from progressively impoverishing creativity. The clash of values and interests, the tension between what is and what some groups feel ought to be, the conflict between vested interests and new strata and groups demanding their share of power, wealth, and status, have been productive of vitality; note for example the contrast between the "frozen world" of the Middle Ages and the burst of creativity that accompanied the thaw that set in with Renaissance civilization.

This is, in effect, the application of John Dewey's theory of consciousness and thought as arising in the wake of obstacles to the interaction of groups.

> Conflict is the gadfly of thought. It stirs us to observation and memory. It instigates to invention. It shocks us out of sheep-like passivity, and sets us at noting and contriving. . . . Conflict is a *sine qua non* of reflection and ingenuity.[2]

Conflict not only generates new norms, new institutions, as I have pointed out elsewhere,[3] it may be said to be stimulating directly in the economic and technological realm. Economic historians often have pointed out that much technological improvement has resulted from the conflict activity of trade unions through the raising of wage levels. A rise in wages usually has led to a substitution of capital investment for labor and hence to an increase in the volume of investment. Thus

---

[1] George Sorel, *Reflections on Violence*, Chapter 2, par. II.

[2] John Dewey, *Human Nature and Conduct*, New York, The Modern Library, 1930, p. 300.

[3] Lewis A. Coser, *The Functions of Social Conflict*, New York, The Free Press, 1956.

the extreme mechanization of coal-mining in the United States has been partly explained by the existence of militant unionism in the American coalfields.[4] A recent investigation by Sidney C. Sufrin[5] points to the effects of union pressure, "goading management into technical improvement and increased capital investment." Very much the same point was made recently by the conservative British *Economist* which reproached British unions for their "moderation" which it declared in part responsible for the stagnation and low productivity of British capitalism; it compared their policy unfavorably with the more aggressive policies of American unions whose constant pressure for higher wages has kept the American economy dynamic.[6]

This point raises the question of the adequacy and relevancy of the "human relations" approach in industrial research and management practice. The "human relations" approach stresses the "collective purpose of the total organization" of the factory, and either denies or attempts to reduce conflicts of interests in industry.[7] But a successful reduction of industrial conflict may have unanticipated dysfunctional consequences for it may destroy an important stimulus for technological innovation.

It often has been observed that the effects of technological change have weighed most heavily upon the worker.[8] Both informal and formal organization of workers represent in part an attempt to mitigate the insecurities attendant upon the impact of unpredictable introduction of change in the factory.[9] But by organizing in unions workers gain a feeling of security through the effective conduct of institutionalized conflict with management and thus exert pressure on management

[4] Cf. McAlister Coleman, *Men and Coal*, New York, Farrar and Rinehart, 1943.

[5] *Union Wages and Labor's Earnings*, Syracuse, Syracuse University Press, 1951.

[6] Quoted by Will Herberg, "When Social Scientists View Labor," *Commentary*, December 1951, XII, 6, pp. 590–596. See also Seymour Melman, *Dynamic Factors in Industrial Productivity*, Oxford, Blackwell, 1956, on the effects of rising wage levels on productivity.

[7] See the criticism of the Mayo approach by Daniel Bell, "Adjusting Men to Machines," *Commentary*, January 1947, pp. 79–88; C. Wright Mills, "The Contribution of Sociology to the Study of Industrial Relations," *Proceedings of the Industrial Relations Research Association*, 1948, pp. 199–222.

[8] See, for example, R. K. Merton, "The Machine, The Workers and The Engineer," *Social Theory and Social Structure*, New York, The Free Press, 1949, pp. 317–328; George Friedmann, *Industrial Society*, New York, 1956.

[9] For informal organization and change, see Roethlisberger and Dickson, *Management and the Worker*, Cambridge, 1939, especially pp. 567–568; for formal organization, see Selig Perlman, *The Theory of the Labor Movement*; on general relations between technology and labor, see Elliot D. Smith and Richard C. Nyman, *Technology and Labor*, New Haven, Yale University Press, 1939.

to increase their returns by the invention of further cost-reducing devices. The search for mutual adjustment, understanding, and "unity" between groups who find themselves in different life situations and have different life chances calls forth the danger that Sorel warns of, namely that the further development of technology would be seriously impaired.

The emergence of invention and of technological change in modern Western society, with its institutionalization of science as an instrument for making and remaking the world, was made possible with the gradual emergence of a pluralistic and hence conflict-charged structure of human relations. In the unitary order of the medieval guild system, "no one was permitted to harm others by methods that enabled him to produce more quickly and more cheaply than they. Technical progress took on the appearance of disloyalty. The ideal was stable conditions in a stable industry."[10]

In the modern Western world, just as in the medieval world, vested interests exert pressure for the maintenance of established routines; yet the modern Western institutional structure allows room for freedom of conflict. The structure no longer being unitary, vested interests find it difficult to resist the continuous stream of change-producing inventions. Invention, as well as its application and utilization, is furthered through the ever-renewed challenge to vested interests, as well as by the conflicts between the vested interests themselves.[11]

Once old forms of traditional and unitary integration broke down, the clash of conflicting interests and values, now no longer constrained by the rigidity of the medieval structure, pressed for new forms of unification and integration. Thus deliberate control and rationalized regulation of "spontaneous" processes was required in military and political, as well as in economic institutions. Bureaucratic forms of organization with their emphasis on calculable, methodical, and disciplined behavior[12] arise at roughly the same period in which the unitary medieval structure broke down. But with the rise of bureaucratic types of organization peculiar new resistances to change made their appearance. The need for reliance on predictability exercises pressure towards the rejection of innovation which is perceived as interference

[10]Henri Pirenne, *Economic and Social History of Medieval Europe*, London, Routledge and Kegan Paul, 1949, p. 186.

[11] See W. E. Ogburn, *Social Change*, New York, B. W. Huebsch, 1923, for the theory of "cultural lag" due to "vested interests."

[12] Cf. Max Weber, "Bureaucracy," *From Max Weber*, Gerth and Mills, ed., pp. 196–244. For the pathology of bureaucracy, see R. K. Merton, "Bureaucratic Structure and Personality," *Social Theory and Social Structure*, op. cit. pp. 151–60.

with routine. Conflicts involving a "trial through battle" are unpredictable in their outcome, and therefore unwelcome to the bureaucracy that must strive towards an ever-widening extension of the area of predictability and calculability of results. But social arrangements that have become habitual and totally patterned are subject to the blight of ritualism. If attention is focused exclusively on the habitual clues, "people may be unfitted by being fit in an unfit fitness,"[13] so that their habitual training becomes an incapacity to adjust to new conditions. To quote Dewey again: "The customary is taken for granted; it operates subconsciously. Breach of wont and use is focal; it forms 'consciousness'."[14] A group or a system that no longer is challenged is no longer capable of a creative response. It may subsist, wedded to the eternal yesterday of precedent and tradition, but it is no longer capable of renewal.[15]

"Only a hitch in the working of habit occasions emotion and provokes thought."[16] Conflict within and between bureaucratic structures provides means for avoiding the ossification and ritualism that threaten their form of organization.[17] Conflict, thought apparently dysfunctional for highly rationalized systems, may actually have important latent functional consequences. By attacking and overcoming the resistance to innovation and change that seems to be an "occupational psychosis" always threatening the bureaucratic office holder, it can help to insure that the system does not stifle in the deadening routine of habituation and that in the planning activity itself creativity and invention can be applied.

We have so far discussed change within systems, but changes of systems are of perhaps even more crucial importance for sociological inquiry. Here the sociology of Karl Marx serves us well. Writes Marx in a polemic against Proudhon:

> Feudal production also had two antagonistic elements, which were
> equally designated by the names of *good side* and *bad side* of feudal-

---

[13] Kenneth Burke, *Permanence and Change*, New York, New Republic, 1936, p. 18.

[14] John Dewey, *The Public and Its Problems*, Chicago, Gateway Books, 1946, p. 100.

[15] This is, of course, a central thesis of Arnold Toynbee's monumental *A Study of History*, O.U.P.

[16] John Dewey, *Human Nature and Conduct, op. cit.*, p. 178.

[17] See, for example, Melville Dalton, "Conflicts Between Staff and Line Managerial Officers," *Am. Soc. R.*, XV (1950), pp. 342–351. The author seems to be unaware of the positive functions of this conflict, yet his data clearly indicate the "innovating potential" of conflict between staff and line.

ism, without regard being had to the fact that it is always the evil side which finishes by overcoming the good side. It is the bad side that produces the movement which makes history, by constituting the struggle. If at the epoch of the reign of feudalism the economists, enthusiastic over the virtues of chivalry, the delightful harmony between rights and duties, the patriarchal life of the towns, the prosperous state of domestic industry in the country, of the development of industry organized in corporations, guilds and fellowships, in fine of all which constitutes the beautiful side of feudalism, had proposed to themselves the problem of eliminating all which cast a shadow upon this lovely picture—serfdom, privilege, anarchy—what would have been the result? All the elements which constituted the struggle would have been annihilated, and the development of the bourgeoisie would have been stifled in the germ. They would have set themselves the absurd problem of eliminating history.[18]

According to Marx, conflict leads not only to ever-changing relations within the existing social structure, but the total social system undergoes transformation through conflict.

During the feudal period, the relations between serf and lord or between burgher and nobility underwent many changes both in law and in fact. Yet conflict finally led to a breakdown of all feudal relations and hence to the rise of a new social system governed by different patterns of social relations.

It is Marx's contention that the negative element, the opposition, conditions the change when conflict between the subgroups of a system becomes so sharpened that at a certain point this system breaks down. Each social system contains elements of strain and of potential conflict; if in the analysis of the social structure of a system these elements are ignored, if the adjustment of patterned relations is the only focus of attention, then it is not possible to anticipate basic social change. Exclusive attention to wont and use, to the customary and habitual, bars access to an understanding of possible latent elements of strain that under certain conditions eventuate in overt conflict and possibly in a basic change of the social structure. This attention should be focused, in Marx's view, on what evades and resists the patterned normative structure and on the elements pointing to new and alternative patterns emerging from the existing structure. What is diagnosed as disease from the point of view of the institutionalized pattern may, in fact, says Marx, be the first birth pang of a new one to come; not wont and use but the break of wont and use is focal. The "matters-of-fact" of a "given state of affairs" when viewed in the light

[18] Karl Marx, *The Poverty of Philosophy*, Chicago, Charles H. Kerr and Co., 1910, p. 132.

of Marx's approach, become limited, transitory; they are regarded a containing the germs of a process that leads beyond them.[19]

Yet, not all social systems contain the same degree of conflict and strain. The sources and incidence of conflicting behavior in each particular system vary according to the type of structure, the patterns of social mobility, of ascribing and achieving status and of allocating scarce power and wealth, as well as the degree to which a specific form of distribution of power, resources, and status is accepted by the component actors within the different subsystems. But if, within any social structure, there exists an excess of claimants over opportunities for adequate reward, there arises strain and conflict.

The distinction between change *of* systems and changes *within* systems is, of course, a relative one. There is always some sort of continuity between a past and a present, or a present and a future social system; societies do not die the way biological organisms do, for it is difficult to assign precise points of birth or death to societies as we do with biological organisms. One may claim that all that can be observed is a change of the organization of social relations; but from one perspective such change may be considered reestablishment of equilibrium whereas from another it may be seen as the formation of a new system.

A natural scientist, describing the function of earthquakes, recently stated admirably what could be considered the function of conflict.

> There is nothing abnormal about an earthquake. An unshakeable earth would be a dead earth. A quake is the earth's way of maintaining its equilibrium, a form of adjustment that enables the crust to yield to stresses that tend to reorganize and redistribute the material of which it is composed. . . . The larger the shift, the more violent the quake, and the more frequent the shifts, the more frequent are the shocks.[20]

Whether the quake is violent or not, it has served to maintain or reestablish the equilibrium of the earth. Yet the shifts may be small

[19] For an understanding of Marx's methodology and its relation to Hegelian philosophy, see Herbert Marcuse, *Reason and Revolution*, N.Y., O.U.P., 1941.

Note the similarity with John Dewey's thought: "Where there is change, there is of necessity numerical plurality, multiplicity, and from variety comes opposition, strife. Change is alteration, or othering, and this means diversity. Diversity means division, and division means two sides and their conflict." *Reconstruction in Philosophy*, N.Y., Mentor Books, 1950, p. 97. See also the able discussion of the deficiencies of Talcott Parsons' sociological theories by David Lockwood, *B.J.S.*, June, 1956.

[20] Waldemar Kaemfert, "Science in Review," *New York Times*, July 27, 1952.

changes of geological formations, or they may be changes in the structural relations between land and water, for example.

At what point the shift is large enough to warrant the conclusion that a change *of* the system has taken place, is hard to determine. Only if one deals with extreme instances are ideal types—such as feudalism, capitalism, and so on—easily applied. A system based on serfdom, for example, may undergo considerable change within—*vide* the effects of the Black Death on the social structure of medieval society; and even an abolition of serfdom may not necessarily be said to mark the end of an old and the emergence of a new system, *vide* nineteenth-century Russia.

If "it is necessary to distinguish clearly between the processes *within* the system and processes of change *of* the system," as Professor Parsons has pointed out,[21] an attempt should be made to establish a heuristic criterion for this distinction. We propose to talk of a change *of* system when all major structural relations, its basic institutions, and its prevailing value system have been drastically altered. (In cases where such a change takes place abruptly, as, for example, the Russian Revolution, there should be no difficulty. It is well to remember, however, that transformations of social systems do not always consist in an abrupt and simultaneous change of all basic institutions. Institutions may change gradually, by mutual adjustment, and it is only over a period of time that the observer will be able to claim that the social system has undergone a basic transformation in its structural relations.) In concrete historical reality, no clear-cut distinctions exist. Change *of* system may be the result (or the sum total) of previous changes *within* the system. This does not, however, detract from the usefulness of the theoretical distinction.

It is precisely Marx's contention that the change from feudalism to a different type of social system can be understood only through an investigation of the stresses and strains *within* the feudal system. Whether given forms of conflict will lead to changes in the social system or to breakdown and to formation of a new system will depend on the rigidity and resistance to change, or inversely on the elasticity of the control mechanisms of the system.

It is apparent, however, that the rigidity of the system and the intensity of conflict within it are not independent of each other. Rigid systems which suppress the incidence of conflict exert pressure towards the emergence of radical cleavages and violent forms of conflict. More

[21] Talcott Parsons, *The Social System*, New York, The Free Press, 1951, p. 481.

I owe much to Prof. Parsons' treatment of this distinction despite a number of major disagreements with his theory of social change.

elastic systems, which allow the open and direct expression of conflict within them and which adjust to the shifting balance of power that these conflicts both indicate and bring about, are less likely to be menaced by basic and explosive alignments within their midst.

In what follows, the distinction between strains, conflicts, and disturbances within a system that lead to a reestablishment of equilibrium, and conflicts that lead to the establishment of new systems and new types of equilibria, will be examined.[22] Such an examination will be most profitably begun by considering what Thorstein Veblen[23] has called "Vested Interests."[24]

Any social system implies an allocation of power, as well as wealth and status positions among individual actors and component subgroups. As has been pointed out, there is never complete concordance between what individuals and groups within a system consider their just due and the system of allocation. Conflict ensues in the effort of various frustrated groups and individuals to increase their share of gratification. Their demands will encounter the resistance of those who previously had established a "vested interest" in a given form of distribution of honor, wealth, and power.

To the vested interests, an attack against their position necessarily

[22] The concept of *equilibrium* is of great value in social science provided it is used, as by Schumpeter, as a point of reference permitting measurement of departures from it. "The concept of a state equilibrium, although no such state may ever be realized, is useful and indeed indispensable for purpose of analyses and diagnosis, as a point of reference" (Joseph A. Schumpeter, *Business Cycle*, N.Y., McGraw Hill, 1939, p. 69). But certain types of sociological functionalism tend to move from this methodological use of the concept to one that has some clearly ideological features. The ideal type of equilibrium, in this illegitimate use, becomes a normative instead of a methodological concept. Attention is focused on the maintenance of a system that is somehow identified with the ethically desirable (see Merton's discussion of this ideological misuse of functionalism is *Social Theory and Social Structure*, *op. cit.*, pp. 38 ff. and 116–117; see also my review of Parsons' Essays, *American Journal of Sociology*, 55, March 1950, pp. 502–504). Such theorizing tends to look at all behavior caused by strains and conflict as "deviancy" from the legitimate pattern, thereby creating the perhaps unintended impression that such behavior is somehow "abnormal" in an ethical sense, and obscuring the fact that some "deviant" behavior actually serves the creation of new patterns rather than a simple rejection of the old.

[23] See especially, *The Vested Interests and the State of the Industrial Arts*, New York, 1919.

[24] Max Lerner ("Vested Interests," *Encyclopedia of the Social Sciences*, XV, p. 240) gives the following definition: "When an activity has been pursued so long that the individuals concerned in it have a prescriptive claim to its exercise and its profit, they are considered to have a vested interest in it."

appears as an attack upon the social order.[25] Those who derive privileges from a given system of allocation of status, wealth, and power will perceive an attack upon these prerogatives as an attack against the system itself.

However, mere "frustration" will not lead to a questioning of the legitimacy of the position of the vested interests, and hence to conflict. Levels of aspiration as well as feelings of deprivation are relative to institutionalized expectations and are established through comparison.[26] When social systems have institutionalized goals and values to govern the conduct of competent actors, but limit access to these goals for certain members of the society, "departures from institutional requirements" are to be expected.[27] Similarly, if certain groups within a social system compare their share in power, wealth, and status honor with that of other groups *and* question the legitimacy of this distribution, discontent is likely to ensue. If there exist no institutionalized provisions for the expression of such discontents, departures from what is required by the norms of the social system may occur. These may be limited to "innovation" or they may consist in the rejection of the institutionalized goals. Such rebellion "involves a genuine transvaluation, where the direct or vicarious experience of frustration leads to full denunciation of previously prized values."[28] Thus it will be well to distinguish between those departures from the norms of a society that consist in mere "deviation" and those that involve the formation of distinctive patterns and new value systems.

[25] Veblen has described this aptly: "The code of proprieties, conventionalities, and usages in vogue at any given time and among any given people has more or less the character of an organic whole; so that any appreciable change in one point of the scheme involves something of a change or readjustment of other points also, if not a reorganization all along the line . . . When an attempted reform involves the suppression or thoroughgoing remodeling of an institution of first-rate importance in the conventional scheme, it is immediately felt that a serious derangement of the entire scheme would result . . . Any of these innovations would, we are told, 'shake the social structure to its base," 'reduce society to chaos,' . . . etc. The aversion to change is in large part an aversion to the bother of making the readjustment which any given change will necessitate" (*The Theory of the Leisure Class*, New York, The Modern Library, pp. 201–203).

[26] See Robert K. Merton and Alice S. Kitt, "Contribution to the Theory of Reference Group Behaviour" for a development of the concept of "relative deprivation" (originally suggested by Stouffer *et al.* in *The American Soldier*) and its incorporation into the framework of a theory of reference groups.

[27] This whole process is exhaustively discussed by Merton in his paper on "Social Structure and Anomie," *Social Theory, op. cit.*

[28] *Ibid.*, p. 145.

What factors lead groups and individuals to question at a certain point the legitimacy of the system of distribution of rewards lies largely outside the scope of the present inquiry. The intervening factors can be sought in the ideological, technological, economic, or any other realm. It is obvious, moreover, that conflict may be a result just as much as a source of change. A new invention, the introduction of a new cultural trait through diffusion, the development of new methods of production or distribution, and such, will have a differential impact within a social system. Some strata will feel it to be detrimental to their material or ideal interests, whereas others will feel their position strengthened through its introduction. Such disturbances in the equilibrium of the system lead to conditions in which groups or individual actors no longer do willingly what they have to do and do willingly what they are not supposed to do. Change, no matter what its source, breeds strain and conflict.

Yet, it may be well to repeat that mere "frustration" and the ensuing strains and tensions do not necessarily lead to group conflict. Individuals under stress may relieve their tension through "acting out" in special safety-valve institutions in as far as they are provided for in the social system; or they may "act out" in a deviant manner that may have serious dysfunctional consequences for the system and bring about change in this way. This, however, does not reduce the frustration from which escape has been sought since it does not attack their source.

If, on the other hand, the strain leads to the emergence of specific new patterns of behavior of whole groups of individuals who pursue "the optimization of gratification"[29] by choosing what they consider appropriate means for the maximization of rewards, social change that reduces the sources of their frustration may come about. This may happen in two ways: if the social system is flexible enough to adjust to conflict situations we will deal with change *within* the system. If, on the other hand, the social system is not able to readjust itself and allows the accumulation of conflict, the "aggressive" groups, imbued with a new system of values that threatens to split the general consensus of the society and imbued with an ideology that "objectifies" their claims, may become powerful enough to overcome the resistance of vested interests and bring about the breakdown of the system and the emergence of a new distribution of social values.[30]

[29] T. Parsons, *The Social System, op. cit.*, p. 498.

[30] R. K. Merton, *Social Theory and Social Structure, op. cit.*, pp. 42–43 and 116–117.

In his *Poverty of Philosophy*, Marx was led to consider the conditions under which economic classes constitute themselves:

> Economic conditions have first transformed the mass of the population into workers. The domination of capital created for this mass a common situation and common interest. This mass was thus already a class as against capital, but not for itself. It is in the struggle . . . that the mass gathers together and constitutes itself as a class for itself. The interests which it defends become class interests.[31]

With this remarkable distinction between class *in itself* and class *for itself* (which unfortunately he didn't elaborate upon in later writings though it informs all of them—if not the writings of most latter-day "Marxists"), Marx illuminates a most important aspect of group formation: group belongingness is established by an objective conflict situation—in this case a conflict of interests;[32] but only by experiencing this antagonism, that is, by becoming aware of it and by acting it out, does the group (or class) establish its identity.

When changes in the equilibrium of a society lead to the formation of new groupings or to the strengthening of existing groupings that set themselves the goal of overcoming resistance of vested interests through conflict, changes in structural relations, as distinct from simple "maladjustment," can be expected.

What Robert Park said about the rise of nationalist and racial movements is more generally applicable:

> They strike me as natural and wholesome disturbances of the social routine, the effect of which is to arouse in those involved a lively sense of common purpose and to give those who feel themselves oppressed the inspiration of a common cause . . . The effect of this

---

[31] Karl Marx, *The Poverty of Philosophy, op. cit.*, pp. 188–189.

[32] This makes it necessary to distinguish between realistic and non-realistic conflict: social conflicts that arise from frustration of specific demands and from estimates of gains of the participants, and that are directed at the presumed frustrating object, may be called realistic conflicts. Non-realistic conflicts, on the other hand, are not occasioned by the rival ends of the antagonists, but by the need for tension release of one or both of them. Some groups may be formed with the mere purpose of releasing tension. Such groups "collectivize" their tensions, so to speak. They can, by definition, only be disruptive rather than creative since they are built on negative rather than positive cathexes. But groups of this kind will remain marginal; their actions cannot bring about social change unless they accompany and strengthen realistic conflict groups. In such cases we deal with an admixture of non-realistic and realistic elements mutually reinforcing each other within the same social movements. Members who join for the mere purpose of tension release are often used for the "dirty work" by the realistic conflict groups.

struggle is to increase the solidarity and improve the morale of the "oppressed" minority.[33]

It is this sense of common purpose arising in and through conflict that is peculiar to the behavior of individuals who meet the challenge of new conditions by a group-forming and value-forming response. Strains that result in no such formations of new conflict groups or strengthening of old ones may contribute to bringing about change, but a type of change that fails to reduce the sources of strain since by definition tension-release behavior does not involve purposive action. Conflict through group action, on the other hand, is likely to result in a "deviancy" that may be the prelude of new patterns and reward system apt to reduce the sources of frustration.

If the tensions that need outlets are continually reproduced within the structure, abreaction through tension-release mechanisms may preserve the system but at the risk of ever-renewed further accumulation of tension. Such accumulation eventuates easily in the eruption of destructive unrealistic conflict. If feelings of dissatisfaction, instead of being suppressed or diverted, are allowed expression against "vested interests," and in this way to lead to the formation of new groupings within the society, the emergence of genuine transvaluations is likely to occur. Sumner saw this very well when he said: "We want to develop symptoms, we don't want to suppress them."[34]

Whether the emergence of such new groupings or the strengthening of old ones with the attendant increase in self-confidence and self-esteem on the part of the participants will lead to a change *of* or *within* the system will depend on the degree of cohesion that the system itself has attained. A well-integrated society will tolerate and even welcome group conflict; only a weakly integrated one must fear it. The great English liberal John Morley said it very well:

> If [the men who are most attached to the reigning order of things] had a larger faith in the stability for which they profess so great an anxiety, they would be more free alike in understanding and temper to deal generously, honestly and effectively with those whom they count imprudent innovators.[35]

[33] Robert E. Park, "Personality and Cultural Conflict," *Publications of the Am. Soc. Soc.*, 25, 1931, pp. 95–110. See p. 107.

[34] Wm. G. Sumner, *War and Other Essays*, p. 241.

[35] John Morley, *On Compromise*, London, Macmillan and Co., 1917, p. 263.

# 4

# Political Class and Ruling Class

*Guido Dorso*

᚛᚛᚛᚛᚛᚛᚛᚛᚛᚛᚛᚛᚛᚛᚛᚛᚛᚛᚛᚛᚛᚛᚛᚛᚛᚛᚛᚛᚛᚛᚛᚛

## EDITORS' COMMENT

With this selection, the work of the Italian political scientist Guido Dorso (1892–1947) reaches American readers for the first time. Unfortunately, because of space restrictions, it has been necessary to abridge the essay "Political Class and Ruling Class." The exclusions pertain chiefly to Dorso's analysis of modern social classes and the competition of political parties. But the fundamental aspects of his theory are presented here without compression.

This is a "grand theory" of political stability and political change, based principally on the European experience that Dorso knew. Although his essay is not about revolution *per se*, an interpretation of political violence is clearly set forth. The reality of political power, according to Dorso, is unabashedly oligarchical. Politics is a contest

SOURCE. Guido Dorso, "Political Class and Ruling Class," from *Dittatura, Classe politica e Classe dirigente* (Turin: Einaudi, 1949), pp. 121–184, excerpted. Reprinted with the permission of the publishers and the Agenzia Letteraria Internazionale, Milan. Copyright 1949 by the Casa Einaudi. Translated by George Armstrong Kelly and Henry Iancovici.

for power, either moderated by the orderly rules of the "political struggle" or intensified by a breakdown of elite exchange. Societies falter when their ruling classes fail to co-opt elements from below at a proper rate. Full-scale revolutions occur when the elite has muffed its mission of providing for the general welfare and when a potentially articulated ruling class is blocked off from positions of authority. These effects are mitigated, but not essentially altered, by the particular traditions of each society.

The reader will not fail to notice that Dorso is working in the peculiarly Italian school initiated by Machiavelli and carried forward by Mosca, Michels, and Pareto. Although sociological analysis is applied in a broad way, the primacy of the "political"—the possession and enjoyment of *political* power—is clear. The political machinery of the British parliamentary system is obviously a realistic norm for the author. He perceives in it a public-spirited refinement of the "political struggle" and the oligarchical principle, constants which lie behind all regimes no matter what "political formulas" they may employ to make their dominance legitimate. Thus the typologies of Aristotle (one, few, and many) and of Montesquieu (republic, monarchy, and despotism), not to mention the more modern categories of writers like Robert Dahl, are brushed aside in favor of a simpler principle.

Dorso went beyond his predecessors Mosca and Pareto in a well-defined sense. Accepting from the latter the notion of the "circulation of elites," he divided the "ruling class" of the former into a "political class" (actually engaged in the leadership of government and opposition) and a ruling class (which supports actual or potential political classes and, when functioning properly, promotes their alternance according to national needs). This creates a three-tiered society in which, ideally, new elites are co-opted to the ruling class without structural damage and appropriate political managers are nominated. Through his class analysis, Dorso reflects the impact of Marxism; by his emphasis on talent and mobility, he prolongs the liberal tradition; and, by adherence to a basic and unchanging notion of the structure of political society, he reveals a conservative strain.

Dorso's scheme is ambiguously an interpretation of actual political life and a norm of performance against which pluralist party democracy must be measured. Despite much Machiavellian tough-talk, Dorso abhors political systems in which the rights of opposition are arbitrarily stifled and attempts to show that this is contrary to the interests of the polity. He was himself a member of the underground resistance to Fascism and a member of the left-center Action Party (whose heroes were Garibaldi and Mazzini) until his premature death. He was also one of a long line of Southerners who pondered and wrote about the "problema del Mezzogiorno." Thus, in continuing the Italian "realist" tradition of political analysis, Dorso was also a democrat. Abhorring both internal violence and elite mismanagement, he sought to rationalize a system of nonviolent competition which, following his predecessors, he called the "political struggle." He, too, in his way, wished for an "end of ideology."

The terms political class, ruling class, subject class, and political struggle translate, respectively classe politica, classe dirigente, classe diretta, and lotta politica. Obviously, they carry certain misleading stresses in the English vocabulary; but there are no convenient or graceful substitutes. We can only caution the reader to make allowance for the fact that these words are not so harsh and Darwinian in Italian as they might appear to be.

The theoretical work of Guido Dorso is further explored at some length by Dante Germino (*Beyond Ideology: The Revival of Political Theory*, New York: Harper & Row, 1967, pp. 109–129). We feel that Germino's praise of Dorso's originality is too hyperbolic. But we have no doubt that this succinct set of propositions relating to stability, change, and violence and summarizing the insights of the "neo-Machiavellian" school merits greater exposure. Whether or not Dorso's analysis of society is empirically viable, it suggests certain insights that should be empirically manageable, as well as a proper sense of the whole. It may be tautological to say that revolution occurs when the ruling class inadequately monitors the political class and when the ascent of certain portions of the subject class to the ruling class is blocked. The ghost of Taine still lingers over this species of interpretation. And yet, if the reader will consult the Eckstein essay included in this volume, he will get a closer appreciation of some of the possibilities for explaining internal war from the perspective of oligarchical breakdown.

# THE POLITICAL CLASS AND
# THE RULING CLASS (Translated by George
# Armstrong Kelly and Henry Iancovici

GUIDO DORSO

## THE THEORY OF THE POLITICAL CLASS

The theory of the political class is rather recent, but its anticipations are ancient. Plato, Sallust, Guicciardini, Machiavelli and Saint-Simon had already hinted at the existence of ruling minorities, but the elaboration of the new doctrine began with the works of Gaetano Mosca and Vilfredo Pareto.

At present the theory is being more fully elaborated, but we can already be sure that people do not attack the theory of the political class on scientific grounds; rather, they offer ideological arguments against it. It is symptomatic that the pre-Marxist socialists, Saint-Simon particularly, were among the first theoreticians of the political class doctrine. However, we cannot ignore that Marxist theory has historically accepted and corroborated the new doctrine by identifying the existence of the political class with the existence of the bourgeoisie, while the political aspect of Marxist ideology has not necessarily contradicted the tenets of the theory of political class. Conservative and liberal writers have embraced the new doctrine; its development toward more strictly scientific ends is in sight; and we can hope to use it for achieving better historical and political results.

In substance, the concept of the political class viewed as an *organized minority* that aims to lead human society and achieve the best possible collective results seems to be the truly vital feature of the new theory. While this feature justifies the husbanding of political power by the political class, the theory also reveals the true relationships that exist between the organized minority and the mass. We shall show how this organized minority comes into being, what its rational functions and its historical deviations are. We shall also show how this inquiry should influence the historical study of each particular country. As yet, it suffices to stress that the study of the political class is critical to our understanding of the most hermetic national movements. Therefore it is destined to have a decisive influence not only on political science but also on historiography.

## POLITICAL CLASS AND RULING CLASS

This basic distinction between the ruling class and the subject class is still not adequate. Had we not been able to deepen the inquiry and introduce new classifications, as happened on occasion, the theory would have reached a stalemate. But, in fact, there is a category of individuals whose social influence is great although they themselves do not in the strict sense belong to the ruling class. Private bankers, important professionals without public careers, famous scientists, intellectuals and industrialists do not belong to the subject class, but they do not strictly belong to the political class. Therefore, it is urgent to introduce new classifications and pay appropriate attention to the terminology, which as yet lacks precision and threatens to confuse the issues.

Saint-Simon had already noticed that there were two power structures in any organized society, one of them possessing the moral and intellectual leadership, and the other the material leadership. To this Mosca added the following: "these two types of power are practiced by two organized minorities which together form the ruling class, the class that we would today call the political class." Pareto, however, distinguished the *governmental elites* from the *non-governmental elites* and his distinction does not bear the Saint-Simonian connotation. In any case, it seems that we can adopt the terms *ruling class* and *political class*. The first term must be understood in its social sense, the second in its strictly political sense.

In a broad sense the term "ruling class" means the organized power structure which enjoys the political, intellectual, and material leadership of the society. The concept also includes the class that is narrowly termed the "political class." The political class, however, is that segment of the ruling class strictly dedicated to political tasks. This segment constitutes a sort of board of directors of the ruling class. In an agrarian society, for example, the great landlord belongs to the ruling class but, as long as he stays on his property, it can hardly be assumed that he also belongs to the political class. And yet a popular representative in any public office belongs to the ruling and political classes at the same time.

Naturally, a stricter definition for the term "ruling class" can also be found: it refers to those who belong neither to the subject class nor to the political class. The need to use the term that way comes up rather rarely, and when it does the context will show it.

These classifications and precise terminologies are necessary not only for deeper understanding of the functions of each class, but also for clarification of the focus of the individual study. Since not infrequently there are instances where political classes do not exactly represent the corresponding ruling classes, precision of vocabulary helps to avoid confusing simple exchanges of political classes with revolutions. Moreover, it is only this classification and suggested terminology that can explain the swell of non-revolutionary opposition within the ranks of the ruling class itself and, generally speaking, the structure and specific function of political parties. The latter must be grasped as extremely important entities in their own right, including large fractions of the subject class, with, at the summit, a fraction of the ruling class as well as the political class.

## THE RULING CLASS AND THE SUBJECT CLASS

There are many relations and linkages between the ruling and subject classes, most of which cannot always be specified.

First of all, the ruling class is a spontaneous formation which, to a certain degree, is mingled with the other, but is clearly differentiated from it beyond a certain point. From gnoseological necessity and for terminology's sake we trace a dividing line between the two great social classes. However there is no precise way to define their boundaries. Besides the fact that the division is performed by a political analyst and may therefore be in error, one must acknowledge that many criteria suggested for this operation have proved to be misleading.

In fact, if we refer to income scales, we risk disbarring people with great moral and intellectual influence from the ruling class. These people might have low salaries or might even be ignored on the tax lists. On the other hand, if we refer to employment and responsibilities, we risk excluding many groups which, without specified responsibility, have an equally great influence upon the masses. However, this influence in itself does not make them a part of the subject class. Therefore one must be content with distinguishing the two classes without any pretense of neat separation, and must view them as forming a continuous spectrum. Thus we accept the view that the two classes are linked across an intermediary gray zone whose dwellers are not specifically ruling or subject, but in continual and perhaps disturbing oscillation. Only thus can we comprehend the influence of the thoroughly modern phenomenon of the petty bourgeoisie in a number of these cases.

In acknowledging our theoretical limits, we must quickly specify that the prime relation between the classes of rulers and subjects concerns recruitment, which normally takes place by co-optation. In the past co-optation was a much more unusual event than it is today. At that time ruling classes were socially more closed—or at least half-closed—than they are now. It would seem that in the modern world access to the ruling class takes place exclusively by the rise of the most active elements from below. Therefore, the "letter of recommendation" from one's elders and betters—a salient requirement for co-optation in the past—has become a rather unimportant asset. But even if the phenomenon of co-optation occurs more easily today—for the expansion of the ruling class now raises minimal obstacles to the prominent elements of the class below—the process has not yet vanished. If it had, the word "revolution" would have been stricken from the political science dictionary, because "revolution" means specifically the violent entry of large numbers of organized groups of the subject class into the ruling class.

Briefly, one might say that exchanges between the two social classes have always taken place. New elements have joined the ruling class and rejuvenated it, while old elements of the ruling class were peeled off and plunged into the masses. Pareto calls this phenomenon "the circulation of *elites*." This phenomenon of social exchange is of utmost importance. One can even say, without fear of reasonable objection, that the political successes of many countries have been due to the normal functioning of this process, while blockages in the collective life of other countries have been due to its dysfunction.

This survey clarifies a fundamental concept that allows us to evaluate the history of a country more succinctly than before. In a certain way the ruling class is the mirror of a nation, its most delicate indicator. When a nation has a superior ruling class, that nation is undoubtedly great. When the nation supports a decadent ruling class, the time has come to assume that the nation is continuously producing decadent elites, which, introduced into the old political system, fail to renovate the ruling class in a way conforming to the historical demands of the country. This is confirmed by revolutionary periods. The historical and logical framework of every revolution is this: a decadent ruling class is supported only by its privileges. This is a ruling class that did not know how to renew itself by co-opting independent groups from the class beneath. It has raised continual obstacles to this inevitable social phenomenon and has therefore withdrawn into a kind of legalism that has slowly created a web of social privilege. And in a challenging role, one can already identify a newly formed ruling class which is lacking only in political power.

Consequently, whenever this historical circumstance occurs, revolution is inevitable. When a revolution takes place and society is renewed by the expulsion of the old decadent elements that no longer performed their social function but only enjoyed social privileges, we can judge the relative success of the revolution. As a matter of fact, if the nation continues its drift, we know it has merely produced another decadent ruling class. However, if the nation soars to a new destiny, its new ruling class is clearly of the first order. The interdependence between the nation and the ruling class represents a permanent factor. It bursts into the clear during revolutionary periods, but its unobtrusive activity never ceases.

The study of the ruling class is necessary for a better understanding of a nation's history, but more is needed. By limiting oneself to what I might call the *official* view of society one runs the risk of offering a unilateral version of events. This version might come remarkably close to reality when the ruling class functions superbly, when the opposition itself is a part of the ruling class, and when its rights are legally recognized. However, it is inadequate during the periods of conflict between the ruling class and the subject class. Here we must go thoroughly into the question by studying and describing that part of the elite (in the etymological sense) struggling to become the legal ruling class and the nation itself. Without this method we might fail to understand the historical process in its dialectical substance. Due to the fact that the perfect functioning of the ruling class is an exception to the rule and that even outstanding ruling classes have had their crises and breakdowns, the study of the entire society is always necessary if one wishes to reach reliable conclusions. This method of study is no doubt quite difficult, especially in the historico-political sense, because while the old ruling class offers abundant documentation about its ideas and structure, frequently adulterated with propaganda, the documents concerning the new ruling class in formation are scarcer and less accessible, and even more so are those regarding the conditions of the people at large. But since the historian is a person who writes about events that have grown cold, he may find that these difficulties are greatly diminished.

The ruling class is linked to the subject class because it has been recruited from that class; it contains in germ all the characteristics of the race. The continual exchange of social cells secures in the least imperfect manner possible a certain correspondence between the nation and the ruling class. It is the task of political analysis through its examination of the present, and of history through the study of the past, to assort and describe these interdependent relations and to stress their anomalies and aberrations.

There is another relation, of no less importance, between the ruling class and the subject class. In fact, due to its very nature, the ruling class has a task and social duty which are projected over the entire society. Its duty is, namely, to be a veritable ruling class. This is to say that the ruling class directs the collective welfare, and not just its personal and particular affairs and interests. Inevitable conflicts arise here. And when they appear, that is, when the ruling class, involved with its own private interests, jeopardizes the interests of the community or obstructs their free development, then privilege, always the basis of the social status of the ruling class, shows its true colors and its lack of justification. Now, the disequilibrium deriving from meaningless privilege can be overcome only by destroying the privilege itself; in other words, the ruling class must be demoted. This has nothing to do with the phenomenon we have already studied—exchanges within the ruling class, that is, the individual demotion of worn-out particles, which are plunged back into the mass.

The flaws of human nature have made it impossible to organize human society except by recourse to oligarchical groups constituting the skeleton of the entire social structure. Oligarchies rule politics, the economy, even humanistic culture; and the oligarchies must be supported. Indeed they have been candidly chosen and will remain legitimate as long as they express the interests of the community, contribute to the collective welfare, and fulfill a social function. Naturally, membership in these oligarchies confers material and moral benefits that are often envied by the masses. But these benefits are the reward for burdensome and difficult functions which the masses are not capable of exercizing directly and which must, therefore, be delegated to the men at the pinnacle of society.

The ruling class has thus to accomplish its social duties, and its sense of responsibility consists especially in knowing how to coordinate it own interests with the general interest, that is, in charging the smallest fee for its oligarchical talents. A ruling class consecrated to a normal exchange of elites and aware of its social responsibilities normalizes the political struggle and will probably bring about the improvement of society. I say "probably." I have introduced this restriction because there are societies which stay stagnant despite a quite active exchange between lower and upper classes. In this case we must renew our inquiry about the features of collective life in general, since the blame for the lack or hindrance of progress cannot be placed on the ruling class. Here the proverb which states that each people gets the government it deserves comes true.

## RELATIONS BETWEEN THE POLITICAL CLASS
## AND THE RULING CLASS

Having examined the relations between the ruling class and the subject class, we must move on to those between the ruling class and the political class. And we shall say unambiguously that they are of the same nature as those existing between the classes of rulers and subjects. In fact, the political class is recruited from within the ruling class and constitutes one of its specialized subdivisions. A continual process of exchange takes place between them. This process is of an even more delicate nature than the one which furnishes the basis of the ruling class. Here is a case that involves selection of the people who are to influence most intensely and directly the progress of the community by means of state action, which tends to encompass the entire social sphere. The society can be only slightly harmed by the error of a manufacturer, but an error in administrative supervision will surely bring about maximum damage to the community.

Therefore, the selection of the political class is of primary interest to the ruling class. In the first place, the political class can harm the particular interests of the ruling class. Secondly, it can provoke a crisis involving the existence of the ruling class through bad government practices. Finally, it can also happen as a result of the economic and social policies adopted by the political class with respect to education, finance, inflation, and speculation that the usual process of selecting the ruling class is changed. Fractions of the petty bourgeoisie may be pushed back into the proletariat, and new proletarians may gain access to the bourgeoisie. Here is the most obvious reason for governmental crises that have no relation whatsoever to the pressure of the lower classes. These are the regulatory crises of the ruling class and their aim is to prevent larger crises in which the subject class would become involved.

When a political class begins to harm the collectivity, it is the responsibility of the ruling class to intervene quickly and change the political class. If the ruling class does not take the necessary steps, or fails in its purpose, we may conclude that the entire ruling class is experiencing a crisis and has to be changed. If the exchange between the ruling class and the subject class is not defective and yet the exchange between the ruling class and the political class is, the entire society is obviously sick and passing through a period of decadence. In fact, in this case it is evident that the cells which continually rise from the lower to the upper classes are decadent and thus unable to modify the ruling class substantially, or at least have no power to modify it up to the point where it will influence the composition of the political class.

That clears up the second aspect of the relationship of immediate exchange between the political class and the ruling class, and the indirect exchange between the political class and the subject class. We see that while the political class has immediate duties of political responsibility toward the subject class, the ruling class has duties of joint political responsibility toward the class beneath it, since it functions, in substance, as the responsible caretaker of the political class. This network of relationships, which some people might regard exclusively as the product of theoretical schematics, does exist, and its silent functioning constitutes the very delicate mechanism by whose means the ruling class can legitimize its oligarchical structure.

When the ruling class begins to aspire to nonpartisanship and political quietism, when much of it wearily dreams of an impossible end to the eternal struggle, that class has unmistakably entered upon a crisis. Its composition begins to grow defective, and its ideas no longer suit the circumstances. It is even symptomatic that the epidemic of political indifference spreads more readily over a ruling class at the dawning of a crisis. This is the first symptom, like a warning bell.

Thus, the relationships of exchange between the political class and the ruling class are of capital importance to the general study of how society functions, because a social crisis begins in the strictly political stratum, spreading from there into society and finally infecting the entire social structure. The more or less extensive widening of the circles—one can almost say the stratigraphic lines—of the crisis are not only a means of measuring it; they also reveal the first functioning of hidden social reserve forces, which calls to mind the function of the hemopoietic organs, whose job is to accelerate their rhythm when hemorrhaging occurs.

## THE COMPOSITION AND STRUCTURE
## OF MODERN SOCIETY

Up to now the terms "political class," "ruling class," "subject class" have been conceived as functioning in a simple pattern. But it is thoroughly clear that without studying the concrete composition of these abstract entities the analysis will be incomplete. Going more deeply into the matter, we shall see that the composition and structure of great human societies are similar but not identical. No doubt it is the differences that provide the distinguishing features of the historico-political process. A more complete notion of the ruling class ought to be derived from that process and those differences. Naturally this discussion would justify a treatise or the editing of a series of treatises. But since that is impossible, I shall limit myself to a set of remarks sufficient to stimulate the reader's thoughts and to support the present argument.

The composition and structure of the most advanced European

and non-European societies is essentially the following: at the top, the remains of the feudal and semi-bourgeois aristocracy and the upper bourgeoisie; at the center, the middle bourgeoisie; beneath them the petty bourgeoisie; and finally the mass of the nation (peasants, workers, artisans, and common people). These human aggregates represent social classes, and we can say that society is articulated through them. Naturally, as we already saw with the ruling class, these units are the invention of our mind. Their boundaries are not rigid or instantly visible; but social classes really do exist and are not mere arbitrary concepts. Therefore, we must seek to identify them, if our wish is to enlarge the general understanding of society and in particular the anatomy and physiology of the ruling class.

Marx, Engels, Schmoller, Schaeffle, Gumplowicz, Ammon, Loria, Bauer, Tarde, van Overbergh, Bücher, and de Greef have all proposed various classifications of social groups, all of them based on different group criteria. The discussion has naturally ended in confusion because each author has tried to impose his own categories to the exclusion of the others. Race has done battle with the ownership of the means of production, and it in turn has been set against the criterion of professional influences, while finally that category has been contrasted with land ownership. However, these theoretical disagreements do not necessarily persuade us to discard the benefits to political criticism and history that come from the hypothesis and study of social classes.

Ever since man undertook the study of himself and human society, the existence of social classes has always been recognized and has been profitable as an object of study. In antiquity classification had a direct institutional importance. The struggle to destroy social barriers has been constant for tens of centuries up to modern times. In our society, class distinctions persist, even if differently aligned. But already the ancient societies—Rome, for example—had slowly produced structural modifications (in the modern sense), which had relegated to the distant past distinctions between patricians and plebians, and had contributed to the creation of new formations alongside the senatorial aristocracy: the class of knights, the military aristocracy of the reign of Caracalla and his successors, the bureaucratic aristocracy under Diocletian and Constantine, the rural bourgeoisie, the financial bourgeoisie, and even an incipient petty bourgeoisie. This happened throughout the entire known world from Britain to Syria and Egypt. It is therefore necessary to admit, with Mosca, that "humanity is divided into social groups, each of which is distinct from the others in beliefs, feelings, habits, and interests unique to it alone" and that "the individuals belonging to one of these groups are united by the consciousness of a common brotherhood and divided from other groups by passions and tendencies that are more or less hostile and antagonistic."

We agree that these groups do not feel, hate and act like individuals and that, above all, their reduction to two basic categories in perpetual conflict is unacceptable. The groups are numerous and they split apart quite frequently and contrary to their real interests. Thus we often have the sense of being in the presence of historical chaos and of observing irrational results. But when the transitory divisions and the logico-political errors that gave rise to them have been ascertained, when the group has recovered from the adverse fate provoked by errors sufficient to neutralize its weight and action, we see clearly that it existed, has continued to exist, and will have to exist so long as the beliefs, feelings, habits and interests that created it provide a source of friction and contrast with other groups based on analogous but different springs of action.

Actually, this fractionalization of social groups occurs more frequently than is usually recognized, and, as we shall soon see, political action is to be explained by the internal cleavage of particular social classes that either place a premium on their feelings at the expense of their interests, or vice versa. But if we do not use methods of classification, we run the risk of understanding nothing about politics and history. We risk giving full credit for events either to the merit of exceptional men or to the monotonous weight of the masses. The real protagonist of history is, however, the political class, and it is neither identified with the masses nor limited to a single individual.

The normality of the interplay between classes, its frequent anomalies, its successive actions and reactions, and the enormous premium for political success in a wide field of error create the real fascination of the political struggle.

In vain would we attempt to penetrate, describe, and study it without theoretical instruments and a proper vocabulary, tools that allow us to give an effective representation of reality, with as little distortion as possible.

We are unable to describe and analyze the feeling, interests, acts, and errors of every particular social individual. Therefore we cannot provide the type of large classifications that take into account all the variants, all the splits, all the idiosyncrasies which occur in the evolving historical process. We cannot designate with utmost precision all the political and logical elements that have shaped the historical outcome and are doomed always to react anew, if only because of original errors and idiosyncrasies of a strictly political kind. . . . [In the passages excluded here, the author gives a more detailed analysis of social

classes: the residual aristocracy, the upper bourgeoisie, the middle bourgeoisie, the petty bourgeoisie, the petty bourgeois intellectuals, the industrial petty bourgeoisie, the merchants, and the rural petty
bourgeoisie.]

## THE POLITICAL CLASS AS A TECHNICAL
## INSTRUMENT OF THE RULING CLASS

The political class is the technical instrument by which the ruling
class exercises its enormous political and social power. It is also a
select oligarchy which denies access to the subject class. In fact, it
is possible that elements belonging to the subject class might achieve
the most important positions in the State, especially in the popularly
based political parties. But it is equally clear that in order to begin
their political ascent these individuals must first cross the "bridge of
donkeys" and make their entry into the ruling class.

Consequently, the same necessity of exchange that we already
described in connection with the ruling class applies to the political
class. The only difference is that this exchange is indirect, in other
words it occurs through the election and co-optation of those elements
of the ruling class that seem most endowed with political capacity
and ability. However, when the political class is inadequate, the ruling
class has the task of speeding up the exchange.

The precise and timely change of the elements of the political
class is perhaps even more necessary and vital than the precise, timely
circulation of ruling-class elements. While the latter type of exchange
is a social mystery that can hardly be influenced, the exchange of
the political class is the duty of the ruling class and, therefore, also
its burden. When a defective ruling-class group prolongs its existence
through periods of collective decadence and causes the crisis of the
political class to become chronic and irreversible, all society suffers
and turns to revolutionary action. Revolution constitutes the dialectical
act by which both the ruling and political classes are changed in a
single stroke. This, however, does not mean that revolution will always
occur when the political and ruling classes are fatigued and incompetent and collective malaise is creeping over the country. Despite
its dialectical connection with the historical process, revolution requires
that the subject class should be capable of compactly presenting new
ruling and political classes in formation. Whenever the subject class
is unfruitful—and this is frequently so—the violent impulses aiming
at the exchange of ruling and political classes take on that "Mexican"
quality which is misnamed as "revolutionary." It is precisely the repe-

tition of so-called *revolutions* that demonstrates the impossibility of *revolution*.

The relationship between the political and the ruling classes is thus sufficiently clear. If the first is the instrument of the political struggle which the second has been constantly involved in defining, it is clear that a first-rate political class cannot be produced by a mediocre ruling class and that the former is only the more sensitive tool for the preservation and prosperity of the latter. But the political class is not only the business manager for the ruling class; it must also govern the country. Its power and, beyond that, its arrogance are accepted as long as its management achieves results that promote a maximum of general welfare. Let us be perfectly plain: there is no precise instrument to measure the general welfare attainable in a given historical period, nor is there one to measure the advantages and defects of political classes. Moreover, the confused swell of political debate and the peculiarities of political reasoning must be frequently added to the crudeness of the instruments. But we know that history has granted extremely long life-spans to certain political classes and that these classes must therefore have responded logically to all the demands that required historical resolution. One cannot conceive the durability of the Roman political class and the greatness of its successes without conceding that there is a law according to which a political class is both the technical tool of the ruling class and, at the same time, the technical and political tool of the country, linked to its success or failure. Only thus is it possible to explain why the Spanish and the English political classes had such opposite fates even though both of them rose at almost the same time. While the former began to decline in less than a century, the latter, still vital, keeps trying to sustain the country it governs and ward off the fickleness of fate.

A political class is no longer exclusively permeated by crass materialism. On the contrary, idealistic motives shape its greatness, and among these motives we must especially acknowledge the pride taken in national defense and organization. And it is precisely these services and credentials which, in the view of the public, justify the oligarchical supremacy that is the *raison d'être* of the political class and which, by submerging the harshness of political struggle, render the problem of elite exchange reasonably innocuous. This exchange takes place subterraneously through the directed activity of the parties and beneath an ideological smoke screen. When it becomes an independent problem, a disease is already clearly infecting the critical joints of the political class, which proves by its abundant disorientation that the ruling class itself has lost its sensitivity and recuperative power. At this point the country enters into gradual crisis and revolutionary trends begin to take shape. The delicate human mechanisms that are so fatiguing to describe no longer function as they should. Everything is debatable or cast in doubt, and the state, its institutions, and the political parties themselves are drained of content.

## THE DEVELOPMENT OF THE RULING CLASS
## AND ITS RELATIONSHIPS WITH THE SUBJECT CLASS

Up to this point the political class has been viewed as a unit, and so, for that matter, has the ruling class. One might be led to believe that the political class is, without nuance, an expression of the ruling class and that both of them rule the country in completely congenial accord. It would thus be sufficient if the political leaders were endowed with at least a minimum of professional honesty in order to prevent their subjects from perceiving the real state of affairs and rebelling against the trivial status that the political class had unquestionably imposed on them. Fortunately for the human race, this is not so: although the treatment of the political class as a self-sufficient unit is a theoretical necessity, it becomes positively harmful at this point in our argument and must be modified in the interests of a fuller grasp of reality. It is precisely during the process when the political class is formed that complex socio-political phenomena intervene to split the ruling class, on the one hand, and, on the other, to split the political class itself in short order.

These phenomena will be seen more clearly when we begin to trace the dynamics of that process and especially when we analyze the political struggle. But even at our present level of inquiry we must specify that the birth of a political class is far from aimless and that the political struggle, as it develops, provokes a split in the ruling class, which, in return, affects the political class and destroys its unity. This does not mean of course that a portion of the ruling class and its counterpart within the political class cease to exist as such and fall back into the subject class. That does not even occur when totalitarian regimes, single parties, or other sorts of public misfortune befall a country, because loss of class is an individual phenomenon depending on factors which no government could possibly create or control totally. Usually, it comes about in cases where attitudinal postures can no longer sustain persons at a determinate social level. And no government has the power to destroy individual attitudes.

Yet, even when a segment of the political class which legally enjoys political power and eminence initiates a fratricidal struggle against the other segment and the fraction of the ruling class that supports it, not only will the unity of the political class vis-à-vis the subject class remain intact, but it is even possible that it might emerge reinforced. This is because the subject class will align itself with the opposition fraction of the political class, strengthening it with the infusion of entirely new elements that possess a great potential of expansion and proselytization. It is therefore clear that the political class is created by means of a split in the ruling class and that in its turn the political class also splits into a governing political class and a political class of opposition. The political struggle depends on the existence of these two fractions of the same oligarchy, and they constitute the supreme security for the interests of the subject class.

We have already said, speaking abstractly, that the relationship between the political class and the subject class consists in the fact that political class action has its rationale in creating the conditions of public welfare, that it is concretely represented in the political struggle between the two fractions of the political class, and that it thrives on historical and political motives which invite the participation of even the subject class in the political struggle. Like all human mechanisms, this one, too, is probably imperfect. Political romanticism and idealism have tried to overcome its flaws by designing abstract political systems which have been justly labeled utopian. The entire history of so-called political doctrines is a graveyard cluttered with generous utopias. Talented people have sketched out these utopias in the vain effort to correct human nature. This will become even clearer when we discuss political formulas. Suffice it now to put the reader on guard against utopian criticisms and corrections, with a warning that if one wants a sounder sense of reality, he should not let himself be taken in by utopian constructions—undeniably seductive but not based on an accurate knowledge of human nature.

The time has perhaps come to stress the semi-utopian character of totalitarian doctrines when they are earnestly rationalized as a cure-all for the defects and inconveniences of the political struggle. It is absurd to propose the coercive unification of the political class, the abolition of the parties through the creation of the so-called State-party, the abolition of the political struggle, or even its absorption within a single party. These irrational and anti-historical attempts are not only foredoomed, but they also produce graver wounds than those they would presume to heal.

The breakup of the ruling class in the very act of giving birth to the political class and its necessary consequence, the simultaneous splitting of the political class, are indispensable conditions of the emergence and development of the political struggle. In its turn, the political struggle is the condition of the legitimacy of power enjoyed by the political class as a whole. It is therefore contradictory and absurd to claim the achievement of a fictitious unity within this human aggregate when its very laws of formation and title of legitimacy are violated in the eyes of the subject class. Totalitarianism is just a political formula whose features are both utopian and directly injurious. In fact, totalitarianism has no other goal but to change the data of the political struggle to the detriment of the opposition. By producing worse defects than those it would like to eliminate, totalitarianism is of great harm to any society where it is allowed to take root. We may confidently assert that when a ruling class gives birth to a dictatorial political class, it is in a deep crisis. Its action raises the price that the country will inevitably have to pay for resolving that crisis.

## GOVERNMENT AND OPPOSITION

The splitting of the political class into two fractions—one of them undertaking the government of the country, the other the duties of opposition—occurs by means of a composition and decomposition of the sub-groups of the ruling class. The governmental political class leans on the governmental ruling class, in other words, a more or less homogeneous conjugation of social subgroups that are interested in achieving a given governmental program. In reaction to this, the remaining parts of the political class organize either a single opposition supported by the remaining social sub-groups or several oppositions, each of which is supported by some of the sub-groups, all unified by the goal of capturing power from the governmental political class.

The struggle between these two sections of the political class, which cannot be completely traced as long as our analysis remains static, normally has for its object the transfer of social sub-groups from the side of the government to the opposition, and exceptionally the provocation of the violent exchange of ruling and political classes. The scope of this struggle depends on factors that cannot be anticipated and whose nature is relative to the design of the "political formula." However, from the static perspective, we can specify that the magnitude of the struggle depends not only on the "political formula," but, above all, on the combined consciousness of the sections of the political class.

In fact, in countries where exchange is well carried out, the governmental political class does not hinder the functioning of the opposition. It adapts itself as far as possible to the mechanism of the political struggle, thus assuring the maintenance of legitimacy by adopting political formulas which, precisely because they protect the rights of the opposition, preserve the fundamental coherence of the political class, even though it functions by means of its contrasts. This is the maximum proper functioning of the political struggle. But its achievement is more the exception than the rule, for it is dominated by a characteristically exceptional meeting of historical and political conditions.

In fact, it is of greatest importance for the exchange between the ruling class and the subject class to function faultlessly so that no one aspiring to rule will ever be trapped within the subject class. Therefore, in giving birth to the political class, the ruling class should rigorously select its candidates. The exchange between the ruling class and the political class should take place without a hitch. Moreover, the processes of the composition and decomposition of the social groups which furnish the bases of the political classes of government and opposition should follow the curve of the psychological variations in the subject class and bear those classes with all due speed toward the political opposition before new fractions of it that are foreign to the traditional composition of the ruling class can form.

Finally, the mechanism of the political struggle should function perfectly, with no delays to hinder the immediate transformation of the opposition political class into a governmental one. Only if this complex and delicate system functions superlatively by absorbing and using in a reasonable and timely fashion all the elements continually released from the subject class can there be achieved that *concordia discors* of the ruling and political classes. Only then can there arise for the service of the centuries those great ruling and political classes which, by securing the welfare and power of a nation, are the wonders of history.

Usually, the ruling class imperfectly operates the mechanism described above. There are social subgroups belonging to the ruling class that are kept in constant opposition. The social groups that support the governmental political class try through various devices to block the aspirations of their adversaries. In that case, the exchange of the political class is defective. Moreover, the political class itself does not function according to that *concordia discors*, which, as we have seen, constitutes the test of unity and legitimacy. The "political formula" which apparently regulates this exchange is seen to be a sham because, in fact, it fails to protect the opposition groups. The whole political struggle emerges distortedly: the privileged social subgroups settle the crisis of the political class by interpretation alone, not by accepting the results of the struggle but by interpreting it exclusively in the interest of their own preservation. Thus they do not resolve these crises, but only prolong them.

In their turn, those non-privileged social sub-groups constantly forced into opposition become convinced that legal political struggle is sterile. From their point of view, the political struggle according to the pattern of the "political formula" is a fiction invented by the governmental political class. Consequently they turn toward the subject class and incite it against their opponents. This is the way that revolutionary oppositions are born. They are always the result of the defective functioning of the political class viewed as a unit, which, in its turn, is the result of the defective functioning of the ruling class in its role of conflict-regulator between the two factions of the political class as mediated by the emotions of the subject class.

If we were to speak of the dynamic aspect of the problem, we should perceive other factors that complicate this mechanism. For present purposes we may be content with shedding light on the origin and function of the political class from a static perspective. Of foremost importance is the function that consists not only in governing the country so as to assure its prosperity and power but also in governing the opposition, which, in substance, means a collaboration involving, in the first place, political contrast and then substitution. It is especially in the exercise of this function that the important variants of the political struggle are determined and that crises and revolutions arise. Here are the circumstances in which political crisis occurs and demands a solution: (1) When a governmental political class operates basically like a *camarilla*, neglecting both the public interest and the respect due the political class of opposition; (2) When the exchange of the governmental political class fails to take place or takes place awkwardly, and the opposition political class is forced into systematic hostility; (3) When the composition and decomposition of the subgroups of the ruling class are delayed and out of phase, and when there is a persisting tendency to interpret crises of the political class as instigations of *camarillas* seeking to impose their mastery on the state. In short, there is political crisis whenever the basic functional mechanism of the ruling class is altered.

If the subject class produces defective elements that cannot improve the quality of the ruling class, so that it, in turn, will not improve the quality of the political class, the country is faced with a serious decay that might last for centuries, until new conditions and new elements maturing within the subject class can bring about political recovery. If, however, the subject class is still able to produce elements suitable for advancement to the ruling class and thence to the political class, there can be only two solutions. Either these elements, entering and mingling with the ruling class, recall it to its function, produce a decomposition and a recomposition of the social sub-groups, and eliminate the *camarilla* that impeded the proper functioning of the political class (political revolution); or, they organize in hetereogeneous groups, engage in combat with the entire ruling class, and appeal directly to the strength of the subject class with the end of destroying the mechanism of the political struggle through the destruction of the traditional makeup of the ruling class (social revolution).

The critical and processual development of the political class is therefore conditioned by multiple factors, among which the vitality of the subject class is always paramount. This is the mine from which the oligarchical components that we have studied are raised. And the proper functioning of the political struggle depends essentially on the political acumen of the ruling class. At this point one might insist that a genuine subject class does not really exist because the class that we have called subject is in the end the dominant force of the political struggle. But this assumption is historically and politically inaccurate, because the subject class is led and governed only by means of the ruling and political classes. It is also scientifically unacceptable, because it would destroy the whole theory that has been so laboriously constructed. In order that the reader should not fall victim to any distortion of reality, one particular truth must be clarified. The functioning of the ruling and political classes not only depends on their composition, but also on the subject class, which has its own role to play in the political struggle. And yet, when this truth is granted and it is further admitted that the subject class has political autonomy at least as it is channeled by way of the two classes whose structures we have indicated, it is no less true that what is of special concern to political science is to study those two classes attentively. For they represent in germ the entire people, and their changes and functioning furnish a sufficient explanation of the successes and ill fortune of the whole country. . . .

[In the remainder of this essay, Dorso goes on to analyze the dynamics and the structure of political parties and the legitimizing role of the "political formula," a notion made famous by Mosca.]

# 5

# Revolution and the Social System

*Chalmers Johnson*

## EDITORS' COMMENT

Chalmers Johnson wrote the following essay as part of a preliminary investigation of revolution which he later developed into a lengthier work entitled *Revolutionary Change* (Boston and Toronto: Little, Brown and Company, 1966). We believe that the essay below is an excellent summary of his views; however, there are a number of refinements expressed in the later work that should be brought to the reader's attention.

Johnson belongs to a long line of equilibrium theorists, going back, at least as far as Aristotle, who treat revolution as a sort of social pathology. In this respect he is to be distinguished from Lewis Coser (see Selection 3 in this volume), who shares with him, to some extent, the structural-functional approach but who regards conflict as a frequent source of political and social vitality.

To describe the *structural* nature of the social system, Johnson relies on the standard concepts of norm, status, and role—the latter two, respectively, being the dynamic and static aspects of the division of labor: "a social system is composed of actions (roles), played from

88

statuses and guided by norms" (*Revolutionary Change*, pp. 44–45). *Functionalism* he defines as "a kind of non-purposive teleology"—that is, when a role in society is functional it serves "either the survival, or the adjustment, or maintenance of the system." When it is not so defined, it becomes "dysfunctional." A properly functioning society is one in *homeostatic equilibrium*, a physiological expression that is described in sociological terms by Anthony Wallace as a series of "co-ordinated actions (including cultural actions . . . ) by all or some [of a social system's] parts, to preserve its own integrity by maintaining a minimally fluctuating life-supporting matrix for its individual members, and [that] will under stress, take emergency measures to preserve the constancy of this matrix" (*Revolutionary Change*, p. 54).

For the student of revolution, several questions are raised by this analysis. How, exactly, *does* an equilibrium theorist deal with the concept of change? Is "equilibrium" simply a benchmark from which to measure change—as Johnson seems to suggest below—or can society countenance some degree of change and yet remain in equilibrium—as he seems to indicate in *Revolutionary Change?* Are the criticisms in Dahrendorf's essay justified? The reader must make his own judgments, but he should ponder the distinction between *automatic* and *conscious* pressures for the alteration and the preservation of a social system. Presumably, the advocate of a homeostatic equilibrium theory should be more at home with the former, and a theorist of power and coercion should be more at home with the latter.

The medical analogy is useful in making this distinction. A normal organism maintains itself by means of automatic self-regulating functions. When its equilibrium is upset sufficiently, and the automatic mechanisms are insufficient, a physician consciously interferes with this system to restore (in some sense) the equilibrium. And he relies to a great degree on physiological homeostasis to assist in the cure. But, the physician is not part of the automatic self-regulating system—his is a conscious interference to restore the system. Obviously, there is a great distinction between the physician who is not part of the system and a ruling elite that is, but something of the flavor of conscious interference in the workings of the equilibrium is hinted at in the following essay—and is developed further in *Revolutionary Change* (see pp. 94–97). There is plenty of room for "pro-system" activity to restore the equilibrium.

In other words, in spite of the gulf between the Johnsons and the Dahrendorfs, there is something that each must borrow from the other's theory. Dahrendorf, to some extent, must borrow a sense of homeostasis: no matter how far one stretches the concept of power, it is not sufficiently pervasive to explain all political and social relation-ships. No matter how clever the physician, without some assistance from self-regulating mechanisms the patient will die. On the other hand, Johnson must borrow the physician—and he does. There are circumstances when society can be saved from revolution only by the conscious activity of the elite *and* can be saved from destruction only by the use of armed force. It is not a coincidence that the "accelerators" mostly relate to some aspect of the condition of the military. There is plenty of room for "pro-system" activity on the part of elites to restore the equilibrium—activity that is conscious, not automatic: it is the physician restoring equilibrium, not the organism adjusting to internal stimuli.

# REVOLUTION AND THE SOCIAL SYSTEM

*Chalmers Johnson*

## I. THE CAUSES OF REVOLUTION

When Hannah Arendt writes in the first paragraph of *On Revolution*, "For revolutions, however one may be tempted to define them, are not mere changes,"[1] she has indicated at the outset the one thing that all revolutions are: changes. Revolution is a form of change within the social system; not *mere* change, but change nonetheless. Revolution is not a unique social phenomenon; there exist functional equivalents of revolution—namely, other forms of social change—and questions directed at discovering the causes of social change and identifying the level in the social system at which social change occurs are relevant to the problem of the causes of revolution. As a kind of social change, revolution is "the most wasteful, the most expensive, the last to be chosen; but also the most powerful, and therefore always appealed to in what men feel to be a last resort."[2]

And what causes social change? We put this question not because we hope to answer it to everyone's satisfaction, but in order to introduce the series of models and assumptions that will be most helpful as a foundation for the analysis of social change.[3] Our point of departure in analyzing social change is the model of a functionally integrated social system—a system whose members cooperate with each other by "playing" various "roles" that, taken together, permit the whole system to "function." This basic model is well known in contemporary social science; it is the primary construct upon which "structural-func-

[1] On Revolution (New York, 1963), p. 13.
[2] George Sawyer Pettee, *The Process of Revolution* (New York, 1938), p. 96.
[3] For an excellent critical summary of all the major theories of social change see J. A. Ponsioen, *The Analysis of Social Change Reconsidered* (The Hague, 1962).

SOURCE. Chalmers Johnson, "Revolution and the Social System," from *Revolution and the Social System* (Stanford: Hoover Institution Studies No. 3, 1964), pp. 3–22, 26–31, excerpted. Reprinted with the permission of the Hoover Institution on War, Revolution and Peace, Stanford University. Copyright 1964 by the Board of Trustees of Leland Stanford Junior University.

tional" analysis rests.[4] Within the framework of this model, we hope to show that revolution is a form of social change undertaken in response to specific conditions of the social system, and that it occurs at a particular stage in the system's efforts to resolve functional difficulties.

One notoriously misunderstood problem with this model of society is that it portrays the social system in a state of equilibrium; it is supposed that the model is useless (or worse) for analyzing social change because of its static bias.[5] Obviously, a changing system is not one in equilibrium; conversely, there is no place for change in an equilibrium system. But this is not an either/or proposition; "equilibrium" is not a real condition but a concept. An equilibrium social system is an ideal type, and the concept of equilibrium is only a reference point for measuring change. No other interpretation of a system's equilibrium, least of all a normative one, is permissible.[6] Since an equilibrium system is not a changing system, a changing system is one that is out of balance. What puts a social system (as here conceived) out of equilibrium?

We believe that society can best be understood as a functionally integrated system. In such a system, if one of the various component structures does not function in the way that it must in order to maintain equilibrium, then first the affected substructure and then, if no remedial action occurs, the entire system will move out of equilibrium. The condition that causes the disequilibrium, and that demands remedial action in order to restore or to a create a new equilibrium, we call *dysfunction*. Dysfunction is a potential condition of any functionally integrated system, and dysfunctional conditions within an imbalanced social system vary in degree of severity over a broad range from slight to mortal. Dysfunctional conditions are caused by pressures (whether they are external or internal is a distinction that is relevant only in an historical case) that compel the members of a substructure to do their work, or view their roles, or imagine their potentialities

[4] The standard works are Marion J. Levy, *The Structure of Society* (Princeton, 1952); Robert K. Merton, *Social Theory and Social Structure* (Glencoe, 1949); and the books of Talcott Parsons. For an early statement of the logic of the approach see A. R. Radcliffe-Brown, "On the Concept of Function in Social Science," *American Anthropologist*, N.S., XXXVII (July–September 1935), 394–402. For a recent application of structural-functional method see William C. Mitchell, *The American Polity* (New York, 1962).

[5] Cf. W. E. Moore, "A Reconsideration of Theories of Social Change," *American Sociological Review*, XXV (December 1960), 811.

[6] This point is made ably by Lewis Coser, "Social Conflict and the Theory of Social Change," *British Journal of Sociology*. VII (September 1957), 206–207, n. 22.

differently from the way that they did under equilibrium conditions. The pressures that cause dysfunction (e.g., technological discoveries, imperialism, and many others discussed below) we call *sources* of dysfunction. In this context, *social change* is action undertaken to alter the structure of the system for the purpose of relieving the condition of dysfunction (in one or more of the system's substructures or, occasionally, throughout the entire structure).

Dysfunction is the condition that demands the response of social change—and of revolution. But what distinguishes revolutionary change from other forms of social change? Two considerations are relevant here: revolution occurs because non-violent evolution is not occurring, and revolution occurs in response to a distinct condition of the system that we call "multiple dysfunction." With regard to the first point, we note that a distinctive characteristic of revolutionary change is the employment of physical violence to relieve dysfunction. "Revolutionary" changes—in the popular sense of changes of great magnitude—that are not initiated by violent alteration of the system are instances of some other form of social change. Big changes are not necessarily revolutionary changes, or else the word merely means "big change." In specifying why revolutionary change is violent, we must refer to the fact that non-violent change has not previously taken place in the dysfunctional system. Social violence is the appropriate response to intransigent resistance; it occurs because known methods of non-violent change are blocked by the ruling elite. That is to say, revolution is politics continued at the level of a violent physical showdown. It takes two to make a revolution, and one of these two is always the status quo elite. The revolutionaries—those recognizing the dysfunctional situation in the face of elite intransigence—are not necessarily the masses; they may be an intrinsic elite (say, a corps of officers) challenging the socially recognized extrinsic elite. Or they may be the masses. (Whatever damage may have to be done to Leninism or to the flamboyantly cynical "iron law of oligarchy," it is an error to suppose that the masses will never rise without guidance.)[7] Of course, if the elite is not intransigent, simple change will occur, dysfunction will be relieved, and no revolution will take place. Therefore the target elite must be blocking change in a revolutionary situation. These considerations say nothing about who will emerge victorious

---

[7] Many jacqueries illustrate this point; Eric Hobsbawm's remarks on the Andalusian anarchist movement offer a concrete example: "Spanish anarchism . . . was overwhelmingly a poor men's movement and it is thus not surprising that it reflected the interests and aspirations of the Andalusian *pueblo* with uncanny closeness." *Primitive Rebels* (Manchester, 1959), p. 83.

when the revolution occurs; that question is related to the condition of one particular subsystem—the army—which will be considered later.

In distinguishing revolutionary change from other, non-violent forms of change in terms of the failure of the latter to relieve dysfunctional conditions, we are oversimplifying actual revolutionary situations. Simple change in response to conditions of dysfunction may be occurring, but it may be an inappropriate or an insufficient response, it may be outrun by spreading dysfunctions or by an accelerator (see below), or it may itself produce other dysfunctions (which may, in turn, produce the "anarchistic" type of revolution, different from the one that simple change sought to forestall). True conservatives may attempt to maintain the continuity of a dysfunctional system (particularly of its integrating myth) by reforming and adjusting the system to changed circumstances. But if they fail to relieve dysfunction to a level at which revolution is inappropriate, or if an accelerator intervenes before such relief is completed, revolution will occur—and it will be directed against them.

It seems hardly necessary to say that dysfunction in the system of elite recruitment is an important element in hastening a revolution. In some instances, a caste-type of elite (e.g., the First and part of the Second Estate) which is no longer the intrinsic elite of the system may, by its actions, promote revolution. In other cases, the elite may be open to rising groups of representatives from the intrinsic elite (even, although rarely, in colonial situations); and such an elite may be implementing policies intended to relieve dysfunction. If only the structure of social mobility within a system is dysfunctional, this can probably be corrected by non-violent change—that is, either by redefining the criteria of the elite or by clipping its powers (e.g., the Lords' Reform). Regardless of the qualities of an elite and of the actions it is taking to relieve dysfunction, if change eventually takes a revolutionary form, the system elite will be attacked violently by the revolutionaries. Such an occurrence is, empirically, a mark of revolution.

The second criterion of revolution we call "multiple dysfunction." At the present stage of knowledge about social systems and social change, it is not possible to measure "amounts" of dysfunctions in a system. If we could, we would be able to describe distinctive conditions of the social system in response to which revolution is the appropriate mode of social change. In lieu of such precision, however, we still require a criterion of "appropriateness." There exists a level of dysfunctional conditions below which revolution (purposive political violence) is not appropriate regardless of how intransigent the elite may be in opposing efforts to relieve it. On the other hand, even if the elite is not intransigent, or is no longer intransigent after a period of initial vacillation, there are levels of dysfunctional conditions that transcend the adjustment capabilities of a system. Revolution will occur in these cases unless the elite acts first and declares its bankruptcy by abdication, resignation, or by otherwise terminating the old order nonviolently. . . .

Social systems may survive extraordinary dislocations without experiencing revolutions so long as certain conditions are met. These conditions are: the existence of the social problems (dysfunctions) must be clearly recognized by the elites as well as by the ordinary members of the system; basic agreement on the need for change must exist; and the sector (substructure) in which the dysfunction prevails must be capable of being isolated within the general context of the social system. If the dysfunction cannot be identified or isolated, it will—like cancer or (as the French Army in Algeria called it) *pourrissement*— metastasize and lead to revolution. It is a people's awareness of the actual, or incipient, metastasis of social ills that causes the "loss of confidence" or "rupture of consensus" that so often presages revolutionary conditions.[8] We suggest as a rule-of-thumb criterion of revolutionary change (in addition to the criterion of elite intransigence in the face of system dysfunction) that dysfunction must "metastasize" beyond one substructure in order for revolution to become appropriate. Generally speaking, no single condition of dysfunction (with the possible exception of agricultural production in certain types of systems) can disintegrate a social system; in a revolutionary situation, more than one of the relatively separable substructures of a system is dysfunctional and, in one type of revolution discussed in Part II, dysfunction is systemic, including the integrative myth. Let us emphasize that this is a rule-of-thumb criterion; we are as yet unable to describe, in the macroscopic terms of the model of the functionally integrated social system, precisely what are revolutionary conditions. This point will be explored further in our discussion of an "accelerator"—i.e., the final aggregate of pressure (source of dysfunction) on a system that leads at once to revolution.

Let us summarize the analysis of revolution to this point. Revolution is one form of social change in response to the presence of dysfunction in the social system. Revolution is the preferred method of change when (a) the level of dysfunctions exceeds the capacities of traditional

---

[8] See, for example, Walter Lippmann's article on the possibility of a Negro rebellion in the United States, *San Francisco Chronicle*, May 28, 1963.

or accepted methods of problem solving; and when (b) the system's elite, in effect, opposes change. ( The second point is analytically necessary because it is possible to conceive of a system that is *completely* dysfunctional without being revolutionary. A natural catastrophe, such as a severe earthquake, might produce this condition.) Conversely, a system elite may resolutely oppose changes advocated by special groups within the system, but no revolutionary situation is generated because the system is basically functional. Revolution is the acceptance of violence in order to bring about change.

The practical importance of these ideas for the study of revolution lies in the usefulness of the concepts of a functionally integrated social system and of its potential for becoming dysfunctional. An investigator will need to discover the *sources* of dysfunction and to estimate the effects of these sources upon a given system. This is a formidable task, but it is also one toward which a great deal has already been accomplished by social scientists. We do not intend to stop here and offer a library-sized footnote on this point, both because that is not our primary purpose in this discussion and because identification of the sources of dysfunction is not the final step in an analysis of the causes of revolution. The sources of dysfunction are numerous. They include: cyclical pressures (hereditary kingship or single party rule without purge may produce dysfunctions), the global diffusion of industrial culture, imperialism, the discovery of new territories, the elaboration of new metaphysical beliefs, technical and scientific discoveries, and so forth.[9] For purposes of the present discussion, our procedure is to assume that such events do affect social systems and do occasionally generate conditions of dysfunction extensive enough to swamp the capacities of the system for adjustment.

If this assumption has been made, it is probably time to come down from the model to specific cases and to insert a small *sabot* into the machinery. For the fact of the matter is that the concepts of multiple dysfunctions and elite intransigence will never, by themselves, reveal what causes a revolution in a concrete case. We may observe that various dysfunction-inducing phenomena—rapid industrialization, relative deprivation, incoherence in the myth, and so

[9] On this subject, cf.: G. L. Arnold, "The Imperial Impact on Backward Countries," *St. Antony's Papers*, II (1957), 104–125; Karl W. Deutsch, "Social Mobilization and Political Development," *American Political Science Review*, LV:3 (September 1961), 493–514; George M. Foster, *Traditional Cultures: And the Impact of Technological Change* (New York, 1962)'; E. J. Hobsbawm, *The Age of Revolution, 1789–1848* (Cleveland and New York, 1962); John H. Kautsky, *Political Change in Underdeveloped Countries* (New York, 1962); and Arnold Toynbee, *The World and the West* (New York, 1953).

forth—are affecting a social system; and we may allege that these pressures cause a given revolution. But the only way we know that these dysfunction-inducing elements cause the revolution is because the revolution has occurred. At the same time, we are frequently confronted with examples of dysfunctional systems—ones in which known dysfunction-inducing elements are present and in which an effective sense of dysfunction does exist—but in which no revolution is occurring. (Note that the distinction is not that some societies are dysfunctional while the population has no subjective awareness of it. It is rather that some dysfunctional systems *with* self-conscious revolutionaries fully mobilized do not experience revolution while other, similarly placed systems do.) The problem is to explain what triggers revolution, *given* sufficient "background" dysfunctions in the system to make revolution probable (e.g., as in contemporary South Africa or Brazil, or Indonesia). It is usual at this point in the analysis of revolution (in either Marxist or non-Marxist studies) to resort to various metaphors of "ripeness," or "tides," or "waves," but let us try to be more specific.

Multiple dysfunction plus elite intransigence plus $X$ equals revolution. And what is $X$? For $X$, let us substitute the concept of "accelerators of dysfunction." This is another rule-of-thumb concept adduced to help us understand the final causes of revolutions; in a truly sophisticated use of structural-functional theory, it ought not to be isolated. By $X$ (or "accelerators of dysfunction") all we mean to identify are particularly intense *sources* of dysfunction that make their effects felt suddenly and powerfully, and that typically constitute the final aggregate in a growing burden of dysfunctional conditions. Accelerators are occurrences that catalyze or throw into relief the already existent revolutionary level of dysfunctions. They do not of themselves cause revolution; but when they do occur in a system already bearing the necessary level of dysfunctions (i.e., in more than one substructure), they will provide the sufficient cause of the immediately following revolution.

As accelerators we have in mind such events as the rise of a prophet or a messiah in a dysfunctional society, causing a revolutionary millenarian movement to develop; or the effects of organizational activities by a revolutionary party that is attempting to create a rebel infrastructure in order to launch a militarized mass insurrection (see Part II below); or, very commonly, the defeat in a foreign war of a system already suffering from multiple dysfunctions. The metaphor which best expresses our present understanding of accelerators is the heart patient who unexpectedly contracts pneumonia—a disease that a healthy man can normally survive—and who then succumbs from the combined effects of the two. A dysfunctional society can similarly experience a long-term gradual secular decline until some occurrence, such as defeat in war, suddenly accelerates or intensifies the burdens under which it labors. We submit that when such an accelerating event occurs the level of dysfunctions will rise dramatically, previous elite efforts (if any) to relieve dysfunctions will be rendered instantly irrelevant, and revolution will take place. Let us consider one such accelerator—defeat in war—in some detail, both because it has played a decisive part in promoting many revolutions and because it is related to one crucial determinant of the success or failure of any given revolutionary attempt—namely, the position of the army.

The intimate connection between defeat in war and the onset of revolution is obvious from many historical examples. The fall of Bonaparte [Napoleon III] and the defeat of the French Army by the Prussians in 1871 created for the first time in modern history the typical situation favorable to the revolutionary capture of political power; this situation was characterized by the neutralization or destruction of the regular army, by loss of confidence on the part of the people of France in any peaceful solution of social ills, and by the vastly increased significance of a military force of armed workers (the Paris National Guard). Defeat in war also accelerated dysfunctional conditions to the flash point in Russia (1905 by the Japanese, and 1917 by the Germans); in Hungary, Germany, and Turkey in 1918; in China and Yugoslavia during World War II;[10] following the defeat of the Red Army in the Ukraine in 1941; in the French, British, and Dutch colonies in east Asia in 1941–42; and external war sufficiently accelerated the dysfunctions in the Irish system to bring the revolution of 1916–23 to the surface. Defeat in war, as an accelerator, shatters the myth of sovereignty, exacts sacrifices—even the supreme sacrifice—from a society's members for an unpopular system, and completes the crippling of an already creaking system; most important, it opens the doors to revolution because of its effects on the army.

The central position of armed forces in revolutions has been hinted at, but not explored, by several writers in the past. Hannah Arendt includes in her list of events that made up the occasion of the first (to her) "true" revolution "the defection of the royal troops before a popular attack."[11] Pettee asserts, in passing, that "there is general agreement that a revolution cannot commence until the army is no

[10] For a discussion of the effects of war on Chinese and Yugoslav societies during World War II see my *Peasant Nationalism and Communist Power* (Stanford, 1962).

[11] *On Revolution*, p. 41.

longer loyal to the old regime";[12] and, more analytically, that "the
force of habit in the dull minds of functionaries and soldiers will keep
a regime going long after it could be voted out of power if voting
were possible."[13] Regarding the Bolshevik Revolution, Lichtheim notes,
"That the revolution ultimately took the form that it did was not
of course entirely due to Lenin. The war provided Lenin with the
opportunity which, had it been postponed even for a few years, would
probably not have recurred."[14] . . .

Possibly the oldest and best-known comment on the relationship
between the army and revolution is Napoleon's rebuke of the king
for failing to use the army fully when the *sans-culottes* stormed the
Tuileries (1792): "Comment a-t-on pu laisser entrer cette canaille?
Il fallait en balayer quatre ou cinq cents avec du canon et le reste
courrait encore."[15] The English equivalent, a "whiff of grapeshot,"
has since entered the language of political violence as the specific anti-
dote to revolution. Katherine Chorley, alone among writers on revolution familiar to me, places primary stress on the position of the army
in a revolutionary situation, and states this as a general principle:

> Insurrections cannot be permanently won against a professional army
> operating its technical resources at full strength. They can be won
> only when the introduction of some extraneous factor cripples the
> striking power of the professional fighting forces for one reason or
> another. The part to be played by the army is, therefore, decisive
> in any revolution, whether social or nationalist.[16]

This is an important principle. By definition, revolution requires
the use of violence by members of the system in order to cause the
system to change. If the old order simply wheezes to a stop and a
new system is formed on the basis of virtually unanimous agreement
among conscious political participants (e.g., as with the end of the
Tokugawa shogunate and its replacement by the Meiji oligarchy),[17]
there has been change but not revolution. Practically speaking, revolution involves armed insurrection, and this implies a clash with profes-
sionally trained and equipped troops at the command of the extrinsic
elite. Both the success or failure of armed insurrection and, in the

[12] *The Process of Revolution*, p. 104.
[13] *Ibid.*, p. 103.
[14] George Lichtheim, *Marxism: An Historical and Critical Study* (London, 1961),
p. 349. Cf. Milovan Djilas, *The New Class* (New York, 1957), pp. 22–23.
[15] Joseph Calmette, *Napoléon I*er* (Paris, 1952), p. 36.
[16] Katherine C. Chorley, *Armies and the Art of Revolution* (London, 1943),
p. 23.
[17] I am aware that qualifications are necessary for this example, but the Meiji
Restoration is more an instance of nonviolent change than of revolution.

age of committed professional revolutionary brotherhoods, commonly even the decision to attempt revolution rest, therefore, upon the attitude (or the revolutionaries' estimate of that attitude) that the armed forces will adopt toward the revolution. The application of science to warfare has created armed forces that are invincible to any force other than a similarly equipped and trained armed force. Regardless of the amount of dysfunction in a system, armed insurrection is futile against a modern army *if* the army can, or will, exploit its capabilities to the full; and to the extent that a given revolution is rationally calculated, its timing as well as its success or failure will depend upon this consideration.

Some revolutions do rest on calculation and will not be launched if there exists no chance of success; in the Sinn Fein revolution, for example, the Irish Republican Brotherhood took the decision secretly, on September 9, 1914, to open revolt against Britain during the war, and this decision led to Easter Week, 1916.[18] Therefore, the study of the determinants of success or failure is also relevant to the problem of cause. But it is equally possible for incapacitation of the army and the decision to revolt to coincide fortuitously. If they coincide, fortuitously or otherwise, the revolution has a good chance of success; if they do not coincide, it will probably fail. Thus, since the success or failure of any revolution depends upon the role of the armed forces, it is important that students of revolution know something about what causes conditions of dysfunction in the military substructure of the social system.

The first generalization to be made about the position of armies in revolutionary situations is that the officer corps and the rank-and-file have radically different attitudes toward the social system. Officers play elite roles in a social system and, as a consequence, are more commonly the targets of revolution than the participants in it. However, if officers are mobilized by one of the sources of dysfunction, they may make an elitist revolution—i.e., a coup d'état (a type of revolution considered in Part II below and, of course, not always one made by officers). Other things being equal, officers' revolutions will always succeed when the officers are in fact commanding the army. They need not worry about armed force being used against them when making their revolution (e.g., as in the installation of the Korean junta in May 1961). Because of this advantage, officers' revolutions are very

---

[18] D. J. Goodspeed, *The Conspirators: A Study of the Coup d'Etat* (London, 1962), p. 45. See also Edgar Holt, *Protest in Arms: The Irish Troubles, 1916–1923* (New York, 1961), and Dorothy Macardle, *The Irish Republic* (London, 1938).

frequent in dysfunctional societies, and they are commonly prompted by relatively insignificant accelerators. . . .

Officers are military leaders, but they are never "apolitical." The "overlapping group memberships" of military officers are more extensive and encompass greater sectors of power than those of most other citizens except for the supreme elite. For this reason there are, of course, many sources of revolutionary mobilization for officers other than defeat in war. . . .

The army rank-and-file, on the other hand, is characterized by having an autonomous morale to the greatest extent that any group can have in an integrated social system. And this fact is of immense relevance to an analysis of the causes of revolution. A revolutionary level of dysfunctions may exist and persist over long periods of time without ever affecting the rank-and-file of the army. Part of the logic of military organization is to cut off troops from civilian interests so that they will accept their officers' orders unquestionably. . . . But defeat in war is the one common occurrence that dissolves well-trained military formations. Chorley emphasizes the consequences of defeat above all others:

> Experience proves that on the whole the rank and file will never disintegrate on their own initiative through the impact of direct political emotion. Some other and stronger solvent is required. The supreme solvent for the distintegration of the rank and file is an unsuccessful war. . . . There can be little doubt that under modern conditions the last stages of an unsuccessful war provide the surest combination of circumstances for a successful revolutionary outbreak.[19]

Defeat in war of a potentially revolutionary dysfunctional system will accelerate the dysfunctions by adding telling new problems to the already burdened system, and it may destroy the ultimate weapon against revolution held by the status quo elite—the army (which may also join the revolution). If the defeated army can be reorganized by the status quo elite before the revolution is victorious, or if undefeated troops can be mobilized, then of course the revolution may still be defeated. But many of the most famous revolutions that have succeeded have occurred in the context of defeat of the status quo regime in external war.

Defeat in war as an accelerator is double-edged. The concept of accelerator itself is not intended to indicate anything necessary about the outcome of revolution; it is a device constructed to help us conceptualize the occurrence of revolution. But the accelerator of defeat

[19] Chorley, op. cit., pp. 108, 38–39.

in war tells us something about why some revolutions occur when they do and also why they may succeed. Not all accelerators will relate to the army, and the success or failure of some revolutions depends upon influences on the army other than the elements that brought the level of dysfunctions to the revolutionary boiling point. . . .

Let us then summarize again the causes of revolution. Multiple dysfunctions plus elite intransigence cause revolution. This is true of all types of revolution. In order to investigate actual revolutions, it is helpful to employ the *ad hoc* concept of "accelerators of dysfunction," so that we may isolate the final dysfunction-inducing element that brings a given revolution into being. One typical accelerator is defeat in war. Success or failure in revolution depends upon whether or not the status quo elite can employ modern armed forces working at their full capacities against the revolutionaries. . . .


II.  THE TYPES OF REVOLUTION

[We have] located revolution within the social system as a form of change that occurs in response to particular conditions of the system. Our problem [now] . . . is to attempt to understand why revolution, when it does occur, takes different forms. Let us try to state this problem clearly. There are varieties of revolution—coups d'état, army revolts, peasant rebellions, revolutionary wars, and so on. Italian society was dysfunctional and its elite intransigent in 1922; Algerian society was similarly dislocated in 1954. The relief of dysfunctional conditions in the one took the form of the March on Rome; in the other, an eight-year revolutionary war ensued. Can we explain why? An explanation of the *cause* of revolution in terms of multiple dysfunctions and elite intransigence will not tell us what kind of revolution is going to occur. However, once we assume that a revolution is going to occur, it is possible to elaborate tentative conceptual principles that will tell us something about the kind of revolution it will be.

At the level of the concrete instance, there are far too many variables to attempt to generalize. There is no substitute for historical and empirical research in order to specify either actual causes or actual forms of specific revolutions. Phrasing the problem in terms of an analogy with the taxonomic classification of the forms of life, we have neither the data nor the space to elaborate typological pigeonholes at the species level. However, we believe that some contribution to the problem of differentiation by type can be made by starting from the top of the taxonomic table and working downward. For "life" in the taxonomic structure, let us substitute "social change." At the level of "kingdom" let us replace "plant" and "animal" with "nonviolent change" and "revolution." And under revolution, let us consider six phyla.

What we are suggesting is that revolutions may be categorized into a six-fold typology conceived to exist at a very high level of abstraction. The six phyla are: jacquerie, millenarian rebellion, anarchistic rebellion, jacobin communist revolution, conspiratorial coup d'état, and militarized mass insurrection. Before proceeding to indicate our criteria of differentiation and to discuss each form in some detail, we must enter a disclaimer about our zoological analogy. The use of the language of taxonomy is not intended to imply the ultimate evolution of each type from the one that precedes it (i.e., phylogeny). Our sole purpose is to indicate difference at a high level of abstraction; precedent for the use of taxonomic terms in this sense is found in the broad, basic divisions of linguistic "families" into phyla.

Our six phyla are distinguished from each other on the basis of four criteria: (1) targets of revolutionary activity; (2) identity of the revolutionaries (masses, elites-leading-masses, and elites); (3) revolutionary goals or "ideology"; and (4) whether or not the revolution is spontaneous or calculated.

Let us elaborate some of these criteria briefly before proceeding to discuss the phyla themselves. By "targets," we mean to imply the question, "Does the revolution have the effect of replacing the *government*, the *regime*, or the *community?*" By community we mean the consciousness of human solidarity that overlays a society technically defined—i.e., people united by the division of labor—and by which men actually perceive their social life. Community does not refer to the inescapable interdependence of men, but to the formal expression by which men understand their complementary relationships with each other. When a man identifies himself as a Kikuyu, a Frenchman, or (in some cases) a Mohammedan, he is referring to the community of which he is a member. The sense of community contributes "integration" to the functional social system.

For purposes of the study of social change, we posit that there are several types of community—e.g., tribal, peasant,[20] theocratic, kinship, national, and so forth—and that there are subvarieties of each type. Since different types of community exist, the form of community may change (by replacement, migration, expansion of the limits of

---

[20] See Robert Redfield, "Peasant Society and Culture," in *The Little Community and Peasant Society and Culture* (Chicago, paper ed., 1960).

the division of labor, etc.) in response to appropriate pressures—e.g., "Ashkenazim" and "Sephardim" may become "Israelis." If this change is accomplished by means of revolution, the particular revolution that accomplishes it must be of the jacobin communist type (e.g., the French Revolution). It is the only form of revolution that "aims" at (or alters) the community. In actual fact, community usually changes gradually and only rarely by revolution.

Most revolutions have as their target the regime—i.e., the level within a community dealing with basic organization, with the "fundamental rules of the game." Democracy, dictatorship, constitutional government, monarchy, oligarchy, and the like are different kinds of regimes. It is quite possible for either non-violent change or revolution to alter the regime without affecting the community (e.g., as in the Cuban revolution), although many such revolutions will be made *because* the community has already changed non-violently (e.g., as in the American Revolution). Finally, some revolutions—notably, jacqueries—intend only to relieve dysfunction by restoring the status quo ante, and this is accomplished by violent change at the level of the government (political and administrative institutions that make and execute decisions for the community). Non-violent change or revolution at the governmental level does not necessarily affect either the regime or the community.[21] It is in the sense of this tri-fold distinction that we employ the criterion of targets.

The criterion of mass or elite is obvious; it refers to who makes the revolution or, more precisely, to who in the system has an effective sense of the existence of dysfunctional conditions in the face of elite intransigence. A coup is always elitist; jacqueries are always mass revolutions. Millenarian rebellions, jacobin communist revolutions, and militarized mass insurrections are all elite-leading-mass revolutions; anarchistic rebellions may be any of the three.

The criterion of revolutionary ideology refers to how revolutionaries propose to relieve dysfunction and, in particular, with what they plan to replace the unsatisfactory government, regime, or community. By ideology, we do not mean the formal, explicit doctrine that may be espoused by the revolutionaries—e.g., fascism, communism, syndicalism, etc. Rather, we refer to a summary analysis of goals under which various actual ideologies can be grouped on the basis of their implicit intent. Thus, we will place certain revolutions in the anarchistic category that did not have a single supporter who called himself

---

[21] The present use of the terms "government," "regime," and "community" follows that of David Easton, "Political Anthropology," in *Biennial Review of Anthropology 1959*, B. J. Siegel, ed. (Stanford, 1959), pp. 228–229.

an "anarchist." If one were to reduce to a name the characteristics of the ideologies appropriate to each phylum, we would propose the following: reformist (jacqueries), eschatological (millenarian), nostalgic (anarchistic), nation-forming (jacobin communist), elitist (conspiratorial coup), and nationalistic (militarized mass insurrection). . . . Finally, the criterion of spontaneity or calculation is to help us distinguish the coup and the militarized mass insurrection from cases that may be similar in all other respects; only these two types are by definition calculated.

There is one particular weakness in this typology that we must identify before discussing the six types. Our criteria of differentiation—targets, identities, ideologies, and spontaneity vs. calculation—do not touch upon the two fundamental factors causing differences in form, namely, the type of system and the sources of dysfunction. If the earlier analysis relating revolution to the social system is approximately accurate, revolutions cannot be meaningfully studied or compared apart from the system in which they occur. To pull revolutions out of the system and to try to compare them without reference to the dysfunctional system destroys the very idea of revolution. However, even if one could conceivably specify types of system as an input into a typology of revolutions, it is doubtful that one could also specify sources of dysfunction and the effects of these sources on various systems; for example, all "traditional" systems are not the same, and "imperialism"—a typical source of dysfunction—varies over time and by agent. It is ultimately the combination of these two inputs—the type of system and the sources of dysfunction—that cause variation; these two elements in all of their complexity must be studied fully in any analysis of a given revolution.

Pointing out this dimension of ultimate variability is a way of drawing attention again to the level of abstraction at which the present typology is pitched. In terms of taxonomic structure, it is a way of reminding the reader that constituents of a phylum also differ from each other analogously to classes, genera, and species. Possibly it reveals a major limitation of the taxonomic classification for our purposes. It may be preferable to imagine the . . . discussion of jacqueries, millenarian movements, and so forth in terms of the study of "ideal types." For surely the reader has already thought of a concrete instance of revolution in which ideology cannot be neatly catalogued; for example, is the ideology of the Kikuyu Mau Mau a millenarian or an anarchistic one, excluding from consideration its urban, politicized supporters? Our grounds for persisting in the attempt to differentiate "phyla" are solely those of utility: whether or not this typology is satisfactory, the very attempt to use it underscores key differences between, for example, the Taiping Rebellion of mid-nineteenth-century China (which I would call millenarian) and the Chinese Communist militarized mass insurrection of 1937–49. There has been and is today a great deal of confusion concerning differences among revolutions and between the two specific Chinese examples mentioned. We submit that it is useless to analyze the causes of revolution in structural-functional terms without raising the question of variability and essaying an answer; since the Jacquerie (1358) and the Bolshevik Revolution can both be subsumed under the earlier discussion of cause, we must at least raise the problem of form, even though we cannot settle it for good. . . .

# 6

# The Concept of a Political Revolution

*Eugene Kamenka*

ꤜꤜꤜꤜꤜꤜꤜꤜꤜꤜꤜꤜꤜꤜꤜꤜꤜꤜꤜꤜꤜꤜꤜꤜꤜꤜꤜꤜꤜꤜꤜ

## EDITORS' COMMENT

There are many ways of categorizing theorists of internal war. In this book, we have paid a great deal of attention to the current methodological dispute between theorists of equilibrium (Johnson, Aristotle, etc.) and theorists of constraint (Dahrendorf, Hobbes, etc.). But, as Kamenka suggests in the following essay (in another context), "there is not a right definition and a wrong definition, there are only fruitful distinctions and less fruitful distinctions, terms useful in one context and useless in another." To understand some of the differences between the essay by Kamenka and the ones by other authors in this volume, some "fruitful distinctions" can be made by examining how theorists of revolution view the nature of historical change. Is it structured or unstructured? Is it random or patterned? Is it accidental or guided? Is it progressive, regressive, cyclical, or nondirectional?

In the work of equilibrium theorists such as Chalmers Johnson we observe that historical change, although patterned (for example, there are six types of revolution), is not directional—there is no sense of an historical event being "progressive" or "reactionary." The sources of dysfunction simply arise from left or right, top or bottom, or from outside of a social system; the sources of change often are accidental. Strictly speaking, the word counterrevolution would be a meaningless term to Johnson—the conspiratorial coup is as much a "revolution" as a militarized mass insurrection.

But this nondirectional view of historical change is also shared by theorists of power, for example, Peter Amann, whom Kamenka discusses, and Ralf Dahrendorf, whose essay appears in this book. To them, the source of conflict is the resistance to a monopoly of power created by the existence of a monopoly of power: "legitimacy amounts at best to a precarious preponderance of power over the resistance it engenders . . . the dialectic of power and resistance determines the rate and direction [note] of change" (See Dahrendorf, Selection 2 in this volume). Again, notice that the terms progressive, reactionary, and counterrevolution do not appear.

If these theorists are nondirectional, what then is a directional view of historical change? Loosely speaking, it implies a theory of progress (or regress), the inevitability (or great likelihood) of certain events and, perhaps, a teleology that is historically instead of functionally defined. Marx, obviously, is such a theorist, and the essays by Trotsky and Mao in this volume give a flavor of this view of history. Whether Debray shares this view of historical change is open to debate, but a good case could certainly be made that he does. Kamenka is a non-Marxist, adhering to a directional view of history, as the following essay illustrates.

Cyclical theories are the third major category of historical change. These views are not widely held today, but we have included in this book an essay by Pitirim A. Sorokin (one of the most respectable contemporary adherents of cyclical theory), who views historical change as the result of shifts between ideational, sensate, and idealistic systems of culture.

If one perceives historical change as progressive, as Kamenka does, it is easy to understand his concept of a "political revolution." Society advances in stages, and revolution is the possible product of a transitional stage in history—never occurring before "Europe" had influenced non-Western societies and never occurring after the "Western" industrial state was fully developed. Because he views history in stages, it makes sense for him to say that certain revolutions are "in" the twentieth century but not "of" it and that communism, as the ideology of backward nations, has really not advanced from 1848.

Revolution, then, because it is a peculiar phenomenon tied to economic and ideological change during a certain stage of history, can be conceptually different from other internal wars (coups, jacqueries, etc.) which theorists of power—not to mention the theorists of equilibrium—lump together. The reader should speculate on the distinctions, in this respect, between Kamenka and James C. Davies—to whom Kamenka is explicitly indebted. Would Davies rule out the possibility of revolution in a modern industrial state? Would Davies accept the notion of counterrevolution?

The reader should also reflect on Kamenka's belief that a convulsive social upheaval—a revolution—is impossible in a modern industrial state (although to him a counterrevolution is possible). The implications of the three categories of historical change for this problem are interesting. A directional theorist, such as Marx, can maintain that the bourgeois state is still in a transitional stage and, hence, is prone to revolution. A directional theorist, such as Kamenka, can maintain that the bourgeois state is not in a transitional but is in a "final" stage—in a sense—and hence, is immune to revolution. (Marx's final stage is also—by definition—immune.)

If a nondirectional theorist wishes to postulate the impossibility of a revolution in a modern industrial state, he must rely on empirical assumptions about the state's capacity for armed repression and ideological mastery—the crucial role of which is emphasized by both equilibrium and coercion theorists in this book—although none of them asserts the invulnerability of the modern state. He must further demonstrate that the mature bourgeois state is different in kind from its ancestors. The cyclical theorist has little comfort for those who suggest the impossibility of revolution in a modern industrial state.

As a final point, the reader should consider precisely what the relationship is between economics and politics in Kamenka's essay—why he is so careful to develop a concept of a *political* revolution yet so ready to tie it to *economic* change. Is he, perhaps, arguing that at lower stages of development, the close relationship between economics and politics was responsible for instability—where "direct power relationships [play] a larger part in the distribution of material welfare?" And, in mature states, stability is the result of the separation between economics and politics in the "era that successfully institutionalized societies' passage from one nonpolitical, social, or economic revolution to another?"

# THE CONCEPT OF A POLITICAL REVOLUTION

## Eugene Kamenka

The twentieth century is and is not the era of revolutions. In the past six decades we have witnessed one upheaval after another: the momentous revolution in Russia and two or three revolutions in China, the rise of Kemal Pasha Atatürk, the collapse of the Austro-Hungarian Empire, the abortive attempts at revolution in Germany and Hungary, the seizure of power by Nazis and Fascists, the "revolution from above" in most of Eastern Europe, the collapse of the old regime in Egypt followed by revolutionary impulses throughout the Arab world, and finally, the revolution in Cuba. In Latin America, the almost institution-alized cycle of revolutions and *coups d'état* remains unbreached; in the old colonial and neo-colonial territories of Asia, Africa, and the Pacific there have been momentous transfers of power, some peaceful, some more violent. The twentieth century, at first sight, seems the century of revolutions and instability *par excellence.*

Yet to many of us whose attitudes are shaped by conditions in the highly industrialized countries of the West, these revolutions and upheavals now seem to be in the twentieth century, but not *of* it. We write, as I myself have written, that the revolution in Russia was successful precisely because Russia under the Czar was not like modern England, or Norway, or Australia, or the United States; we tend to agree with Karl Kautsky in treating the Austro-Hungarian Empire as a grotesque survival from the past, notable not for its fall, but for its astonishing ability to totter on into the twentieth century. Consciously or unconsciously, sweepingly or cautiously, we liken the social struggles in Asia, Africa, and Latin America to the social strug-gles of eighteenth- and nineteenth-century Europe and not to the prob-lems confronting advanced industrial societies in the modern age of technology. Communism, *the* revolutionary movement of our time,

Source. Eugene Kamenka, "The Concept of a Political Revolution," from C. J. Friedrich (ed.), *Nomos VIII: Revolution* (New York: Atherton Press, 1966), pp. 122–135. Reprinted by permission of the publishers, Atherton Press, Inc. Copyright 1966 by the Atherton Press, New York. All rights reserved.

smacks to us of 1848; we see it and the revolutionary ideology in general, as the understandable, whether regrettable or commendable, ideology of backward nations. The aim of all this fuss is not really to change the course of development in the twentieth century, but to catch up with it.

The revolutions that seem to us in some sense not "of" the twentieth century are, of course, *political* revolutions—the only kind of revolutions I am concerned with in this paper. One can also speak of the industrial revolution, the scientific revolution, the computer revolution, the Freudian revolution, or, perhaps, of the annual revolution in female fashions. These revolutions are very much *of* the twentieth century: indeed, the more men see such revolutions as part of the regular life of their country, the less prone they seem to be to turn to political revolutions for salvation. Viewed in terms of the historical development of Western society, which we see as now setting the fundamental economic objectives and values pursued in contemporary history, the twentieth century is notable not as the era that gave the world political revolutions, but as the era that successfully institutionalized society's passage from one nonpolitical, social or economic revolution to another.

What is a political revolution? When Aristotle spoke of revolutions, he used the term *metabole*, change, and where appropriate, *metabole kai stasis*, change and uprising. But what sort of change, and how important is the element of uprising or violence? Aristotle thought the change had to be one in the *type* of political organization, e.g., from monarchy to oligarchy, from oligarchy to democracy, and so on. Today, we are perhaps somewhat less confident than Aristotle was that the political changes that amount to a change in type, or in the *essence* of the social order, can so readily be detected among other changes; at the same time, we tend to pay even greater attention than he does to the ideology, the beliefs and habits, involved in the existence of a social order. As a preliminary approach to the problem of isolating and describing the meaning of the term "revolution," we might therefore suggest the following: Revolution is a sharp, sudden change in the social location of political power, expressing itself in the radical transformation of the process of government, of the official foundations of sovereignty or legitimacy and of the conception of the social order. Such transformations, it has usually been believed, could not normally occur without violence, but if they did, they would still, though bloodless, be revolutions. The concept of a sharp, sudden change is no doubt a relative concept; what appears to the participants as the slow, gradual evolution of a new style of life may, to later generations, seem a sudden and revolutionary change. At the same time, acknowledged revolutions are rarely sharp and sudden enough to take place at a clearly defined point in time, or to reveal themselves unequivocally as revolutions at the very moment of the formal transfer of power. The violent outburst that heralds the beginning of the revolution for the chronicler may be understandable only as the product of important, if less spectacular, social changes that preceded it; the task of distinguishing a revolutionary outbreak from *coup d'état* or a rebellion may be impossible until we see how the new masters use their new-won power. But unless we confine the term "revolution" to the field of *convulsive* changes we shall find revolution everywhere, all the time.

The history of the term "revolution" as a political concept has been traced for us in a scholarly work by the German sociologist Eugen Rosenstock-Huessy.[1] The men of the Italian Renaissance had used "revolution" (*rivoluzioni*) to describe the motion of the planets under the iron laws of the celestial spheres. In transposing the term into the field of politics, they meant to recognize in the rise and fall of princes a superhuman, astral force—the revolving wheel of fortune that raised up one prince or government and threw down another. This concept of a revolution as a total, fundamental and *objective* transformation, as a natural catastrophe, Rosenstock-Huessy calls the *naturalistic* concept. It persisted according to him, right up to the French Revolution. When the Duc de Liancourt informed Louis XVI of the storming of the Bastille, the King exclaimed, "But good God! That is a revolt!" "No, Sire," replied the Duc, "c'est la révolution"—meaning that this was a force of nature completely beyond human control.[2]

With the French Revolution, Rosenstock argues, a new concept of revolution, the *romantic* concept, comes to the fore. Revolution is now seen as the heroic, romantic deed, as the assertion of human sub-

---

[1] Eugen Rosenstock-Huessy, *Revolution als politischer Begriff in der Neuzeit* (Breslau: 1931). There is a short summary of Rosenstock's argument in Sigmund Neumann, "The International Civil War," *World Politics*, 1 (1948–1949), pp. 333–350. For a brief but independent confirmation of some of Rosenstock's findings, see Arthur Hatto, "Revolution: An Enquiry into the Usefulness of an Historical Term," *Mind*, 58 (1949), pp. 495–517.

[2] Cited by Neumann, *op. cit.*, p. 336. The naturalistic concept of revolution retained the cyclical conception of astronomy and of Classical political philosophy; the term "revolution" was associated with a concept of restoration, of the wheel of fortune returning to its original mark. It is for this reason, as Hatto points out (*op. cit.*, p. 505) that Clarendon called the events in England in 1660 a "revolution," that is, a *return* to the rightful order of things. For the opposing party, 1688 was the return or restoration, occurring, as they were delighted to note, precisely one hundred years after the expulsion of the Papists from England. The year 1688 was thus their "revolution": the Glorious Revolution that marked the restoration of their fortunes.

jectivity, of man as the master of history. Before the Revolution Voltaire and Condorcet has laid down the elements of this view; Robespierre became its spokesman; the barricades of 1848 and the Blanquist faction in the Paris Commune were its visible expression. But in reality, the romantic period in Europe was short-lived. By 1850 it had lost most of its force. In the Italian *Risorgimento*, the realist Cavour replaced the romantic Mazzini; Germany moved into the age of Bismarck; the Republican opposition in the France of the Second Empire falls under the sway of the Comtean positivist Gambetta.[3] We enter a new period in the history of the idea of revolution, the general trend of which is only confirmed by the defeat of the Paris Commune. It is the period of the *realist* concept of revolutions.

Rosenstock-Huessy is in the Hegelian tradition; he sees the realist phase as the dialectical negation and synthesis (*Aufhebung*) of the two previous phases. Revolution is no longer seen as an unpredictable result of superhuman forces; to that extent, naturalism is overcome. But revolutions are seen as dependent on objective conditions; they come when the time is ripe for them. To that extent, naturalism is preserved. Neither are revolutions the mere product of human will, they can occur only in a revolutionary situation. Thus, romanticism is overcome. But for the revolutionary situation to become effective, there must be a class ready to do its work, or a decided leadership able to recognize, articulate, and direct the revolutionary forces of the time. Thus, romanticism, the importance of subjectivity, is also preserved. It is because Karl Marx, the outstanding "realist," combined and yet transcended the naturalistic and the romantic views of revolution, that he and his disciples could claim to be neither the astrologers nor the poets of revolution, but its scientists.

The realist theory of revolutions has yet one more important component, which die-hard Hegelians, no doubt, might seek to interpret as the *Aufhebung* of cyclical repetition and lawless leaps into the future. This is the concept of progress. Revolutions were the milestones in humanity's inexorable march toward true freedom and true universality. Each revolution, Marx and Engels write in the *German Ideology*, is the work of a particular class, but during the revolution it appears as the representative of the whole society; as we pass from aristocracy to *bourgeoisie* and from *bourgeoisie* to proletariat, we pass to an ever-broadening base of social power; each revolution is thus truly nearer universality than the last.

The ascription of responsibility in history is governed by much

---

[3] Cf. David Thomson, "Scientific Thought and Revolutionary Movements," *Impact of Science on Society*, VI (1955), pp. 23–24.

the same psychological mechanisms as the ascription of responsibility in morals and law. A revolution, like a street accident, results from the interaction of a number of factors, each of them necessary but not sufficient to produce the result. We are constantly tempted to pick out as *the* cause the factor that we consider unusual or improper, the factor that lies outside the normal range of our expectations. The young Marx, accustomed to think of governments and social structures as rigid, and greatly impressed with the comparatively recent consciousness of the far-reaching economic changes taking place in society, saw revolution as caused by these changes. By the turn of the century, there was a new generation of Anglo-American thinkers, accustomed to think of far-reaching economic changes as the norm of social life: To them, *the* cause of revolutions seemed the rigidity of governments, the lack of social mobility and political flexibility, repression, and administrative incompetence.[4]

Though the emphases differ, the position is basically the same. Revolution, says Marx, is the bursting of the integument by the repressed forces of economic and social development; revolution, say later sociologists as different as Ward, Ellwood, Pareto, and Brooks Adams,[5] is the conflict between advancing classes or groups or interests in a society and the rigid structure or elite that holds them back.

Karl Marx, who saw revolutions as the violent conflicts between classes, defined these classes as purely economic groups, whose behavior and attitude were determined by their relationship to the means of production. Contemporary sociologists have been very strongly aware not only of the difficulties of Marx's class position in general, but of its particular weaknesses in dealing with revolutions. The leaders of the French revolution, for the most part, were not merchants, but

---

[4] Cf. the passage in L. F. Ward's *Pure Sociology* (p. 230): "Only the labile is truly stable, just as in the domain of living things only the plastic is enduring. For lability is not an exact synonym of instability, but embodies, besides, the idea of flexibility and susceptibility to change without destruction or loss. It is that quality in institutions which enables them to change and still persist, which converts their equilibrium into a moving equilibrium, and which makes possible their adaptation to both internal and external modification. . . . When a society makes for itself a procrustean bed, it is simply preparing the way for its own destruction by the on-moving agencies of social dynamics." Charles A. Ellwood puts the position even more strongly: the causes of revolution are the causes of social rigidity—the breakdown of those habits and institutions (free discussion, public criticism, etc.) that make a government responsive to the need or demand for social transitions. See Ellwood, "A Psychological Theory of Revolutions," *American Journal of Sociology*, II (1905–1906), p. 53.

[5] V. Pareto, *The Mind and Society*, Vols. III and IV, esp. pp. 2050–2059, 2170–2203, and 2227; Brooks Adams, *The Theory of Social Revolution, passim.*

lawyers, notaries, and bailiffs—professional men. The Russian Revolution in 1917 depended heavily for its success on the leadership of that very special noneconomic class, the intelligentsia, and on the fact that a significant number of peasants had been converted, for a period, into soldiers. In these circumstances, most modern writers on revolution have turned, consciously or unconsciously, to Max Weber's conception of class as composed of those who share the same chance in life (*Lebenschance*)—a definition that enables us to cope with intellectuals and, in certain circumstances, with racial or national conflicts and the politics of minorities.

The conception of revolution as connected with members of a Weberian class seeking to improve their life chance, throws into relief once more the role of social rigidity in the production of revolutions and the mitigating influence that we might expect from the existence of a fairly high degree of social mobility, or from the strong belief in its possibility. Members of a class may ascend as individuals; they may ascend collectively as the result of objective conditions; or they may seek the revolutionary path of destroying the privileges of an upper class and reducing its life chances until it ceases to exist as a separate class—normally in the belief that a gain in average life chances will result. Collective ascent as the result of objective conditions is usually slow, but it can be extremely significant. Few people would doubt that the gradual collective ascent of the working classes of Western Europe and North America between 1815 and 1914 did a very great deal indeed to contain and even discredit revolutionary forces and movements. The extent and significance of individual ascent is much more the subject of controversy; but again, one might reasonably assert that the significant chance of individual ascent offered by the assisted migration schemes in England from the 1860's to the 1880's played a marked role in averting the revolutionary situation, or at least the sustained atmosphere of revolt, that might have resulted from the agricultural depression.

An important allied point about revolution was first hinted at by Karl Marx in *Wage Labour and Capital*[6] and put quite decisively by Alexis de Tocqueville a few years later:

---

[6] "A noticeable increase in wages presupposes a rapid growth of productive capital. The rapid growth of productive capital brings about an equally rapid growth of wealth, luxury, social wants, social enjoyments. Thus, although the enjoyments of the workers have risen, the social satisfaction that they give has fallen in comparison with the increased enjoyments of the capitalist, which are inaccessible to the worker, in comparison with the state of development of society in general." Marx and Engels, *Selected Works*, Vol. I (Moscow: 1955), p. 94.

Revolutions are not always brought about by a gradual decline from bad to worse. Nations that have endured patiently and almost unconsciously the most overwhelming oppression often burst into rebellion against the yoke the moment that it grows lighter. The regime which is destroyed by a revolution is almost always an improvement on its immediate predecessor. . . . Evils which are patiently endured when they seem inevitable become intolerable when once the idea of escape from them is suggested.[7]

The final sentence is the crucial one. Part of the difference between a revolutionary uprising and a rebellion is the difference in the beliefs and expectations of those involved; rebels seek the redress of grievances, the return to a former state of comparative justice or prosperity; it is amazing, when we look back, just how limited the demands of that Great Peasant Rebellion in Germany in 1525 actually were, and how ready its leaders were to accept the authority of princes and kings. Revolutionaries, on the other hand, have great expectations; they think in terms of a new order, of progress, of changing times that need changing systems of government. For nearly two thousand years, China witnessed civil wars, rebellions, secessions, and *coups d'état;* but until the European revolutions came, there had been not one revolution in China. For revolutions, as Crane Brinton found,[8] require among other things an economically advancing society, the conception of progress, of the human ability to bring about fundamental social change, which seems, as far as we can tell, to be exclusively associated with the conception of a market economy. Rebellions and *coups d'état* occur everywhere; revolutions, it is fascinating to note, seem to have occurred only in *cities* and, until comparatively recently, in Western societies. The revolutions in other types of social structures, I shall argue, rest on the permeation of Western economy and ideology; they are revolutions by contact and imitation.

Revolutions are not produced by the forces of the market economy alone; they require the belief in human power and in the possibility of vast material improvement, but they require also anger and the prospects of success. They require, that is, the support of a significant section of people not normally given to revolt. This tends to occur when two requirements are fulfilled. First, there must have been a strong rise in people's expectations, such as an economically advancing society normally produces, which is suddenly vitiated by a sharp decline in satisfactions. As James C. Davies puts it:

[7] Alexis de Tocqueville, *The Old Regime and the Revolution,* transl. by John Bonner (New York: 1856), p. 214.

[8] Crane Brinton, *Anatomy of Revolution,* rev. ed. (London: 1953), pp. 277 f. ("Some tentative uniformities").

Revolutions are most likely to occur when a prolonged period of economic and social development is followed by a short period of sharp reversal. People then subjectively fear that ground gained with great effort will be quite lost; their mood then becomes revolutionary.[9]

Davies attempts to show that this was in fact what happened just before Dorr's (unsuccessful) nineteenth-century rebellion in Rhode Island in 1840–42, in the period preceding the Russian Revolution, and in postwar Egypt before the fall of Farouk. Revolutions, he concludes, do not take place in a society where there is the continued, unimpeded opportunity to satisfy new needs, new hopes and new expectations; neither do they take place in a society in which there are no hopes, no expectations, but only hardship and hunger as long as men can remember.

The second requirement is related to the need for prospects of success, but is often intimately connected with the economic reversal that satisfies the first requirement. In every revolution that I can think of, the state against which the revolutionaries fought had been strikingly weakened by financial failure, administrative incompetence, lack of self-confidence and, in a very high number of cases, by defeat in war.

This latter point should not surprise. For if revolutions are the milestones on the way to the development of an advanced industrialized economy, they are also bloody battles, desperate struggles against the authority and power of the previously existing state. As Borkenau puts it:

> Every great revolution has destroyed the State apparatus which it found. After much vacillation and experimentation, every revolution has set another apparatus in its place, in most cases of quite a different character from the one destroyed; for the changes in the state order which a revolution produces are no less important than the changes in the social order. The revolutionary process itself is in the first instance a struggle for political power. And whatever may be the deeper driving-forces of a revolution, the struggle for the State always appears as its immediate content (!); indeed to such an extent that the transformation of the social order often appears not as the goal of the revolution, but simply as means used by revolutionaries to conquer or to exercise power.[10]

Contemporary political thinkers molded in the background of Western democracy are extremely conscious, in recent years, of the ruthless internal logic of revolutions, of the fraudulence of their claim

---

[9] James C. Davies, "Toward a Theory of Revolution," *American Sociological Review*, 27 (1962), p. 5.

[10] F. Borkenau, "State and Revolution in the Paris Commune, the Russian Revolution, and the Spanish Civil War," in *Sociological Review*, 29 (1937), p. 41.

to transfer power to "the people." Most of us today would accept what Borkenau calls "the law of the twofold development of revolutions. They begin as anarchistic movements against the bureaucratic state organization, which they inevitably destroy; they continue by setting in its place another, in most cases stronger, bureaucratic organization, which suppresses all free mass movements."[11] The Thermidorian reaction seems to us no longer a possible danger that revolutions must avoid, but a necessary consequence of the very nature of the revolutionary ideology and the revolutionary struggle. So clear, and so apparently inevitable, is the centralizing, dictatorial trend of revolutions that for the first time in human history we actually find revolution cynically used as a *means* for welding together a diffuse society, for creating centralized authority and power.

It is tempting, in these circumstances, to merge into one concept the successful rebellion, the revolution, and the *coup d'état*. Peter Amann, in a recent paper,[12] tries to do just this. Revolution, as he defines it, "prevails when the State's monopoly of power is effectively challenged and persists until a monopoly of power is re-established."[13] This approach, he argues, avoids such traditional problems as that of distinguishing a revolution from a *coup d'état*, the uncertain differentiation between wars of independence, civil wars and revolutions, and the difficulty of deciding how much social change is necessary before a movement may be called a revolution. At the same time, the definition recognizes the possibility of suspended revolutions, where we have the prolonged co-existence of two antagonistic governmental power centers, e.g., the Army and the Government in the Weimar Republic or in the post-Peron Frondizi regime in Argentina.

Such simplifications are always attractive and, in a sense, they are not wrong. Words have no natural definitions; social events have no clearly manifest essential character. *Eadem sed aliter* is the motto of history and of nature. The distinctions we make, the connections and similarities we emphasize, are made for a purpose, an explanatory purpose. For some purposes, we may be interested only in the breakdown of the governmental monopoly of public power; for these purposes Amann's use of the word "revolution" may well be a useful shorthand. For other purposes—and they are the ones with which I and most students of revolution are concerned—it misses crucial distinctions. It is, I think, important to recognize the role of rising expecta-

---

[11] *Ibid.*, p. 67.

[12] Peter Amann, "Revolution: A Redefinition," *Political Science Quarterly*, 77 (1962), pp. 36–53.

[13] *Ibid.*, p. 39.

tions and of ideology in revolutions, to be able to say that revolution is different from peasant uprisings and slave rebellions in respects crucial to understanding the process, and that there have been no revolutions in Asia and Africa until this century. To understand why this is so, we need a concept of revolution that is no doubt trickier to work with, but that has also far greater explanatory power, that the formalized concept that Amann proposes.

We have noted the naked emergence, in the twentieth century, of the centralizing motif in revolutions—the open preoccupation with power that lends plausibility to Amann's suggested redefinition. But even here there is a crucial distinction between, say, the Indonesian Revolution on the one hand and the old Chinese Triad movement to "overthrow the Ch'ing and restore the Ming" on the other.[14] Revolution has come to Asia because Europe has come to Asia; the change of power is no longer seen as a restoration, but as a leap forward, a leap forward into the universalized, industrialized society of the West. The Indonesian rebellion against the Dutch was utterly different from the Jewish rebellion against the Romans: it was not merely a movement of national liberation from foreign masters, but a struggle for *control* over political, social, and economic processes that were now recognized as the key to the future. In this sense, it seems to me, the movements of national liberation and the more or less peaceful transfers of power in Asian, African, and Pacific countries have to be seen not only as revolutions, but as *revolutions within the history of Europe*, the transfer of social power from one governing class to a new class. It is only because Asia, Africa, and the Pacific have entered the history of Europe that such true revolutions have become possible to them. It is because Turkey had entered the history of Europe that Kemal Pasha Atatürk's *coup d'état* aspired to become a revolution.

In the advanced, industrial countries of the West, on the other hand, one is inclined to say that the age of revolutions is over. As R. S. Parker put it recently:

> If . . . we consider preindustrial societies where the population pressed hard on the means of subsistence, we invariably expect to find direct power relations playing a larger part in the distribution of material welfare. . . . Comparatively speaking, high average living standards and the economic and social mobility that go with them in a country like Australia conduce, other things being equal, to a

[14] The T'ai-p'ing T'ien-kuo rebellion of 1850—64 marks the transition; on the one hand, it drew on the traditions of southern separatism and hostility to the Ch'ing (the Manchus), on the other hand it drew from European missionary influence and the penetration of European trade a messianic character that laid some of the groundwork for the revolutionary movement in China.

general acceptance of the economic processes of bargaining and exchange, and reduced need for the exercise of power in arranging the allocation of material values.[15]

For the first time in human history technological advance has become so great that society can, as Toynbee notes in his *Reconsiderations*,[16] support a vast proliferation of bureaucracy without a sharp decrease in the sub-bureaucratic standard of living; the cyclical law of the rebellion against bureaucratic rule no longer applies. At the same time, the ideology of the market has found its political counterpart in the procedures of representative government. While popular political control is no doubt as imperfect as the consumer control extolled by capitalist apologetics, it is nevertheless there. Representative government *has* produced, in conjunction with the radically "capitalized" society, a comparatively flexible, responsive social structure able to make the transitions for which revolution and uprising were needed in the past.

This is not to say that the present political structure of advanced industrial societies has no tendencies that might lead to rigidity, or that a sharp discrepancy between people's economic expectations and their economic satisfactions might not once more arise, producing a decidedly rebellious, revolutionary mood. But from the standpoint of the classical conception of revolutions, there will be fundamental differences in any such future situations. The concept of universality has been exhausted, for all practical purposes, in the attaining of representative government and reasonable economic affluence. The revolution of the future in advanced, democratic, industrialized society could only be a counterrevolution, a seizure of power by a group intent on re-establishing despotic rule and a status society. The intensification of military struggle or of population pressures on food resources could make such a possibility seem far more real than it does today; but they could hardly convert such a coup from its obvious place with Roman dictatorships to an affinity with the French, the Russian, or even the Chinese and Indonesian Revolutions.

In the Communist world, future revolutions in my sense of the word do not seem to us impossible. The Hungarian revolt was indeed part of a tradition that goes back to the French, Polish, and Russian Revolutions; it might even have ended, if successful, more happily than any of these. For the revolutionary in the Communist world the problem is the concentration of power in the hands of the modern

---

[15] R. S. Parker, "Power in Australia," a seminar paper delivered in the Institute of Advanced Studies, Australian National University, on October 8, 1962, and circulated to participants in the seminar on "The Sociology of Power," pp. 2–3.

[16] See Arnold Toynbee, *A Study of History*, Vol. XII (London: 1961), esp. pp. 200–209.

state, the comparatively blurred nature of the class against which he is rebelling, and the fact that his revolution—unlike previous revolutions directed against idle aristocrats, absentee landlords, and broken-down bureaucracies—would be against a class playing a significant role in the process of production.

The problems of social theory will not be solved by any careful, preliminary analysis of concepts. The definition of revolution is not the beginning but the end of an inquiry into social upheaval, social change, and the translocation of power. There is not a right definition and a wrong definition, there are only fruitful distinctions and less fruitful distinctions, terms useful in one context and useless in another. In this paper I have tried to suggest that we should not abandon too readily the economic strand in the realist conception of revolutions. The Leninist emphasis on revolutionary theory as a manual for the seizure of power has led many contemporary sociologists to seek to treat revolution in static terms, as a situation in which the state monopoly of power is being effectively challenged. This emphasizes the undoubted connections between revolutions, rebellions, civil wars, wars of liberation, and *coups d'état;* it is useful in deflating revolutionary pretensions about the elimination of power in human affairs and bringing out the centralizing tendencies inherent in bitter conflict. But this static, cross-sectional treatment of societies in the throes of conflict seems to me totally inadequate as a foundation for examining the causes and more general consequences of such conflicts, for understanding when and why they are likely to occur. For these purposes, we do need to distinguish between a *coup d'état* and a revolution, between the inauguration of a new dynasty and the inauguration of a new social order. The distinctions cannot be made sharply; social events run together, they vacillate between one category and another, they end where no one dreamed at the beginning they would end. Kemal Pasha's *coup d'état,* I have suggested, aspired, through its association with the Young Turks, to become a revolution; and for some purposes it may best be understood as such. The transfer of power in India, with its momentous revolutionary implications, has perhaps not succeeded in realizing them; one might easily query whether the India of 1963 is a new India in comparison with the India of 1938. Nevertheless, distinctions that can be blurred, or that can fail to be helpful in some situations, may still be vital to understanding the general picture. To do this, I have suggested, we need a *dynamic* concept of revolutions, a concept of political revolutions that sees them in their intimate relationship to the more general class of social revolutions of which they are part rather than to the allied classes of rebellions, uprisings, and wars.

# 7

# Fluctuations of Internal Disturbances

*Pitirim A. Sorokin*

## EDITORS' COMMENT

Despite the nature of the subject matter, most essays in this book exhibit a degree of measured optimism—from obviously different viewpoints. Beneath the theories of equilibrium are necessary assumptions about the stability of an integrated culture. Beneath the theories of power are necessary assumptions about man's technical abilities to control his fellow creatures. Beneath Marxist theory lies a faith in some form of ultimate human triumph. Revolutions are either controllable aberrations, in the final analysis, or are necessary and contributory episodes on the road to human freedom. Of course, counterrevolutions can occur, but they are almost, by definition, against the trend of history—or, again, are controllable annoyances. Sorokin dissents. To him, civil disturbances are frequent, normal, inevitable and, in most cases, unjustified.

The following selection is comprised of slightly more than a chapter from the abridged version of *Social and Cultural Dynamics*, which is a massive enterprise that the interested reader must consult if he wishes to examine Sorokin's theories and assumptions in detail. This essay is no substitute for the complete work, but it does point to a number of interesting findings that the student of civil violence should not ignore. Anyone interested in the statistical methodology must refer to the original, but here we observe that Professor Sorokin not only has been judicious in his handling of quantitative data but also quite bold in the scope of its application.

This short introduction cannot begin to do justice to Sorokin's overall theory of history and culture, but a brief outline is necessary for an understanding of the following essay—which otherwise might prove confusing. Sorokin believes that every human culture can be described best by identifying its most fundamental ideological assumption—its *Weltanschauung,* or major premise. This premise provides what he calls the logico-meaningful integrating factor, which governs how men think in a given culture and, hence, how they act: that is, how they organize their society, justify their politics, explain their wars, create their art, and worship their deities. Once identified, this premise can be used to explain not only the nature of a culture but the dynamics of cultural change.

Although there are a number of subcategories, there are only three major premises to be found in Western history: ideational, sensate, and idealistic. (Sorokin suggests that they are also the only premises in Oriental cultures, but he does not systematically analyze the East in this work.) Ideational mentality is based on an ultimate truth. "Reality is perceived as non-sensate and non-material everlasting Being (*Sein*)." Needs are spiritual—its adherents are either basically ascetic or are filled with missionary zeal. Sensate mentality "views reality as only that which is presented to the sense organs . . . . The Sensate reality is thought of as a Becoming, Process, Change, Flux, Evolution, Progress, Transformation. Its needs and aims are mainly physical, and maximum satisfaction is sought of these needs." Idealistic mentality is a logically integrated and balanced mixture of the two. (*Social and Cultural Dynamics,* Boston: Porter Sargent, 1957, p. 27.)

These major premises explain the integration of a culture, but also they explain the transformation from one culture to another, since Sorokin concludes that there has been a repeating cycle ("rhythm") in Western history of the sequence: ideational, idealistic, sensate, ideational, and so on. From the standpoint of internal war, the maximum amount of disturbance (both in frequency and intensity) comes during periods of change from one culture to another—and Western society is now entering such a period of change as our current sensate culture disintegrates—presumably, paving the way for a new ideational phase.

Thus, Kerensky's former secretary has erected one of the most interesting contemporary theories of ideology—diametrically opposed to the more widely acknowledged theories of Marx and Karl Mannheim. To Sorokin, ideas are not the product of social and economic relationships, but social and economic relationships are the result of a ruling *Weltanschauung*. The prevailing ideology is not the interest of the ruling class or, in any way, the product of a social class; it is prior to the class structure and permeates all levels of the culture. Major social upheavals are not the product of a shift in "objective" economic forces but the result of the decay of the major premise and the growth of a new one. Ideas are not only related to objective social reality but they rule it.

A major corollary to this rejection of the Marxist view of ideology is a total rejection of any economically based views of progress or direction in history. Not only is there no correlation in Sorkin's findings between internal violence and the rise or decline of a society (or the well-being of its citizens) but the economic progress of the past two centuries and its product, the modern industrial state, are merely a somewhat different result of the same sensate ideology which has existed in the past—and which is now breaking down. If Sorokin is to be believed, all the premises of stability which Kamenka has found in advanced industrial society are false. The optimism of an equilibrium theorist is ill-founded (since basic value changes cannot be adopted to a culture based on a different ideology), and the theorist of power cannot assume the possibility of the permanence of the values of manipulation—since this becomes irrelevant if the very concept of what constitutes power in our sensate culture is rendered absurd to the participants in the society by a shift from sensate to ideational mentality. By operating on the most fundamental of levels, Sorokin is able to perceive vast similarities existing throughout history—and the possibility of a repetition of history's more sordid aspects.

# FLUCTUATIONS OF INTERNAL DISTURBANCES

Pitirim A. Sorokin

## 1. METHODS

The material of this study includes most of *the recorded internal disturbances of importance,* from the relatively small disorders to the biggest revolutions, which have taken place in the life history of Greece, Rome, France, Germany (Central Europe), England, Italy, Spain, the Netherlands, Byzantium, Poland, Lithuania, and Russia. The very fact of its mention in the annals of history is considered a sign of the importance of an internal disturbance. Quite insignificant disorders which do not affect the life of the country in any appreciable way usually pass by without leaving any traces in the records of history.

Each of the disturbances is studied in the four quantitative aspects that seem most important: (1) the proportional extent of the *social* (not merely geographical) area of the disturbance (social space); (2) the proportion of the population actively involved in the disturbance (for or against it); (3) the duration of the disturbance; (4) the proportional intensity (the amount and sharpness of violence and the importance of effects) of the disturbance. Our concept of the magnitude of disturbance is composed as nearly as possible of the combination of these four variables. They do not embrace all the aspects of the disturbance, but they seem to embrace its most significant quantitative aspects. *Other conditions being equal, the greater the proportional extent of the social area of the disturbance, the greater the proportion of the population involved in it, the greater its intensity and the longer its duration, then the greater is the comparative magnitude of the disturbance.* As such, this magnitude aims to estimate, and does estimate, only those aspects which enter into it as an element or a variable;

Source. Pitirim A. Sorokin, "Quantitative Measurement of Internal Disturbances," from *Social and Cultural Dynamics,* one-volume abridgment (Boston: Porter Sargent, 1957), pp. 573–604, excerpted. Reprinted by permission of the publishers. Copyright 1957 by Pitirim A. Sorokin.

it does not aim to estimate other aspects of it, especially the qualitative one. . . .

[The predominant *qualitative* nature and the main objective of the disturbances are divided into five classes].

A. predominantly political disturbances, the main objective of which is a change in the existing political regime.

B. predominantly socioeconomic disturbances, directed toward a modification of the existing social and economic order.

C. national and separatistic disturbances, the main objective of which is national independence, or autonomy, or the elimination of disfranchisements, or the achievement of some other privileges and advantages.

D. religious disturbances.

F. disturbances with specific objectives—like some personal change in the government; resistance to a specific law, or tax, or other concrete measure—and disturbances without any single more dominant objective but with two or more equally strong objectives.

These qualitative pigeonholings are to be regarded, of course, as very approximate. It can hardly be questioned that any social disturbance has several reasons and several objectives. On the other hand some movements are marked by the fact that they show one of these characteristics more conspicuously than the others. In many disturbances such "predominant color" is lacking; therefore they are lumped together into a group called "mixed." . . .

Altogether there are 84 disturbances in the history of Greece; 170 in that of Rome; 49 for Byzantium; 173 for France; 150 for Germany; 162 for England; 251 for Italy; 235 or 242 (if seven disturbances which were wars rather than disturbances be included) for Spain; 103 for the Netherlands; 167 for Russia; 78 for Poland and Lithuania. A total of 1622 to 1629 disturbances is listed for all these countries

. . . . .

## 2. CONCLUSIONS

(A) The first important conclusion concerns the *frequency of occurrence of important social disturbances in the life of social bodies.* Usually it is thought that they are fairly infrequent events. Meanwhile the data at hand show—and show consistently for all the countries studied—that on the average one notable social disturbance happens in about six years, for some countries in five years, for others in seventeen years. If, instead of taking the average time span per significant social disturbance, we ask ourselves what is the average number of years without a disturbance per years with a disturbance, then the results will be still more striking. They indicate that the relationship between the years with disturbances and those without them fluctuates between one to two and one to eight, depending upon the country. On the average in most of the countries studied, to one year with a significant social disturbance there have been only about five peaceful years, free from inner social tensions and storms. Table 1 gives more exact data in the field.

Even with the relatively wide deviation of Byzantium from the record of other countries (which is due in all probability to a less careful recording of the disturbances in the history of that country) the averages for the occurrence of disturbances (in years) and for the ratio of years without disturbance to years with disturbance are remarkably close. And this in spite of the enormous difference between countries and the times in which they have been making their history! The importance of these figures is that the occurrence of social disturbances is far from being so infrequent on the average as is usually thought. On the average, in about every six to eight years one social disturbance may be expected. In this sense disturbances are "normal" occurrences in the life process of social groups.

The following figures are, of course, averages. Such would be the average frequency of disturbances if they were distributed evenly in the course of time. But such evenness is lacking. Some periods have abundant disturbances, which sometimes continue for many years; other times are free from important social storms. Therefore, the actual distribution of disturbances in the course of time is somewhat different from those averages.

Once in a while, although only rarely, periods have occurred when there was no disturbance during the whole of a quarter century. In a few such periods—all countries and for all the time studied, there are hardly more than ten cases—internal peace existed for about half a century. All in all, each generation is likely to have one or more important social disturbances during its life span.

(B) Another suggestion follows from Table 1. It is a fairly common opinion that *there are nations "inherently" disorderly and inclined to anarchy and disturbances, and nations which are, by God's will or for racial or some other reasons, destined to be orderly and free from social convulsions.* Most of the conservative proponents of this theory include their own nation in the "orderly" class; most of the radicals, who are Don Quixotes of revolution, in the "revolutionary." During the last few years there have been not infrequent occasions for hearing that, for instance, "these Slavs and Russians are anarchists by nature, while we (the British, the French, the Americans, etc.),

TABLE 1    Frequency of Important Social Disturbances

| Country | Number of Years Studied | Number of Disturbances in Period | Average Occurrence of Disturbances (in Years) | Number of Years with Disturbance | Average Ratio of Years without to Years with Disturbances |
|---|---|---|---|---|---|
| Ancient Greece (600 B.C. to 146 B.C.) | 454 | 84 | 5.4 | 122 | (2.7) |
| Rome (509 B.C. to A.D. 476) | 985 | 170 | 5.8 | 219 | (3.5) |
| Byzantinum (532–1390) | 858 | 49 | 17.5 | 89 | (8.6) |
| France (531–1933) | 1402 | 173 | 8.1 | 246 | (4.7) |
| Germany and Austria (709–1933) | 1124 | 150 | 7.5 | 204 | (4.5) |
| England (656–1933) | 1277 | 162 | 7.9 | 247 | (4.2) |
| Italy (526–1933) | 1407 | 251 | 5.6 | 365 | (2.9) |
| Spain (467–1933) | 1466 | 242 | 6.1 | 424 | (2.4) |
| The Netherlands (678–1933) | 1255 | 103 | 12.1 | 263 | (3.8) |
| Russia (946–1933) | 987 | 167 | 5.9 | 280 | (2.6) |
| Poland and Lithuania (1031–1794) | 763 | 78 | 9.8 | 146 | (4.3) |

thank heaven! are an orderly nation." Variations on this theme have been numerous and ingenious. *A glance at Table 1 is sufficient to dissipate these theories. All nations are orderly and disorderly, according to the times.* At the best, some of them show somewhat less inclination to social disturbances than others. But the difference is not serious, and even this small discrepancy is likely to decrease if we should deal with their completed history, as for example with that of Greece and Rome.

This last means that, as we shall see, there is an observable tendency for a few of the countries (but not all) to have their disturbances decrease at the later stages of their history, after their climax is over, and the glory and the fame are in the past. For instance, the Netherlands show a low disturbancy during the last two or three centuries, and a high one during the time that they were engaged in making a place for themselves under the sun. Something similar we see in

Greece, Rome, and Poland and Lithuania. This will be discussed later in more detail. For the present, the above data and these hints are sufficient to dissipate the myth of orderly and disorderly nations "by nature." The difference between people in this respect is small and does not warrant any such theory.

The partisans of orderly and disorderly nations may, however, find refuge in the contention that though the incidence of disturbances is common to all nations, they nevertheless differ radically in that revolutions proceed in the orderly nations without any, or with little, violence, while in the disorderly nations they are aways violent, bloody, and cruel. During these last few years such arguments have been heard many times. Is such a claim valid? The answer is given by Table 2, which lists the percentages of the disturbances among the nations studied, according to the degree of their intensity and violence. From the standpoint of intensity all the revolutions are divided into five classes, beginning with Class I, the "pure and bloodless" disturbances, and passing in order to Class V, the most violent among the disturbances in both the quantitative and qualitative aspects. In other words, our indicators of the intensity of disturbances are very near to being in fact what might be called the indicators of the violence, cruelty, and bloodiness of the disturbances. This is particularly true of the first three classes.

Table 2 shows that there are some differences between the nations

TABLE 2   Intensity of Revolutions by Countries—by Class

| Countries | I | | II | | III | | IV | | V | | Total | |
|---|---|---|---|---|---|---|---|---|---|---|---|---|
| | No. | Per Cent | No. | Per Cent | No. | Per Cent | No. | Per Cent | No. | Per Cent | No. | Per Cent |
| Greece | 1 | 1.2 | 11 | 3.1 | 30 | **35.7** | 24 | 28.5 | 18 | 21.4 | 84 | 100 |
| Rome | 2 | 1.2 | 49 | 28.8 | 79 | **46.5** | 19 | 11.2 | 21 | 12.5 | 170 | 100 |
| Byzantium | 2 | 4.0 | 1 | 2.0 | 10 | 20.4 | 36 | **73.6** | 0 | 0 | 49 | 100 |
| France | 17 | 9.9 | 43 | 24.5 | 74 | **43.0** | 33 | 19.2 | 6 | 3.4 | 173 | 100 |
| Germany and Austria | 12 | 8.0 | 24 | 16.0 | 73 | **48.7** | 39 | 26.0 | 2 | 1.3 | 150 | 100 |
| England | 15 | 9.2 | 41 | 25.3 | 51 | 31.5 | 52 | **32.2** | 3 | 1.8 | 162 | 100 |
| Italy | 13 | 5.1 | 35 | 13.9 | 88 | 35.1 | 112 | **44.7** | 3 | 1.2 | 251 | 100 |
| Spain | 4 | 1.7 | 46 | 19.5 | 132 | **56.2** | 43 | 18.3 | 10 | 4.2 | 235 | 100 |
| The Netherlands | 2 | 1.9 | 17 | 16.5 | 58 | **56.4** | 20 | 19.4 | 6 | 5.8 | 103 | 100 |
| Russia | 8 | 4.7 | 98 | **59.0** | 36 | 21.4 | 19 | 11.3 | 6 | 3.6 | 167 | 100 |
| Poland and Lithuania | 5 | 6.4 | 5 | 6.4 | 55 | **70.5** | 13 | 16.7 | 0 | 0 | 78 | 100 |
| Total | 81 | | 370 | | 686 | | 410 | | 75 | | 1622 | |

in this respect, but they are neither great nor consistent. This means that England and France, for instance, show the highest percentage of disturbances of those in Class I (the least violent) and in this point seem to be at the top of the list of the least violent countries. When, however, we find the predominant type of disturbances there, we see that their "mode" falls into Class IV and Class III, while the "mode" for all the other countries falls either into Class II, III, or IV. This means that all in all the English and French disturbances cannot be regarded in any way as less violent than, for instance, the Russian or German or Spanish or Dutch or the Roman.

On the basis of the data, first place in this respect seems to belong to Greece, whose percentage of Class V disturbances is excessive. However strange it may appear in the light of the contemporary Russian Revolution with its endless cruelties, so far the Russian disturbances seem not to have been more violent than those of other countries: 64 per cent of all the Russian disturbances fall into classes I and II, and only 36 percent into the remaining more violent classes. Such an indicator is not shown by any other country among those studied. Other countries, generally speaking, occupy about the same position in this respect. All this means that the contention discussed is also a myth based on a mere wish and imagination. Together with the preceding data these results are enough to dissipate the legend of "orderly" and "disorderly" peoples.

Another conclusion suggested by Table 2 is that only about 5 per cent of all 1622 disturbances studied occurred without violence and about 23 percent with slight violence. More than 70 per cent were accomplished and followed by violence and bloodshed on a considerable scale. This means that *those who dream of a "bloodless revolution" have little chance (some five chances out of one hundred) to accomplish their dream.* He who aspires for a disturbance must be ready to see violence and to be a witness or victim or perpetrator of it. This is true for all nations and groups.

(C) The third item concerns the *duration* of the disturbances. From this standpoint there are ten different classes, beginning with the disturbances which lasted only a few days and ending with those which lasted for more than twenty-five years. The questions arise: What is the proportion of short and long disturbances? What is the predominant type of their duration? Are there appreciable differences in this respect between the disturbances of various countries?

These questions are answered by Table 3, which gives the actual and the per cent figures for the duration of the disturbances studied.

From these data it follows that for the majority of the countries taken separately *the predominant type of disturbance is of Class II, that is, of a few weeks' duration.* Only in Germany and Austria, and

TABLE 3    Duration of Revolutions by Countries—by Class

| Countries | I | | II | | III | | IV | | V to VIII | | IX to X | | Total |
|---|---|---|---|---|---|---|---|---|---|---|---|---|---|
| | No. | Per Cent | No. | Per Cent | No. | Per Cent | No. | Per Cent | No. | Per Cent | No. | Per Cent | No. |
| Greece | 22 | 26.2 | 36 | **42.8** | 12 | 14.3 | 3 | 3.6 | 10 | 11.9 | 1 | 1.2 | 84 |
| Rome | 42 | 24.7 | 88 | **51.8** | 21 | 12.3 | 9 | 5.3 | 10 | 5.9 | 0 | 0 | 170 |
| Byzantium | 8 | 16.3 | 22 | **44.9** | 7 | 14.3 | 1 | 2.0 | 11 | 22.5 | 0 | 0 | 49 |
| France | 28 | 16.3 | 69 | **39.5** | 34 | 19.8 | 10 | 5.9 | 32 | 18.6 | 0 | 0 | 173 |
| Germany and Austria | 20 | 13.4 | 40 | 26.6 | 53 | **35.4** | 10 | 6.6 | 26 | 17.4 | 1 | 0.6 | 150 |
| England | 28 | 17.3 | 67 | **41.4** | 33 | 20.4 | 8 | 4.9 | 25 | 15.4 | 1 | 0.6 | 162 |
| Italy | 85 | **33.7** | 67 | 26.5 | 44 | 17.7 | 17 | 6.9 | 37 | 14.8 | 1 | 0.4 | 251 |
| Spain | 45 | 19.1 | 108 | **46.0** | 23 | 9.8 | 22 | 9.3 | 36 | 15.3 | 1 | 0.4 | 235 |
| The Netherlands | 7 | 6.8 | 24 | 23.3 | 37 | **35.9** | 4 | 3.9 | 28 | 27.2 | 3 | 2.9 | 103 |
| Russia | 30 | 18.5 | 74 | **44.0** | 24 | 14.3 | 4 | 2.4 | 32 | 19.0 | 3 | 1.8 | 167 |
| Total | 315 | 20.4 | 595 | **38.5** | 288 | 18.6 | 88 | 5.6 | 247 | 15.2 | 11 | 0.7 | 1544 |

the Netherlands is the predominant type that with a duration of several months, while in Italy it is that of a few days. Next come the disturbances with durations of a few days and a few months (Classes I and II). Then the proportion of disturbances of longer duration decreases as the duration increases; disturbances with durations of above ten years are lacking altogether in the history of several countries, in others they are below 1 per cent of all the disturbances. Only in the Netherlands and in Russia are they above 1 per cent. In general, disturbances with a duration of less than one year compose about 80 per cent of all the disturbances. Disturbances with a duration of more than one year make about 15 per cent of the total. Thus *most of the internal crises in the life process of a social body* (like sicknesses in the life process of an individual) *come and pass their acute stage within a period of a few weeks.* Only a small proportion last for one year or more.

The same data show again that, although differences exist in regard to the duration of disturbances in various countries, they are not fundamental. On the contrary, the proportionate duration of the specified disturbances is closely similar in most of the countries studied, especially if disturbances with a duration of about one year or less are taken. The main deviations occur in the records of Byzantium and the Netherlands; but even they are not conspicuously great. This suggests again that there is no particularly strong basis for qualifying some nations as "bent to disorders," and some others as "bent to be orderly." This uniformity suggests also that the occurrence of the disturbances, their frequency, and their duration seem to be controlled by forces and conditions which lie very deep, far below the specific cultural and other circumstances, in which these countries differ markedly. What I imply by the phrase "deep factors" is that a social disturbance is perhaps an immanent trait of sociocultural life itself, and in this sense is inescapable and in its essentials is manifested similarly in all the social bodies. Here, probably, we meet again the same fact of the immanent self-regulation of social processes which any thoughtful investigator of such processes often comes across.

Finally, it is enough to glance at Greece, Rome, and Byzantium—the countries which existed a long time ago—and at those existing now, in order to see that there is no important difference between the duration of their disturbances. We cannot say that they were uniformly longer or shorter in the countries of the past compared with those of the present. Likewise, if the detailed data are examined for the duration of disturbances in the same country, beginning with the earliest and ending with the latest, they also show no uniform trend, in fact almost no trend at all. Here we strike, then, the first blow at the popular opinion that in the course of time disturbances tend to disappear, and to become shorter, less violent, and less inevitable. We find nothing corresponding to this pleasant view in the data of their duration.

(D) In spite of all the vicissitudes and changing conditions within the system of the indicators accepted, the magnitude of the disturbances fluctuates from century to century much less than is usually expected. If we take all the European countries studied from the sixth to the twentieth century, the amplitude of fluctuation of the magnitude of the disturbances is between 414.65 and 882.90; that is, in the most turbulent century the disturbances are only a little more than twice greater than in the most orderly century.

If we take the indicators of the quarter centuries, the difference is naturally greater, the maximum figure being here 300.46 and the minimum figure 53.81, the maximum exceeding the minimum by five to six times. Such swings are not exceedingly wild. They indicate some permanently working forces, inherently connected with the essence of the social life itself, which do not permit either a complete elimination or the unlimited growth of disturbances. As soon as the curve of disturbances approaches either the minimum or the maximum level, a reaction sets in and sends its course in the opposite direction.

(E) *In these "reactions" we observe several times, although not always, that when the curve approaches especially close to the mini-*

*mum or maximum limits, the counteraction also becomes especially strong.*

We do not need a mystical or numerological interpretation when, as so often (though not always), we see that the further and the more sharply a curve swings in one direction the stronger is the reaction which sends it back again. It is simply that the swing from order to disorder, and the reverse, seems to have a limit, as do almost all sociocultural phenomena, and as physicochemical and biological processes apparently do. Besides indicating the comparatively narrow limits of the maximum and the minimum fluctuation of our indicators, the above suggests that deep within social life are forces, possibly two opposing sets, that manifest themselves in such pulsations. When one set of forces becomes too strong, other forces, in some way or for some reason, are set in motion in the opposite direction.

(F) *The indicators for either quarter century or century periods show no continuous trend, either toward bigger and better "orderly progress" or toward ever-increasing disorderliness.* The curve fluctuates, that is all one can say. The popular theory that social change tends to become more and more orderly, more and more free from violence as "civilization progresses," is, then, nothing but a "pleasant myth." One reason why so utterly improbable a theory was accepted by so many scholars as well as by the public in general is shown by Table 4; the third quarter of the nineteenth century was more orderly than the three quarters preceding it; the fourth quarter (85.61) was more orderly than any of the preceding forty-three quarters from the sixth to the twentieth century, only two quarter centuries, 1726–1750 (53.81) and 626–650 (84.98), being slightly more orderly. Social conditions like these naturally are conductive to the popularity of such theories.

(G) *According to Table 4, there is hardly any definite periodicity in the ups and downs of internal disturbances.* Their tempo, as well as their rhythm, is varied. From one period to the next *piano* or *pianissimo* replaces *forte*, and the reverse.

So all the fashionable theories which try to interpret sociocultural processes by a mechanistic principle and to ascribe a definite periodicity to these are wrong, in this field as well as in most others.

(H) Tables 4 and 5 [together with Figure 1] shows which of the centuries and quarter centuries in the history of the greater part of the European continent have been particularly stormy and which particularly quiet. The turbulent centuries from the sixth to the twentieth were the thirteenth, fourteenth, twelfth, nineteenth, fifteenth, eighth, and eleventh. The maximum of disturbances fall within the thirteenth and then the fourteenth; the minimum fall within the eighteenth, seventh, sixth, and sixteenth centuries.

TABLE 4   Total Measure of Internal Disturbances of Europe from 525 to 1925 by Quarter Centuries

| Period | Total of the Indicators | Number of the Countries | Average |
|---|---|---|---|
| 525 to 550 A.D. | 458.89 | 4 | 114.72 |
| 551 to 575 | 641.13 | | 160.28 |
| 576 to 600 | 684.79 | | 171.20 |
| 601 to 625 | 623.93 | | 154.98 |
| 626 to 650 | 339.91 | | 84.98 |
| 651 to 675 | 521.16 | 5 | 104.23 |
| 676 to 700 | 684.01 | 6 | 114.00 |
| 701 to 725 | 1507.40 | 7 | 215.34 |
| 726 to 750 | 1223.55 | | 174.79 |
| 751 to 775 | 1294.82 | | 184.97 |
| 776 to 800 | 1112.14 | | 158.88 |
| 801 to 825 | 726.74 | | 103.82 |
| 826 to 850 | 1763.45 | | 251.92 |
| 851 to 875 | 667.41 | | 95.34 |
| 876 to 900 | 969.95 | | 138.57 |
| 901 to 925 | 782.69 | | 111.78 |
| 926 to 950 | 1264.73 | 8 | 158.09 |
| 950 to 975 | 1112.55 | 9 | 123.62 |
| 976 to 1000 | 1295.44 | | 143.94 |
| 1001 to 1025 | 1772.17 | | 196.91 |
| 1026 to 1050 | 1478.97 | | 164.33 |
| 1051 to 1075 | 1737.84 | | 193.09 |
| 1076 to 1100 | 1256.18 | | 139.57 |
| 1101 to 1125 | 1284.37 | | 142.71 |
| 1126 to 1150 | 1734.30 | | 192.70 |
| 1151 to 1175 | 1887.16 | | 209.68 |
| 1176 to 1200 | 1963.97 | | 218.22 |
| 1201 to 1225 | 2176.65 | | 241.85 |
| 1226 to 1250 | 1648.26 | | 183.14 |
| 1251 to 1275 | 2010.18 | | 223.35 |
| 1276 to 1300 | 2111.01 | | 234.56 |
| 1301 to 1325 A.D. | 2100.43 | | 233.37 |
| 1326 to 1350 | 1812.87 | | 201.43 |
| 1351 to 1375 | 1283.90 | | 142.66 |
| 1376 to 1400 | 2245.87 | | 249.54 |
| 1401 to 1425 | 1297.70 | 8 | 162.21 |
| 1426 to 1450 | 1752.89 | | 219.11 |
| 1451 to 1475 | 1549.73 | | 193.72 |
| 1476 to 1500 | 1386.70 | | 173.34 |
| 1501 to 1525 | 918.60 | | 114.83 |
| 1526 to 1550 | 947.05 | | 118.38 |
| 1551 to 1575 | 864.78 | | 108.10 |
| 1576 to 1600 | 1349.67 | | 168.71 |

Table 4    Total Measure of Internal Disturbances of Europe from 525 to 1925 by Quarter Centuries

| Period | Total of the Indicators | Number of the Countries | Average |
|---|---|---|---|
| 1601 to 1625 | 1081.28 | | 135.16 |
| 1626 to 1650 | 1808.24 | | 226.03 |
| 1651 to 1675 | 1226.00 | | 153.23 |
| 1676 to 1700 | 728.66 | | 91.08 |
| 1701 to 1725 | 890.13 | | 111.27 |
| 1726 to 1750 | 430.44 | | 53.81 |
| 1751 to 1775 | 871.36 | | 108.92 |
| 1776 to 1800 | 1132.69 | | 141.56 |
| 1801 to 1825 | 1085.92 | 7 | 155.13 |
| 1826 to 1850 | 2703.23 | | 386.18 |
| 1851 to 1875 | 979.91 | | 139.99 |
| 1876 to 1900 | 599.37 | | 85.61 |
| 1901 to 1925 | 2071.28 | | 295.89 |

Table 5.    Total Measure of Internal Disturbances of Europe by Centuries

| Century | Average | Century | Average |
|---|---|---|---|
| VI[a] | 446.20 | XIII | 882.90 |
| VII | 458.19 | XIV | 827.00 |
| VIII | 733.98 | XV | 748.38 |
| IX | 589.65 | XVI | 509.56 |
| X | 537.43 | XVII | 605.50 |
| XI | 693.90 | XVIII | 415.56 |
| XII | 763.31 | XIX | 766.91 |

[a] Three quarters only.

If quarter-century periods are taken, the most turbulent periods were: 1826–1850; 1901–1925; 826–850; 1201–1225; and 1301–1325. The most orderly periods were: 1726–1750; 1876–1900; 1676–1700; 851–875; 601–625. The most orderly and turbulent quarter-century periods for each of the seven countries separately studied were indicated above. Almost every country had one or more twenty-five-year periods with practically no important disturbances.

(I) Table 4 shows, as mentioned, that the *last quarter of the nineteenth century was remarkably orderly;* of fifty-six quarter centuries from 525 to 1925 only two had a slightly lower figure of disturbances. Shall we wonder that in that orderly "capitalistic" milieu

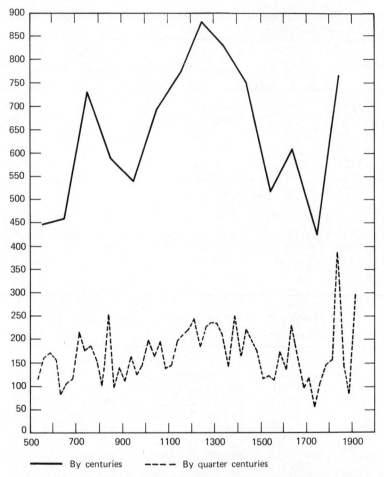

By centuries    ---- By quarter centuries

Fɪɢ. 1.    Movement of internal disturbances in Europe.

theories of assured "orderly progress" sprang up and were generally accepted? *At its height, therefore, the "capitalistic regime," which it is now the fashion to curse, was the most orderly of social systems and gave the greatest assurance of internal and external peace and of Sensate liberty and freedom for individuals.* In the light of this datum it is childish rather to ascribe to it all the vices of both anarchy and militarism and to strive to establish internal and external peace and the maximum of Sensate liberty by destroying capitalism and creating socialism, fascism, communism, Hitlerism, and other "isms" of today.

(J) The data show, further, *where we now stand on the historical road.* The indicators are not carried beyond 1925. If they were, the

data for the first of the twentieth century would be still more conspicuous and definite. Even as it stands, the figures show that *after
the very peaceful final quarter of the nineteenth century, Europe entered the stormy period of the twentieth.* The indicator for the first
quarter of the twentieth century is exceptionally high. From 525 to
1925 only one quarter century shows itself more turbulent than the
1901–1925 period. We are in a rising tide of internal disturbances.
Since 1925 there have been a large number of disturbances, and of
great magnitude, in Germany and Austria, France, and Spain; and
the number of smaller disturbances in England, Italy, and Russia is
also great. *On its face value, as the figure shows, the first quarter
of the twentieth century, 1901–1925, was not only the bloodiest period
in the entire history of the international conflicts of mankind but also,
when internal disturbances are considered, was one of the very turbulent periods.* Such is the unavoidable conclusion from our data on war
and disturbances.

This, then, is the latest point of "social progress and evolution"
to which we have come. This conclusion will certainly startle all the
manufacturers and all the consumers of the "sweet" theories that civilization is progressive through a process of orderly change toward universal peace. They will undoubtedly ponder over it a little; and it
would be very useful for them, no matter who they are—for the
partisans of these theories are not, in the main, simple and ignorant
people, but rather "highbrows and authorities"—to consider whether
they have not been believing in their own wishes rather than heeding
ugly facts, and whether they have not been too confident and too
light-hearted in their theories and conclusions. *The twentieth century,
so far, has been the bloodiest and the most turbulent period—and therefore one of the cruelest and least humanitarian—in the history of
Western civilization and perhaps in the chronicles of mankind in
general.*

(K) If we inquire as to whether the movement of internal disturbances for the eight European countries studied is connected directly
and synchronously with the movement of international war, the answer
must be in the negative. Comparing the curve of war movement with
the curve of the disturbances, both by century and quarter-century
periods, we see that *so far as century periods are concerned, each
process has had a course independent of the other, without either positive or negative association.* While war indicators increase by casualties
and by army's strength from the twelfth to the seventeenth century
inclusive, the indicators of disturbances show no such tendency; they
tend rather to decrease from the fourteenth to the nineteenth century.

But while the indicator of war in the nineteenth century declines, the indicator of disturbances, on the contrary, rises greatly. Thus, their movements for these centuries were rather opposite or "compensatory." But for the centuries from the twelfth to the fourteenth and from the seventeenth to the eighteenth their course was parallel rather than compensatory.

Finally, both increase in the first quarter of the twentieth century. Thus, there is no evident consistency in the relation between the two indicators for the century period.

In a desire to elucidate the problem somewhat more, the annual and the quarter-century indicators of both processes in the history of Greece, Rome, and Russia were subjected to a detailed statistical analysis. No definitely consistent relationship between the two variables was found. There did seem to be a slight indication that *disturbances tend to occur more frequently during and around years of war, being more frequent in war years, and in the years immediately preceding and following wars, and becoming rarer as we move further in either direction from the years of war.* For instance, of all the 207 years with disturbances in Rome studied, 96, or 45 per cent, occurred during years of war, 19 within one year before or after a war, 11 within two years before or after a war, 9 within three years, 11 within four years, 7 within five years, 5 within six years, 4 within seven years, 3 within eight years, then 4, 3, 4, and 4 within 9, 10, 11, and 12 years, respectively, after a war; 180 disturbances out of 207 are distributed in this way, while the remaining 27 cases of disturbances occurred at a still greater distance from a war.

Considering, however, that war occurred in 41 per cent of the total number of years of Roman history, this result is less conclusive than may appear at first glance. In the history of Russia, 35 of the 70 disturbances from 1450 to 1925, or 50 per cent, occurred in years of war. War occurred, however, in about 46 per cent of all the years studied. The result is again very inconclusive, failing to show any definite and uniform association between the processes studied.

Such an ambiguous and indefinite result is perhaps due to the fact that in our analysis we did not divide the wars into victorious and unsuccessful. Mere common sense, together with slight historical observation, seems to suggest that victorious wars are much less likely than unsuccessful wars to be followed or preceded by internal disturbances. During and after World War I, revolutions took place in Bulgaria, Turkey, Germany, Austria, and Russia—that is, in the defeated countries—while England, France, Italy, and Serbia, or the United States of America, did not have any revolution or disturbance that led to the overthrow of the existing regime or was as great as those disturbances in the defeated countries. Likewise, Russia, after her defeat in the Russo-Japanese War of 1904–1905, had a revolution, during 1905–1906, while Japan had no disturbance. After being defeated in war in 1912, Turkey had a revolution and deposed Abdul-Hamid, while nothing like this happened in the victorious countries. Likewise, France had a revolution after being defeated in the Franco-Prussian War; and one might give a long list of such cases from recent as well as from remote periods.

If this consideration has any importance, then it is clear why our analysis showed no more definite relationship between the variables. We put together all the wars, successful as well as unsuccessful, and so, of course, obscured any consistent relationship which may have existed between them. It was advisable, therefore, to try to discover the connection between the movement of disturbances and the movement of successful and unsuccessful wars.

Such a study, however, proved very difficult. Many disturbances have been of a purely local nature, small in magnitude and somewhat undefined as to the exact time and duration of their occurrence. Many disturbances by peasants and workers have been a kind of unrest or milling around spread over a number of years, with only occasional outbursts here and there. Then there were several "palace revolutions" involving only a small faction without any active participation by the masses.

Finally, wars are often indefinite in result, without victor or vanquished. All this makes a comparison of all wars listed with disturbances impracticable and incapable of yielding definite results.

In view of this fact, another procedure seemed advisable, namely, to take only the biggest wars and biggest revolutions during recent centuries, for which data are comparatively accurate. However, even this method is not irreproachable; some of the biggest disturbances happened in time of war, and quite an insignificant war, while some of the biggest wars were synchronous with disturbances of a purely local character and insignificant magnitude. Even in the few cases when a defeat in war seemed to have been followed by a big disturbance, some specific circumstance, like the death of the king, occurred at the same time, making it impossible to decide whether the unsuccessful war or the death of the ruler was the really important factor in causing the disturbance. And there are dozens of such "obscuring" circumstances. All this material should be kept in mind.

There follow the approximate results of a study of several samples from several countries. In Russia since 1600 there have been 14 great disturbances. Of these 14, 4 occurred during or immediately after big and unsuccessful wars, 6 in a period of peace, and 1 during a successful war. Three others occurred in somewhat indefinite circumstances.

Thus the relationship is quite indefinite. If, on the other hand, we take the biggest wars for the same period, the results are about the same. Some of these big wars continued for a number of years, like the Napoleonic Wars, or the northern wars of Peter the Great. For a number of years they were unsuccessful, and for a number, successful; but in neither phase were they followed by any disturbance of importance. In the unsuccessful Crimean War of 1853–1856 there was only one, relatively very small, disturbance, in 1854–1855, among the soldiers. Another unsuccessful war, the Russo-Japanese, 1904–1905, was followed by a great revolution. The World War, 1914–1917, was followed by a great revolution. In brief, the results of the study are very indefinite.

The history of France from 1600 on gives similar results. From 1600 to 1925 we find 13 great disturbances. Seven of these occurred in peaceful times when, except for two quite insignificant colonial expeditions, no war was going on. Among the 7 great disturbances were those of 1830 and 1848; 3 big disturbances definitely happened during or immediately after unsuccessful wars. The remaining 3 occurred in somewhat indefinite circumstances, during wartime, but when success or defeat was somewhat uncertain. When, on the other hand, we take all the big wars from 1600 to 1925, we find at least 25 wars of comparatively large magnitude. During 17 of these, at least, not less than 5 being unsuccessful, none of the great internal conflicts above mentioned occurred, either while hostilities continued or immediately after the close of the campaign. During each of the remaining 8 wars a big disturbance occurred, 4 of these disturbances being losing wars, 1 successful, and the remaining 3 only partially successful or of indefinite outcome.

These results seem to corroborate all the previous ones. Two other samples from two other countries lead to similar conclusions. On the basis of all these data, one must say that, *contrary to expectations, the data do not definitely show a positive association between unsuccessful wars and big disturbances nor between victorious wars and the absence of such. At best they yield only a very slight association between unsuccessful wars and disturbances.* As a study of the presence or absence of association between war in general and disturbances did not disclose any close uniform relationship between these, one has to conclude, at least until more refined analysis makes the question clear, *that the two processes proceed fairly independently of each other and that no direct nor quite tangible interdependence is shown.*

This means that the widely held opinion that there is a close dependence between these processes, and especially between unsuccessful wars and disturbances, needs some limitations, reservations, and toning down. The mere occurrence of an unsuccessful war as such is not sufficient to produce an important disturbance, if the country is not disorganized, mentally and morally, or otherwise. On the contrary, as has happened several times—to the Romans in the Punic Wars, the Russians in the "Fatherland War" with Napoleon, and to Belgium when invaded by the Germans—defeat, great danger, and privations, instead of demoralizing and disorganizing the invaded and defeated country, may make it strong as iron. Instead of an explosion of internal disturbances being caused by such conditions, these latter may decrease or entirely disappear. Only in a country with weak "nerves" and discipline and little solidarity may disturbances be started by successful or by unsuccessful wars or without any war whatsoever, by almost any incident or insignificant event.

Taking all this into consideration, it is clear that war, as such, no matter whether successful or not, is neither a necessary nor a sufficient condition for starting or reinforcing internal disturbances. Conversely, an important internal disturbance is neither necessary to start a war nor sufficient to start or greatly to increase one.

Data from various other countries studied corroborate this hypothesis. In Greece, for instance, the curves of war and disturbances are parallel for several periods, reach their maximum in the same centuries, the fourth and fifth, and then decline; but in Rome the direction of movement of one curve for several centuries is practically opposite to that of the other; the third century B.C. has the highest indicator of war and the lowest indicator of disturbances, while the first century A.D. has the lowest indicator of war and one of the highest of internal disturbances; a similiar relationship is found in several other periods. Data for other countries also show the same contrast in the movement of the two curves, parallel during some periods, moving in opposite directions in others, and similarly with the total indicators of both processes, for all the European countries studied, as we have seen. So much for the direct relationship of the two processes to each other. *As we shall see, they are related to each other, but only in the identity of the main factor—the transition factor—that causes both processes.* But from the identity of their main cause, it does not follow that they must be either synchronous or must be the direct cause of each other.

(L) We must touch upon the problem already discussed when we traced the movement of the curve of the magnitude of war in relation to the periods of blossoming and decay in the history of the countries studied. Do internal disturbances tend to increase regularly in periods of bloom and well-being or of decay, or do they occur erratically, regardless of these periods? Taking the indicators of disturbances by centuries, the results can be summed up as follows.

In Greece the disturbances reached their peak mainly in the fifth and fourth centuries B.C., when the power, culture, and social life of Greece were at their summit. In Rome the peak of the disturbances occurred in the first century B.C., the second highest point in the third century A.D., and the third and fourth highest in the fourth and first centuries A.D. If the two centuries just before and after the birth of Christ can be regarded as the summit of Roman power and culture, these had already begun to decline by the third and fourth centuries A.D. On the other hand, the curve of disturbances is low in the fifth century A.D. and the third and fourth B.C., the fourth and third centuries B.C. being the periods of most vigorous growth, and fifth A.D. decidedly one of decline.

The data on Byzantium are likewise inconsistent. On the one hand resplendent periods of prosperity, when culture was at its height, have a low indicator of disturbances. Such are the "Golden Age" of the sixth century, especially the time of Justinian (527–565), and the period extending, roughly, from the beginning of the Macedonian dynasty in 867 to the end of the tenth century. On the other hand, centuries of decline like the thirteenth and, to some extent, the twelfth, have also low indicators, the thirteenth even much lower than the more flourishing tenth century. Then we find the highest indicators of disturbances in the seventh and eighth centuries, which were disastrous and agonizing, in spite of the activities and reforms of such rulers as Leo the Isaurian (717–741), and in the tenth, which all in all seems to have been a healthy and prosperous period. This means that here again we find no uniform and consistent relation between periods of decline and a decrease in disturbance.

We must conclude that *in periods either of blossoming or of decline, disturbances have sometimes increased in number and have sometimes decreased.*

If this conclusion is valid, there must be various kinds of disturbances. Some seem to be like the tensions of childbearing and of healthy growth, which are often associated with pain and with internal disturbances of the organism. Others are disturbances of illness or of senility. The former occur when the growth of the social group, the nation, is sound and rapid. The growing vital forces cannot be contained in the old network of social relations, and therefore disturb or disrupt it here and there.

Disturbances during social decline and disorganization result from the waning of the vital and creative forces of a given society or from some extraordinarily unfortunate combination of external circumstances, which makes an orderly life impossible for the group. Such disturbances are attempts, mostly blind and desperate, to "do something" to get rid of impossible conditions; and so occur during periods of decline and decay. A more detailed study of many great revolutions indicates that not all, nor perhaps even most, but at least many of them, occurred in just such periods of disorganization and decline.

(M) Does the fact that disturbances occur in both periods really mean that no "uniformity" can be found in that "diversity"? Is it not possible to find in that diversity—almost opposition—of periods of bloom and decline something which belongs to both periods and in which both are similar? If so, might not this be the common factor "producing" disturbances in both periods?

With this idea in mind let us glance more attentively at the indicators, by centuries, of disturbances—first at the indicators for all the European countries studied and then at the indicators for separate countries. We find the following interesting phenomena. For the sixth and seventh centuries indicators are low (446.20 and 458.19). For the eighth century the indicator is very high (733.98); in the ninth, tenth, and eleventh centuries there is a considerable drop (589.65, 537.43, and 693.90 respectively); and it rises considerably in the twelfth century and reaches the highest points in the thirteenth and fourteenth centuries (882.90 and 827.00), followed by a decline in the fifteenth (748.38), during which century the curve is still high but notably lower than before; then they greatly decline in the sixteenth (509.56) and stay low in the seventeenth (605.50) and the eighteenth, when up to the last quarter of the eighteenth they give the lowest point (415.56). The curve then begins to rise and jumps greatly in the nineteenth century (766.91). Notwithstanding a temporary sharp decline in the last quarter of the nineteenth century, it flares up in the first half of the twentieth. Thus we have *three main peaks; in the eighth, in the thirteenth and fourteenth centuries, and in the nineteenth and twentieth. After each peak the wave of disturbances subsides and remains low till the next peak.*

Have these facts a meaning, and can an interpretation be found to fit them that will be satisfactory from a logical standpoint also? The answer is given by the whole character of this work, namely, all three peak periods are the periods of transition, either in the whole culture of Europe and in its system of social relationships, or in the system of social relationships only. We know already that the thirteenth and fourteenth centuries were those of the greatest transition of European culture and society from the Ideational to the Sensate form[1] and from the feudal to the modern systems of social relationships (from predominantly familistic to coercive-contractual; from theocracy to the secular regime, from Ideational freedom to Sensate; from the feudal regime to the national monarchies, and so on).

In all these respects, these centuries were the greatest turning point in all European history; with the greatest breakdown of the system of social values and of social relationships. Therefore the curve of the disturbances reaches the highest point during these centuries. They would be expected logically to be centuries of disturbances, and they were such in fact. The hypothesis of transition, with its breakdown of the system of values and relationships, as set forth in the preceding part in regard to war movement, accounts for this peak.

Can it account for the peaks of the eighth and the nineteenth and twentieth centuries? As for the nineteenth and especially the twentieth century, it accounts for it easily; we have seen that the twentieth century is transitional in all the compartments of European culture. As for the end of the eighteenth and the first part of the nineteenth century (which is responsible for the comparatively high indicator for the nineteenth century), we know also that this was the period of the "liquidation of the postmedieval relationships" in the system of social organization, and especially the period of transition from predominantly compulsory to the predominantly contractual relationships. This shift was accomplished roughly in the period opened by the French Revolution in 1789 and the first few decades of the nineteenth century. Such a transition from one fundamental type of social relationship to another had to call forth, according to the hypothesis, a rise of the curve of disturbances; and this curve did indeed rise. Beginning roughly with the second part of the nineteenth century, Europe settled definitely into the comfortable new contractual house, and the fever of disturbances subsided. But toward the twentieth century, Sensate culture itself began to show signs of disintegration, and with it the contractual system of social relationships was disturbed. Both entered the sharp stage of transition. Hence the rapid rise of the curve in the twentieth century.

Finally, as to the eighth-century peak, it also agrees with the hypothesis. It was the period of the so-called Carolingian Renaissance. If it did not mean a fundamental change in the culture, which remained Ideational before and after it, it accomplished nevertheless

---

[1] The terms around which Sorokin's general sociocultural theory is constructed; polar opposites meaning, generally speaking, transcendental and materialistic.

some important modifications in it. Its transitional character was, however, mainly in the system of social relationships; in the forms of
social, economic, and political organization or reorganization; and in
this field it was a genuinely transitional period. As such, it had to give
rise to disturbances; and it certainly did.

Thus all the three main peaks seem to be well accounted for by
the hypothesis of transition. The same hypothesis accounts for the
comparatively low level of disturbances in the other centuries: from
the ninth to the twelfth; from the fifteenth to the eighteenth inclusive
(except its last decade); and from the second part of the nineteenth
to the beginning of the twentieth century. These were the settled periods in the type of dominant culture, as well as in that of the system
of social relationships. Even a slight rise of the curve in the seventeenth
century is accountable from this standpoint; it was the last stand of
the Ideational culture and its satellites to regain its dominance. The
effort failed, and the question was definitely settled.

Thus the hypothesis of the transition accounts for these tidal waves
of disturbances. It means that, *other conditions being equal, during
the periods when the existing culture, or the system of social relationships, or both, undergo a rapid transformation, the internal disturbances in the respective societies increase; when they are strong and
crystallized, the internal disturbances tend to decrease and stay at
a low level.* This proposition is but a different version of the statement
regarding the main factor of war and peace given in a preceding
chapter.

We have seen that disturbances occur in periods of bloom and
of decline, in periods of prosperity and of poverty, and in periods when
society moves upward with particular rapidity and during the phase
of its rapid downward movement.

This "inconsistency" is quite consistent in the light of the above
hypothesis. Indeed, the established social order and cultural system
may be, and is, as easily unsettled in periods of rapid enrichment,
vigorous blossoming, as in periods of catastrophe and decline.

Whatever factors lead to a rise and decline of each main form
of culture and system of social relationship (and in passing I may
say that the main factors calling forth change are "immanent" or
"inherent" in cultural and social life itself, and that these factors in
the course of time will bring any sociocultural order to confusion),
*the main and the indispensable condition for an eruption of internal
disturbances is that the social system or the cultural system or both
shall be unsettled.* This datum seems to fit the facts much better than
most of the popular theories. These theories, that ascribe internal dis-

turbances either to growing poverty and "hard material conditions" or, on the contrary, to material progress, and that correlate them either with periods of decay or with periods of bloom, are sharply contradicted by relevant facts as well as by the bulk of the indicators. However hard living conditions may be in a given society, if the framework of its relationships and values is unshattered, no disturbances will be forthcoming. The members of such a society may be dying of starvation and yet not revolt; or, anyhow, make fewer attempts to revolt than members of a perfectly comfortable society in which the sociocultural system of values is loose. If one can imagine a society where everyone has the standard of living of a millionaire but sociocultural relationships are not crystallized and the main values are not compatible, such a society would be more turbulent and disorderly than one where even the main physiological needs are barely satisfied but where the sociocultural framework is strong and definite and the members of the society believe in the same values and live by them.

This hypothesis not only explains the movement of the indicators for the countries taken together, but also explains many of the ups and downs of the indicators for separate countries.

The reader may test its validity by indicators of disturbances and by the historical data on the conditions of the network of sociocultural values and relationships. *It is not my contention that the factor stressed explains all the ups and downs in the curves of disturbances.* But I do claim that the factor of the status of the sociocultural network of relationships and values is enough in itself to "explain" the main "ups and downs" of the curves in all the societies studied.

(N) In view of all this it is easier to understand the facts emphasized in the previous chapters. Let us recall them.

The first is that inner tensions and disturbances seem to be phenomena inseparably connected with the existence and functioning of social bodies. These are no less "natural" and "common" than storms in ordinary weather conditions.

Second, disturbances occur much oftener than is usually realized. Only rarely does it happen that two or three decades in the life history of a vast social body pass without them. On the average of from four to seven years, as a rule, one considerable social disturbance may be expected. This fact confirms our conclusions that they are inseparable from the very existence and functioning of social bodies.

Their "causes" are as deep in social life as the "causes" of internal peace. A set of special conditions, like a poor government, a selfish aristocracy, stupid mob-mindedness, poverty and war, may play a secondary role in reinforcing or weakening, accelerating or retarding, disturbances, but these are only secondary factors. Even without them, disturbances, like storms, would frequently occur. They have occurred under stupid and under wise governments, under conditions of war and of peace, in monarchies and republics, in democracies and aristocracies, in prosperity and poverty, in ages of "enlightenment" and of "ignorance," in urbanized and industrial as well as in rural and nonindustrialized countries; and in other most diverse circumstances. To continue, therefore, to look upon them as something exceptional, abnormal, accidental, and incidental to social life itself is no more scientific than to look at indispositions, sicknesses, painful experiences, as incidental.

In stressing these facts before, I have indicated that they suggest that we must look far deeper for the "causes" of disturbances than is usually done. Now we have the deep, the inherent, causes before us. Since the main cause of these is the status of the sociocultural framework of relationships and of values, and since sooner or later, on account of immanent change inherent in sociocultural system, such a system is bound to be unsettled, "withered," and broken, the sociocultural order of every society is bound to have periods of transition and with them rising tides of disturbances. On the other hand, any new system, if only it survives, will surely become crystallized and settled. This means that any society will also have periods when the wave of disturbances subsides, and hence the similarity of all societies in these respects, and the similarity of all the societies studied in the frequency and the magnitude of disturbances.

(O) Another important problem in the field of internal disturbances, as of any other important social process, is to *what extent the direction, and particularly the quantitative direction, of the process is the same in various countries of the same "cultural continent" during the same period.* In other words, do disturbances, for instance, increase simultaneously in all the countries, or in several of these, or do they increase in some while decreasing in others? The answer, in the field studied, is given by the above figures.

All this means that the forces generating disturbances rarely, if ever, work in one country only. For good or bad, they seem to work in the areas of several countries simultaneously. Disturbances started in one country usually spread over or are independently originated in several others. So it was in the past and so it is in the present.

# 8

# Toward A Theory of Revolution

*James C. Davies*

## EDITORS' COMMENT

The following essay, if only because of the number of references to it in the literature on revolution, must be regarded as one of the most influential recent pieces on the study of internal warfare. This influence is the product not only of Davies' intelligent combination of the Marx and Tocqueville observations on the causes of revolution into a useful shorthand description but is also a result of his interest in one of the most fundamental of problems: Are revolutions caused by "objective" conditions, or "subjective" attitudes? How do these factors influence each other? What is the mixture between them, and are they independent or dependent variables?

These questions prevade the literature on the subject of revolution. In this book widely separated theorists such as Hobbes, Kamenka, Chalmers Johnson, Eckstein, and even Trotsky explicitly discuss the interaction between objective and subjective factors. Although Davies does not pretend to have a definitive answer, he does have some interesting insights and raises a number of even more interesting questions.

Davies clearly argues that attitudes, not objective conditions (almost by definition) create the proto-revolutionary situation. Interestingly enough, attitudes which lead to civil violence are to him evaluations of future, not present conditions (except insofar as present conditions indicate the future). What is at work here is a series of extrapolations. First, there is an extrapolation of progress (and the possibility of progress) from the experience of social progress. This is followed by an extrapolation of regress (and the probability of regress) from a (to Davies) short-term reversal. The idea of the possibility of progress combined with the probability of regress creates the explosion.

Second, it is obvious from this line of reasoning that objective events have an enormous effect on attitudes. The rising expectations of a society or a class are tied largely to measurable economic progress (although he includes noneconomic factors as well), and the expectations of a reversal are also tied to objective factors—for example, economic depression or repressive political actions, like "Bloody Sunday" in Russia—or accidental objective political occurrences, such as the loss of a war by Egypt.

The reader should compare Davies' analysis with that of Harry Eckstein (see selection 9 in this volume), since Eckstein argues that there may well be no direct or necessary relationship between objective conditions and subjective attitudes. The reader should also compare both of these essays with the works of Marx and Engels (especially, *The German Ideology*), or Karl Mannheim (especially, *Ideology and Utopia*). For the structural-behavioral arguments, the problem of "class consciousness," and the whole range of debates over consent and legitimacy are all part of one large question of ideology and its political consequences. And the role of ideas in the creation of revolutionary conditions is an area where scholarship has yet to penetrate very far. There have been hints and suggestions—and an almost universal acknowledgment of the importance of the question—but still one is left with the feeling that the area is comparatively unharvested.

One of the reasons for this primitiveness is the extreme difficulty of measuring attitudes, as Davies points out near the end of his essay. He is hopeful about using objective data to indicate attitudes, but the reader may be left with the feeling that Davies himself is lamenting the primitiveness of the art and is appealing for thoughts and suggestions on the subject which, if possible, would lend considerable strength to his type of analysis. Davies' own pursuit of the subject can be assessed in his more recent essay: "The J-Curve of Rising and Declining Satisfactions as a Cause of Some Great Revolutions and a Contained Rebellion" (in H. D. Graham and T. R. Gurr, eds., *Violence in America*. New York: Signet Books, 1969).

# TOWARD A THEORY OF REVOLUTION

James C. Davies

In exhorting proletarians of all nations to unite in revolution, because they had nothing to lose but their chains, Marx and Engels most succinctly presented that theory of revolution which is recognized as their brain child. But this most famed thesis, that progressive degradation of the industrial working class would finally reach the point of despair and inevitable revolt, is not the only one that Marx fathered. In at least one essay he gave life to a quite antithetical idea. He described, as a precondition of widespread unrest, not progressive degradation of the proletariat but rather an improvement in workers' economic condition which did not keep pace with the growing welfare of capitalists and therefore produced social tension.

> A noticeable increase in wages presupposes a rapid growth of productive capital. The rapid growth of productive capital brings about an equally rapid growth of wealth, luxury, social wants, social enjoyments. Thus, although the enjoyments of the workers have risen, the social satisfaction that they give has fallen in comparison with the increased enjoyments of the capitalist, which are inaccessible to the worker, in comparison with the state of development of society in general. Our desires and pleasures spring from society; we measure them, therefore, by society and not by the objects which serve for their satisfaction. Because they are of a social nature, they are of a relative nature.[1]

Marx's qualification here of his more frequent belief that degradation produces revolution is expressed as the main thesis by de Tocqueville in his study of the French Revolution. After a long review of

[1] Karl Marx and Frederick Engels, "Wage Labour and Capital," *Selected Works in Two Volumes,* Moscow; Foreign Languages Publishing House, 1955, Vol. 1, p. 94.

Source. James C. Davies, "Toward a Theory of Revolution," from *American Sociological Review,* XXVII, 1 (February 1962), pp. 5–19, excerpted. Reprinted with the permission of the author and the American Sociological Association. Copyright 1962 by the American Sociological Association.

economic and social decline in the seventeenth century and dynamic
growth in the eighteenth, de Tocqueville concludes:

> So it would appear that the French found their condition the more
> unsupportable in proportion to its improvement. . . . Revolutions are
> not always brought about by a gradual decline from bad to worse.
> Nations that have endured patiently and almost unconsciously the
> most overwhelming oppression often burst into rebellion against the
> yoke the moment it begins to grow lighter. The regime which is
> destroyed by a revolution is almost always an improvement on its
> immediate predecessor. . . . Evils which are patiently endured when
> they seem inevitable become intolerable when once the idea of escape
> from them is suggested.[2]

On the basis of de Tocqueville and Marx, we can choose one
of these ideas or the other, which makes it hard to decide just when
revolutions are more likely to occur—when there has been social and
economic progress or when there has been regress. It appears that
both ideas have explanatory and possibly predictive value, if they are
juxtaposed and put in the proper time sequence.

Revolutions are most likely to occur when a prolonged period
of objective economic and social development is followed by a short
period of sharp reversal.[3] The all-important effect on the minds of
people in a particular society is to produce, during the former period,

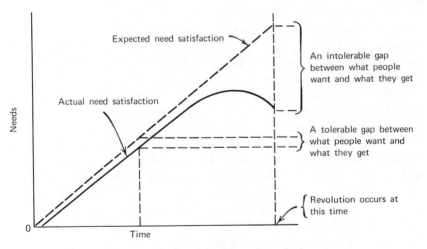

FIG. 1.   Need satisfaction and revolution.

[2] A. de Tocqueville, *The Old Regime and the French Revolution* (trans. by
John Bonner), N.Y.: Harper & Bros., 1856, p. 214.
[3] Revolutions are here defined as a change in the basic power structure of
a polity accompanied by substantial violence.

an expectation of continued ability to satisfy needs—which continue to rise—and, during the latter, a mental state of anxiety and frustration when manifest reality breaks away from anticipated reality. The actual state of socioeconomic development is less significant than the expectation that past progress, now blocked, can and must continue in the future [see Figure 1].

Political stability and instability are ultimately dependent on a state of mind, a mood, in a society. Satisfied or apathetic people who are poor in goods, status, and power can remain politically quiet and their opposites can revolt, just as, correlatively and more probably, dissatisfied poor can revolt and satisfied rich oppose revolution. It is the dissatisfied state of mind rather than the tangible provision of "adequate" or "inadequate" supplies of food, equality, or liberty which produces the revolution. In actuality, there must be a joining of forces between dissatisfied, frustrated people who differ in their degree of objective, tangible welfare and status. Well-fed, well-educated, high-status individuals who rebel in the face of apathy among the objectively deprived can accomplish at most a coup d'état. The objectively deprived, when faced with solid opposition of people of wealth, status, and power, will be smashed in their rebellion as were peasants and Anabaptists by German noblemen in 1525 and East Germans by the Communist elite in 1953.

Before appraising this general notion in light of a series of revolutions, a word is in order as to why revolutions ordinarily do not occur when a society is generally impoverished—when, as de Tocqueville put it, evils that seem inevitable are patiently endured. They are endured in the extreme case because the physical and mental energies of people are totally employed in the process of merely staying alive. The Minnesota starvation studies conducted during World War II[4] indicate clearly the constant pre-occupation of very hungry individuals with fantasies and thoughts of food. In extremis, as the Minnesota research poignantly demonstrates, the individual withdraws into a life of his own, withdraws from society, withdraws from any significant kind of activity unrelated to staying alive. Reports of behavior in Nazi concentration camps indicate the same preoccupation.[5] In less extreme and barbarous circumstances, where minimal survival is possible but little more, the preoccupation of individuals with staying alive is only

[4] The full report is Ancel Keys et al., The Biology of Human Starvation, Minneapolis: University of Minnesota Press, 1950. See J. Brozek, "Semi-starvation and Nutritional Rehabilitation," Journal of Clinical Nutrition, 1 (January, 1953), pp. 107–118, for a brief analysis.

[5] E. A. Cohen, Human Behavior in the Concentration Camp, New York: W. W. Norton & Co., 1953, pp. 123–125, 131–140.

mitigated. Social action takes place for the most part on a local, face-to-face basis. In such circumstances the family is a—perhaps the major—solidary unit[6] and even the local community exists primarily to the extent families need to act together to secure their separate survival. Such was life on the American frontier in the sixteenth through nineteenth centuries. In very much attenuated form, but with a substantial degree of social isolation persisting, such evidently is rural life even today. This is clearly related to a relatively low level of political participation in elections.[7] As Zawadzki and Lazarsfeld have indicated,[8] preoccupation with physical survival, even in industrial areas, is a force strongly militating against the establishment of the community-sense and consensus on joint political action which are necessary to induce a revolutionary state of mind. Far from making people into revolutionaries, enduring poverty makes for concern with one's solitary self or solitary family at best and resignation or mute despair at worst. When it is a choice between losing their chains or their lives, people will mostly choose to keep their chains, a fact which Marx seems to have overlooked.[9]

It is when the chains have been loosened somewhat, so that they can be cast off without a high probability of losing life, that people are put in a condition of proto-rebelliousness. I use the term proto-rebelliousness because the mood of discontent may be dissipated before a violent outbreak occurs. The causes for such dissipation may be natural or social (including economic and political). A bad crop year that threatens a return to chronic hunger may be succeeded by a year of natural abundance. Recovery from sharp economic dislocation may take the steam from the boiler of rebellion. The slow, grudging grant of reforms, which has been the political history of England since at least the Industrial Revolution, may effectively and continously prevent the degree of frustration that produces revolt.

A revolutionary state of mind requires the continued, even ha-

[6] For community life in such poverty, in Mezzogiorno Italy, see E. C. Banfield, *The Moral Basis of a Backward Society*, Glencoe, Ill.: The Free Press, 1958. The author emphasizes that the nuclear family is a solidary, consensual, moral unit (see p. 85) but even within it, consensus appears to break down, in outbreaks of pure, individual amorality—notably between parents and children. (See p. 117.)

[7] See Angus Campbell *et al.*, *The American Voter*, New York: John Wiley & Sons, 1960, Chapter 15, "Agrarian Political Behavior."

[8] B. Zawadzki and P. F. Lazarsfeld, "The Psychological Consequences of Unemployment," *Journal of Social Psychology*, 6 (May, 1935), pp. 224–251.

[9] A remarkable and awesome exception to this phenomenon occurred occasionally in some Nazi concentration camps, for example, in a Buchenwald revolt against capricious rule by criminal prisoners. During this revolt, one hundred criminal prisoners were killed by political prisoners. See Cohen, *op. cit.*, p. 200.

bitual but dynamic expectation of greater opportunity to satisfy basic needs, which may range from merely physical (food, clothing, shelter, health, and safety from bodily harm) to social (the affectional ties of family and friends) to the need for equal dignity and justice. But the necessary additional ingredient is a persistent, unrelenting threat to the satisfaction of these needs: not a threat which actually returns people to a state of sheer survival but which puts them in the mental state where they believe they will not be able to satisfy one or more basic needs. Although physical deprivation in some degree may be threatened on the eve of all revolutions, it need not be the prime factor, as it surely was not in the American Revolution of 1775. The crucial factor is the vague or specific fear that ground gained over a long period of time will be quickly lost. This fear does not generate if there is continued opportunity to satisfy continually emerging needs; it generates when the existing government suppresses or is blamed for suppressing such opportunity.

[Two] rebellions or revolutions are given considerable attention in the sections that follow: the Russian Revolution of 1917, and the Egyptian Revolution of 1952. Brief mention is then made of several other major civil disturbances, all of which appear to fit the J-curve pattern.[10] After considering these specific disturbances, some general theoretical and research problems are discussed.

No claim is made that all rebellions follow the pattern, but just that the ones here presented do. All of these are "progressive" revolutions in behalf of greater equality and liberty. The question is open whether the pattern occurs in such markedly retrogressive revolutions as Nazism in Germany or the 1861 Southern rebellion in the United States. It will surely be necessary to examine other progressive revolutions before one can judge how universal the J-curve is. And it will be necessary, in the interests of scientific validation, to examine cases of serious civil disturbance that fell short of producing profound revolution—such as the Sepoy Rebellion of 1857 in India, the Pullman Strike of 1894 in America, the Boxer Rebellion of 1900 in China, and the Great Depression of the 1920s and 1930s as it was experienced in Austria, France, Great Britain, and the United States. The explanation for such still-born rebellions—for revolutions that might have occurred—is inevitably more complicated than for those that come to term in the "normal" course of political gestation. . . .

[10] This curve is of course not to be confused with its prior and altogether different use by Floyd Allport in his study of social conformity. See F. H. Allport, "The J-Curve Hypothesis of Conforming Behavior," *Journal of Social Psychology*, 5 (May, 1934), pp. 141–183.

## THE RUSSIAN REVOLUTION OF 1917

In Russia's tangled history it is hard to decide when began the final upsurge of expectations that, when frustrated, produced the cataclysmic events of 1917. One can truly say that the real beginning was the slow modernization process begun by Peter the Great over two hundred years before the revolution. And surely the rationalist currents from France that slowly penetrated Russian intellectual life during the reign of Catherine the Great a hundred years before the revolution were necessary, lineal antecedents of the 1917 revolution.

Without denying that there was an accumulation of forces over at least a 200-year period, we may nonetheless date the final upsurge as beginning with the 1861 emancipation of serfs and reaching a crest in the 1905 revolution.

The chronic and growing unrest of serfs before their emancipation in 1861 is an ironic commentary on the Marxian notion that human beings are what social institutions make them. Although serfdom had been shaping their personality since 1647, peasants became increasingly restive in the second quarter of the nineteenth century.[11] The continued discontent of peasants after emancipation is an equally ironic commentary on the belief that relieving one profound frustration produces enduring contentment. Peasants rather quickly got over their joy at being untied from the soil after two hundred years. Instead of declining, rural violence increased.[12] Having gained freedom but not much free land, peasants now had to rent or buy land to survive: virtual personal slavery was exchanged for financial servitude. Land pressure grew, reflected in a doubling of land prices between 1868 and 1897.

It is hard thus to tell whether the economic plight of peasants was much lessened after emancipation. A 1903 government study indicated that even with a normal harvest, average food intake per peasant was 30 per cent below the minimum for health. The only sure contrary item of evidence is that the peasant population grew, indicating at least increased ability of the land to support life. . . .

The land-population pressure pushed people into towns and cities, where the rapid growth of industry truly afforded the chance for economic betterment. One estimate of net annual income for a peasant

---

[11] Jacqueries rose from an average of 8 per year in 1826–30 to 34 per year in 1845–49. T. G. Masaryk, *The Spirit of Russia*, London: Allen and Unwin, Ltd., 1919, Vol. I, p. 130.

[12] Jacqueries averaged 350 per year for the first three years after emancipation. *Ibid.*, pp. 140–141.

family of five in the rich blackearth area in the late nineteenth century was 82 rubles. In contrast, a "good" wage for a male factory worker was about 168 rubles per year. It was this difference in the degree of poverty that produced almost a doubling of the urban population between 1878 and 1897. The number of industrial workers increased almost as rapidly. The city and the factory gave new hope. Strikes in the 1880s were met with brutal suppression but also with the beginning of factory legislation, including the requirement that wages be paid regularly and the abolition of child labor. The burgeoning proletariat remained comparatively contented until the eve of the 1905 revolution.[13]

There is additional, non-economic evidence to support the view that 1861 to 1905 was the period of rising expectations that preceded the 1917 revolution. The administration of justice before the emancipation had largely been carried out by noblemen and landowners who embodied the law for their peasants. In 1864 justice was in principle no longer delegated to such private individuals. Trials became public, the jury system was introduced, and judges got tenure. Corporal punishment was alleviated by the elimination of running the gauntlet, lashing, and branding; caning persisted until 1904. Public joy at these reforms was widespread. For the intelligentsia, there was increased opportunity to think and write and to criticize established institutions, even sacrosanct absolutism itself.

But Tsarist autocracy had not quite abandoned the scene. Having inclined but not bowed, in granting the inevitable emancipation as an act not of justice but grace, it sought to maintain its absolutist principle by conceding reform without accepting anything like democratic authority. Radical political and economic criticism surged higher. Some strong efforts to raise the somewhat lowered floodgates began as early as 1866, after an unsucessful attempt was made on the life of Alexander II, in whose name serfs had just gained emancipation. When the attempt succeeded fifteen years later, there was increasing state action under Alexander III to limit constantly rising expectations. By suppression and concession, the last Alexander succeeded in dying naturally in 1894.

When it became apparent that Nicholas II shared his father's

[13] The proportion of workers who struck from 1895 through 1902 varied between 1.7 per cent and 4.0 per cent per year. In 1903 the proportion rose to 5.1 per cent but dropped a year later to 1.5 per cent. In 1905 the proportion rose to 163.8 per cent, indicating that the total working force struck, on the average, closer to twice than to once during that portentous year. In 1906 the proportion dropped to 65.8 per cent; in 1907 to 41.9 per cent; and by 1909 was down to a "normal" 3.5 per cent. *Ibid.*, p. 175n.

ideas but not his forcefulness, opposition of the intelligentsia to absolutism joined with the demands of peasants and workers, who remained
loyal to the Tsar but demanded economic reforms. Starting in 1904,
there developed a "League of Deliverance" that coordinated efforts
of at least seventeen other revolutionary, proletarian, or nationalist
groups within the empire. Consensus on the need for drastic reform,
both political and economic, established a many-ringed circus of groups
sharing the same tent. These groups were geographically distributed
from Finland to Armenia and ideologically from liberal constitutional-
ists to revolutionaries made prudent by the contrast between their
own small forces and the power of Tsardom.

Events of 1904–5 mark the general downward turning point of
expectations, which people increasingly saw frustrated by the continuation of Tsardom. Two major and related occurrences made 1905 the
point of no return. The first took place on the Bloody Sunday of January 22, 1905, when peaceful proletarian petitioners marched on the
St. Petersburg palace and were killed by the hundreds. The myth
that the Tsar was the gracious protector of his subjects, however sur-
rounded he might be by malicious advisers, was quite shattered. The
reaction was immediate, bitter, and prolonged and was not at all confined to the working class. Employers, merchants, and white-collar
officials joined in the burgeoning of strikes which brought the economy
to a virtual standstill in October. Some employers even continued to
pay wages to strikers. University students and faculties joined the
revolution. After the great October strike, the peasants ominously sided
with the workers and engaged in riots and assaults on landowners.
Until peasants became involved, even some landowners had sided with
the revolution.

The other major occurrence was the disastrous defeat of the Russian army and navy in the 1904–5 war with Japan. Fundamentally
an imperialist venture aspiring to hegemony over the people of Asia,
the war was not regarded as a people's but as a Tsar's war, to save
and spread absolutism. The military defeat itself probably had less
portent than the return of shattered soldiers from a fight that was
not for them. Hundreds of thousands, wounded or not, returned from
the war as a visible, vocal, and ugly reminder to the entire populace
of the weakness and selfishness of Tsarist absolutism.

The years from 1905 to 1917 formed an almost relentless proces-
sion of increasing misery and despair. Promising at last a constitutional
government, the Tsar, in October, 1905, issued from on high a proclamation renouncing absolutism, granting law-making power to a duma,
and guaranteeing freedom of speech, assembly, and association. The

first two dumas, of 1906 and 1907, were dissolved for recalcitrance. The third was made pliant by reduced representation of workers and peasants and by the prosecution and conviction of protestants in the first two. The brief period of a free press was succeeded in 1907 by a reinstatement of censorship and confiscation of prohibited publications. Trial of offenders against the Tsar was now conducted by courts martial. Whereas there had been only 26 executions of the death sentence, in the 13 years of Alexander III's firm rule (1881–94), there were 4,449 in the years 1905–10, in six years of Nicholas II's soft regimen.[14]

But this "white terror," which caused despair among the workers and intelligentsia in the cities, was not the only face of misery. For the peasants, there was a bad harvest in 1906 followed by continued crop failures in several areas in 1907. To forestall action by the dumas, Stolypin decreed a series of agrarian reforms designed to break up the power of the rural communes by individualizing land ownership. Between these acts of God and government, peasants were so pre-occu-

FIG. 2.    The Russian Revolution.

pied with hunger or self-aggrandizement as to be dulled in their sensitivity to the revolutionary appeals of radical organizers.

After more than five years of degrading terror and misery, in 1910 the country appeared to have reached a condition of exhaustion. Political strikes had fallen off to a new low. As the economy recovered, the insouciance of hopelessness set in. Amongst the intelligentsia the mood was hedonism, or despair that often ended in suicide. Industrialists aligned themselves with the government. Workers worked. But an upturn of expectations, inadequately quashed by the police, was evidenced by a recrudescence of political strikes which, in the first

[14] *Ibid.*, p. 189n.

half of 1914—on the eve of war—approached the peak of 1905. They sharply diminished during 1915 but grew again in 1916 and became a general strike in February 1917.

Figure 2 indicates the lesser waves in the tidal wave whose first trough is at the end of serfdom in 1861 and whose second is at the end of Tsardom in 1917. This fifty-six year period appears to constitute a single long phase in which popular gratification at the termination of one institution (serfdom) rather quickly was replaced with rising expectations which resulted from intensified industrialization and which were incompatible with the continuation of the inequitable and capricious power structure of Tsarist society. The small trough of frustration during the repression that followed the assassination of Alexander II seems to have only briefly interrupted the rise in popular demand for more goods and more power. The trough in 1904 indicates the consequences of war with Japan. The 1905–6 trough reflects the repression of January 22, and after, and is followed by economic recovery. The final downturn, after the first year of war, was a consequence of the dislocations of the German attack on all kinds of concerted activities other than production for the prosecution of the war. Patriotism and governmental repression for a time smothered discontent. The inflation that developed in 1916 when goods, including food, became severely scarce began to make workers self-consciously discontented. The conduct of the war, including the growing brutality against reluctant, ill-provisioned troops, and the enormous loss of life, produced the same bitter frustration in the army. When civilian discontent reached the breaking point in February, 1917, it did not take long for it to spread rapidly into the armed forces. Thus began the second phase of the revolution that really started in 1905 and ended in death to the Tsar and Tsardom—but not to absolutism—when the Bolsheviks gained ascendancy over the moderates in October. A centuries-long history of absolutism appears to have made this post-Tsarist phase of it tragically inevitable.

## THE EGYPTIAN REVOLUTION OF 1952

The final slow upsurge of expectations in Egypt that culminated in the revolution began when that society became a nation in 1922, with the British grant of limited independence. British troops remained in Egypt to protect not only the Suez Canal but also, ostensibly, to prevent foreign aggression. The presence of foreign troops served only to heighten nationalist expectations, which were excited by the Wafd, the political organization that formed public opinion on national rather than religious grounds and helped establish a fairly unified community—in striking contrast to late-nineteenth century Russia.

But nationalist aspirations were not the only rising expectations in Egypt of the 1920s and 1930s. World War I had spurred industrialization, which opened opportunities for peasants to improve, somewhat, their way of life by working for wages in the cities and also opened great opportunities for entrepreneurs to get rich. The moderately wealthy got immoderately so in commodity market speculation, finance, and manufacture, and the uprooted peasants who were now employed, or at any rate living, in cities were relieved of at least the notion that poverty and boredom must be the will of Allah. But the incongruity of a money-based modern semi-feudality that was like a chariot with a gasoline engine evidently escaped the attention of ordinary people. The generation of the 1930s could see more rapid progress, even for themselves, than their parents had even envisioned. If conditions remained poor, they could always be blamed on the British, whose economic and military power remained visible and strong.

Economic progress continued, though unevenly, during World War II. Conventional exports, mostly cotton, actually declined, not even reaching depression levels until 1945, but direct employment by Allied military forces reached a peak of over 200,000 during the most intense part of the African war. Exports after the war rose steadily until 1948, dipped, and then rose sharply to a peak in 1951 as a consequence of the Korean war. But in 1945 over 250,000 wage earners[15]— probably over a third of the working force—became jobless. The cost of living by 1945 had risen to three times the index of 1937. Manual laborers were hit by unemployment; white collar workers and professionals probably more by inflation than unemployment. Meanwhile the number of millionaires in pounds sterling had increased eight times during the war.[16]

Frustrations, exacerbated during the war by German and thereafter by Soviet propaganda, were at first deflected against the British but gradually shifted closer to home. Egyptian agitators began quoting the Koran in favor of a just, equalitarian society and against great differences in individual wealth. There was an ominous series of strikes, mostly in the textile mills, from 1946–8.

At least two factors stand out in the postponement of revolution. The first was the insatiable postwar world demand for cotton and textiles and the second was the surge of solidarity with king and coun-

[15] C. Issawi, *Egypt at Mid-Century: An Economic Survey*, London: Oxford University Press, 1954, p. 262. J. & S. Lacouture in their *Egypt in Transition*, New York: Criterion Books, 1958, p. 100, give a figure of over 300,000.

[16] J. and S. Lacouture, *op. cit.*, p. 99.

try that followed the 1948 invasion of the new state of Israel. Israel now supplemented England as an object of deflected frustration. The diastrous defeat a year later, by a new nation with but a fifteenth of Egypt's population, was the beginning of the end. This little war had struck the peasant at his hearth, when a shortage of wheat and of oil for stoves provided a daily reminder of a weak and corrupt government. The defeat frustrated popular hopes for national glory and—with even more portent—humiliated the army and solidified it against the bureaucracy and the palace which had profiteered at the expense of national honor. In 1950 began for the first time a direct and open propaganda attack against the king himself. A series of peasant uprisings, even on the lands of the king, took place in 1951 along with some 49 strikes in the cities. The skyrocketing demand for cotton after the start of the Korean War in June, 1950 was followed by a collapse in March, 1952. The uncontrollable or uncontrolled riots in Cairo,

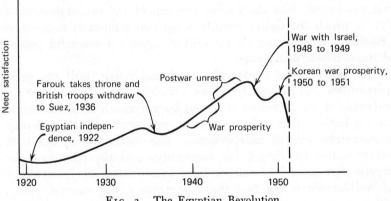

FIG. 3.   The Egyptian Revolution.

on January 26, 1952, marked the fiery start of the revolution. The officers' coup in the early morning of July 23 only made it official [See Figure 3].

The J-curve of rising expectations followed by their effective frustration is applicable to other revolutions and rebellions than just the [two] already considered. . . .

The American Revolution itself fits the J-curve and deserves more than the brief mention here given. Again prolonged economic growth and political autonomy produced continually rising expectations. They became acutely frustrated when, following the French and Indian War (which had cost England so much and the colonies so little), England began a series of largely economic regulations having the same purpose as those directed against New York in the preceding century. From the 1763 Proclamation (closing to settlement land west of the Appalachians) to the Coercive Acts of April, 1774 (which among other things, in response to the December, 1773 Boston Tea Party, closed tight the port of Boston), Americans were beset with unaccustomed manifestations of British power and began to resist forcibly in 1775, on the Lexington-Concord road. A significant decline in trade with England in 1772[17] may have hastened the maturation of colonial rebelliousness.

The curve also fits the French Revolution, which again merits more mention than space here permits. Growing rural prosperity, marked by steadily rising land values in the eighteenth century, had progressed to the point where a third of French land was owned by peasant-proprietors. There were the beginnings of long-scale manufacture in the factory system. Constant pressure by the bourgeoisie against the state for reforms was met with considerable hospitality by a government already shifting from its old landed-aristocratic and clerical base to the growing middle class. Counter to these trends, which would *per se* avoid revolution, was the feudal reaction of the mid-eighteenth century, in which the dying nobility sought in numerous nagging ways to retain and reactivate its perquisites against a resentful peasantry and importunate bourgeoisie.

But expectations apparently continued rising until the growing opportunities and prosperity rather abruptly halted, about 1787. The fiscal crisis of the government is well known, much of it a consequence of a 1.5 billion livre deficit following intervention against Britain in the American war of independence. The threat to tax the nobility severely—after its virtual tax immunity—and the bourgeoisie more severely may indeed be said to have precipitated the revolution. But less well-known is the fact that 1787 was a bad harvest year and 1788 even worse; that by July, 1789 bread prices were higher than they had been in over 70 years; that an ill-timed trade treaty with England depressed the prices of French textiles; that a concurrent bumper grape crop depressed wine prices—all with the result of making desperate the plight of the large segment of the population now dependent on other producers for food. They had little money to buy even less bread. Nobles and bourgeoisie were alienated from the government by the threat of taxation; workers and some peasants by the threat of starvation. A long period of halting but real progress for virtually all segments of the population was now abruptly ended in consequence of the government's efforts to meet its deficit and of eco-

[17] See U.S. Bureau of the Census, *Historical Statistics of the United States, Colonial Times to 1957,* Washington, D.C., 1960, p. 757.

nomic crisis resulting from poor crops and poor tariff policy.[18] . .

One negative case—of a revolution that did not occur—is the depression of the 1930s in the United States. It was severe enough, at least on economic grounds, to have produced a revolution. Total national private production income in 1932 reverted to what it had been in 1916. Farm income in the same year was as low as in 1900; manufacturing as low as in 1913. Construction had not been as low since 1908. Mining and quarrying was back at the 1909 level.[19] For much of the population, two decades of economic progress had been wiped out. There were more than sporadic demonstrations of unemployed, hunger marchers, and veterans. In New York City, at least 29 people died of starvation. Poor people could vividly contrast their own past condition with the present—and their own present condition with that of those who were not seriously suffering. There were clearly audible rumbles of revolt. Why, then, no revolution?

Several forces worked strongly against it. Among the most depressed, the mood was one of apathy and despair, like that observed in Austria by Zawadzki and Lazarsfeld. It was not until the 1936 election that there was an increased turnout in the national election. The great majority of the public shared a set of values which since 1776 had been official dogma—not the dissident program of an alienated intelligentsia. People by and large were in agreement, whether or not they had succeeded economically, in a belief in individual hard work, self-reliance, and the promise of success. (Among workers, this non-class orientation had greatly impeded the establishment of trade unions, for example.) Those least hit by the depression—the upper-middle class businessmen, clergymen, lawyers, and intellectuals—remained rather solidly committed not only to equalitarian values and to the established economic system but also to constitutional processes. There was no such widespread or profound alienation as that which had cracked the loyalty of the nobility, clergy, bourgeoisie, armed forces, and intelligentsia in Russia. And the national political leadership that emerged had constitutionalism almost bred in its bones. The major threat to constitutionalism came in Louisiana; this leadership was unable to capture a national party organization, in part because Huey Long's arbitrariness and demagogy were mistrusted.

The major reason that revolution did not nonetheless develop probably remains the vigor with which the national government attacked

---

[18] See G. Lefebvre, *The Coming of the French Revolution*, Princeton: Princeton University Press, 1947, pp. 101–109, 145–148, 196.

[19] See U.S. Bureau of the Census, *Historical Statistics of the United States: 1789–1945*, Washington, D.C.: 1949, p. 14.

the depression in 1933, when it became no longer possible to blame the government. The ambivalent popular hostility to the business community was contained by both the action of government against the depression and the government's practice of publicly and successfully eliciting the cooperation of businessmen during the crucial months of 1933. A failure then of cooperation could have intensified rather than lessened popular hostility to business. There was no longer an economic or a political class that could be the object of widespread intense hatred because of its indifference or hostility to the downtrodden. Had Roosevelt adopted a demagogic stance in the 1932 campaign and gained the loyalty to himself personally of the Army and the F.B.I., there might have been a Nazi-type "revolution," with a potpourri of equalitarian reform, nationalism, imperialism, and domestic scapegoats. Because of a conservatism in America stemming from strong and long attachment to a value system shared by all classes, an anticapitalist, leftist revolution in the 1930s is very difficult to imagine.

## SOME CONCLUSIONS

The notion that revolutions need both a period of rising expectations and a succeeding period in which they are frustrated qualifies substantially the main Marxian notion that revolutions occur after progressive degradation and the de Tocqueville notion that they occur when conditions are improving. By putting de Tocqueville before Marx but without abandoning either theory, we are better able to plot the antecedents of at least the disturbances here described.

Half of the general, if not common, sense of this revised notion lies in the utter improbability of a revolution occurring in a society where there is the continued, unimpeded opportunity to satisfy new needs, new hopes, new expectations. . . . Would the Russian Revolution have taken place if the Tsarist autocracy had, quite out of character, truly granted the popular demands for constitutional democracy in 1905? Would the Cairo riots of January, 1952 and the subsequent coup actually have occurred if Britain had departed from Egypt and if the Egyptian monarchy had established an equitable tax system and in other ways alleviated the poverty of urban masses and the shame of the military?

The other half of the sense of the notion has to do with the improbability of revolution taking place where there has been no hope, no period in which expectations have risen. Such a stability of expectations presupposes a static state of human aspirations that sometimes exists but is rare. Stability of expectations is not a stable social condition. Such was the case of American Indians (at least from our perspective) and perhaps Africans before white men with Bibles, guns, and other goods interrupted the stability of African society. Egypt was in such a condition, vis-à-vis modern aspirations, before Europe became interested in building a canal. Such stasis was the case in Nazi concentration camps, where conformism reached the point of inmates cooperating with guards even when the inmates were told to lie down so that they could be shot.[20] But in the latter case there was a society with externally induced complete despair, and even in these camps there were occasional rebellions of sheer desperation. It is of course true that in a society less regimented than concentration camps, the rise of expectations can be frustrated successfully, thereby defeating rebellion just as the satisfaction of expectations does. This, however, requires the uninhibited exercise of brute force as it was used in suppressing the Hungarian rebellion of 1956. Failing the continued ability and persistent will of a ruling power to use such force, there appears to be no sure way to avoid revolution short of an effective, affirmative, and continuous response on the part of established governments to the almost continuously emerging needs of the governed.

To be predictive, my notion requires the assessment of the state of mind—or more precisely, the mood—of a people. This is always difficult, even by techniques of systematic public opinion analysis. Respondents interviewed in a country with a repressive government are not likely to be responsive. But there has been considerable progress in gathering first-hand data about the state of mind of peoples in politically unstable circumstances. One instance of this involved interviewing in West Berlin, during and after the 1948 blockade, as reported by Buchanan and Cantril. They were able to ascertain, however crudely, the sense of security that people in Berlin felt. There was a significant increase in security after the blockade.[21]

Another instance comes out of the middle Eastern study conducted by the Columbia University Bureau of Applied Social Research and reported by Lerner.[22] By directly asking respondents whether they

---

[20] Eugen Kogon, *The Theory and Practice of Hell*, New York: Farrar, Straus & Co., 1950, pp. 284–286.

[21] W. Buchanan, "Mass Communication in Reverse," *International Social Science Bulletin*, 5 (1953), pp. 577–583, at p. 578. The full study is W. Buchanan and H. Cantril, *How Nations See Each Other*, Urbana: University of Illinois Press, 1953, esp. pp. 85–90.

[22] Daniel Lerner, *The Passing of Traditional Society*, Glencoe, Ill.: Free Press, 1958.

were happy or unhappy with the way things had turned out in their life, the interviewers turned up data indicating marked differences in the frequency of a sense of unhappiness between countries and between "traditional," "transitional," and "modern" individuals in these countries.[23] There is no technical reason why such comparisons could not be made chronologically as well as they have been geographically.

Other than interview data are available with which we can, from past experience, make reasonable inferences about the mood of a people. It was surely the sense for the relevance of such data that led Thomas Masaryk before the first World War to gather facts about peasant uprisings and industrial strikes and about the writings and actions of the intelligentsia in nineteenth-century Russia. In the present report, I have used not only such data—in the collection of which other social scientists have been less assiduous than Masaryk—but also such indexes as comparative size of vote as between Rhode Island and the United States, employment, exports, and cost of living. Some such indexes, like strikes and cost of living, may be rather closely related to the mood of a people; others, like value of exports, are much cruder indications. Lest we shy away from the gathering of crude data, we should bear in mind that Durkheim developed his remarkable insights into modern society in large part by his analysis of suicide rates. He was unable to rely on the interviewing technique. We need not always ask people whether they are grievously frustrated by their government; their actions can tell us as well and sometimes better.

In his *Anatomy of Revolution*, Crane Brinton describes "some tentative uniformities" that he discovered in the Puritan, American, French, and Russian revolutions.[24] The uniformities were: an economically advancing society, class antagonism, desertion of intellectuals, inefficient government, a ruling class that has lost self-confidence, financial failure of government, and the inept use of force against rebels. All but the last two of these are long-range phenomena that lend themselves to studies over extended time periods. The first two lend themselves to statistical analysis. If they serve the purpose, techniques of content analysis could be used to ascertain trends in alienation of intellectuals. Less rigorous methods would perhaps serve better to ascertain the effectiveness of government and the self-confidence of rulers. Because tensions and frustrations are present at all times in every society, what is most seriously needed are data that cover

---

[23] *Ibid.*, pp. 101–103.

[24] See the revised Vintage Books edition of 1965, pp. 250–252.

an extended time period in a particular society, so that one can say there is evidence that tension is greater or less than it was N years or months previously.

We need also to know how long is a long cycle of rising expectations and how long is a brief cycle of frustration. We noted a brief period of frustration in Russia after the 1881 assassination of Alexander II and a longer period after the 1904 beginning of the Russo-Japanese War. Why did not the revolution occur at either of these times rather than in 1917? Had expectations before these two times not risen high enough? Had the subsequent decline not been sufficiently sharp and deep? Measuring techniques have not yet been devised to answer these questions. But their unavailability now does not forecast their eternal inaccessibility. Physicists devised useful temperature scales long before they came as close to absolute zero as they have recently in laboratory conditions. The far more complex problems of scaling in social science inescapably are harder to solve.

We therefore are still not at the point of being able to predict revolution, but the closer we can get to data indicating by inference the prevailing mood in a society, the closer we will be to understanding the change from gratification to frustration in the people's minds. That is the part of the anatomy, we are forever being told with truth and futility, in which wars and revolutions always start. We should eventually be able to escape the embarrassment that may have come to Lenin six weeks after he made the statement in Switzerland, in January, 1917, that he doubted whether "we, the old [will] live to see the decisive battles of the coming revolution."[25]

[25] Quoted in E. H. Carr, *A History of Soviet Russia*, Vol. I, *The Bolshevik Revolution: 1917–23*, London: Macmillan, 1950, p. 69.

# 9

# On the Etiology of Internal Wars

*Harry Eckstein*

〈〈〈〈〈〈〈〈〈〈〈〈〈〈〈〈〈〈〈〈〈〈〈〈〈〈〈〈〈〈〈〈〈〈〈〈〈〈〈〈〈〈〈〈〈〈

## EDITORS' COMMENT

If Louis XVI had not dismissed Necker, if Kerensky had taken Russia out of the war, if Hindenburg had resisted the advice of von Papen. . . . It is always fun to speculate about what might have been done to avert a revolution—to be Monday-morning quarterbacks of the moves of governments that were presented with crises which later proved fatal to the regime. This speculation raises one fundamental question. Just what *can* elites do in the face of a rising tide of revolution—how much should one attribute the success of a revolution to the failures of the elite? In the following essay, Harry Eckstein confronts this problem, among others, in an interesting survey of the contemporary writing on revolution.

　To some extent, virtually all authors included in this book attribute some of the success of a revolution to the failures of elites. Even Trotsky in the *Russian Revolution* (in a section not reprinted here) analyzes this problem in such a way that the reader is left with the impression that at least one Marxist is very nervous about this point. Although Trotsky must assert that historical forces, not individual decisions, were responsible for the Revolution, he devotes too much space to a discussion of royal personality for the reader to believe that he is indifferent to the decisions and actions of the elites.

Eugene Kamenka, in the essay reprinted in this volume, asserts that the government, as a focus of attack by any political revolutionary movement, necessarily imposes severe constraints on the form which a revolution must take: the more organized the government, the more organized the revolution. Hence, in a modern state, revolution becomes a matter of tactics—and the analysis of revolution, a matter of comparative tactics. In Eckstein's analysis, taking off from this point, it is not surprising, therefore, to find a strong flavor of game theory, since the realm of tactics is quite easily adapted to game-theory analysis.

To Eckstein, in effect, revolution is a contest, each side having its options, its resources, its strategies. And the paradigm which he constructs at the conclusion of his essay is very much in line with this analysis. One can view revolution as a balance of forces; the course of a revolution (even the scope of a revolution in Rosenau's sense) is the product of this balance. Nor is the contest necessarily an unequal one. Eckstein, by implication, does not side with the theorists who assert that revolution is impossible in an advanced industrial state. Indeed, he suggests that there are severe limitations on the resources of the incumbents in any of this kind. The reader might speculate as to where the advantage (if any) should lie. Before the detractors of game theory are deterred from reading this essay, let us observe that, perhaps, the contest approach is more useful when applied to a revolutionary situation than, say, to international relations.

Eckstein makes one set of assertions which distinguishes him from most other theorists of revolution. He perceives attitudes in a society as independent variables—they are not necessarily the product of objective social conditions—although, obviously, they can be affected by these conditions. In this respect, Eckstein disagrees with the analysis of James C. Davies (see Selection 8 in this volume). Clearly, the structural-behavioral distinction, or the objective-subjective distinction which is its philosophical counterpart, is an ancient problem. With respect to theorists of revolution, it has been really an insurmountable problem since, in the experience of elites, objective conditions have been easier to handle than subjective opinions: witness the lamentations of Hobbes or Burke. And Eckstein has little remedy to offer to a beleaguered Nicholas II or Louis XVI. Here is an area where gamesmanship and the balance of forces are extraordinarily difficult to conceptualize: All that any theorist has been able to do thus far, given Eckstein's assumptions, is to describe the symptoms without having cures to recommend. All one can do is to indicate the general relationship between ideas and conditions—and to manipulate conditions.

Nor is this a problem which bedevils only incumbents. The attempts on the part of revolutionaries to develop class or group consciousness and to manipulate ideas indicate the great importance of the latter. Yet, at present, theory has little to say on this subject.

# ON THE ETIOLOGY OF INTERNAL WARS

## Harry Eckstein

The term "internal war" denotes any resort to violence within a political order to change its constitution, rulers, or policies. It is not a new concept; distinctions between external and internal war (*guerre extérieure* and *guerre intérieure*) were made already in the nineteenth century by writers on political violence. Nor does it mean quite the same thing as certain more commonly used terms, such as revolution, civil war, revolt, rebellion, uprising, guerrilla warfare, mutiny, *jacquerie, coup d'état,* terrorism, or insurrection. It stands for the genus of which the others are species. . . .

[Because of the problems of typology], it can do no harm and might do much good to consider internal wars as all of a piece at the beginning of inquiry and to introduce distinctions only as they become necessary or advisable. In this way, the possibilities of developing general theories are increased, as is the likelihood that the distinctions made will be important and precise. In any event, that is how I shall proceed here, showing at the end how a general theory about the genus "internal war" can be adapted to give an account of special cases.

The theoretical issues raised by internal wars can be classified according to the phases through which such wars pass. They include problems about their preconditions, the way they can be effectively waged, the courses they tend to take, the outcomes they tend to have, and their long-run effects on society.

Curiously enough, the later the phase, the less there is to read about the issues involved. Despite the protracted normative argument between pro-revolutionaries and anti-revolutionaries, initiated by Paine and Burke, almost nothing careful and systematic has been written about the long-run social effects of internal wars, least of all perhaps about some of the most poignant and practical problems they raise:

SOURCE. Harry Eckstein, "On the Etiology of Internal Wars," from *History and Theory*, IV, 2 (1965), pp. 133–163, excerpted. Reprinted by permission of the author and Wesleyan University Press. Copyright 1965 by Wesleyan University.

how political legitimacy and social harmony may be restored after violent disruption, what makes internal wars acute or chronic, and what the comparative costs (and probabilities) are of revolutionary and evolutionary transformations. Little more is available on the determinants of success or failure in internal wars. A fair amount has been written about the dynamic processes of revolutions, above all in the comparative historical studies already mentioned and in a very few more recent books, like Crozier's *The Rebels*. But in regard to etiology, to "causes," we are absolutely inundated with print.

This abundance of etiological studies is not, however, an unmixed blessing. If studying other aspects of internal wars poses the basic problem of thinking of theoretical possibilities, studying their etiology poses a difficulty equally great: how to choose among a rare abundance of hypotheses which cannot all be equally valid nor all be readily combined. This problem exists because most propositions about the causes of internal wars have been developed in historical studies of particular cases (or very limited numbers of cases) rather than in broadly comparative, let alone genuinely social-scientific, studies. In historical case-studies one is likely to attach significance to any aspect of pre-revolutionary society that one intuits to be significant, and so long as one does not conjure up data out of nothing one's hypotheses cannot be invalidated on the basis of the case in question.

That most studied of all internal wars, the French Revolution, provides a case in point—as well as examples in abundance of the many social, personal, and environmental forces to which the occurrence of internal wars might be attributed. Scarcely anything in the French *ancien régime* has not been blamed, by one writer or another for the revolution, and all of their interpretations, however contradictory, are based on solid facts.

Some interpreters have blamed the outbreak of the French Revolution on intellectual causes, that is to say, on the ideas, techniques, and the great public influence of the *philosophes* (who were indeed very influential). This is the standard theory of post-revolutionary conservative theorists, from Chateaubriand to Taine, men who felt, in essence, that in pre-revolutionary France a sound society was corrupted by a seductive and corrosive philosophy.

Other writers have blamed the revolution mainly on economic conditions, although it is difficult to find very many who single out as crucial the same conditions. The revolution has been attributed to sheer grinding poverty among the lower classes (who were certainly poor); to financial profligacy and mismanagement on the part of the government (of which it was in fact guilty); to the extortionate taxation inflicted on the peasants (and peasant taxation verged upon brutality); to short-term setbacks (which actually occurred and caused great hardship) like the bad harvest of 1788, the hard winter of 1788–89, and the still winds of 1789 which prevented flour from being milled and made worse an already acute shortage of bread; to the over-abundant wine harvests of the 1780's (one of the first historic instances of the harmful effects of overproduction); to the increased wealth and power of the bourgeoisie in a society still dominated to a significant extent by aristocrats, the growth of the Parisian proletariat and its supposedly increasing political consciousness, and the threatened abrogation of the financial privileges of the aristocracy, particularly their exemption from taxation—all unquestionable facts producing manifest problems.

Still another set of writers locates the crucial cause of the revolution in aspects of social structure. Much has been made, and with sufficient reason, of the fact that in the last years of the *ancien régime* there occurred a hardening in the lines of upward mobility in French society—for example, a decline in grants of patents of nobility to commoners and the imposition of stringent social requirements for certain judicial and administrative positions and the purchase of officerships in the army. This, many have argued (following Mosca's and Pareto's famous theory of the circulation of elites), engendered that fatal yearning for an aristocracy of wealth and talent to which the *philosophes* gave expression. Much has also been made, with equal reason, of popular dissatisfaction with the parasitic life of the higher nobility, with its large pensions and puny duties, its life of hunting, love-making, watchmaking, and interminable conversation. And much has been attributed to the vulnerability of the privileged classes to the very propagandists who wanted to alter the system that supported them ("How," asked Taine, "could people who talked so much resist people who talked so well?"), reflected in the Anglomania which swept through the higher aristocracy toward the end of the *ancien régime* and in the rush of many aristocrats to the cause of the Americans in their war of independence.

There are also certain well-founded "political" explanations of the French Revolution: that the revolution was really caused by the violation of the tacit "contract" on which the powers of the monarchy rested (a contract by which the aristocracy surrendered its powers to the monarchy in return for receiving certain inviolable privileges), or that the revolution was simply a successful political conspiracy by the Jacobins, based on efficient political organization. Personalities, needless to say, get their due as well: the revolution has been blamed, for example, on the character, or lack of character, of Louis XVI (who was in fact weak, vacillating and inconsistent), the supposed immoral-ity of the Queen (who indeed was the subject, justly or not, of many scandals), the effect on the public of the dismissal of Necker, and, of course, on the "genius," good or evil, of unquestionable geniuses like Mirabeau, Danton, Marat, and Robespierre. . . .

How can this embarrassment of interpretative riches (one hesitates to say theoretical riches) be reduced? If the examination of any single case allows one to determine only whether an interpretation of it is based on facts, then broad comparative studies in space and/or time are needed to establish the significance of the facts on which the interpretations are based. Was a blockage in the channels of social mobility a significant precondition of the French Revolution? We can be reasonably confident that it was only if it can be shown that elite circulation and political stability are generally related. . . .

This is the simplest conceivable methodology, and easy to indicate abstractly. But actually to find the broad general relationships on the basis of which particular interpretations can be assessed is not so easy. For this purpose we need a tremendous amount of historical work that comparative historiographers of internal wars have hardly even begun to do. There are so many possibilities to be tested against so many cases. A general etiology of internal wars, at this stage, can only be a remote end of inquiry, and neither limited comparative studies nor interpretations of particular instances of internal war should pretend otherwise.

But even prior to undertaking that work, theoretical reflection can introduce some order into the chaos that internal war studies present. Most important, it can produce useful judgments as to the more economic lines to pursue in empirical inquiry. We can in a small way approach an etiology of internal wars by classifying the theoretical possibilities available, indicating the analytical choices they require and do not require to be made, and attempting to determine what lines of analysis are most likely to prove rewarding. Where the theoretical possibilities are as varied and chaotic as in the case of internal war, such reflection, to organize and restrict inquiry, is a necessary preliminary to the more definitive work of rigorously testing well-formulated propositions.

Perhaps the first thing that becomes apparent when one tries to classify causal explanations of the sort sketched above is that many of the explanations do not really require a choice to be made by the analyst. The propositions do not always contradict one another; often, in fact, they are complementary, differing only because they refer to different points in the time-sequence leading to revolution, or because they refer to different kinds of causality, or because they single out one factor among many of equal significance.

The most important distinction to make in this connection is between preconditions and precipitants of internal wars. A "precipitant" of internal war is an event which actually starts the war ("occasions" it), much as turning the flintwheel of a cigarette lighter ignites a flame. "Preconditions" of internal war, on the other hand, are those circumstances which make it possible for the precipitants to bring about political violence, as the general structure of a lighter makes it possible to produce a flame by turning the flintwheel. Some of the causal explanations of the French Revolution already mentioned clearly fall into the first category, while others fall equally clearly into the second; and between explanations singling out precipitants and explanations emphasizing preconditions of internal war there obviously is no genuine contradiction. . . .

The greatest service that the distinction between precipitants and preconditions of internal war can render, however, is to shift attention from aspects of internal war which defy analysis to those which are amenable to systematic inquiry. Phenomena which precipitate internal war are almost always unique and ephemeral in character. A bad harvest, a stupid or careless ruler, moral indiscretion in high places, an ill-advised policy: how could such data be incorporated into general theories? They are results of the vagaries of personality, of forces external to the determinate interrelations of society, of all those unique and fortuitous aspects of concrete life which are the despair of social scientists and the meat and drink of narrative historians.

Closely related, the distinction between precipitants and preconditions of internal wars will also help one to avoid what is perhaps the most misleading theory about their causes: an unqualified conspiracy theory of internal war. To be sure, conspiracy seems to play an essential role in certain types of internal war, particularly those previously referred to as *coups* and palace revolutions. As well, one undoubtedly finds conspiratorial organizations in every internal war of any consequence—in one case Jacobins, in others fascists, in still others communists. This is precisely what tempts so many to attribute internal wars solely or mainly to conspirators, and thus to regard them, in the manner of Malaparte, essentially as matters of technique—plotting on one hand and intelligence and suppression on the other. In many cases, however, the conspirators seem to do little more than turn the flintwheel in volatile situations, or indeed not even as much as that; sometimes they merely turn the revolutionary conflagration to their own purposes. Internal wars do not always have a clear aim, a tight organization, a distinct shape and tendency from the outset. Many seem to be characterized in their early stages by nothing so much as amorphousness. They are formless matter waiting to be shaped, and if there is an art of revolution, it involves, largely at least, not making or subduing it, but capitalizing on the unallocated political resources it provides. . . .

Certain kinds of precipitants of internal war have a special importance of their own, however, in what one might call "practical etiology"—the anticipation of internal wars for policy purposes. A precipitant may be found so frequently on the eve of internal wars that its existence can be treated as a particularly urgent danger signal, particularly if its effects are delayed sufficiently to allow some adaptation to the danger. As far as we know, both of these conditions are satisfied by economic precipitants of internal war. The point deserves some elaboration, particularly in view of the persistent emphasis on economic conditions in writings on internal war.

It now seems generally agreed that persistent poverty in a society rarely leads to political violence. Quite the contrary. As Edwards points out, following an argument already developed by de Tocqueville, economic oppression, indeed all kinds of oppression, seems to wane rather than increase in pre-revolutionary periods.[1] Brinton makes the same point. While not under-estimating the amount of poverty in the societies he analyzes in *The Anatomy of Revolution,* he does point out that all of these societies were enconomically progressive rather than retrograde. . . . Even some Marxists seem to share this view. Trotsky, for example, once remarked that if poverty and oppression were a precipitant of revolution the lower classes would always be in revolt, and obviously he had a point.

It is equally difficult to establish a close link between economic improvement and internal war. Pre-revolutionary periods may often be [in the long-term sense] economically progressive, but economic progress is not always (or even often) connected with internal war. . . . The moment one focuses on short-term tendencies, a fairly frequently repeated pattern emerges—and one which tells us why it is that some writers adhere stubbornly to the immiseration theory of internal war and others, with just as much conviction, to the economic progress theory. It so happens that before many internal wars one finds both economic improvement and immiseration; more precisely, many internal wars are preceded by long-term improvements followed by serious short-term setbacks.[2] The bad harvests and unfavorable weather conditions in pre-revolutionary France, the American recession of 1774–1775, the bad Russian winter of 1916–1917 (not

---

[1] Edwards, *The Natural History of Revolutions* (Chicago, 1927), 33.
[2] See James C. Davies, "Toward a Theory of Revolution," *American Sociological Review,* 27 (1962), 5–19.

to mention the economic impact of the war on Russia) and the marked rise of unemployment in Egypt before Naguib's *coup* are cases in point. All dealt serious short-term blows to economic life and all followed long periods of economic progress, especially for those previously "repressed."

It is this dual pattern which really seems to be lethal, and it is not difficult to see why. In times of prolonged and marked economic progress, people become accustomed to new economic standards and form new economic expectations, which previously they could scarcely imagine. Confidently expecting continuous progress, they also tend to take risks (like accumulating debts) which they might not take otherwise. All this greatly exaggerates the impact of serious temporary setbacks; both psychologically and economically the costs of such setbacks are bound to be greater than if they occurred after long periods of stagnation or very gradual progress. . . .

We can profitably relegate to a secondary role most of those greatly varying, unique, and largely fortuitous events which occasion the outbreak of internal wars. But even if we do, a great variety of hypotheses remains—great enough if we confine ourselves to general treatments of internal war, and greater still if we deal with hypotheses formulated to deal with particular cases. In this connection, it might be useful to supplement the explanations of particular revolutions listed above with a sample of propositions frequently found in the more general literature on internal war. These include:[3]

(a) *Hypotheses emphasizing "intellectual" factors:*

1. Internal wars result from the failure of a regime to perform adequately the function of political socialization.
2. Internal wars are due to the coexistence in a society of conflicting social "myths."
3. Internal wars result from the existence in a society of unrealizable values or corrosive social philosophies.
4. Internal wars are caused by the alienation (desertion, transfer of allegiance) of the intellectuals.

(b) *Hypotheses emphasizing economic factors:*

1. Internal wars are generated by growing poverty.

[3] The hypotheses come from a large variety of sources, including: Lasswell and Kaplan, *Power and Society* (New Haven, 1950); L. P. Edwards, *The Natural History of Revolution* (Chicago, 1937); George S. Pettee, *The Process of Revolution* (New York, 1938); Crane Brinton, *The Anatomy of Revolution* (New York, 1938; Rudé, *The Crowd in the French Revolution* (Oxford, 1959); Trotsky, *The History of the Russian Revolution* (Ann Arbor, Michigan, 1957); De Grazia, *The Political Community* (Chicago, 1948); Gaetano Mosca, *The Ruling Class* (New York, 1939); and Vilfredo Pareto, *The Mind and Society* (New York, 1935).

2. Internal wars result from rapid economic progress.
3. Internal wars are due to severe imbalances between the production and distribution of goods.
4. Internal wars are caused by a combination of long-term economic improvement and short-term setbacks.

(c) *Hypotheses emphasizing aspects of social structure:*

1. Internal wars are due to the inadequate circulation of elites (that is, inadequate recruitment into the elite of the able and powerful members of the non-elite).
2. Internal wars result from too much recruitment of members of the non-elite into the elite, breaking down the internal cohesion of the elite.
3. Internal war is a reflection of *anomie* resulting from great social mobility.
4. Internal war is a reflection of frustration arising from little general social mobility—from general social stagnation.
5. Internal wars result from the appearance in societies of new social classes.

(d) *Hypotheses emphasizing political factors:*

1. Internal wars are due to the estrangement of rulers from the societies they rule.
2. Internal war is simply a response to bad government (government which performs inadequately the function of goal-attainment).
3. Internal wars are due, not to the attacks of the governed on those who govern, but to divisions among the governing classes.
4. Internal wars are responses to oppressive government.
5. Internal wars are due to excessive toleration of alienated groups.

(e) *Hypotheses emphasizing no particular aspects of societies, but general characteristics of social process:*

1. Political violence is generated by rapid social change.
2. Political violence results from erratic and/or uneven rates of social change, whether rapid or not.
3. Internal war occurs when a state is somehow "out of adjustment" to society.

From this sample of propositions, all of them at least plausible, we can get some idea of the overwhelming ambiguities that general studies of the pre-conditions of internal war have created to supplement those originating in case studies. These ambiguities arise most obviously from the fact that many of the propositions are manifestly contradictory; less obviously, from the sheer variety and disparity of factors included, not all of which, surely, can be equally significant, or necessary, in the etiology of internal wars. For this reason, even when precipitants are subtracted, a considerable range of choices between theories remains to be made.

One crucial choice that needs to be made is whether to put emphasis upon characteristics of the insurgents or incumbents, upon the side that rebels or the side that is rebelled against. Not surprisingly, the existing literature concentrates very largely on the rebels, treating internal war as due mainly to changes in the non-elite strata of society to which no adequate adjustment is made by the elite. This would seem to be only natural; after all, it is the rebels who rebel. At least some writings suggest, however, that characteristics of the incumbents and the classes that are usually their props must be considered jointly with characteristics of the insurgents, indeed perhaps even emphasized more strongly. Pareto, for example, while attributing revolution partly to blockages in a society's social mobility patterns, considered it equally necessary that certain internal changes should occur in an elite if revolution was to be possible; in essence, he felt that no elite which preserved its capacity for timely and effective violence, or for effective manipulation, could be successfully assailed, or perhaps assailed at all. One must, according to this view, seek the origins of internal war not only in a gain of strength by the non-elite, but also in the loss of it on the part of the elite. Brinton makes the same point: revolutions, in his view, follow the loss of common values, of internal cohesion, of a sure sense of destiny and superiority and, not least, of political efficiency in elites, and thus must be considered results as much as causes of their disintegration. And in Edwards' and Pettee's studies as well, revolutions emerge as affairs of the elites (if not always directly of the actual rulers): the crucial roles in them are played by intellectuals, by men rich and powerful but "cramped" by their lack of status or other perquisites, and by the gross inefficiency of the ruling apparatus.

Significantly enough, this view is stated perhaps more often in the writings of actual revolutionaries than in those of students of revolution. Trotsky, for example, believed that revolution requires three elements: the political consciousness of a revolutionary class, the discontent of the "intermediate layers" of society, and, just as important, a ruling class which has "lost faith in itself," which is torn by the conflicts of groups and cliques, which has lost its capacity for practical action and rests its hopes in "miracles or miracle workers."[4]

[4] Trotsky, *The Russian Revolution*, 311.

The joint consideration of insurgent and incumbent patterns thus would seem to be the logical way to proceed in the early stages of inquiry into the causes of revolution. But one should not overlook the possibility that sufficient explanations of the occurrence of many internal wars might be found in elite characteristics alone. A ruling elite may decay, may become torn by severe conflict, may be reluctant to use power, may come to lack vital political skills—and thus make it perfectly possible for a relatively weak, even disorganized, opposition of a sort that may exist in any political system to rise against it and destroy it. Indeed, there are theories which maintain that internal wars are always caused solely or primarily by changes in elite characteristics, and that one can practically ignore the insurgents in attempting to account for the occurrence of internal wars.

One such theory is propounded in Mosca's *The Ruling Class.* If the elementary needs of human life are satisfied, argued Mosca, one thing above all will cause men to rebel against their rulers, and that is their feeling that the rulers live in a totally different environment, that they are "separated" from their subjects in some profound sense. In other words, the estrangement of the elite from the non-elite is inseparable from the alienation of the latter; only the elite itself, consequently, can undermine its political position. . . .

This interpretation certainly makes sense in light of French experience: the French Revolution was far more an attack upon the refined and parasitic court nobility than upon the coarse, and little less parasitic, provincial nobility. It makes sense also in the case of Britain, for the British nobility (in the main) always preserved close ties to the soil and to the manner and morals of its tenantry; Squire Western is the embodiment of that fact. That is why it was for so long the butt of jokes among the more sophisticated, and shorter-lived, continental aristocracies. . . .

More examples of the instability that ensues from the estrangement of elites are furnished in profusion by the westernized elites of many currently under-developed areas. The elites referred to in this case are not those who learn Western skills yet remain identified with their native context; rather it is the westernized in lifeways, the visitors to the Riviera and the riders in Cadillacs, who try to lead a life totally different from that of their people. For such estranged elites, living abroad may indeed be a course preferable to the imitation of alien ways at home; at any rate, they are in that case rather less conspicuous.

It is worth noting that in the postwar period internal wars have been relatively rare in two kinds of societies: either thoroughly modernized countries or very underdeveloped countries whose elites have remained tied closely to the traditional ways and structures of life.[5] Of course, a generalization of this kind is becoming increasingly harder to test, since the number of societies without a gulf between highly modernized elites and much less modernized masses seems to be rapidly shrinking. Nevertheless the notion is given credibility by the fact that, while transitional societies seem to suffer more from internal wars than either traditional or modern societies—as one would expect upon many hypotheses—a very few seem to have strikingly low rates of violence compared to the rest. Egypt is one example, and Pakistan another. These societies seem to differ from the rest in one main respect. They have had "secondary" revolutions, so to speak, in which men of rather humble origins and popular ways (colonels' regimes) have unseated previously victorious transitional elites.

All this is not meant to validate the idea that elite estrangement is the main cause of internal war but only to show why it should be taken very seriously. The possible consequences of elite estrangement are not, however, the only reason for emphasizing studies of the incumbents at least as much as studies of insurgents in the etiology of internal wars. Another is the fact that internal wars are almost invariably preceded by important functional failures on the part of elites. Above all is this true of difficulties in financial administration—perhaps because finance impinges on the ability of governments to perform all their functions. And finally, insurgent groups seem rarely to come even to the point of fighting without some support from alienated members of incumbent elites. On this point, agreement in the literature on internal war is practically unanimous.

A second strategic choice to be made in constructing an etiology of internal wars is between structural and behavioral hypotheses. A structural hypotheses singles out, so to speak, "objective" social conditions as crucial for the occurrence of internal war: aspects of a society's "setting," such as economic conditions, social stratification and mobility, or geographic and demographic factors. A behavioral hypothesis, on the other hand, emphasizes attitudes and their formation—not setting, but "orientations" (such as degrees of strain and *anomie* in societies, the processes by which tension and aggression are generated, and the processes by which human beings are "socialized" into their communities). The great majority of propositions regarding the causes of internal war are, on the basis of these definitions, structural in character. . . .

[5] Cases in point are the stable, highly developed democracies on the one hand, and countries like Ethiopia and Somalia on the other.

Which approach is preferable? Despite the fact that there is a danger that the behavioral approach might lead to naive conspiracy theory (the belief that internal wars are always the results of insidious indoctrination by subversive elements, and could therefore always occur or always be avoided) the arguments against a primary emphasis on structural theories are very strong.

One such argument derives from the general experience of modern social science. Purely structural theories have generally been found difficult to sustain wherever they have been applied, and one fundamental reason for this is that patterns of attitudes, while responsive to the settings in which men are placed, seem also to be, to an extent, autonomous of objective conditions, able to survive changes in these conditions or to change without clearly corresponding objective changes. This is one of the basic insights underlying the sociological theory of action, which, to be sure, assigns an important role to the situations in which human action occurs, but treats "culture" largely as a separate variable and attaches particularly great significance to agencies of socialization and acculturation. It underlies as well the relatively successful use of mediational models, rather than simple S-R models, in behavioral psychology.

No doubt this point should be much elaborated.[6] But one can make a cogent case for stressing behavioral theories of the causes of internal wars without going lengthily into the general nature and past experiences of social science.

The most obvious case for behavioral theories of internal war derives from the very fact that so many different objective social conditions seem capable of generating it. We may have available many interpretative accounts of internal wars simply because an enormous variety of objective conditions can create internal-war potential. Certain internal wars do seem to have followed economic improvement, others seem to have followed closely the Marxist model of internal wars; however, many more have followed some combination of the two. Some internal wars have in fact been preceded by great, others by little social mobility; some regimes have been more oppressive and others more liberal in the immediate pre-revolutionary period, some both and some neither. Is it not reasonable to conclude that one should not seek explanations of the occurrence of internal wars in specific social conditions, but rather in the ways in which social conditions may be perceived? Instead of looking for direct connections between

---

[6] Useful summaries of action and behavior theories can be found in Roland Young, ed., *Approaches to the Study of Politics* (Evanston, Illinois, 1958), 217–243 and 285–301.

social conditions and internal war, should one not look rather for the ways in which an existing cognitive and value system may change, so that conditions perceived as tolerable at one point are perceived as intolerable at another; or, concomitantly, look for the ways in which old systems of orientation are in some cases maintained rather than adapted in the face of social change, so that changes which one society absorbs without trouble create profound difficulties in another?

The point is not that objective conditions are unrelated to internal war. Rather it is that orientations mediate between social setting and political behavior, and—because they are not simply mirrors of environment—so that different objective conditions may lead to similar political activities, or similar conditions to different activities in different contexts; that in a single context a considerable change in political activity may occur without significant changes in objective conditions or changes in objective conditions without changes in activity. What should be avoided is linking aspects of social setting *directly* to internal war or *mechanically* to orientations. Internal wars are best conceived as responses to political disorientation (such as "cognitive dissonance," *anomie*, and strains in the definition of political roles), particularly in regard to a society's norms of legitimacy; and political disorientation may follow from a considerable variety of conditions, due to the variable nature of the orientations themselves and of the agencies that implant them in different societies.

One conspicuous point of agreement in comparative studies of revolution gives further credence to this argument. This is that revolutions are invariably preceded by the "transfer of allegiance" of a society's intellectuals and the development by them of a new political "myth." If intellectuals have any obvious "functions," in the sense social scientists understand the term function, they are surely these: to socialize the members of a society outside of the domestic context, in schools and adult learning situations; to reinforce and nationalize attitudes acquired in all social contexts; and to provide meaning to life and guidelines to behavior by means of conscious doctrines where events have robbed men of their less conscious bearings. Intellectuals are particularly important in the education of adolescents and young people, and it has been shown quite definitely that political socialization occurs (or fails) mainly in the years between early childhood and full maturity.[7] It could also be shown that among revolutionaries the young tend to predominate, sometimes quite remarkably. Together these points go far to explain why the alienation of intellectuals is, in

[7] For evidence, see Herbert H. Hyman, *Political Socialization* (Glencoe, Illinois, 1959).

Edward's language, a "master-symptom" of revolution: a condition that makes revolutionary momentum irreversible.

Another point that speaks for behavioral propositions is that internal wars can, and often do, become chronic . . . . In such cases, internal wars result not from specifiable objective conditions, and not even from the loss of legitimacy by a particular regime, but from a general lack of receptivity of legitimacy of any kind. Violence becomes a political style that is self-perpetuating, unless itself "disoriented." . . .

To give still more support to the argument for behavioral theories there is the object lesson provided by the sad history of Marxist theory. Marxism singles out certain objective social conditions as underlying internal wars. It also singles out certain social groups as indispensable to the making of internal war. But Marxist revolutions themselves have been made neither under the social conditions nor by the groups emphasized in the theory. What is more, these revolutions have been made in a large variety of conditions, with a large variety of means, by organizations constituted in a large variety of ways. This is true even if one can show that the appeal of Marxism is greatest in transitional societies, for the term transition, in its very nature, denotes not a particular social state but a great many different points on whatever continuum social development may involve.

This argument has a close bearing upon a third strategic choice to be made in analyzing of internal war. Even if one emphasizes behavioral characteristics in theories of internal wars, one must, as I have said, always relate these characteristics to the social setting. The question is how to do this. Should one, in the manner of most of the hypotheses listed above, develop propositions emphasizing particular social conditions or, in the manner of a few of them, select propositions about general characteristics of social process? In the first case, one would relate internal war to particular socio-economic changes, in the second to characteristics of the general phenomenon of social change itself, such as rapid change or erratic change in any sectors of society, or conditions that may result from any social change whatever, such as imbalances between social segments (e.g., between elites of wealth and elites of status) or incongruities among the authority patterns of a society.

The proper choice between these alternatives is already implied in the arguments of the previous section. If many particular social conditions may be connected with internal wars, then clearly one should stress broad propositions about social processes and balances that can comprehend a variety of such conditions. The same position results if disorientation is conceived, in large part, as a breakdown in mutualities and complementarities of behavior. Not least, there is overwhelming evidence to show that "*anomie*," the feeling that one lacks guidelines to behavior, is increased by rapidity of change in any direction (for example, by rapid economic betterment no less than rapid economic deterioration) and that "strain," the feeling that one's roles make inconsistent demands, is aggravated by uneven or incongruent changes in different social sectors (for example, when the economic sector of society becomes significantly modern while the political remains largely traditional).

What has been said about economic conditions preceding internal wars fits the argument particularly well. It is not just that cases can be found to support both immiseration and improvement theories of revolution, hence the view that internal wars are related to economic changes as such, not to change in any particular direction; more suggestive still is the fact that internal wars most frequently follow an irregular—an anomalous—course of economic change, long-term trends being interrupted by abrupt and short-lived reversals. Such a course exhibits at least two of the general characteristics of social processes that would, upon earlier arguments, seem to be related to the occurrence of internal wars: rapidity of change and eccentricity of change . . . .

Undoubtedly there is a danger that broad formulations concerning general social processes will turn into empty and untestable generalizations, trivialities like the much-repeated proposition that political violence tends to accompany social or economic change. But this danger is avoidable; one can, after all, be specific and informative about general social processes as well as about their substantive content.

So far I have tried to make two related points. The first is that one is most likely to gain understanding of the forces impelling societies toward internal war if one avoids preoccupation with the more visible precipitants of internal wars, including conspiracies, and directs one's efforts to the analysis of their preconditions, stressing disorientative general social processes and particularly taking into account elite behavior, performance, and cohesion. The second point is in a sense the converse of this: that existing etiologies of internal wars are chaotic and inadequate precisely because studies have so far concentrated on precipitants rather than preconditions, insurgents rather than incumbents, and particular aspects of social structure rather than the effects on orientations of general social processes.

An important point must now be added. Even if we had better knowledge of the forces which push societies toward political violence, a crucial problem relating to the etiology of internal wars would remain, one that is generally ignored in the studies available to us. This problem concerns forces that might countervail those previously discussed: "obstacles" to internal war, as against forces which propel societies toward violence. . . .

*Repression*

The most obvious obstacle to internal war is, of course, the incumbent regime. It goes almost without saying that by using repression the established authorities can lessen the chances of violent attack upon themselves, or even reduce them to nil. Internal wars, after all, are not made by impersonal forces working in impersonal ways, but by men acting under the stress of external forces. This much at least there is in the conspiracy theory of revolution: wholly spontaneous riots by wholly unstructured and undirected mobs may occur, but hardly very frequently or with much effect. Actual cases of internal war generally contain some element of subversion, some structure for forming political will and acting upon decisions, however primitive and changeable. On this point, if no other, the great enemies of revolution (Burke, Chateaubriand, Taine) are at one with the great revolutionaries (Lenin, Trotsky); it is also this point, rather than some subtle idea, which underlies Pareto's and Brinton's argument that revolutions are due to elites as much as non-elites. And anything with a structure can of course be detected and repressed, through not always very easily.

The matter, however, is not quite so simple. Repression can be a two-edged sword. Unless it is based upon extremely good intelligence, and unless its application is sensible, ruthless, and continuous, its effects may be quite opposite to those intended. Incompetent repression leads to a combination of disaffection and contempt for the elite. Also, repression may only make the enemies of a regime more competent in the arts of conspiracy; certainly it tends to make them more experienced in the skills of clandestine organization and *sub rosa* communication. No wonder that botched and bungled repression is often a characteristic of pre-revolutionary societies. The French *ancien régime*, for example, had a political censorship, but it only managed to make French writers into masters of the hidden meaning, and whet the appetite of the public for their subversive books. "In our country," a French aristocrat said, "authors compete with one another for the honors of the bonfire"; even the Queen seems to have spent many delicious evenings reading the forbidden Encyclopedia with her ladies.[8] Russia, under the later Czars, was practically a model of repressive bumbledom; her policy of exile, for example, created close-knit communities of revolutionaries more

---

[8] For much information relevant to this point, see Hyppolite Taine, *Origines de la France Contemporaine*, rev. ed., 12 vols. (Paris, 1899–1914), Vol. I.

than it destroyed their cohesion. The worst situation of all seems to arise when a regime, having driven its opponents underground, inflamed their enmity, heightened their contempt, and cemented their organization, suddenly relaxes its repression and attempts a liberal policy.

From this standpoint, repression may be both an obstacle to and precipitant of internal war. Repression is of course least likely to prevent internal war in societies which, unlike totalitarian regimes, have a low capacity for coercion. In such societies, adjustive and diversionary mechanisms seem to check revolutionary potential far better. Indeed, they may in any society.

*Diversions and Concessions*

Diversionary mechanisms are all those social patterns and practices which channel psychic energies away from revolutionary objectives—which provide other outlets for aggressions or otherwise absorb emotional tensions. If Elie Halévy's theory is correct, then English non-conformist evangelicalism, especially the Methodist movement, furnishes an excellent case in point.[9] Halévy, being French, was deeply puzzled by the fact that England did not have any serious revolution in the early nineteenth century, despite conditions which, on their face, seem to have contained very great revolutionary potential—conditions resulting from the industrial revolution and from the fact of endemic revolution throughout the Western world. His solution was that English evangelicalism, more than anything else, performed a series of functions which greatly lowered the revolutionary level of British politics. Among these functions were the provision of outlets for emotional expression and the inculcation of a philosophy which reconciled the lower classes to their condition, made that condition seem inevitable, and make patient submission to it a sacred obligation. In England, at least at the time in question, religion seems indeed to have been the opiate of the people, as Marx and Engels, no less than later and different-minded historians, seem to have realized.

England may have been spared major political violence since the seventeenth century for other reasons too: for example, because at least twice in English history, just when she seemed to be on the very brink of civil war, external war opportunely occurred, unifying the country as external wars will: at the time of the Napoleonic wars, and again in 1914 after the mutiny in the Curragh threatened to de-

[9] Elie Halévy, *A History of the English People*, 6 vols. (London, 1960), Vol. I.

velop into something much more serious. Indeed, diverting popular attention from domestic troubles by starting foreign wars is one of the most venerable dodges of statecraft. This too, however, is a weapon that cuts two ways. Military adventures are excellent diversions, and military successes can marvellously cement disjoined societies, but military failure, on the evidence, can hardly fail to hasten revolution in such cases. Russia may well have entered the first World War to distract domestic unrest, but if so, the outcome was revolution rather than the contrary. . . .

Adjustive mechanisms reduce, or manage, tensions, rather than providing for them surrogate outlets. Concessions are perhaps the most obvious of such mechanisms. It is banal, but probably true, to say that timely concessions have been the most effective weapons in the arsenal of the British ruling class, and one of Halévy's more cogent points about the pacific effects of evangelicalism on nineteenth-century England is that it made the elite extraordinarily willing to ameliorate the lot of the masses. It enjoined upon them philanthropy as a sacred duty and educated them in the trusteeship theory of wealth—remember Wesley's counsel "gain all you can, save all you can, give all you can"—at the same time as it made the masses extraordinarily willing to suffer their burdens in peace. (For this reason, we can of course regard all functioning institutions for adjusting conflict as barriers to internal war.) But concessions too may work in two directions, no less than repression and certain diversionary tactics. They may only lead to further and greater demands, further and greater expectations of success, and must therefore, like repression, be continuous, and continuously greater, to succeed. "There is no better way [than a conciliatory policy]" according to Clemenceau, "of making the opposite party ask for more and more. Every man or every power whose action consists solely in surrender can only finish by self-annihilation. Everything that lives resists . . ."[10]

## Facilities for Violence

A final set of obstacles to internal war are conditions that affect the capacities of alienated groups to use violence at all, or, more often in real life, to use it with fair prospects of success. These conditions do not always prevent violence. But they can prevent its success. For this very reason, they help determine the likelihood of decisions to use violence at all. What are some of these conditions?

Perhaps the first to come to mind is terrain. While practically

[10] Quoted in G. Sorel, *Reflections on Violence* (New York, 1915), 71.

all kinds of terrain can be used, in different ways, for purposes of rebellion, not all can be used to equal advantage. The ideal, from the viewpoint of the insurgents, seems to be an area which is relatively isolated, mountainous, overgrown, criss-crossed by natural obstacles (hedges, ditches, etc.), and near the sea or other sources of external supply—terrain which affords secure bases to the insurgents in their own territory, gives them the advantage of familiarity with local conditions, and allows ready access to them of external supporters.[11]

The communications facilities of a society are another relevant condition. Marx, among many others, seems to have realized this when he argued that urbanization increases the likelihood of revolution, if only in that it makes men accessible to one another and thus makes revolutionary organization easier to achieve. "Since the collective revolutionary mentality is formed by conversation and propaganda," writes the French historian Lefebvre, "all means that bring men together favor it."[12] In this case, a condition which may heighten the chances of successful internal war (bad communications) may also discourage its outbreak. There may be nothing more mysterious to the celebrated peaceability of peasants, as compared to city-dwellers, than the physical difficulty in rural life, especially if fairly primitive, to form a "collective revolutionary mentality."

Terrain and communications are physical obstacles to (or facilities for) internal war. There are human obstacles as well. For example, internal wars seem rarely to occur, even if other conditions favor them, if a regime's instruments of violence remain loyal. This applies above all to the armed forces. Trotsky for one, and Lenin for another, considered the attitude of the army absolutely decisive for any revolution;[13] so did Le Bon.[14] Pettee, on the other hand, dissents, but for a rather subtle reason: not because he considers the attitude of the armed forces insignificant, but because he feels that armies never fail to join revolutions when all other causes of revolution are present, and that they never fail to oppose them when this is not the case.[15] We could enlarge this point to read that internal wars are unlikely

---

[11] For examples of how much terrain benefits insurgents, see Peter Paret, *Internal War and Pacification: The Vendée, 1793–1796* (Princeton, 1961); W. E. D. Allen, *Guerrilla War in Abyssinia* (London, 1951), 19; Chalmers Johnson, "Civilian Loyalties and Guerrilla Conflict," *World Politics*, July 1962; and Ernesto Guevara, *Che Guevara on Guerrilla War* (New York, 1961)—among many others.

[12] G. Lefebvre, "Foules Révolutionnaires," *Annales Historiques de la Révolution Francaise*, 1934, 23.

[13] Trotsky, *The Russian Revolution*, 116.

[14] Gustave Le Bon, *The Psychology of Revolution* (New York, 1913), 29.

[15] G. S. Pettee, *The Process of Revolution*, 105.

wherever the cohesion of an elite is intact, for the simple reason that insurgent formations require leadership and other skills, and are unlikely to obtain them on a large scale without some significant break in the ranks of an elite. Even if elites do not always "cause" their own downfall by becoming rigid or foreign to their people, they can certainly hasten their own demise by being internally at odds. From this standpoint, if not from that of Mosca's theory, elite cohesion is a factor which should be classified among the obstacles to internal war, as well as among their causes.

A final human obstacle to internal war—perhaps the greatest of all—is lack of wide popular support for rebellion. It seems generally accepted among modern writers on internal war, indeed it is the chief dogma of modern revolutionaries, that without great popular support the insurgents in an internal war can hardly hope to win (and with it are hardly likely to lose)—unless by means of a *coup d'état.* So vital is this factor that some writers think that the distinctive characteristic of internal war is the combination of violent techniques with psychological warfare, the latter designed, of course, to win the active support of the non-combatants; this is asserted in the much repeated pseudo-formula of the French theorists of *guerre révolutionnaire:* revolutionary warfare = partisan war + psychological warfare.[16] To be sure, psychological warfare occurs nowadays also in international wars. Its role in these, however, is not nearly so crucial as in internal war; it is incidental in one case but seems to be decisive in the other.

One reason for this is that in internal wars, unlike international wars, there is generally a great disparity in capacity for military effort between the incumbents and insurgents. The former tend to be in a much stronger position—not always, of course, for this is where the loyalties of the established instrumentalities of violence enter the picture, but more often than not. The insurgents are therefore forced, in the normal case, to supplement their capabilities by taking what advantage they can of terrain and the cooperation of the non-combatant population. Like terrain itself, a well-disposed population affords a secure base of operations to rebels, as well as providing them with indispensable logistical support. Rebels who can count on popular support can lose themselves in the population (according to Mao "the populace is for revolutionaries what water is for fish"), count on the population for secrecy (in wars in which intelligence is practically the whole

---

[16] G. Bonnet, *Les guerres insurrectionelles* (Paris, 1958), 60. The point that in guerrilla warfare almost everything turns on popular support is argued in many sources, most strongly perhaps in C. A. Johnson, "Civilian Loyalties and Guerrilla Conflict," *World Politics,* July 1962.

art of defense), and reconstitute their forces by easy recruitment; if they can do all of these things, they can be practically certain of victory, short of a resort to genocide by the incumbents . . . .

Needless to say, these arguments do not amount to anything like a finished etiology of internal wars. My concern here has been with preliminary, but fundamental and neglected, questions of strategy in theory-building, no more. Nevertheless, taking it all in all, this study does imply something more than that certain lines of inquiry are more promising than others in internal-war studies. When its arguments are added up, there emerges at least a considerable clue to the *form* that an adequate etiology of internal wars should take, even if little of a very specific nature can as yet be said about content. We have arrived at a paradigm, if not a fully-fledged theory.

Two points can serve as summary, as well as to spell out the nature of the paradigm I have in mind. One is that internal-war potential (the likelihood that internal war in some form will be precipitated) should be conceived formally as a ratio between positive forces making for internal war and negative forces working against it—with the *possibility* that internal war of some kind may be fomented no matter what the overall [negative] potential, and that the *probability* of its occurrence increases as internal-war potential rises. This is certainly elementary, but it is in fact far more usual, in both general theories and specific interpretations of internal war, to speak of revolutionary or pacifying forces alone, and to depict rebelliousness as either absolutely present or absolutely lacking in societies. The other, and more important point, is that the forces involved should be conceived in both cases as functions of four factors. The positive forces are produced by the *inefficacy of elites* (lack of cohesion and of expected performance), *disorienting social processes* (delegitimization), *subversion* (attempts deliberately to activate disorientation, to form new political orientations and to impede the efficacy of elites), and the *facilities* available to potential insurgents. Countervailing these factors are four others: the *facilities* of incumbents, *effective repression* (not any kind of repression), *adjustive concessions* and *diversionary mechanisms*— the first referring to the incumbents' perceived capacity to fight if internal war occurs, the others to preventative actions.

This summation provides at least the minimum that one expects from paradigms: a formal approach to study and a checklist of factors that should be particularly considered whether one is interpreting specific cases or constructing general theory. But a minimum is not much. It is necessary to go further, particularly in the direction of determining the relative values of the factors and their relations to one another.

After being stated, the variables must be ordered. Consequently, to conclude, I should like to add some suggestions that indicate how one might proceed from the mere cataloguing of promising variables toward their systematization.

In the first place, it seems, from what has been said about possible obstacles to internal war, that the negative forces vary within a much smaller range than the positive ones, so that beyond a point, internal-war potential can be reduced only with geometrically decreasing effectiveness, if at all. Take, for example, adjustive concessions. These cannot be indefinitely increased, for, in the end, they would be tantamount to surrender, and long before that point, would only serve to increase the insurgents' capabilities (not to mention the probable effects on the insurgents' demands and the incumbents' cohesion). Repression is intrinsically limited as well, among other reasons because it requires repressors and because its use will tend to intensify alienation; as in the case of concessions there may be an optimum of repression, but a maximum of it is as bad as none at all. And one can doubt the efficacy of diversions where disorientation is very widespread and goes very deep; besides, intrinsic limitations operate in the case of this factor too, for a society that lives on diversions to the extent of, say, the Roman Empire is for that very reason in decay. The factors that make for internal-war potential clearly are less inherently circumscribed. More clearly still, certain of them, like the crucial facility of popular support, belong to the realm of zero-sums, so that an increase of forces on the positive side implies a concomitant decrease on the other. In this sense, the variables involved in internal war potential have a certain hierarchical order (an order of "potency"): one set is more significant than the other.

Such an order seems to exist within each set as well. For example, no one rebels simply because he has appropriate facilities—otherwise, the military and police would be everywhere and constantly in rebellion. At the very least, internal war presupposes some degree of subversion as well as brute capabilities. Subversion in turn, however, presupposes something that can be subverted—disorientations to activate and to reshape toward new legitimizations. And much evidence suggests that, whatever forces may be at work in a society, in whatever fashion, disorientation and subversion are both unlikely where the elite performs well, is highly cohesive, and is deeply enough attuned to the general spirit of social life to provide the mutualities and complementarities that settled social orientations require—granted that certain social processes make this extremely improbable. Per contra, elite inefficacy in itself always invites challenge, from within or without, no matter what other forces may be at work in the non-elite; in one form (incohesion), it implies the likelihood of internecine elite conflict, in others the probability of alienation of the non-elite. If disorientation arising from other sources is added, the brew obviously becomes more lethal (and its explosion tends to take a different form), with or without much concerted subversion. The latter, and insurgent facilities, are essentially extra additives, the more so since insurgents can hardly lack facilities on some scale where elite inefficacy and political disorientation are great; these factors may intensify internal-war potential, but do not create it.

The factors that reduce internal-war potential can be arranged (with rather more ambiguity, to be sure) in a similar order of potency. The essential criterion that establishes their weight is the extent to which they are intrinsically limited, either because they can become self-defeating or because they are zero-sums that do not allow increases on the positive side to be balanced by increases on the other. Diversions, while certainly not unlimited, are probably the most potent of the factors, for they can apparently be carried very far before they thoroughly devitalize societies. Repression and concessions seem to have a much lower optimum point. It is difficult at present to say which of them is the less potent; in all probability, however, it is repression— if only because concessions may increase the legitimation of authority among potential dissidents (that is, serve as surrogates for other kinds of elite "performance") while acts of repression, as well as being inherently self-denials of legitimacy, are well-tailored to cope only with the less potent factor of subversion. Incumbent facilities, finally, while being by all odds the most ambiguous factor, seem to belong somewhere between diversions on one hand and concessions on the other. The reasons for this are three: First, since the most vital of them are zero-sums, they can be, in a sense, either very weak or very potent, a decrease in them implying a corresponding increase in insurgent facilities and the reverse holding as well (a sort of inherent limitation different from that operating in the case of the other factors). Secondly, it seems, on the evidence, more difficult for incumbents to regain lost facilities (especially lost loyalties) than for insurgents to multiply their stock of them, even if "logical" reasons for this are not readily apparent. And thirdly, while an increase in incumbent facilities most clearly reduces one of the positive factors, that factor happens to be least potent of the four.

The catalogue of forces making for internal-war potentials thus takes on a certain preliminary order—even if this order is as yet far from precise.

A further element of order can be introduced into the list of variables by noting that, to an extent, they can be paired with one another, specific negative and positive forces being particularly closely related. This is manifest in the case of insurgent and incumbent facilities—clearest of all where the facilities in question are zero-sums. All else being equal, it is obviously not the absolute value of facilities on either side that matters, but the ratio of the facilities concerned. Just as obviously, as already stated, there is a special relation between subversion and repression. Disorientation or elite inefficacy can hardly be repressed; only subversion can.[17] Less manifestly, but pretty clearly still, adjustive concessions bear a particular relation to certain elite failures, particularly in performance, and diversions can, to an extent, provide gratifications that alleviate the psychic stresses of disorientation; but neither is likely to counteract anything else.

One final point that bears more indirectly upon the ordering of the variables listed above requires consideration. It is an appropriate theme on which to conclude, for it is the point with which we started. Throughout the discussion, no distinction has been made between types of internal war, and this not without reasons. The fact remains, however, that internal wars, although in some ways similar, are in most respects greatly various. An adequate etiology of internal wars should therefore be able to tell one more than whether internal war in some form will occur in a society. It should also enable one to account for the specific forms internal wars take in different circumstances. . . .

The point is that two things can be done with the paradigm I have sketched. By weighing the general balance of positive and negative forces, one can arrive at an assessment of the overall degree of internal-war potential in a society. By considering the *particular* forces, combinations of forces, and ratios of forces that are strong or weak—the forces that are especially instrumental in determining the overall result—one can arrive at definite ideas of what kinds of internal war are likely to occur (quite apart from the possibility that the general degree of internal-war potential may itself set limits to the varieties that internal war can take). For example, where elite inefficacy, especially incohesion, greatly predominates among the positive forces, something like what many have called palace revolution is a very likely result. Where disorientation is very great but other positive factors are negligible, one might expect relatively unorganized, sporadic rioting as the normal response. Where subversion looms large relative

---

[17] To avoid misunderstanding, it should be clearly understood that repression here refers not to putting down rebels in internal wars but preventative actions by the incumbents.

to other factors, *coups*, *Putsches* or terrorism are more likely. Where incumbent and insurgent facilities are rather equally matched and elite cohesion is particularly tenuous, the stage is probably set for full-scale civil war. One could, in fact, contrive a useful, although very complex, typology of internal wars by working out probable results for the various possible constellations of factors included in the paradigm; and one could similarly take any typology otherwise worked out and produce for it a set of appropriately corresponding combinations of the factors.

The signal advantage of this procedure is that it avoids what defaces the whole corpus of historical studies of internal war available to us, the *ad hoc* piling up of unrelated theories, and prevents also the most conspicuous flaw of unhistorical, abstract models of revolutionary processes, the disregarding of special forces in particular cases. As well, the procedure I suggest can deal coherently with another eminently historical and theoretical matter, the transformation of many internal wars in the course of their development—the revolutionary "process." It can do so simply by applying typological theories dynamically. For the constellations of forces that provide initial impetus to internal wars are likely to undergo constant transformation in their course, much as such constellations may vary in the pre-revolutionary period. Subversion may become more intense, more purposeful; the balance of facilities may shift; incumbent elites may become more cohesive or disunited under fire; mild disorientation may become severe as authority is challenged and society disrupted by violence; the insurgents may win power, but at the cost of their own cohesion and without being able to provide effective new legitimations—and thus internal wars may proceed from stage to stage, from type to type, in unique or characteristic, continuous or spasmodic, dynamic patterns.

# 10

# Internal War as an International Event

*James N. Rosenau*

≪≪≪≪≪≪≪≪≪≪≪≪≪≪≪≪≪≪≪ ≪≪≪≪≪≪≪≪≪≪≪≪≪≪≪≪≪≪

## EDITORS' COMMENT

The following essay is an example of the growing literature on the interaction between domestic violence and the international system. It is taken from a collection of essays on this subject, edited by Professor Rosenau and entitled *International Aspects of Civil Strife*. As the title of this essay implies, his analysis of internal war is made from the viewpoint of the international system—or from the viewpoint of the actors in that system—and, therefore, tends to be a description of *policy* reaction to civil violence in another country. Rosenau's typology of internal war, for instance, is based on the objectives of the insurgents—of prime concern to the foreign policy maker—not on the class of the participants nor on the "progressive" or counterrevolutionary ideologies *per se*. Contrast his typology with that of Chalmers Johnson, for example.

We suggest that the reader compare Rosenau's essay to the Kelly article on Spain (see Selection 17) and that he compare the dynamics of a bipolar and a tripolar system as it relates to intervention and foreign perceptions. While making this comparison, he might ponder the role which nuclear weapons have played in the contemporary world. Have there been changes recently in the international attitudes towards intervention which might account for some of the differences? And, finally, do not some contemporary interventions (perhaps, for example, Vietnam) actually take place more in a tripolar than in a bipolar atmosphere?

Rosenau asks one question which the student of politics finds increasingly important these days: What is so different about violence? Although his answer is reached somewhat from the standpoint of foreign policy making, his observations have wider implications, since violence seems to be the political problem par excellence.

He really is talking about change—violent change as opposed to nonviolent change—and the most important distinction he makes is the *unpredictability* of violence, coupled with the assumption that predictability and manageability rank high on the policymaker's list of values. Perhaps he is saying that violent conditions cannot be controlled or countered by other than violent methods. The *amorality* of violence which he describes is, possibly, a universalizing force cutting through all particular legal and moral structures which men have erected: violence is the most universal of languages. In this book, the essays by Gouldner, Kelly-Miller, and Kelly (Spain) illustrate this assumption remarkably well—since international and domestic restraints are more easily destroyed by the example of violence than, perhaps, by any other force; it is a more ruthless taskmaster than the "cash nexus" ever was. Violence, by its own nature, has an internal logic—as Kamenka shows in his essay in this volume; revolutions by the very nature of conflict must become organized and centralized. As Thucydides put it:

> For in peace and prosperity, as well cities as private men are better minded because they be not plunged into necessity of doing anything against their will. But war, taking away the affluence of daily necessaries, is a most violent master, and conformeth most men's passions to the present occasion.

Thus amorality and unpredictability are united by violence. In nonviolent change, presumably, the norms of the society and the context of the change are much more manageable, and many aspects can be discounted in advance. But with violent change, the outcome is seldom discernible far in advance of events—hence, not only its "explosiveness," but its contagion.

The reader should recognize that Rosenau's illuminating essay was written more than half a decade ago and should expect from it neither speculative prophecy nor analyses of more recent events.

# INTERNAL WAR AS AN INTERNATIONAL EVENT

James N. Rosenau

International life is nourished and shaped by developments within nation-states as well as by relations among them. The stability and structure of international relationships are, to be sure, primarily determined by the accommodations and conflicts that mark the never-ending interactions of chiefs of state, foreign ministers, and other officials. But, irrespective of the skills of policy-makers and the dynamics of their interaction, the international system is also affected by the events and trends which comprise the domestic life of nations. If officials abroad attach importance to changes within a society, or if the internal changes lead that society's officials to press new values upon the rest of the world, then these domestic developments are certain to have external consequences. This inquiry focuses on the international repercussions of one particular kind of activity which can be—and increasingly seems to be—a mode of far-reaching and rapid change within societies: namely, political violence, by which is meant the use of force, legitimately (by incumbents) or otherwise (by insurgents), to control political behavior and accomplish political objectives. . . .

To achieve a balanced assessment [of the international repercussions of internal violence], preconceptions about the nature of violence must be set aside in favor of . . . [an] exploratory approach. Instead of building on ready assumptions, we need to break them down and examine their component parts, to identify the relevant variables and isolate the range within which they operate. More precisely, we need to consider such basic questions as these: What conditions maximize the external effects of internal violence and under what circumstances are the repercussions only of a minimal kind? What are the characteristics of an internal war that arouse the concern of foreign offices and the interest of foreign publics? What characteristics are likely

SOURCE. James N. Rosenau, "Internal War as an International Event," from James N. Rosenau (ed.), *International Aspects of Civil Strife* (Princeton: Princeton University Press, 1964), pp. 45–91, excerpted. Reprinted with permission of the author and publishers. Copyright 1964 by the Princeton University Press.

to produce changes in the structure and stability of the international system? Are variations in the scope of violence accompanied by corresponding changes in the system? Is the duration of an internal war a relevant variable? Does the manner in which it begins shape its external consequences? In what ways does internal violence differ from other forms of intrasocietal change that have intersocietal consequences?

# I

The last of these questions is perhaps the most troublesome. On the other hand, it is clearly true that violence is not the only form of internal social change that can have wide international repercussions. The endless ramifications of changes in Great Britain that culminated in its readiness to consider affiliation with the European Common Market would seem to be a case in point. So would any national election in which victory goes to a party that has pledged sharp and thorough going policy revisions. Economic recessions in the United States, decisions of leaders in Asia and Africa to accept proffers of Soviet arms, and potential Chinese and French acquisition of nuclear capabilities are examples of other types of nonviolent change which do or can have noticeable effects upon world politics. The more one ponders the question, the more one wonders about the wisdom of regarding violence as a significant variable in the linkage between intrasocietal developments and intersocietal consequences: If any internal change can have international repercussions, how will these differ if the change occurs peacefully rather than violently? If violence is merely one form of social change, a rapid and extreme form at one end of a continuum, are not change and societal stability rather than violence the key variables insofar as international repercussions are concerned? . . .

On the other hand, notwithstanding the force of the foregoing illustrations and questions, one cannot resist the impression that internal violence is a unique form of change; that it can lead to special consequences for the international system; that, indeed, the external repercussions of the changes [occurring violently in a nation] would, other things being equal, prove to be greater and more profound than those . . . [occurring non-violently in another] nation. Such an impression is inescapable in the light of twentieth-century world politics. Leaving aside the repercussions of international war, it does not take much familiarity with recent history to discover that many of the widest and most lasting changes in the international system can be traced back to internal wars. What nonviolent intrasocietal development, for example, had such an immediate and sharp impact upon intersocietal structure as did the civil war in China? Similarly, the 1946–1950 guerrilla war in Greece, the 1947 *coup d'état* in Czechoslovakia, the stalemated, three-way war in the Congo, the successful revolt led by Castro in Cuba, the unsuccessful 1956 rebellion in Hungary, and the African and Asian wars for independence from colonial rule stand out as events in the postwar world that have proved most unsettling or decisive for the international system. One could, to be sure, add a few non-violent episodes to this list, but these additions would not be so numerous, or seem so far-reaching in their effects, as those in which the use of force was a central or pervasive phenomenon. Or, if these examples do not support the impression that internal wars foster wider and more enduring external consequences than other kinds of intrasocietal change, consider the differential effects which followed from the 1917 advent of communism in Russia and the 1945–1951 advent of socialism in England—episodes which can certainly be regarded as, respectively, the most violent and the most peaceful political upheavals of this century. . . .

Historical examples in support of any general proposition about international politics, however, can always be found. More is required than a simple comparison of the effects of the British and Soviet experiences if the impression that internal violence can foster especially extensive international repercussions is to be elevated to the level of an assumption in the ensuing analysis. Such a procedure necessitates identification of those characteristics of violence or of the reactions to it which are unique, which set it apart as a form of social change that has widespread consequences beyond national boundaries. Three characteristics would seem to meet this specification. In order of increasing importance—and for want of better terms—they are the morbidity and the amorality of reactions to violence, and its "explosiveness"—that is, its rapidity and uncertainty. Let us briefly examine each characteristic.

Perhaps more than any other human activity, violence exerts a strong hold over people's curiosity. There is abundant evidence of man's propensity to be fascinated by the plight rather than the pleasure of his neighbors, to take a morbid interest in their catastrophes while ignoring their normal routines. Presumably this tendency for violence to evoke morbidity also obtains on an international scale. Presumably it means, at the very least, that internal wars are likely to receive more sustained and elaborate attention and publicity abroad than any other socio-political events wh:ch occur within a country. . . . The world's news media share [the public's] morbid concern for violence.

In the case of Algeria, they clearly gave more prominent and extensive coverage to the plastic bombs that exploded in the Casbah than to the offers and counteroffers that crossed the conference table in Evian.

It is, of course, possible to exaggerate the importance of the magnetism of violence. Neither man's morbid propensities nor the publicity they foster are so all-powerful as to be prime movers in the course of events. Certainly the vast differences between the consequences of the British and Russian upheavals can hardly be explained in this way. The wide publicity which attends internal wars is not as potent a source of change in the international system as are the altered foreign policies and new alignments which they initiate.

On the other hand, this unique characteristic of violence can be underestimated. . . . Widespread publicity regarding the purpose, course, and outcome of such conflicts may, for example, serve as a stimulant to similar activity in other societies. Such repercussions are especially likely when insurgents are spectacularly successful in their use of violence, for then groups abroad with similar goals or grievances, encouraged by the accounts of how such methods produced governmental acquiescence, may be emboldened to resort to similar tactics. Student riots are a good illustration of this process. They frequently occur in waves—as do other types of internal wars—and the connection between one riot and those occurring elsewhere in the international system is often made quite explicit by its leaders. . . .

Nor is the contagion confined to activists. Widespread publicity can also serve to arouse otherwise apathetic publics abroad, thus enabling the insurgents—if the publicity is favorable to their cause—to procure aid more effectively from external sources. The extensive and laudatory publicity which Castro's uprising received in the United States proved to be a major factor in the overthrow of the Batista regime. Among other things, widespread American sympathy for Castro contributed to the neutralization of the United States' diplomatic posture toward Cuba and, in March 1958, to the cancellation of military aid to Batista. . . .

A second aspect which differentiates violence from other forms of behavoir is the amorality of reactions to it. Whatever the law may say about the right of one person to intervene in the affairs of others, it has little relevance when these affairs are marked by violence. . . . This unique dimension of violence also obtains on an international scale. Whereas both nations and international organizations are quite circumspect in their manner of intervening in the affairs of a peaceful society, caution and discretion are readily abandoned when that society collapses into—or otherwise experiences—violence. Efforts to influence the outcomes of elections in other societies, for example, are ordinarily carried out in a judicious, if not secretive, manner. Other nations usually have strong preferences about which party they want to win at the polls, but rarely will they proclaim these preferences unqualifiedly, and even less frequently will they run the risk of seeming to intervene in the campaign. When the form of change is of a violent nature, however, the situation becomes amoral; all concerned accept the principle that both nations and international organizations are entitled to adopt publicly—even vociferously—a position of partiality with respect to the conflict. Elections are inviolable and intervention in them is wrong, but internal wars are everybody's business and overt concern about them is justifiable. Indeed, occasionally nations are unable to avoid involvement in an internal war even though they desire to remain aloof from it. Some of the neutral nations of Asia and Africa, for instance, were strongly pressed to render judgements about the Hungarian uprising of 1956.

There is, of course, an extensive body of international laws on the inviolability of national sovereignty and the illegality of nations intervening in each other's affairs. Implicitly, however, even the law recognizes the amorality of internal wars. The rules and norms of intervention become obscure, "more difficult to classify,"[1] when violence marks the affairs of the society in which intervention occurs. Internal wars are, as noted below, too explosive for policymakers to be guided by legal rather than political considerations in their reactions to them. Law takes precedence when vital national interests are not challenged or when it coincides with such interests. Internal wars are challenging in this way, however, and thus nations, like the observer of a knife fight between two gangs, react to them either by intervening or by fleeing, depending upon which course is the most self-serving. In such situations, consequently, the law loses force and the distinction between intervention and nonintervention tends to be obliterated. As one observer put it in a discussion of Cuba's internal wars, "Some forms of 'nonintervention' are nothing more than acquiescence in someone else's intervention, and some forms of 'intervention' are so wrong and futile that they amount in their practical effect to nonintervention". . . . [2]

[In the case of] . . . international organizations, a new legitimacy has emerged to justify recent interventions in the affairs of war-torn

---

[1] Richard A. Falk, "American Intervention in Cuba and the Rule of Law," *Ohio State Law Journal*, XXII (Summer 1961), p. 567. . . .

[2] Theodore Draper, *Castro's Revolution: Myths and Realities* (New York: Frederick A. Praeger, 1962), p. 113.

societies. The role of the United Nations in the Congo and of the OAS in Cuba represents a degree of intervention which was not contemplated when both organizations were founded. Article 2 of the United Nations Charter, for example, explicitly notes that the U.N. is not authorized "to intervene in matters which are essentially within the domestic jurisdiction of any state." Yet, this did not prevent the U.N. from intervening in the Congo in order to prevent Great Power confrontation in Africa. Rather, such action required an adjustment of international morality and the development of the principle that U.N. intervention was legitimate when peace had to be restored and order maintained.

Again a word of caution is in order. The international amorality fostered by internal wars can also be exaggerated and it is important to emphasize that this reaction to violence is unique only in degree. Nations also intervene in each other's nonviolent affairs. Programs of economic aid to peaceful societies are a form of intervention, as are propaganda campaigns, cultural exchange programs, and a host of other techniques which nations employ to shape the contents of attitudes and to control the course of events within one another's sphere of jurisdiction. . . . [And] it would . . . be naïve to imply that internal war is the only condition under which political considerations take precedence over legal ones. International relations, like all human relations, can range from full compliance to noncompliance with shared norms. Internal wars are distinguished by their capacity to evoke external reactions which fall toward the noncompliant extreme of the continuum—by a lack of restraint and a depth of commitment on the part of interested nations, characteristics which are not a part of situations in which normative compliance prevails. With nations overtly involved and deeply committed, it follows that internal war situations are likely to foster more extensive and enduring international repercussions than are nonviolent ones.

But why should internal wars conduce to international amorality? This question brings us to the third characteristic that distinguishes internal violence as a source of external repercussions. Internal wars constitute a form of social change which unfolds rapidly toward an uncertain outcome. This rapidity and uncertainly of violence—what we have labeled its "explosiveness"—encourage unrestrained and overt reactions abroad because they introduce conditions which place the course of events beyond the control of other nations. No situation is more threatening to nations than one whose outcome has become so uncertain as to have moved beyond their control. In order to maintain their identity and fulfill their aspirations, nations must maximize control over the outside world by adjusting their goals and behavior to their capacities and to developments which occur abroad. . . . [3]

Ordinarily, it is possible for nations to maximize, through rational calculation, their control over changes in the international environment. The capacity to control may not be sufficient to achieve the desired ends, and the controlling nation may even be subjected to more control than it exercises. Nevertheless, in most situations the leaders of a nation can calculate which courses of action are likely to result in optimum adjustment to the changes occurring abroad. Internal wars, however, present policy-makers with a unique problem. Events unfold too quickly and in directions that are too unclear for officials to calculate their responses rationally. A sudden shift of public sentiment in the war-torn society, a quick turn in the tide of battle, an intervention by another nation, an ambush of key insurgent leaders or an assassination of the chief of state, an assertion of superiority by one side and a contrary claim by the other, an uneasy lull in the fighting, a tenuous stalemate while both sides probe each other's ambiguous terms for ending the conflict, a lack of information on whether the historic ties that previously bound the war-torn society are surviving and whether the end of hostilities will mean the restoration of stability—these are but a few of the unpredictable conditions that distinguish internal wars from other kinds of situations over which policy-makers must attempt to exert control. Faced with the potentiality of so much change at any moment, unclear as to what the next stage of the war will be, foreign policy-makers understandably become especially sensitive to violence in other societies. Maximum control over social change is not easy to exercise under any conditions—even those involving slow and sequential change—so that rapid and uncertain change may well require additional commitments (including a readiness to resort to amoral action) if interests are to be protected and some degree of control maintained.

It must be emphasized that we are not positing rapidity and uncertainty as separate characteristics of violence. A variety of nonviolent situations unfold rapidly or are marked by uncertainly. In one sense, for example, an election involves rapid change. One day a party is in power, the next day it is voted out, and shortly thereafter the winning party takes over the reins of government. Yet, elections are generally not also characterized by uncertainty. How the electorate will

[3] The maintenance of calculated control over the external environment may be viewed as the very essence of foreign policy. This conception is elaborately presented in my monograph, *Calculated Control as a Unifying Concept in the Study of International Politics and Foreign Policy* (Princeton: Center of International Studies, Research Monograph No. 15, 1963). . . .

cast a majority of its votes is an unknown factor, but policy-makers abroad can usually anticipate what each party will do if elected and thus they can be ready to respond to any rapid changes that occur in the situation. Contrariwise, many nonviolent situations are marked by uncertain futures. What the result will be of efforts to modernize underdeveloped countries, for instance, is never clear and a host of outcomes always seem possible. Usually, however, such situations do not also unfold rapidly, and thus policy-makers are given time to adjust to developments they were unable to anticipate. . . . In short, nonviolent changes in societies are rarely both rapid and uncertain. Internal wars, on the other hand, are normally distinguished by the presence of both characteristics, and it is this explosive combination which makes their international repercussions so extensive.

That these characteristics must combine for internal wars to have external consequences is further demonstrated by the atypical case in which violence is not accompanied by uncertainty. Ordinarily, for example, there are few international repercussions when a military *coup d'état* occurs in societies where the overthrow of one right-wing dictator by another has become a traditional form of change. Under these circumstances other nations do not become particularly concerned about the situation because, irrespective of which faction wins the struggle, the policies of the war-torn society are not expected to change. In other words, traditional *coups d'état* pose no problem for foreign policy-makers because the techniques of maximizing control with respect to them are known and have been previously tested.

## II

Now that we have determined that violence does possess unique characteristics which, relatively speaking, differentiate it from other forms of internal change having external effects, let us turn to an exploration of certain aspects of internal wars which underlie variations in their international repercussions. In particular we shall be concerned with the differential effects fostered by the scope, duration, and origin of internal violence. These variables will be examined first in terms of their effects upon other nations and then in relation to the structure and stability of the international system.[4] The scope, duration, and

---

[4] In assessing the external effects of internal wars, we have been forced to make the simplifying assumption that policy-makers in all nations will react similarly to events in war-torn societies. Empirically, of course, the reactions of officials may be as varied as the goals, histories, and structures of the countries for whom they speak and act. In addition, throughout the analysis it is presumed that the international system is organized along loose bipolar lines, a presumption which means that the presentation is primarily applicable to internal wars in the post-World War II era. . . .

origin of internal wars, in other words, will be treated as independent variables—as causes—and developments in other nations or in the international system as dependent variables—as effects. . . .

By the *scope* of an internal war we do not mean the number of persons or communities actively involved in combat. Nor are we referring to the intensity of the violence or the form which it takes. Such variables are central from the standpoint of combat strategy and postwar internal stability, but they do not seem particularly crucial with respect to the international repercussions of a conflict. When viewed from an international perspective, they would seem to be subsumed by the purposes for which an internal war is perceived as being waged, and it is this variable which we shall treat as the key measure of scope. Aside from humanitarian considerations, other nations are mainly concerned about the posture which a war-torn society will take toward the outside world once order is restored and a government is able to govern. Hence it is the goals which the contesting forces are perceived as pursuing, and not their perceived size nor the perceived intensity of their struggle, which arouse anxiety among foreign leaders and publics. Normally, to be sure, the more encompassing the goals of a war, the larger will be the number of persons and communities involved in it and the greater will be their commitments and efforts. We have chosen to focus on perceived goal variations as the primary measure of scope, however, because from an international perspective the exceptions to this rule can be as important as the rule itself. A small band of rebels fighting to remodel the socio-economic bases of a society, for example, is likely to stimulate more interest abroad than will a large mob which riots in order to satisfy a highly particular grievance such as a shortage of food or a resumption of nuclear testing.

Although a host of purposes can initiate and sustain internal violence, and while the purposes can, as noted below, sh'ft during the course of conflict, the goals of warring factions can be fruitfully viewed as giving rise to three main kinds of internal wars, which we shall designate as personnel, authority, and structural wars. Empirically, of course, no war corresponds exactly to any of the three kinds. These are ideal types which sufficiently approximate particular situations to serve as useful tools of analysis. They can be differentiated as follows:

> PERSONNEL wars are those which are perceived as being fought over the occupancy of existing roles in the existing structure of political authority, with no aspiration on the part of the insurgents to alter either the other substructures of the society or its major domestic

and foreign policies. Latin American *coups d'état* in which one junta replaces another are examples of personnel wars.

AUTHORITY wars are those which are perceived as being fought over the arrangement (as well as the occupancy) of the roles in the structure of political authority, but with no aspiration on the part of the insurgents to alter either the other substructures of the society or its major domestic and foreign policies. Struggles to achieve independence from colonial regimes, or those based on efforts to replace dictatorships with democracies, would ordinarily be classified as authority wars.

STRUCTURAL wars are those which are perceived as being not only contests over personnel and the structure of political authority, but also as struggles over other substructures of the society (such as the system of ownership, the educational system, etc.) or its major domestic and foreign policies. A war involving a Communist faction exemplifies a structural war, as does an agrarian revolt and possibly the present situation in the Union of South Africa. It is difficult to imagine structural wars which are not also personnel and authority wars, and thus this is the most comprehensive type.

It does not take much reflection about this formulation to recognize that a direct relationship exists between the scope of an internal war and its external repercussions—namely, the wider the scope of a conflict, the greater will be its repercussions.[5] This linkage would seem to obtain both geographically and in terms of the degree to which

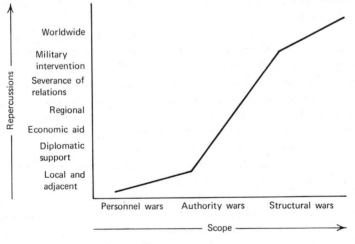

DIAGRAM 1.

[5] It must be emphasized that this linkage and its graphic presentation in Diagram 1 have been derived from deductive reasoning and not from systematic empirical inquiry. Along with the other linkages and diagrams presented below, it should be regarded more as a hypothesis than as an established finding.

nations become involved in an internal war: the wider the scope of a conflict, the greater will be the tendency for more nations in more parts of the world to resort to more varied and direct techniques of exercising control with respect to it. As can be seen in Diagram 1, however, the association between scope and repercussions is not constant even though it is direct. As one variable increases so does the other, but the rate of increase varies, with the sharpest change in the slope occurring between personnel and authority wars. The reasons for this S-like pattern can be readily outlined. The international repercussions of personnel wars will ordinarily be minimal and confined to nearby nations because such conflicts encompass issues which have only local significance. The contending factions in a personnel war will, by definition, adhere to a common posture toward the great questions of world politics, so that the hostilities will not create much uncertainty abroad and more distant nations will not care particularly which faction triumphs. However, in order to justify the resort to violence, the two factions are likely to accentuate their differences on local matters, and when these include external issues such as boundary disputes or price wars, officials of adjacent or nearby societies will become sensitive to the struggle and concerned about its outcome. Furthermore, the contending factions in such a war are much more likely to turn to neighboring countries for the kind of logistical assistance—such as arms, bases, and even political asylum—that more distant nations cannot easily supply.

Now let us suppose that the scope of the war expands to a contest between an authoritarian regime and a democratically oriented group of insurgents. In such a case the likelihood of other nations' developing an interest in the course of the conflict increases sharply as a universal value (self-government) rather than local issues becomes central to the fighting. To the extent that this value is of pressing concern to other nations, either as a matter of contention at home or as a key feature of policies abroad, then to that extent they will develop a stake in the outcome of the hostilities. Authoritarian regimes elsewhere in the world, for example, are likely to become fearful that an authority war may be contagious, that the aims or successes of the insurgents may encourage dissident groups within their own society to take similar action. (Portugal's reactions in the U.N. to wars of independence in British territories have clearly reflected concern about the situation in Angola and exemplify international repercussions of this sort.) Conversely, insurgents in authority wars are likely to attract the sympathy, if not the overt support, of newly independent nations or of those with foreign policies in which self-government is a core value. In addition, because distant diplomatic support may be as important in authority wars as close logistic support, warring factions will engage in more wide-ranging activities abroad than they do in personnel wars, thus further expanding the international repercussions of such conflicts.

As an increasing number of universal values divides the combatants in an internal war, the conflict is likely to have greater relevance for the internal affairs and foreign policies of other nations. Thus they are likely to attach more significance to the course and outcome of a structural war than of any other kind. Such a reaction is fostered partially by the possibility that the insurgents in a structural war are likely, if they triumph, to effect drastic alterations in socio-economic policies at home and thereby challenge other countries to do the same for their own populations. Structural wars, in other words, are more contagious than any other type. More segments of a population can find more reasons to emulate the insurgents than is the case in authority or personnel wars. Whereas contagion in an authority war is usually limited to intellectuals and middle-class groups who care about the value of self-government, the infectiousness of a structural war can extend to peasants, workers, and other groups whose way of life is at issue in the conflict.

The extensiveness of reactions to structural wars also originates with officials abroad. Their sensitivity to this type of conflict is likely to be heightened not only by a fear of unrest at home, but also by a concern about the foreign policies which the war-torn society will pursue when the hostilities are over. Structural wars are especially conducive to such uncertainty because they are, virtually by definition, fought over some of the same socio-economic values which are at issue in the ideological struggle between East and West. Hence there is always the possibility—and this is why policy-makers abroad, irrespective of the side they favor in the conflict, become especially sensitive to it—that in their desire to overhaul basic societal structures the insurgents may, upon gaining power, adopt a radically new posture toward the external world, including a retreat into neutrality or even an entrance into a new alliance system. Such extreme consequences do not ordinarily accompany the downfall of governments in the other types of internal wars. . . .

Since other nations tend to anticipate that insurgents in a structural war will adopt new policies subsequent to the seizure of power, their responses to this type of conflict are likely to be more amoral and varied than to any other type. Having a special stake in either preventing or promoting victory by the insurgents, other nations will be disposed to employ a wide range of techniques, including covert military intervention, to maximize control over the outcome of the struggle. Lesser internal wars may evoke external statements of concern, threats of economic reprisal, and calls for U.N. action; but structural wars are characterized by the breaking of official ties, the imposition of embargoes, and the commitment of arms or troops to battle. American reactions to events in Cuba provide a cogent illustration of how increases in the scope of a war foster corresponding extensions in the form and degree of external intervention. While Castro was fighting an authority war against Batista, U.S. intervention took the form of permitting the shipment of supplies to the former and canceling military aid to the latter. But when the conflict became a structural one, with Castro in the role of incumbent rather than insurgent, the U.S. responded by suspending sugar quotas, severing diplomatic relations, and, ultimately, mounting a refugee invasion of the island. Similarly, rebels fighting for independence from colonial regimes rarely receive large-scale aid from abroad, but wherever Communist guerrillas are active, as in Greece in the late 1940's or in Southeast Asia more recently, the response of both East and West includes tactical weapons, military advisers, and helicopter pilots—not because of the kind of war that the guerrillas are waging, but because they are Communists who will alter the policies of the war-torn society if they are triumphant.

Of course, the purposes and postwar commitments of the insurgents in a structural war may not always be explicit or discernible. Frequently, in order to triumph in a prolonged struggle, insurgent movements must appeal to a wide variety of diverse and conflicting publics at home and abroad. Building such a coalition is a delicate process. As the behavior of American political parties in an election campaign clearly demonstrates, the mobilization of support among overlapping interests requires a minimum of specificity about intentions and a maximum of generalization about aspirations. To avoid offending any potential sources of assistance, domestic or foreign, the insurgents are unlikely to make detailed pronouncements about how they will proceed when they triumph. Rather, if they are not already inextricably linked to an outside nation or bloc, they will be inclined to espouse ambiguous values, such as freedom and self-government, and to claim, perhaps correctly, that prosecuting the conflict does not allow time for postwar planning. In short, structural conflicts often appear to be authority wars, a fact which foreign policy-makers recognize and which thereby narrows the difference between the international repercussions fostered by each type. The pattern depicted in Diagram 1 levels off at the top not so much because authority and structural wars are essentially the same, as because diplomats abroad may well regard them as similar. U.S. intervention in Cuba's war against Batista illustrates this point. Rightly or wrongly, American officials responded cautiously to the conflict—although they might have been expected to champion democratic rule in Cuba more vigorously—because, among other reasons, they were unsure of Castro's motives and the scope of the war he was waging.

Let us now turn to a second aspect of internal wars, their *duration*. A number of observers have proceeded on the assumption that the international consequences of such conflicts are directly related to this variable. Samuel Huntington, for example, asserts that "the longer the domestic violence continues [in a society], . . . the more likely are foreign governments to become involved on one side or another."[6] Empirically such an assumption seems entirely warranted. Certainly the internal wars of this century which have had the widest impact on world politics—such as those in Russia, Spain, China, and Cuba—lasted several years, whereas those which have not greatly affected the international system—such as the frequent *coups d'état* in Latin America—ended soon after they began. Similarly, there are many instances in which internal wars produced wider repercussions as they progressed through time. The Algerian conflict, to cite a recent example, was strictly an internal French affair at the outset, but the longer it lasted, the greater became the involvement of other nations in its outcome. What the dynamics of this relationship are, however, is far from clear. In what way does the length of a war matter insofar as its international consequences are concerned? Is the linkage a simple and direct one, with each increase in duration fostering an increase in consequence? Are the effects of internal violence cumulative? Or are there particular stages in an internal war which, when they are entered, have unique characteristics that alter and intensify responses abroad? . . .

Time is a reflection of two aspects of internal wars—the relative capabilities of the combatants, and the compatibility of their goals. Violence will persist as long as neither side is able to eliminate the other or force it to negotiate a settlement. Negotiated settlements, however, are primarily a function of the compatibility of the objectives of the losing side with any armistice terms that may be offered. If the differences between the warring factions are great, then the imbalance of capabilities must be correspondingly large before one side will be ready to accede to the peace terms of the other. Indeed, if they are divided by completely incompatible aims, then the capability bal-

[6] Samuel P. Huntington, "Patterns of Violence in World Politics," in Samuel P. Huntington (ed.), *Changing Patterns of Military Politics* (New York: Free Press of Glencoe, 1962), p. 44. . . .

ance becomes irrelevant to the duration of the conflict as the losing side assumes a "fight to the finish" attitude.

Long wars, in other words, are those in which either balanced capabilities prevent a military conclusion or incompatible goals inhibit a political resolution; conversely, short conflicts are characterized by imbalanced capabilities or compatible objectives. Neither of these two factors, however, remains constant during the course of the fighting, and it is the changes in them which create the linkage between the duration and the external repercussions of internal wars. Capabilities tend to change in the direction of greater balance and goals in the direction of greater incompatibility. The latter change reflects the processes of polarization: as time passes each side accumulates more and more grievances against the other and then revises its military and postwar objectives to account for the new grievances, with the result that both sides become increasingly less willing to negotiate a reconciliation of their differences.[7] Capabilities tend to balance as time passes, because each side, spurred on by its intensified inclination to achieve a total victory, procures new supplies and support by making new commitments—at home and abroad—which increasingly offset those obtained by the other. If both the insurgents and incumbents survive the initial days of combat, internal wars are almost bound to pass into a prolonged stage marked by stalemate and irreconcilability. At such a point in a conflict, with both warring factions continuously revising their goals and extending their commitments, other nations are certain to become increasingly interested and involved in the course of the war. Each goal revision and each new commitment deepens their uncertainty about the outcome of the hostilities and the subsequent posture of the war-torn society. As time passes, therefore, the international repercussions of internal wars are destined to mount as other nations increase their support for one of the factions or press more vigorously for negotiations between them.

Interestingly, the external consequences of internal violence reach a climax toward the end of the fighting and not during the prolonged stalemate. Stalemates tend to be stable and uneventful: the hostilities of the war-torn society are in balance, with each side knowing the limits of what it and the other side can accomplish. . . . As internal wars move out of stalemate and near an end, however, uncertainty mounts—both at home and abroad—with the knowledge that the war-torn society is soon to reassemble and redirect itself. And the actual cessation of hostilities, rather than bringing a relaxation of internal tensions and a decline of external reactions, is in fact the point of

[7] For a stimulating analysis of the process of polarization, see James S. Coleman, *Community Conflict* (Glencoe: Free Press, 1957), pp. 9–14.

greatest uncertainty. Neither officials abroad nor participants at home are able to anticipate what will transpire when, with the conflict formally concluded, the two warring factions are forced to live side by side. . . .

The wounds of internal wars do not heal easily. The reconstruction of individual and group ties tends to proceed less smoothly and at an even slower pace than after international wars. In the latter case, relations between—not within—societies have disintegrated. Stretching across cultural and national boundaries, these intersocietal ties were not very strong prior to the outbreak of conflict, encompassing only a small portion of the lives of individuals and groups. . . . Being long-range and tenuous, therefore, the relations destroyed in an international war are, relatively speaking, susceptible to quick and full restoration. Unless the victorious nation permanently subjugates the defeated one, ties again become remote and partial when the former withdraws its occupying forces from the latter and, under these circumstances, hostility can diminish and memories can fade. . . . The ties broken down in an internal war, on the other hand, cannot be reassembled so speedily or fully. In this kind of conflict, disintegration occurs in the close-at-hand relations that constitute the daily routine of life. Instead of the enemy being distant and unknown, he may be one's colleague or boss, possibly one's brother. Instead of serving time-honored loyalties, the conflict has caused them to be abandoned and betrayed, replacing them with suspicion and deceit. Furthermore, the longer and the more intensely the fighting has been waged, the deeper and more poisonous will be the wounds opened in intrasocietal relations. If the hostilities last more than a few weeks, and if the war grows in scope, socio-economic, ethnic, ideological, and religious differences are bound to be exacerbated. And, as the hostilities become ever wider, family ties are likely to be affected, as are relations within neighborhoods, factories, villages, and cities. To heal the wounds of internal war, in other words, is to recreate an old social system or to create a new one, and such a process is inevitably slow and painful. Victors and vanquished must live side by side and be constantly reminded of what each did to the other. Little wonder, then, that decades elapse before the scars of internal wars disappear. No better example can be cited than the persistent manifestations in American life today of the schisms created by the Civil War of a century ago.

In sum, even if one side in an internal war has clearly trounced the other, and even if a formal conclusion has been proclaimed or signed, it is never quite clear whether the conflict is actually over. The immediate postwar situation is at best unstable and at worst it threatens to explode again into violence. Both at home and abroad, all concerned have good reason to wonder whether the violence has so scarred the society that its members cannot maintain peaceful relations with each other. . . .

If the situation within war-torn societies is most fluid as their conflicts seem to approach an end, the involvement of other nations is also likely to reach a climax at this time. In the first place, they must decide whether or not a conflict is over and, if they decide that it is, must then establish some kind of relation with the victor. Aloofness and neutrality are no longer possible inasmuch as the outward forms of normalcy require a return to international morality and diplomatic protocol. If the settlement is a negotiated one, nations that supplied the antagonists must turn to overt diplomatic participation in order to protect the interests which their supplies were designed to promote. If the war ends through a total victory by one side, then the nations which supported the victors must seek to obtain fulfillment of the obligations which their support was intended to incur; conversely, those that supported the vanquished will probably feel compelled to salvage what they can from the situation and, in any event, they must come to terms with the faction which they sought to defeat. Secondly, the no-war-no-peace phase that marks the culmination of internal wars is the point at which the future domestic and foreign policies of a war-torn society begin to take shape. Shaky as its existence may be, the new regime turns to making choices which can be crucial to other nations: the choice between breaking or reconfirming old alliances, establishing or resisting new ones, expanding or contracting trade relations, altering or reinstating the distribution of wealth and land, adopting democratic institutions to solidify political support or curbing opposition through authoritarian means. Turning points such as these can, through indirect contagion or official contacts, undermine or enhance the ability of other nations to maximize control over both their internal and external environments, and thus it seems probable that their involvement in a war-torn society will increase as its violence diminishes. International reactions to recent wars in Hungary, Laos, the Congo, and Cuba certainly reflect such a pattern. Indeed, the only exceptions to it are *coups d'état*, where the inception and termination of conflict are too close together for any pattern to develop.

The association between the duration of internal violence and its external repercussions does not, however, follow the same pattern for all types of conflict. Although in all cases the linkage is a direct one, the pattern does vary according to the scope of the war. Diagram 2 presents generalized patterns for personnel, authority, and structural wars. Here it can be seen that while all three types foster sharply

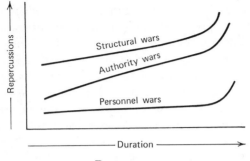

DIAGRAM 2.

increased international repercussions as they near a conclusion, the external effects of authority wars evolve at a different pace than do those of personnel and structural wars. The last two are widely separated quantitatively, but qualitatively they are highly similar. Until the closing phase of conflict, the repercussions abroad produced by both types increase at a slow rate—structural wars, because their external effects are already high when they commence; and personnel wars, because the geographic range of their consequences is limited. A personnel war would, of course, have sharply increased effects abroad if its warring factions revised their goals to include substantive policy issues, but such a change would mean that the conflict had escalated into an authority or structural type and thus the evolution of its effects could no longer be traced along the same slope. The international repercussions of authority wars, on the other hand, increase at a fast rate through time. The slope for this type of conflict is much steeper than for the other two because authority wars can start as localized struggles, but, if they do, they quickly arouse concern abroad as the fact that a fight for self-government is being waged becomes widely known. Castro's fight to oust Batista, for example, followed this pattern until it escalated into a structural conflict, and so did most of the recent wars for independence from colonial rule in Africa.

The foregoing analysis of scope and duration as independent variables has been cast in terms of societies which lack the structure and experience to effect peaceful change and which therefore, through the processes of polarization, collapse into violence of their own accord. Internal wars, however, do not always begin in this way and variations in their *origins* can foster differences in their repercussions abroad. Most notably, violence in societies can stem from external instigation as well as from internal collapse. Although, as previously noted, little is to be gained from efforts to estimate whether collapse is a more prevalent cause of internal war than instigation, we cannot ignore the implications of the fact that intrasocietal conflict does originate in the latter way. The "just wars of national liberation" promoted by the Communists are the outstanding example of instigated violence and their occurrence is enough to necessitate distinguishing the origin of internal wars as an independent variable. The distinction between instigation and collapse is, of course, a relative one. The origins of internal war can be placed on a continuum, and where a particular conflict falls depends on how intra- and extra-societal factors combine to precipitate it. . . .

From an international perspective, cases of violence due to instigation and those that are due to collapse differ in the extent to which they produce repercussions at the outset of hostilities. When other nations perceive that an internal war has been externally instigated, they are likely to attach particular significance to the conflict and react immediately. If a society collapses into violence of its own accord, on the other hand, policy-makers abroad proceed cautiously until the situation clarifies. In such a case, time must usually elapse before the nature and direction of the war become clear. Not until then can policy-makers abroad identify both their own and their competitors' stake in the conflict. That is, the motives of other nations toward a situation which has collapsed into violence can hardly be manifest at the outset because they evolve only as the potentialities of the conflict emerge. Furthermore, since ordinarily other nations do not actively intervene at the outset of violence in a collapsed society, they must accept the terms and patterns of warfare which have been established by the time of their entry and thus they are limited in their ability to control the course and results of the fighting. In an instigated war, however, the threat—or opportunity—is clearly discernible from the start to policy-makers abroad. More importantly, it is clear from the outset that something in addition to an explosive situation has developed, that, indeed, another power or bloc is attempting to expand its influence over the war-torn society by promoting chaos within it. Clear, too, is the realization that by participating in the war at its inception the instigating power has a much greater chance of controlling the direction and outcome of the fighting than if it took no part until a later stage in the conflict. Thus other nations are likely to react sooner and more vigorously to instigated wars than to those which result from collapse. The U.S. response to the Greek war instigated by the Communists in 1947, for example, was quick and direct (the Truman Doctrine) in contrast to the cautious, wait-and-see attitude that characterized the American reaction when Algeria collapsed into violence in 1954. Similarly, the responses of other Western Hemisphere nations to rioting fomented by Castro's agents in one of them have been considerably quicker and sharper since 1958 than was the case when Castro initiated violence in his own country in 1956.

After the initial flurry of participation in an instigated war, of course, such a conflict tends to stabilize as it passes into the stalemate stage. Consequently, with the situation balanced as a result of their quick response, other nations are able to cut back on the extent and vigor of their intervention in it—or at least they can do so as long as the stalemate continues. Then, for the same reasons noted above in the case of wars that result from collapse, the involvement of other nations reaches a peak again as the conflict nears a military or nego- tiated conclusion. . . . [This] pattern characterizes both authority and structural wars that are instigated from abroad, but it does not obtain in the case of personnel wars, since an outside power would have no reason to initiate such a conflict.

## III

Thus far, the international repercussions of internal war have been analyzed in terms of the reactions of "other nations." There is, however, another set of repercussions which need to be noted—namely, those affecting the international system as a whole. While our treat- ment of the motives and responses of other nations is admittedly a simplified one—their reactions to intrasocietal violence are certainly more varied and complex than we have indicated—it has facilitated identification of the major aspects of internal war which have external consequences, and it therefore enables us to move on to consider briefly these larger questions: Do internal wars necessarily alter the structure of the international system and reduce its stability? Are there ways in which such conflicts actually make the system more stable? Do variations in the scope, duration, and origin of internal wars foster corresponding changes in the system's structure and stability? Do in- ternal wars have effects upon smaller international systems (such as a region or a bloc of nations) similar to those they have upon the global system?

For analytic purposes, let us regard the structure of the interna- tional system—or of any smaller system composed of two or more national or supranational actors—as comprising those relations and interactions between nations which recur with sufficient frequency for a pattern to be discernible. Thus, for example, antagonism between the United States and the U.S.S.R. is a structural element of the system, as is the North Atlantic Treaty Organization, the avoidance of align- ment of many nations in Asia and Africa, the rivalry of India and

Pakistan, the cordiality of China and Albania, the foreign aid programs of nations and international organizations, the European Common Market, and so on. The system is lacking in structure, on the other hand, to the extent that international events are unique or transient. Efforts to exert military control over space illustrate an activity within the system which has yet to acquire structure, while the crash of a plane carrying the Secretary-General of the United Nations is a unique event which is not part of a recurring pattern. It follows that when a pattern alters or ceases to exist, or when a new one comes into being, the structure of the international system can be said to have changed. Ordinarily the creation of a new alliance exemplifies structural change, since it usually means that some nations—the allies—modify their mode of interacting with each other. The system also undergoes structural change when a new nation is established, when an old one revises its basic foreign policies, or when a nation's capabilities grow or diminish to the point where other members of the system alter their responses to it. . . . Unless otherwise noted, the ensuing discussion will focus on . . . [the current] global system, which has been appropriately labeled one of loose bipolarity.

Although a gross oversimplification, let us define the stability of the system in terms of the readiness of either bloc to employ military action in order to preserve or alter its structural elements. The system tends toward stability when the blocs are inclined to employ peaceful means of competition, and toward instability when the probability of warfare between the blocs increases. . . .

The relevance of the foregoing formulation to the international repercussions of internal wars is obvious. It suggests that only structural wars can produce change in the interaction patterns which comprise the international system, since such change occurs only when the victorious faction alters the foreign policies of the war-torn society to the extent of shifting it from one bloc to the other or from one bloc to a position of neutrality. Not every structural war, of course, produces such change: if the *status quo* faction prevails, the structure of the system will be maintained even though such an outcome may prove quite unsettling for it in other ways. Personnel and authority wars, on the other hand, can never effect structural change because in neither type are the factions committed to profound policy alterations.

Our discussion further implies that the impact of an internal war upon the structure of the system is not determined by its duration. Lengthy wars may render the system more unstable, since their continuance tends to increase the involvement of a greater number of other nations; but they will not affect its structure as long as their scope does not escalate into substantive policy matters. Contrariwise, short wars can result in major structural change if their scope is sufficiently extensive. The *coups d'état* which took Czechoslovakia into the Eastern bloc in 1947 and Iraq from a pro-Western to a neutral status in 1958 clearly illustrate this point. The contrast between these examples and the similar shifts that resulted from the prolonged wars in China and in Algeria sharply demonstrates the absence of a linkage between the duration of internal violence and its structural repercussions.

For similar reasons, it seems clear that the manner in which a war originates does not affect its impact upon the structure of the system. Externally instigated wars are especially conducive to instability, as noted above, but they will be no greater a source of structural change than those that originate through internal collapse as long as their scope is confined to the personnel and authority of government.

At a subsystemic level—within the blocs and among the neutrals—significant structural change may be fostered by those aspects of internal war which do not produce alterations at the global level. A conflict's duration, for instance, can have important consequences for the solidarity and capabilities of a bloc, with the amount of structural change increasing the longer the hostilities continue. Consider the 1956 uprising in Hungary: each day that passed further weakened ties within the Soviet bloc and, even though the rebellion was crushed and the global structure preserved, the structure of the bloc has not been the same since that climactic episode. Perhaps an even more striking example of subsystemic structural change is the 1946–1949 war in Greece: it did not result in alterations of the global structure, but its length facilitated the establishment of a pattern of American foreign aid to beleaguered nations which has certainly had profound consequences in terms of the relative strength of the two blocs. Similarly, the longer the Algerian conflict lasted, the more it weakened the ability of the Western bloc to build military defenses in Europe. The structure of relations among uncommitted nations can also be affected by the duration of a conflict. As the war persisted in the Congo, for example, certain groups of nations—the "radicals" and the "conservatives"—increasingly came to recognize common interests in the conflict and, consequently, the members of each group tended to draw closer together in an effort to adopt a unified stance toward the two blocs as well as toward the Congo. Indeed, this hardening of alignments acquired formal structure when both groups convened conferences to ratify a set of policy resolutions, the conservatives at

Brazzaville in December 1960 and the radicals at Casablanca in January 1961.

From the viewpoint once again of the global system, it should be noted that internal wars which result in structural change at this level do not necessarily lessen international stability. To be sure, conflicts which portend the shift of the war-torn society from one bloc to the other are likely, for reasons noted below, to heighten the readiness of both blocs to resort to military action, i.e., to promote instability. There is, nevertheless, one type of internal war which will probably have structural repercussions without a corresponding increase in interbloc tension—namely, a brief *coup d'état* which is not externally instigated and as a result of which the war-torn society shifts from a bloc alignment to a neutral status. Under these circumstances, neither bloc has time to intervene in the conflict and the one suffering the loss of a member is not likely to be so dismayed by the shift to neutrality as to employ military means to reverse the outcome. The 1958 coup in Iraq is illustrative in this respect. Upon seizing power General Kassim severed relations with the Bagdad Pact and took his country out of the Western bloc into neutrality, but the stability of the global system was not greatly affected by these events. The United States did respond shortly thereafter with the dispatch of troops to nearby Lebanon, but these were soon withdrawn as clarification of the local situation revealed that Iraq had not taken up membership in the Communist bloc. . . .

The longer a war involving a possible shift to neutrality lasts, the more likely are the two blocs to develop contradictory stakes in the outcome and thus to intensify their readiness to resort to military action. Indeed, lengthy structural wars, plus all types of instigated ones, constitute the only conditions under which international stability is endangered. As the preceding analysis has shown, other types of conflicts can have a variety of external repercussions: foreign publics will develop sympathies for one or another side; officials abroad will be concerned about the welfare of their citizens and property in the war-torn society; diplomatic sanctions may be employed and economic aid programs may be curtailed or expanded. Yet high involvement, even active intervention, by other nations in internal wars does not necessarily mean an increase in tension between the two blocs. Both East and West, for example, are likely to be attentive to an authority war in a neutral country, partly because they have particular economic, regional, or ideological interests in it, but mainly because neither side can allow the other to develop advantageous relations with the winning faction. Such a conflict, however, is not so ominous for the structure of the system as to invite irrevocable commitments by the blocs. Competition is instead confined to such acts as inviting official visits, granting formal recognition, offering long-term assistance—in short, to control techniques which have become accepted features of cold war maneuvering and which therefore do not lessen the stability of the system.

To be sure, if an authority war breaks out within one of the blocs, its leadership is likely to react swiftly and extensively—even to the point of military interventions—in order to preserve bloc solidarity. But the unaffected bloc, although hopeful it may benefit from the disruption of its adversary, is not likely to respond in a similar manner and become overly committed in a situation which does not involve its vital interests. Thus, for example, the Hungarian uprising of 1956 did not noticeably lessen the stability of the global system, because only one of the blocs made an extensive military response to it. Not only was there no increase in the readiness of the West to resort to military action in Hungary, but the bloc's leadership took great pains to demonstrate its restraint and to prevent any incidents which might convey a contrary impression. . . .

For two reasons . . . the kinds of internal wars which conduce to international instability can be expected to recur in the future, possibly with even greater frequency and intensity. In the first place, as has often been observed, the acquisition of long-range nuclear weapons by both blocs has reduced the effectiveness of direct military threats and has therefore reinforced Communist efforts to expand their influence by instigating or taking advantage of intrasocietal violence in the uncommitted world. Secondly, the susceptibility of the uncommitted nations to internal war is, quite apart from what the Soviet bloc may do, likely to increase rather than decrease as dynamic social changes accompany their efforts to modernize. As Huntington notes: "Without a constitutional tradition of peaceful change some form of violence is virtually inevitable. In the underdeveloped areas the alternatives, broadly speaking, are not constitutional change or violent change, but gradual change through a succession of reform *coups d'état* or tumultuous change through revolutionary wars or revolutionary *coups d'état*."[8] But, to repeat, the Soviet bloc is not likely to stand aside while violence persists in the uncommitted world. Rather, as one observer has cogently put it:

> The close proximity of Communist power all along the vulnerable arc from Iran to Korea invites external support of internal disorder,

[8] *Op. cit.*, p. 39.

and the external and internal threats feed upon each other. Potential and half-promised intervention from powerful neighbors stimulates the rise of underground movements, invites local Communist aid to them, and inhibits popular expressions of resistance against them. Once formed, such movements offer pretexts for increasing intervention in the interest of liberation.[9]

Nor is the West likely to remain detached from future structural conflicts in the uncommitted world. Its postwar military strategy has also been rendered obsolete by the nuclear standoff. Having found its newest and deadliest weapons insufficient to prevent the Soviet bloc from capitalizing on internal wars in Asia and Africa, the West's readiness to intervene actively in such conflicts has also increased. Each Communist success in this regard, whether instigated or not, has stiffened Western resolve to contest the cold war in this way. Furthermore, greater resolve has been accompanied by the acquisition of means to implement it. Recent years have witnessed the development of elaborate counter-guerrilla strategies and capabilities on the part of the West. Since the new arsenal of internal war weapons includes a capacity to airlift guerrillas or troops quickly into battle anywhere on the globe, from Vietnam to the Congo, bloc confrontation in the internal wars of neutral countries is likely to occur with increasing frequency and intensity in the foreseeable future. . . .

[9] Russell Rhyne, "Patterns of Subversion by Violence," *The Annals*, Vol. 341 May 1962), p. 73.

# 11

# Internal War and International Systems: Perspectives on Method

*George A. Kelly and Linda B. Miller*

≪≪≪≪≪≪≪≪≪≪≪≪≪≪≪≪≪≪≪≪≪≪≪≪≪≪≪≪≪≪≪≪≪≪≪≪≪≪

## EDITORS' COMMENT

Despite the fact that internal violence has been a persisting and unexceptional political phenomenon of world history and was, in fact, so coronated by Aristotle in Book V of his *Politics*, most contemporary political research has tended to treat it as aberrant, pathological and, in the widest sense, antipolitical. Theories of political integration are far in advance of those of political disintegration. Although normative political philosophy is obviously concerned with the overcoming of strife within the commonwealth, it is peculiar that research calling itself empirical should be necessarily so oriented. One of the motives behind the present essay has been to restore the hypothesis that domestic violence can, under certain conditions, be regarded as "natural" much in the same way as organized warfare among states. In such a view the hard and fast separation between internal political systems and international ones tends to become blurred and the impacts of each are exchanged by a variety of procedures.

Thus, the themes of this speculative study concern both the treatment of organized political violence as a fact and the interpenetrability of civil and international techniques and doctrines of violence. The authors happen to share the prescriptive goal of political philosophy, best expressed in Kant's imperative *there shall be no war*, but they eschew the familiar exercise of attempting to counsel decision-makers in the state as to how factional violence can best be quelled. Rather, their interest is to describe neutrally the forms and functions of internal violence in various international systems.

They are interested also in the historical dimension of internal war and the impact of cultures and time-spans on its practice. This question goes beyond the mere observation that domestic political violence is something more than exceptional or dysfunctional. For it introduces the notion that styles of violence and the scope of internal war will vary with ideology, levels of technology, and the types of international system that support or absorb the insurgencies. The general technique chosen for this preliminary inquiry is Raymond Aron's "historical sociology" and its methodological assumptions, whose brilliant applications are already familiar to many readers through Aron's *Peace and War* (New York: Praeger, 1967).

It is important to grasp the range and limitations of this approach in political analysis. No claim is made to what the modern philosophy of science calls *prediction and explanation*. Through a generally inductive pattern of historical examination one seeks to establish the most durable concepts and "rules" by which the observer may reasonably expect to order and understand the chaos of events that we nevertheless feel free to call a "civilization" or a "system." This is more an exercise of clarification and ratiocination than of prophecy, and it necessarily implies an intellectual tension between political typologies and the ultimately inscrutable movement of history. To use Kant's language, the generalizations that emerge from "historical sociology" are used only "regulatively"; they are not "laws" that could be constitutive of the political universe.

Hence, it follows that politics still depends on a philosophy that is established by methods beyond political research and analysis. But, by the same token, there can be no "philosophy of history" in the old sense. We strive only to establish the concepts and categories within which the process of political history can be understood and meaningfully communicated and reject any search for the meaning of history itself. We confess thereby a certain relativism and are disposed to cleave to the patterns of thought emanating from the vocabulary of our own civilization, but we test these conclusions in two fundamental ways: (1) by the normal trials of logic and method; and (2) by the durability of certain patterns, standards, and ideas (suggesting the possibility of a wide human communication).

The essay below is less an excursion in methodology than an effort to assert certain basic themes and problems relevant to placing internal warfare in an transnational context. However rudimentary the present study may be, the authors feel that it is important to state their views in a time when modern Pythagoreanism is strangling historical method in what are today called the social sciences and used to be called the moral sciences. "Historical sociology" is no less empirical in thrust than other schematic efforts that have been made to deal with internal warfare. Though more difficult and less promising of "hard results," it may be a surer method than the indiscriminate and unhistorical agglutination of statistical guesswork.

# INTERNAL WAR AND INTERNATIONAL SYSTEMS: PERSPECTIVES ON METHOD

GEORGE A. KELLY AND LINDA B. MILLER

Contemporary research on internal war thus far has failed to yield widely accepted theories of the phenomenon. The modest purpose of this essay is to suggest certain connections between the perspectives of political theory, comparative politics, and international relations that might enhance our systematic understanding of civil strife. Our special concern will be to build bridges between "history" and "analysis" and to indicate ways in which "types" of internal wars may be viewed as products of both particular social systems and the surrounding milieu. Persuaded that our subject may be encompassed neither by manipulating gelid paradigms nor by holding the environment constant, we propose an extension of "historical sociology"—itself a methodology of international politics—to the study of internal war.

## THE STUDY OF INTERNAL WAR

The fact that internal war has become a pressing concern for policy in the last two decades undoubtedly hampers our comprehension of it; yet, in any era, it deals with a supreme political drama. Traditionally, the breakdown of civil society means the collapse of the common experiment in the "good life," the detonation of public order, and the path back to the state of nature. So liberal a thinker as Kant, who hailed the French Revolution with a "wishful participation that borders closely on enthusiasm," nevertheless held that "all instigation to rebellion is the worst and most punishable crime in a commonwealth."[1]

[1] Cf. Immanuel Kant, "An Old Question Raised Again: Is the Human Race Constantly Progressing?" in Lewis White Beck (ed.), *Kant on History* (New York, 1963), p. 144; "On the Common Saying: This May Be True in Theory but Is Useless is Practice," in C. J. Friedrich (ed.), *The Philosophy of Kant* (New York, 1949), p. 423.

SOURCE. George A. Kelly and Linda B. Miller, "Internal War and International Systems: Perspectives on Method," Harvard University Center for International Affairs Occasional Paper No. 21, Cambridge, Mass., August 1969. Reprinted with permission of the publishers. Copyright 1969 by the President and Fellows of Harvard College.

Revolution was a peremptory challenge to sedimentary layers of civilization and to the "Idea" of civil justice and public domestication. The factional rupture of man's miracle, the socio-political commonwealth, is a subject of power and passion, tragedy and irony.

It is also a subject fraught with immense difficulties of method, notably those that relate to observation, close comparison, and typification. The problem is part actual, part formal. In the latter sense, we have a subject intersecting the established fields of politics and sociology, and sub-fields like the history of warfare.

The typologies from a political or sociological point of view are diverse and fluctuating. We are far from certain what term or terms are suitable. Often, the concepts chosen will migrate according to empirical circumstance or research design, or else will be usurped by partisanship or "policy science." Even should we settle on a fairly neutral epithet like "internal war," we confront a thicket of stipulations whose paternity is usually discipline-oriented or problem-inspired.

Within a single project, for example, Harry Eckstein calls internal war "any attempt to alter state policy, rulers, or institutions by the use of violence, in societies where violent competition is not the norm and where well-defined institutional patterns exist,"[2] while Andrew Janos prefers to speak of "a violent conflict between parties subject to a common authority and of such dimensions that its incidence will affect the exercise or structure of authority in society."[3] Important differences flow from these definitions. On the whole Eckstein's is the more restrictive. The problem of language cannot fail to raise substantive issues, as we perceive when we "bracket" such concepts as "norm of violent competition," "well-defined institutional patterns," or "authority in society." Indeed, as Eckstein himself admits, the book of essays to which he plays reluctant midwife reveals a glaring lack of common ground.

Unfortunately, scholars do not always clarify at what point the concept "war" is held to pertain, whether it is a species of the genus "conflict" or whether they are somehow opposed. Logically, one would suppose that "war" is the appropriate term, given a state of violence above a certain threshold, when that violence has collective political and social ends. Yet it is questionable whether any kind of violence that does not impugn or threaten the central exercise of political au-

---

[2] Harry Eckstein (ed.), *Internal War: Problems and Approaches* (New York, 1964), p. 12. But see his "On the Etiology of Internal War," *History and Theory*, IV, 2 (1965), p. 133.

[3] Andrew C. Janos, "Authority and Violence: The Political Framework of Internal War," in Harry Eckstein (ed.), *Internal War*, p. 130.

thority (whose forms, as we must recognize, have varied tremendously over time and space) should be regarded as pertinent. Moreover, political authority may be threatened and altered by fundamentally nonviolent but illegal acts, in which case legality is tortuously redefined (cf. the "Glorious Revolution" of 1688). Our essential point is that war is a condition of expectation of violence (if needed) implicitly "declared" against *de facto* political authority by a collective insurgency that is prepared to go to the limit of replacing that authority if its primary goals are not attained. Nevertheless, the heteromorphism between typologies of kinds and intensities of violent socio-political change and of their instrumental forms (not to mention the problem of "unsuccessful events") makes it close to impossible to build concep tual structures for these phenomena.

Our picture is further clouded by the ambiguous, sometimes careless use of words like "conflict," "struggle," "resistance and constraint," and "force," to cover a spectrum of physical violence, subversion, sedition, psychological opposition, or sometimes merely inevitable and intractable antagonism. As a contemporary sociologist correctly insists: "indiscriminate lumping of warfare with other forms of conflict will at times lead to untenable conclusions."[4] Certain types of "conflict" may be "functional" in preventing "violence;" "violence" may even be "functional" in certain cases of "conflict resolution," we are told.

An additional problem concerns the perspective of inquiry. Three cultural or psychological hindrances to the study of internal war deserve mention. The first and easiest to describe is that we are members of a national society deeply preoccupied with the curtailment of local violence in the world. A portion of the social science community has been involved directly in recommending measures and policies for reducing these disturbances in the pursuit of either national power or a peaceful world, or both. Perhaps progress demands that we defer asking a central question of policy science: "how can internal wars be dealt with?" and begin to concentrate on the question: "what is an internal war?" In introducing his new *Archiv für Sozialwissenschaft und Sozialpolitik* to the public Max Weber wrote: "Inevitably, problems of social *policy* will . . . find expression in the columns of this journal . . . alongside those of social *science*. But we would not dream of pretending that such discussions can be described as 'science,' and we shall see to it that they are not confused with it."[5] A detachment of this kind is required for the study of internal war.

[4] Lewis Coser, *The Functions of Social Conflict* (New York, 1964), p. 88.
[5] Max Weber, *Gesammelte Aufsätze zur Wissenschaftslehre* (Tübingen, 1923), p. 157.

A second obstacle derives from our participation in an *historical* national community which, at least since its own trauma of internal war a century ago, has been taught to abhor violent cleavage and which, at high levels of social theorizing, has produced elaborate paradigms of consensus and conciliation, thereby manifesting a firm tendency to regard social values as amenable to peaceful adjudication.[6]

Finally, our membership in a monumental Western civilization, secular in values, liberal in political convictions, and broadly hedonistic in its interpretation of the bases of social and political life—what might be called the mainstream inheritance of post-Enlightenment Western man—complicates our attitudes. Our secular value system generally, though not entirely, discourages transcendental justifications of civil violence, although it may accumulate such justifications on the international plane. Our liberalism enjoins us to regard ideological factionalism, as distinct from "consensual competitiveness" (party or group politics) as perverse. Our hedonism leads to premises by which the stability of society is explained in terms of the distribution of material benefits.

If these assertions are reasonable, they describe a special impediment to our understanding of internal violence, especially in non-Western contexts. To be sure, there are contrary values within modern Western civilization, as evidenced not only by a profusion of social theory but also by the vivid fact that our civilization itself has been in a state of "internal war" for the past hundred or more years. The challenges of Communism and Fascism grew in Western soil, both transcending and permeating the membranes of the nation-state and transplanting themselves to other cultures. If it is granted that the tradition whose barest outlines have been suggested is dominant in Western thought, some inferences about our approach to internal violence may be developed.

We require a disciplinary context in which the question of internal war as both a *quid facti* and a *quid juris* can be treated. In our view, what Raymond Aron and others, notably Stanley Hoffmann, have termed "historical sociology"[7] provides such a context. It is not just

---

[6] See Jessie Bernard, "Where is the Modern Sociology of Conflict?", *American Journal of Sociology*, LVI, 1 (1950), pp. 11–16.

[7] Raymond Aron discusses his uses of this method in "Conflict and War from the Viewpoint of Historical Sociology," in *The Nature of Conflict* (Paris: UNESCO, 1957), pp. 190–197. See especially, p. 190: "The mere story of events teaches us nothing unless it is given form and meaning by reference to concepts; unless it entails effort to distinguish the essential from the subsidiary, and deep-lying trends from accidents; and unless it seeks to compare the means, differing from age to age, by which international relations and wars are conducted."

a technique for putting flesh on paradigmatic bones or looking at the temporal context of occurrences. It is also a therapeutic acquisition of historical sense. Its value as a methodological instrument emerges from a discussion of the relationship between domestic and international politics, a relationship deeply influenced by internal wars.

## SYSTEMS OF INTERACTION

From time immemorial, it is the distinction between "foreign" and "domestic" that has put politics in two almost watertight compartments and has guided theory at its highest level. Of course, there is a firm reality in which this distinction is grounded. Yet we are all too aware today, in a troubled and permeable world, of the frequent artificiality in the separation of foreign and domestic politics. We can no longer be confident that this strategy of analysis tells us what we need to know about the vital structures of political action, or that it permits us to cope with the shadowland of continuities between the two types of politics. From the perspective of the performance of domestic systems, we can scarcely neglect impinging international forces, in the great states because they are intimately involved in critical transactions, in the small states because they are weak and dependent. The inter-penetration is equally evident when we adopt the global overview.

In a definition more scrupulous than operational, Stanley Hoffmann argues:

> An international system is a pattern of relations among the basic units of world politics, characterized by the scope of the objectives pursued by those units and of the tasks performed among them, as well as by the means used to achieve those goals and perform those tasks. This pattern is largely determined by the structure of the world, the nature of the forces that operate across or *within the major units, and the capabilities, patterns of power, and political cultures of those units* . . . [our italics].[8]

This description makes of the international system a comprehensive nexus of inner and outer. Arguing the point in reverse, we might affirm that *only conceptually* can there be a purely "internal" war, although, as affected by the variables of goals, scope, and duration, there are obviously greater and lesser degrees of inner-outer permeability in such wars.

One study that analyzed and classified over fifty cases of contem-

[8] Stanley Hoffmann, "International Systems and International Law," in *The State of War* (New York, 1965), p. 90.

porary local violence concludes that the boundary between international and internal war is frail.[9] Reflection on past events leads to the supposition that such frailty may not be novel. Thucydides was probably the first to give a maximum description:

> Practically the whole of the Hellenic world was convulsed, with rival parties in every state—democratic leaders trying to bring in the Athenians, and oligarchs trying to bring in the Spartans. In peacetime, there would have been no excuse and no desire for calling them in, but in time of war, when each party could always count upon an alliance which would do harm to its opponents and at the same time strengthen its own position, it became a natural thing for anyone who wanted a change of government to call in help from outside.[10]

The predilection for external involvement in internal wars transcends historical epochs, as participants in a recent symposium on internal war quickly acknowledged.[11] Understandably, the question of a proper balance between the study of "internal" variables and "external" determinants in the evolution of internal war preoccupies many observers. It becomes increasingly difficult to maintain, even in theory, the classical discrimination between Caesar (an international system lacking a common authority and ordered by the "right of the strongest") and God (a domestic system premised on common values and internal coherence).

Additional obfuscation is created by the use of the terms domestic and international *systems*. At least two meanings of "system" are current: one suggests "an assemblage of substances that is in or tends toward equilibrium;" a second implies "an aggregation or assembly of objects (i.e. sovereign actors) joined in regular action or interdependence." While it would be totally unrealistic to request a change in vocabulary, the curious should be warned that a penetrability of the two kinds of systems does not refer to a relationship between homologous concepts.

Often, in an analysis of a domestic "system," external influences are treated as contained within the system boundaries (sacrificing precision to schematics), while, in Hoffmann's definition of an international system, given above, the domestic is subsumed within the

---

[9] See ACDA/WEC-98: "The Control of Local Conflict: A Design Study on Arms Control and Limited War in the Developing Areas" (4 volumes, Washington, June 30, 1967), II, pp. 132–133.

[10] Thucydides, *The Peloponnesian War* (trans. Rex Warner, Harmondsworth, 1954), III, 5, p. 208.

[11] Cf. James N. Rosenau (ed.), *International Aspects of Civil Strife* (Princeton, 1964), p. 7.

global.[12] The two meanings of system can be related to the traditional division of political methodology. The "equilibrium" definition is surely a "modern" way of stating the formula of the common pursuit of the "good life" in a political society and the prime questions, both normative and empirical, that surround it. The "regular action" definition corresponds to the international problem of security, coercion, and the "state of war." The gulf is not bridged, and we are also aware of a transparent continuity between "classical" and modern inquiry in this regard.

While it would be fatuous to discard the obviously legitimate discriminations between international and domestic systems, or international and domestic events, neither should we ignore their analogical relationship. There are many ways of underscoring this continuity. One is Hans Morgenthau's thesis that all politics is based on power, and the view of the state as a fundamentally coercive organization. We choose to make the transition, however, at a slightly narrower level of generalizing, which is by means of the concepts of *war and peace*, understood as historical and social phenomena. Territorial sovereignties combat each other in "interstate" war, but they are often frequently divided internally in other kinds of war.

Let us recall at this point Aron's two critical variables for defining the performance of an international system: the polarization of the actors and the intensity of the dispute over the basic doctrine and organization of political legitimacy. This categorization provides us with two pairs of ideal types—"bipolar" and "multipolar" (we except for this purpose the possibility of "unipolar" or universal monarchy) and "homogeneous" and "heterogeneous."[13] Hoffmann prefers the terms "bipolar" and "balance-of-power," and "revolutionary" and "moderate," but the implications are virtually unchanged. The Aron-Hoffmann ideal types are not independent variables; analysis reveals that they affect one another in ways that produce certain ex-

---

[12] The metaphor of a "social system" was itself adapted from the organic systems of biology, notably by the anthropologist Radcliffe-Brown. This view has worn somewhat thin; as a contemporary cultural anthropologist writes: "Social systems are not nearly as integrated as organic systems, and the processes working within them are not as cyclical and repetitive. . . . Moreover, social systems are open to the influence of changes in environment, and to changes due to relations with other social systems, as organic systems are not." Max Gluckman, *Order and Rebellion in Tribal Africa* (New York, 1963), p. 38.

[13] Raymond Aron, *Paix et guerre entre les nations* (Paris, 1962), especially pp. 108–113, 137–148, 154–156. For the second set of concepts, Aron credits Panoyis Papaligouras, *Théorie de la société internationale* (Geneva, 1941).

pected constellations. A comprehensive explanation of internal war at the intra-state level would lead to a similar conclusion.

There is another variable (if we can call it that) which insures both the linkage of systems analysis with empirical politics and the virtual impossibility of constructing predictive paradigms. The set of results obtained from the time-dimension constitutes this variable. In history it encompasses much of what Aron calls "sociology," including all aspects of cultural and technological change (i.e., "progress") that bear on political relationships. In the field of international politics it would have its most adequate expression through the effects of multiplied social communication, the magnification of war technology, and the related notions of the "expansion" and "saturation" of an originally Europocentric system of diplomatic activity. Further analysis would, of course, have to make some fine discriminations with regard to these notions: "expansion" and "saturation" obviously are not identical. But for our purposes, it is important to note that from the Renaissance to the present this process has been cumulative and irreversible, leading today to a world where "there is no event, in Korea or in Laos, that does not make itself felt in the Soviet Union or the United States. The diplomatic universe is like an echo chamber: the noises of men and things are amplified to infinity."[14]

Although "systems" patterns may repeat themselves, history, in the sense just described, does not or has not. Any overview of international systems must respect the fact of this "non-recurrence of recurrences." It should also be possible to make a similar statement about the configurations of domestic politics, up to and including the kinds of system that provide for an outbreak of internal war.

Let us pursue our line of comparison further by considering Aron's "operational" definition of international system:

> I call "international system" the totality constituted by political units which maintain regular and reciprocal relations and all of which are susceptible to being involved in a general war. Those units which the leaders of the principal states must account for in their calculations of force [in Aron's terminology: instrumental physical action] are members of an international system in the fullest sense.[15]

The system is composed of two elements: its susceptible participants and its major actors, whose forces must be "calculated." Internal wars also should be thus classified, for it is of preponderate importance to the system within which they occur whether they take place in a

---

[14] Raymond Aron, *Paix et guerre*, p. 371.
[15] *Ibid.*, p. 103.

major or a minor state, and it may make little or no difference if they erupt outside the effective range of the system—at least from the point of view of that system.

The familiarity of terminology just reviewed makes no further explanation or illustration necessary. We shall now suggest that the "types" of international system described have their parallels within the domestic order. In theory, the mechanism of the "balance-of-power" system has close resemblances to the "equilibrium" paradigm of the domestic socio-political order, as discussed in the works of Talcott Parsons, David Easton, and others. Given the "value-sharing" emphasis of his social theory, Easton's "aspect of a political system that consists of its members seen as a group of persons bound together by a political division of labor"[16] might seem to have only the most frivolous similarity to an international system "in which the main components behave so as to curb each other's ambitions and opportunities, to preserve an approximate equilibrium of power between them, and to reduce the level of violence."[17] But if we set aside preconceived notions of what distinguishes domestic and international systems, we will see a connection between Parsons' "set of common value patterns with the internalized need disposition structure of the constituent personalities"[18] and Hoffmann's "code of international legitimacy that has, at a minimum, agreed rules of competition and that originates in the measure of similarity among the regimes."[19] Furthermore, if we approach the subject in this way, we are not so abruptly put off by the burning political question of sovereignty.

The "sovereigns" become those effective units of force that direct the performance of each kind of system with a degree of autonomy. In Hoffmann's discussion the "balance-of-power" system is also the prototype of a "moderate" system; and indeed some similar kind of moderation underlies the conditions of a tolerable civil community— itself a kind of regulated competition braced up by prescriptive values. If it is argued that any international system, even the optimal, lives in the shadow of violence, we may reply that this shadow also falls across the face of the civil society more often than we would like to suppose. We could even say that the restraints on warfare characteristically imposed by balance-of-power politics resemble, albeit at

---

[16] David Easton, *A Systems Analysis of Political Life* (New York, 1965), p. 177.

[17] Stanley Hoffmann, *Gulliver's Troubles* (New York, 1968), p. 13.

[18] Talcott Parsons, *The Social System* (New York, 1964), p. 42.

[19] Stanley Hoffmann, *Gulliver's Troubles*, p. 13.

a much more serious threshold, the coercive and persuasive techniques used to restrain civil violence.

These observations suggest what our second set of comparisons will be. We find an equivalent correlation between the idea of a polarized and heterogeneous international system (called "revolutionary" by Hoffmann)[20] and that of a domestic society where the condition of internal war is incipient or actual. This observation is almost redundant, for it is obvious that the actuality of the "state of war" tends toward a bipolar cleavage. Individual societies, too, know their "cold wars" or armed truces.

## IMAGES OF WAR SYSTEMS

Our appreciation of the linkages between "revolutionary" domestic and international environments is enriched by the insights of the classical Western political theorists. Philosophers like Hobbes and Rousseau were fond of drawing the analogy between a presumptive "state of war" (the antithesis of political life), in which each man was the executor of the law of nature, and the condition of international conflict reigning among sovereign states. The idea, even if analogical, is useful, since it parallels the similitudes we are attempting to establish. Following a favored expression, let us call this pattern the "first image." It is the image of *anarchy*, a true war "of all against all." But international war, in our experience, is not anarchy; it is a bipolar conflict between "A" and "B." Whatever pattern of violence the hypothetical brutish man in the state of nature (or, if one follows Rousseau, the fallen pre-political state) may be involved in, it is not the dual struggle of armies. Our "second image" is now before us. It is the image of *cleavage*. General wars of modernity are characteristically wars of cleavage. Societies enduring internal wars, in the maximum sense of that concept, are also cleft: they polarize into the competing legitimacies of incumbent and insurgent; they are far from being in a condition of general anarchy.[21]

Were Hobbes and Rousseau really being perversely philosophical and negligent in regarding the real facts of the case? While it is true that as a consequence of their highly individualistic approach to politi-

---

[20] Cf. *Ibid.*, p. 14.

[21] Kant straddles the two images in a significantly ambiguous manner when he writes: "if a state, by internal rebellion, should fall into two parts, each of which pretended to be a separate state making claim to the whole . . . it is then in a state of anarchy." "Perpetual Peace," I, 5, in *Kant on History* (ed. L. W. Beck, New York, 1964), p. 89.

cal phenomena, they were concerned with the philosophical dichotomy of society and anarchy, they found little in the history of their times to suggest that this was an artificial distinction. When Hobbes surveyed the chaos of the English Civil War, he saw not two armies arrayed for battle along continuous fronts, but rather a "dissolute condition of masterless men, without subjection to laws, and a coercive power to tie their hands from rapine and revenge."[22] When Rousseau examined the international coalition wars of his age, he saw states not as fixed allies but as partners of pure convenience, comparable to men in the "state of war." "Independence, denied to men, takes refuge in societies; and these great bodies, delivered to their own impulses, produce shocks which, in the degree that their masses prevail over the [force of] individuals, are the more terrible."[23] The situation Rousseau describes is, in fact, analogous to what Hoffmann calls a revolutionary, but multipolar, system. For actual descriptive use "anarchy" is such a maximal and abstract concept that we shall hereafter substitute the term "dysarchy" (the anarchy of groups), which emphasizes diffused factionalism rather than absolute lawlessness.

Without engaging in historical digression, there is at least presumptive evidence that in dealing with wartorn domestic or international systems we must conjure with two basic "ideal types": *dysarchy* and *cleavage*. In international systems *cleavage* appears to become the more important pattern both as ideological intensity (the struggle to define political legitimacy) increases and as technological penetration and destructive war-potential lead toward a more extended and "saturated" system. As we shall argue presently, this cleavage tends to be reproduced in the domestic societies as well. One of these variables, "heterogeneity," is recurrent; the other, "saturation," is historical and cumulative: the employment of the concept must make recognition of this fact. We would emphasize that the scope of cleavage is magnified in the modern world due to "saturation."

If within the parameters of the present international system the notion of dysarchy seems less fruitful, it is of considerable consequence when we examine the domestic systems where civil violence has been pronounced. We do not mean that the states in question lack governments or the trappings of sovereignty: we would suggest that numerous internal wars are in part a consequence of the fact that such nations are socially incoherent, that their governments lack range, force, and

---

[22] Thomas Hobbes, *Leviathan* (ed. Michael Oakeshott, New York, 1962), xviii, p. 141.

[23] "Etat de guerre," C. E. Vaughan (ed.), *Jean-Jacques Rousseau: The Political Writings* (2 volumes, New York, 1962), I, p. 296.

adequate legitimacy, and that the situation approaches the dysarchic rather than the cleft model. Much of the tension of our present "saturated" international system derives from the fact that many dysarchic political units are overlaid with a pattern of international cleavage. Thus the war that has plagued the Indochinese peninsula for the past generation reveals both "dysarchic" and "cleft" tendencies.

All internal wars will, in fact, have or at least commence with pronounced dysarchic tendencies; thus they "devour their own children." The idea is well expressed by the sociologist Nicholas Timasheff: "While the government is *one* by necessity, and is more or less united [this itself may be a sometimes unwarranted presumption], the revolutionary opposition may be united or divided into two or more factions competing or fighting with one another. Whereas in [external] war there are two clear-cut parties, revolution may receive the shape of the *bellum contra omnes*."[24]

Indeed, this tendency is clearly evident in history's most monumental instances of internal rupture, where the head is dizzied by the succession of constitutionals, "monarchiens," Feuillants, Girondins, Montagnards or of Kadets, Mensheviks, SR's, and Bolsheviks. Yet the total effect of these major upheavals is the cleavage of society, the clash of two great principles and forces. And even if many internal wars remain dysarchic in conduct and significance, we may hypothesize that the more they become proxies of strife in the international system and invite intervention, the more they tend to polarize.

It also may be true that the dysarchy type is further divisible in terms of whether a society is breaking down (what we shall call *anomic*) or in the preliminary stages of political and authoritative consolidation (what we shall call *pre-integrated*). The collapse and disappearance of societies is not the most conspicuous feature of the present world for the political scientist, although it is critical to the anthropologist. Yet, it obsessed our ancestors of the Renaissance and Enlightenment, who were imbued with classical history—*vide*, the melancholy lament of Rousseau: "If Sparta and Rome perished, what nation could hope to live forever."[25] Sometimes it might truly be said that an old society crumbles while a new one rises from its fragments: modern Turkey may not be a bad example. In any case, both possibilities should be considered. Such models correspond in our analogy to the terminal periods of historical multipolar international systems.

[24] N. S. Timasheff, *War and Revolution* (New York, 1965), p. 140.
[25] *Contrat Social*, II, xi, in Vaughan, II, p. 91; cf. Montesquieu, *De l'Esprit des Lois*, XI, vi.

The typology developed thus far can be expressed as follows:

I. Paradigm of equilibrium, "moderate" system.
II. Paradigm of conflict, "revolutionary" system.
   1. Cleavage: polarized, heterogeneous.
   2. Dysarchy: fragmented, legitimacy in doubt.
      a. "Pre-integrated," *terminus a quo.*
      b. "Anomic," *terminus ad quem.*

The virtues of a typology are formal and instrumental. Formally, the principal attributes to be sought are simplicity, comprehensiveness, and absence of redundancy. Instrumentally, we must seek to achieve the clarification of reality. The formal qualities of our present classifications are, we believe, easily defensible. But we do not propose within the limits of this essay to test these correspondences empirically. Obviously, problems loom along the way in manipulating the inner-outer combinations that emerge; they have a descriptive, not explanatory, value. Clearly, some means of expressing the intensity of interaction (perhaps even a sense of "causal" direction) will have to be elaborated. In addition, the temporal boundaries of both "social" and "international" systems will have to be carefully stipulated. Finally, this device will be more useful for some kinds of investigation than for others. Nevertheless, in attempting to trace the outlines of an historical sociology of internal war, we have the advantages of a rough parallelism of categories and an inherently dynamic frame of reference.

For present purposes it suffices to stress that (1) both international systems and domestic systems may be analyzed as potential *war* systems; (2) the nature of the violence may be analyzed in terms of certain correlative configurations; and (3) under given circumstances we shall wish to analyze the modes and consequences of the interpenetrability.


WAR AND REVOLUTION

Our analysis would be deficient without a consideration of the connection between internal and external violence *per se*. Four possibilities are evident. Either the frequencies and intensities of internal and international wars vary in some kind of direct proportion, vary inversely, vary "arhythmically" (i.e., connectedly but with a temporal lag), or appear to have no causal relationship with one another. Fortunately, one study—of massive proportions—exists that offers some guidance, namely Pitirim Sorokin's extraordinary tabulation of the wars and internal disturbances of Europe beginning with classical antiquity and extending through the first quarter of the present century.[26]

In terms of our present inquiry, Sorokin's conclusions are faintly indecisive. He notes that:

(1) Most of the internal crises . . . come and pass their acute stage within a period of a few weeks. (p. 479).

(2) There is hardly any periodicity in the ups and downs of internal disturbance. (p. 482).

(3) There may be a very slight tendency for disturbances to occur more frequently in a period of (international) war and in the years nearest wars; but the tendency is neither strong, consistent, nor quite tangible. (p. 489).

(4) Disturbances have occurred not only in the periods of the decay and decline of society, but in its periods of blossoming and healthy growth. (p. 495).

(5) The forces generating disturbances rarely, if ever, work in one country only. (p. 506).

Significantly, no conspicuous correlation between internal disturbance and international violence is established, nor is it anywhere suggested that positive inferences can be drawn from the one to the other. In terms of specific politics, the gradients often move at cross-purposes; at best it can be said that there is an "arhythmical" lag between these curves when European civilization as a whole is considered. The pristine separation between the domestic problem of the "good life" and the international problem of the "state of war" is thus maintained. Of course, it may be a natural sociological bias to see internal social events as, in the main, internally generated. Yet, there are certain observations that tend to expose the transnational linkages of internal war, especially within a "common" civilization (Sorokin's frame of reference). "Civilizations" contain motives or factors of revolutionary disturbance which either transcend the authority problems of the individual political units included or else may be regarded as pertinent to other, more osmotic and extensive "systems," cultural and economic. Unlike an international "war system," which must be described in terms of the component political units, the idea

[26] Pitirim Sorokin, *Social and Cultural Dynamics*, Vol. III: *Fluctuation of Social Relationships, War and Revolution* (New York, 1937), pp. 383–506. Sorokin's work undeniably presents problems for our type of analysis, because of a certain subjectivity of the data and categories and the questionable availability of certain data; massiveness of scope; and, most importantly, its discrimination of disturbances by duration and intensity rather than by any independent assessment of their political relevance. Also, we may judge Sorokin's master scheme of differentiation between Ideational and Sensate cultures to be beyond our present concern.

of generalized "civilizational" disturbance describes antagonisms carried by the printed page, trade, disease, or religion that do not, so to speak, stop at the *douane*.

This concept (which in Sorokin is statistically derived, and not genuinely "causal") permits us to formulate certain generalizations that bring the connection between international and domestic systems into a kind of focus, at least for recent history. Thus, in referring to the period of the French Revolution, Sorokin can claim: "Such a transition from one fundamental type of social relationship to another had to call forth . . . a rise of the curb of disturbances." (p. 497). Again, he remarks: "the last quarter of the nineteenth century was remarkably orderly" (p. 486), and: "The twentieth century, so far, has been the bloodiest period and one of the most turbulent periods . . . in the history of Western civilization." (p. 487).

As we know, the first and third of these periods were accompanied by massive and violent international shocks, whereas the second was comparatively stable internally and peaceable externally. Yet Sorokin's quarter-century segments are very deceptive. If the period 1875–1900 places us beyond the Franco-Prussian and First Balkan Wars, it still contains Prince Bismarck's departure from the Prussian chancellorship and the economic depressions and industrial turbulence of the late eighties and early nineties, both fateful for the future. To a large degree the explosions of the twentieth century were nourished in the nineteenth. A period of suppressed or "managed" heterogeneity mortgages the future for the present and, as such, is scarcely a legitimate Golden Age. Time is a funnel through which political violence builds: thus it may be impermissible to assert the "peaceableness" of a short period of history unless we are well aware of its subterranean discordancies, their rate of flow, and the long-range efficacy of the dikes that politics constructs to contain them. Clearly, while the short-range management of the period seems to have been effective in controlling both internal disturbance and international violence, the relationship between the two remains obscure.

We must also inquire whether international war may have a negative correlation with internal violence. War can be a paramount builder of nations as well as a salient destroyer. Richelieu used the Thirty Years' War to hammer out the mold of a modern French state. Germany and Italy achieved their belated unifications with the assistance of armed conflict. The uprising against France contributed most of the sinews of today's Algerian republic. These images suggest the solidarity of the "inside" against the "outside." A common (but empirically untestable) prudential maxim is that the statesman can reunite his country by taking it into war. But it seems that the bases of such unity might have to pre-exist the stateman's act or there would be considerable danger of achieving the opposite result.

Hobbes goes further by suggesting that the perpetual risk of international war is a fair price to pay for political stability within, that the anarchy of states is much less to be deplored than the anarchy of persons:

> . . . in all times kings and persons of sovereign authority, because of their independency, are in continual jealousies and in the state and posture of gladiators, having their weapons pointing and their eyes fixed on one another: that is, their forts, garrisons, and guns upon the frontiers of their kingdoms, and continual spies upon their neighbors, which is a posture of war. But because they uphold thereby the industry of their subjects, there does not follow from it that misery which accompanies the liberty of particular men.[27]

Hobbes is arguing that a border bristling with guns guards the orderly process of civil society within. Similar views, albeit romanticized, can be found in Hegel.[28] The observation of Hobbes, possibly erroneous or banal in itself, leads to two quite interesting problems regarding the shape of the history that we have been analyzing. First, it may be true in the pattern of international politics that Hobbes is discussing—essentially a multipolar and homogeneous setting based on "natural," not ideological hostility—that an inverse relationship between internal solidarity and international peril is not farfetched. (We can state with some assurance that this is much less likely to be so in a world of heterogeneous cleavage and *Weltanschauung* confrontation.) Second, in our own hazardous world where the "bristling cannons" are actually trained on the substance of society, it is often implicitly granted that a fair quantity of internal warfare in the minor units of the system is scarcely too high a price to pay if it compensates for or symbolizes at an acceptable level of violence that "cleft" armed confrontation which is beyond all magnitude of dread. In this sense, the technological and political balance of forces seem to have reversed "Hobbes's choice."

We reach the tentative conclusion that there is likely to be a much closer affiliation between internal and international violence

---

[27] Hobbes, *Leviathan*, p. 101. The unvarnished notion that national solidarity promotes international discord is, of course, a political commonplace; cf. Reinhold Niebuhr, *Moral Man and Immoral Society* (New York, 1960), p. 16: ". . . the whole history of mankind bears testimony to the fact that the power which prevents anarchy in intragroup relations encourages anarchy in intergroup relations."

[28] Cf. Hegel, *Philosophy of Right* (ed. and transl. T. M. Knox, Oxford, 1945), paragraph 324, pp. 209–210.

when the legitimacy of the "rules" of international politics is at stake, i.e., when the system is "heterogeneous" or determined by ideological cleavage, than when a more flexible, consensually limited diplomacy prevails. Since "heterogeneity" is inevitably involved with the question of social authority in the political order as well as with the contention of ideologically antagonistic states over the definition of a "legitimate" world, there is a natural relationship between inner and outer tensions. Canons of international non-interference will be especially honored in the breach in a system whose major forces endorse opposed postulates of unilateral systemic change. Moreover, in competitions of "ideas" or fundamental organizing principles of society there are no natural political frontiers. *Weltanschauung* explosions in the domestic systems of great states usually do resist containment. In homogeneous systems, there is presumptively a reciprocal interest of the major states to deal collaboratively with internal uprisings, rather than to take sides by proxy, although the temptation to do the latter may be considerable in any actual system.[29] Once more the hypothetical nature of these arguments needs to be stressed. They must stand or fall both on the accuracy of our perception of observed events and on the acuteness of the rapprochement between conceptual and actual historical systems.

## REVOLUTIONS AND THEIR BOUNDARIES

Classifying varieties of internal war is not only an important but a difficult task because, as we have shown, internal war is enmeshed in the historical dimension of social theorizing. The elusive quality of "revolution" introduces a further complication, for its use in political discourse has varied with history and with linguistic development. The "nature and purpose" of revolutions have been germane to politics ever since Aristotle's pioneering treatment. We could agree with Chalmers Johnson in accepting Sigmund Neumann's definition as a point of departure: "a sweeping, fundamental change in political organization, social structure, economic property control and the predominant

---

[29] Modern defenders of the balance-of-power system often are prone to ignore the very serious and destabilizing interference committed by their hero-diplomats, especially in the latter half of the nineteenth century. Subversion is not new; but in the balance-of-power system there was a tendency to restrict it to secondary areas of confrontation: Mexico, the Balkans, etc. But Antonio. Gramsci was not far wrong when he wrote (*The Modern Prince and Other Writings* [New York, 1957], p. 151): "It must *never* be forgotten that, in the struggle between nations, it is in the interest of each nation that the other should be weakened by internal struggles and that the parties are precisely the elements of internal struggles."

myth of a social order, thus indicating a major break in the continuity of development,"[30] provided that Tocqueville's famous caution about transrevolutionary continuity is respected.

At the same time, we must render our judgment on what a revolution is not. It is not what Sir Lewis Namier claims it to be:

> A gale blows down whatever it encounters, and does not distinguish. Revolutions are anonymous, undenominational, and inarticulate . . . [R]evolutions are not made; they occur . . . If . . . corrosion of the moral and mental bases of government coincides with a period of social upheaval, and the conviction spreads, even to the rulers themselves, that the ramshackle building cannot last, government disintegrates and revolution ensues. Revolutions, as distinct from mere revolts, usually start at the centre of government, in the capital; but the nature of the actual outbreak and its purpose almost invariably escape analysis . . . .[31]

Namier's romantic language tends to obscure rather than illuminate the accessibility of revolution to social science research and is therefore not discriminating enough for our needs. On the other hand, Franz Borkenau's observation, that revolutions customarily direct their destructive force against the prevailing state apparatus, usually replacing it with a structure still more formidable, seems useful.[32] A true revolution is scarcely imaginable without a well-articulated state to attack. Though a revolution is characteristically a moment of the reallocation of the power of society, its political dimension needs special emphasis.

From this rudimentary base we should like to develop two special points. Revolution in the modern political vocabulary customarily describes an event of fairly recent historical currency. The *idea* of revolution is intimately linked to the idea of secular progress and to the actual historical expectation of utopias. This development, long in the making, was finally affirmed in the late eighteenth century, first in literature, then in fact. The antithesis to revolution in this respect

[30] Sigmund Neumann, "The International Civil War," *World Politics*, I, 3 (April 1949), pp. 333–334n., cited in Chalmers Johnson, "Revolution and the Social System," Hoover Institution Studies (Stanford, 1964), p. 2.

[31] L. B. Namier, "1848: Seed-Plot of History" (excerpt from *Vanished Supremacies* [London, 1958]), in Melvin Kranzberg (ed.) 1848: *A Turning Point* (Boston, 1959), pp. 64–65.

[32] Franz Borkenau, "State and Revolution in the Paris Commune, the Russian Revolution, and the Spanish Civil War," *Sociological Review*, XXIX (1937), p. 41. Cf. Karl Marx, *The Eighteenth Brumaire of Louis Bonaparte* (New York, 1963), p. 122: "All revolutions [have] perfected this [political] machine instead of smashing it. The parties that contended in turn for domination regarded the possession of this huge state edifice as the principal spoils of the victor."

is usually called "revolt" or "rebellion," words with which the Middle Ages are studded. Eugene Kamenka puts it this way:

> Part of the difference between a revolutionary uprising and a rebellion is the difference in the beliefs and expectations of those involved; rebels seek the redress of grievances, the return to a former state of justice or prosperity . . . Revolutionaries, on the other hand, have great expectations; they think in terms of a new order, of progress, of changing times that need changing systems of government.[33]

This discrimination does not seem to be challenged by the fact that the most portentous revolution of modernity, the French, encompasses both elements, depending on the classes and ideologies being examined.

Of course there are other significant dimensions to the modern revolutionary experience. But this one clearly sets apart old and new. To those who insist that this process is best understood as a secularization of traditional chiliastic norms of the oppressed and consequently not a fundamental novelty, we would reply that: (1) The unleashing of large numbers of people on behalf of the tangible secular city and not the city of God, accompanied by the external transmutation of "wars of religion" into "wars of ideology" is itself a fact of capital significance; and that (2) the new development reveals the special power to propel elites as well as the masses. The greatest importance of the present distinction lies in establishing the concept of a "Western revolutionary tradition," whose utility will be examined shortly.

A second discrimination useful to the present context is that between orders of magnitude. Internal disorders may be unusually bitter, deep, and protracted or they may resemble a comic-opera *coup*. For the former we reserve the word "revolution." Yet there are also revolutions of varying scope, measured according to whether they occur within relatively insignificant political units or within major states, where their incidence is susceptible to provoking an outward thrust or to threatening the structure of the prevailing international system. Evidently the Turkish and Mexican Revolutions of the present century were quite profound experiences of social violence and change, but

---

[33] Eugene Kamenka, "The Concept of a Political Revolution," *Nomos VIII: Revolution* (New York, 1966), p. 129. It might be plausibly argued that "rebellion" so defined has supplied a fair amount of the physical shock of significant modern "revolutions" despite its ideological regressiveness. See, in general, Barrington Moore, Jr., *Social Origins of Dictatorship and Democracy* (Boston, 1966); and cf. M. Gluckman, *Order and Rebellion in Tribal Africa*, p. 127: ". . . in African political life men were rebels and never revolutionaries." By another set of distinctions, probably originating in Max Stirner's *The Ego and His Own* and familiarized by Albert Camus' *The Rebel* (*L'homme révolté*), rebellion is seen as a personal act and revolution as a collective one.

neither generated much impact upon world politics; the same cannot be said for the Bolshevik Revolution.

A simple and familiar terminology of "petty" and "great" seems applicable to revolutions: we define the latter as events whose incidence is closely related to international systemic change. Clearly we are adopting an instrumental and not a formal definition of revolutions, passing no judgment on their internal intensity. At the same time, we are not claiming that certain revolutions directly *cause* systemic change, because it would be fatuous not to regard these factors as intervening reciprocally in a complex way; we are merely attesting the critical character of the relationship. The preceding clarifications prepare the way for a generalized effort to relate modern revolutions and their effects to an historical sociology of international politics. It is necessary to explore both the issue of the "boundaries" of revolutions and the question of typologies of internal war in an international setting.

Political analysis, as we have pointed out, commonly treats revolutions as self-contained domestic events waged over principles of social authority and political power. It is to the craft of history that we must turn in order to discover fully developed arguments for the thesis of transnational revolution. In the past decade or so, an illuminating debate has been conducted by historians of the French Revolution regarding the origins and boundaries of that phenomenon. On one side of the issue, R. R. Palmer, with somewhat modified support from Jacques Godechot, has argued "that this whole [Atlantic] civilization was swept in the last four decades of the eighteenth century by a single revolutionary movement, which manifested itself in different ways and with varying success in different countries, yet in all of them showed similar objectives and principles."[34] On the opposite side, George Rudé, with nuanced support from the late Georges Lefebvre, has written: "none [of the other contemporary conflicts] was 'democratic,' in so far as none transferred, or was intended to transfer, the weight of political authority to the people at large; and none went on, by progressive stages, to effect a thorough transformation of existing society. This happened only in France. . . ."[35]

Our purpose is not to enter this thorny fray, but rather to raise

[34] P. R. Palmer, *The Age of Democratic Revolution* (Princeton, 1959), I, p. 4. Cf. Jacques Godechot, *France and the Atlantic Revolution of the Eighteenth Century, 1770–1799* (trans. Herbert H. Rowen, New York, 1965), pp. 7–26.

[35] George Rudé, *Revolutionary Europe, 1783–1815* (New York, 1966), p. 65. Cf. Georges Lefebvre, *The French Revolution From its Origin to 1793* (trans. Elizabeth M. Evanson, New York, 1962), pp. 88–91.

the significance of the issue for political analysis. As we might expect, the "Atlanticists" adduce evidence not only of complementarity but of transnational linkage, especially of economic and ideological factors, for their interpretation; while the "nationalists" insist especially on the uniqueness of French social and political conditions, notably the "passion for equality" (Lefebvre *via* Tocqueville) and the peculiar class constellation in France which thwarted an alliance between the aristocracy and the upper bourgeoisie (the doomed experiment of Mounier, Malouet and others). Naturally there are pitfalls of hidden prejudice in both interpretations: we cannot dismiss the contact between cold-war "Atlanticism" and an old revolution or fail to recall the political feelings of Lefebvre and Rudé.

Yet the main issue concerns the relative fermature or permeability of societies on the eve of political upheaval and the patterns of transmissibility of the revolutionary impulse. If the "Atlanticists" are sound in positing a sequence of transnational economic shock waves throughout the environment, and if this position, once established, can be generalized for other revolutionary eras (which seems likely, given the increasing volume of international transactions as we move closer to our own time), then "closed" comparative economic studies of revolutions, such as J. C. Davies's "J-Curve" thesis (itself based on a harmonization of Marx and Tocqueville),[36] will need to account for it. If the "nationalists" have the better part of the argument, then the more appropriate model of investigation will place greater emphasis on the revolutionary core-country than on the transnational revolutionary environment.[37]

It is possible—indeed likely, in our opinion—that both dimensions are important and will vary according to circumstances. Thus the French Revolution was followed by a general European war, whereas a war of similar political magnitude was among the major causes of the Bolshevik Revolution.[38] Was the Russian Revolution more "transnationally" affected than the French? For our present purpose, it is not helpful to debate the "Atlantic" question. Rather we should note that all serious commentators agree: once the French explosion had oc-

---

[36] James C. Davies, "Toward a Theory of Revolution," *American Sociological Review*, XXVII, 1 (February 1962), p. 6. The "J-Curve" refers of course to a J in the prone position which expresses the literal progress of economic satisfaction.

[37] Chalmers Johnson has made one interesting attempt to bridge these two kinds of interpretations with his dysfunction-accelerator image; but again it is clear that his main emphasis is on the internal milieu. "Revolution and the Social System," pp. 5–13.

[38] Cf. Alexander Kerensky, *The Catastrophe* (New York, 1927), p. vii.

curred, it swiftly overran its national limits in the war of 1792, carrying revolutionary ideology and social unrest to all parts of Europe. In these events, the character of the international system and its assumptions of legitimacy were changed; even if a world was "restored" in 1815, that world thereafter was scarred by a defensively ideological conservatism and a heterogeneous revolutionary underground in the major states of Europe.

The debate over "transnational revolutions" may be conducted along lines other than those we have mentioned. The Marxists who made the Bolshevik Revolution, with their experiences of cosmopolitan exile and their universalist vision of imperialism and class struggle, saw Russia as a means to an end, and also as a revolutionary core-country.[39] The special flavor of the Bolshevik Revolution, according to Trotsky, derived from the fact that "by becoming worldwide, capitalist development thereby snapped those threads which in the past epoch bound the fate of the social revolution with the fate of one or another more highly developed capitalist country." Thus, "the Russian proletariat found itself placed by history in a position which compelled it to accomplish the revolution before this could be accomplished by its older and much stronger European brothers."[40] This observation suggests new departures in transnational analysis, to be played off against the equally strong "nationalist" elements of interpretation that accompany the "great revolutions" in Russia and in China.

## STRUCTURAL WAR

The problem of typologies demands additional discussion. The words are familiar—revolution, rebellion, revolt, insurrection, insurgency, civil war, putsch, coup d'état, etc.—but subject to varied interpretations. Chalmers Johnson, in an interesting attempt at classification of "revolution," develops six types that are based on the interplay of four criteria: (1) the targets of revolutionary activity; (2) the identity

[39] Thus, for example, Trotsky writes: "The not infrequent disputes among Russian historians of the newest school as to how far Russia was ripe for present-day imperialist policies often fell into mere scholasticism, because they look upon Russia in the international arena as isolated, as an independent factor, whereas she was but one link in a system. . . . The semicomprador Russian bourgeoisie had world-imperialistic interests in the same sense in which an agent working on percentages lives by the interests of his employer. . . ." *The Russian Revolution* (selected and edited by F. W. Dupee, New York, 1959), p. 14.

[40] Trotsky, "The First Five Years of the Communist International: 1919–1924," in Isaac Deutscher (ed.), *The Age of Permanent Revolution: A Trotsky Anthology* (New York, 1964), pp. 127, 129–130.

of the revolutionaries (masses, elites-leading-masses, and elites); (3) the goals or "ideology" of the revolution; and (4) the spontaneity or calculation of the revolution.[41] Despite the seriousness of Johnson's effort at conceptualization, a brittle set of types with dubious explanatory value emerges.

One of the conspicuous difficulties with his effort is that he creates an analytical scheme into which the historical and cultural dimension of revolutionary experience continually keeps intruding in a disorderly way. For example, "millenarianism" is perhaps not the most cogent category of modernity, except insofar as elements of it persist in other sorts of uprisings. Historically, a so-called "Jacobin-Communist revolution" is an anomaly, though its *exemplaria* are clearly related to the historical factors of urbanization and centralization of political authority. The "militarized mass insurrection" is clearly an historical category modelled on Mao's "agricultural strategy" and the special problem of creating a revolutionary army to combat and exhaust the coercive power of regular forces in a zone consistent with its needs of maneuver.

The lesson that we draw from Johnson's attempt is that since history can as little be excluded from the understanding of the types of internal warfare as it can be eliminated from the study of international politics *tout court*,[42] the acknowledgement of an historical dimension of interpretation must be explicit in order to enable observers to render more accurate judgments on the phenomena being studied. History, in this sense, includes the progressive spread and "saturation" of diplomatic interests and transactions from their original core and the consequent cross-fertilization of regional civilizations by the Western and "modernizing" thrust.

In an earlier portion of this essay we postulated (following Raymond Aron) the three critical variables of international systems: polarity, intensity of ideological discord ("homogeneity-heterogeneity"), and a broad, irreversible historical dimension represented as the widening and completion of the diplomatic system under a well-known sequence of technological impacts. It is the third of these factors that we refer to above. We must now ask whether some typological scheme of internal war can be related to the historical process and if so whether it can then be related to the analytical components of historical systems.

In the scattered writings on internal war there is one set of cate-

[41] Chalmers Johnson, "Revolution and the Social System," pp. 27–28.
[42] See Martin Wight, "Why is There No International Theory?" in Herbert Butterfield and Martin Wight (eds.), *Diplomatic Investigations* (Cambridge, Mass., 1966), p. 33, where the case is surely overstated.

gories that offers at least a partial answer. It is Rosenau's proposal that internal wars be visualized according to three main ideal types, which he designates as "personnel wars," "authority wars," and "structural wars." In Rosenau's scheme, personnel wars are "those which are perceived as being fought over the occupancy of existing roles in the existing structure of political authority. . . ." Authority wars are "those which are perceived as being fought over the arrangement (as well as the occupancy) of the roles in the structure of political authority . . ." and structural wars are "those which are perceived as being not only contests over personnel and the structure of political authority, but also as struggles over other substructures of the society . . . or its major domestic and foreign policies."[43]

These categories are not "historical" in Rosenau's usage. Perhaps they partake too easily of the structural-functional language of modern social science.[44] Nevertheless, we believe that there is a considerable opportunity to use these concepts historically and in a manner that helps to bridge the gulf between the "inner" and "outer" aspects of the revolutionary phenomenon. Two other features of Rosenau's "types" deserve notice. They are continuous in sequence, which raises the problem of transition from one to another, and they proceed from lesser to greater inclusiveness, which means that an "authority war" will also be a "personnel war" and that both types are included in a "structural war," at least for conceptual purposes.

The utility of Rosenau's scheme for our analysis stems from the evident correlations between "revolution" and "structural war." The link between the two is confirmed by recalling a famous passage from

[43] James N. Rosenau, "Internal War as International Event," in *International Aspects of Civil Strife*, p. 63.

[44] In some ways, the proximity of Rosenau's concepts to structural-functional or "systems" modes of analysis helps to tie differing perspectives together. For example, the present triad somewhat recalls David Easton's discrimination of authorities, regime, and political community—"political community" being the consciousness and mechanics of communal solidarity, "regime" being the forms by which political authority is constituted and "authorities" being the specific political and administrative institutions (*A Systems Analysis of Political Life*, pp. 171–219). We see that "structural wars" closely involve the first, "authority wars," the second, and "personnel wars" the third. On this point, see Chalmers Johnson, *Revolutionary Change* (Boston, 1966), p. 141. No doubt the "newness" of this kind of analysis should not be overstressed. Aristotle's *Politics* (Book V, 1301b) had already distinguished between "changing the state into some other" and "having no objection to the already established regime . . . but choosing to have the sole management in it." Our intention here is not to commend the Rosenau typology uncritically; it raises obvious problems with regard to analytic indicators, historical applicability, and transitional criteria. But the notion seems a promising start.

Edmund Burke's pamphlet, "Thoughts on French Affairs." Burke opposed the French Revolution and its admirers in England because he perceived in it something disturbingly novel. The great Whig statesman's obsessive concern with the radical and "conspiratorial" dimensions of the event may be ignored for our present purposes. Burke wrote:

> There have been many internal revolutions in the government of both countries, both as to persons and forms, in which the neighbouring states have had little or no concern. Whatever the government might be with respect to those persons and those forms, the stationary interests of the nation concerned have most commonly influenced the old; and the revolution, turning on matters of local grievance, or of local accommodation, did not extend beyond its territory.
>
> The present revolution in France seems to me to be quite of another character and description; and to bear little resemblance or analogy to any of those which have been brought about in Europe, upon principles merely political. *It is a revolution of doctrine and theoretic dogma. . . .*[45]

Burke's brilliant analysis thus describes the irruption of a certain kind of internal war into history. Today most scholars would be inclined to place less emphasis on the ideocentric nature of the event and much more on its social origins and implications. Nonetheless, the category of "structural war" manages to encompass both perspectives. The novelty of the French Revolution is that it is basically a "structural war." The internal revolutions "in which the neighboring states have had little or no concern" were no more than "authority wars." Burke was referring here to a type of civil strife fought over local liberties and authority relations that were not an immediate peril to a relatively homogeneous kind of international system based on dynastic thrusting and parrying.[46]

---

[45] Edmund Burke, "Thoughts on French Affairs," in *Reflections on the French Revolution* (London, 1955), pp. 287–288. Burke's arch-enemy Paine agreed, but put the matter differently: "The revolutions that have taken place in other European countries have been excited by personal hatred. The rage was against the man, and he became the victim. But, in the instance of France, we see a revolution generated in the rational contemplation of the rights of man, and distinguishing from the beginning between persons and principles." Thomas Paine, *The Rights of Man*, Part I, in P. S. Foner (ed.), *The Complete Writings of Thomas Paine* (2 volumes, New York, 1945), II, p. 258.

[46] It is not our purpose to defend the political duplicity based on the "right of the stronger" of the eighteenth century. Yet, in the light of what was to come after, it is permissible to speak of restraint: Clausewitz wrote in the first chapter of *Vom Kriege* that "theory was beginning to move in this direction (war as a rational act) when the events of the war with Napoleon taught us better." See Karl von Clausewitz, *War, Politics and Power* (trans. and ed. Edward M. Collins, Chicago, 1962), p. 65.

Burke also discovered similarities between the French Revolution and the Protestant Reformation. Both had in common the tendency "to introduce other interests into all countries than those which arose from their locality and natural circumstances."[47] If, following Burke, there is such an antecedent, it may then be asked why we insist on the French Revolution's originality as a "structural war." The answer, given earlier, is that it is also a full-fledged secular war; the first "structural war" of modern civilization. If we take an intermediate example, the English Civil War of 1642–1648, we may generalize that its political components were those of an "authority war" (definition of the Constitution), while its "structural" characteristics were intimately related to religious turbulence. In point of fact, the English Civil War did not have serious repercussions on the prevailing international system, except as a sidelight of the Thirty Years' War. Cromwell fought the Dutch, another Protestant power, while receiving the prudent homages of Louis XIII and Cardinal Mazarin: unlikely tendencies for a revolutionary system.

What Burke is saying, if we may translate, is that "structural wars" are characterized not only by deep social cleavage and "theoretic dogma," but by an associated momentum that causes them to spill over into the international system and threaten its outlines. This propensity distinguishes them from mere "personnel" and "authority wars" long familiar to Europe and largely relevant to local circumstances. Rosenau comments in the same vein:

> As an increasing number of universal values divides the combatants in an internal war, the conflict is likely to have greater relevance for the internal affairs and foreign policies of other nations. Thus they are likely to attach more significance to the course and outcome of a structural war than of any other kind. Such a reaction is fostered partially by the possibility that the insurgents in a structural war are likely, if they triumph, to effect drastic alterations in socio-economic policies at home and thereby challenge other countries to do the same for their own populations.[48]

Of course, saying does not make it so. A wide field of investigation remains for empirical research. But we find this distinction to be a fruitful advance in the conceptualization of revolutionary disorders. It remains to be said that "great revolutions" produce the Burkean effect, while "petty revolutions" have a much smaller scope of repercussion. Are these petty revolutions any less "structural"? Two discriminations are worthy of note. The first is that "petty revolutions" are normally posterior to and in some degree inspired by "great revolutions."

[47] Burke, "Thoughts on French Affairs," p. 288.
[48] Rosenau, "Internal War as an International Event," p. 66.

The second is that they are likely to occur within the social orbit of the secondary units of Aron's international system and thus to provoke, *ceteris paribus*, a correspondingly restricted response within the system. It is probable that their domestic effects need be no less structural.

## THE ESCALATION OF INTERNAL WAR

The criteria for assessing processes of transition from one type of internal war to another constitutes an inherent difficulty in any conceptual scheme. Rosenau's categories are no exception, as the author himself acknowledges. A few remarks will serve to outline the dimensions of this problem.

A violent *coup d'état* is clearly a "personnel war," a sudden illegal transfer of offices and political power. But the latter term seems more useful to us, because *coup d'état* has come to refer almost exclusively to the mere exchange of governing elites by an act of force, without further reference to the uses of political power by those elites over a period of time. Of course, it is possible to imagine that a sequence of events beginning as a "personnel war" may acquire wider dimensions as the seizure of power is being consolidated. The interpretation of this process will vary greatly, depending on whether one takes an "ideological" or "neo-Machiavellian" view of the proceedings. In any case, *coup* is then merely a technique, to be judged on the one hand by the "least expense" principle and on the other by the criterion of social preparation for radically new authority. Sequential categories like Rosenau's direct our attention to the process that exceeds the initial and successful act of political violence.

More critical is the nature of the transition between "authority" and "structural" wars, since there is a likely implication of "spillover" into the international system, where critical judgments by foreign statesmen are apt to become involved. Rosenau refers at some length to Cuba as a case-type of this "escalation." We see what was initially a "regime" or "authority" conflict reaching "structural" proportions as a result of the interplay of greater foreign forces and the determination of an ideologically diffuse regime to consolidate its security by navigating the perilous straits of great-power politics.[49] Unfortunately, neither Cuba nor any single case exemplifies the complex mechanics of transition in a given international system.

It is apparent that the circumstances in which internal wars "spill

[49] Our interpretation is indebted to Andrés Suarez, *Cuba: Castroism and Communism, 1959–1966* (Cambridge, Mass., 1967).

over" may often be other than "structural," although structural issues will customarily spill back into such conflicts. Minor political disturbances in "client states," in symbolic or strategic zones may alert great-power concern and stimulate crises. Such reactiveness could encourage "structural" consequences where these were not implicit in the original situation; the process may be fueled by the fear that inaction would, at least in the longer term, be worse. [50]

These comments raise the vital issue of intervention in internal wars. From the perspective of an historical sociology of international relations, two sets of questions are significant. Clearly, the definitional bog that mars much discussion of intervention is related to the indiscriminate use of the term to describe the varied activities of a military, economic or political character that may be undertaken by a diversified group of state actors, international organizations, corporations or individuals. The highly-charged issue of intervention is not often elucidated by asking, what is intervention?

For our purposes, we might inquire, what acts in the context of internal wars are perceived or construed as interventionary in a given historical setting? What consequences of these acts are feared and for what reasons? These questions, deceptively simple at first glance, increase in complexity as observers attempt to demarcate the temporal and spatial boundaries of international systems or to correlate typologies of internal war with categories of third-party interposition. In the contemporary international system, the methodological difficulties are aggravated by the dual nature of some third parties, especially international organization, which may intervene in internal wars and also attempt to regulate the interventionary acts of others.[51] This complication does not disappear if we adopt the continuum of structural-authority-personnel wars, a classification that tries to cut across historical

---

[50] In 1958 internal tension in Lebanon, which was basically of the "personnel" variety (although it quickly absorbed overtones of the cold war), elicited the presence of U.S. Marines. The British have been no less dilatory in response to troubles in Kuwait; and the French behaved similarly in Gabon (where prestige in the Franco-African bloc, rather than the balances of the Bank of France was threatened). The nature of responses in current times can be connected to both "bipolarity" and the "saturation of the system" as well as to the more traditional interdiction and protection of material and ideal resources.

[51] Sometimes the saliency of an intervening body must be measured by the power and preferences of the natural "intervenors" in it (e.g., the U.N.); sometimes ad hoc bodies may be structured around these "intervenors" in an attempt to preserve their dialogue and moderate their actions (e.g., the Non-Intervention Committee in the Spanish Civil War). Of course, such bodies can as easily disguise or justify self-intervention as curtail or neutralize it.

periods, instead of a scheme more deeply embedded in a particular epoch.[52]

A second set of questions that may yield comparative insights takes as its point of departure the assumption that internal wars and the international system affect each other according to mechanisms that permit separation for analytic purposes. We may ask: To what extent do the asymmetrical power bases of insurgents and incumbents affect the competitive process of seeking external support? To what extent are the choices for potential intervenors limited by existing diplomatic practices or legal norms? To what extent does the existing state of technology or the quality of material resources shape the character of specific interventions?

The experience of the postwar era is instructive when approached through the questions posed. In the present historical setting, which combines the tensions generated by nuclear weapons and decolonization with the maintenance of the state system in a formal sense, acts perceived or construed as interventionary in internal wars include an extensive catalogue of non-military activities, as well as the more conventional uses of force. Economic and propaganda instruments are familiar modes for states wishing to affect the course of internal wars in the less industrialized sectors of Asia, Africa, Latin America and the Middle East. The chief consequence feared is the escalation of local conflict into regional or perhaps global confrontations between nuclear-armed adversaries. Thus the stakes in contemporary internal wars are raised by the *potential* level of conflict, despite the well-known inhibitions on intervention that affect the calculations of third parties, especially the superpowers.

The transfer of traditional forms of interstate rivalry into newer channels is reflected in the emergence of internal war and revolution as surrogates for international war. The "structural" component of contemporary internal wars, wars that invite a wide range of "interventionary" behavior, permits us to distinguish these conflicts from those of earlier systems in which the technological resources for intervenors were less extensive. The much lamented obsolescence of legal dicta inherited from the Europocentric era of international relations underscores the uniqueness of the present period. The results for observers have become apparent. The heterogeneity and polarization of

---

[52] One example of time-bound categories is the spectrum of colonial wars, postcolonial breakdowns of law and order, and proxy wars or internal conflicts involving forms of external aggression or subversion, all prevalent in recent decades. For a fuller exposition, see Linda B. Miller, *World Order and Local Disorder: The United Nations and Internal Conflicts* (Princeton, 1967). Also, on the general subject, see "Intervention and World Politics," special number of the *Journal of International Affairs*, XXII, 2 (1968).

the international system make it difficult to predict the incentives that will influence third parties to undertake or resist interventions in internal wars. The line between internal and international wars has become increasingly difficult to draw, given the diminished relevance of national boundaries for military strategy and ideological commitment. Internal wars continue to be viewed at home and abroad as parts of larger conflicts of a racial, anti-colonial-anti-imperial, or cold war character, despite the decline of the bipolar diplomatic strategic configuration that gave such attitudes legitimacy.

Research designed to offer even tentative answers to the questions we have posed may help to explain the processes whereby the options of foreign aid, subversion, mediation, or recognition of an insurgent regime are selected or rejected by third parties.[53] Such research may also clarify the shifts in the relationship of international law and organization to world politics, shifts mirrored in the present unclear status of intervention in legal theory and state practice.

## INTERNAL WAR AND GLOBAL SYSTEM

Some basic themes in an historical sociology of internal war have been traced in terms of the development of Western technology and ideology and the expansion of the Europocentric international system. But some conventional appraisals of the distinctions between the "Western" historical experience and the experience of other civilizations may require re-evaluation. These include the conceptions of "structural war" and of the "saturation" of the international system. Is revolution a specific donation of Western culture?[54]

It would appear to be a fact that the French Revolution—whether treated as "unique" or as part of an "Atlantic" context—played the "structural" role we describe. It also seems true that this seed, once planted in the bodies politic of Western Europe, proved ineradicable and highly eligible for export together with European empire and technology. Moreover, we have good reason to presume that such structural

[53] The argument that these four responses are the most significant reactions to internal wars is found in George Modelski, "The International Relations of Internal War," in James N. Rosenau (ed.), *International Aspects of Civil Strife*, pp. 14–44.

[54] For example, as C. J. Friedrich writes (*An Introduction to Political Theory*, Boston, 1967, p. 33): "The attitude to revolution found in our Western society is quite distinctive and quite different from that of other political societies and civilizations." Eugene Kamenka ("The Concept of a Political Revolution," p. 129) corroborates more specifically: "For nearly two thousand years, China witnessed civil wars, rebellions, secessions, and coups d'état, but until the European revolutions came, there had not been one revolution in China. . . . Rebellions and coups d'état occur everywhere; revolutions, it is fascinating to note, seem to have occurred only in cities and, until comparatively recently, in Western society."

war, because of its universalizing tendencies, not only invades the social milieu but may also explode vigorously into the international arena, affecting the conflicts between states. Nonetheless, it is not basically clear why such an event should have happened exclusively in the pre-industrial West or whether social structures and ideologies peculiar to Christendom and a *Siècle des Lumières* were needed to produce it. Left to their own devices, would the culture patterns of other civilizations have failed to give rise to structural war? Modern revolution surely had its older antecedents (political centralization, population pressures, bourgeois ideology, religious conflict): did corresponding forces not exist elsewhere exclusive of the impact of European ideas?

The expansion of the European core is a political fact. The eighteenth century heralded the repulse of the Turk and the gradual but decisive impingement of European power on the coasts of Asia. By the nineteenth century the viability of all independent sub-systems of diplomacy had been shattered. The age of Europeanizing empire was established. Yet in the course of this "saturation" and in the following movement of decolonization it is not altogether clear to what extent a future cosmopolitanism based on European values was inaugurated. Western civilization evidently did not convert the great social substrate of these areas or leaven them so as to ordain the reactions of all future elites. Greece and Rome have indeed gone to their graves, but the Islamic, Sinic, and Indic civilizations are still active concerns.

Technology may be a Western invention, but it is not necessarily the essence of the Western soul or belief system; it may prove highly adaptable for others without sacrifice of themselves.[55] In short, we may see a resurgence of the dormant cores of other self-conscious "systems" and a rollback of the system we have "completed." Western class ideologies will thus be superseded by doctrines of indigenous manu-

---

[55] On this point, see, for example, Werner Heisenberg, *Physics and Philosophy* (New York, 1958), p. 200: ". . . modern science penetrates into those large areas of our present world in which new doctrines were established only a few decades ago as foundations for new and powerful societies. There modern science is confronted both with the content of the doctrines, which go back to the European philosophical ideas of the nineteenth century (Hegel and Marx), and with the phenomenon of uncompromising belief. Since modern physics must play a great role in these countries because of its practical applicability, it can scarcely be avoided that the narrowness of the doctrines is felt by those who have really understood modern physics and its philosophical meaning. Therefore, at this point an interaction between science and the general trend of thought may take place. Of course the influence of science should not be over-rated. . . ." Also, Jacques Ellul, *The Technological Society* (New York, 1964), p. 116: "The people of these countries have no need to be Westernized. Technique, to be used, does not require a 'civilized' man. Technique, whatever hand uses it, produces its effect more or less totally in proportion to the individual's more or less total absorption in it."

facture or at least masked so as to resemble a local product. To say that the globe is becoming "Westernized" is at best ambiguous.[56] Thus we will probably have to conjure with the impact of actual, refurbished or mythologized non-Western revolutionary traditions. If today we find it increasingly inaccurate to speak simply in terms of "bourgeois" or "Marxist" uprisings transferred to Islam, China, or India, tomorrow we will need new explanations of these events that are not so obviously culture-bound. The mere notion of nationalisms patterned on those of the nineteenth century European experience, or of "rifts" and "schisms" in world revolutionary movements may no longer be adequate to capture the pith of these events.[57] We will require a more "cubist" perspective on the internal genesis of world violence, not neglecting the obvious fact that clashes of major cultures have been decisive sources of revolutionary shock.

Reduced to the most pragmatic level, as one commentator has expressed it: "The attempt to generalize from 'Western' political warfare experience and apply so-called 'lessons' to non-Western theatres with radically different culture patterns, such as those of Asia and Africa, is almost certain to lead to serious planning and operational blunders."[58] In all probability, there is enough mechanical similarity to "personnel" and, conceivably, "authority" wars the world over to enable us to envision them as repetitive persistencies of political struggle relative to the efficacy and vulnerability of political regimes that must balance between the demands of liberty and order in a wide variety of cultural patterns.[59] Structural wars, as we have argued, pose more difficult problems for both theorists and policy-makers.

[56] As one scholar declares in a *futurible:* "[I hypothesize] that in the year 2000 the American world system that has been developed during the last twenty years will be in a state of disintegration and decay. . . . Among those that will play a prominent role . . . will be China on mainland Asia, Indonesia in Southeast Asia, Brazil in Latin America, and I do not know what in the Middle East and Africa." Samuel P. Huntington, "Political Development and the Decline of the American System," *Daedalus*, XCVI, 3 (Summer 1967), p. 928. If this is the image of the future, there is no reason to infer these centers of power will not project their indigenous patterns of culture, diplomacy, and revolution, albeit mixed with the experience of the West.

[57] In his recent stimulating study, *Political Order in Changing Societies* (New Haven, 1968), Samuel P. Huntington introduces numerous discriminations between "Western" and "Eastern" revolutions, pp. 266 ff.

[58] Paul Blackstock, *The Strategy of Subversion* (Chicago, 1964), p. 162.

[59] The form and stakes of these kinds of wars seem to be universal; a major question for historical sociology is whether their occurrence is, so to speak, regular and "functional." But the questions regarding structural war—which is dubiously functional—are (1) its problematic relation to the cumulative experience of large, self-aware societies; and (2) its presumed singularly European genesis (here provisionally questioned).

In our view, historical sociology furnishes two basic approaches to this issue. One, the more integrative, would tend to see societies as driven by basically similar needs and motivated by essentially like impulses. The question then, on a trans-cultural comparative basis, is how to isolate those factors, demographic, sociological, or frankly culturally stimulated, that account for the differences in development and reaction, including the intensity and universality of revolutionary experience.[60]

A second approach would concede insurmountable difficulties in comparative method and would favor the study of isolable cultural wholes, concentrating on the aspects of their historical field of revolutionary development that are native and those that are borrowed and, especially, on the impingement of social-revolutionary world views on one another. This method of study in political science is underdeveloped because it is curtailed by the metaphysics of "our" philosophy of history, the Europocentricity of international relations, and the provincialism or segmentation of area studies.

In moving from the familiar Western European sphere to other cultures, it would be useful to take a look at revolutionary ideologies that have characterized structural upheavals in places most sensitive to the European influence. Russia itself (whether neo-Byzantine, Tsarist, or Soviet) has long been described as "in Europe, but not of Europe"—a Janus-faced culture imbedded in both inherited and acquired experience. Although it was the locus of the first great socialist revolution, Russia absorbed its Marxism into a preformed channel that exalted the primitive so-called communism of the *mir* and *obshchina* and a populist revolutionary tradition obsessed with the overleaping of the dismal bourgeois-capitalist stage of Western Europe.[61] In view of this mythology, or utopianizing of the facts, Marxism was already seriously distorted when it descended on Russia.

Another case of interest is the Algerian revolution. When the

[60] Barrington Moore, Jr. has ambitiously undertaken such an attempt in his recent *Social Origins of Dictatorship and Democracy;* it is "classical" in the sense that similar criteria are applied to very different national cultures, even though the crucial *differentiae* are often culturally explained. Its main statement is (p. 453): "The process of modernization begins with peasant revolutions that fail. It culminates during the twentieth century with peasant revolutions that succeed." Thus, elements of comparison and non-comparability are heuristically joined by a positivistic notion of "development" and assumptions about the time-stream of events. It is an important effort to deal with the problem just raised.

[61] Cf. Franco Venturi, *The Roots of Revolution* (New York: 1966), pp. 5–7, 151, 248–249; Martin Malia, *Alexander Herzen and the Birth of Russian Socialism, 1812–1855* (Cambridge, Mass., 1961), pp. 305–406.

FLN revolted in 1954, its leadership was largely composed of French-speaking, Frenchified subversives. Their propaganda was quasi-Marxist and Jacobin as well as nationalistic. Surprisingly, a very important Islamic substrate of revolutionary impetus and techniques was largely ignored by Western observers.[62] Despite close ties with Europe and an important economic infrastructure created by the French, Algeria is still searching for self-justification and its own mood and substance, as its extraordinary belligerency toward distant Israel reveals. The subsequently rewritten history of its war of independence may very well stress this aspect.

Finally, there is China. Is the Sino-Soviet struggle really a fight for the possession of the holy writ of Marxism, a Western philosophy? Conceivably; for, after all, the Europeans honor Christ and the Japanese Buddha. No doubt, Marxism is a prize to be possessed. Yet the stakes are predominantly cultural ones. The Soviets are perhaps not mistaken in claiming that the CCP is infected with "the artificially cultivated idea of China as the center of the world."[63] In any case, the Maoists seem to have wedded a vociferous but rather deviant "Marxism-Leninism" to a considerable treasury of national values. As one observer writes: "Mao Tse-Tung has followed Lao Tzu and the ancient Book of Changes rather than the Western tradition in adapting what he calls the 'algebra of revolution,' by which he won power, to the task of seeing that succeeding generations 'never change.' "[64]

Franz Schurmann, in his highly praised work on Chinese ideology and organization, establishes China's communist revolution as the termination of a series of rebellions begun in the eighteenth century, not necessarily as a result of European impact.[65] He makes the further point that "the Sino-Soviet dispute is not only a conflict between two powers, but one between two different revolutionary models."[66] Although he explains the structure of Chinese communism in terms of the breakdown of traditional patterns and explains ideology as a fusion of "a pure ideology essentially derived from Marxism and Leninism" and a practical ideology "enriched by . . . long experiences

---

[62] See René Delisle, "Les origines du F.L.N.," *La NEF*, XII-XIII (Oct. 1962–Jan. 1963), pp. 19–32.

[63] *Kommunist*, April 1968, reported by TASS agency.

[64] See W. A. C. Adie, "China: Government by Permanent Rebellion," *Government and Opposition*, II, 2 (Jan.–Apr. 1967), pp. 219–239.

[65] Franz Schurmann, *Ideology and Organization in Communist China* (Berkeley and Los Angeles, 1967), p. xxxi.

[66] *Ibid.*, p. xxxix.

in revolutionary struggle," he suggests that the practical ideology (Mao's 'thought') has "elements in it which link it up with deeper Chinese cultural traditions . . . specifically . . . the earlier religious ideas of Heaven, so closely associated with rebellion."[67]

The "sinification of Marxism" may come to be seen increasingly as no mere species of a genus, but as a full-blown syncretism of its own. Once it is proclaimed that "Asia, Africa, and Latin America are the regions in which the contradictions of the world are concentrated"[68] and that the model for uprisings there has little to do with Marx's European perspective, we are well on the way to the assertion of non-European revolutionary traditions. Frantz Fanon's psychology of violent outrage goes half-way to this point, as does the modern Garibaldism of Che Guevara and his disciple Debray.[69] Marx and Engels did indeed declare in the *Manifesto* that each proletariat would have to deal with its national situation separately, but there are notable elements of both Maoism and Castroism that would have shocked their vision of the revolutionary enterprise.

In any case, the Marxist heresies, of which the first was the Russian, currently grapple for paradigmatic pre-eminence and, failing that, fortify their claims with national and cultural ammunition. As the world swings ambiguously between its "East-West" and "North-South" poles of conflict, creating doctrines and resuscitating revolutionary myths obscure to the expansive European system, historical sociologists will need to chart these "logics of revolution" both as fact and as ideology without succumbing to any undue confidence that the world is one, in sickness or in health.

---

[67] *Ibid.*, pp. 23, 50. Cf. Robert Jay Lifton, *Revolutionary Immortality: Mao Tse-tung and the Chinese Cultural Revolution* (New York, 1968), pp. 36–37, referring to the August 18, 1966 launching of the Red Guards: "An event of this kind is meant to convey *a blending of the immortal cultural and racial substance of the Chinese as a people with the equally immortal Communist revolution.*"

[68] *Jen-Minh Jih-Pao*, October 22, 1963.

[69] Régis Debray, "Le Castroisme: La longue marche de l'Amérique Latine," *Les Temps Modernes* (Jan. 1965), pp. 1127–1228, where the author claims Marxist sanction for his novel departures in theory. For Africa, cf. Gérard Chaliand, *Lutte armée en Afrique* (Paris, 1967), p. 110: ". . . national liberation and social revolution are not merchandise for export; they are—more and more every day—the product of a local and national elaboration, more or less influenced by favorable and unfavorable outside factors, but essentially determined and conditioned by the historical reality of each people."

# 12

# The War Between the Cities

*Alvin W. Gouldner*

≪≪≪≪≪≪≪≪≪≪≪≪≪≪≪≪≪≪≪≪≪≪≪≪≪≪≪≪≪≪≪≪≪≪≪≪≪≪≪≪≪

## EDITORS' COMMENT

" 'O Tyrtaeus . . . tell us then: do you clearly recognize, as we do, two distinct kinds of war?' . . . [For] there are two kinds, the one being that which we call 'civil,' which is of all wars the most bitter . . . while the other kind . . . is that which we engage in when we quarrel with foreigners and aliens—a kind much milder than the former" (The Athenian in Plato's *Laws* 620CD).

Alvin Gouldner in his essay below examines these two kinds of war and finds that they are not necessarily as distinct or as unrelated as the Athenian, perhaps, would make us believe. He suggests that the "grid of domestic and international tensions" which plagued ancient Hellas created a unity of violence, tying international and civil war inseparably together. The sources of this combination were the domestic structure of the *polis* (divided between rich and poor) and an international system, growing increasingly bipolar.

Gouldner argues that external warfare was necessary to the internal stability of the polis, since it supplied slaves and booty which prevented an economic crisis from arising between the rich and the poor. But, when this external warfare found its culmination in the Peloponnesian conflict, a war created by the political rivalry of Athens and Sparta, the internal stability of the polis was destroyed, not enhanced, since Sparta and Athens, respectively, gave political expression to the universal Greek division between the rich (the few) and the poor (the many). The international and internal divisions thus reenforced each other in a sort of "feedback" which made the Peloponnesian cataclysm the result of a deadly paradox: external war was needed for internal stability, but the form which external war took destroyed internal stability. As Thucydides describes it,

> . . . quarrels arose everywhere between the patrons of the commons, that sought to bring in the Athenians, and the few, that desired to bring in the Lacedaemonians. Now in times of peace they could have had no pretense nor would have been so forward to call them in; but being war and confederates to be had for either party, both to hurt their enemies and strengthen themselves, such as desired alteration got them to come in.

In modern experience, internal war can be a reflection of international divisions, and the shape of the system can have important effects on the outcome of a civil war, as the essays in this volume by Rosenau and Kelly (Spain) show. But the situation in Hellas was quite different from contemporary analyses—actually, there is nothing in modern history quite like the Peloponnesian war. Since the rise of the modern state system, there have been numerous systemwide wars, countless interventions in civil wars, caused as the result of international polarity or war, and international wars that have been caused by states falling into revolution, but never has a system-wide war occurred simultaneously with widespread internal wars *which were a reflection of the polarity of the system*. There have been many hints at the possibility of such an occurrence. The Thirty Years War was the closest modern counterpart—but, even in that nightmare, most cities fought and died as cities. The wars surrounding the French Revolution had something of the flavor of this situation, as Rudé's article indicates, but the five great powers retained a remarkable cohesiveness throughout. The closest contemporary possibility can be found at the close of World War I. If the Marxist revolution been more successful in Germany and if "White-Red" civil war had broken out all over Europe—with each side having a powerful national champion and with conflict persisting for two decades—the modern world might have shared with the Greeks an appreciation of the *real* potential for interaction between international and internal warfare.

The reader of the various essays on internal war and international systems that appear in this book might well ask why the Greek situation was so different. Many social scientists today suggest that, when people have many roles within a society, the result is stabilizing. But in ancient Hellas this phenomenon had precisely the opposite effect. Men perceived themselves as members of a class, citizens of a polis, and as *Greeks*. The fact that they perceived themselves as Greeks, however, in this case, proved destabilizing since it was not strong enough to prevent a "Grecian civil war," yet it *was* strong enough to weaken their loyalty to the polis. It enabled them to perceive sufficient culturewide similarities and interests, so that the *dēmos* throughout the cities of Greece could identify with the political fortunes of Athens and the oligarchic faction could identify with the interests of Sparta. If the Greeks had not had this feeling of widespread cultural affinities, their loyalty to the polis would probably have been sufficient to prevent international warfare from being compounded by the horrors of civil war—which the Athenian above found "most bitter."

In modern times, there has been sufficient division between the states and sufficient cohesion inside the states, so that international bipolarity has not been compounded with the breakup of the state on a massive scale. Spain was not replicated throughout Europe. If Europeans had thought of themselves more as members of one culture and, hence, less as members of separate cultures, perhaps, Spain might have been replicated.

International warfare in ancient Greece was very much institutionalized as a result of its laws, customs, and even seasons. Civil war was not institutionalized, and much of its nightmare came from its unpredictibility, as Thucydides clearly documented and Hobbes later explained (see Selection 1). In a negative sense, there is no clearer illustration of the problems of Greece than Stanley Hoffmann's comment on Hobbes:  As the Athenian above put it, "it is much milder"—

> While Hobbes explains how insecurity incites men to crawl out of their state of nature to set up the Leviathan, he does not invite Leviathans to follow suit. Here is the key of the paradox: in the international competition, it is the state itself that serves as a cushion. Even though international politics, in the sense of constraining power, is not a state of peace, even though it is a condition in which the nasty features of human nature (repressed within civil society by the setting up of the Leviathan) can, so to speak, re-emerge at their worst, nevertheless the international state of war is bearable (*The State of War*, Frederic A. Praeger, New York: 1965, p. 60)—

and much milder it was until the interaction between domestic and international forces made it impossible for the state to serve as a cushion.

# THE WAR BETWEEN THE CITIES

## Alvin W. Gouldner

While in their moments of despair the Greeks might blame their trouble on the gods, there is another level on which they know better. When Homer has Zeus complain that men unjustly attribute their misfortunes to the gods, we have to remember that it is, after all, "Homer" who is talking. In having Zeus speak in this way, Homer attests to the Greek disposition to blame the gods and, at the very same time, he reveals their counterdisposition toward self-blame. The Greeks not only recognize but make a point of insisting that much of their suffering comes from themselves; from their own decisions, their own stiff-necked pride, willful blindness, envy, and soaring ambition. . . .

The Greeks see their world as having an inner flaw and see themselves as the killers of their own dream. To understand this Greek vision of the world as doomed by an inner defect, we need an overview of the dynamics of Greek civilization and a glimpse of its movement as a system. We need to connect the internal tensions of the *polis* with the strains in the relations among city-states. We need to see how this grid of domestic and international tensions traps Hellenic civilization as a whole in that inescapable net to which Aeschylus so frequently refers. . . .

### THE GREEK STATE

Although hereditary kingships had all but disappeared by the eighth century B.C., until the end of the seventh century the *polis* was commonly governed by an oligarchy which restricted political privileges primarily to the large landholders and the well-to-do. . . . At the beginning of the sixth century, in response to growing class conflict, Solon's reforms in Athens began the development toward democracy. This trend continues and by Pericles' time full power is seen to derive

SOURCE. Alvin W. Gouldner, "The War Between the Cities," from *Enter Plato* (New York: Basic Books, 1965), pp. 133–161, excerpted. Reprinted with permission of the publishers. Copyright 1965 by Basic Books, Inc., Publishers, New York.

from, if it does in practice always reside in, the Assembly or *ekklēsia*. Greek democracy is, in principle, direct and not representative, each male citizen having one vote in the Assembly which meets at stated intervals and which, in time, comes to have the final decision on all important matters. Only a fraction of the citizenry, however, usually attends meetings of the Assembly. Since rural citizens are loath to leave their farms and since many are often at war, it is rare that more than two thousand to three thousand Athenians—most of them townsmen— sit in the Assembly.

Athenian democracy, however, is not as direct as some friendly stereotypes suggest, and in part for that reason is not as irresponsible and capricious as some hostile stereotypes maintain. While it is true that the *ekklēsia* controls basic decisions, it nonetheless is led by a representative council, the *boulē*, which actually presides over the day-to-day conduct of foreign affairs and civic defense. The president of the Assembly cannot initiate discussion of any matter that has not been first referred to the *boulē*. The five hundred members of the *boulē* are elected annually by lot, and every reputable Athenian of even moderate means can expect, if he so wishes, to be a member at least once during his life. Over the *boulē*, in turn, there are fifty *prytaneis* who function as its executive committee; and over the *prytaneis* are the *epistatai*, each of whom sits for a day as chairman of the executive committee and who is in effect the president of the republic. The pyramid of power, then, is: *ekklēsia*, *boulē*, *prytaneis*, and *epistatai*.

The administration of civic affairs is shared widely by the male citizens who hold office briefly and then retire. Many minor tasks of civic administration are performed by unpaid volunteers, lesser officials are chosen by lot, and generals are elected by vote of the Assembly. By the middle of the fifth century, the basic principle underlying political leadership is that "no one [is] better qualified than anyone else by breeding, intellectual power, or specific training to direct public policy."[1]

A full-time bureaucracy is scarcely existent. There is, for example, no public prosecutor, and individual citizens themselves initiate legal action concerning both private and civic wrongs. There is no police force or professional military group in the modern sense. The Athenian police consists of a group of mounted Scythian slaves, while the military forces consist of every able-bodied citizen, each of whom is usually expected to provide his own weapons and supplies and is liable to

---

[1] J. S. Morrison, "The Place of Protagoras in Athenian Public Life," *The Classical Quarterly* (January–April 1941), p. 8.

military duty until age sixty. In short, political decision-making and military power are in the hands of the male citizenry as a whole. The state is, in principle, the citizenry in arms.

Ordinary citizens do not think of the Athenian state in a Germanic abstract or personified way; the state is neither conceived as "the republic" nor even as "Attica" but as "the Athenians"—the community of male citizens. The state is thus not yet clearly distinguishable or set apart from its citizens, and, under these circumstances, it cannot be expected that clear distinctions will be made between the polity and the society or between the political and the social aspects of the community.

The Greek state is in part tacitly modeled after the $\overline{oi}kos$. It is, consequently, the state's duty to provide for and to protect its members in all important respects and, in particular, to do so, minimally, by maintaining its own autonomy and, maximally and preferably, by establishing its hegemony over other states.

The state is not only *in loco* $\overline{oi}kos$ in terms of its obligations, but also in its rights vis-à-vis its members. Until about the end of the fifth century, there is in principle scarcely any limit on the claims that the state can make upon its citizenry. Their fortunates and their persons are regarded as dependent upon the fortunes of the state to which, in turn, they have diffuse obligations of obedience regardless of the demands made: Socrates obeys even when he is directed to drink the hemlock. A man's entire life and character are seen as drawing sustenance from the city, which is regarded as the chief educative influence on him: "A city teaches a man," says Simonides of Ceos, later to be echoed by Socrates. The laws of the city are commonly regarded as the standard of right and wrong, and there is a tendency to view the legal and the ethical as identical. This, in turn, suggests that there is yet little distinction made between the citizen's private life and his public life. . . .

CITIZEN AND STATE

The nature of the Greek city-state, and the character of the problems that it faces, are better seen when the full magnitude of the support and benefits which it provides its citizens is seen. A mere listing of those provided by Athens during various periods is impressive: the state distributes grain to citizens during times of famine and highly inflated corn prices; it provides pensions for disabled soldiers and for their orphans (indeed orphans are maintained until their eighteenth birthday, when males would be given their military equipment freely and poor girls—if comely, it seems—their dowries); and during some periods the conduct of state-financed public religious sacrifices provides the poorer citizen with an average of one meat dinner a week; citizens are paid three obols or one-half drachma per day for their frequent service as *hēliastai* on juries. If one is correct in inferring from certain passages in Aristophanes that a laborer could support a wife and one child on three obols a day, then Hasebroek is not far wrong in stating that "in the fourth century all full citizens were in receipt of a 'sufficient amount of food and money to secure them their livelihood,"[2] while thousands of other citizens had annual incomes from captured territories which were distributed among them. The "glory that was Greece" was a glory born in the ancient approximation of the welfare state.

As the franchise and other opportunities for political participation are pulled down into the lower reaches of the class structure and as political rights and duties are extended to the masses of the *dēmos*, the civic offices requiring extensive time and energies increase in number and can no longer be manned by those able to support themselves from independent incomes. Not only is there a need to maintain the five hundred members of the *boulē*, but there are also a total of six thousand *hēliastai*, half of whom hear cases during any day, five hundred wardens of the arsenal, and about ten thousand citizens who perform a host of other official duties either in Athens or abroad. Glotz estimates that public affairs require the full attention of about a third of the citizenry at a time when half the citizens do not have an annual income of their own of two hundred drachmae.[3]

If citizens faithfully perform their extensive civic duties, they are unable to support themselves; if they attend to their trades to support themselves they have neither the time to perform their public duties nor to protect their political prerogatives. To resolve this dilemma, Pericles arranges payments (*misthoi*) to all citizens who renounce their professions in order to serve the state. These payments, of course, are not merely a response to the need of the *dēmos*, but also to its political power. The poorer classes use their franchise to better their economic positions by voting themselves various benefits. At certain periods, then, the Athenian citizen can and sometimes does live off the state. To suggest, however, as some writers have, that they are living off the "dole" is mistakenly to equate the *polis* with the

    [2] J. Hasebroek, trans. L. M. Fraser and D. C. Macgregor, *Trade and Politics in Ancient Greece* (London: G. Bell, 1933), p. 35.

    [3] G. Glotz, *The Greek City* (London: Routledge and Kegan Paul, 1950), p. 126.

modern welfare state. Despite significant similarities between the two, such a view is mistaken because it forgets that the Greek citizens *are* the state; they are not a dispirited group of unemployed but men actively engaged in full-time politics, civic administration, and frequent military service. They are not a pariah group but an elite who feel that what they receive from the state is only a just perquisite enabling them to devote themselves to its affairs. Rather than being a kind of unemployment compensation, the income and the other benefits provided citizens are more akin to the dividends paid to stockholders of the modern private corporation. This analogy is far from a limping one, for it is "the ineradicable idea of the Greek that [state] surpluses should be divided between citizens. . . ."[4]

It is precisely because the advantages accruing to citizens are so substantial that they are jealous about restricting citizenship to a narrowly limited body. Until about the middle of the fifth century, only someone born of an Athenian father could be a citizen, and in 451 B.C. it is required that both his parents must be Athenian if he is to be a citizen. The citizenry are as loath to share their prerogatives as the managerial group in the modern corporation.

We will not be far wrong, then, in thinking of the *polis* as a private corporation: indeed, Aeschines—Demosthenes' political opponent—uses a similar metaphor, complaining that certain of the political sessions "proceed not as deliberative assemblies, but rather as meetings of shareholders after a distribution of surpluses." Yet if the citizenry are akin to the stockholders of a private corporation, this is a corporation whose stock can often be obtained only by inheritance and which is not always freely purchasable on an "exchange." The *polis* is a closed corporation. It is administered for the benefit of its citizens, who are both its managers and shareholders, and who are often scarcely a majority of the people in the city.

The Greek conception of citizenship embraces diverging values and interests. From one standpoint, citizenship is regarded as a matter of ascription; it is a right which depends primarily upon birth and is not contigent upon residence and is not earned. In this view, citizenship is a kind of property right. There is, however, another view which also influences access to citizenship in very exceptional circumstances. This regards citizenship as a privilege which could be earned, particularly by risking one's life in the military service of the city. Greek democracy, however, commonly takes the direction of extending the political privileges of those who are already defined as citizens rather

[4] H. Michell, *The Economics of Ancient Greece* (Cambridge: Cambridge University Press, 1940), p. 366.

than of extending citizenship itself to those who did not have it; it does not normally make it possible for outsiders to achieve citizenship by performing some routine service or by attainments that comply with certain universal standards. . . .

The conception of citizenship as a privilege capable of being earned through one's routine services and performances—although consistent with crucial elements in the Greek value system—is used only rarely; the dominant view regards citizenship as a form of property and a birthright. Those already privileged decline to share their advantages with others outside their own charmed circle. If this undermines the loyalty of those excluded and makes the citizens a narrowly vulnerable elite, this is a price that they are commonly willing to pay for their advantages. They pay another price as well, the betrayal of their own deeply ingrained achievement values, especially of their own conception of *aretē*, or excellence, which in all its forms always emphasizes that a man's worth is dependent on his own attainments. When the exclusive conception of citizenship begins to break down, it does so not because of a new determination to uphold achievement values but primarily because of venality: rich *metoikoi* can and do buy their way into the citizenry.

## STATE FINANCING

That the Greek state exists primarily for the benefit of its citizens and at the expense of its slaves, resident aliens, and subjects becomes all the more evident if we examine the sources from which the state derives its financing. The Athenian state's surplus during the Empire, Michell tells us, "was created from the tribute of the allies, the receipts from the mines of Laurium, custom duties, and harbor duties, and taxes on *Metics* and foreigners."[5] . . . [An additional] source of public financing at Athens, during the period of democracy, is the taxation of the rich. While Athenians commonly dislike and avoid direct taxation, there are a variety of civic services which the rich are expected to finance. Among these are the *leitourgiai* which, if originally volunteered by the citizen as a way of enhancing his prestige, come, in time, to be regular impositions upon the rich. Among these are the costs of certain religious festivals, the dramas, and the choruses and dances. That these expenses could be draining is suggested in a speech written by Lysias in which one citizen-plaintiff complains that he has spent more than sixty thousand drachmae in nine years. There are, too, the *eisphora*, special taxes on capital levied during times of emer-

---

[5] *Ibid.*, p. 370.

gency. Finally, there are the recurrent costs of outfitting or repairing a man-of-war, or *trières*, which also fall on the rich; these become especially onerous during the Peloponnesian War, even though the state itself pays the initial cost of building and rigging the ship.

Without doubt the endemic tensions between the rich and poor—the "few" and the "many"—derive, in important part, from this system of taxation. . . . [And this] conflict . . . over taxation rests on the poor citizen's political power in the Assembly, [which] in its turn, leads the rich to oppose democracy and to seek to supplant it with an oligarchy which restricts the franchise. The economic pressure on the rich, along with the resentment of the older families toward the *nouveaux riches*, contributes to the growing alienation of sectors of the upper class. By the end of the fifth century, antidemocratic beliefs are prevalent among them and conspiracies and revolts which they initiate against the Democracy begin to occur. "[A]ll the world over," says the "Old Oligarch" writing about the last quarter of the fifth century B.C., "the cream of society is in opposition to the democracy. . . . [T]here is no state in which the best element is friendly to the people. It is the worst element which in every state favours the democracy."[6]

The economic and the status tensions of the older landed gentry are also severely exacerbated by the prevalence of wars and, in particular, by the Peloponnesian War, which lasts twenty-seven years. War brings direct economic loss through physical damage to landed property; when Athens withdraws behind its walls, the invading Spartans and their allies are free to ravage the countryside, to harry the fields, to burn the crops and houses, and to drive off the livestock. This, in turn, intensifies the poorer peasants' feeling against the gentry, for they could not afford capital repairs and once again they are overburdened with debts and mortgages. The landed gentry is thus politically and economically damaged by war and is, consequently, more inclined toward peace. . . .

Not only might the well-to-do be taxed and outvoted during the Democracy, but their military honor and privilege are also undermined as Athens' military power becomes increasingly naval in character. With Athens' growing reliance on her naval power, the "rowers who guard the state"—the *"rhyppapai,"* as they come to be known popularity from their rhythmic rowing chant—in turn acquire increased political influence. . . . As Adkins notes, "the poor man, not the rich, mans the navy, the most important striking force of the state, and, his

[6] "The Old Oligarch" (Or pseudo-Xenophon), "The Constitution of the Athenians," F. R. B. Godolphin, ed., *The Greek Historians*, Vol. 2 (New York. Random House, 1942), pp. 634–643.

equipment being provided for him, can meet the rich on at least equal terms on that score."[7]

In the last years of the Peloponnesian War the maintenance and repair of ships costs more than can be afforded by a single rich citizen, and groups of two or more citizens, a *synarchia*, are set up for this purpose. By the middle of the fourth century B.C. the size of the ship-maintaining unit is made even larger and comes to consist of sixty members. The growing intensity and costs of war undermine the wealth of the landed gentry as well as the status claims of the rich in general, insofar as the latter are traditionally justified by their contribution to military activities.

## WAR AND THE CLASS STRUCTURE

At this point, we may begin to discern some of the relationships between Athens' military adventures abroad and her class struggles and political conflicts at home. During the period of the Delian League, Athens' main source of state financing, and thus of the benefits she provides her citizens, derives from the annual tribute paid by her allies. This had first been fixed at 460 talents, with a surplus of some 3,000 talents accumulating by about 453 B.C. However, with the defeat of Athens at the end of the Peloponnesian War the tribute is eliminated, and in consequence, state financing based upon taxation of the rich assumes more significance. This, in turn, conduces to greater tensions between rich and poor.

The wealthier groups are caught in a grinding cross-pressure in which they face the dilemma of either foreign war or civil war. To avoid being taxed by the *dēmos*, the rich are constrained either to satisfy the demands of the *dēmos* by allowing or leading military adventures from which booty and tribute can be obtained or undercutting the demands of the *dēmos* by eliminating their political power through the overthrow of the Democracy. The first solution means war abroad and the possible pillage of country properties; the second solution invites civil war at home. For both rich and poor citizens, however, war abroad is preferable to war at home and indeed the threat of civil war at home is conducive to conflict between the cities. War diverts the poor from the resources of the rich; it unites both classes against a foreign enemy and provides both a common gain—if they win. Victory produces not only tribute but opportunities for booty as well; it provides new land which is important to the endemically

---

[7] A. W. Adkins, *Merit and Responsibility: A Study in Greek Values* (Oxford: Clarendon Press, 1960), p. 197.

land-hungry citizens and thus reduces discontent and pressure against the landed gentry; it insures control of overseas food supplies which are almost always important to Athens because of her insufficient food production; and it also permits fresh supplies of cheap slaves. Class tensions, within the city and in the countryside, are in some part resolved by war or, more precisely, by victory in war. Defeat, of course, is another matter and results in a continuation and, indeed, an exacerbation of internal class conflicts.

In some ways, the Greek system of stratification is conducive to war but inhibitive to victory. Aside from the debilitating costs on disunity between rich and poor, a city's military position is imperiled by its class system in two other ways: First, her slaves are sometimes a locus of instability; they might revolt or flee during war, in effect contributing to the strength of the enemy. These military costs of slavery are not, however, borne equally by the major contenders in the Peloponnesian War. Sparta, for example, is more disadvantaged by its slave system than is Athens, for a substantial part of her military force is always pinned down at home against the danger of Helot rebellion while Athens, at most fearing desertion rather rebellion from her slaves, can deploy a larger part of her fighting men abroad. Secondly, since payments to the citizens are in part dependent on the size of the state's surpluses, there is always some question about dividing a surplus or using it to strengthen the city's forces by building more *triēreis*. Defense spending and welfare spending even then compete with one another. The rich, however, cannot wholeheartedly reject the policy of dividing the surplus since, if they do so, this induces the poor to press for increased taxation of the rich. Further, since the rich have to pay for maintaining and repairing the ships after they have been built, a division of the surplus means fewer *triēreis* which have to be kept in condition.

To say that military victory eases the internal conflicts of the city means that war and social disorder between the cities are conducive to social order within the city. In some degree, war is necessary for the internal stability of the *polis*. And there is war aplenty. According to P. A. Sorokin's estimates, during the 375 years between 500 and 126 B.C., some 235 of them or about 63 percent, have an occurrence of war. "[I]n the history of Greece," says Sorokin, "frequency of war was much higher than many are wont to think."[8]

"To the Greek mind the normal condition of things was war between state and state, not peaceable coexistence."[9] In addition to the

---

[8] P. A. Sorokin, *Social and Cultural Dynamics*, Vol. 3 (New York: American Book Company, 1937), p. 294.

[9] Hasebroek, *Op. cit.*, p. 118.

many full-scale wars between cities, piracy and privateering—which are common in most periods of Greek history—provide for the continual and institutionalized conduct of conflict by private parties. Citizens of one state are often the legitimate prey of those in another; foreigners are frequently exposed to seizure on the high seas or coastal waters unless protected by special treaty between cities or by personal privilege. . . . Not peace but war is the condition reckoned as normal; peace is viewed as a time between wars rather than war being viewed as a disruption of peace. Although the ravages of the Peloponnesian War make many long for peace, peace is not viewed as a humane ideal but as a matter of self-interest and, even in 425 B.C., many Athenians still believe that victory in war would ensure their prosperity and enhance their power.

This view of the classical conception of war as the continual and normal state of affairs is by no means a modern ethnocentric projection into the past. In his *Laws*, Plato himself has Cleinias remark, "For what men in general term peace . . . [is] only a name; in reality every city is in a natural state of war with every other, not indeed proclaimed by heralds, but everlasting."[10] In its turn, war is regarded by Plato as having shaped not only Sparta's but also Athens' basic institutions and, indeed, as being their major objective. When Plato has the Athenian remark, in the *Laws*, that it is better to arrange wars for the sake of peace than peace for the sake of wars, Cleinias rejoins that "there is truth, Stranger, in that remark of yours; and yet I am greatly mistaken if war is not the entire aim and object of our own institutions, and also of the Lacedaemonian." To which the Athenian replies, "I dare say. . . ."[11]

It is this prevalence of war and the continuing hope for war's prizes, of war as an ongoing way of life and not simply as the glorious memory of an outmoded Homeric past, that deeply shapes the character of the Greek citizenry. If by the time of the Peloponnesian War the Athenian masses are far from a warrior elite lusting after immortality through heroic military exploits, if their personal taste for battle has dulled and they are no longer so ready to "face the blood and the slaughter [and] go close against the enemy and fight with [their] hands,"[12] they yet remain greedy for the spoils of war.

[10] Plato, *Laws*. 626 AB; Benjamin Jowett, Trans. and ed., *The Dialogues of Plato* (New York: Random House, 1937). All subsequent quotations from Plato will be from this edition. . . . References to this volume . . . refer to the pages in Stephens' text which are given in the margin of Jowett's translation. . . .

[11] *Ibid.*, 628 E-629 A.

[12] From the poet Tyrtaeus of Sparta, in R. Lattimore, trans., *Greek Lyrics* (Chicago: University of Chicago Press, 1955), p. 14.

## SLAVERY AND WAR

Endemic war binds the citizens ever more closely to slavery, and slavery, in turn, makes war ever more necessary. An elite engaged in frequent wars cannot take part in the routine conduct of economic affairs; they must be able to live without working if only because they spend so much of their time in the field. Indeed this is one of the reasons that Xenophon adduces for relieving the aliens of military duties; for "the trouble of quitting trades and homesteads is no trifle,"[13] he observes. The citizen elite need slaves to help maintain their establishments during their military service, and they need to fight so that they can maintain the slave supply. Slavery and war in Greece are interdependent, each enabling the other to be carried on.

Greek slavery is, indeed, intrinsically inhibitive of the maintenance of a system of peaceful international order among the city-states, because a stable international order tends to reduce the number and to increase the price of slaves. . . . Maintenance of a cheap slave supply requires large areas of social disorder between the city-states; it requires kidnapping, piracy, privateering, and above all war. Slavery is thus one of the major inhibitants to the spread of a peaceful international order in Hellenic civilization. Conversely, international disorder is actually useful for the maintenance of Greek slavery, because it allows those outside the basic political unit, the *polis*, to be preyed upon and to be subjugated as slaves. And without the slaves there can be no citizen elite.

The citizen soldiery is the main group in Greek society which can live off unearned income: from payments by the state, from *klērouchiai*, from rents on land that it alone is privileged to own. During certain periods, it is a castelike group whose members are forbidden by law to marry foreigners, membership in which is a jealously guarded birthright, and which has a monopoly of legal and political control.

To be sure, there are many relatively poor citizens—for if they are all "stockholders," each does not hold the same amount of stock—and this is one of the sources of the city's internal tensions. These tensions are all the more aggravated because poverty and routine, continous work are discrepant with their conception of the ideal citizen. A central objective of Xenophon's proposed economic reforms is to

---

[13] Xenophon, *Ways and Means*, "A Pamphlet on Revenues," in Godolphin, *op. cit.*, p. 646.

avoid work and to enable every citizen to "be supplied with ample maintenance at the public expense."[14] . . .

The ideal citizen is a man of leisure, rich enough to devote himself to the management of the affairs of the *polis* and to its aggrandizement. The citizenry are an elite of politics and war who cannot live as they think themselves entitled to unless others are there to play their parts. The system is a seamless whole: there can be no masters unless there are others who live under constraint.

It is impossible to have an adequate understanding of the Hellenic wars without seeing them in relation to slavery and to the classical system of social stratification common to the city-states. Not only is the Greek class system conductive to war, it also shapes the strategies by which they are fought and influences the conditions under which peace might be sought. When the cities are at peace, they aid one another in maintaining their own slave systems as, for example, in 462 B.C., when Athens sends Cimon with a hoplite army to help Sparta put down a major revolt of the Helots. Conversely, when the cities are at war they incite their enemies' slaves to rebellion or desertion, as in 425 B.C., when Athens seizes a harbor on the west coast of the Peloponnese and Sparta becomes greatly concerned that this will be a locus for spreading rebellion among her Messenian Helots and begins to think of peace.

In the peace treaty signed in 421 B.C. it is agreed that, "Should the slave-class rise in rebellion, the Athenians will assist the Lacedae-monians with all their might. . . ."[15] Something less than a century later, the members of the Hellenic League show that it remains one of the prime functions of international concord among the Greek cities to maintain the established system of stratification by agreeing that there should be "no confiscation of property, no redistribution of land, no cancellation of debts, no freeing of slaves for the purposes of revolution."[16]

Powerful groups in the various cities feel a common interest not only in maintaining slavery but, also, in bolstering the larger system of stratification. The tensions of war and, in particular, of defeat in war, exacerbate the strains inherent in the cities' class system; after the Peloponnesian War, in particular, both internecine conflicts and wars between the cities grow in brutality. The poorer classes want the city to be rich enough to support them. The upper classes find

[14] *Ibid.*, p. 652.
[15] M. I. Finley, ed., *Slavery in Classical Antiquity*, "Views and Controversies" (Cambridge: Heffner, 1960), p. 65.
[16] *Ibid.*, p. 65.

themselves economically drained and politically damaged by wars, yet they continue to need war as a way of diverting the *dēmos* from taxing them.

## HELLENIC UNITY AND ATHENIAN EXPANSION

One basic solution to this problem is, of course, to promote Greek unity. Stabilizing the relations between the cities and consolidating their forces, the cities can then make a common assault on the "barbarian" empires in the Near East. In this connection, it is notable that Plato objects to the enslavement of Greeks by Greeks because it weakens Hellenic civilization as a whole in its contest with the barbarians. "Do you think it right that Hellenes should enslave Hellenic states, or allow others to enslave them, if they can help?" he asks. "Should not their custom be to spare them, considering the danger which there is that the whole race may one day fall under the yoke of the barbarians?"[17]

Greek unity, however, cannot be attained unless another problem is first solved. This problem is the old one of each of the city-states jealously guarding its autonomy so that none will relinquish leadership to another voluntarily. They could not be unified except by the domination of some more powerful state. Up until the Peloponnesian War, Athens comes closest to consolidating an empire that could provide the power center for an Hellenic peace, but she is finally thwarted by two things: first, by Sparta and her allies, of course, and secondly, by her own inability to assimilate her friends within the subject populace of the empire. In particular, Athens is usually unwilling to consolidate their friendship by giving them citizenship (as Rome later does) because she so jealously guards the prerogatives of citizenship. The exclusive and narrow conception of "community" with which the Athenians operate undermines, to a great extent, their own empire.

It is clear, however, that Athens drifts toward a policy of expansion through conquest and domination. In the fifth century the young Athenian swears an oath that he will recognize "no bounds to Attica save beyond the corn and barley fields, the vineyards and the olive groves"; and by the fourth century he swears, "I will not leave my country smaller, but I will leave it greater and stronger than I received it."[18] . . .

## ATHENS AND THE HELLENIC CLASS STRUCTURE

Athens' expansion is not, however, motivated only by her citizens' avarice. Her power is based not on the needs of Athens alone, seen

[17] Plato, *Republic*, 469 B.
[18] Glotz, *Op. cit.*, p. 133.

as a separate social system, but is sustained by larger forces set in motion by the class system common to Hellenic civilization as a whole. The war between the cities, especially the Peloponnesian War, is rooted in the class struggles between the few and the many, the oligarchs and democrats.

No one has made this plainer than Thucydides. The Spartans, he tells us, pride themselves on their oligarchical character; they boast that in Sparta "the many do not rule the few, but rather the few the many, owing their position to nothing else than to superiority in the field."[19] Normally, Sparta's policy is not to exact tribute from her allies (in part because she already has a rich "internal" empire in Messenia consisting of some twenty Helots for every citizen), "but merely to secure their subservience to her interests by establishing oligarchies among them . . ."[20] Of Athens, Thucydides says that "in all cities the people is your friend, and either does not revolt with the oligarchy, or, if forced to do so, becomes at once the enemy of the insurgents; so that in the war with the hostile city you have the masses on your side."[21] In the Peloponnesian War the whole Hellenic world is convulsed, says Thucydides, by this interlocking of class conflict and intercity warfare, "[s]truggles being everywhere made by the popular chiefs to bring in the Athenians, and by the oligarchs to introduce the Lacedaemonians."[22]

What Sparta or Athens become in their international role does not depend solely on their own peculiar internal pressures and character; it constitutes a response to class cleavages and to conflicts that pervade all of Hellas and cut across the various city-states. It is not simply that Sparta imposes oligarchy upon the cities or that Athens imposes democracy. . . . The class-rooted sources of oligarchy in the cities throughout Hellas create and support Sparta, in part making her what she becomes; the class-rooted sources of democracy throughout the Hellenic cities create and sustain Athens also, making her, in some part, what she becomes in power and political character.

This interpretation need not at all commit us to the view that Athens, always and everywhere, supports democracy and the *dēmos* in other cities, or that she gives support only to democratic cities. Athenian interests of state, the exigencies she faces as a power contending with Persia and Sparta, demand that she give independent consideration to the unity of her empire, and this occasionally leads her to

<hr />

[19] Thucydides, trans. R. Crawley, *The Peloponnesian War* (Garden City: Doubleday, n.d.), p. 300.

[20] *Ibid.*, p. 23.

[21] *Ibid.*, p. 189.

[22] *Ibid.*, p. 207.

support oligarchic governments and factions. Yet there is no question that in the classical period the Athenian disposition is predominantly prodemocratic, that she relies upon the loyalty of the *dēmos* in the subject cities, and that where there is internal strife in a city or some question of its loyalty to Athens, she commonly throws her power behind the democratic faction. . . .

Certainly, neither Sparta nor Athens can reverse their roles; . . . each becomes a magnet attracting different class and different political forces. . . . [And] time and again, it is clear from Thucydides' account that the initiative is taken not by Sparta or Athens but by the class-rooted groups in the various cities. It is often they who appeal to and they who seek to ally themselves with one side or the other, rather than having this rule imposed upon them. "Since the fifth century," notes Glotz, "democrats everywhere had fallen into the habit of appealing to Athens for help."[23] It is particularly notable that when, toward the end of the Peloponnesian War, the Athenian democracy is overthrown from within by the conspiracy of the Four Hundred, the Athenian army still at Samos then joins with the Samian *dēmos* to overthrow the oligarchy and restore democracy to Athens. Here, clearly, it is not Athens which is imposing democracy on a tributary, but, rather, it is the latter which, joining with other forces, seeks to defend democracy and to bring it back to Athens.

The power of the Athenian empire is as much created by the need of its subjects as by the greed of its rulers. Despite the shortsighted and overweening ambition of the Athenians, they play a role in Hellenic civilization that transcends their own selfishness and is larger than they know. Although she exacts a price, Athens gives a service in return: she gives protection not only to her own but to the Hellenic *dēmos*, buffering them from their own upper classes. Athens' drive toward empire, her ability to endure the twenty-seven years of the Peloponnesian War against a legion of foes, is empowered and vitalized because she manipulates, exploits and, also, because she gives authentic expression and aid to the Hellenic *dēmos* in their struggles against their own local oligarchical factions.

To hold that the character and strength of the Athenian empire rests on these class forces throughout Hellas does not commit us to a view that Athens is—or is not—popular among the majority of her subjects. . . . Even if all social classes in the subject cities had been polled and a majority in each had been found—because of their commitment to the idea of civic autonomy—to be opposed or hostile to Athens, it would still be significant to know whether the *dēmos* was

[23] Glotz, *Op. cit.*, p. 326.

as strongly opposed as the upper classes. It is, in short, still relevant and important to determine whether all classes in the subject cities are equally committed to civic autonomy and equally hostile to Athens.

On this point, the evidence is clear enough: Plato notes in his seventh *Epistle* that the Athenians "maintained their empire for seventy years, because they possessed in the various cities men who were their friends."[24] Among whom were these friends, the *dēmos* or "the better sort of people"? Certainly not the latter, if the testimony of the Old Oligarch is to be believed.

> [E]missaries from Athens come out, and, according to common opinion, calumniate and vent their hatred upon the better sort of people, this is done on the principle that the ruler cannot help being hated by those whom he rules; but that if wealth and respectability are to wield power in the subject cities the empire of the Athenian People has but a short lease of existence. This explains why the better people are punished with infamy, robbed of their money, driven from their homes, and put to death, while the baser sort are promoted to honour.[25] . . .

The point must be reiterated, then, that in some part the Athenian Empire becomes as strong as it does because of the Panhellenic class conflicts between the *dēmos* and the elite and because of the support Athens receives from and gives to the *dēmos*. . . .

[Yet] Athens could never make itself Hellas' tribune of freedom; for she was fighting not for an abstract freedom or even for civic autonomy alone; the Athenians fought for such freedom as masters wish, the cherished right to have and to hold slaves without which they are masters no more. Fighting for their liberties and *their* ancient way of life, the citizens of Athens—like those in other places and later times—were never capable of renouncing their vested interests and prerogatives; they were caged within the barricade of their own institutional commitments. Like men under a sentence of death, they would not risk all in a desperate break with their own privileged past, and hoping against hope for a last minute reprieve that history never granted, they were dragged toward their fate.

Had Athens' restless groping toward empire succeeded, she might have unified Hellas by imposing an Athenian peace. Suppressing the internecine slaughter among Greeks, she might have marshaled their forces and led them in a commonly profitable attack upon the East. As Rome later did, Athens might have established a peace through domination; but Athens failed. . . .

[24] L. A. Post, trans., *Thirteen Epistles of Plato* (London: Oxford, 1925), the seventh *Epistle*, 332C.

[25] "The Old Oligarch," *Op. cit.*, p. 636.

## THE POWER VACUUM IN GREECE

The question of Greek unity and, in particular, the question of who will lead this unity, is posed in its most desperate form when both the great powers of Greece are smashed: when Athens is defeated by Sparta and when, with classic retribution, Sparta herself is defeated, first in 394 B.C. at the naval battle of Knidos, and some twenty-five years later and much more surprisingly to the Greek world when this Behemoth of Hellas meets a military genius, Thebes' Epaminondas, who trades on Sparta's inability to improvise and who crushes her finally on land.

These culminating events within Greece must also be placed in the larger context of the developing relationship between Greece and Persia. Persia's power in Greece increases during the Peloponnesian War and especially after 412 B.C. when, in hostility to the democracy at Athens, Persia opens her purse to Sparta. Indeed, it is Persian funds that finance the fleets with which Sparta finally starves Athens into submission. . . .

The inherent dilemma of Hellenic international politics is this: since none of the cities would agree voluntarily to the leadership of another, unity in Hellas can be won only if one city dominates all the others; yet for a city to win such dominance, she is commonly forced to seek aid from and therefore compromise with the Persians—as Sparta has and, indeed, as Epaminondas also does later. The desire to remove Persian influence motivates the Greeks toward unity, but this unity could be imposed only by a city with sufficient resources. These, however, are often sought from Persia, which is implacably opposed to Greek unity and whose defeat is, in any event, the whole point of such unity.

It is in this way that two policies—that of war against Persia and that of Hellenic unity—become fused into two sides of the same coin. War against Persia becomes an international and a domestic necessity for the Greek cities. It is needed in order to remove Persia's disunifying influence in Greece. It is needed in order to sack Persia so that the internal class tensions within each Greek city can be reduced; so that the *dēmoi* will have no motive for taxing their own rich, so that the rich will have no motive for violently curbing the *dēmoi*; and so that the two will not rend the city with class war. Conversely unity among the cities is needed so that the war against Persia can be prosecuted successfully. In order to establish this unity in Greece, however, the Hellenic power vacuum will have to be filled; some city strong enough to impose unity will have to be found.

It is in this context that various elements in Greece begin to search for a political power strong enough to unify Greece and to spearhead the Hellenic push against the East. It is in this context that there is increasing expression of a need for strong men to lead the cities and the idea of a powerful monarchy is rejuvenated. It is in this context, also, that the movement for Panhellenic unity begins to spread and to find its spokesmen.

The sophist Gorgias first raises the theme of Panhellenism at the Olympics, perhaps about 408 B.C., and Lysias takes it up again in 384, shortly after the King's Peace. The fullest and most significant expression of Panhellenism is voiced by the publicist and rhetorican Isocrates. Isocrates at first thinks to solve the problem of Hellenic leadership by calling for unity between Sparta and Athens. Since, however, the two are in his view to unite under Athens' leadership, it soon becomes clear that this strategy is hopeless. Isocrates then begins to look outside the core of Greek culture for a strong man who can dominate Hellas, turning at various times to Jason of Pherae, Dionysius I of Syracuse, and, finally, to Philip of Macedonia.

In his *Panegyricus,* Isocrates berates both the Spartans and the Athenians for their "utter madness, not only because we risk our lives fighting as we do over trifles when we might enjoy in security a wealth of possessions, but also because we continually impoverish our own territory while neglecting to exploit that of Asia."[26] The time for war against Persia is now opportune, he pleads; the king's satellites are in revolt and his territories are being overrun by his other enemies. Greece, he points out, is being devastated by wars and factionalism; it is being destroyed by disorganization and anarchy, with homeless men wandering through the land and with many obliged to enlist in foreign armies in order to live. Those who take up the call and march eastward, Isocrates promises, will enjoy a fame undying: "[H]ow great must we think will be the name and the fame and the glory which they will enjoy during their lives, or, if they die in battle, will leave behind them, . . . what encomiums should we expect these men to win who have conquered the whole of Asia?"[27] In the end, Isocrates returns again to the promise of pillage, inciting the Greeks with a conjured fantasy of the riches to be won: "[T]ry to picture to yourselves what vast prosperity we should attain if we should bring the war which now involves ourselves against the peoples of the continent, and bring the prosperity of Asia across to Europe."[28] . . .

[26] Isocrates, i. 203. Trans. G. Norlin, 3 vols. (London: Heinemann, 1928).
[27] *Ibid.,* i. 239.
[28] *Ibid.,* i. 241.

[In the Macedonian conquest], Hellas . . . at last found a solution to her travail. Only a temporary solution, to be sure; but history knows nothing of permanent solutions. Like all solutions, this, too, was purchased at a price; the price that was paid is what is called, in retrospect, the "decline" of Greek civilization. If this price seems high, what was the alternative? Surely the indefinite continuation of war within and between the cities augured no better.

The only constructive alternative—necessary if not sufficient— would have been a radical overhauling of Greek institutions, especially of its system of stratification and its narrowly exclusive image of community, a change which would have opened the city to the great number who lived in but were not of it. Yet, magnanimous though it may be, can we expect the ancient Greeks to have been wiser than ourselves? Can we expect them to have paid this price when, more than two thousand years later, there are still many who are unwilling to pay a like price, who refuse to open their communities to the outsiders who live among them, who refuse to change their customs in more than trivial ways and who blindly believe that, if only they cling tenaciously enough to their past, history will do for their social system what it has never done for another, give it a grant of immortality.

# 13

# Revolutionary War in Europe

*George Rudé*

≪≮≪≮≪≮≪≮≪≮≪≮≪≮≪≮≪≮≪≮≪≮≪≮≪≮≪≮≪≮≪≮≪≮≪≮≪≮≪≮≪≮≪≮≪≮≪≮

## EDITORS' COMMENT

In 1791 Edmund Burke composed a memoir for the Pitt ministry, published after his death as *Thoughts on French Affairs*. Here, among other passages of shrewd analysis and cold invective, the scandalized Jeremiah of conservative Europe wrote: "A system of French conspiracy is gaining grounds in every country. This system, happening to be founded on principles the most delusive indeed, but the most flattering to the the natural propensities of the unthinking multitude, and to the speculations of all those who think, without thinking very profoundly, must daily extend its influence," In the selection given below, George Rudé, one of the most creative contemporary scholars of the French Revolution, gives a masterful summary of the means by which the "French system" spread in Europe and what resistances and complicities the revolutionary effort to bring "liberty" to other "subject peoples" by force of arms encountered.

Obviously, there can be no question in an anthology of this nature of doing justice to the single most important internal war of modern and, probably, world history. The significant writings on the subject fill libraries and have fueled factions to this day. The enormously important sociological evaluations of the events of the period, beginning with Von Stein and Tocqueville, extending through the magistral writing of Jaurès and, later, Mathiez and Lefebvre, and blossoming today in the splendid works by Albert Soboul, Richard Cobb, Charles Tilly, and others, glut the student's appetite. Rudé himself has contributed the remarkable study *The Crowd in the French Revolution* and a number of fine essays.

In this section we have decided to concentrate for lively variety on the significant question of revolutionary spillover or transmission. Here, as in many areas, the French Revolution is a *locus classicus*. Although the development of events inside France between 1788 and 1792 is so complex as to seem virtually anarchic when one studies the play of factions, leaders, and classes, the translation of what Burke called "theoretic dogma" into a doctrine of war and international politics, is at least on the surface much clearer. The historic and limited, if often cruel, clash of dynastic interests was to be supplanted by a theory of liberation based on the rights of man and of the citizen. The people were to rise and assert their natural liberties; the rulers were to tremble. As Condorcet and other lesser diplomatists quickly put it, the conflict between France and Austria (and, soon, Prussia) of 1792 was to be a "war against the palaces, with peace to the cottages." The Constitution of 1791 had declared that henceforth France would fight only defensive wars. But it had also said that the Declaration of Rights applied not just to Frenchmen, but to all mankind. Thus an aggressive France could also be mankind's defender against centuries of abuse and tyranny.

Assuredly, the French revolutionists had certain reasons for being provoked into war (circles surrounding the beleaguered Louis XVI actively promoted it), but there cannot be much dispute that the ascendant leaders of the Gironde saw this as a holy war that would scourge Europe while it conveniently established their power at home. As far as their own fortunes were concerned, they were poor calculators: their mismanagement of military operations helped to cost them their eminence and, in some cases, their heads. Robespierre was more realistic in wishing to impose revolutionary unity on the nation before taking it into a foreign adventure.

In any case, it was paradoxically the government of the Committee of Public Safety that inherited the war after Danton had given it new energy, and it was these Jacobins of the Left who brought the doctrines of "revolutionary army" and "revolutionary war" to a maximum of effectiveness. Napoleon and his marshals were trained in this school.

When the French armies crossed into neighboring territories, they were confronted with theoretical and practical problems. The theoretical question was how to "liberate" the occupied peoples not only from their hereditary oppressors but from their inbred slavish political habits. The practical question was how to affirm the authority, security, and logistics of the invading forces. As can be imagined, philosophy often had to take a back seat to the demands of warfare and strategy.

Nevertheless, in greatly varying proportions, there were always social and economic groups—usually aspiring bourgeois and intellectuals—that welcomed the advance of the French for self-interested or dizzily cosmopolitan motives. There were also "Jacobins" and sympathizers in places where French troops never marched (for example, England and Ireland). In Wallonia, Flanders, the Rhineland, Northern Italy, and in other communities the organizations of townspeople collaborated with the French liberators and requested annexation or, at least, parallel constitutions of their own. But it can be doubted whether the masses of people had a similar wish to be liberated. In any event, we witness here the portentious sight of a cosmopolitan ideology, based at least loosely on class conflict and carried abroad under national banners.

Rudé brilliantly covers the many different circumstances with the expert eye of a synthesizer, assessing the comparative power of the penetration of the French ideology and the reasons for it. Simultaneously, he supports his arguments for the relative uniqueness of the French Revolution, its limitations as a missionary creed, and the varying but general unpreparedness of other societies to receive such a radical and democratic imprint—a point already made in 1791 by Robespierre. This species of interpretation runs counter to the famous thesis of "Atlantic" or "democratic" revolution in the eighteenth century, promoted by the historians R. R. Palmer and Jacques Godechot. Because the French uprising *generated* a good deal of foreign revolutionary activity as well as a substantial amount of popular resistance and because its radicalism limited its appeal—according to Rudé—it is something more than merely the most vivid case of Atlantic turbulence. Views on this question are well covered in Peter Amann (ed.), *The Eighteenth-Century Revolution: French or Western?* (Boston: Heath, 1963).

# REVOLUTIONARY WAR IN EUROPE

GEORGE RUDÉ

Even before the revolution in France, political movements were taking place in a number of European countries whose purpose was to challenge, in one form or another, the accepted traditions, institutions and loyalties of the old aristocratic society. Such movements we noted in the Austrian Netherlands (Belgium), the United Provinces (Holland), England, Ireland, Switzerland, and even in Austria and Poland. In none of these countries, however—with the possible exception of England—did these movements, whether promoted by "enlightened" monarchs, middle-class "patriots," or (more rarely) by the common people themselves, achieve any substantial results. In France, and in France alone, did a revolution take place in 1789 that was not only to overthrow governments and political institutions but to uproot and radically transform the social order itself.

Yet it is hardly surprising that the events taking place in France during the next ten years should have given a fresh edge and stimulus to the earlier movements and in some cases, given them a new revolutionary content. This happened sometimes by the propagation of the French revolutionary ideas; sometimes by the impact or occupation of France's crusading armies; and, to a greater or a lesser extent, by the action taken against their rulers by the people of the countries concerned. The eventual outcome was so to transform the Europe of the Old Regime that, at the close of the revolutionary and Napoleonic era in 1815, there was hardly a country west of Russia and Turkey and north of the Pyrenees whose society and political institutions had not been profoundly affected. From this result and the events that precede it some historians have concluded that the French Revolution was not so much a unique and particular phenomenon as merely one "phase" of a far wider convulsion that they have variously termed a

SOURCE. George Rudé, "Europe and the French Revolution," from *Revolutionary Europe, 1783–1815* (New York: Harper & Row, 1964), pp. 179–200, 220–222. Reprinted with permission of the publishers, Harper & Row and William Collins & Sons, Publishers, London. Copyright 1964 by George Rudé.

"western," "Atlantic," or "world" revolution.[1] (This is an important question to which we shall return, ahead.)

One early result of the French Revolution was to divide European society into two distinct and mutually hostile groups—its supporters or "patriots" on the one hand, and its opponents or "counter-revolutionaries" on the other. But this was not immediately apparent, as the fall of the Bastille and other early episodes were generally well received. There were, of course, exceptions: the Empress Catherine of Russia, the Kings of Spain and Sweden, and Edmund Burke in England were resolutely hostile almost from the start. Yet the more usual and immediate reaction was one of enthusiasm, relief, benevolent neutrality, or even a sort of malicious glee. "Liberal" Emperors like Joseph II and his successor, Leopold II, of Austria, though brothers of the Queen of France and as such anxious for her future, were not at first unduly disturbed. English dissenters, liberal Polish noblemen, and reformers everywhere, whether aristocratic or plebeian, drew hope and courage from the successful challenge to "despotism" in France. More remarkable still was the chorus of enthusiasm voiced in intellectual and artistic circles from Madrid to St. Petersburg: by English poets and scientists (Blake, Burns, Coleridge, Southey, Wordsworth, Priestley and Telford); by German poets and philosophers (Wieland, Klopstock, Fichte, Kant, Hegel and Herder); by Italian *illuminati*, rationalists and Free Masons; by Beethoven in Germany and Pestalozzi in Switzerland. Many of them changed sides later; but, at this stage, they might have applauded Wordsworth's poetic raptures and echoed Samuel Romilly's opinion (shared by Charles Fox) that the revolution in France was "the most glorious event, and the happiest for mankind, that has ever taken place since human affairs have been recorded." In some countries, as in England, there were other reasons for the general satisfaction expressed at the turn of events in France. France was the traditional enemy and her present convulsions would, it was supposed, weaken her for years to come as a commercial rival and active belligerent. Many thoughtful Frenchmen recognized this possibility and some told Arthur Young, even before the fall of the Bastille,

---

[1] The case has been argued by R. R. Palmer in "The Revolution of the West, 1763–1801," *Political Science Quarterly*, March 1954, and in *The Age of the Democratic Revolution*, vol. 1, *The Challenge*, pp. 4–6; by J. Godechot in *La Grande Nation* (2 vols. Paris, 1956), 1, 7–37 and *Les Revolutions* (1770–1799) (Paris, 1963); and by Godechot and Palmer in a joint contribution to the 10th Congress of Historical Sciences (Rome, 1955) entitled "Le Problème de l'Atlantique du XVIIIe au XXe siècle," *Relazioni del X Congresso Internazionale di Scienze Storiche* (Florence, n.d.), 172–239. See also P. Amann, ed., *The Eighteenth-Century Revolution: French or Western?* (Boston, 1963).

that "the English must be well contented at our confusion." This was certainly the view of Pitt's government; and Lord Grenville, then Home Secretary, wrote in September that the French would not "for many years be in a situation to molest the invaluable peace which we now enjoy." Pitt himself was expressing similar opinions until 1792.

So, for one reason or another, the French Revolution got off to a good start and, during 1789 and the greater part of 1790, there was a general readiness to let it take its course and comparatively little was said about the dangerous explosive consequences it might have for France's neighbours. But subsequent events and the construction put on them abroad were soon after to change this mood, among the privileged and propertied classes in particular, into one apprehension and concern. The French Revolution, it now appeared, was very different from the American: the drastic land reforms, the expropriation of the estates of the Church, the emigration of nobles and moderates and the tales that they told, all served to alarm conservative opinion. Meanwhile, democrats and reformers from other countries—large numbers of Belgians, Dutchmen and Germans; fewer English, Scots and Irish; and occasional Italians, Spaniards and Russians—had arrived in Paris, imbibed the new revolutionary ideas and, returning to or corresponding with their homelands, started clubs and newspapers in the image of the French; while the French press itself, like the paper edited by Camille Desmoulins, began to concern itself increasingly with the problem of France's fellow-"patriots" abroad. All this alarmed respectable society even more; so that when Edmund Burke, in November 1790, published his *Reflections on the Revolution in France*, he found a ready audience that bought up 30,000 copies and eleven editions of his work in little over a year. Unlike the majority of the intellectuals of his day, Burke condemned the Revolution from the start and as a whole. Far from welcoming it as a necessary means of curing France of age-old ills, he deplored the uprooting of the past, preached the sanctity of property and tradition and the virtues of gradual change, and even extolled the merits of the French higher clergy and Queen Marie Antoinette. With the "rights of man," he argued, the French were preparing to tear down the whole social fabric, not only in France but elsewhere, and to rush blindly along a path of total renovation. "It is with infinite caution," he asserted, "that any man should venture upon pulling down an edifice, which has answered in any tolerable degree for ages the common purposes of society, or on building it up again without having models and patterns of approved utility before his eyes." The author was congratulated on his work by the Empress Catherine; he found a host of admirers and imitators abroad—among them, Friedrich von Gentz in Germany and Mallet du Pan in Switzerland; and the *Reflections* became the almost unchallanged Bible of counter-revolution in every European country.

But naturally Burke met with hostility as well as support; and, in England, none of his critics challenged his defence of the Old Regime in France and his championship of conservative gradualism with greater vigour and success than Thomas Paine, already distinguished as a radical pamphleteer of the American Revolution. In his *Rights of Man* (1791), Paine replied to Burke's apologia of the French Court in a memorable phrase: "He pities the plumage, but forgets the dying bird"; and, striking at the core of his opponent's argument, he claimed that "the vanity and presumption of governing beyond the grave is the most ridiculous and insolent of tyranies." The book was badly received by the English propertied classes, particularly as Paine went on, in a second volume, to make a frontal assault on the British monarchy and established Church; but it was eagerly read by reformers, Protestant dissenters, democrats, London craftsmen and the skilled factory-hands of the new industrial north: its sales were prodigious and may have reached a million copies. So now the great "debate" on the French Revolution had started, and political opinion everywhere tended to divide into supporters and admirers of the French—generally to be found (though by no means universally) among the professional and manufacturing or trading middle class and urban craftsmen—and those who, fearing that property or religion or monarchy was everywhere endangered, became their most resolute opponents. The counter-revolution, thus launched, took a variety of guises differing from country to country. It might confine itself (as for long in England) to harrying and persecuting local "patriots" and democrats and blocking reform; to inciting "King and Church" riots among peasants and urban workers against the Revolution's supporters, as in Birmingham, Manchester, Brussels, Naples, and Madrid; or it might engage in open intervention against the Revolution in France itself, either by subsidizing the activities of French *émigrés* and their agents, or by joining military coalitions to restore the old order in France. In all countries outside France and her neighbours, it tended to promote a religious revival, to discredit Enlightenment and discourage reform. We shall return to some of these aspects later; here we are more immediately concerned with the impact of the French Revolution on the democratic and revolutionary movements in Europe.

It is hardly surprising that this impact should have varied greatly from one country to another. Some countries, like Russia and Turkey, were far removed from France's borders, and their traditions and social development made them almost totally immune to the penetration of revolutionary ideas. Others, like Bavaria and parts of Belgium, were protected from contagion by a pious peasantry and clerical domination. Spain, though sharing a common frontier with France, was similarly placed and had, morever, but a small educated middle class to act as the main channel for the new ideas. England's evolution had been very different, but she was made the most resistant by her relatively high standard of living, her island-position and her traditional enmity to France. There were countries, on the other hand, whose geographical position, cultural traditions and social evolution made them susceptible to French revolutionary ideas and to the penetration of her armies. Such countries were Holland, Belgium, the Rhineland, Switzerland and Italy; and, although all countries felt the impact of the events in France, it was in these alone that revolutions modelled on the French took place; yet even in these, as we shall see, no revolutionary government survived once French military protection had been withdrawn.

England was one of those countries in which the French Revolution, at its outbreak, evoked an enthusiastic response. There were various reasons for this: she had a free press; her rulers were delighted rather than outraged by the French challenge to "despotism;" religious dissenters, parliamentary reformers and Whig opposition Lords all saw some political advantage to be gained from events across the Channel; and, not least, she was going through the first throes and disturbances of an Industrial Revolution. Burke's onslaught naturally took its toll of early admirers; but even after opinion had begun to harden against the French, they found their supporters among a combination of social elements including middle-class radicals and reformers, Whig aristocrats, and spokesmen for the London craftsmen and industrial workers of the north. They engaged in varied activities. In London, Dr. Richard Price used the platform of the Revolution Society (founded to commemorate the "Glorious Revolution" of 1688) to extol the virtues of the French, and the Society sent a congratulatory address to the Constituent Assembly in Paris. Under the stimulus of French events, old reform societies revived and new ones came into being. Major Cartwright's Society for Promoting Constitutional Information, founded in 1780 and long since moribund, gained a new lease of life in 1791 and came under the more radical influence of John Horne Tooke and Thomas Paine. Constitutional and Reform Societies sprang up in Manchester, Sheffield, Norwich, Leeds, Nottingham and other cities, corresponded with France and collected boots and comforts for the French armies. The Foxite Whigs founded a more moderate Society of the Friends of the People and engaged in lengthy duels with Pitt and Grenville in the Houses of Parliament. And, most significant of all, a London Corresponding Society was started by Thomas Hardy in January 1792, which not only corresponded with the French and with its numerous affiliates at home, but acted as a centre for radical agitation in England: composed of craftsmen and small tradesmen, it was the first political association of workingmen to be formed in any country. Thus, in England, more than in any other country outside France, the Revolution left its mark on the industrial workers. Yet it was not deep enough at this stage to survive persecution and war. After 1792, Pitt's government took active steps to suppress the "Jacobins" and reform societies in both England and Scotland: the severest punishment was that meted out to the Scottish "martyrs"—Muir, Palmer, Margarot and others—who were transported to Botany Bay for their part in convening a British Convention in 1793. London juries were less harsh than the Scottish Courts of Judiciary, but the radical movement gradually subsided and lay dormant for nearly fifteen years. A final flicker appeared, however, in the mutinies of Spithead and the Nore in 1797. Primarily, these were seamen's revolts against low wages, brutal discipline and filthy food; but Parker, leader at the Nore, was a member of the United Irishmen, and the central committee formed on Parker's ship proposed to sail to the Texel and petition the French National Convention for protection. But it is equally significant that not a single ship obeyed the signal to sail and that the Spithead mutineers actually demanded to be sent against the French once their grievances had been met. For, by this time, the first phase of popular "Jacobinism" in England was all but spent.

Strangely enough, "Jacobinism" stood a greater chance of success in Ireland than it ever did in England or Scotland. It might be supposed that the Irish, being predominantly peasants and Catholics like the Spanish and Bavarians, would have been less likely to become infected with the ideas of the Enlightenment and the French Revolution than the English or the Scots. This would have been true enough had it not been for the fact that the Irish rebellion, temporarily appeased by the concessions of 1782-4, broke out again, under cover of the European war, in 1794. It took two forms: the national independence movement of the United Irishmen, led by the Catholic Lord Edward Fitzgerald and the Protestant Wolfe Tone: and the massive agrarian revolt of the land-hungry Irish peasantry. The aristocratic and middle-class leaders were undoubtedly men of the Enlightenment: they had read Rousseau, they preached the "rights of man" and religious toleration, and Tone and Fitzgerald came to France to discuss their plans with the National Convention. The Catholic peasants, too—such was their hatred for the traditional enemy across St. George's Channel—burned candles for the victory of French arms and prepared to welcome a French invasion. Hoche's first attempt to land in the winter of 1796–7 was premature and proved abortive. A second attempt was planned for the spring of 1798; but the British government got the wind of the plans and arrested the rebel leaders as they were about to sail for France. The present rebellion, intended to coincide with a landing that failed to take place, broke out in June and was pitilessly repressed. When General Humbert's fleet at last arrived in September 1798, it was already too late. It was the last attempt, and England escaped (perhaps less miraculously than it appeared at the time) from the greatest danger she had to face before Napoleon's invasion-threat of 1805.

Poland, too, though her social structure quite unfitted her to follow in the path of the French Revolution, was profoundly affected by the events taking place in France. France had long been allied to Poland and of all countries was the one to which Poles concerned for their country's survival looked with the greatest expectancy for aid to resist the predatory ambitions of her Russian, Prussian and Austrian neighbours. The outbreak of revolution in France was greeted with varying degrees of enthusiasm by Polish intellectuals, liberal members of the *szlachta* (nobility) and even by their King, Catherine's one-time lover and *protégé*, Stanislas Poniatowski. As with the Irish, it was the fear of foreign domination that brought them into the French revolutionary camp; but the Poles went further. They formed a "philosophical" club at Prince Radziwill's home, which earned them Catherine's irate epithet of "Jacobin", and, by a political *coup d'état*, compelled the diet in May 1791 to adopt a constitution in many respects similar to that adopted the same year by the French. It introduced important innovations: the diet was declared representative of "the nation as a whole;" the *liberum veto*, which had long obstructed all legislative and executive initiative, was abolished; the throne was made hereditary and judges elective. Yet the constitution, the creation of liberal nobles, remained essentially aristocratic. No more than a handful of bourgeois were admitted to the diet and, more important, the social order remained as little altered by these reforms as that of Russia and Prussia had been by those of their respective "enlightened despots:" the peasants, it is true, were placed under the protection of the law, but serfdom remained. Yet even these minor reforms were too much for the conservative magnates, who invited Catherine to send in a Russian army to compel Stanislas to withdraw the constitution; the second partition of Poland by her three powerful neighbours followed soon after. It was this second national humiliation that prompted the patriot Kosciusko to launch an insurrection in the spring of 1794. This time, something like a national-popular movement developed and Kosciusko was supported by the craftsmen and working people of Warsaw. But the French were both unable and unwilling to lend support (they had, by now, lost all sympathy with the liberal aristocrats of Poland), a third partition followed, and Poland for some years disappeared from the map.

A country whose society and institutions were similar to those of Poland was Hungary. She, too, had her "national" troubles: we have noted her disputes with Maria Theresa and, above all, with the Emperor Joseph II. But Hungarian nationalism, in so far as it existed at all, was skin-deep: the great noble families normally spoke German and only paraded their attachment to the Magyar tongue and traditions in order to win popular sympathy for their private vendettas with the Habsburg monarchy, which had encroached on their "liberties." The leaders of the aristocratic revolt against Joseph quoted from Rousseau and Voltaire but, when Leopold succeeded Joseph, they insisted that serfdom be restored on their estates as the price of their allegiance. The Hungarian nobility, however, continued to parade revolutionary sentiments and, in 1793, the diet drew up a constitutional act and a Declaration of Rights of Man in imitation of the French; yet they were meekly withdrawn when the new Emperor, Francis II, who had turned his back on the liberal experiments of his predecessors, opposed them. In fact, in Hungary as in Austria, the only genuine "Jacobins," who not only believed in democracy but had a social as well as a political programme, were small groups of middle-class officers, writers, lawyers, professors and civil servants—men like Lacskovicz, a former officer, and Condorcet's friend Martinovicz—who had been trained as much in the school of "Josephism" as of the Enlightenment and the French Revolution. Martinovicz and his six fellow "conspirators" were executed in May 1795, a few months after two of his Austrian counter-parts had been hanged in Vienna. They failed because they were divorced from the people and were unable to turn to political account the land-hunger and war-weariness of the peasantry; but their ideas survived and it is they rather than the rebellious noblemen of 1788–90 that were the real forerunners of Hungary's first national revolution in 1848.

Of the countries bordering France, none was so little affected by her example as Spain. Spanish institutions and society in the eighteenth century were, in some respects, similar to the French. But her middle class was weaker and less mature; her peasantry was poorer, less literate and more closely subjected to the domination of priest and *señor;* her nobility had, in consequence, less inducement than the French to compete for control of the central government; and, above all, the country was sharply divided between a relatively prosperous north and east and a poverty-striken centre and south. For these and other reasons, the Enlightenment had made little headway outside the main urban centres, there had been no "aristocratic revolt," and the French Revolution had, even at its inception, roused little sympathy and support. In addition, the Spanish government and Church resorted from the start to a systematic repression of "patriots" and imposed a blanket of silence on all news from France: even Burke's *Reflections* were suspect for the problems that they raised and were for long condemned by the Inquisition! In consequence, there was little that Spanish democrats could do other than to emigrate across the border, and small groups of "Jacobins" gathered on French soil, at Bayonne and elsewhere. Even when French armies began, in 1793, to occupy Spanish towns and provinces, they met with a remarkable ideological resistance. A veritable crusade for "Religion, King and Country" was preached against the godless French and won popular support even in large cities like Barcelona and Madrid. In 1797 and 1798, there were popular revolts against rising food prices in Guadalajara, Seville and Asturias; but, by then, Spain was France's ally against England. The significant point to note is that war with Britain was more unpopular than war with France and that Spain provides an early example of that militant "Church and King" conservatism that, in Catholic peasant communities in particular, proved to be an important auxiliary to the armies of France's enemies.

"Jacobinism" made little headway (though it existed) in Russia, the Balkans or the Scandinavian countries—still less in such distant outposts as Constantinople, Aleppo and Smyrna—and it only remains to consider here the early impact of the Revolution on the peoples adjacent to France's eastern and south-eastern borders. Of these . . . the Dutch, the Belgians and Genevans had already become involved, before July 1789, in political disputes with their rulers. The Dutch Patriots, when abandoned by their French allies before the Orangist victory of 1787, had closed down their clubs and societies; but these reappeared two years later with the news of the outbreak of revolution in France. However, the Dutch Patriots were cautious and relatively inactive; and, in January 1793, after Belgium had been invaded by French armies, the French representative in Amsterdam reported to the Ministry of Foreign Affairs in Paris that the Patriot party was non-existent at the Hague and weak in Rotterdam and Amsterdam. Besides, unlike the Jacobins in France, it was largely composed of rich merchants and manufacturers who, though dissatisfied with both Stadholder and city regents, had retained a healthy respect for property and feared for their businesses and fortunes. Consequently, the Patriots showed little inclination to support the French armies when they occupied Dutch Brabant for a while in February 1793. In the following weeks, as Dumouriez withdrew through Belgium before deserting to the Austrians, Patriot activity revived. But two of the seven provinces— Zeeland and Guelderland—remained obstinately attached to the Stadholder's cause: and, even elsewhere, the majority of simple townsmen and country-dwellers appeared to see the French as the mere allies of the bourgeoisie. So, contrary to the early hopes of the French, the long-awaited Dutch Patriot revolution held fire and only broke out when the French occupied the country in January 1795.

In Belgium . . . something like a national revolt against Joseph II's innovations had begun in 1787. In its opening stages, it took the form of an "aristocratic revolt" led by the Estates party of Van der Noot; but soon a rival leadership appeared in the moderate democratic party of J.-F. Vonck. As in England and the United Provinces, the outbreak of revolution in France was received with great enthusiasm throughout the country; but here it also acted as a stimulus to open rebellion. Vonck entered immediately into contact with the new authorities in Paris; "patriot" volunteers were enrolled in Brabant and in the neighbouring independent bishopric of Liège; the people rose in Liège and drove out their bishop; a "patriot" army under General Vandermersch expelled the Austrians from Ghent and Brussels; and, in December, the Austrians, having offered little resistance, withdrew from the Belgian provinces. Thus the Belgians, having attained their national independence, looked like they were following in the footsteps of the French; and the Vonckists prepared to reorganize their institutions on more democratic lines. But events in France, while momentarily strengthening the democrats at the expense of their rivals, also had the effect of driving a deeper wedge between the Belgian parties and of dividing the country in two. The Estates party had the solid backing of the Catholic Church and the merchant guilds; with their support they managed, in January, to proclaim a United States of Belgium, based on the more conservative American model and not on the French, as desired by their rivals. A "witch-hunt" was launched against the Vonckists, whose moderate reformist aims were represented as part of a sinister plot to destroy Belgium's traditions and fundamental "liberties." In Brussels, which in December had hailed the "patriots" and volunteers, a popular insurrection broke out against them in March. The houses of wealthy Vonckists were pillaged and destroyed; the volunteers were stoned and disarmed; and one "patriot" leader was forced to his knees and made to declare: "I recognize, by order of the Brussels people, that the Patriotic Society of which I am a member is nothing but a band of rogues." Many of the democrats were arrested, others sought refuge in France. Thus an "aristocratic revolt," when faced with the consequences of a national revolutionary uprising, had turned to counter-revolution. Profiting by these divisions, the Austrian armies returned in December 1790, re-installed the prince-bishop of Liège and restored the *status quo* in the Belgian provinces. With their patrician rivals removed from office, many of the democrats returned from exile to await their own and their country's "liberation" at the hands of the French.

The Swiss cantons and their associated territories were composed of rural areas, some of which enjoyed a sort of primitive democracy, and city-states governed by bishops and merchant aristocracies. This oligarchic form of rule had already . . . been challenged in the 1760's, with temporary success, in the city of Geneva. The revolution in France helped to develop the democratic movements and to spread it to other cantons. In 1790, a Helvetian Club was formed in Paris among the Swiss refugees and democrats resident in the capital; they ran their own newspaper, disseminated revolutionary propaganda in the cantons, and invited their countrymen at home to follow their example. The Swiss Germans also caught the contagion from the neighbouring French—but German-speaking—province of Alsace. In Basel the "patriots," led by Peter Ochs and Gobel (later Constitutional Bishop of Paris), stirred up such an agitation among the peasants that the bishop took fright and called in Austrian troops to restore order; but after the first French victories in this region, the democrats voted for union with France, and a part of the bishop's territories became the new French department of Mont-Terrible (March 1793). Peasant insurrections also occurred in the rural districts of Vaud and Valais, but were sternly repressed and their leaders hanged. In Geneva, the democrats, robbed of their earlier partial victory by French intervention (1782), took power again in December 1792 and extended full rights of citizenship to all, including both Burghers and Natives. A revolutionary committee was set up to govern the city, Jacobin clubs were formed (there were fifty in 1793), a Revolutionary Tribunal was installed, and a "reign of terror" followed, in the course of which patricians were imprisoned and executed, or merely heavily taxed. But while this was the most advanced stage that the revolution ever reached in Switzerland, it was probably in German-speaking Zurich that the French Revolution had its largest following: among them were such distinguished local notables as the painter Fuseli, the educational reformer Pestalozzi, and the Rolands' friend, the Protestant pastor Lavater. They formed a revolutionary club which, in 1794, launched a comprehensive programme of political and social reform. The "conspirators" were rounded up and 260 persons were imprisoned or exiled. But the agitation continued and spread to the neighbouring rural districts of Glarus and St. Gall; and, in September 1798, the peasants of St. Gall compelled their abbot to agree to commute a part of their feudal obligations for a small monetary payment. It was, in fact, a strength of the Swiss revolutionary movement that, in several cantons, in contrast with that in the Dutch and Belgian provinces, it was compounded of both middle-class urban and peasant elements.

German reactions to the French Revolution were, at the outset, similar to the English, but they were more varied and the results proved more lasting. Apart from a small number of large sovereign states like Prussia, Bavaria and Saxony, Germany was composed of a congeries of Free Cities and petty principalities, both lay and ecclesiastical, virtually sovereign but still owing some allegiance to the moribund Holy Roman Empire: the Rhineland states alone, with a population of 1,300,000, had no fewer than 97 separate rulers—dukes, margraves, landgraves, Imperial knights and ecclesiastical electors and princes. The confusion and multiplicity of political institutions were almost matched by those of social rank, the middle classes were generally excluded from public affairs, and serfdom was prevalent outside the western regions and the single state of Baden in the south. Yet in sharp contrast with these tenacious survivals from the medieval past was the vigour of Germany's intellectual life and institutions. No other country had more and better universities; none had so thriving a press (1,225 journals were launched in the 1780's alone); and few countries, if any, had produced so rich a crop of literary and scholarly talent as Germany in the past thirty years. It was the age of the *Aufklärung* (Enlightenment), Goethe's and Schiller's romantic period of *Sturm und Drang* ("Storm and Stress"), and of a profound literary and cultural revival. Among "enlightened" ideas, those of Montesquieu and Rousseau had taken root and, particularly since the American Revolution, had been eagerly discussed in the press, the universities, Masonic lodges, literary clubs and groups of *illuminati*. In such circles the Revolution met with an almost unanimous response. The fall of the Bastille was hailed by Johannes von Müller, Swiss historian and secretary to the Archbishop of Mainz, as the happiest occasion since the fall of the Roman Empire and by the historian Herder as the most momentous since the Reformation. Among poets acclaiming the event were the venerable Klopstock, Wieland, Bürger, Hölderlin, Tieck and Wackenroder; Goethe and Schiller, however, though not outspokenly hostile, remained comparatively unmoved. Other supporters included, among philosophers, Kant, Hegel, Fichte and Schlegel; and, among political journalists, Schlözer at Göttingen and Archenholz and Nicolai at Berlin. Hamburg, Klopstock's city, celebrated with odes and banquets; and even rulers like the Duke of Brunswick, the Duke and Duchess of Gotha and Prince Henry of Prussia joined in the chorus of praise.

Already, there were a few dissentient voices, including old-style Whigs like Rehberg and Brandes at Göttingen. These were inevitably joined by others as the Revolution developed: as the end of "despotism" and "privilege" was followed by the sale of Church lands, emigration, the fall and execution of the King, Terror, Jacobin dictatorship and democratic experiment; and as Burke's *Reflections* began to exercise its spell over more conservative minds. An early convert was Schlözer who, after the October "days" at Versailles, began to lament the "mindless tyranny of the mob." Johannes von Müller, so enthusiastic at the start, was wavering in 1790 and, by 1793, was declaiming against "those madmen and monsters in France". Even more thorough was the conversion of Friedrich von Gentz who, having been an admirer of Rousseau and Mirabeau, was won over by Burke and, next to Burke himself, became the leading oracle of the counter-revolutionary crusade against France. To others, more radical, it was the Terror or the execution of Louis that brought disillusionment—among them, Wieland, Jean-Paul Richter, Schleiermacher, Klopstock and Hegel; while Goethe and Schiller, though by no means indifferent, maintained their Olympian detachment. Some, however, never fully lost their enthusiasm— the poets Bürger, Tieck and Wackenroder; the philosophers Herder, Fichte and (more hesitantly) Kant; and Georg Forster, librarian of the University of Mainz, who not only condoned the execution of the King and welcomed the Republic, but became a leading figure in the revolution at Mainz that followed its occupation by General Custine's troops in the autumn of 1792.

In the long run, the attitude of the intellectuals was, no doubt, of considerable importance for Germany's future. But of more immediate significance was the impact of the Revolution in other quarters— on the bourgeoisie, politicians and peasants in a number of cities and states. Of these, none were more exposed to the French "contagion"

than those in the Rhineland provinces, adjoining France's eastern border. The dominions of the Electors of Cologne, Treves and Mainz and
of the rulers of Baden and the Bavarian Palatinate were caught, as
it were, in pincers between the revolutions in Alsace and Liège. In
Baden, peasant disturbance was minor and quickly suppressed; in the
Palatinate, there were mutinies at Landau and Zweibrücken, and peasants revolted against the hunting rights of the nobility and refused
to pay their dues. The ecclesiastical principalities of Cologne, Treves
and Mainz were more deeply affected, partly through the influence
of Elogius Schneider, ex-Franciscan and former professor at Bonn, who,
expelled by the Elector of Treves, took a university post across the
border at Strasbourg, where he became a leading political figure. In
Cologne, the Third Estate, taking their cue from the French, demanded
an end of fiscal inequality; at Bonn, the "patriots" formed a revolutionary club; while in Mainz, whose Elector made himself doubly unpopular by following Austria and Prussia into war with France (April
1792), townsmen rioted against rising prices and peasants against their
landlord's exactions. So here, as in the Swiss cantons, the victorious
French armies of 1792 and 1794 were to find a situation that favoured
their political and military aims.

Beyond the Rhine, the French impact was less direct and was
only fully felt in Napoleon's time. In Saxony, peasants protested
against the *corvée* and feudal dues; but Saxony, like Mecklenburg
in the north, was among those areas that emerged relatively unscathed
from the whole Revolutionary and Napoleonic experience. Bavaria was
hardly affected until the Directory, when Munich was for a while
occupied by the French, and the *illuminati* and their leader, Montgelas,
began to exercise considerable influence at Court. Hamburg, as we
saw, greeted the Revolution with banquets; and, a year later, the liberal
Hamburg merchants, inspired by Georg Sieveking, a wealthy mer-
chant-prince and patron of letters, celebrated the Feast of the Federation and continued to do so for some years to come. But the French
connection was valued as much for commercial as for political reasons;
and once Hamburg found herself (at the Empire's bidding) at war
with France alongside the English, enthusiasm for England began to
eclipse that for France; and later, having been annexed by Napoleon,
Hamburg was one of the few German states to revolt against his rule.
In Prussia, the impact of the Revolution went deeper and was more lasting. Frederick the Great's successor, Frederick William II, was a weak
and indolent ruler and his reign saw an aristocratic and clerical revival.
Yet the French found allies at Court: Prince Henry and Hertzberg,
Frederick's old foreign minister, who led a peace-party that helped

to shorten the war that broke out with France in 1792. The liberal bourgeoisie, though wavering, was never entirely hostile to the Revolution; the younger officers were said to be infected with French ideas; and, in Silesia, between 1794 and 1796, secret societies were formed by a group including a business man, an army captain and two government officials. Silesia was also the scene of considerable popular disturbance: in the winter of 1792, peasants refused to pay dues to the Junkers; soon after, weavers rioted over wages and called on the French to come to their aid. In 1793, there were riots in Breslau and a bloody revolt among Silesian Poles; and, in 1796, a general "spirit of revolt" among Silesian peasants was attributed to the agitation carried on by troops demobilized after the war with France. In the long run, the greater part of Germany emerged radically transformed from the Revolutionary and Napoleonic period; but, in these earlier years, it was not the south, the north or the centre but these peripheral frontier regions—the Rhenish and Silesian provinces—that were the most deeply affected.

In Italy, too, there were factors that favoured the progress of French revolutionary ideas: a large educated, and mainly anti-clerical, middle class, already steeped in the teachings of the Enlightenment; widespread resentment at the alien domination of Austrians in the north and centre and Spaniards in the south; a nobility that, in many respects, shared the advanced views and political aspirations of the educated middle class; and a seething mass of peasant discontent. After the initial enthusiasm, the weaknesses, however, became equally evident. There was the difficulty, in a country so divided, of concerting the scattered efforts of the various groups which, in response to the revolutionary doctrines of the French, began to think in terms of national unity and liberation. There was, too, the even greater problem of how to find a common political meeting-ground between the wealthy middle-class or aristocratic "Jacobins" and the impoverished peasants and urban masses. The first of these difficulties would begin to be overcome when Bonaparte himself pointed the way by imposing something like a unified system of administration over the greater part of the Italian peninsula; the second would prove a more intractable problem in the poor and Catholic south than in the more prosperous and anticlerical north. The northern Kingdom of Piedmont and Sardinia had, moreover, the additional advantage, from the point of view of would-be revolutionaries, of lying close to the French border and of enclosing the province of Savoy, where a movement for union with France had already long been in existence. Savoy was the first Italian province to rebel and, in 1789, peasants who had won

freedom from manorial dues refused to pay their landlords any compensation. Soon after, in neighbouring Piedmont, peasants rioting for
land-reform declared themselves to be citizens of France; while, in
Turin, its capital, there was a "Jacobin" attempt to overthrow the
government in 1794. Francophile sympathies also united the educated
classes and the common people at Bologna and in other parts of the
north; but, further south, free-thinking bourgeois, *illuminati* and middle-class "Jacobins" tended to stand alone, or even to be the object
of deep popular hatred and suspicion. In Naples, the Masonic lodges
and "Patriot" societies were probably stronger and more numerous
than anywhere else in Italy; but when the local "Jacobins" attempted
to lead an insurrection against their rulers in 1794, the common people
remained obstinately aloof. Not surprisingly, the Church and governing
circles were able, as in Spain and Belgium, to exploit these antipathies
and turn them to their own advantage. In January 1793, we find
a French envoy, Hugo de Bassville, being massacred in the course
of a popular riot; and, in Naples, the city poor, if hostile to "Jacobinism," which they associated with the middle-class rich, were all the
more responsive to the call of "Church and King."[2]

The reaction of Europe to the first years of the revolution in
France was, then, an extremely varied one. Leaving aside for the moment the counter-revolution and the attitudes of governments, how
can we briefly summarize the impact of the Revolution on the countries
of Europe on the eve of France's military expansion and conquests?
On the one hand, there were countries like Turkey, Russia, Spain,
the Balkans, Austria, and Hungary, and the Scandinavian states which,
in spite of local pockets of "Jacobinism," remained at this stage at
least, largely untouched by the revolution in France. There were countries like England and Scotland where the initial support for French
revolutionary ideas had, by 1795, died a natural death, or had been
stamped out or driven underground by repression and the impact of
war. There were others like Poland and Ireland where, for quite exceptional reasons, the French Revolution had met with a remarkable degree of support; but, lying beyond the range of French military assistance, their rebellions were easily crushed. Among France's closer
neighbours, Holland's abortive Patriot "revolution" of 1787 had been
given a new shot in the arm by the events in France, but showed
little sign of developing into open revolt by the spring of 1793. In
Belgium alone, a revolutionary situation was already present by the

---

[2] See E. J. Hobsbawm, *Primitive Rebels* (Manchester, 1954), pp. 112–113; and
*The Age of Revolution* (London, 1962), pp. 82–3.

summer of 1789, and, in Liège and Brabant in particular, was brought to a head by the impact of the revolution in France; but, subsequently, the democratic movement had been weakened by internal counterrevolution and the restoration of Austrian authority. Finally, the impact of the French Revolution had been considerable in parts of Germany and Switzerland and most of Italy; but, as in Holland, enthusiasm for French ideas had been largely confined to the urban middle class and educated circles and it was only in a handful of Swiss cantons, in the German Rhineland and Prussian Silesia and in the Italian provinces of Piedmont and Savoy that anything like a popular revolutionary movement had, by 1793, sprung up in the wake of the events in France. . . .

Are we dealing here with an essentially *French* revolution with its offshoots in other western countries; or are Professors Godechot and Palmer correct in suggesting that all these revolutions, the French and the American included, are merely "phases" of a more general "democratic" revolution of the West? There might perhaps be some point in attaching a general label of this kind to all the revolutions taking place in Europe and America from, say, 1550 to 1850—covering not only the American and the French, but the Dutch of the sixteenth, the English of the seventeenth, and various South American and European revolutions of the early nineteenth century. All of these raise, in one form or another, common problems relating to feudalism and capitalism, democracy and national sovereignty. In this wider context, the American Revolution of the 1760's and seventies may appear to be as closely linked with the English Revolution of 120 years before as with the French of twenty years after; and the German and Italian revolutions are seen in full flood rather than at their earliest beginnings. But if one chooses merely to consider the revolutions of the eighteenth century, one is struck rather by differences than similarities and by the small number that can claim to be revolutions in their own right. In Europe, the only "democratic" (or, more accurately, "liberal") revolutions taking place at this time in any way independent of the French were those in Liège, Brussels and Geneva; but the first two of these had been defeated by 1790 and only revived as the result of French military occupation. Revolutionary movements were also germinating, inspired by the French example, in the Rhineland, Piedmont and parts of Switzerland; but they only came to a head on the approach of France's armies. Elsewhere in Western Europe, revolutions, though owing something to local "patriots" and local conditions, were largely imposed by the French. In fact, of 29 constitutions adopted in European countries other than France between 1791 and 1802, all except three (two Genevan and one Polish) were the outcome of French intervention.[3] So strictly speaking, outside America, and perhaps the tiny state of Geneva, the only revolution in its own right was the French.

Even more important perhaps is the fact that the revolution in France went much further than elsewhere—not only in the sense that it was more violent, more radical, more democratic and more protracted, but that it posed problems and aroused classes that other European revolutions (and the American, for that matter) left largely untouched. This was partly due to a different historical development in these countries from that in France and partly to the fact that the French after July 1794 (when they began to impose their ideas on their neighbours) were no longer interested in promoting the democratic ideals of 1793—and ruthlessly crushed the Piedmontese when they attempted to do so. If we are only concerned with the spread of the ideas of the Enlightenment, the permanent legislation of the revolutionary assemblies and the liberal "principles of 1789," then the similarities between the revolutions in France and in these other countries are strikingly close: all went, with greater or lesser thoroughness, through a common bourgeois revolution, which destroyed the old feudal institutions and obligations, expropriated the estates of the Church, abolished serfdom, legal inequalities and the privileged order, and declared careers to be "open to talent"; and this process continued, though in a muted form, in Germany and Poland under the Empire. Important as this is, it leaves out an essential element of the French Revolution: the active participation of the common people from 1789 onwards and all the consequences that flowed from it. John Adams, it may be remembered, criticized the Dutch Patriots of 1787 for having been "too inattentive to the sense of the common people"; and they continued to be so. And this was by no means a failure peculiar to the Dutch: Belgian, Roman and Neapolitan "Jacobins" were equally divorced from the people and made little serious effort to bridge the gap. In some of these countries, it is true, there were temporary movements in which both "patriots" and peasants or urban poor took part and in which the latter classes voiced the slogans and ideas of their bourgeois allies; but these were exceptional and short-lived. In France alone, owing to the particular circumstances in which the revolution developed and broke out (and certainly not to any innate Gallic quality!), the "Fourth Estate" became the indispensable ally of the Third, exacted its reward, and even built up a distinctive political movement

[3] H. B. Hill, "The Constitutions of Continental Europe, 1789–1813," *Journal of Modern History*, VIII (1936), 82.

of its own. So in France we have such phenomena as the peasant "revolution," the *sans-culotte* movement of 1793, the Jacobin Dictatorship, the *levée en masse* and *armées révolutionnaires*, and the social experiments and Republic of the Year II. These factors reappeared, often in more advanced forms, in the European revolutions of the nineteenth century; but, with minor exceptions, they did not in those of the 1790's—and still less so under the Consulate and Empire. In this sense, the revolution in France, though casting its shadow all over Europe, remained quite peculiar and unique.

# 14

# The Revolution of February 1848

*Lorenz Von Stein*

≪-≪-≪-≪-≪-≪-≪-≪-≪-≪-≪-≪-≪-≪-≪-≪-≪-≪-≪-≪-≪-≪-≪-≪-≪-≪-≪-≪-≪-≪-≪-≪-≪-

## EDITORS' COMMENT

Virtually unknown to English-speaking students and ignored in most intellectual histories of the nineteenth century, Lorenz von Stein (1815–1890) is, nonetheless, the founder of German sociology and the inventor of the operational concept of the *proletariat*. For his pioneering explorations of the class dimension of various phases of revolution in France, he surely merits a place beside Alexis de Tocqueville as an ancestral social theorist. One wonders what would have been his position with posterity if *he* had written *Democracy in America!* But the plain fact is that, aside from Kaethe Mengelberg's introduction to the new (unfortunately abridged) translation of *The History of the Social Movement in France*, from which this excerpt is taken, an article by J. Weiss in the *International Review of Social History* (VII, 1, 1963), and a rather hurried treatment by Herbert Marcuse in *Reason and Revolution*, Von Stein is no more than an archive among us. Therefore, we are doubly gratified to include in this anthology his brief case study of the revolutionary event that he was able to observe most closely at the great watershed of modern class conflict in 1848.

Von Stein began his academic career in Schleswig and spent the last thirty years of his life as a Professor of Political Economy in Vienna. The present work and two preceding studies on *Socialism and Communism in Contemporary France* are the product of four years spent in Paris when the scholar was still very young, in his late twenties. Von Stein moved in the same circles of socialist intellectual ferment that stimulated the youthful Karl Marx. In fact, the *Social Movement* reflects the most radical period in the intellectual life of a thinker who would later become a constitutional and public policy advisor to the Austrian monarchy and to the Meiji reformers of Japan.

There is a rather strong consensus among scholars that Marx and Engels got quite a lot from Von Stein—naturally, without acknowledgment—including their sociological grasp of the proletariat as the universal revolutionary class, which Marx had derived speculatively from his Hegelian and Feuerbachian studies. However, because of the common atmosphere in which Marx and Von Stein elaborated their theories, the indebtedness cannot be precisely determined. What is manifest is how both thinkers assimilated their wide knowledge of French socialist ideas to a general framework of Hegelian philosophy.

Hegel had postulated the philosophical state as a guarantor of freedom and as a moderator of the friction-ridden and group-interested clashes of civil society. In Von Stein's hands this notion furnishes the takeoff for a sociological transformation: (1) in theory, state and society are absolutely dichotomized, the former (under ideal circumstances) becoming the sphere of freedom and the epitome of the general interest, the latter being the perpetual arena of class struggle; (2) in practice, however, the state is always captured by a factional interest of civil society—a ruling class—and is bent to its purposes. Thus the real state is far from free and far from supreme, as Hegel had proclaimed. Of course, the rise of industrial property and of an industrial working class had done much to provoke these revisions in thought.

Von Stein postulates "natural laws" of social change, in which a theory of revolution, based on the unending dialectic of state and society, is prominent. "Since the higher class of society is unable to change the (existing) state," Stein writes (*Social Movement*, p. 58), "or to eliminate the state altogether, or to resist its power, it aims if possible at taking exclusive control of government power." Modern society has affirmed this cleavage by sharpening the distinction between the property-holders and the propertyless. Mutually exclusive demands lead inevitably to struggle. "This struggle between the two major social classes is the *revolution;* the prerequisite for it is the acquisition of property through labor by members of the dependent class; its goal is the realization of the idea of justice, its objective a corresponding new constitution" (*Ibid*, p. 77). Such is the essence of bourgeois revolution. But Von Stein permits himself to speculate that there is a further stage of *social revolution* in which "the proletariat asks the ruling class, in the name of equality, for something which this class neither desires to offer nor possibly can offer" (*Ibid*, p. 89). Unlike Marx, Von Stein refuses to grant finality or historical virtue to this clash: there remains eternally the problem of the state and its unilateral possession.

These are the terms in which the following excerpt covering the February 1848 revolution, the ultimate work of the industrial bourgeoisie, should be understood. From the perspective of the aspiring ruling class, it was a battle for the unrestricted political rights associated with the nature of an industrial society and its subjacent property relationships. The strictly *social* (or proletarian) part of the revolution was yet to come. It is of considerable interest to compare Von Stein's arguments in this and surrounding chapters with Marx's analysis of the "abstract universality" of extensive suffrage in his essay, "On the Jewish Question" (1843).

# THE REVOLUTION OF FEBRUARY 1848

## Lorenz Von Stein

The February Revolution is the most significant event in the whole history of modern Europe. It proved with elemental power that neither the highest form of monarchy nor the greatest danger of the social revolution will prevent the property-owning class of industrial society from destroying any personal government which does not respect the principle of popular representation.

If one studies the history of this revolution from its early beginnings, . . . one discovers that, considered as a single event, it had three very definite, essentially different phases. The difference among these phases is not superficial. It is deeply embedded in the conditions of French history. . . . The monarchy was well aware of being the object of increasing antagonism on the part of the ruling class and its interests. But this time it was determined to dare the utmost. This led to the decisive struggle, which was partly provoked by the monarchy itself. It was only natural that the organ threatened directly was the first to take a stand against the monarchy in this struggle. This was . . . the minority of the Chamber. The minority knew very well that according to the letter of the law it had to submit to the absolutist majority; it knew that, as long as the mode of election remained unchanged, a victory over the majority was hardly—if at all— possible. The minority, therefore, wanted an electoral reform. But there was no way of obtaining it by the usual procedure. In order to increase its influence in the Chamber, the minority had to demonstrate to the King and to the country the support it commanded outside the Chamber among the population at large. Only thus could it again lend emphasis to its position in the Chamber. The minority was hopeful that through an impressive and lasting display of its strength it might gain a victory over the majority and its system by means of the electoral reform without having to take recourse to other measures.

SOURCE. Lorenz von Stein, "The Revolution of February 1848," from Kaethe Mengelberg (ed. and trans.), *History of the Social Movement in France, 1789–1850* (Totowa, N.J.: Bedminster Press, 1964), pp. 339–350. Reprinted with permission of the publishers. Copyright 1964 by the Bedminster Press.

With this aim in view it proceeded systematically though cautiously. . . . Since early 1847 members of the party had held—after the model of the British—large banquets in all parts of France, whose objective was the discussion of electoral reform. These banquets were neither popular assemblies nor clubs; even the form these meetings took indicated that the minority did not represent the masses but merely the property-owning class. Only the well-to-do had admission, because only they could afford to pay the price. The banquets therefore were not principally but factually a protest of the property-owning class against their exclusion from political power by the personal government of the King. They were not intended and were not supposed to represent both classes of the industrial society; they were supposed to demonstrate to the government that the property-owning class was represented by the minority in the Chamber, that this position was contrary to public opinion, and that this class was no longer willing to tolerate it. In fact, the reform-banquets did succeed in showing all this; they were a perfectly legal but determined declaration of war of the ruling class against personal government.

Unanimously supported by the ruling class, the constitutional minority entered the Chamber in 1848. Its representatives were determined to oust the Cabinet of Guizot, the representative of personal government, and to replace it by a parliamentary government. The government knew this; instead of avoiding the inevitable showdown it chose to face it. The King declared himself in his speech from the throne, just as Charles I had done, against the efforts of the minority, particularly against the agitation of the reform-banquets, which had been organized to strengthen the opposition. . . . This involved not only a condemnation of the minority itself, but also of its attempts to establish a constitutional government by gaining a majority through an electoral reform. It was a declaration of war by the monarchy against the ruling class of society and its representatives. . . . Thus began the first period of the Revolution, the struggle of the minority of the Chamber against the Cabinet. After the debate was opened, the main leaders of the opposition came into the foreground. With a display of great intellectual effort they raised their voice against the existing system of government. One brilliant and powerful attack followed the other. . . . Lamartine deplored and predicted . . . a settlement by violent revolutionary means; . . . Ledru-Rollin threatened and goaded, fighting disdainfully and yet furiously against a majority which he knew would never yield. . . . These are the most powerful and striking illustrations of the conditions prevailing in Europe and in France before the Revolution; they survive as monuments of that period during which the monarchy wanted to sacrifice the liberty of Europe in order to preserve the dynasty; . . . the speeches showed that the public funds were exhausted, that the principles of administrative procedures were disregarded, and that the elements of freedom were destroyed and banned in order to tie the people to the majority of the Chamber, subservient to the personal government. It is understandable that the powerful storm which destroyed the monarchy also obliterated the memory of this grandiose parliamentary battle, which did not yet want to attack the monarchy as an institution. But the historiography of future generations will reconsider this period in order to evaluate what the July Monarchy had dared and tolerated to transform the constitutional government into a legitimate personal rule which stood in contradiction to the spirit of the nation.

The Cabinet of Guizot kept silent in the face of these powerful attacks. . . . Guizot knew that the aim of the unified opposition was to gain a few votes from the bribed majority; he knew that the opposition would not succeed, . . . and he assumed that it would stop there. He was right insofar as the parliamentary opposition was concerned. The rebuttal to debate was accepted without discussion; this rebuttal repeated, almost verbatim, the arguments of the King. It condemned the reform movement, and with it the minority, and with the minority the whole concept of a parliamentary government, the constitutional rule of the property-owning class. . . . The majority was victorious, the Cabinet was saved, the opposition . . . accepted defeat. The other members of the Chamber, the majority of the Cabinet, had dissociated themselves definitely from the majority of the ruling social class, and pseudo-constitutionalism became the acknowledged principle of government.

At this instant the Chamber withdrew from the battle; the Chamber was no longer of importance. . . . The first period of the Revolution was over. Now began the second stage, during which the parliamentary representatives were no longer the main actors. The actors were now that part of the nation who had attended the reform-banquets; they now confronted the King directly, without a political intermediary. They were the property-owning class, who now had to step in to demand participation in government which the minority had failed to obtain. . . . The address of the majority had been accepted on February 14th. There was much excitement; the Deputies of the Left did not know any more what to do. This was the time when the so-called bourgeoisie itself had to appear on the scene. Secretary Duchatel had stated that he was going to suppress the banquets by applying a law of 1790. To prohibit the banquets was to take away from the property-owning class the organ through which it had so far succeeded in upholding the opposition in the Chamber against the absolute monarchy but through which—after the defeat of the minority—it now needed to express its views independently. The Cabinet of the Government, by planning to prohibit the banquets, went now into direct opposition to the ruling class of society; thus began the second phase of the battle. . . . As an answer to the declaration of the Secretary, the 12th *arrondissement* of Paris arranged a spectacular reform-banquet; 92 Deputies of the Left stated that they would participate, as did 3 Peers; . . . the Left of the Chamber thus rejoined the ruling class, . . . the bourgeoisie felt that they could not yield any further without submitting to the autocratic monarchy. About 10,000 members of the National Guard, interpreting the situation . . . correctly, joined and offered their support to the banquet. . . . The two great elements which were to compete for the power of the state, the monarchy and the ruling class, stood ready, facing each other. Nobody spoke about the Chamber any more.

What followed, on February 21st, is of particular importance, because it illustrates clearly the profound ignorance of the King, as well as of the leaders of the opposition, with regard to the nature and dynamics of contemporary society. The monarchy assumed that it had merely to deal with the leaders of the opposition in the Chamber and that the approaching rebellion would collapse with their resignation. The government therefore displayed its apparently enormous strength before the eyes of Odilon Barrot, the leader of the opposition. . . . It demonstrated that he was legally in the wrong in resisting the decisions of the legally ruling majority of the Chamber, and that, by continuing his resistance, he would plunge the country into a revolution beyond control. The Government persuaded him that it was capable of defeating the rebellion with one big stroke and then, after the victory, . . . it would destroy the remnants of still existing rights. Odilon Barrot lost courage. He, for his part, also assumed that the whole movement depended on the Deputies. He had not understood that these deputies were never of any significance by themselves and that all parliamentary activities were nothing else but an expression of the demands which the ruling class, according to its nature, had to raise. He therefore could not see that this class had to take up the battle by itself, regardless of the position of the deputies, and that this was not a continuation of the parliamentary quarrel but an inevitable struggle imposed by the laws of society. Odilon Barrot and four-fifths of the deputies withdrew from the banquet; as late as the 21st an order was issued to cancel the banquet. The Government believed that it had finally won a decisive victory.

And yet the street fighting began on February 22nd; . . . the whole city of Paris arose, the National Guard took up its arms, Government troops filled the streets and public squares; . . . the next day the decisive battle became inevitable. . . . The ruling class felt that this battle was fought for its rights against the pseudo-constitutionality of the monarchy. On the 23rd, the whole National Guard was under arms; one legion after the other joined the insurrection. The slogan of the revolutionaries was: "Long live the Reform! Down with Guizot!" That was the essence of the struggle as understood by the bourgeoisie proper; monarchy and the Charter were left untouched; a government was wanted which, under the protection of the monarchy, would accept the rule of the property-owning class. The Army wavered; it did not attack the National Guard. . . . The King, still stubborn and incredulous, finally recognized that he had to give in. Guizot was dismissed; the King considered appointing somebody else. He did not yet understand what had happened; he assumed that a change of Cabinets would be satisfactory. On the evening of February 23rd, the ruling class had definitely gained the upper hand. The main demand was the one for reform. The King had not yielded on this point; it would have destroyed his whole system. He rather wanted to take the utmost risks. But at this point it was already clear that the victorious bourgeoisie would wrest the reform law from the King. . . .

At 10 o'clock at night, a new column of workers and members of the National Guard . . . ran into the famous battalion of the 14th regiment, which fired a volley of shots and thus renewed the already abating battle. It is easily possible that misfortune or misinformation caused such a turn of events. But in this instance it was apt to be decisive. The King, when he ascended the throne, had confirmed the sacredness of the Charter by oath; he had used the eighteen years of his rule to destroy it. Who could assure the people that his present royal promise would not be just as invalid? Peace depended upon trust in the king; the only basis for the monarchy, after the victory of the bourgeoisie, was one of faith in the royal word. Never had distrust against a king been more justified than in this instance. At the moment when he was defeated and ready to give in, how could he have murdered the harmless population of the capital? If such was the case, if royal promises could not be trusted at all any more, if the people were betrayed, then there was no other way out except to destroy the incorrigible monarchy itself. Thus the shooting echoed in the hearts of the Parisians. At this moment, the second period of the struggle came to a close with the victory of the ruling class; the ruling class had lost confidence in the monarchy; . . . the struggle for reform receded, . . . and on February 24th the amorphous masses of the people began to attack the monarchy, and with it the rule of large capital over the other classes, as well as the existing order of society.

This was the third day of that remarkable Revolution. The second important element of industrial society, labor, stepped into the foreground. Labor was aware of the fact that the exclusive rule of capital was destroyed through the monarchy, that, on the other hand, capital desired above all to regain through a revolution its own ruling position under the monarchy. It understood that monarchy without a constitution would suppress both classes of society; it also understood that a constitutional monarchy, obeying the ruling and property-owning class, at least had to further suppress the subjected laboring class. Labor, therefore, arrived at the conclusion that monarchy is under any condition an antagonist of the working class. It realized that monarchy would become stronger than society as a whole by the defeat of the ruling class; therefore it aligned itself with the ruling class. But it knew just as well that through the defeat of monarchy by the ruling class the rule of the latter would be infinitely strengthened. Therefore, labor did not want to stop the revolution at this victory of the bourgeoisie. As long as the first part of the battle was being fought it restrained itself; but when, after February 24th, the second part began, labor came into the foreground; and as soon as that happened, the issue was no longer restricted to the struggle between genuine constitutionalism versus pseudo-constitutionalism, but became a struggle of monarchy versus the abolition of monarchy.

One question arises here which we still have to explore: If monarchy is the most natural and the simplest basic form of government for industrial society, how did it happen that during the revolution the victorious bourgeoisie abandoned the monarchy under attack by the proletariat at a moment when it could have obtained from it anything it asked? . . . The answer to this question is given by the history of the French monarchy itself. Ever so often since 1789, the ruling class had attempted to lay the foundation for a constitutional monarchy similar to the British. The ruling class had been deceived so often that it finally identified monarchy with political repression. . . . Through the reign of Louis-Philippe, confidence, not only in the king but also in monarchy as such, had been undermined. . . . This is why the ruling class could not defend the monarchy when it was attacked by the laboring class. . . . The ruling class did not want to destroy the monarchy, but the lack of trust resulted in a lack of determination at a moment when only trust could have saved it. . . . Thus complete confusion followed on February 24th, when the ruling class was overpowered by the proletariat and the Chamber of Deputies by the *Hôtel de Ville*. The monarchy collapsed not because its enemies were all-powerful, but because its natural friends had been completely alienated. . . .

Thus the February Revolution came to a close. It ended with the abolition of the monarchy. However, this was, in fact, only a negative result. With it the basic form of the old Constitution was destroyed, but a new one was not yet put into effect. It was the end of past history but not yet the beginning of a new era. . . . What was going to happen after the power of the state, through the abolition of monarchy, had fallen back into the hands of the people? . . .

Popular sovereignty, prescribed by political democracy and realized by the ideal republic, identifies the state with the aggregate of its members. . . . The will of the state is the joint will of all individuals, and each of their wills is an independent will. Under popular sovereignty the reasons for the will of the state are therefore the same as those of the individuals; these are based on the assumption that the individual believes he is furthering his own well-being by realizing his own will. Therefore, we call these reasons his interest. . . . In a state based on popular sovereignty, the unity of the joint will is secured only through the identity of the interests of all individuals. If individuals or whole segments of the population have differing and opposing interests which can be realized by the will of the state, the inner unity of the will of the state will necessarily be destroyed. Popular sovereignty, therefore, begins to develop an inner contradiction. As long as the differentiation of interests remains casual and transitory, the disruption of the will of the state is merely temporary. . . . If contradictory interests did not exist within the community, popular sovereignty might be realized, without danger, by the ideal republic and democracy.

The science of society shows that property is the material basis of personal development. Preservation and the growth of property not only correspond to the material interests of men, but are also required for the development of the human personality. Property appears to be only the pursuit of material goods but actually is also the pursuit of personal interests; the interests of property become the truly justified interest also of those who are free and independent. This interest demands that the labor of others be utilized for the increase of private property of the ruling class. But the work of one individual for the growth of property of another individual means dependence. Thus it appears that the personal interest of those who own property must necessarily entail the dependence of the laborers. The laborer, on his part also free to pursue his aspirations, demands not only that this dependence be allayed, but that he too receive a share of property as large as possible, because such property is the prerequisite of his personal fulfillment. . . . Hence there are in each state two sets of interests mutually exclusive, although both are a logical consequence of the inner nature of the personality. . . . Since the highest evolution of the state depends upon the growth of all individuals, the high value of property is a decisive reason why the state must preserve and foster the growth of property of those who already own it, and at the same time foster the acquisition of property by those who do not own it. These two interests are not extraneous to the state but inherent in the community, and are inseparable from the concept of the state. The absolute contradiction reflected by these two interests is the germ of disruption of the will of the state. . . .

As soon as one conceives that the state based on popular sovereignty . . . has a will and is capable of acting, the unity collapses and dissolves into its opposing elements. The concept of "the people" does not suffice to explain or to solve the growing contradiction: what really emerges from the antagonism between owners and non-owners . . . and what wields control over the state is the order of society and the conflict of its interests, which always have and always will dominate the state. . . .

If we assume that the state, embodied in the monarchy, loses its own representative—just as it did in France through the February Revolution—and that the power of the state or sovereignty reverts to the community, what consequence will this have? Is—as constitutions state and as the popular saying goes—popular sovereignty thereby established? It is indeed established, but only as a principle. It expresses the fact that the community is the only sovereign. In reality, however, in any positive action of the state, the will of the state is determined by those forces which have created the inevitable opposition of interests, the order of society. It is this social order which rules under popular sovereignty. The life of any republic is determined by the following rule: as soon as popular sovereignty is accepted as a principle in a country without a monarchy, the sovereignty of society becomes the true basis of state order. . . .

The science of society, of its elements and laws, gains more practical significance the closer a nation moves—be it through inner conviction or through circumstances—toward the abolition of monarchy. Only this science can then explain the forms which the state may develop; only this science can discover and predict the dangers which the abolition of monarchy brings about; only this science will enable us to understand the importance of governmental laws and governmental measures, the significance of the popular excitement and the struggles which necessarily follow the abolition of monarchy.

If it is true that the social order always controls the state—inasmuch as the ruling class of society gains control of the state by the constitution and the administration, while the dependent class is excluded from power—it may be asked in which respect the rule of society in the republic differs from that in the monarchy, and whether the position of the social elements is different under these two systems of government. . . .

After the monarchy is overthrown and the people as a whole gain sovereignty, the ruling class of society—according to the laws of society—takes political power into its hands. No constitution, not even universal suffrage, can change this inevitable consequence. . . . Since what we want is determined by our interests, and since those who own property have an interest in the preservation and growth of property rights, it follows that through the subjugation of the state by the ruling class the interests of property become the principle of the state represented by this class. The sovereignty of society— which is the true meaning of the term popular sovereignty—manifests itself as the sovereignty of the property-owning class over the property-less class. The republic, therefore, necessarily represents the domination of the interests of the property owners over the interests of the propertyless. . . . This rule of the interests of property owners—set in action by popular sovereignty—is in direct contradiction to the idea of the state, . . . because the interests of the propertyless class become suppressed not only in fact but also by law; the lower class is no longer protected by monarchy, and is too weak to build up any resistance by itself.

The inherent aspirations of the individual toward freedom in the state as well as in society assert themselves the more as the subjugated class is further removed from its potentialities through the rule of the upper class. The contradiction inherent in the concept of the state develops into an open antagonism in the life of the people. Both classes become more aware of it; hatred and scorn grow on one side, arrogance and fear on the other. The rule of the property-owning class creates the hostile opposition of the two social elements of the state, each of which wants to gain control over the government.

The conflict usually results in the definite rule of one class over the other, after a series of revolutions which, as the science of society shows, are violent attempts on the part of the lower class to gain control over the state. During these revolutions, sometimes the one, sometimes the other class is victorious. But since the exclusive rule of one class is in contradiction to the idea of the state, . . . the existence of the state is threatened in either case.

If popular sovereignty can be interpreted as the rule of society over the state, this sovereignty necessarily results in a continuous battle between the social classes and their opposing interests. The final victory of one class over the other . . . inevitably leads to the ruin of the nation and the state. . . . Does this not suggest . . . that any form of government is irreconcilable with universal freedom? Proudhon, after many doubts, reached this conclusion. Plato had drawn a picture of the Republic as an image of an idea to which there was no counterpart in reality; Thomas More transplanted it to Utopia, and Rousseau, who considered political democracy just as impossible as monarchy, stated that the Republic was possible only among the Gods. As long as the existence of the state was an unchallenged fact, these opinions could be quietly ignored. But now the nations begin to doubt, to investigate and to reconsider the situation. Can the social sciences offer them only this deplorable answer? Is there no solution and reconciliation for this apparently total contradiction? There is such a solution. But one has to have the courage to search for it by an analysis of this contradiction.

Up to now we have interpreted the concept of ownership in a general way as the basis of the order of society and the state. From this . . . concept we arrived at an apparently absolute contradiction. We have characterized the absolute antagonism between the classes under a sovereign society as the beginning of the decline. . . . The possibility of realizing popular sovereignty depends upon the possibility of eliminating the antagonism between the classes . . . by developing opportunities making it possible to rise from the status of the property-less to that of property owner.

Thus the question arises whether the inner nature of ownership and the distribution of property, which controls everything, offer such a solution. Unless they do, the above contradiction is insoluble and all historical developments come to a permanent stagnation or a quick dissolution.

A closer examination of the concept of ownership reveals that it is composed of several elements. In a narrow sense, ownership means the possession of tangible goods which we call property; however, these are the result of labor; this is the second element in the concept of ownership: possessions cannot be acquired except by labor. Acquisition, or ownership through labor, represents the third element in the concept of ownership. . . . The concept of ownership, therefore, is composed of the elements of property, labor and acquisition. These three elements have a definite interrelationship. According to the concept of ownership, neither one is conceivable without the other two; there can be no property without labor and acquisition, no labor without acquisition and property, no acquisition without property and labor. The concept of ownership in a society in which it is generally accepted requires that property cannot persist without labor and acquisition, and labor not without acquisition and property. As long as property depends upon labor and acquisition, and as long as working people gain property through acquisition, the economy corresponds to the concept of ownership, and society, ruled by property-owners, includes two classes: those who come to work and gain acquisition through their property and those who gain property through work and acquisition.

But it is possible for men to disrupt this natural relationship. Since property is not only an economic concept but also a legal one, each individual owner may keep his property for himself or consume it without using it for work and acquisition. Secondly, the whole class of property owners can introduce laws and establish institutions which will obstruct the acquisition of property; it can eliminate the process of labor as a means of acquiring property. The property-owning class has the power, because property, as a prerequisite of labor and acquisition, is the most powerful of the three elements in the concept of ownership and rules over the other two. The property-owning class wants to do so because everybody prefers unearned and secure income to the uncertainty of acquisition; it carries this out by separating property from acquisition.

Thus a contradiction develops between the economic order and the concept of ownership, which presupposes that the acquisition of property through work is the basis for the growth of the individual personality. This contradiction cannot persist. The complete separation of property from acquisitive labor has to be overcome and replaced by a reciprocal relationship, if it is true that the idea of personality grows out of the various elements of ownership and if world history is the history of this development. This, however, cannot happen suddenly or by mere chance. On the contrary, a continuous and organic progress has to take place, unfolding the gradual harmony of both. . . .

And now let us return to France. What happened after the proclamation of the Republic in 1848? A constitution was created whose stability and duration, indeed, depended upon the relationship that prevailed at that time between property and acquisitive labor in French society. . . . This particular French Republic differed from all previous Republics to the extent that this relationship had changed. . . .

# 15

# The Art of Revolution

*L. D. Trotsky*

≪≪≪≪≪≪≪≪≪≪≪≪≪≪≪≪≪≪≪≪≪≪≪≪≪≪≪≪≪≪≪≪≪≪≪

## EDITORS' COMMENT

Lev Davidovitch Trotsky, *né* Bronstein, is one of the greatest historical and political writers of our century, as well as being one of its most influential and flamboyant personalities. His *History of the Russian Revolution*, finished in 1930 while he was in political and physical exile, is a monument to the drama, sweep, and optimism of the events in which he so closely participated. If less interesting in detail than the contemporary accounts of John Reed and Nicolai Sukhanov, who were relative bystanders, his account is far more durable in capturing the rhythm and meaning of the great uprising. It is penetrated by a faith in what Trotsky was to call, in his so-called "testament" of 1940, "the communist future of humanity." Although describing specific events and not a scheme of human development, Trotsky, with some justice, could be termed the Condorcet of the Russian Revolution. Both saw history as something massive, anonymous, and progressive. Both also shared the fate of "devoured children."

The facts of Trotsky's life are well known (see Isaac Deutscher's trilogy) and need not be rehearsed here. Trotsky's importance as a revolutionary leader from the abortive uprising of 1905, in which he served briefly as president of the first St. Petersburg Soviet, needs no defense. Captured by the authorities, he escaped and fled abroad. Always a Marxist, he was never officially a Bolshevik until July 1917, when Lenin implored him to join the party leadership. Previously, he had been a Menshevik and had later dominated the small but intellectually powerful group of "Interdistrictites" (*Mezhrayontsi*). Trotsky's role in the events he describes here was capital—as writer, planner, orator, organizer, and later as creator of the Red Army. Yet of all the figures who militated in the turbulence of 1917, he is the most anonymous in the pages of his own account. The danger is separated from the dance.

From the many surviving descriptions of Trotsky, his personality emerges as introspective, brilliant, volatile, intellectual, and practical—held in nervous equilibrium by revolutionary faith and discipline. His literary sensitivity and skill were of the first order. But his contemporaries were perhaps struck most by his verbal eloquence. His colleague Lunacharsky declared without nuance in his *Revolutionary Silhouettes:* "I consider Trotsky probably the greatest orator of our times." This was also the quality observed by that connoisseur of political heroes, André Malraux, who met Trotsky in France in 1934: "As soon as I got accustomed to that ravishing phantom in eyeglasses, I felt that his whole force of character proceeded from a mouth whose flat lips were tense, extremely defined, and sculptured in the Asian style. . . . The principal quality of his voice is its total domination over his words. . . ." Beyond this rhetorical power, there is no doubt that Trotsky possessed superior moral and physical courage.

The *History of the Russian Revolution* does not pretend to a "treacherous impartiality," but is far from being a mere Marxist tract. Max Eastman is near the truth when he claims that "this is the first time the scientific history of a great event has been written by a man who played a dominant part in it." Trotsky's own methodological ambitions are these: "an honest study of the facts, a determination of their real connections, an exposure of the causal laws of their movement" (Preface to the work). To be sure, the frame of reference is the Marxist theory of dialectical materialism and historical class struggle; but it will be noted that Trotsky argues from fact to theory, commenting abundantly on "mistakes," and is far from being the logical doctrinaire that one might expect. This is no Livian historical myth of the creation of a Third Rome, but is a piece of exemplary scholarship that is guided by purpose.

In interpreting the success of the Bolsheviks (a determined group of "hardly more than 25,000 or 30,000 at the most") in making themselves masters of an empire, Trotsky pays due justice to the decadence of the ruling aristocracy and to the incoherence and ineptitude of the middle class leadership. He is also impressed with the self-generating process by which a revolution squanders all its resources, bypassing the transient solutions of yesterday or the day before. In this respect he saw a close parallel with the French Revolution:

> At a given moment each group exhausted its political possibilities and could advance no farther against powerful reality: internal economic conditions, international pressure, new mass currents that were the consequence, etc. In such conditions, each step taken initiated results contrary to the ones hoped for (Letter of 1938, quoted in Pierre Naville, *Trotsky vivante*, Paris: Julliard, 1962, pp. 123–24).

This notion of momentum or chain reaction was at the core of Trotsky's famous and little understood theory of the "permanent revolution."

The excerpt published below includes some of Trotsky's preliminary observations about the Russian revolution and a large portion of the famous chapter, "The Art of Revolution," which describes the theoretical mechanics of the Bolshevik takeover. Many of his general remarks on the strategy and nature of revolution can be found in the selection, including an analysis of the elitist and populist components of the uprising, a consideration of the political role of the proletariat and peasantry and, implicitly, a discussion of theory and practice.

# THE ART OF REVOLUTION

## L. D. TROTSKY

The Russian proletariat learned its first steps in the political circumstances created by a despotic state. Strikes forbidden by law, underground circles, illegal proclamations, street demonstrations, encounters with the police and with troops—such was the school created by the combination of a swiftly developing capitalism with an absolutism slowly surrendering its positions. The concentration of the workers in colossal enterprises, the intense character of governmental persecution, and finally the impulsiveness of a young and fresh proletariat, brought it about that the political strike, so rare in western Europe, became in Russia the fundamental method of struggle. The figures of strikes from the beginning of the present century are a most impressive index of the political history of Russia. With every desire not to burden our text with figures, we cannot refrain from introducing a table of political strikes in Russia for the period 1903 to 1917. The figures, reduced to their simplest expression, relate only to enterprises undergoing factory inspection. The railroads, mining industries, mechanical and small enterprises in general, to say nothing of agriculture, for various reasons do not enter into the count. But the changes in the strike curve in the different periods emerge no less clearly for this.

We have before us a curve—the only one of its kind—of the political temperature of a nation carrying in its womb a great revolution. In a backward country with a small proletariat—for in all the enterprises undergoing factory inspection there were only about $1\frac{1}{2}$ million workers in 1905, about 2 million in 1917—the strike movement attains such dimensions as it never knew before anywhere in the world. With the weakness of the petty bourgeois democracy, the scatteredness and political blindness of the peasant movement, the revolutionary strike of the workers becomes the battering ram which the awakening

SOURCE. Lev Davidovitch Trotsky, "The Art of Revolution," from *History of the Russian Revolution*, 3 Vols., tr. Max Eastman (New York: Simon & Schuster, 1932), I, pp. 33–51; III, pp. 167–182, excerpted.

nation directs against the walls of absolutism. Participants in political strikes in 1905 numbering 1,843,000—workers participating in several strikes are here, of course counted twice—that number alone would permit us to put our finger on the revolutionary year in our table, if we knew nothing else about the Russian political calendar.

| Year | Number in thousands of participants in political strikes |
|---|---|
| 1903 | 87[a] |
| 1904 | 25[a] |
| 1905 | 1,843 |
| 1906 | 651 |
| 1907 | 540 |
| 1908 | 93 |
| 1909 | 8 |
| 1910 | 4 |
| 1911 | 8 |
| 1912 | 550 |
| 1913 | 502 |
| 1914 (first half) | 1,059 |
| 1915 | 156 |
| 1916 | 310 |
| 1917 (January–February) | 575 |

[a] The figures for 1903 and 1904 refer to all strikes, the economic undoubtedly predominating.

For 1904, the first year of the Russo-Japanese war, the factory inspection indicates in all only 25,000 strikers. In 1905, political and economic strikes together involved 2,863,000 men—115 times more than in the previous year. This remarkable fact by itself would suggest the thought that a proletariat, impelled by the course of events to improvise such unheard-of revolutionary activities, must at whatever cost produce from its depths an organization corresponding to the dimensions of the struggle and the colossal tasks. This organization was the soviets—brought into being by the first revolution, and made the instrument of the general strike and the struggle for power.

Beaten in the December uprising of 1905, the proletariat during the next two years makes heroic efforts to defend a part of the conquered positions. These years, as our strike figures show, still belong directly to the revolution, but they are the years of ebb. The four following years (1908-11) emerge in our mirror of strike statistics as the years of victorious counter-revolution. An industrial crisis coincident with this still further exhausts the proletariat, already bled white. The depth of the fall is symmetrical with the height of the rise. National convulsions find their reflection in these simple figures.

The industrial boom beginning in 1910 lifted the workers to their feet, and gave a new impulse to their energy. The figures for 1912-14 almost repeat those for 1905–07, but in the opposite order: not from above downwards, but from below up. On a new and higher historical basis—there are more workers now, and they have more experience—a new revolutionary offensive begins. The first half-year of 1914 clearly approaches in the number of political strikes the culminating point of the year of the first revolution. But war breaks out and sharply interrupts this process. The first war months are marked by political inertness in the working class, but already in the spring of 1915 the numbness begins to pass. A new cycle of political strikes opens, a cycle which in February 1917 will culminate in the insurrection of soldiers and workers.

The sharp ebbs and flows of the mass struggle had left the Russian proletariat after a few years almost unrecognizable. Factories which two or three years ago would strike unanimously over some single arbitrary police action, today have completely lost their revolutionary color, and accept the most monstrous crimes of the authorities without resistance. Great defeats discourage people for a long time. The consciously revolutionary elements lose their power over the masses. Prejudices and superstitions not yet burnt out come back to life. Gray immigrants from the village during these times dilute the workers' ranks. Sceptics ironically shake their heads. So it was in the years 1907-11. But molecular processes in the masses are healing the psychological wounds of defeat. A new turn of events, or an underlying economic impulse, opens a new political cycle. The revolutionary elements again find their audience. The struggle reopens on a higher level.

In order to understand the two chief tendencies in the Russian working class, it is important to have in mind that Menshevism finally took shape in the years of ebb and reaction. It relied chiefly upon a thin layer of workers who had broken with the revolution. Whereas Bolshevism, cruelly shattered in the period of the reaction, began to rise swiftly on the crest of a new revolutionary tide in the years before the war. "The most energetic and audacious element, ready for tireless struggle, for resistance and continual organization, is that element, those organizations, and those people who are concentrated around Lenin." In these words the Police Department estimated the work of the Bolsheviks during the years preceding the war.

In July 1914, while the diplomats were driving the last nail into the cross designed for the crucifixion of Europe, Petrograd was boiling like a revolutionary cauldron. The President of the French Republic, Poincaré, had to lay his wreath on the tomb of Alexander III amid the last echoes of a street fight and the first murmurs of a patriotic demonstration.

Would the mass offensive of 1912-14 have led directly to an overthrow of tzarism if the war had not broken out? It is hardly possible to answer that question with certainty. The process would inexorably have led to a revolution, but through what stages would the revolution in those circumstances have had to go? Would it not have experienced another defeat? How much time would have been needed by the workers in order to arouse the peasantry and win the army? In all these directions only guesses are possible. The war, at any rate, gave the process at first a backward movement, but only to accelerate it more powerfully in the next period and guarantee its overwhelming victory.

.   .   .   .   .

The Russian proletariat found its revolutionary audacity not only in itself. Its very position as minority of the nation suggests that it could not have given its struggle a sufficient scope—certainly not enough to take its place at the head of the state—if it had not found a mighty support in the thick of the people. Such a support was guaranteed to it by the agrarian problem.

The belated half-liberation of the peasants in 1861 had found agricultural industry almost on the same level as two hundred years before. The preservation of the old area of communal land—somewhat filched from during the reform—together with the archaic methods of land culture, automatically sharpened a crisis caused by the rural excess population, which was at the same time a crisis in the three-field system. The peasantry felt still more caught in a trap because the process was not taking place in the seventeenth but in the nineteenth century—that is, in the conditions of an advanced money economy which made demands upon the wooden plow that could only be met by a tractor. Here too we see a drawing together of separate stages of the historic process, and as a result an extreme sharpening of contradictions. The learned agronomes and economists had been preaching that the old area with rational cultivation would be amply sufficient— that is to say, they proposed to the peasant to make a jump to a higher level of technique and culture without disturbing the landlord, the bailiff, or the tzar. But no economic regime, least of all an agricultural regime, the most tardy of all, has ever disappeared before exhausting all its possibilities. Before feeling compelled to pass over to a more intensive economic culture, the peasant had to make a last attempt to broaden his three fields. This could obviously be achieved only at the expense of non-peasant lands. Choking in the narrowness of his land area, under the smarting whip of the treasury and the market, the muzhik was inexorably forced to attempt to get rid of the landlord once for all.

On the eve of the first revolution the whole stretch of arable land within the limits of European Russia was estimated at 280 million dessiatins. The communal allotments constituted about 140 million. The crown lands, above 5 million. Church and monastery lands, about $2\frac{1}{2}$ million. Of the privately owned land, 70 million dessiatins belonged to the 30,000 great landlords, each of whom owned about 500 dessiatins. This 70 million was about what would have belonged to 10 million peasant families. These land statistics constitute the finished program of a peasant war.

The landlords were not settled with in the first revolution. Not all the peasants rose. The movement in the country did not coincide with that in the cities. The peasant army wavered, and finally supplied sufficient forces for putting down the workers. As soon as the Semenovsky Guard regiment had settled with the Moscow insurrection, the monarchy abandoned all thought of cutting down the landed estates, as also its own autocratic rights.

However, the defeated revolution did not pass without leaving traces in the village. The government abolished the old land redemption payments and opened the way to a broader colonization of Siberia. The frightened landlords not only made considerable concessions in the matter of rentals, but also began a large-scale selling of their landed estates. These fruits of the revolution were enjoyed by the better-off peasants, who were able to rent and buy the landlords' land.

However, the broadest gates were opened for the emerging of capitalist farmers from the peasant class by the law of November 9, 1906, the chief reform introduced by the victorious counter-revolution. Giving the right even to a small minority of the peasants of any commune, against the will of the majority, to cut out from the communal land a section to be owned independently, the law of November 9 constituted an explosive capitalist shell directed against the commune. The president of the Council of Ministers, Stolypin, described the essence of this governmental policy towards the peasants as "banking on the strong ones." This meant: encourage the upper circles of the peasantry to get hold of the communal land by buying up these "liberated" sections, and convert these new capitalist farmers into a support for the existing regime. It was easier to propose such a task, however, than to achieve it. In this attempt to substitute the kulak problem for the peasant problem, the counter-revolution was destined to break its neck.

By January 1, 1916, 2½ million home-owners had made good their personal possession of 17 million dessiatins. Two more million home-owners were demanding the allotment to them of 14 million dessiatins. This looked like a colossal success for the reform. But the majority of the homesteads were completely incapable of sustaining life, and represented only material for natural selection. At that time when the more backward landlords and small peasants were selling on a large scale—the former their estates, the latter their bits of land—there emerged in the capacity of principal purchaser a new peasant bourgeoisie. Agriculture entered upon a state of indubitable capitalist boom. The export of agricultural products from Russia rose between 1908 and 1912 from 1 billion roubles to 1½ billion. This meant that broad masses of the peasantry had been proletarianized, and the upper circles of the village were throwing on the market more and more grain.

To replace the compulsory communal ties of the peasantry, there developed very swiftly a voluntary cooperation, which succeeded in penetrating quite deeply into the peasant masses in the course of a few years, and immediately became a subject of liberal and democratic idealization. Real power in the cooperatives belonged, however, only to the rich peasants, whose interests in the last analysis they served. The Narodnik intelligentsia, by concentrating its chief forces in peasant cooperation, finally succeeded in shifting its love for the people on to good solid bourgeois rails. In this way was prepared, partially at least, the political bloc of the "anti-capitalist" party of the Social Revolutionaries with the Kadets, the capitalist party *par excellence.*

Liberalism, although preserving the appearance of opposition to the agrarian policy of the reaction, nevertheless looked with great hopes upon this capitalist destruction of the communes. "In the country a very powerful petty bourgeoisie is arising," wrote the liberal Prince Troubetskoy, "in its whole make and essence alien alike to the ideals of the united nobility and to the socialist dreams."

But this admirable medal had its other side. There was arising from the destroyed communes not only a "very powerful bourgeoisie," but also its antithesis. The number of peasants selling tracts of land they could not live on had risen by the beginning of the war to a million, which means no less than five million souls added to the proletarian population. A sufficiently explosive material was also supplied by the millions of peasant-paupers to whom nothing remained but to hang on to their hungry allotments. In consequence those contradictions kept reproducing themselves among the peasants which had so early undermined the development of bourgeois society as a whole in Russia. The new rural bourgeoisie, which was to create a support for the old and more powerful proprietors, turned out to be as hostilely opposed to the fundamental masses of the peasantry as the old proprietors had been to the people as a whole. Before it could become a support to the existing order, this peasant bourgeoisie had need of some order of its own wherewith to cling to its conquered positions. In these circumstances it is no wonder that the agrarian problem continued a sharp one in all the State Dumas. Everyone felt that the last word had not yet been spoken. The peasant deputy Petrichenko once declared from the tribune of the Duma: "No matter how long you debate you won't create a new planet—that means that you will have to give us the land." This peasant was neither a Bolshevik, nor a Social Revolutionary. On the contrary, he was a Right deputy, a monarchist.

The agrarian movement, having, like the strike movement of the workers, died down toward the end of 1907, partially revives in 1908, and grows stronger during the following years. The struggle, to be sure, is transferred to a considerable degree within the commune: that is just what the reaction had figured on politically. There are not infrequent armed conflicts among peasants during the division of the communal land. But the struggle against the landlord also does not disappear. The peasants are more frequently setting fire to the landlord's manors, harvests, haystacks, seizing on the way also those individual tracts which had been cut off against the will of the communal peasants.

The war found the peasantry in this condition. The government carried away from the country about 10 million workers and about 2 million horses. The weak homesteads grew still weaker. The number of peasants who could not sow their fields increased. But in the second year of the war the middle peasants also began to go under. Peasant hostility toward the war sharpened from month to month. In October 1916, the Petrograd Gendarme Administration reported that in the villages they had already ceased to believe in the success of the war—the report being based on the words of insurance agents, teachers, traders, etc. "All are waiting and impatiently demanding: When will this cursed war finally end?" And that is not all:

> Political questions are being talked about everywhere and resolutions adopted directed against the landlords and merchants. Nuclei of various organizations are being formed. . . . As yet there is no uniting center, but there is reason to suppose that the peasants will unite

by way of the cooperatives which are daily growing throughout all
Russia.

There is some exaggeration here. In some things the gendarme has
run ahead a little, but the fundamentals are indubitably correct.

The possessing classes could not but foresee that the village was
going to present its bill. But they drove away these black thoughts,
hoping to wriggle out of it somehow. On this theme the inquisitive
French ambassador Paléologue had a chat during the war days with
the former Minister of Agriculture Krivoshein, the former Premier
Kokovtsev, the great landlord Count Bobrinsky, the President of the
State Duma Rodzianko, the great industrialist Putilov, and other
distinguished people. Here is what was unveiled before him in this
conversation: In order to carry into action a radical land reform it
would require the work of a standing army of 300,000 surveyors for
no less than fifteen years; but during this time the number of homesteads would increase to 30 million, and consequently all these preliminary calculations by the time they were made would prove invalid.
To introduce a land reform thus seemed in the eyes of these landlords,
officials and bankers something like squaring the circle. It is hardly
necessary to say that a like mathematical scrupulousness was completely alien to the peasant. He thought that first of all the thing
to do was to smoke out the landlord, and then see.

If the village nevertheless remained comparatively peaceful during
the war, that was because its active forces were at the front. The
soldiers did not forget about the land—whenever at least they were
not thinking about death—and in the trenches the muzhik's thoughts
about the future were saturated with the smell of powder. But all
the same the peasantry, even after learning to handle firearms, could
never of its own force have achieved the agrarian democratic revolution—that is, its own revolution. It had to have leadership. For the
first time in world history the peasant was destined to find a leader
in the person of the worker. In that lies the fundamental, and you
may say the whole, difference between the Russian revolution and
all those preceding it.

In England serfdom had disappeared in actual fact by the end
of the fourteenth century—that is, two centuries before it arose in
Russia, and four and a half centuries before it was abolished. The
expropriation of the landed property of the peasants dragged along
in England through one Reformation and two revolutions to the nineteenth century. The capitalist development, not forced from the outside,
thus had sufficient time to liquidate the independent peasant long
before the proletariat awoke to political life.

In France the struggle with royal absolutism, the aristocracy, and the princes of the church, compelled the bourgeoisie in various of its layers, and in several installments, to achieve a radical agrarian revolution at the beginning of the eighteenth century. For long after that an independant peasantry constituted the support of the bourgeois order, and in 1871 it helped the bourgeoisie put down the Paris Commune.

In Germany the bourgeoisie proved incapable of a revolutionary solution of the agrarian problem, and in 1848 betrayed the peasants to the landlords, just as Luther some three centuries before in the peasant wars had betrayed them to the princes. On the other hand, the German proletariat was still too weak in the middle of the nineteenth century to take the leadership of the peasantry. As a result the capitalist development of Germany got sufficient time, although not so long a period as in England, to subordinate agriculture, as it emerged from the uncompleted bourgeois revolution, to its own interests.

The peasant reform of 1861 was carried out in Russia by an aristocratic and bureaucratic monarchy under pressure of the demands of a bourgeois society, but with the bourgeoisie completely powerless politically. The character of this peasant emancipation was such that the forced capitalistic transformation of the country inevitably converted the agrarian problem into a problem of revolution. The Russian bourgeois dreamed of an agrarian evolution on the French plan, or the Danish, or the American—anything you want, only not the Russian. He neglected however, to supply himself in good season with a French history or an American social structure. The democratic intelligentsia, notwithstanding its revolutionary past, took its stand in the decisive hour with the liberal bourgeoisie and the landlord, and not with the revolutionary village. In these circumstances only the working class could stand at the head of the peasant revolution.

The law of combined development of backward countries—in the sense of a peculiar mixture of backward elements with the most modern factors—here rises before us in its most finished form, and offers a key to the fundamental riddle of the Russian revolution. If the agrarian problem, as a heritage from the barbarism of the old Russian history, had been solved by the bourgeoisie, if it could have been solved by them, the Russian proletariat could not possibly have come to power in 1917. In order to realize the Soviet state, there was required a drawing together and mutual penetration of two factors belonging to completely different historic species: a peasant war—that is, a movement characteristic of the dawn of bourgeois development—and a pro-

letarian insurrection, the movement signalizing its decline. That is
the essence of 1917. . . .

. . . . .

People do not make revolution eagerly any more than they do
war. There is this difference, however, that in war compulsion plays
the decisive role, in revolution there is no compulsion except that of
circumstances. A revolution takes place only when there is no other
way out. And the insurrection, which rises above a revolution like
a peak in the mountain chain of its events, can no more be evoked
at will than revolution as a whole. The masses advance and retreat
several times before they make up their minds to the final assault.

Conspiracy is ordinarily contrasted to insurrection as the deliberate
undertaking of a minority to a spontaneous movement of the majority.
And it is true that a victorious insurrection, which can only be the
act of a class called to stand at the head of the nation, is widely separated both in method and historic significance from a governmental
overturn accomplished by conspirators acting in concealment from the
masses.

In every class society there are enough contradictions so that a
conspiracy can take root in its cracks. Historic experience proves, however, that a certain degree of social disease is necessary—as in Spain,
for instance, or Portugal, or South America—to supply continual nour-
ishment for a regime of conspiracies. A pure conspiracy even when
victorious can only replace one clique of the same ruling class by
another—or still less, merely alter the governmental personages. Only
mass insurrection has ever brought the victory of one social regime
over another. Periodical conspiracies are commonly an expression of
social stagnation and decay, but popular insurrections on the contrary
come usually as a result of some swift growth which has broken down
the old equilibrium of the nation. The chronic "revolutions" of the
South American republics have nothing in common with the Permanent Revolution; they are in a sense the very opposite thing.

This does not mean, however, that popular insurrection and conspiracy are in all circumstances mutually exclusive. An element of
conspiracy almost always enters to some degree into any insurrection.
Being historically conditioned by a certain stage in the growth of a
revolution, a mass insurrection is never purely spontaneous. Even when
it flashes out unexpectedly to a majority of its own participants, it has
been fertilized by those ideas in which the insurrectionaries see a way
out of the difficulties of existence. But a mass insurrection can be
foreseen and prepared. It can be organized in advance. In this case the

conspiracy is subordinate to the insurrection, serves it, smoothes its path, hastens its victory. The higher the political level of a revolutionary movement and the more serious its leadership, the greater will be the place occupied by conspiracy in a popular insurrection.

It is very necessary to understand the relations between insurrection and conspiracy, both as they oppose and as they supplement each other. It is especially so, because the very use of the word conspiracy, even in Marxian literature, contains a superficial contradiction due to the fact that it sometimes implies an independent undertaking initiated by the minority, at others a preparation by the minority of a majority insurrection.

History testifies, to be sure, that in certain conditions a popular insurrection can be victorious even without a conspiracy. Arising "spontaneously" out of the universal indignation, the scattered protests, demonstrations, strikes, street fights, an insurrection can draw in a part of the army, paralyze the forces of the enemy, and overthrow the old power. To a certain degree this is what happened in February 1917 in Russia. Approximately the same picture is presented by the development of the German and Austro-Hungarian revolutions of the autumn of 1918. Since in these events there was no party at the head of the insurrectionaries imbued through and through with the interests and aims of the insurrection, its victory had inevitably to transfer the power to those parties which up to the last moment had been opposing it.

To overthrow the old power is one thing; to take the power in one's own hands is another. The bourgeoisie may win the power in a revolution not because it is revolutionary, but because it is bourgeois. It has in its possession property, education, the press, a network of strategic positions, a hierarchy of institutions. Quite otherwise with the proletariat. Deprived in the nature of things of all social advantages, an insurrectionary proletariat can count only on its numbers, its solidarity, its cadres, its official staff.

Just as a blacksmith cannot seize the red hot iron in his naked hand, so the proletariat cannot directly seize the power; it has to have an organization accommodated to this task. The coordination of the mass insurrection with the conspiracy, the subordination of the conspiracy to the insurrection, the organization of the insurrection through the conspiracy, constitutes that complex and responsible department of revolutionary politics which Marx and Engels called "the art of insurrection." It presupposes a correct general leadership of the masses, a flexible orientation in changing conditions, a thought-out plan of attack, cautiousness in technical preparation, and a daring blow.

Historians and politicians usually give the name of *spontaneous insurrection* to a movement of the masses united by a common hostility against the old regime, but not having a clear aim, deliberated methods of struggle, or a leadership consciously showing the way to victory. This spontaneous insurrection is condescendingly recognized by official historians—at least those of democratic temper—as a necessary evil, the responsibility for which falls upon the old regime. The real reason for their attitude of indulgence is that "spontaneous" insurrection cannot transcend the framework of the bourgeois regime.

The social democrats take a similar position. They do not reject revolution at large as a social catastrophe, any more than they reject earthquakes, volcanic eruptions, eclipses and epidemics of the plague. What they do reject—calling it "Blanquism," or still worse, Bolshevism—is the conscious preparation of an overturn, the plan, the conspiracy. In other words, the social democrats are ready to sanction—and that only *ex post facto*—those overturns which hand the power to the bourgeoisie, but they implacably condemn those methods which might alone bring the power to the proletariat. Under this pretended objectivism they conceal a policy of defense of the capitalist society.

From his observations and reflections upon the failure of the many insurrections he witnessed or took part in, Auguste Blanqui derived a number of tactical rules which if violated will make the victory of any insurrection extremely difficult, if not impossible. Blanqui demanded these things: a timely creation of correct revolutionary detachments, their centralized command and adequate equipment, a well calculated placement of barricades, their definite construction, and a systematic, not a mere episodic, defense of them. All these rules, deriving from the military problems of the insurrection, must of course change with social conditions and military technique, but in themselves they are not by any means "Blanquism" in the sense that this word approaches the German "putschism," or revolutionary adventurism.

Insurrection is an art, and like all arts it has its laws. The rules of Blanqui were the demands of a military revolutionary realism. Blanqui's mistake lay not in his direct but his inverse theorem. From the fact that tactical weakness condemns an insurrection to defeat, Blanqui inferred that an observance of the rules of insurrectionary tactics would itself guarantee the victory. Only from this point on is it legitimate to contrast Blanquism with Marxism. Conspiracy does not take the place of insurrection. An active minority of the proletariat, no matter how well organized, cannot seize the power regardless of the general conditions of the country. In this point history has condemned Blanquism. But only in this. His affirmative theorem retains all its force.

In order to conquer the power, the proletariat needs more than a spontaneous insurrection. It needs a suitable organization, it needs a plan; it needs a conspiracy. Such is the Leninist view of this question.

Engels's criticism of the fetishism of the barricade was based upon the evolution of military technique and of technique in general. The insurrectionary tactic of Blanquism corresponded to the character of the old Paris, the semi-handicraft proletariat, the narrow streets and the military system of Louis Philippe. Blanqui's mistake in principle was to identify revolution with insurrection. His technical mistake was to identify insurrection with the barricade. The Marxian criticism has been directed against both mistakes. Although at one with Blanquism in regarding insurrection as an art, Engels discovered not only the subordinate place occupied by insurrection in a revolution, but also the declining role of the barricade in an insurrection. Engels' criticism had nothing in common with a renunciation of the revolutionary methods in favor of pure parliamentarism, as the philistines of the German Social Democracy, in cooperation with the Hohenzollern censorship, attempted in their day to pretend. For Engels the question about barricades remained a question about one of the technical elements of an uprising. The reformists have attempted to infer from his rejection of the decisive importance of the barricade a rejection of revolutionary violence in general. That is about the same as to infer the destruction of militarism from considerations of the probable decline in importance of trenches in future warfare.

The organization by means of which the proletariat can both overthrow the old power and replace it, is the soviets. This afterwards became a matter of historic experience, but was up to the October revolution a theoretical prognosis—resting, to be sure, upon the preliminary experience of 1905. The soviets are organs of preparation of the masses for insurrection, organs of insurrection, and after the victory organs of government.

However, the soviets by themselves do not settle the question. They may serve different goals according to the program and leadership. The soviets receive their program from the party. Whereas the soviets in revolutionary conditions—and apart from revolution they are impossible—comprise the whole class with the exception of its altogether backward, inert or demoralized strata, the revolutionary party represents the brain of the class. The problem of conquering the power can be solved only by a definite combination of party with soviets—or with other mass organizations more or less equivalent to soviets.

When headed by a revolutionary party the soviet consciously and in good season strives towards a conquest of power. Accommodating itself to changes in the political situation and the mood of the masses, it gets ready the military bases of the insurrection, unites the shock troops upon a single scheme of action, works out a plan for the offensive and for the final assault. And this means bringing organized conspiracy into mass insurrection.

The Bolsheviks were compelled more than once, and long before the October revolution, to refute accusations of conspiratism and Blanquism directed against them by their enemies. Moreover, nobody waged a more implacable struggle against the system of pure conspiracy than Lenin. The opportunists of the international social democracy more than once defended the old Social Revolutionary tactic of individual terror directed against the agents of tzarism, when this tactic was ruthlessly criticized by the Bolsheviks with their insistence upon mass insurrection as opposed to the individual adventurism of the intelligentsia. But in refuting all varieties of Blanquism and anarchism, Lenin did not for one moment bow down to any "sacred" spontaneousness of the masses. He thought out before anybody else, and more deeply, the correlation between the objective and subjective factors in a revolution, between the spontaneous movement and the policy of the party, between the popular masses and the progressive class, between the proletariat and its vanguard, between the soviets and the party, between insurrection and conspiracy.

But if it is true than an insurrection cannot be evoked at will, and that nevertheless in order to win it must be organized in advance, then the revolutionary leaders are presented with a task of correct diagnosis. They must feel out the growing insurrection in good season and supplement it with a conspiracy. The interference of the midwife in labor pains—however this image may have been abused—remains the clearest illustration of this conscious intrusion into an elemental process. Herzen once accused his friend Bakunin of invariably in all his revolutionary enterprises taking the second month of pregnancy for the ninth. Herzen himself was rather inclined to deny even in the ninth that pregnancy existed. In February the question of determining the date of birth hardly arose at all, since the insurrection flared up unexpectedly without centralized leadership. But exactly for this reason the power did not go to those who had accomplished the insurrection, but to those who had applied the brakes. It was quite otherwise with the second insurrection. This was consciously prepared by the Bolshevik party. The problem of correctly seizing the moment to give the signal for the attack was thus laid upon the Bolshevik staff.

*Moment* here is not to be taken too literally as meaning a definite day and hour. Physical births also present a considerable period of uncertainty—their limits interesting not only to the art of a midwife, but also to the casuistics of the Surrogate's Court. Between the moment when an attempt to summon an insurrection must inevitably prove premature and lead to a revolutionary miscarriage, and the moment when a favorable situation must be considered hopelessly missed, there exists a certain period—it may be measured in weeks, and sometimes in a few months—in the course of which an insurrection may be carried out with more or less chance of success. To discriminate this comparatively short period and then choose the definite moment—now in the more accurate sense of the very day and hour—for the last blow, constitutes and most responsible task of the revolutionary leaders. It can with full justice be called the key problem, for it unites the policy of revolution with the technique of insurrection—and it is needless to add that insurrection, like war, is a continuation of politics with other instruments.

Intuition and experience are necessary for revolutionary leadership, just as for all other kinds of creative activity. But much more than that is needed. The art of the magician can also successfully rely upon intuition and experience. Political magic is adequate, however, only for epochs and periods in which routine predominates. An epoch of mighty historic upheavals has no use for witch-doctors. Here experience, even illumined by intuition, is not enough. Here you must have a synthetic doctrine comprehending the interactions of the chief historic forces. Here you must have a materialistic method permitting you to discover, behind the moving shadows of program and slogan, the actual movement of social bodies.

The fundamental premise of a revolution is that the existing social structure has become incapable of solving the urgent problems of development of the nation. A revolution becomes possible, however, only in case the society contains a new class capable of taking the lead in solving the problems presented by history. The process of preparing a revolution consists of making the objective problems involved in the contradictions of industry and of classes find their way into the consciousness of living human masses, change this consciousness and create new correlations of human forces.

The ruling classes, as a result of their practically manifested incapacity to get the country out of its blind alley, lose faith in themselves; the old parties fall to pieces; a bitter struggle of groups and cliques prevails; hopes are placed in miracles or miracle workers. All this constitutes one of the political premises of a revolution, a very important although a passive one.

A bitter hostility to the existing order and a readiness to venture upon the most heroic efforts and sacrifices in order to bring the country out upon an upward road—this is a new political consciousness of the revolutionary class, and constitutes the most important active premise of a revolution.

These two fundamental camps, however—the big property holders and the proletariat—do not exhaust the population of a country. Between them lie broad layers of the petty bourgeoisie, showing all the colors of the economic and political rainbow. The discontent of these intermediate layers, their disappointment with the policy of the ruling class, their impatience and indignation, their readiness to support a bold revolutionary initiative on the part of the proletariat, constitute the third political premise of a revolution. It is partly passive—in that it neutralizes the upper strata of the petty bourgeoisie—but partly also active, for it impels the lower strata directly into the struggle side by side with the workers.

That these premises condition each other is obvious. The more decisively and confidently the proletariat acts, the better will it succeed in bringing after it the intermediate layer, the more isolated will be the ruling class, and the more acute its demoralization. And, on the other hand, a demoralization of the rulers will pour water into the mill of the revolutionary class.

The proletariat can become imbued with the confidence necessary for a governmental overthrow only if a clear prospect opens before it, only if it has had an opportunity to test out in action a correlation of forces which is changing to its advantage; only if it feels above it a far-sighted, firm and confident leadership. This brings us to the last premise—by no means the last in importance—of the conquest of power; the revolutionary party as a tightly welded and tempered vanguard of the class.

Thanks to a favorable combination of historic conditions both domestic and international, the Russian proletariat was headed by a party of extraordinary political clarity and unexampled revolutionary temper. Only this permitted that small and young class to carry out a historic task of unprecedented proportions. It is indeed the general testimony of history—the Paris Commune, the German and Austrian revolutions of 1918, the soviet revolutions in Hungary and Bavaria, the Italian revolution of 1919, the German crisis of 1923, the Chinese revolution of 1925–27, the Spanish revolution of 1931—that up to now the weakest link in the chain of necessary conditions has been the party. The hardest thing of all is for the working-class to create a revolutionary organization capable of rising to the height of its historic task. In the older and more civilized countries powerful forces work toward the weakening and demoralization of the revolutionary vanguard. An important constituent part of this work is the struggle of the social democrats against "Blanquism," by which name they designate the revolutionary essence of Marxism.

Notwithstanding the number of great social and political crises, a coincidence of all the conditions necessary to a victorious and stable proletarian revolution has so far occurred but once in history: in Russia in October 1917. A revolutionary situation is not long-lived. The least stable of the premises of a revolution is the mood of the petty bourgeoisie. At a time of national crisis the petty bourgeoisie follows that class which inspires confidence not only in words but deeds. Although capable of impulsive enthusiasm and even of revolutionary fury, the petty bourgeoisie lacks endurance, easily loses heart under reverses, and passes from elated hope to discouragement. And these sharp and swift changes in the mood of the petty bourgeoisie lend their instability to every revolutionary situation. If the proletarian party is not decisive enough to convert the hopes and expectations of the popular masses into revolutionary action in good season, the flood tide is quickly followed by an ebb: the intermediate strata turn away their eyes from the revolution and seek a savior in the opposing camp. And just as at flood tide the proletariat draws after it the petty bourgeoisie, so during the ebb the petty bourgeoisie draws after it considerable layers of the proletariat. Such is the dialectic of the communist and fascist waves observable in the political evolution of Europe since the war.

Attempting to ground themselves upon the assertion of Marx that no regime withdraws from the stage of history until it has exhausted all its possibilities, the Mensheviks denied the legitimacy of a struggle for proletarian dictatorship in backward Russia where capitalism had far from exhausted itself. This argument contained two mistakes, both fatal. Capitalism is not a national but a world-wide system. The imperialist war and its consequences demonstrated that the capitalist system had exhausted itself on a world scale. The revolution in Russia was a breaking point of the weakest link in the system of world-wide capitalism.

But the falsity of this Menshevik conception appears also from a national point of view. From the standpoint of economic abstraction, it is indeed possible to affirm that capitalism in Russia has not exhausted its possibilities. But economic processes do not take place in the ether, but in a concrete historical medium. Capitalism is not an abstraction, but a living system of class relations requiring above all things a state power. That the monarchy, under whose protection Russian capitalism developed, had exhausted its possibilities is not denied even by the Mensheviks. The February revolution tried to build up an intermediate state regime. We have followed its history: in the course of eight months it exhausted itself completely. What sort of state order could in these conditions guarantee the further development of Russian capitalism?

"The bourgeois republic, defended only by socialists of moderate tendencies, finding no longer any support in the masses . . . could not maintain itself. Its whole essence had evaporated. There remained only an external shell." This accurate definition belongs to Miliukov. The fate of this evaporated system was necessarily, according to his words, the same as that of the tzarist monarchy: "Both prepared the ground for a revolution, and on the day of revolution neither could find a single defender."

As early as July and August Miliukov characterized the situation by presenting a choice between two names: Kornilov or Lenin? But Kornilov had now made his experiment and it had ended in a miserable failure. For the regime of Kerensky there was certainly no place left. With all the varieties of mood, says Sukhanov, "the one thing upon which all united was hate for the Kerensky regime." Just as the tzarist monarchy had toward the end become impossible in the eyes of the upper circle of the nobility and even the grand dukes, so the government of Kerensky became odious even to the direct inspirers of his regime, the "grand dukes" of the compromisist upper crust. In this universal dissatisfaction, this sharp political nerve-tension of all classes, we have one of the symptoms of a ripe revolutionary situation. In the same way every muscle, nerve and fiber of an organism is intolerably tensed just before an abscess bursts.

The resolution of the July congress of the Bolsheviks, while warning the workers against premature encounters, had at the same time pointed out that the battle must be joined "whenever the general national crisis and the deep mass enthusiasm have created conditions favorable to the going over of the poor people of the city and country to the side of the workers." That moment arrived in September and October.

The insurrection was thenceforth able to believe in its success, for it could rely upon a genuine majority of the people. This, of course, is not to be understood in a formal sense. If a referendum could have been taken on the question of insurrection, it would have given extremely contradictory and uncertain results. An inner readiness to support a revolution is far from identical with an ability clearly to formulate the necessity of it. Moreover, the answer would have depended to a vast degree upon the manner in which the question was presented, the institution which conducted the referendum—or, to put 't more simply, the class which held the power.

There is a limit to the application of democratic methods. You can inquire of all the passengers as to what type of car they like to ride in, but it is impossible to question them as to whether to apply the brakes when the train is at full speed and accident threatens. If the saving operation is carried out skillfully, however, and in time, the approval of the passengers is guaranteed in advance.

Parliamentary consultations of the people are carried out at a single moment, whereas during a revolution the different layers of the population arrive at the same conclusion one after another and with inevitable, although sometimes very slight, intervals. At the moment when the advanced detachment is burning with revolutionary impatience, the backward layers have only begun to move. In Petrograd and Moscow all the mass organizations were under the leadership of the Bolsheviks. In Tambov province, which has over three million population—that is, a little less than both capitals put together—a Bolshevik faction first appeared in the soviet only a short time before the October revolution.

The syllogisms of the objective development are far from coinciding—day by day—with the syllogisms of the thought process of the masses. And when a great practical decision becomes unpostponable, in the course of events, that is the very moment when a referendum is impossible. The difference in level and mood of the different layers of the people is overcome in action. The advance layers bring after them the wavering and isolate the opposing. The majority is not counted up, but won over. Insurrection comes into being at exactly that moment when direct action alone offers a way out of the contradictions.

Although lacking the power to draw by themselves the necessary political inferences from their war against the landlords, the peasants had by the very fact of the agrarian insurrection already adhered to the insurrection of the cities, had evoked it and were demanding it. They expressed their will not with the white ballot, but with the red cock—a more serious referendum. Within those limits in which the support of the peasantry was necessary for the establishment of a soviet dictatorship, the support was already at hand. "The dictatorship"—as Lenin answered the doubters—"would give land to the peasants and all power to the peasant committees in the localities. How can you in your right mind doubt that the peasant would support that dictatorship?" In order that the soldiers, peasants and oppressed nationalities, floundering in the snow-storm of an elective ballot should recognize the Bolsheviks in action, it was necessary that the Bolsheviks seize the power.

But what correlation of forces was necessary in order that the proletariat should seize the power?" To have at the decisive moment, at the decisive point, an overwhelming superiority of force," wrote Lenin later, interpreting the October revolution,"—this law of military success is also the law of political success, especially in that seething and bitter war of classes which is called revolution. The capitals, or generally speaking, the biggest centers of trade and industry . . . decide to a considerable degree the political fate of the people—that is, of course, on condition that the centers are supported by sufficient local rural forces, although this support need not be immediate." It was in this dynamic sense that Lenin spoke of the majority of the people, and that was the sole real meaning of the concept of majority.

The enemy democrats comforted themselves with the thought that the people following the Bolsheviks were mere raw material, mere historic clay. The potters were still to be these same democrats acting in cooperation with the educated bourgeoisie. "Can't those people see," asked a Menshevik paper, "that the Petrograd proletariat and garrison were never before so isolated from all other social strata?" The misfortune of the proletariat and the garrison was that they were "isolated" from those classes from whom they intended to take the power!

But was it really possible to rely upon the sympathy and support of the dark masses in the provinces and at the front? "Their Bolshevism," wrote Sukhanov scornfully, "was nothing but hatred for the coalition and longing for land and peace." As though that were little! Hatred for the coalition meant a desire to take the power from the bourgeoisie. Longing for land and peace was the colossal program which the peasant and soldier intended to carry out under the leadership of the workers. The insignificance of the democrats, even the most leftward, resulted from this very distrust—the distrust of "educated" sceptics—in those dark masses who grasp a phenomenon wholesale, not bothering about details and nuances. This intellectual, pseudo-aristocratic, squeamish attitude toward the people was foreign to Bolshevism, hostile to its very nature. The Bolsheviks were not lily-handed, literary friends of the masses, not pedants. They were not afraid of those backward strata now for the first time lifting themselves out of the dregs. The Bolsheviks took the people as preceding history had created them, and as they were called to achieve the revolution. The Bolsheviks saw it as their mission to stand at the head of that people. Those against the insurrection were "everybody"—except the Bolsheviks. But the Bolsheviks were the people. . . .

# 16

# Revolution from Above and Fascism

*Barrington Moore, Jr.*

⟪⟨⟨⟨⟨⟨⟨⟨⟨⟨⟨⟨⟨⟨⟨⟨⟨⟨⟨⟨⟨⟨⟨⟨⟨⟨⟨⟨⟨⟨⟨⟨⟨⟨⟨⟨⟨⟨⟨⟨⟨⟨⟨⟨⟨⟨⟨⟨⟨⟨⟨

## EDITORS' COMMENT

The following essay, reprinted from Barrington Moore, Jr.'s *Social Origins of Dictatorship and Democracy*, discusses the political effects which result from one particular form of modernization. "Revolution from above," as the reader will discover, does not refer to a counter-revolution or to a reactionary coup but, instead, to what some might call a "progressive" revolution—the modernization of a nation by a traditional or a semitraditional ruling elite. Moore suggests in *Social Origins* that for the modern world this course is one of three major alternatives: the bourgeois revolution and the communist-agrarian revolution being the other paths by which a nation casts off its traditions sufficiently to become industrialized.

In an essay reprinted in this volume (see Selection 6), Eugene Kamenka develops the concept of a "political revolution"—a social upheaval which changes the structure of the government but which has its origins in rapid economic development. Moore would agree, by and large, with Kamenka's definition; both writers have a progressive view of history, and both are impressed by the close relation between economic change and political upheaval. But Moore goes much beyond Kamenka (and most other theorists of the economic basis of historical change) by placing a heavy reliance on the role of the countryside in the formation of the type of society which emerges from the modernization process. In the following essay, he argues that the origins of fascism are to be found in an alliance between the industrial and the agricultural elites in an attempt to maintain their economic position—a situation which could not have arisen in a society that had experienced a bourgeois revolution, nor in a society where the bourgeoisie was too weak to form an effective alliance with the rural landlord.

The difference between this form of capitalistic development and a democratic capitalistic development is to be found in a combination of historical accidents and rural feudal conditions. At the risk of vastly oversimplifying Moore's arguments, one can summarize his views as follows: democracy in Europe was the result of a persistent competition between crown and manor, the commercialization of agriculture, and the competition between commercialized agricultural interests and the interests of the towns. Or, to reverse the argument, the persistence of a highly extractive agricultural system, the prevalence of either crown or manor in a society, and the unification of interests between industrial and agricultural elites generally led to a repressive society. There is more than just the flavor of Lewis Coser in these arguments— that conflict and competition produce a progressive, in this case democratic, society. Violence, to Moore, is a functional element of democratic modernization.

Moore's analysis not only raises the problem of how much effect economic forces have on politics but also the question of how much effect the constraints of past culture have on any society. Although he explicitly rejects the notion that Germany, Japan, and Italy were doomed to fascism centuries before its actual occurrence, nevertheless, there is present in his essay a strong sense of the past—the medieval and early postmedieval past. He certainly finds the origins of Nazism in the nineteenth-century social structure, and one might gain the impression that its development was inevitable from Bismarck on. However, on careful reading, it appears that he stops short of this thesis— since, despite all the forces of economics and history, Moore is aware of the accidental and the fortuitous in shaping the history of nations. In fact, that England did not become a fascist state, he argues, was the result of a number of historical accidents and unique conditions.

This essay is a most pessimistic chapter in a very pessimistic book, since Moore's overall assumption is that modernization cannot occur without violent revolution or extreme repression: that one form of force or another is necessary to bring about any major form of political or economic change. He, therefore, anticipates much human suffering for the developing nations—suffering from violence and repression if they proceed rapidly through the stages of development and suffering from deprivation if they do not.

Another point raised is the role of nationalism in averting civil disorders. The conscious use by elites of the real or imaginary threat of foreign powers or the use of imperialist ideologies to develop internal cohesion are very important factors in the Revolution from above. In this sense—in this *negative* sense—the international dimensions of internal conflict are once more illustrated.

Finally, the reader should compare Moore's assertions in this essay about economic and social forces with the ones of theorists who place much emphasis on the role of ideology in social change, since Moore believes that the role of ideas is minor in the sense that they are largely reflective of social conditions.

# REVOLUTION FROM ABOVE AND FASCISM

BARRINGTON MOORE, JR.

The second main route to the world of modern industry we have called the capitalist and reactionary one, exemplified most clearly by Germany and Japan. There capitalism took hold quite firmly in both agriculture and industry and turned them into industrial countries. But it did so without a popular revolutionary upheaval. What tendencies there were in this direction were weak, far weaker in Japan than in Germany, and in both were diverted and crushed. Though not the only cause, agrarian conditions and the specific types of capitalist transformation that took place in the countryside contributed very heavily to these defeats and the feebleness behind any impulse toward Western democratic forms.

There are certain forms of capitalist transformation in the countryside that may succeed economically, in the sense of yielding good profits, but which are for fairly obvious reasons unfavorable to the growth of free institutions of the nineteenth-century Western variety. Though these forms shade into each other, it is easy to distinguish two general types. A landed upper class may, as in Japan, maintain intact the preexisting peasant society, introducing just enough changes in rural society to ensure that the peasants generate a sufficient surplus that it can appropriate and market at a profit. Or a landed upper class may devise wholly new social arrangements along the lines of plantation slavery. Straightforward slavery in modern times is likely to be the creation of a class of colonizing intruders into tropical areas. In parts of eastern Europe, however, indigenous nobilities were able to reintroduce serfdom, which reattached the peasants to the soil in ways that produced somewhat similar results. This was a halfway form between the two others.

Both the system of maintaining peasant society intact but squeez-

SOURCE. Barrington Moore, Jr., "Revolution from Above and Fascism," from *Social Origins of Dictatorship and Democracy* (Boston: Beacon Press, 1966), pp. 433–452. Reprinted with permission of the publishers, Beacon Press and Penguin Books, Ltd. Copyright 1966 by Barrington Moore, Jr.

ing more out of it and the use of servile or semiservice labor on large
units of cultivation require strong political methods to extract the surplus, keep the labor force in its place, and in general make the system
work. Not all of these methods are of course political in the narrow
sense. Particularly where the peasant society is preserved, there are
all sorts of attempts to use traditional relationships and attitudes as
the basis of the landlords' position. Since these political methods have
important consequences, it will be helpful to give them a name.
Economists distinguish between labor-intensive and capital-intensive
types of agriculture, depending on whether the system uses large
amounts of labor or capital. It may also be helpful to speak of labor-
repressive systems, of which slavery is but an extreme type. The difficulty with such a notion is that one may legitimately ask precisely
what type has not been labor-repressive. The distinction I am trying
to suggest is one between the use of political mechanisms (using the
term "political" broadly as just indicated) on the one hand and reliance
on the labor market, on the other hand, to ensure an adequate labor
force for working the soil and the creation of an agricultural surplus
for consumption by other classes. Those at the bottom suffer severely
in both cases.

To make the conception of a labor-repressive agricultural system
useful, it would be well to stipulate that large numbers of people are
kept at work in this fashion. It is also advisable to state explicitly
what it does not include, for example, the American family farm of
the midnineteenth century. There may have been exploitation of the
labor of family members in this case, but it was done apparently
mainly by the head of the household himself with minimal assistance
from the outside. Again, a system of hired agricultural laborers where
the workers had considerable real freedom to refuse jobs and move
about, a condition rarely met in actual practice, would not fall under
this rubric. Finally, precommercial and preindustrial agrarian systems
are not necessarily labor-repressive if there is a rough balance between
the overlord's contribution to justice and security and the cultivator's
contribution in the form of crops. Whether this balance can be pinned
down in any objective sense is a moot point best discussed . . . in
connection with the causes of peasant revolutions. Here we need only
remark that the establishment of labor-repressive agrarian systems in
the course of modernization does not necessarily produce greater suffering among the peasants than other forms. Japanese peasants had an
easier time of it than did English ones. Our problem here is in any
case a different one: how and why labor-repressive agrarian systems
provide an unfavorable soil for the growth of democracy and an important part of the institutional complex leading to fascism.

In discussing the rural origins of parliamentary democracy, we noticed that a limited degree of independence from the monarchy constituted one of the favorable conditions, though one that did not occur everywhere. While a system of labor-repressive agriculture may be started in opposition to the central authority, it is likely to fuse with the monarchy at a later point in search of political support. This situation can also lead to the preservation of a military ethic among the nobility in a manner unfavorable to the growth of democratic institutions. The evolution of the Prussian state constitutes the clearest example. Since we have referred to these developments at several points in this work, it will be appropriate to sketch them very briefly here.

In northeastern Germany the manorial reaction of the fifteenth and sixteenth centuries, about which we shall have still more to say in quite another context, broke off the development toward the liberation of the peasantry from feudal obligations and the closely connected development of town life that in England and France eventually culminated in Western democracy. A fundamental cause was the growth of grain exports, though it was not the sole one. The Prussian nobility expanded its holdings at the expense of the peasantry which, under the Teutonic Order, had been close to freedom, and reduced them to serfdom. As part of the same process, the nobility reduced the towns to dependence by short-circuiting them with their exports. Afterward, the Hohenzollern rulers managed to destroy the independence of the nobility and crush the Estates, playing nobles and townsmen off against one another, thereby checking the aristocratic component in the move toward parliamentary government. The result in the seventeenth and eighteenth centuries was the "Sparta of the North," a militarized fusion of royal bureaucracy and landed aristocracy.[1]

From the side of the landed aristocracy came the conceptions of inherent superiority in the ruling class and a sensitivity to matters of status, prominent traits well into the twentieth century. Fed by new sources, these conceptions could later be vulgarized and made appealing to the German population as a whole in doctrines of racial superiority. The royal bureaucracy introduced, against considerable aristocratic resistance, the ideal of complete and unreflecting obedience to an institution over and above class and individual—prior to the nineteenth century it would be anarchronistic to speak of the nation. Prussian discipline, obedience, and admiration for the hard qualities of the soldier come mainly from the Hohenzollern efforts to create a centralized monarchy.

All this does not of course mean that some inexorable fate drove

---

[1] See Rosenberg, *Bureaucracy*; Carsten, *Origins of Prussia*.

Germany toward fascism from the sixteenth century onward, that the process never could have been reversed. Other factors had to intervene, some very important ones, as industrialization began to gather momentum during the nineteenth century. About these it will be necessary to speak in a moment. There are also significant variants and substitutions within the general pattern that has led to fascism, subalternatives one might say if one wished to be very precise and technical, within the major alternative of conservative modernization through revolution from above. In Japan the notion of total commitment to authority apparently came out of the feudal, rather than the monarchical, side of the equation.[2] Again in Italy, where fascism was invented, there was no powerful national monarchy. Mussolini had to go all the way back to ancient Rome for the corresponding symbolism.

At a later stage in the course of modernization, a new and crucial factor is likely to appear in the form of a rough working coalition between influential sectors of the landed upper classes and the emerging commercial and manufacturing interests. By and large, this was a nineteenth-century political configuration, though it continued on into the twentieth. Marx and Engels in their discussion of the abortive 1848 revolution in Germany, wrong though they were on the other major features, put their finger on this decisive ingredient: a commercial and industrial class which is too weak and dependent to take power and rule in its own right and which therefore throws itself into the arms of the landed aristocracy and the royal bureaucracy, exchanging the right to rule for the right to make money.[3] It is necessary to add that, even if the commercial and industrial element is weak, it must be strong enough (or soon become strong enough) to be a worthwhile political ally. Otherwise a peasant revolution leading to communism may intervene. This happened in both Russia and China after unsuccessful efforts to establish such a coalition. There also appears to be another ingredient that enters the situation somewhat later than the formation of this coalition: sooner or later systems of labor-repressive agriculture are liable to run into difficulties produced by competition from more technically advanced ones in other countries. The competition of American wheat exports created difficulties in many parts of Europe after the end of our Civil War. In the context of a reactionary coalition, such competition intensifies authoritarian and reactionary trends among a landed upper class that finds its economic basis sinking and therefore turns to political levers to preserve its rule.

[2] Sansom, *History of Japan*, I. 368.
[3] See Marx, *Selected Works*, II, "Germany: Revolution and Counter-Revolution," written mainly by Engels.

Where the coalition succeeds in establishing itself, there has followed a prolonged period of conservative and even authoritarian government, which, however, falls far short of fascism. The historical boundaries of such systems are often somewhat blurred. At a rather generous estimate, one might hold that to this species belong the period from the Stein-Hardenberg reforms in Germany to the end of the First World War and, in Japan, from the fall of the Tokugawa Shogunate to 1918. These authoritarian governments acquired some democratic features: notably a parliament with limited powers. Their history may be punctuated with attempts to extend democracy which, toward the end, succeeded in establishing unstable democracies (the Weimar Republic, Japan in the twenties, Italy under Giolitti). Eventually the door to fascist regimes was opened by the failure of these democracies to cope with the severe problems of the day and reluctance or inability to bring about fundamental structural changes. One factor, but only one, in the social anatomy of these governments has been the retention of a very substantial share in political power by the landed elite, due to the absence of a revolutionary breakthrough by the peasants in combination with urban strata.

Some of the semiparliamentary governments that arose on this basis carried out a more or less peaceful economic and political revolution from above that took them a long distance toward becoming modern industrial countries. Germany travelled the furthest in this direction, Japan only somewhat less so, Italy a great deal less, Spain very little. Now, in the course of modernization by a revolution from above, such a government has to carry out many of the same tasks performed elsewhere with the help of a revolution from below. The notion that a violent popular revolution is somehow necessary in order to sweep away "feudal" obstacles to industrialization is pure nonsense, as the course of German and Japanese history demonstrates. On the other hand, the political consequences from dismounting the old order from above are decidedly different. As they proceeded with conservative modernization, these semiparliamentary governments tried to preserve as much of the original social structure as they could, fitting large sections into the new building wherever possible. The results had some resemblance to present-day Victorian houses with modern electrical kitchens but insufficient bathrooms and leaky pipes hidden decorously behind newly plastered walls. Ultimately the makeshifts collapsed.

One very important series of measures was the rationalization of the political order. This meant the breakup of traditional and long established territorial divisions, such as the feudal *han* in Japan or independent states and principalities in Germany and Italy. Except in Japan, the breakup was not complete. But in the course of time a central government did establish strong authority and a uniform administrative system, and a more or less uniform law code and system of courts appeared. Again, in varying degrees, the state managed to create a sufficiently powerful military machine to be able to make the wishes of its rulers felt in the arena of international politics. Economically the establishment of a strong central government and the elimination of internal barriers to trade meant an increase in the size of the effective economic unit. Without such an increase in size, the division of labor necessary for an industrial society could not exist, unless all countries were willing to trade peacefully with one another. As the first country to industrialize, England had been able to draw on most of the accessible world for material and markets, a situation that gradually deteriorated during the nineteenth century when others caught up and sought to use the state to guarantee their markets and sources of supply.

Still another aspect of the rationalization of the political order has to do with the making of citizens in a new type of society. Literacy and rudimentary technical skills are necessary for the masses. Setting up a national system of education is very likely to bring on a conflict with religious authorities. Loyalty to a new abstraction, the state, must also replace religious loyalties if they transcend national boundaries or compete with one another so vigorously as to destroy internal peace. Japan had less of a problem here than Germany, Italy, or Spain. Yet even in Japan, as the somewhat artificial revival of *Shintó* indicates, there were substantial difficulties. In overcoming such difficulties, the existence of a foreign enemy can be quite useful. Then patriotic and conservative appeals to the military traditions of the landed aristocracy can overcome localist tendencies among this important group and push into the background any too insistent demands of the lower strata for an unwarranted share in the benefits of the new order. In carrying out the task of rationalizing and extending the political order, these nine-teenth-century governments were doing work that royal absolutism had already accomplished in other countries.

One striking fact about the course of conservative modernization is the appearance of a galaxy of distinguished political leaders: Cavour in Italy; in Germany, Stein, Hardenberg, and Bismarck, the most famous of them all; in Japan the statesmen of the Meiji era. Though the reasons are obscure, it seems unlikely that the appearance of a similar leadership in similar circumstances could be pure coincidence. All were conservatives in the political spectrum of their time and country, devoted to the monarchy, willing and able to use it as an instrument of reform, modernization, and national unification. Though all were aristocrats, they were dissidents or outsiders of a sort in relation to the old order. To the extent that their aristocratic background contributed habits of command and a flair for politics, one may perhaps detect a contribution of the agrarian *anciens régimes* to the construction of a new society. But there were strong contrary pulls here too. To the extent that these men were aliens within the aristocracy, one may see the incapacity of this stratum to meet the challenge of the modern world merely with its own intellectual and political resources.

The most successful of the conservative regimes accomplished a great deal, not only in tearing down the old order but in establishing a new one. The state aided industrial construction in several important ways. It served as an engine of primary capitalist accumulation, gathering resources and directing them toward the building of an industrial plant. In the taming of the labor force it again played an important role, by no means entirely a repressive one. Armaments served as an important stimulus for industry. So did protectionist tariff policies. All of these measures at some point involved taking resources or people out of agriculture. Therefore they imposed from time to time a serious strain on the coalition between those sectors of the upper strata in business and in agriculture that was the main feature of the political system. Without the threat of foreign dangers, sometimes real, sometimes perhaps imaginary, sometimes as in the case of Bismarck deliberately manufactured for domestic purposes, the landed interests might well have balked, to the point of endangering the whole process. The foreign threat alone, however, need not bear the whole weight of explaining this behavior.[4] Material and other rewards—the "payoff" in the language of gangsters and game theory—were quite substantial for both partners as long as they succeeded in keeping the peasants and industrial labor in place. Where there was substantial economic progress, the industrial workers were able to make significant gains, as in Germany, where *Sozialpolitik* was invented. It was in those countries that remained more backward, Italy to some extent, probably Spain to a greater extent, that there was more of a tendency to cannibalize the indigenous population.

Certain conditions seem to have been necessary for the successes of conservative modernization. First, it takes very able leadership to drag along the less perceptive reactionary elements, concentrated

[4] For a brilliant analysis of the situation in Germany toward the end of the nineteenth century see Kehr, *Schlachtflottenbau.* Weber, "Entwickelungstendenzen in der Lage der Ostelbischen Landarbeiter," in *Gesammelte Aufsätze,* esp. 471–476, brings out very clearly the position of the Junkers.

among, though not necessarily confined to, the landed classes. In the beginning, Japan had to suppress a real rebellion, the Satsuma revolt, to control these elements. Reactionaries can always advance the plausible argument that modernizing leaders are making changes and concessions that will merely arouse the appetites of the lower classes and bring on a revolution.[5] Similarly, the leadership must have at hand or be able to construct a sufficiently powerful bureaucratic apparatus, including the agencies of repression, the military and the police (compare the German saying *Gegen Demokraten helfen nur Soldaten*), in order to free itself from the influence of both extreme reactionary and popular or radical pressures in the society. The government has to become separate from society, something that can happen rather more easily than simplified versions of Marxism would allow us to believe.

In the short run, a strong conservative government has distinct advantages. It can both encourage and control economic growth. It can see to it that the lower classes who pay the costs under all forms of modernization do not make too much trouble. But Germany and, even more, Japan were trying to solve a problem that was inherently insoluble, to modernize without changing their social structures. The only way out of this dilemma was militarism, which united the upper classes. Militarism intensified a climate of international conflict, which in turn made industrial advance all the more imperative, even if in Germany a Bismarck could for a time hold the situation in check, partly because militarism had not yet become a mass phenomenon. To carry out thoroughgoing structural reforms, i.e., to make the transition to a paying commercial agriculture without the repression of those who worked the soil and to do the same in industry, in a word, to use modern technology rationally for human welfare was beyond the political vision of these governments. Ultimately these systems crashed in an attempt at foreign expansion, but not until they had tried to make reaction popular in the form of fascism.

Before discussing this final phase, it may be instructive to glance at unsuccessful reactionary trends in other countries. As mentioned above, this reactionary syndrome can be found at some point in all the cases I have examined. To see why it has failed in other countries may sharpen awareness of the reasons behind its successes. A brief

---

[5] Such arguments were also very prominent in England as part of the reaction to the French Revolution. Many have been collected in Turberville, *House of Lords*. Tory reform could work in nineteenth-century England, however, at least partly because it was a sham battle anyway: the bourgeoisie had won, and only the more obtuse could fail to see their power.

look at these trends in such widely differing countries as England, Russia, and India may serve to bring out important underlying similarities concealed beneath a variety of historical experiences.

Beginning in the latter years of the French Revolution and lasting until about 1822, English society passed through a reactionary phase that recalls both the cases just discussed and contemporary problems of American democracy. During most of these years England was fighting against a revolutionary regime and its heirs, sometimes, it may have seemed, for national survival itself. As in our own time, the advocates of domestic reform were identified with a foreign enemy represented as the incarnation of all that was evil. Again, as in our own time, the violence, repressions, and betrayals of the revolutionary movement in France sickened and discouraged its English supporters, making easier and more plausible the work of reactionaries eager to stamp out the sparks that floated across the channel. Writing in the 1920s the great French historian Elie Halévy, certainly not a man given to dramatic exaggeration, asserted, "A reign of terror was established throughout England by the nobility and middle class—a terror more formidable, though more silent, than the noisy demonstrations [of the radicals]."[6] The events of the four decades and more that have passed since Halévy wrote these lines have dulled our senses and lowered our standards. No one writing now would be likely to refer to this phase as a reign of terror. The number of direct victims of repression was small. In the "massacre" of Peterloo (1819)—a derisive reference to Wellington's more famous victory of Waterloo—only eleven persons were killed. Nevertheless the gathering movement to reform Parliament was placed outside the law, the press muzzled, associations that smacked of radicalism forbidden, a rash of reason trials initiated, spies and *agents provocateurs* let loose among the people, the Habeas Corpus suspended *after* the war with Napoleon had ended. Repression and suffering were real and widespread, only partly mitigated by some continued articulate opposition: an aristocrat such as Charles James Fox (d. 1806) who spoke up courageously in Parliament, here and there a judge or a jury that refused to convict on treason or other charges.[7]

[6] Halévy, *History of the English People*, II, 19.
[7] An excellent and detailed description of what life was like for the lower classes in England during this period may be found in Thompson, *Making of Working Class*. The main governmental measures and some of their effects can be traced through Cole and Postgate, *British People*, 132–134, 148–149, 157–159, 190–193. For some valuable additional details see Halévy, *History of the English People*, II, 23–25. Aristocratic opposition to repression may be found in Trevelyan, *History of England*, III, 89–92, and Turberville, *House of Lords*, 98–100.

Why was this reactionary upsurge no more than a passing phase in England? Why did not England continue along this road to become another Germany? Anglo-Saxon liberties, Magna Charta, Parliament and such rhetoric will not do for an answer. Parliament voted repressive measures by huge majorities.

An important part of the answer may be found in the fact that, a century before, certain extremist Englishmen had chopped off the head of their monarch to shatter the magic of royal absolutism in England. At a deeper level of causation, England's whole previous history, her reliance on a navy instead of an army, on unpaid justices of the peace instead of royal officials, had put in the hands of the central government a repressive apparatus weaker than that possessed by the strong continental monarchies. Thus the materials with which to construct a German system were missing or but feebly developed. Still, by now we have seen enough great social and political changes out of unpromising beginnings to suspect that the institutions could have been created if circumstances had been more favorable. But fortunately for human liberties they were not. The push toward industrialism had begun much earlier in England and was to render unnecessary for the English bourgeoisie any great dependence on the crown and the landed aristocracy. Finally, the landed upper classes themselves did not need to repress the peasants. Mainly they wanted to get them out of the way in order to go over to commercial farming; by and large, economic measures would be enough to provide the labor force they needed. Succeeding economically in this particular fashion, they had little need to resort to repressive political measures to continue their leadership. Therefore in England manufacturing and agrarian interests competed with one another for popular favor during the rest of the nineteenth century, gradually extending the suffrage while jealously opposing and knocking down each other's more selfish measures (Reform Bill of 1832, abolition of the Corn Laws in 1846, gentry support for factory legislation, etc.).

In the English phase of reaction there were hints of fascist possibilities, particularly in some of the antiradical riots. But these were no more than hints. The time was still too early. Fascist symptoms we can see very much more clearly in another part of the world at a later point in time—during a brief phase of extremism in Russia after 1905. This was extreme even by Russian standards of the day; one could make a strong case for the thesis that Russian reactionaries invented fascism. Thus this phase of Russian history is especially illuminating because it shows that the fascist syndrome (1) can appear in response to the strains of advancing industrialism independently of a specific social and cultural background; (2) that it may have many roots in agrarian life; (3) that it appears partly in response to a weak push toward parliamentary democracy; (4) but cannot flourish without industrialism or in an overwhelmingly agrarian background—points, to be sure, all suggested by the recent histories of China and Japan too, though it is illuminating to find stronger confirmation in Russian history.

Shortly before the Revolution of 1905 the tiny Russian commercial and industrial class showed some signs of discontent with the repressive tsarist autocracy and a willingness to flirt with liberal constitutional notions. Workers' strikes, however, and the promise contained in the Imperial Manifesto of October 17, 1905, to meet some of the demands of the strikers, brought the industrialists safely back within the tsarist camp.[8] Against this background appeared the Black Hundreds movement. Drawing partly on American experience, they made "lynch" into a Russian word and asked for the application of *zakon lyncha,* lynch law. They resorted to violence in storm-trooper style to suppress "treason" and "sedition." If Russia could destroy the "kikes" and foreigners, their propaganda asserted, everyone could live happily in a return to "true Russian" ways. This anti-Semitic nativism had considerable appeal to backward, precapitalist, petty bourgeois elements in the cities and among the smaller nobility. However, in still backward peasant Russia of the early twentieth century, this form of rightist extremism was unable to find a firm popular basis. Among the peasants it succeeded mainly in areas of mixed nationality, where the explanation of all evil as being due to Jews and foreigners made some sense in terms of peasant experience.[9] As everyone knows, to the extent that they were politically active, the Russian peasants were revolutionary and eventually the major force in exploding the old regime.

In India, which is equally if not more backward, similar movements have likewise failed to obtain a firm basis among the masses. To be sure, Subhas Chandra Bose, who died in 1945, expressed dictatorial sentiments, worked for the Axis, and had a very large popular following. Though his fascist sympathies were consistent with other aspects of his public record and do not seem to be the outcome of momentary enthusiasm or opportunism, Subhas Chandra Bose has gone down in Indian tradition mainly as an extreme and perhaps misguided anti-British patriot.[10] There has also been a scattering of nativist Hindu

---

[8] Gitermann, *Geschichte Russlands,* III, 403, 409–410; Berlin, *Russkaya burzhauziya,* 226–227, 236.

[9] Levitskii, "Pravyya partii," *Obshchestvennoye dvizheniye v Rossii,* III, 347–472. See esp. 432, 370–376, 401, 353–355.

[10] See Samra, "Subhas Chandra Bose," in Park and Tinker, eds, *Leadership and Political Institutions,* 66–86, esp. 78–79.

political organizations, some of which developed the autocratic discipline of the European totalitarian party. They have reached the peak of their influence so far in the chaos and riots surrounding Partition, during which they helped to promote anti-Muslim riots and served as defense organs for Hindu communities against Muslim attacks, led, presumably, by similar organizations on the Muslim side. Their programs lack economic content and appear to be mainly a form of militant, xenophobic Hinduism, seeking to combat the stereotype that Hindus are pacific, divided by caste, and weak. So far their electoral appeal has been very small.[11]

One possible reason for the weakness of the Hindu variant of fascism to date may be the fragmentation of the Hindu world along caste, class, and ethnic lines. Thus a characteristically fascist appeal addressed to one segment would antagonize others, while a more general appeal, by taking on some color of universal panhumanism, begins to lose its fascist qualities. In this connection it is worth noticing that nearly all the extremist Hindu groups have opposed untouchability and other social disabilities of caste.[12] The main reason, however, is probably the simple fact that Gandhi had already preempted the anti-foreign and anticapitalist sentiment of huge masses of the population: peasants and artisans in the cottage industries. Under the conditions created by the British occupation, he was able to tie these sentiments to the interests of a large section of the business class. On the other hand, the landed elite generally stood aloof. Thus reactionary trends have been strong in India and have helped to delay economic progress since Independence. But as a mass phenomenon the larger movements belong to an historical species distinct from fascism.

Though it might be equally profitable to undertake a parallel consideration of democratic failures that preceded fascism in Germany, Japan, and Italy, it is enough for present purposes to notice that fascism is inconceivable without democracy or what is sometimes more turgidly called the entrance of the masses onto the historical stage. Fascism was an attempt to make reaction and conservatism popular and plebeian, through which conservatism, of course, lost the substantial connection it did have with freedom. . . .

The conception of objective law vanished under fascism. Among its most significant features was a violent rejection of humanitarian ideals, including any notion of potential human equality. The fascist outlook stressed not only the inevitability of hierarchy, discipline, and

---

[11] Lambert, "Hindu Communal Groups," in Park and Tinker, eds, *Leadership and Political Institutions*, 211–224.

[12] Lambert, "Hindu Communal Groups," 219.

obedience, but also posited that they were values in their own right. Romantic conceptions of comradeship qualify this outlook but slightly; it is comradeship in submission. Another feature was the stress on violence. This stress goes far beyond any cold, rational appreciation of the factual importance of violence in politics to a mystical worship of "hardness" for its own sake. Blood and death often acquire overtones of erotic attraction, though in its less exalted moments fascism was thoroughly "healthy" and "normal," promising return to a cosy bourgeois, and even prebourgeois, peasant womb.[13]

Plebeian anticapitalism thus appears as the feature that most clearly distinguishes twentieth-century fascism from its predecessors, the nineteenth-century conservative and semiparliamentary regimes. It is a product of both the intrusion of capitalism into the rural economy and of strains arising in the postcompetitive phase of capitalist industry. Hence fascism developed most fully in Germany where capitalist industrial growth had gone the furthest within the framework of a conservative revolution from above. It came to light as only a weak secondary trend in such backward areas as Russia, China, and India. Prior to World War II, it failed to take much root in England and the United States where capitalism worked reasonably well or where efforts to correct its shortcomings could be attempted within the democratic framework and succeed with the help of a prolonged war boom. Most of the anti-capitalist opposition to big business had to be shelved in practice, though one should not make the opposite error of regarding fascist leaders as merely the agents of big business. The attraction of fascism for the lower middle class in the cities, threatened by capitalism, has often been pointed out; here we may confine ourselves to a brief review of the evidence on its varying relationships to the peasantry in different countries. In Germany the effort to establish a massive conservative base in the countryside long antedates the Nazis. As Professor Alexander Gerschenkron points out, the basic elements of Nazi doctrine appear quite distinctly in the Junkers' generally successful efforts, by means of the Agrarian League established in 1894, to win the support of the peasants in non-Junker areas of smaller farms. *Führer* worship, the idea of a corporative state, militarism, anti-Semitism, in a setting closely related to the Nazi distinction between "predatory" and "productive" capital, were devices used to appeal to anticapitalist sentiments among the peasantry.[14] There are a good many indications that in subsequent years down to the depression the substan-

---

[13] To say that fascism was atavistic does not distinguish it sufficiently. So are revolutionary movements, as I have tried to show in some detail in the next chapter.

[14] *Bread and Democracy*, 53, 55.

tial and prosperous peasants were slowly losing ground to dwarf peasants. The depression constituted a deep and general crisis, to which the main rural response was National Socialism. Rural support for the Nazis came to an average of 37.4 per cent, practically identical with that in the country as a whole in the last relatively free election of July 31, 1932.[15]

If one looks at a map of Germany showing the distribution of the Nazi vote in the rural areas and compares this map with others showing the distribution of land values, types of cultivation,[16] or of the areas of small, medium, and large farms,[17] the first impression will be that Nazism in the countryside shows no consistent relationship with any of these. However, as one studies the maps more closely, one can discern substantial evidence to the effect that the Nazis succeeded most in their appeal to the peasant whose holding was relatively small and unprofitable *for the particular area in which it existed*.[18]

To the small peasant, suffering under the advance of capitalism with its problems of prices and mortgages that seemed to be controlled by hostile city middlemen and bankers, Nazi propaganda presented the romantic image of the idealized peasant, "the free man on free land." The peasant became the key figure in the ideology of the radical right as elaborated by the Nazis. The Nazis were fond of stressing the point that, for the peasant, land is more than a means with which to earn a living; it has all the sentimental overtones of *Heimat*, to which the peasant feels himself far more closely connected than the white collar worker with his office or the industrial worker with his shop. Physiocratic and liberal notions found themselves jumbled together in these doctrines of the radical right.[19] A firm stock of small and middle peasants," said Hitler in *Mein Kampf*, "has still been at all times the best protection against social evils as we have them now."

---

[15] For the rural vote see the map of Germany showing the distribution of Nazi voting for rural areas, July 1932, with *Stadtkreise* removed, in Loomis and Beegle, "Spread of German Nazism," 726. For the percentage of the Nazi vote in Germany as a whole, consult the election statistics from 1919 to 1933 assembled in Dittmann, *Das politische Deutschland.*

[16] Compare Loomis-Beegle map above with map inserts VIII, VIIIa, and I, in Sering, ed. *Deutsche Landwirtschaft.*

[17] Printed as appendices in *Statistik des Statistik Reichs* and in less detail but on a single page as map insert IV in Sering, ed., *Deutsche Landwirtschaft.*

[18] See Loomis and Beegle, "Spread of German Nazism," 726, 727. Further evidence pointing in the same direction is summarized and cited in Bracher, et al., *Machtergreifung,* 389–390.

[19] Bracher et al., *Machtergreifung,* 390–391.

Such a peasantry constitutes the only way through which a nation can secure its daily bread. He goes on, "Industry and commerce retreat from their unhealthy leading position and fit into the general framework of a national economy based on need and equality. Both are then no longer the basis for feeding the nation, but only a help in this."[20]

For our purposes there is nothing to be gained by examining the fate of these notions after the Nazis came to power. While a few starts were made here and there, most of them were junked because they contradicted the requirements of a powerful war economy, necessarily based on industry. The notion of a retreat from industry was only the most obviously absurd feature.[21]

In Japan, as in Germany, pseudoradical anticapitalism gained a considerable foothold among the Japanese peasantry. There too the original impulse came from the landed upper classes. On the other hand, its more extreme forms, such as the assassins' bands among junior military officers, though they claimed to speak for the peasants, do not seem to have had a strong following among them. Extremism was in any case absorbed into the more general framework of "respectable" Japanese conservatism and military aggression, for which the peasantry provided a mass basis. . . .

Italian fascism displays the same pseudoradical and propeasant features found in Germany and Japan. In Italy, on the other hand, these notions were more of an opportunistic growth, a cynical decoration put on to take advantage of circumstances. Cynical opportunism was present in Germany and Japan too, of course, but seems to have been much more blatant in Italy.

Immediately after the 1914 war, there was a bitter struggle in the north Italian countryside between Socialist and Christian-Democratic trade unions on the one hand and the big landowners on the other. At this point, i.e., 1919–1920, Mussolini, according to Ignazio Silone, paid no attention to the countryside, did not believe in a fascist conquest of the land, and thought fascism would always be an urban movement.[22] But the struggle between the land-owners and the unions, representing the interests of hired labor and tenants, gave fascism an unexpected opportunity to fish in troubled waters. Presenting them-

[20] *Mein Kampf*, 151–152. For the main factual aspects of Nazi policy see also Schweitzer, "Nazification," in *Third Reich*, 576–594.

[21] For the fate of the agrarian program, consult Wunderlich, *Farm Labor*, pt. III, "The Period of National Socialism."

[22] Silone, *Fascismus*, 107.

selves as the saviors of civilization against Bolshevism, *fasci*-bands of idealists, demobilized army officers, and just plain toughs—broke up rural union headquarters, often with the connivance of the police, and during 1921 destroyed the leftist movement in the countryside. Among those who streamed into fascist ranks were peasants who had climbed into the middle ranks of landowners, and even tenants who hated the monopolistic practices of the unions.[23] During the summer of this year Mussolini made his famous observation that "if Fascism does not wish to die or, worse still, to commit suicide, it must now provide itself with a doctrine. . . . I do wish that during the two months which are still to elapse before our National Assembly meets, the philosophy of Fascism could be created."[24]

Only later did Italian fascist leaders begin to declare that fascism was "ruralizing" Italy, championing the cause of the peasants, or that it was primarily a "rural phenomenon." These claims were nonsense. The number of owner-operators dropped by 500,000 between 1921 and 1931; that of cash-and-share tenants rose by about 400,000. Essentially fascism protected big agriculture and big industry at the expense of the agricultural laborer, small peasant, and consumer.[25]

As we look back at fascism and its antecedents, we can see that the glorification of the peasantry appears as a reactionary symptom in both Western and Asiatic civilization at a time when the peasant economy is facing severe difficulties. . . . To say that such ideas are merely foisted on the peasants by the upper classes is not true. Because the ideas find an echo in peasant experience, they may win wide acceptance, the wider, it seems, the more industrialized and modern the country is.

As evidence against the evaluation that such glorification constitutes a reactionary symptom, one might be tempted to cite Jefferson's praise of the small farmer and John Stuart Mill's defense of peasant farming. Both thinkers, however, in the characteristic fashion of early liberal capitalism, were defending not so much peasants as small independent property owners. There is in their thought none of the militant chauvinism and glorification of hierarchy and submission found in the later versions, though there are occasional overtones of a romantic attitude toward rural life. Even so, their attitude toward agrarian problems and rural society does indicate the limits that liberal thinkers

---

[23] Schmidt, *Plough and Sword*, 34–38; Silone, *Fascismus*, 109; Salvemini, *Fascist Dictatorship*, 67, 73.

[24] Quoted by Schmidt, *Plough and Sword*, 39–40.

[25] For figures and details see Schmidt, *Plough and Sword*, v, 132–134, 66–67, 71, 113.

had reached at their respective points in time. For such ideas to serve reactionary purposes in the twentieth century, they have had to take on a new coloring and appear in a new context; the defense of hard work and small property in the twentieth century has an entirely different political meaning from what it had in the middle of the nineteenth or the latter part of the eighteenth centuries.

# 17

# The International System and Non-Intervention in Spain, 1936–1937

*George Armstrong Kelly*

‹‹‹‹‹‹‹‹‹‹‹‹‹‹‹‹‹‹‹‹‹‹‹‹‹‹‹‹‹‹‹‹‹‹‹‹‹‹‹‹‹‹‹‹‹‹‹‹‹‹‹‹

## EDITORS' COMMENT

"Nonintervention," Talleyrand once wrote," is an abstract and metaphysical term meaning practically the same thing as intervention." So it was in 1936 when, as a consequence of motives and assessments which the essay below explores, France and Great Britain determined to "sanitize" Europe from the contagion of the civil conflict in Spain. For there can be no doubt that "nonintervention" in practice meant the discouragement of the material and moral hopes of the Spanish Republic. Although it is far from certain that different policies by the Western liberal democracies in this instance could have contributed to preserving peace honorably in Europe (this may have been impossible after Hitler's renunciation of the Versailles treaty in 1935), it cannot be seriously disputed that the nonintervention scheme altered the political destiny of a European state for more than a generation.

The present essay makes no pretense of describing the Spanish crisis or the European crisis in detail. In order to do that, the complex dimension of the internal cleavages in Spain would have to be added, as well as the significance of the Spanish Civil War as one of a long and dismal set of events that entangled European diplomacy—beginning with the world depression and the Manchurian crisis and ending with Munich and the rape of Czechoslovakia. Fortunately, the primary historical evidence for this period is lavish. We have access to a great deal of material on Spain, to the diplomatic archives of Germany, Italy, the United States and, most recently of Great Britain. These documents are fortified by numerous memoirs of the leading personalities, including a few from the Russian side, and by the testimony of French statesmen close to the question (important French archives were burned prior to the fall of Paris in 1940). Altogether, this is an abundant subject for historical and political research. Among the many good studies on the Spanish background of the crisis, we mention five available in English that will provide a fundamental grasp of the situation:

Gerald Brenan, *The Spanish Labyrinth* (Cambridge: Cambridge University Press, 1943).

Franz Borkenau, *The Spanish Cockpit* (London: Faber & Faber, 1937).

Hugh Thomas, *The Spanish Civil War* (New York: Harper, 1961).

Gabriel Jackson, *The Spanish Republic and the Civil War, 1931–39* (Princeton: Princeton University Press, 1965).

George Orwell, *Homage to Catalonia* (New York: Harcourt, Brace, 1952).

The bibliography included in the notes to this article, as well as the much greater wealth of sources that the student can instantly compile from research in the major books, will provide more than a long winter's reading and reflection.

The methodological and explanatory problems posed here relate to the interaction between international politics and the irruption of certain kinds of internal war. This is the same kind of subject matter that is broadly breached in the Rosenau and Kelly-Miller essays and that is more specifically treated in George Rudé's study of the foreign consequences of the French Revolution and in Gouldner's study of the Greek city-states. The present author has attempted to mediate here, critically and analytically, between the richness of diplomatic event and the theoretical application of international systems models as posited by Aron's "historical sociology." Since, in the case of Spain, we find (1) a particular international constellation easily reducible to abstract description, (2) a preponderate instance of internal warfare, (3) heavy inputs of foreign intervention and, (4) an international mechanism articulated to constrain or affect the interaction, this is a fairly ideal historical laboratory for the study of the problem. Hopefully, other case histories might be constructed on a similar basis. Needless to say, the theoretical interest of the Spanish Civil War crisis and the response of the international system also go beyond the questions treated here; two areas that come immediately to mind are (a) diplomatic style and the policy process, and (b) the implementation of arms control agreements. But the present essay is mainly intended to provide food for thought within the stated ambitions of this volume.

For further observations on intervention, the reader should consult: Special Number on "Intervention and World Politics," *Journal of International Affairs,* Summer 1968.

# THE INTERNATIONAL SYSTEM AND NONINTERVENTION IN SPAIN, 1936–1937

GEORGE ARMSTRONG KELLY

The following is a study of foreign involvement, by direction and indirection, in the process of one of the most famous internal wars of modern history. Its purpose is to explore the international system of the period, its susceptibilities, and the consequences that ensued from the convergence of the policies of the major actors upon a situation fully capable of illuminating them.

## THE INTERNATIONAL SYSTEM

An international system is the effective range of a core of state actors who establish the mechanics of world diplomacy and whose antagonism can lead to general, i.e., system-wide, war.[1] In the 1930's the system included the major powers of Europe plus, inferentially, a distant Japan and a withdrawn United States. Descriptively, the system was of a peculiar character, whose principal outlines we shall proceed to trace:

1. It was in process of becoming a *tripolar* system, in other words a configuration in which the states were magnetized toward three incor-

[1] Compare Raymond Aron, *Peace and War*, trans. Richard Howard and Annette Baker Fox (New York and Washington, 1967), p. 94: *"I call an international system the ensemble constituted by political units that maintain regular relations with each other and that are all capable of being implicated in a generalized war. Units taken into account, in their calculation of forces, by those governing the principal states, are full-fledged members of an international system."*

porating principles with the endemic possibility of conflict among the three blocs, either between two of them with one remaining neutral or by virtue of a coalition of two against one.[2] This represented a degeneration and tightening of the characteristically multipolar European state system of other times.

2. The system was also *heterogeneous:*[3] it featured not only the persistent marginal inter-state quarrels over extension of power, but also deep challenges to the legitimacy of the prevailing (liberal-parliamentary) political order. This division, also tripolar, had directed and reinforced the procedure of bloc coalescence.

3. The result was the formation (as yet not perceived by most of the statesmen of the "protecting powers") of a coalescent tripolar heterogeneous system,[4] a condition which may be supposed perilous, possibly terminal, for a given pattern of international order. The three blocs were, to use ideological shorthand: the democratic, the fascist, and the communist (as yet limited to one country).

4. It would appear natural in a situation of triadic bloc formation

[2] There are some interesting observations on triadic problems in John W. Thibaut and Harold H. Kelley, *The Social Psychology of Groups* (New York, 1963): see especially Chapter XI, "Interdependence in Larger Groups," for an analysis of coalition-forming. Morton A. Kaplan gives passing mention to tripolarity in his "Models of International Systems," *American Political Science Review* (September 1957), p. 689: "An important condition for stability concerns the number of essential national actors. If there are only three, and if they are relatively equal in capability, the probability that two would combine to eliminate the third is relatively great." This statement somewhat neglects the contradictory tensions of a heterogeneous situation. See also, William S. Riker, *The Theory of Political Coalitions* (New Haven, 1962).

[3] On the concept of heterogeneity, see Aron, *Peace and War*, pp. 99–104.

[4] R. N. Rosecrance, in *Action and Reaction in World Politics* (Boston, 1963) chooses to designate the interwar international system as bipolar. "The result was the eventual consummation of a bipolar system: The Fascist actors recognized the similarity of their objectives relatively early; the democratic actors (and the Soviet Union) only became aware of their need to stand together when the Fascist challenge reached its height. . ." (p. 258). We disagree totally. A general war system is, of course, by definition bipolar, but the tripolarity of the 1930's was not even resolved in the first two years of the war. A propos is Raymond Aron's description: "Before 1939 the international system was *heterogeneous*. A complex heterogeneity, moreover, since three regimes were in conflict, profoundly hostile to one another, each of them inclined to put its two adversaries 'in the same sack.' To the Communists, fascism and parliamentary government were only two modes of capitalism. To the Western powers, communism and fascism represented two versions of totalitarianism. To the fascists, parliamentary government and communism, expressions of democratic thought, marked two stages in degeneration, that of plutocracy and that of despotic levelling. But under duress each of these regimes consented to acknowledge elements of relationship with one of its adversaries" *Op. cit.*, p. 115.

that two of the members of the system might be described as "revisionist" and one as "conservative." At the same time there must be inaccessible differences between the two revisionist actors; their dispute will not be markedly less grave than the one between either of them and the "moderates." By the same token (given the assumption that more than three sovereignties are capable of acting with influence in the system), there will be a necessary connection between tripolarity and heterogeneity. "Homogeneous" actors would tend to avoid the "terminal compression" of the triad[5] through the exercise of tactical flexibility—it being preferable to preserve the system by marginal adjustment than to shatter it in general war.

5. A system forming as we have described it will be almost intolerably tense and fragile. The reasons we advance in theory for this fragility were well borne out in practice by the international events from 1936 on. One deserving special mention—and with severe effects lingering into our present time—is the harsh contradiction between the "terminal" tripolar system of 1936-1941, which did not even vanish with the coming of the war (until Hitler had attacked his two opponents in succession) and the eventual enforced bipolarity of general war (democracies and the U.S.S.R. against the fascist states). The resolution of the triad by necessity led to a duality of expediency which later, upon the elimination of one of its members, broke almost instantly into another dyad that had been prefigured in the original triad.

General war, of necessity, approximates duality,[6] since everything significant tends to be drawn into it. And even if it does not begin thus (World War I), it will create a more and more heterogeneous pattern as war aims grow more totalistic. Superimpose on this a tenacious and preexistent triadic relationship, and one has a highly abstract but lucid portrait of the origin of our contemporary difficulties.

6. We may add the following characteristics of tension in the period 1936-1939 to our previous analysis:

(a) The severe ideological mistrust of the three parties.

(b) The totalistic political ambitions of the revisionist parties.

(c) The clear preponderance of any coalition of two against one.

---

[5] "Terminal," as implying the breakdown of the system into war, owing to the impossibility of sustained equilibrium, disaggregation into a more multiple system, or coalescence in a balanced bipolarity.

[6] See Aron, p. 139: "If a generalized war breaks out between two, each is more influenced by one of the actors than by the others. In other words, if generalized war breaks out, a multipolar configuration tends of itself to approach a bipolar configuration."

(d) The temptation/restraint pattern with regard to preventive war or precautionary action, based on the one hand on the sheer advantage of coalition, and on the other on the mistrust of any partnership.

(e) The great advantages of aggressive risk-taking in cases where another party manifests a special reticence to act.

(f) The considerable possibilities of misunderstanding, either because of malfunctioning of diplomatic communications or because of ideological misassessment of the designs of the competing blocs.

(g) The natural disabilities of the middle or "peace-keeping" member of the triad, who will find tactical coalition with either of the extremes repugnant.

7. The problems of what we have termed the "moderate force" in this type of situation will be especially anguishing. While it would seem in a normal triadic configuration that extremes cannot meet and that each extreme would seek the "moderate" member as a partner, this will perhaps not be so in a heterogeneous system where the extremes share a common interest in drastic revision that the stabilizing member cannot accept. The moderates will be thrust on the defensive and jeopardized by quarrels for which they have no appetite. They will find it difficult to assert their available power directly in the interest of sustaining an equilibrium. But if they adopt a policy of inaction they will suffer loss of prestige and dynamism that further tempts the revisionists.

8. In the 1930's the international system had other problems besides the advancing doom of heterogeneous tripolarity; it was unstable in other ways. Though the two challengers to prevailing political legitimacy represented socio-political ideologies, a rigid bloc competition had also arisen because of revisionist reaction to the shortsighted system of Versailles and the pervasive economic disorder of the Great Depression, which the "peace-preserving" powers had been unable to remedy by collective action. There was, furthermore, a fundamentally misleading antithesis between the notions of collective security and the traditional balance of power which had been allowed to captivate political thinking. The role of the nations and the role of world order had not been reconciled, in part because the League had been founded on a disequilibrated system. There was the additional paradox of being pledged to "peaceful settlement," with its connotations of pacifism and nonintervention, and to "collective security against aggression" at the same time. The League, which had been spawned both from utopian ideals and from the desire to perpetuate an unbalanced system, was gradually abandoned for purposes of serious European diplomacy. The temptations become too great to use the League either for concealment

of power behind principle or for abdication of international peace-keeping responsibility when the burden seemed too great. Prefigured by the Ethiopian fiasco, Spain represents the point at which the democracies ceased to use the League at all.[7]

9. To this picture we must add the flesh and blood of men and public policy. The democracies were unfortunate in their faltering leadership and divided opinion. Irresolution and dissention vied with the desire to proclaim weak initiatives as acts of statesmanship. This fault is not necessarily a consequence of the parliamentary system, which has proved its mettle in time of danger. But it surely may be attributed to the difficulties of moderation, described above, and to various sorts of social demoralization that had been festering since the war. Two chief misestimates of the statesmen should be pointed out: (a) the conflict of policies which were synthesized finally in nonintervention and later in appeasement, based on the notion that an active balancing role in the European crisis could not be hazarded; and (b) the misinterpretation of the coalescing tripolar system, based most often on the assumption that Germany and Italy could be persuaded to become responsible actors and that any joint action with the U.S.S.R. for the restoration of the balance was worse than the other possible consequences.

## POLICIES AND PRACTICES OF THE POWERS

Though the Spanish political situation was, inpart, a reflection of the wider European ideological struggle, most serious historians agree that the war was due to local causes, not to the existence of any internationally organized "Red plot" or "Fascist plot."[8] However, once the rebellion had broken out, both the Republicans and the Nationalists made haste to solicit military aid in friendly countries, bringing international war into Spain by their own initiative. The fascist states had

[7] See F. P. Walters, *A History of the League of Nations*. (2 Vols., Oxford, 1952), II, pp. 692 ff.

[8] Hugh Thomas, *The Spanish Civil War* (New York, 1961), p. 209; David T. Cattell, *Soviet Diplomacy and the Spanish Civil War* (Berkeley and Los Angeles, 1957), p. 44; Manfred Merkes, *Die deutsche Politik gegenüber den spanischen Bürgerkrieg, 1936-1939* (Bonn, 1961), p. 17; and Salvador de Madariaga, *Spain: A Modern History* (New York, 1958), p. 482, agree generally on this point. Patricia van der Esch, *Prelude to War: The International Repercussions of the Spanish Civil War, 1936-1939* (The Hague, 1951), p. 26, offers a dissent. Anthony Eden, *Facing the Dictators* (Cambridge, Massachusetts, 1962), p. 446, offers the following judgment: "The powers without sought to profit from the struggle as it developed. They did not and could not promote it, nor was the rebellion once it came just another Fascist plot."

been at least somewhat geared to act in such an emergency;[9] but, hoping at that time for a *coup d'état* rather than a protracted conflict, they had assuredly not prepared for what was to follow. Germany and Italy granted almost immediate aviation and technical assistance to the Rebels.[10] The Soviet Union, after preliminary shipments of food, clothing, and fuel, responded in kind to the pleas of the Republican government when it became apparent that arms were needed for the defense of the capital. Fascist aid began arriving by the beginning of August, according to many eyewitness reports;[11] the first Soviet tanks and guns were unloaded at Alicante during the middle of October.[12] Significant Italian manpower began to reach the Rebels in immediate response to the Soviet intervention and grew to a total commitment of about 50,000–55,000 soldiers and an outlay of at least 7.5 billion lire, including the shipment of 763 aircraft and the assistance of 91 submarines and warships.[13]

Germany, more modest and cunning in her commitment, was

[9] General Sanjurjo, the leader of the general's uprising who was killed when the plane bringing him from Portugal crashed at takeoff, had held consultations in Berlin with high officials of the military and Foreign Office in early 1936. Similar approaches had been made in Rome.

[10] Joachim von Ribbentrop renders Hitler's explanation of his decision to intervene in *Zwischen London und Moskau*, (Frankfurt a/M., 1953), pp. 88–89. It was taken on July 26, 1936. The Italians had acquiesced on July 24. (See Thomas, p. 218). For the official Russian interpretation of Hitler's decision to intervene in Spain, see I. M. Maisky, *Ispanskiye Tetradi* (Moscow, 1962), p. 20. See also the report of the American counsul in Seville, August 9, 1936, quoted by Thomas, p. 259.

[11] By means of the German Junkers 52 aircraft 10,500 troops of Franco's Army of Morocco were transported from Africa to Spain in July and August, and 9700 in September (Thomas, p. 244n). Large amounts of German aid were airlifted to reinforce them in Seville, which had fallen immediately to the Rebels. Shortly thereafter the Portuguese border was open to the dispatch of German arms. See also, Thomas, pp. 229–230, and references.

[12] Stalin apparently decided to send military aid to the Republicans in the third week of September, mainly purchased and shipped through the agencies of the Comintern. The first volunteers of the International Brigades arrived at Albacete on October 14. Twelve cargo vessels from Odessa carrying arms and supplies for Spain passed the Turkish straits between October 1 and October 24. See *German Foreign Policy Documents*, Series D. (1937–1945) III, p. 126; Thomas, pp. 304–305; Walter Krivitsky, *I Was Stalin's Agent* (London, 1939), pp. 101–105; Adolfo Lizon Gadea, *Brigadas Internacionales en España* (Madrid, 1940), pp. 8–9.

[13] The following figures and information are furnished primarily by Thomas, pp. 634–643 ("Appendix III: Foreign Intervention in the Spanish War"), which is itself based on a number of sources, conspicuously the estimate on Soviet military aid supplied by the German attaché in Ankara. We have found additional useful information in Galeazzo Ciano, *Diary 1937–38* (London, 1952), in Krivitsky, *op. cit.*, and in 'Henri Rabassaire,' *Espagne, creuset politique* (Paris, 1938), "Note sur l'apport étranger," p. 143.

to send the highly trained "Condor Legion" of 6000 men (to which were appended 30 antitank companies) as well as about 10,000 other effectives, mostly of the technical services. Total German expenditures on war material for Spain amounted to more than 500 million reichs-marks (43 million pounds). To the total number of foreign troops committed on the Rebel side we must add about 10,000 Portuguese soldiers.

Soviet, Comintern, and miscellaneous Western aid is estimated at the approximate equivalent of 81 million pounds (as opposed to a total of about 123 million pounds for Franco). But, in all likelihood, these resources were not applied as efficiently as the Italo-German ones: a ratio of about 1:2 in effective assistance would seem reasonable. About 40,000 men served in the International Brigades (all non-Soviet, and never more than 18,000 committed at one time); in addition, there were about 2000 Soviet technicians and political officers.[14] The Republicans received from abroad about 450 aircraft (half-Soviet, half-French in provenance). They obtained little or no outside naval support. Russian aid appears to have reached its maximum in the early months of 1937 (prior to the installation of the control mechanism) and dropped off very sharply after September;[15] Italo-German aid reached a steady flow by the last month of 1936 and maintained a fairly even level until the outcome of the war was assured in late 1938.[16]

Though a considerable portion of Comintern aid to Republican Spain was purchased and procured in the Western countries (even including Germany), the democratic governments officially furnished no assistance to the Loyalists except for a first headlong dispatch of French aircraft and equipment (otherwise justified by a Franco-Spanish arms purchase agreement of 1934) before the advent of the nonintervention policy.[17] Nevertheless, Western ships (principally

[14] Krivitsky, p. 114.

[15] According to the figures of the German attaché, cited by Thomas, *loc. cit.*

[16] Ciano, *Diary:* "August 30 (1937) . . . Decided in principle to send 5000 men to Spain." (p. 6) "September 15. Franco is asking for four submarines to be put at his disposal. Two will go at once and the other two shortly." (p. 13) "March 26 (1938) . . . . They want a billion lires worth of goods, payment to be mostly in kind and very problematical." (p. 94). Re: Germany, cf. Thomas, p. 566: "The refurbishment of the Condor Legion and other supplies sent by Germany to Nationalist Spain (after the exhaustion of the Republican offensive on the Ebro in July–September 1938) was the most important act of foreign intervention in the course of the Spanish Civil War." The Germans received extensive mining concessions from Franco for their timely assistance (see *GFPD*, III, pp. 195–196).

[17] See Pierre Cot's testimony in *Les événements survenus en France de 1933 à 1945*, Vol. 1: "Témoignoges et documents" (1951), p. 274; also Blum's (pp. 215–219). Britain prohibited all export of war material to Spain on August 15 (the date of the Franco-British exchange of letters declaring the policy of nonintervention).

British, French, Dutch and Scandinavian) were primary carriers of cargo to Republican ports. During lapses in the control agreements the Pyrenean border was open to arms traffic from France, and an unestimated amount of smuggling went on. The Rebels enjoyed similar advantages from proximity to the Portuguese border.[18]

As we shall see, the nonintervention pledge and the "control of arms" in the Spanish civil war were both largely observed in the breach by the interested foreign parties. We shall come to the measures and mechanisms presently, but first we will do well to flesh out our abstract description of the system with a brief summary of the policies of the major powers.

*England* understood full well the local origins of the Spanish Civil War, but the British deduced from this that it would end in the indecisive manner of previous Spanish imbroglios if foreign interference could be dissuaded.[19] It was the vain hope of British policy to reach a conclusive reconciliation of moderates on both sides of the struggle through the example of a "hands off" policy. The Spanish Republicans were uncomfortably leftist for the Baldwin government and the Foreign Office; there was some active sympathy for the Rebels in ruling circles;[20] and the Labour opposition was split by pacifist (and, here and there, pro-German) conviction.

But, above all, the British were not interested in the ideological aspects of the conflict: they were determined, first of all, that all means should be employed to prevent any international *casus belli*,[21] and, secondly, that whatever the outcome of the war, historic British inter-

---

[18] Dr. Salazar remarked on August 1 that he would help the Rebels "with all available means." *GFPD*, III, pp. 25, 53.

[19] See *The Economist*, April 10, 1937, p. 67: "On the assumption that the foreign driving force is going to die out of the Spanish Civil War, we may go on to assume that . . . [it] will end in the same way as its predecessors; and these have [always] ended in the patching up of some sort of an armistice, after which the troops on either side have melted away and have resisted all attempts to call them back to the colours."

[20] Some members of the Government, like Mr. Alan Lennox-Boyd, were outspokenly pro-Franco. Even the maverick Winston Churchill—and other Tories—did not recognize the dangers of withholding support to Republican Spain until much too late, in 1938. Mr. Alfred Duff Cooper favored Italian appeasement: "The Italo-German alliance was an anomaly. The Germans and Austrians were the traditional enemies of the Italians; the English and French, who had contributed so much to their liberation, were their historic friends. . . ." *Old Men Forget* (New York, 1954) p. 211.

[21] Eden, p. 451: "There were forceful reasons why Britain must favor nonintervention. First, because if the fighting in Spain were once internationalized, its consequences would be uncontrollable. . . ." Lord Plymouth, English president of the Nonintervention Committee, stated in its seventh meeting that "the primary

ests in the Mediterranean and in Spanish investment and commerce should be protected.[22] As Franco came gradually closer to victory and the Germans wrung commercial hegemony in Spain from him, the Board of Trade placed heavy pressure on Whitehall to react to this reality.

There were three other determinants of the situation: (1) a divided public opinion, which, in 1936, was about to be shaken by the dynastic crisis; (2) a historical reflex against any direct interference in Spanish affairs as judged by national interest;[23] and (3) a continuing belief that international cooperation from the totalitarian powers could be secured if their aggressive activities were winked at.

One observer of the time stated the situation acutely: "London. . . seeks to compromise, to exhaust the adversaries in their equilibrium, to concede the preponderance of neither, and especially: to let none of the adversaries escape the responsibility of international collaboration."[24] This *was* a policy, but the means for effecting it honorably were no longer within England's reach. Nonintervention was the outcome of grave misjudgments of the system, the prestige of collective security, and national capacities. When Chamberlain came to power, moreover, the die was cast for a policy of Italian appeasement.

By 1936, *France* had exhausted her diplomatic virtue. A tense

---

concern of the United Kingdom in consenting to the establishment of the committee in London has been to avoid the extension of the civil war beyond the Spanish frontiers . . ." The Russians, viewing the situation through their ideological screen of interpretation, apparently saw the origins of nonintervention as a precarious compromise between "advanced" (i.e. working-class) public opinion in England and the reactionary and pro-Franco tendencies of the Baldwin government. Maisky, *Ispanskiye Tetradi*, p. 22.

[22] See 'Rabassaire,' *op. cit.*, pp. 18–19, esp.; "More than half of Spanish exports went to the British Empire, the United States, and France, and only ten per cent to Germany. The war has changed these proportions." Also, Thomas, p. 210n: "In 1935, the United Kingdom took nearly 50% of Spanish exports (11 million pounds out of 23 million pounds) and provided 17% of her imports." Eden writes, *op. cit.*, p. 475: "It was important to us that the winning side should not grant territorial prizes or negotiate closer military relations with other powers."

[23] Castlereagh, in 1820, regarding Spain: "There is no portion of Europe of equal magnitude in which such a revolution could have happened less likely to menace other states with that direct and imminent danger which has always been regarded—at least in this country—as alone constituting the case which would justify external interference." Quoted from René Albrecht-Carrié, *Italy from Napoleon to Mussolini* (New York, 1950), p. 252. Eden, p. 451: ". . . the British Government had no wish to be involved in a Spanish civil war, nor were they convinced that, whatever its outcome, the Spaniards would feel any gratitude to those who had intervened."

[24] 'Rabassaire,' p. 21.

domestic situation had resulted from the polarization of politics and the creeping effects of the depression in 1934–36. The weakness of her defense arrangements was pulling France up short. Nevertheless, a government of the Left, headed by the Socialist Léon Blum, and superficially much resembling the Spanish Republican government, was in power.

When the Spanish crisis broke, the Republicans immediately appealed to France for assistance, and Blum was inclined to give it.[25] By the end of ten days a combination of events had talked him out of his first reaction and persuaded him of the wisdom of nonintervention: (1) the threat of civil disorder; (2) heated dissension within his Cabinet;[26] (3) military unpreparedness;[27] and (4) British refusal to second any French initiative or apply the Locarno guarantee to the frontiers of France.[28]

Whether or not under British pressure,[29] M. Blum demurred and became the sponsor for a plan of organized nonintervention, even though the French knew by this time of German and Italian involvement.[30] In short, France was compelled to choose and choose quickly. Though she had a supreme interest in not allowing three hostile powers

[25] See *Les événements survenus*, pp. 217–219.

[26] Thomas, p. 225. "At four in the afternoon [of July 25], the French Cabinet met. Daladier [the Defense Minister] and Delbos [the Foreign Minister] were the spokesmen for a refusal to Spain, Cot [Secretary of State for Air] for acceptance."

[27] *Les événements survenus*, pp. 216–217. The opinion of Daladier and the military chiefs (Army especially: Admiral Darlan served as Blum's unofficial emissary to sound out Lord Chatfield of the British Admiralty on the possibilities of support for assistance to the Spanish Republic).

[28] André Géraud ("Pertinax") writes: "At the beginning of August M. Léon Blum was informed that the guarantee given by Great Britain to maintain the frontiers of France would not remain valid in the event of independent French action beyond the Pyrenees." In the preface to E. N. Dzelepy, *The Spanish Plot* (London, 1937), p. vii. See also, Albrecht-Carrié, *France, Europe and the Two World Wars* (Geneva, 1960), p. 302. Thomas (p. 258) personally corroborated this hypothesis to his satisfaction.

[29] Albrecht-Carrié, *op. cit. supra*, feels that there was British pressure in abundance and that the idea of non-intervention was hatched in the Foreign Office. So, naturally, did Sr. Alvarez del Vayo, Republican Spanish Foreign Minister; see his *Freedom's Battle* (New York, 1940), p. 44. Léon Blum himself declared in September 1936: "We put pressure behind this measure so as to avoid serious and immense international complications." (*La tribune des nations*, September 10, 1936). In his testimony to the post-war parliamentary committee of inquiry (*Les événements survenus*, p. 219) he continued to defend his decision. He is also quoted by Miss van der Esch (p. 72) as saying: "In the Spanish affair it is from London that the initiatives have come for more than a year, and it is the positions taken there which have, in the last analysis, determined or guided the positions of Paris."

[30] Italy quickly dispatched eleven Savoia 81 bombers to aid the Rebels in Morocco. Two of these made a forced landing in French Morocco and one crashed

to become established on her major borders and, thus, a reciprocity of interest with the U.S.S.R. as regards Spain, the British alliance was her mainstay and, for better or worse, she could not jeopardize it. From this point on, she became the stalking-horse for her partner's diplomacy.

The *Soviet Union* was forced to balance two contradictory policies.[31] In the first place, as the world leader of Socialism she could not afford to allow the battle with the fascists and their proxy to go by default; the "popular front" tactic of 1935 pointed directly toward assistance to the Republicans. But also, there was the matter of higher diplomacy: The U.S.S.R. was attempting to break out of her isolation and, for tactical purposes, cultivate closer relations with the democratic governments. Her treaty with France was the best *entrée* to the international system that Soviet Russia could show. If British and French diplomacy remained platitudinous and yielding, she was, in a sense, chained to their pattern of weak response.[32] Thus, schizophrenically, she joined the nonintervention agreement and continued to intervene as widely as she thought necessary to keep the Rebels from a speedy victory and so as to reap propaganda advantages. Maxim Litvinov squarely tied his arguments to the prior action of France:

> The Soviet Union associated itself with the declaration on non-intervention in Spanish affairs only because a friendly country feared that an international conflict might otherwise ensue. It did so in spite of its opinion that the principle of neutrality does not apply in a case where mutineers are fighting against the lawful government. . . .[33]

---

at Saida in Algeria. Though their colors were painted out, the French government had certain knowledge of their identity in the first week of August 1936. However, the French themselves were rushing aid to the Republicans prior to the embargo date of August 15.

[31] Our interpretation of Soviet motives is chiefly indebted to the two studies by David T. Cattell, *Soviet Diplomacy*, cited above, and *Communism and the Spanish Civil War* (Berkeley and Los Angeles, 1955).

[32] Cattell, *Communism*, p. 75: "To Russia [as opposed to Germany and Italy] it was important and essential that in breaking the agreement she should not in any way alienate her potential partners, the Western democracies, and that the West should not lose faith in Russia as an ally because she failed to abide by the pact."

[33] Excerpt from speech delivered at the XVII Plenary Session of the League of Nations, September 28, 1936. Text reproduced in Maxim Litvinov, *Against Aggression* (London, 1939), pp. 56–57. If we are to believe Soviet ambassador I. M. Maisky, the U.S.S.R. was so eager to cooperate with the democracies that it could accept their Spanish position in return for other, unspecified, forms of collaboration. See his *Kto pomogal Gitleru?* (Moscow, 1963), p. 60. Maisky states the U.S.S.R.'s reasons (obviously quite *ex post facto*) for participation in the Non-Intervention Committee in his *Ispanskiye Tetradi*, p. 26.

On October 28, 1936, in the Nonintervention Committee, the Russians declared their "will to exercise the same rights as the other powers."[34] Exercise them they did, but they remained behind the facade of nonintervention and actively sought to draw the reluctant democracies away from dead center. The measure of their skill in appeasing leftist appetites in the West was the creation of the International Brigades, which no Soviet citizens were permitted to join. Essential Soviet policy, then, was both precautionary and contradictory. The motive was to play for better stakes by turning the Spanish civil conflict into a war of attrition. Rebuffed by the democracies, Stalin finally purged the spokesmen for the "popular front" and turned to the idea of tactical collaboration with Hitler.[35]

*Germany* had much to gain by playing her Spanish cards right. The outbreak of the rebellion provided opportunities to extend her political, military, and economic influence; to outflank the historic enemy France; to discredit the democracies, the League and the collective security principle; to insure the Italian alliance; and to satisfy a pathological fear of Communism.[36] The *coup* of the Spanish generals was not organized at German instigation; but once it had been engineered, Hitler was determined to support it massively and generously. The question of the character of the intervention remained. Here the Germans were more discriminating than the Italians, being at the moment less besotted with ideas of prestige and glory.[37] But there were tangible advantages to be won by encouraging a war that would go

---

[34] A reiteration of the language of the note to the Committee dated October 7, 1936, N.I.C. document no. 81: "The Soviet Government is . . . compelled to declare that if violations of the Agreement for Non-Intervention are not immediately stopped the Soviet Government will consider itself free from the obligations arising out of the Agreement." Kagan (Maisky's deputy) to Lord Plymouth.

[35] It is still far from clear how the patterns and rhythms of Stalin's tortuous diplomacy evolved in the period 1936–39 and what the exact domestic connections may have been. Was Munich the turning point, as many have instinctively felt? George Kennan is convinced that a Russian accommodation with the West was always chimerical; see *Russia and the West under Lenin and Stalin* (Boston, 1961), pp. 308–313. But General André Beaufre, a junior participant in the Anglo-Franco-Soviet military talks of 1939, feels that Stalin did not opt for the Nazi pact until very late in the game; see his *1940: The Fall of France* (London, 1967), p. 140.

[36] Ribbentrop, p. 89: "[Hitler] elucidated for my benefit—and here again I saw that the global components were still uppermost in his total thinking—that Germany must not under any circumstances countenance a Communist Spain. As a National Socialist he had the duty to do everything to prevent it."

[37] See *Kölnische Zeitung*, May 31, 1939: "In contrast to Italy . . . Germany awaited a Franco victory and the end of her self-imposed tasks before disclosing all that the German ["Condor"] legion . . . had performed."

only gradually in Franco's favor:[38] Germany could steadily reduce Spain to an economic satellite,[39] buy time to bring her war plans to fulfilment, and guarantee a more favorable situation in the Mediterranean. Membership in the nonintervention scheme was regarded as a good obfuscating and delaying tactic, an additional platform for fulmination against the Soviet Union, a means for testing the weakness of the democracies, and an access to an available instrument for ending the war if such should ever be desired.[40] There was no intention of being deterred by any of the committee's restrictions, though it might be used diplomatically to inhibit the U.S.S.R.

*Italy's* intervention in Spain, which rose swiftly to massive and blatant proportions, was no more carefully plotted than the German, and what planning took place was uncoordinated between the two countries.[41] However, it soon became abundantly clear that the destinies of the two powers had been closely linked by the Spanish adventure.[42]

Mussolini's Italy, like Hitler's Germany and Salazar's Portugal, had a pathological fear of seeing a "Communist state" edified in Spain. Moreover, in her ambition to dominate the Mediterranean, Italy per-

[38] Hitler to the generals and Foreign Minister on November 5, 1937: "A hundred per cent victory for Franco . . . is not desirable from the German point of view. Rather we are interested in a continuance of the war and in keeping up the tension in the Mediterranean." Quoted from *GFPD* by William L. Shirer, *The Rise and Fall of the Third Reich* (New York, 1960), p. 297n.

[39] See Thomas, pp. 229–230, 566.

[40] Ernst von Weizsäcker, then political secretary to the Foreign Office, suggests that non-intervention was pushed by his Ministry for internal political reasons: "participation in these international discussions in London also had a certain internal value in Germany. Hitler and Göring could no longer act in quite such a free-and-easy manner and without consulting the Foreign Office. The Foreign Office was now able to gain some influence in the formulation of policy." *Memoirs* (London, 1951), p. 113.

[41] This seems clear from the German documents, the various sources collected by Thomas (pp. 214–218), and from the study of Manfred Merkes, *op. cit., passim.* Grandi was instructed by Ciano "to do his best to give the [Non-Intervention] Committee's activity a purely platonic character." *GFPD*, III, p. 75. Ribbentrop had instructions to let the Italians take the lead.

[42] Germany and Italy began immediately to coordinate their diplomatic machinery with regard to Spain. Close contact was kept with the Franco regime, which both countries recognized on November 18, 1936. The representatives on the Nonintervention Committee were instructed by their Foreign Offices to work closely, though Ribbentrop detested Grandi ("eine ausgesprochene Intrigantannatur"). For the complications of Italo-German relations during the crisis of the Ethiopian War, see especially Elizabeth Wiskemann, *The Rome-Berlin Axis* (New York, 1949), pp. 41–52. The evolving relationship was completed by Mussolini's acquiescence in the *Anschluss.*

ceived the strategic profit of having a dependent regime on her western flank. Though a whole generation of Italian diplomats had been brought up on the axiom of collaboration with Britain in Mediterranean matters, Mussolini cared not a fig for this kind of prudence, nor did his anglophobic son-in-law Ciano.

But primarily the feeling was chauvinistic, pompous, militant. Mussolini reveled in the idea that his troops were playing an essential and valorous part in the war.[43] He decorated returning "volunteers" publicly, in contrast to the German discretion. Count Dino Grandi said bluntly to the Nonintervention Committee on March 23, 1937 that "the Italian volunteers will not leave Spanish territory until General Franco has gained a complete and final victory.[44] The democracies hid their eyes.[45]

Mussolini's parodical *hubris* left bad effects on his nation. Tied irreparably to Germany as a result of Spain, he bequeathed the Axis a fatigued and tottering war machine which gained him little glory and little influence in the totalitarian alliance.

Though not a major power, *Portugal* deserves brief mention because of its proximity to the conflict, its ideological preferences, and its conduct as a small-power weathervane. Opposed to Communism and liberalism alike, the regime of Dr. Salazar cooperated actively with the Rebels and their supporters, facilitating the transshipment of fascist arms and playing an obstructionist role in the Nonintervention Committee. However, he did not extend diplomatic recognition to the Franco government until the spring of 1938.[46]

Interestingly, no power desired the Spanish conflict to boil up into general war. However, the totalitarian states regarded war as inevitable and only to be delayed until their moment of maximum preparedness,[47] whereas the democracies hoped that war might be indefinitely deferred. This gave the revisionists great flexibility in their Spanish maneuvering. They quickly learned—from the noninterven-

---

[43] *La Stampa* of Turin blared on July 20, 1937: "While the diplomats play for time, the legionaries cut the Gordian knot with their swords."

[44] Quoted from J. Alvarez del Vayo, *Freedom's Battle*, p. 46.

[45] England, in particular, conducted extensive informal negotiations with Italy during this period, and signed a so-called "gentlemen's agreement" for stability in the Mediterranean on December 31, 1936. Two days later a substantial shipment of Italian troops arrived in Spain.

[46] See Antonio de Oliviera Salazar, *Doctrine and Action: Internal and Foreign Policy of the New Portugal, 1928–1939* (London, 1939), especially the speech to the National Assembly of April 28, 1939, pp. 356 ff.

[47] See Ciano, *Diary, 1937–38*, entry for October 5, 1937: "Germany is not ready. In three years she will be" (p. 18).

tion appeal—that they could broaden their spectrum of provocation without running great risks of a *casus belli*. Each pledge broken, each merchant ship sunk, each airplane delivered, each lie accepted confirmed them in this judgment.

In late 1936 the war scare was general in European diplomatic circles: the diplomats had a close memory of 1914.[48] Mr. Eden cleaves to this judgment in his memoirs; so does M. Blum in his testimony before a committee of the French National Assembly charged with inquiry into national unpreparedness. The fear was real, and it elicited some regrettable reactions. The Axis powers sensed this fear, which mitigated a portion of their own fear, and prepared to take advantage of it. As Manfred Merkes relates:

> The [German] ambassador in Paris reported on December 28 [1936] on the seriousness of the situation: "There is a nervosity prevailing here in political circles which has not been felt since the end of the [First World] War." But Neurath [then German Foreign Minister] was the world of calm. "We have no need to be caught up in this nervosity bordering on hysteria shown by the French government."[49]

Spain was essentially a game of skill and nerve, with the whole system symmetrically involved. The democracies had the least sinew, and instead of reserving their options, they played the card of nonintervention.

## THE IMPLEMENTATION OF NONINTERVENTION

Léon Blum, as we have said, was personally inclined to aid the Spanish Republicans. His Cabinet, however, was sharply divided and the French Right was bitterly opposed. Moreover, the British let it be known that their Locarno guarantees of the frontiers of France would be considered null if the French undertook independent action beyond the Pyrenees..[50] M. Blum ceded and became, in fact, the official sponsor of nonintervention. This policy was declared on August 15, 1936 in an official exchange of notes by the French and British governments, pledging to refrain from all interference, direct or indirect, in the internal affairs of Spain and to embargo all shipments of war materials to the country, subject to the adherence of Italy, Germany, Portugal and the Soviet

---

[48] See Viscount Grey of Falloden, *Twenty-Five Years, 1892–1916* (New York, 1925), II, p. 32: "The abyss was not generally seen even when the governments came to the edge of it. . . . In a crisis people cannot change their settled views on general matters; they are too busy with the particulars of the moment."

[49] Merkes, p. 77.

[50] See note 28, above.

Union[51] These latter countries—Portugal most grudgingly—finally entered the agreement, but obviously with the intention of being bound by it only as national interest might dictate. As the German *chargé* in Rome reported, it would be possible "not to abide by the declaration anyway."[52] The decision on embargoes was especially hurtful to the Spanish Republic, which had poor weapons and the uncertain remnant of an army but abundant gold and currency reserves.[53]

Thus began the unsupervised phase of the internationally organized nonintervention system in the Spanish conflict. We shall examine its evolution briefly.

Twenty-seven countries finally expressed adherence to the principle of non-intervention in separate diplomatic notes. An analysis of the language indicates that the commitments were to be interpreted as *bona fide*, although each power reserved itself an operative escape clause. By the turn of 1937, the engaged nations had supplemented their declarations with the passage of comprehensive domestic legislation forbidding the export of war materials (in the case of the conspicuous interventionist nations this action had been completed before the beginning of September 1936). In most instances, the punitive mechanisms were essentially weak or lacking.[54]

On September 9, apparently at the suggestion of Italy,[55] the engaged states sent representatives to the first meeting of a Nonintervention Committee in London. Most of the participants were the regularly accredited ambassadors to the Court of St. James.[56] This body was strictly informal and *de facto*. It had no status according to international treaty and no formal connection with the League, where Germany was not a member and Italy had, since Ethiopian sanctions,

---

[51] See the accounts in Norman J. Padelford, *International Law and Diplomacy in the Spanish Civil Strife* (New York, 1939), p. 57; Thomas, pp. 277–278; Patricia van der Esch, pp. 79–83; Merkes, pp. 106–107.

[52] *GFPD*, III, p. 60.

[53] Republican Spain boasted the sixth largest gold reserves in the world (2,258,569,908 pesetas, of which 70% was in gold pounds sterling). On October 25, 1936, about three-fifths of this amount was dispatched to the Russians in Odessa for safekeeping and pre-payment.

[54] Documents and analysis in Padelford, pp. 60–69, and Appendix III, pp. 233–310.

[55] According to Thomas, p. 264. But compare I. M. Maisky, *Ispanskiye Tetradi*, who says that the idea came from the French government (p. 24). The Committee held 29 plenary meetings and 103 subcommittee meetings before its demise in 1938 (Maisky, p. 29).

[56] See Maisky, *ibid.* (pp. 68–86), for interesting verbal portraits of the leading figures.

refused to participate.[57] Neither Spanish party had members or observers on the Committee; it was thus itself "interventionist" in the fullest sense. The mission of the group was to oversee the observance of the principle of nonintervention and serve as a forum for negotiating the instrumentalities of the accord. Anthony Eden described nonintervention as follows to the House of Commons on October 29, 1936: "[It] is a device, admittedly a device, by means of which we hope to limit the risks of war. It is an improvised safety curtain."[58]

Little pretense was made by the democracies that the non-intervention scheme should bear on the outcome of the conflict in Spain. It was frankly intended to limit the war territorially and in intensity. Lord Plymouth's words to the Non-Intervention Committee may be considered typical of a host of declarations made by Eden, Blum, Viénot, Delbos, Lord Cranborne and others:

> The chief concern of the United Kingdom Government in consenting to the establishment in London of the Committee had been to prevent the civil war from spreading beyond the Spanish frontiers and to secure a measure of co-operation among the Powers in what threatened to become a most dangerous international situation.[59]

Even Litvinov, in clarifying the Soviet motives for participation, evoked similar reasons: the French alliance and the French fear of war.[60]

Was this really nonintervention? In a literal sense, it was intervention to deny support to a legitimate and recognized state in its struggle for self-preservation. It was also intervention in the sense of being a connivance to ignore external interference in the affairs of that state. Finally, it was, in a broad way, intervention to hasten the deterioration of the system of which the democracies had styled themselves the guardians. For it was an organization of "non-security" destined to whet the appetites of the dictators and confirm their opinion of democratic ineptitude and loss of vitality.

In passing our harsh verdict we have the advantage of hindsight; but we also have sympathy for the dilemma as Raymond Aron has expressed it: "In such a circumstance it is easier for the moralist to blame these maneuvers than for the politician to find a substitute for

---

[57] See Padelford, p. 93.

[58] Quoted in Eden, *Facing the Dictators*, p. 463.

[59] Words addressed to the seventh meeting of the N.I.C., quoted by Giuseppe Vedovato, *Il Non Intervento in Spagna* (Florence, n.d., probably 1938), p. 24. See also, Eden (*op. cit.*, p. 451): "There were forceful reasons why Britain must favor non-intervention. First, because if the fighting in Spain were once internationalized, its consequences would be uncontrollable. . . ."

[60] See note 33, above.

them."[61] Nonetheless, we know today that the democratic statesmen turned out to be terribly wrong. They misunderstood their opponents and they misunderstood the system. Fundamentally, nonintervention was wrong on two basic counts: (1) had the British and French been able to pursue the policy effectively, i.e., literally inhibit the flow of arms to Spain from all quarters by their own action, this by itself would have created as many provocative incidents as any other conceivable policy; (2) since it became quickly evident that exhortation alone was not going to limit foreign participation in the Spanish war and since Britain and France were not willing to take major risks to "make" their policy work, they would have done better to allow themselves greater flexibility of action in Spain.

With regard to the latter point, Blum especially appears to have believed that Spain was an all-or-nothing proposition: either intervention escalating into international war or a formal declaration of nonintervention in which other powers would be asked to join.[62] But surely there were middle solutions available. One can at least reserve his options till the proper mode of action becomes clearer. And a bloc interested above all in the restoration of stability need not commit its full power to the support of a disputant; it can attempt to apply sufficient power to render certain actions by an aggressor unprofitable. The British Navy, in particular, was in a position to offer this kind of limited and controlled response to the fascist buildup in Spain. This was indeed the very measure which the Germans feared and managed successfully to neutralize by diplomatic action in late 1936.

## COMMITTEE AND CONTROL

Once nonintervention had been implemented by formal arrangement, and, for better or worse, twenty-seven European powers had acceded to the principle in an approximate form,[63] Britain and France became

---

[61] Aron, *Peace and War*, p. 116.

[62] See Eden, p. 457: "Blum asked what [other] method was open except the use of force with all its possible consequences. He explained that to avoid this, and the equal recognition of the two forces in Spain, the French Government had concluded the Non-Intervention Agreement."

[63] Padelford, *op. cit.*, has scrupulously collected the texts of these national declarations and submitted them to comparative legal analysis, pp. 57–60 and Appendix I, pp. 205–230. The twenty-seven countries were: Albania, Austria, Belgium, Bulgaria, Czechoslovakia, Denmark, Estonia, Finland, France, Germany, Greece, Hungary, Irish Free State, Italy, Latvia, Lithuania, Luxembourg, the Netherlands, Norway, Poland, Portugal, Rumania, Sweden, Turkey, the United Kingdom, the U.S.S.R., and Yugoslavia.

tied to their own initiative. There was no going back, and no alternative but for the officials responsible for foreign affairs in Paris and London to proclaim the scheme a success in their parliaments or before the League.[64] It had been inadvertently made the cornerstone of the Franco-British alliance. By November Eden feared that "a breakdown of the [Nonintervention] Committee would have had baleful consequences, perhaps even on the Anglo-French alliance, which I regarded as indispensable to our joint survival and that of freedom in Europe."[65] This was a precarious reed on which to lean an alliance. To be trapped in the nonuse of power is not the best policy for perilous times.

Most of the deliberations of the Committee were undertaken by a subcommittee, chosen at the second meeting of September 14, in which Belgium, Czechoslovakia, England, France, Germany, Italy, the Soviet Union and Sweden were represented. Lord Plymouth of Great Britain was named President, and Mr. Francis Hemming, also English, became the Executive Secretary (i.e., director of research and operations).[66] Portugal joined the subcommittee tardily. With her exception, the smaller powers played an insignificant role.

The rules of procedure established by the Committee made it virtually impossible to administer any responsible grievance system. In fact, prescriptive action was virtually paralyzed: propaganda harangue became the normal standard of business. Though the Committee was probably wise in refusing to hear complaints emanating from private sources or from nonmember governments, it shielded itself from the implications of the evidence brought before it, and declared its incompetence even to censure noncompliance. No provision was made for public exposure of violations, either through news or government channels; no recourse to legal appeal was provided; no mechanism of sanctions was instituted or anticipated.

In international law the Committee had a shaky foundation. It shunned the responsibilities of exposure and admonition, and depended on the domestic legislation of the interventionist countries for its power to restrain. After a short while the major diplomatic efforts of the

---

[64] See Eden's speech to the League Council on May 28, 1937, quoted by Cattell, *Soviet Diplomacy*, p. 76: ". . . it would be impossible to deny that real progress has been made . . . and in these days, when the possibilities of international collaboration are so frequently decried, it is well to recall this fact."

[65] Eden, p. 467.

[66] Lord Plymouth quickly replaced Mr. W. S. Morrison, the original British delegate. Mr. Hemming's work was applauded from all sides, even by the Russians (see Maisky, *Ispanskiye Tetradi*, pp. 84–86). He was the author of the voluminous "Hemming Report," summarizing the national measures taken to embargo various war materials (*British Parliamentary Paper*, Spain No. 2, 1936, Cmd. 5300).

democracies were devoted to calming tempers and seeking to prevent Germany, Italy and Portugal, on the one hand, and Soviet Russia, on the other, from walking out of the Committee.[67] In the meantime, the expostulations of Republican Spain were carefully muffled at the League, and that body was tacitly abandoned by the Great Powers as a useful forum.

Patricia Van der Esch, in her discussion of the subject, divides the activities of the Nonintervention Committee into four phases:[68] (a) the battle over proofs of intervention (September 1936—January 1937); (b) the construction and implementation of the naval and frontier control scheme (February 1937—July 1937); (c) the debate over extending the nonintervention agreement to volunteers (early 1937); and (d) debate over the withdrawal of foreign armies from Spain (mainly 1938). In terms of our analysis, the earlier period is of much greater importance than the inevitable train of events that followed, and the question of the volunteers chiefly reduplicates the question of armaments.[69] Hence, we shall concentrate on the first two items and add some observations about the Nyon Naval Conference, which provides a useful contrast to the futility of the London procedures. The post-July 1937 evolution of the Nonintervention Committee is both instructive and poignant; but, by this time, the Spanish question had lost center-stage prominence and become a function of other European disturbances which its mishandling had done so much to encourage.

On the first period of nonintervention few words need to be spent. Committee activity was largely devoted to the hearings of charges and countercharges by the members. In general, the accusations of Italian intervention presented by the Soviet delegate, I. M. Maisky, on behalf of the Spanish government were more tangible than the Italo-German protestations; however, the Committee refused to forward or endorse the charges, pleading its incompetence. Léon Blum, in an anxious and double-edged speech, reassured the French Chamber of Deputies on December 5, 1936, that "the noninvolvement policy, despite affronts, surprises, deceptions, and anguishes that it has caused, has at least

---

[67] If, in the words of Cattell (*Soviet Diplomacy*), the democracies "were secretly apprehensive lest the Soviet Union leave the Committee and break up the Non-Intervention Agreement" (p. 47), they also dreaded "any action that might upset the frail bonds [sic] of the Committee by furnishing Germany and Italy with a pretext for leaving" (p. 74).

[68] *Op. cit.*, p. 72.

[69] The embargo on the shipment of war materials was, in theory, extended to the departure of volunteers from the territory of member states to Spain on February 16, 1937. It proved totally unenforceable.

diminished risks and skirted dangers. . . ."[70] Eden, on his part, was moved to contemplate a more active position:

> It is . . . my conviction that unless we cry a halt in Spain, we shall have trouble this year in one of the other danger points I have referred to. It follows that to be firm in Spain is to gain time, and to gain time is what we want.[71]

If there is a culprit or victim of this tragic misunderstanding, it is not the British Foreign Secretary, who at least dimly perceived some of the main issues at stake. But his successive Prime Ministers (Baldwin and Chamberlain), his Cabinet colleagues, and the public had a false understanding of the problem. The British Cabinet debated blockade proposals on January 8, 1937, and turned them down. This would not have aided the legitimate Spanish government (which had naturally swerved leftward in the absence of democratic encouragement), but it would have put some "teeth" into the pious thought of nonintervention and penalized the fascist arms-running, which was heavily dependent on sea delivery.

Soviet aid had stemmed Franco at the Battle of Madrid in December 1936, and the scene was possibly set for a war of attrition if fascist assistance could be reduced. For this reason, the U.S.S.R. worked hard in support of an international sea and frontier control arrangement in early 1937.[72] The democracies, eager to salvage the substance of nonintervention without alienating the fascist states, sought to water down the Soviet demands and make them palatable to their opponents.

A conjuncture of the battlefield helped to bring a multilateral control arrangement temporarily into being. On February 8 the Nationalists won the significant victory of Málaga, which produced a wave of Italo-German optimism about the outcome of the war. Germany, in fact, preferred not to conclude hostilities too swiftly and Mussolini wished for a string of glorious Italian victories. For this reason, the fascists were confirmed in a decision taken in the last days of December 1936 to go slow on aid,[73] fearing also that the Russians might increase their effort. This judgment allowed a nonintervention control plan to be devised and accepted by all the powers.

[70] Quoted by Vedovato, p. 43.

[71] Eden, pp. 487–488.

[72] The idea of control was first suggested by the Soviets in connection with the Portuguese border on October 12, 1936. Later, the British and French discussed a wider application of the idea and laid it before the Committee on November 2. The Soviets grew especially interested in the scheme after the Madrid front had been stabilized at the turn of 1937. See Maisky, *Tetradi*, pp. 87–94; Merkes, pp. 107–115; van der Esch, pp. 76–78; Padelford, pp. 77–79.

[73] See *GFPD*, III, pp. 165, 222–225.

Born of British initiative the previous December and, in modification, finally receiving the support of all the powers, physical control was agreed on in principle by the Committee on February 13, just five days after Málaga. It consisted of three separate types of verification: (1) frontier control, to be accomplished by an international inspectorate along the Franco-Spanish border and in Gibraltar, and by British observers on the Luso-Spanish frontier; (2) port control, which compelled merchant vessels of the nations subscribing to nonintervention to take on inspectors at prescribed points before preceeding to Spanish destinations and (3) naval control, apportioned by zone to the navies of Germany, Italy, France, and England, whereby arms-running would be intercepted in international waters off the coasts of Spain.[74] The instrument of agreement was signed on March 8, 1937, but did not come into full effect until April 20, because of the difficulties of recruiting inspection personnel, appropriating money, and passing domestic legislation for the task. However, on February 27, the French closed their border to arms traffic. Seven new agencies had to be created for the administration and operation of the control scheme, including an inspectorate of 685 observers exclusive of those in Portugal. Each of these bodies was assigned a complicated set of functions.[75]

In mid-March the Spanish Republicans had won a morale-boosting battle at Guadalajara, in which large Italian forces were engaged on the Nationalist side. This gave the fascist powers (and especially prestige-thirsty Italy) second thoughts about the virtues of control. But the plan could not be dynamited abruptly or casually. The hoped-for incident arrived on May 29, when the German battleship *Deutschland,* lying at anchor in Palma, was damaged by a Republican bomb intended for a Nationalist ship. The Germans shelled the undefended city of Almeria in retaliation and finally, after a game of diplomatic charades, withdrew from the naval patrol together with Italy on June 23, further aggravated by an alleged firing on the crusier *Leipzig.*[76]

[74] Full text of the instrument is published as *British Parliamentary Paper,* Spain No. 1 (1937), Cmd. 5399, "Resolution adopted by the Committee relating to a Scheme of Observation of the Spanish Frontiers by Land and Sea," London, March 8, 1937.

[75] See Padelford, pp. 79–87. Besides the original Nonintervention Committee, the other bodies were: an International Nonintervention Board; two regional Chief Administrators; a group of local Administrators and Deputy Administrators; a corps of Observing Officers; a Naval Patrol; an International Fund; and an Accounting Officer (auditor) of the Fund.

[76] A detailed account of these events can be found in Van der Esch (pp. 79–83), and in Merkes (pp. 114–120).

At this point the French and British offered to assume the entire burden of the naval patrol, a solution that the fascist states could not countenance. Their counterproposal was the granting of belligerent rights to both parties in the civil war,[77] which would indeed have made further naval patrolling unnecessary and given the Franco regime a considerable quota of international respectability. A British plan of July 14 combined the limited recognition of dual belligerency with a scheme for the withdrawal of all foreign volunteers. Much debated and amended during the year to follow, this idea formed the substance of the agreement assented to by the full Committee on July 5, 1938. Long before this time, however, naval control had lapsed utterly, and the outcome of the war was now abundantly clear to all.

The weary atrophy of the nonintervention system need not concern us here: it broke down of its own accord in November 1938, after its operating subcommittee had failed to meet for five months. Spain was by this time a forgotten backwater of the European confrontation.

We must backtrack briefly, however, to the Nyon Naval Conference of September 10, 1937. Largely unmoved by the deterioration of the international system, the British, with their maritime pride, might have been expected to react sharply to the frequent sinking of their merchant vessels by "unidentified" (but obviously Italian) submarines. The pace of naval aggressions had quickened enormously, beginning in March of the year; a rash of submarine attacks commenced in August. Professor Padelford has recorded seventy-eight separate assaults on shipping of the non-interventionist powers between March and September 1937 (49 surface, 24 air, 5 submarine).[78] The French were only slightly less disturbed. For once, outside the premises of organized nonintervention, the two countries of the Entente Cordiale acted with some resolution by inviting all Mediterranean states, except Spain, plus Germany and the U.S.S.R. to a conference on maritime piracy at Nyon, Switzerland. Germany and Italy refused to attend.

[77] One of the peculiarities of the international reaction to the Spanish crisis had been the literal suppression of Loyalist belligerent rights (including purchase of arms in foreign countries) at the outset, and the consequent dilemma of being unable to accord belligerent rights to both parties until much later in the struggle for fear of sabotaging the nonintervention experiment. On the subject of insurgency and belligerent rights, see Padelford, pp. 1–9, 196–200, and Charles Rousseau, "La non-intervention en Espagne," *Revue de droit international et de législation comparative*, No. 3, 1938, pp. 510–520. Also the remarks of J. Alvarez del Vayo, *Freedom's Battle* (New York, 1940), p. 44.

[78] Figure reached by addition of incidents recorded in Padelford, Appendix XV, pp. 663–674.

The Conference passed a strong resolution on July 14, instructing the French and British navies to patrol the western Mediterranean and attack any suspicious submarines.[79] Ciano, as we now know, was deeply worried by the unexpectedly stiff response, and attempted tardily to insinuate Italy into the agreement. Unfortunately, Chamberlain (now Prime Minister), hopeful of the results of appeasement, let the fascists completely off the hook four days later.[80] Little positive was thus accomplished and the maritime aggressions redoubled a few months later. But we may read into the Nyon experience the judgment that Franco-British resolution (or ambivalent threat), if applied earlier in the Spanish crisis, could have borne fruit.

By the time the control scheme was sabotaged by Italy and Germany, the deleterious effects of non-intervention should have been clear to anyone. Further attempts made to sustain the procedure had some useful humanitarian consequences for exchange of prisoners but were otherwise a pathetic epilogue to an initial series of fundamental policy errors. But as yet, even, the danger to the European equilibrium was only dimly perceived, and it cannot be claimed that the democracies ever seriously used nonintervention as a device to "buy time" or prepare for the worst. By contrast, the Germans, having had exactly the war they wanted in Spain (not too dangerous, not too swift in outcome, not too expensive), were preparing relentlessly for the big showdown.

## ANALYSIS OF NONINTERVENTION

The fundamental defects of nonintervention may be considered under four categories:

### 1. Structural Flaws

The nonintervention scheme was anomalously created by those same powers who were dedicated to the principle of collective security through the League. By removing the Spanish question from that forum and improvising a new body of consultation, the democracies undermined international organization and helped to destroy their remaining prestige as guardians of the system which had fostered it.

---

[79] The text of the Nyon Agreements of September 14 and 17, 1937, is contained in Padelford, pp. 603–609. For the Nyon background, see Thomas, pp. 476–478.

[80] Ciano, *Diary, 1937–1938*, p. 15: "September 21 . . . we agree to a technical conference to modify the Nyon clauses in accordance with our wishes. It is a fine victory. From suspected pirates to policemen of the Mediterranean—and the Russians, whose ships we were sinking, excluded!"

The new Committee, unlike the League, had no international status or powers *de jure*. Violations of the subscribed agreements of the Nonintervention Committee could not be construed as violations of international law. Withdrawal from or disruption of the scheme not only carried no penalties but also little pejorative implication. On the other hand, the sponsoring powers (France and England) became chained to the consequences of their initiative and doomed to "make the system work," in fact or in fiction.

What powers of compulsion the Committee did possess by vague implication were distributed back to the participant states in the form of domestic injunction or punitive legislation. The potential criminals were appointed their own judges.

The Committee, despite its name, was itself "interventionist," being deeply involved in the internal affairs of a national state without the permission or representation of that state in its acts and deliberations.

Finally, the Committee was of an *ad hoc* variety, born from response to the confusion and peril of a particular event, divorced from all regular guidelines of international stabilization. There was, to use George Liska's phrase, no insurance of a "reliable, if conditional, preponderance on the side of the *status quo*."[81] Rather, the attempt was made to enlist the support of the revisionist powers in a new and embryonic form of European concert. To a certain degree, all international initiatives of this type will be *ad hoc* (that is, after aggression has occurred), but when they are separated from preexisting criteria of international obligation, the inference is that they have superseded these criteria.

### 2. *Non-Intervention as a Conflict-Limiting Device*

In the first instance, it is perfectly clear that general war did not occur while the nonintervention scheme was in literal operation; but, as we now know, no power wanted such a war for at least three years.[82] Neither can one justly claim that nonintervention prevented the Spanish war from escalating. Territorially it was suited to containment (barring direct French armed intervention), and the multiplicity of maritime incidents that did occur suggests the improbability of a *casus belli* at sea during this period. The most that even Professor Padelford, an ardent champion of the legal beauties of nonintervention, will claim for it is "that it perhaps was instrumental in preventing

[81]George Liska, *International Equilibrium* (Cambridge, Mass., 1957), p. 92.
[82] Ciano, *Diary, 1937–1938*, p. 18. Entry for October 5, 1937.

the civil strife from becoming international war."[83] He did not, however, have the advantage of seeing the German Documents or the Ciano diaries, which strongly suggest the contrary.

As we now know, the relaxation of the collective security obligation practiced by the democracies toward the legitimate Spanish state in 1936 in no way prohibited the early eruption of aggressive incidents elsewhere in Europe, and in certain ways did much to encourage them. Joint Italian and German policy in support of the Spanish Nationalists cemented the fascist bloc and insured that Italy would abandon her historic interest in Austria at the time of the Anschluss in 1937. It is no less clear that Chamberlain's policy from June 1937 on demonstrated to the Axis chancelleries that they enjoyed *carte blanche* in Spain without any threat of war.

The non-intervention control scheme did comparatively little to hinder the shipment of arms and effectives to Spain in its brief duration, but it was capable of creating conceivable war provocations almost as serious as any that would have accompanied a free situation. Following the German shelling of the undefended city of Almeria, the Spanish Republican Minister of War, Don Idalecio Prieto, a right-wing Socialist, proposed the unrestricted bombing of German warships, and was restrained only by his left-leaning cabinet colleagues and the remonstrances of Moscow, whose greatest fear of the moment was the escalation of the war.[84] If the *casus belli* was desired by any power, it was not hard to find.

Finally, the tangles of legalistic precedent and disputation were designed to blind the democracies to the strategic implications of their policy. Aggression could subsequently be practiced by the totalitarian states with the ammunition of law books and demographic charts in response to this liberal susceptibility, until at last unambiguous war alone could suffice.

### 3. *The Partiality of Non-Intervention*

Without applying impossible moral criteria to the motives of states in a competitive international order, it would not have been unreasonable to ask of nonintervention that it penalize the legitimate party in Spain no more than the rebellious party. Yet, according to every just estimate, this is precisely what it did not do. It impeded Italo-German aid much less than Soviet aid, because of the factor of distance and policies of border control. It refused prescribed international succour to a member state of the collective security system. Both Eden

[83] Padelford, p. 120.
[84] Thomas recounts the incident, pp. 441–442.

and Blum professed to be convinced at an early stage that "had there been no Nonintervention Agreement, the Spanish Government would have suffered more than the rebels."[85] But this is to be doubted, or is only true at a few precise moments in the crisis. One also doubts that Germany and Italy were prepared, in the absence of any negotiated restraint, to extend aid to the Franco regime on a much larger scale than they did; Italy's war potential was, in fact, gravely strained by the Spanish involvement. At the same time, the Republicans were well fixed to purchase arms in the West if these had not been embargoed. Alvarez del Vayo was later to lament: "Today no one should be able to deny that the collapse of the Spanish Republic was due to Non-Intervention."[86] Whether or not this is true, we may trust Professor Padelford's rather parenthetical judgment: ". . . it cannot be gainsaid that in practice the accords operated in such a way as to weaken the established government and to confer advantages upon the insurgents."[87]

## 4. Technical Defects and Peculiarities of the Control System

As we have indicated, the full-functioning arms control system lasted only from mid-April to mid-June 1937. The inspection was far from perfect and failed to deter the passage of arms to Spain—especially on the fascist side. We will briefly mention the following loopholes and susceptibilities:

(a) Cargoes carried in ships under Spanish or non-European flags were inviolable. These vessels accounted for twenty per cent of the sea traffic to Spain during the period.[88] There was no provision against the sale or leasing of hulls to non-participants in the agreement.[89] Furthermore, embargoed materials could be either transshipped to Spanish destinations from their points of origin or clandestinely transferred to noninspectable vessels in international waters.[90]

(b) Vessels of participant nations could breach the agreement by simply flying Spanish or other flags when under threat of search. The patrol vessels, in cases of suspicion, were not authorized to enforce search.[91]

(c) "There was no air control; this would allow Italy and Ger-

---

[85] Eden, p. 459.

[86] Op. cit., p. 70. See also, his speech to the League, September 25, 1936. Journal Officiel, S.D.N., Supplément Spécial, No. 155, p. 47.

[87] Padelford, p. 120.

[88] Cattell, Soviet Diplomacy, p. 101.

[89] Padelford, p. 93. Also, Eden, quoted by the Times (London), July 20, 1937.

[90] Padelford, p. 92.

[91] Ibid., p. 85.

many to fly planes directly to Spain, a method closed to the Soviet Union because of distance."[92]

(d) No sanctions were provided for. Out of a total of 111 offenses alleged—of which none involved a Soviet ship—no action whatever was taken, or could be taken, by the Non-Intervention Board or the Non-Intervention Committee.[93] No public report was ever made on the findings of the British observers in Portugal.[94] Yet this was one of the main paths of Axis aid, a path smoothed, as we know now, by the full cooperation of Dr. Salazar.

(e) The control arrangement, representing a complex application of resources and expertise for limited results, allowed insincere participants to seek advantages in the asymmetrical disruption of its components. Sea delivery was of the essence to the fascists; the Comintern depended heavily on the French border for delivery. In June 1937 Germany attempted to disrupt sea control, while the land frontier surveillance continued to operate owing to the more prudent reflexes of the sponsoring powers.

The preceding observations are intended to show that the complications of attempting to enforce nonintervention made control an inadequate remedy for the vices of the uncontrolled system. The difficulties of nonintervention were inherent in its conception and could be no more than marginally corrected by a control machinery.[95]

The conclusion is unavoidable: nonintervention sapped the resistance of a security system that could be sustained only if the democracies preserved their latitude of action and the will to act. If the various initiatives were, in the words of Padelford, "important experiments in and contributions to international cooperation and administration, and significant attempts to bring some of the international aspects of civil war within the realm of international regulation and law,"[96] this was for future, lawful-minded generations to decide. For the present, they were a measure of the democracies' failure to police the system which they had built.

[92] Cattell, *Soviet Diplomacy*, p. 68.
[93] *Ibid.* p. 85.
[94] Padelford, pp. 78–79.
[95] The Chairman and Secretary of the Nonintervention Board reported to the Committee on August 25, 1937 that the Naval Patrol had been a failure and suggested that it be abandoned. The land control had broken down long before. In effect, the Nyon Agreements had superseded the sea control.
[96] Padelford, p. 52.

# 18

# Problems of Strategy in China's Revolutionary War

*Mao Tse-tung*

❮❮❮❮❮❮❮❮❮❮❮❮❮❮❮❮❮❮❮❮❮❮❮❮❮❮❮❮❮❮❮❮❮❮❮❮❮❮❮❮❮❮❮❮❮❮❮❮❮❮❮

## EDITORS' COMMENT

In the wake of the Chinese "cultural revolution," Mao Tse-tung has become one of the great enigmas of Western Pekinologists. He has been subjected to psychoanalysis, literary criticism, and the more standard forms of inquiry; but neither he, nor Chinese communism, nor the modern dynamics of power and social change in the Middle Kingdom has been satisfactorily penetrated by our scholarship. Fortunately, there is no necessity to wrestle with these vexing questions in introducing an essay written more than thirty years ago. In judging this article, we can agree with retired French air force General Lionel Max Chassin that Mao showed "a wide breadth of view and a profound realism" (*The Communist Conquest of China*, Cambridge: Harvard University Press, 1965, p. 31).

Until recent years, when Mao became determined to promote revolutionary anarchy to the detriment of his old standard of disciplined order, Western military analysts had grudgingly conceded his genius.

393

Mao's contribution to the doctrine and practice of communism does not directly concern us here except that the reader should carefully observe the emphasis on obedience and pedagogy in the essay reproduced below. What stands out in the analysis of internal warfare is Mao's obvious mastery of the techniques of consolidating and increasing power in a situation of massive civil confusion. In this respect, there has scarcely been a harder or more productive thinker and commander.

In commenting on the essay "Problems of Strategy in China's Revolutionary War," two kinds of clarification are important. We need to know the events surrounding the time when it was written, and we must debunk certain widespread but unverified impressions about the nature of Chinese communism. Above all, it is important to recognize that Mao Tse-tung has never been a detached military philosopher but that he has written many particular essays to describe the balance of forces in the Chinese revolution, its relation to world revolutionary forces, and the situation that responds to the archetypal Leninist question: *What is to be done?* If the writings of Mao are now broadcast as a creed and a doctrine for all revolutionary movements of the "Third World," they were, in their time, specific analyses and exhortations designed for the practical use of the Chinese Red Army.

The present essay is dated December 1936. This is an especially portentous date in the Chinese revolutionary chronology. Between October 1934 and October 1935, Mao and his companion leaders had, amid combats and perils, brought the bulk of the Chinese communist military and political apparatus through a 6000-mile march to its new redoubt in Shensi province. During the journey a force of 100,000 men had shrunk to 20,000; but its will and discipline remained intact. By February 1936, the Communists had recovered from the extraordinary rigor of the "Long March," and a year later their effectives had increased to 80,000 as a direct result of their political operations in the new territory. In the same period, the frequency of incidents in the undeclared war between Japan and China was mounting in the northern regions. Chiang Kai-shek exercised only loose control over his commanders in the north, but ordered them to attack the Communists. The generals, led by Marshal Chang Hsueh-liang demurred, preferring to direct their strength against the Japanese enemy. In December 1936, Chiang flew from Nanking to Sian to bend his subordinates to his will. Instead, he was "kidnapped" by his recalcitrant lieutenants and forced to come to terms with the Communists in the national effort. Shortly after Chiang's release (on December 26, 1936) Mao wrote to him that he "owed his safe departure from Sian to the mediation of the Communist Party."

Both Mao and Chiang knew full well, even at this time, that the future of China was involved in a fight to the death between their respective forces and political principles. But there is every evidence that in 1937 each thought that the indispensable condition for control and predominance was to demonstrate effectiveness in the war against Japan. The Yugoslav parallel is not without interest here. At any rate, the internal problem soon became ambiguously a complex triangular confrontation, whose dimensions are fairly expressed in Mao's essays written after 1937.

Despite the threat of the Japanese in 1936, however, the principal problem remained that of internal warfare against Nanking. The procedures were determined by the three "laws of war" with which Mao begins the following essay. Altogether, it is clear that the "law of China's revolutionary war," based on the four analytical "characteristics" expressed later on, dominate and, in a sense, supersede the more general aspects of conflict. Here, in germ, is the military and national seed of the rift that would sprout much later within the Communist bloc.

It is commonly believed that Mao's deviation from Soviet doctrines of revolution followed from the Long March. In a sense, this problem is meaningless; in another sense it is illusory. Mao began to *succeed* after the Long March. But he had already been deeply interested in the scope of the Hunan peasant insurrections in 1927, and by 1928 he had grasped the importance of organized military units and secure base areas (see Stuart R. Schram, *Mao Tse-tung: Basic Tactics*, New York: Praeger, 1966, pp. 19–22). Lenin and the Russian revolutionary experience had already hinted at some of "Maoism." What Mao lacked before 1936 were not the rudiments of doctrine, but the availability of a field of successful experiment. This became possible after his brilliant march to the North. Indeed, his strategic reflections on guerrilla warfare date from the earlier period and, as is now widely recognized, never constituted a *ne plus ultra* but, instead, a matter of convenience, in his military thinking.

If one had honestly to assign a priority of ideas in the military doctrine of Mao Tse-tung, he would no doubt arrive at the following order: (1) Chinese nationalism, (2) Leninist bolshevism, and (3) a cognizance of the skills of guerrilla warfare, resulting (combined with communism) in the idea that men and their morale are the decisive factor in war, not mere supremacy of material force. The nationalism speaks for itself: that is, the will to war against the Japanese and the frequent references in Mao's writings to Sun Tzu and other Chinese classics of strategy. Balanced against this predominant tradition is the obvious influence of Leninism, sensed not only in the common appreciation of imperialism but also in the military strain that comes originally from Clausewitz. As the distinguished scholar Benjamin Schwartz writes: "Marxism was carried into China in the wake of the messianic message and the concrete political program of Lenin" (*Chinese Communism and the Rise of Mao*, Cambridge: Harvard University Press, 1958, p. 27). As for the particular mode of warfare that Mao's army practiced, it was politically instrumental. Mao had fully emerged from his guerrilla stage before launching the final blows against the Kuomintang. Too often his writings on guerrilla strategy are read as universal *dicta*, when they were actually intended to direct and inspire his forces at a particular stage of the combat

It is Mao's total political strategy rather than his opportunist guerrilla strategy which prevailed in the great Chinese Civil War. His forging of a disciplined and ideological regular army was more than equal to Cromwell's accomplishment in the seventeenth century. But above all, he knew how to capitalize on the fact that China was, in the proportion of 80 percent, a peasant nation, although only 20 percent of the people owned land. That is the basic fact of the Chinese revolution.

# PROBLEMS OF STRATEGY
# IN CHINA'S REVOLUTIONARY WAR

Mao Tse-Tung

## CHAPTER I: HOW TO STUDY WAR

1. *The Laws of War Are Developmental*

The laws of war are a problem which anyone directing a war must study and solve.

The laws of revolutionary war are a problem which anyone directing a revolutionary war must study and solve.

The laws of China's revolutionary war are a problem which anyone directing China's revolutionary war must study and solve.

We are now engaged in a war; our war is a revolutionary war; and our revolutionary war is being waged in this semicolonial and semi-feudal country of China. Therefore, we must study not only the laws of war in general, but the specific laws of revolutionary war, and the even more specific laws of revolutionary war in China.

It is well known that when you do anything, unless you understand its actual circumstances, its nature and its relations to other things, you will not know the laws governing it, or know how to do it, or be able to do it well.

War is the highest form of struggle for resolving contradictions, when they have developed to a certain stage, between classes, nations, states, or political groups, and it has existed ever since the emergence of private property and of classes. Unless you understand the actual circumstances of war, its nature and its relations to other things, you will not know the laws of war, or know how to direct war, or be able to win victory.

*Revolutionary war*, whether a revolutionary class war or a revolutionary national war, has its own specific circumstances and nature, in addition to the circumstances and nature of war in general. There-

Source. Mao Tse-tung, "Problems of Strategy in China's Revolutionary War," from *Selected Military Writings* (Peking: Foreign Language Press, 1966), pp. 77–152, excerpted.

fore, besides the general laws of war, it has specific laws of its own. Unless you understand its specific circumstances and nature, unless you understand its specific laws, you will not be able to direct a revolutionary war and wage it successfully.

*China's revolutionary war*, whether civil war or national war, is waged in the specific environment of China and so has its own specific circumstances and nature distinguishing it both from war in general and from revolutionary war in general. Therefore, besides the laws of war in general and of revolutionary war in general, it has specific laws of its own. Unless you understand them, you will not be able to win in China's revolutionary war.

Therefore, we must study the laws of war in general, we must also study the laws of revolutionary war, and, finally, we must study the laws of China's revolutionary war.

Some people hold a wrong view, which we refuted long ago. They say that it is enough merely to study the laws of war in general, or, to put it more concretely, that it is enough merely to follow the military manuals published by the reactionary Chinese government or the reactionary military academies in China. They do not see that these manuals give merely the laws of war in general and moreover are wholly copied from abroad, and that if we copy and apply them exactly without the slightest change in form or content, we shall be "cutting the feet to fit the shoes" and be defeated. Their argument is: why should knowledge which has been acquired at the cost of blood be of no use? They fail to see that although we must cherish the earlier experience thus acquired, we must also cherish experience acquired at the cost of our own blood.

Others hold a second wrong view, which we also refuted long ago. They say that it is enough merely to study the experience of revolutionary war in Russia, or, to put it more concretely, that it is enough merely to follow the laws by which the civil war in the Soviet Union was directed and the military manuals published by Soviet military organizations. They do not see that these laws and manuals embody the specific characteristics of the civil war and the Red Army in the Soviet Union, and that if we copy and apply them without allowing any change, we shall also be "cutting the feet to fit the shoes" and be defeated. Their argument is: since our war, like the war in the Soviet Union, is a revolutionary war, and since the Soviet Union won victory, how then can there be any alternative but to follow the Soviet example? They fail to see that while we should set special store by the war experience of the Soviet Union, because it is the most recent experience of revolutionary war and was acquired under the guidance of Lenin and Stalin, we should likewise cherish the experience of China's revolutionary war, because there are many factors that are specific to the Chinese revolution and the Chinese Red Army.

Still others hold a third wrong view, which we likewise refuted long ago. They say that the most valuable experience is that of the Northern Expedition of 1926–27[1] and that we must learn from it, or, to put it more concretely, that we must imitate the Northern Expedition in driving straight ahead to seize the big cities. They fail to see that while the experience of the Northern Expedition should be studied, it should not be copied and applied mechanically, because the circumstances of our present war are different. We should take from the Northern Expedition only what still applies today, and work out something of our own in the light of present conditions.

Thus the different laws for directing different wars are determined by the different circumstances of those wars—differences in their time, place and nature. As regards the time factor, both war and the laws for directing wars develop; each historical stage has its special characteristics, and hence the laws of war in each historical stage have their special characteristics and cannot be mechanically applied in another stage. As for the nature of war, since revolutionary war and counter-revolutionary war both have their special characteristics, the laws governing them also have their own characteristics, and those applying to one cannot be mechanically transferred to the other. As for the factor of place, since each country or nation, especially a large country or nation, has its own characteristics, the laws of war for each country or nation also have their own characteristics, and here, too, those applying to one cannot be mechanically transferred to the other. In studying the laws for directing wars that occur at different historical stages, that differ in nature and that are waged in different places and by different nations, we must fix our attention on the characteristics and development of each, and must oppose a mechanical approach to the problem of war.

Nor is this all. It signifies progress and development in a commander who is initially capable of commanding only a small formation, if he becomes capable of commanding a big one. There is also a difference between operating in one locality and in many. It likewise signifies progress and development in a commander who is initially capable of operating only in a locality he knows well, if he becomes capable of operating in many other localities. Owing to technical, tactical and

[1] The Northern Expedition was the punitive war against the Northern warlords launched by the revolutionary army which marched north from Kwangtung Province in May–July 1926. . . .

strategic developments on the enemy side and on our own, the circumstances also differ from stage to stage within a given war. It signifies still more progress and development in a commander who is capable of exercising command in a war at its lower stages, if he becomes capable of exercising command in its higher stages. A commander who remains capable of commanding only a formation of a certain size, only in a certain locality and at a certain stage in the development of a war shows that he has made no progress and has not developed. There are some people who, contented with a single skill or a peep-hole view, never make any progress; they may play some role in the revolution at a given place and time, but not a significant one. We need directors of war who can play a significant role. All the laws for directing war develop as history develops and as war develops; nothing is changeless.

### 2. *The Aim of War Is to Eliminate War*

War, this monster of mutual slaughter among men, will be finally eliminated by the progress of human society, and in the not too distant future too. But there is only one way to eliminate it and that is to oppose war with war, to oppose counter-revolutionary war with revolutionary war, to oppose national counter-revolutionary war with national revolutionary war, and to oppose counter-revolutionary class war with revolutionary class war. History knows only two kinds of war, just and unjust. We support just wars and oppose unjust wars. All counter-revolutionary wars are unjust. All revolutionary wars are just. Mankind's era of wars will be brought to an end by our own efforts, and beyond doubt the war we wage is part of the final battle. But also beyond doubt the war we face will be part of the biggest and most ruthless of all wars. The biggest and most ruthless of unjust counter-revolutionary wars is hanging over us, and the vast majority of mankind will be ravaged unless we raise the banner of a just war. The banner of mankind's just war is the banner of mankind's salvation. The banner of China's just war is the banner of China's salvation. A war waged by the great majority of mankind and of the Chinese people is beyond doubt a just war, a most lofty and glorious undertaking for the salvation of mankind and China, and a bridge to a new era in world history. When human society advances to the point where classes and states are eliminated, there will be no more wars, counter-revolutionary or revolutionary, unjust or just; that will be the era of perpetual peace for mankind. Our study of the laws of revolutionary war springs from the desire to eliminate all wars; herein lies the distinction between us Communists and all the exploiting classes.

### 3. Strategy Is the Study of the Laws of a War Situation as a Whole

Wherever there is war, there is a war situation as a whole. The war situation as a whole may cover the entire world, may cover an entire country, or may cover an independent guerrilla zone or an independent major operational front. Any war situation which acquires a comprehensive consideration of its various aspects and stages forms a war situation as a whole.

The task of the science of strategy is to study those laws for directing a war that govern a war situation as a whole. The task of the science of campaigns and the science of tactics[2] is to study those laws for directing a war that govern a partial situation.

Why is it necessary for the commander of a campaign or a tactical operation to understand the laws of strategy to some degree? Because an understanding of the whole facilitates the handling of the part, and because the part is subordinate to the whole. The view that strategic victory is determined by tactical successes alone is wrong because it overlooks the fact that victory or defeat in a war is first and foremost a question of whether the situation as a whole and its various stages are properly taken into account. If there are serious defects or mistakes in taking the situation as a whole and its various stages into account, the war is sure to be lost. "One careless move loses the whole game" refers to a move affecting the situation as a whole, a move decisive for the whole situation, and not to a move of a partial nature, a move which is not decisive for the whole situation. As in chess, so in war.

But the situation as a whole cannot be detached from its parts and become independent of them, for it is made up of all its parts. Sometimes certain parts may suffer destruction or defeat without seriously affecting the situation as a whole, because they are not decisive for it. Some defeats or failures in tactical operations or campaigns do not lead to deterioration in the war situation as a whole, because they are not of decisive significance. But the loss of most of the campaigns making up the war situation as a whole, or of one or two decisive campaigns, immediately changes the whole situation. Here, "most of the campaigns" or "one or two campaigns" are decisive. In the history of war, there are instances where defeat in a single battle nullified all the advantages of a series of victories, and there are also instances

---

[2] The science of strategy, the science of campaigns and the science of tactics are all components of Chinese military science. The science of strategy deals with the laws that govern the war situation as a whole. The science of campaigns deals with the laws that govern campaigns and is applied in directing campaigns. The science of tactics deals with the laws that govern battles and is applied in directing battles.

where victory in a single battle after many defeats opened up a new situation. In those instances the "series of victories" and the "many defeats" were partial in nature and not decisive for the situation as a whole, while "defeat in a single battle" or "victory in a single battle" played the decisive role. All this explains the importance of taking into account the situation as a whole. What is most important for the person in over-all command is to concentrate on attending to the war situation as a whole. The main point is that, according to the circumstances, he should concern himself with the problems of the grouping of his military units and formations, the relations between campaigns, the relations between various operational stages, and the relations between our activities as a whole and the enemy's activities as a whole—all these problems demand his greatest care and effort, and if he ignores them and immerses himself in secondary problems, he can hardly avoid setbacks.

The relationship between the whole and the part holds not only for the relationship between strategy and campaign but also for that between campaign and tactics. Examples are to be found in the relation between the operations of a division and those of its regiments and battalions, and in the relation between the operations of a company and those of its platoons and squads. The commanding officer at any level should centre his attention on the most important and decisive problem or action in the whole situation he is handling, and not on other problems or actions.

What is important or decisive should be determined not by general or abstract considerations, but according to the concrete circumstances. In a military operation the direction and point of assault should be selected according to the actual situation of the enemy, the terrain, and the strength of our own forces at the moment. One must see to it that the soldiers do not overeat when supplies are abundant, and take care that they do not go hungry when supplies are short. In the White areas the mere leakage of a piece of information may cause defeat in a subsequent engagement, but in the Red areas such leakage is often not a very serious matter. It is necessary for the high commanders to participate personally in certain battles but not in others. For a military school, the most important question is the selection of a director and instructors and the adoption of a training programme. For a mass meeting, the main thing is mobilizing the masses to attend and putting forward suitable slogans. And so on and so forth. In a word, the principle is to centre our attention on the important links that have a bearing on the situation as a whole.

The only way to study the laws governing a war situation as

a whole is to do some hard thinking. For what pertains to the situation as a whole is not visible to the eye, and we can understand it only by hard thinking; there is no other way. But because the situation as a whole is made up of parts, people with experience of the parts, experience of campaigns and tactics, can understand matters of a higher order provided they are willing to think hard. The problems of strategy include the following:

> Giving proper consideration to the relation between the enemy and ourselves.
>
> Giving proper consideration to the relation between various campaigns or between various operational stages.
>
> Giving proper consideration to those parts which have a bearing on (are decisive for) the situation as a whole.
>
> Giving proper consideration to the special features contained in the general situation.
>
> Giving proper consideration to the relation between the front and the rear.
>
> Giving proper consideration to the distinction as well as the connection between losses and replacements, between fighting and resting, between concentration and dispersion, between attack and defense, between advance and retreat, between concealment and exposure, between the main attack and supplementary attacks, between assault and containing action, between centralized command and decentralized command, between protracted war and war of quick decision, between positional war and mobile war, between our own forces and friendly forces, between one military arm and another, between higher and lower levels, between cadres and the rank and file, between old and new soldiers, between senior and junior cadres, between old and new cadres, between Red areas and White areas, between old Red areas and new ones, between the central district and the borders of a given base area, between the warm season and the cold season, between victory and defeat, between large and small troop formations, between the regular army and the guerrilla forces, between destroying the enemy and winning over the masses, between expanding the Red Army and consolidating it, between military work and political work, between past and present tasks, between present and future tasks, between tasks arising from one set of circumstances and tasks arising from another, between fixed fronts and fluid fronts, between civil war and national war, between one historical stage and another, etc., etc. . . .

## 4. *The Important Thing Is To Be Good at Learning*

Why have we organized the Red Army? For the purpose of defeating the enemy. Why do we study the laws of war? For the purpose of applying them in war.

To learn is no easy matter and to apply what one has learned is even harder. Many people appear impressive when discoursing on military science in classrooms or in books, but when it comes to actual fighting, some win battles and others lose them. Both the history of war and our own experience in war have proved this point.

Where then does the crux lie?

In real life, we cannot ask for "ever-victorious generals," who are few and far between in history. What we can ask for is generals who are brave and sagacious and who normally win their battles in the course of a war, generals who combine wisdom with courage. To become both wise and courageous one must acquire a method, a method to be employed in learning as well as in applying what has been learned.

What method? The method is to familiarize ourselves with all aspects of the enemy situation and our own, to discover the laws governing the actions of both sides and to make use of these laws in our own operations.

The military manuals issued in many countries point both to the necessity of a "flexible application of principles according to circumstances" and to the measures to be taken in case of defeat. They point to the former in order to warn a commander against subjectively committing mistakes through too rigid an application of principles, and to the latter in order to enable him to cope with the situation after he has committed subjective mistakes or after unexpected and irresistible changes have occurred in the objective circumstances.

Why are subjective mistakes made? Because the way the forces in a war or a battle are disposed or directed does not fit the conditions of the given time and place, because subjective direction does not correspond to, or is at variance with, the objective conditions, in other words, because the contradiction between the subjective and the objective has not been resolved. People can hardly avoid such situations whatever they are doing, but some people prove themselves more competent than others. As in any job we demand a comparatively high degree of competence, so in war we demand more victories or, conversely, fewer defeats. Here the crux is to bring the subjective and the objective into proper correspondence with each other.

Take an example in tactics. If the point chosen for attack is one of the enemy's flanks and it is located precisely where his weak spot happens to be, and in consequence the assault succeeds, then the subjective corresponds with the objective, that is, the commander's reconnaissance, judgement and decision have corresponded with the enemy's actual situation and dispositions. If the point chosen for attack is on another flank or in the centre and the attack hits a snag and makes no headway, then such correspondence is lacking. If the attack is properly timed, if the reserves are used neither too late nor too early, and if all the other dispositions and operations in the battle are such as to favour us and not the enemy, then the subjective direction throughout the battle completely corresponds with the objective situation. Such complete correspondence is extremely rare in a war or a battle, in which the belligerents are groups of live human beings bearing arms and keeping their secrets from each other; this is quite unlike handling inanimate objects or routine matters. But if the direction given by the commander corresponds in the main with the actual situation, that is, if the decisive elements in the direction correspond with the actual situation, then there is a basis for victory.

A commander's correct dispositions stem from his correct decisions, his correct decisions stem from his correct judgments and his correct judgments stem from a thorough and necessary reconnaissance and from pondering on and piecing together the data of various kinds gathered through reconnaissance. He applies all possible and necessary methods of reconnaissance, and ponders on the information gathered about the enemy's situation, discarding the dross and selecting the essential, eliminating the false and retaining the true, proceeding from the one to the other and from the outside to the inside; then, he takes the conditions on his own side into account, and makes a study of both sides and their interrelations, thereby forming his judgments, making up his mind and working out his plans. Such is the complete process of knowing a situation which a military man goes through before he formulates a strategic plan, a campaign plan or a battle plan. But instead of doing this, a careless military man bases his military plans on his own wishful thinking, and hence his plans are fanciful and do not correspond with reality. A rash military man relying solely upon enthusiasm is bound to be tricked by the enemy, or lured on by some superficial or partial aspect of the enemy's situation, or swayed by irresponsible suggestions from subordinates that are not based on real knowledge or deep insight, and so he runs his head against a brick wall, because he does not know or does not want to know that every military plan must be based on the necessary reconnaissance and on careful consideration of the enemy's situation, his own situation, and their interrelations.

The process of knowing a situation goes on not only before the formulation of a military plan but also after. In carrying out the plan from the moment it is put into effect to the end of the operation, there is another process of knowing the situation, namely, the process of practice. In the course of this process, it is necessary to examine anew whether the plan worked out in the preceding process corresponds with reality. If it does not correspond with reality, or if it does not fully do so, then in the light of our new knowledge, it becomes necessary to form new judgments, make new decisions and change the original plan so as to meet the new situation. The plan is partially changed in almost every operation, and sometimes it is even changed completely. A rash man who does not understand the need for such alterations or is unwilling to make them, but who acts blindly, will inevitably run his head against a brick wall.

The above applies to a strategic action, a campaign or a battle. Provided he is modest and willing to learn, an experienced military man will be able to familiarize himself with the character of his own forces (commanders, men, arms, supplies, etc., and their sum total) with the character of the enemy forces (likewise, commanders, men, arms, supplies, etc., and their sum total) and with all other conditions related to the war, such as politics, economics, geography and weather; such a military man will have a better grasp in directing a war or an operation and will be more likely to win victories. He will achieve this because, over a long period of time, he has come to know the situation on the enemy side and his own, discovered the laws of action, and resolved the contradictions between the subjective and the objective. This process of knowing is extremely important; without such a long period of experience, it would be difficult to understand and grasp the laws of an entire war. Neither a beginner nor a person who fights only on paper can become a really able high-ranking commander; only one who has learned through actual fighting in war can do so.

All military laws and military theories which are in the nature of principles are the experience of past wars summed up by people in former days or in our own times. We should seriously study these lessons, paid for in blood, which are a heritage of past wars. That is one point. But there is another. We should put these conclusions to the test of our own experience, assimilating what is useful, rejecting what is useless, and adding what is specifically our own. The latter is very important, for otherwise we cannot direct a war.

Reading is learning, but applying is also learning and the more important kind of learning at that. Our chief method is to learn warfare through warfare. A person who has had no opportunity to go to school can also learn warfare—he can learn through fighting in war. A revolutionary war is a mass undertaking; it is often not a matter of first learning and then doing, but of doing and then learning, for doing is itself learning. There is a gap between the ordinary civilian and the soldier, but it is no Great Wall, and it can quickly be closed, and the way to close it is to take part in revolution, in war. By saying that it is not easy to learn and to apply, we mean that it is hard to learn thoroughly and to apply skilfully. By saying that civilians can very quickly become soldiers, we mean that it is not difficult to cross the threshold. To put the two statements together, we may cite the Chinese adage, "Nothing in the world is difficult for one who sets his mind to it." To cross the threshold is not difficult, and mastery, too, is possible provided one sets one's mind to the task and is good at learning.

The laws of war, like the laws governing all other things, are reflections in our minds of objective realities; everything outside of the mind is objective reality. Consequently what has to be learned and known includes the state of affairs on the enemy side and that on our side, both of which should be regarded as the object of study, while the mind (the capacity to think) alone is the subject performing the study. Some people are good at knowing themselves and poor at knowing their enemy, and some are the other way round; neither can solve the problem of learning and applying the laws of war. There is a saying in the book of Sun Wu Tzu, the great military scientist of ancient China, "Know the enemy and know yourself, and you can fight a hundred battles with no danger of defeat,"[3] which refers both to the stage of learning and to the stage of application, both to knowing the laws of the development of objective reality and to deciding on our own action in accordance with these laws in order to overcome the enemy facing us. We should not take this saying lightly.

War is the highest form of struggle between nations, states, classes, or political groups, and all the laws of war are applied by warring nations, states, classes, or political groups for the purpose of achieving victory for themselves. Unquestionably, victory or defeat in war is determined mainly by the military, political, economic and natural conditions on both sides. But not by these alone. It is also determined by each side's subjective ability in directing the war. In his endeavour to win a war, a military man cannot overstep the limitations imposed by the material conditions; within these limitations, however, he can and must strive for victory. The stage of action for a military man is built upon objective material conditions, but on that stage he can

[3] Sun Wu Tzu, or Sun Wu, also known as Sun Tzu, was a famous Chinese soldier and military scientist in the 5th century b.c., who wrote *Sun Tzu*, a treatise on war containing thirteen chapters. This quotation is from Chapter 3, "The Strategy of Attack."

direct the performance of many a drama, full of sound and colour, power and grandeur. Therefore, given the objective material foundations, *i.e.*, the military, political, economic and natural conditions, our Red Army commanders must display their prowess and marshal all their forces to crush the national and class enemies and to transform this evil world. Here is where our subjective ability in directing war can and must be exercised. We do not permit any of our Red Army commanders to become a blundering hothead; we decidedly want every Red Army commander to become a hero who is both brave and sagacious, who possesses both all-conquering courage and the ability to remain master of the situation throughout the changes and vicissitudes of the entire war. Swimming in the ocean of war, he not only must not flounder but must make sure of reaching the opposite shore with measured strokes. The laws for directing war constitute the art of swimming in the ocean of war.

So much for our methods.

## CHAPTER II:   THE CHINESE COMMUNIST PARTY AND CHINA'S REVOLUTIONARY WAR

China's revolutionary war, which began in 1924, has passed through two stages, the first from 1924 to 1927, and the second from 1927 to 1936; the stage of national revolutionary war against Japan will now commence. In all three of its stages this revolutionary war has been, is, and will be fought under the leadership of the Chinese proletariat and its party, the Chinese Communist Party. The chief enemies in China's revolutionary war are imperialism and the feudal forces. Although the Chinese bourgeoisie may take part in the revolutionary war at certain historical junctures, yet its selfishness and lack of political and economic independence render it both unwilling and unable to lead China's revolutionary war on to the road of complete victory. The masses of China's peasantry and urban petty bourgeoisie wish to take an active part in the revolutionary war and to carry it to complete victory. They are the main forces in the revolutionary war, but, being small-scale producers, they are limited in their political outlook (and some of the unemployed masses have anarchist views), so that they are unable to give correct leadership in the war. Therefore, in an era when the proletariat has already appeared on the political stage, the responsibility for leading China's revolutionary war inevitably falls on the shoulders of the Chinese Communist Party. In this era, any revolutionary war will definitely end in defeat if it lacks, or runs counter to, the leadership of the proletariat and the Communist

Party. Of all the social strata and political groupings in semi-colonial China, the proletariat and the Communist Party are the ones most free from narrow-mindedness and selfishness, are politically the most far-sighted, the best organized and the readiest to learn with an open mind from the experience of the vanguard class, the proletariat, and its political party throughout the world and to make use of this experience in their own cause. Hence only the proletariat and the Communist Party can lead the peasantry, the urban petty bourgeoisie and bourgeoisie, can overcome the narrow-mindedness of the peasantry and the petty bourgeoisie, the destructiveness of the unemployed masses, and also (provided the Communist Party does not err in its policy) the vacillation and lack of thoroughness of the bourgeoisie—and can lead the revolution and the war on to the road of victory.

The revolutionary war of 1924–27 was waged, basically speaking in conditions in which the international proletariat and the Chinese proletariat and their parties exerted political influence on the Chinese national bourgeoisie and its parties and entered into political co-operation with them. However, this revolutionary war failed at the critical juncture, first of all because the big bourgeoisie turned traitor, and at the same time because the opportunists within the revolutionary ranks voluntarily surrendered the leadership of the revolution.

The Agrarian Revolutionary War, lasting from 1927 to the present, has been waged under new conditions. The enemy in this war is not imperialism alone but also the alliance of the big bourgeoisie and the big landlords. And the national bourgeoisie has become a tail to the big bourgeoisie. This revolutionary war is led by the Communist Party alone, which has established absolute leadership over it. This absolute leadership is the most important condition enabling the revolutionary war to be carried through firmly to the end. Without it, it is inconceivable that the revolutionary war could have been carried on with such perseverance.

The Chinese Communist Party has led China's revolutionary war courageously and resolutely, and for fifteen long years has demonstrated to the whole nation that it is the people's friend, fighting at all times in the forefront of the revolutionary war in defence of the people's interests and for their freedom and liberation.

By its arduous struggles and by the martyrdom of hundreds of thousands of its heroic members and tens of thousands of its heroic cadres, the Communist Party of China has played a great educative role among hundreds of millions of people throughout the country. The Party's great historic achievements in its revolutionary struggles have provided the prerequisite for the survival and salvation of China at this critical juncture when she is being invaded by a national enemy; and this prerequisite is the existence of a political leadership enjoying the confidence of the vast majority of the people and chosen by them after long years of testing. Today, the people accept what the Communist Party says more readily than what any other political party says. Were it not for the arduous struggles of the Chinese Communist Party in the last fifteen years, it would be impossible to save China in the face of the new menace of subjugation.

Besides the errors of the Right opportunism of Chen Tu-hsiu[4] and the "Left" opportunism of Li Li-san,[5] the Chinese Communist Party has committed two other errors in the course of the revolutionary war. The first error was the "Left" opportunism of 1931–34.[6] which resulted in serious losses in the Agrarian Revolutionary War so that, instead of our defeating the enemy's fifth campaign of "encirclement and suppression," we lost our base areas and the Red Army was weakened. This error was corrected at the enlarged meeting of the Political Bureau of the Central Committee at Tsunyi in January 1935. The second was the Right opportunism of Chang Kuo-tao in 1935–36[7] which

[4] Chen Tu-hsiu was a radical democrat around the time of the May 4th Movement. Later, under the influence of the October Socialist Revolution he became one of the founders of the Chinese Communist Party. . . . The capitulationists, represented by Chen Tu-hsiu, "voluntarily gave up the Party's leadership of the peasant masses, urban petty bourgeoisie and middle bourgeoisie, and in particular gave up the Party's leadership of the armed forces, thus causing the defeat of the revolution" ("The Present Situation and Our Tasks," *Selected Works of Mao Tse-tung*, Eng. ed., FLP, Peking, 1961, Vol. IV, p. 171). . . .

[5] The "Left" opportunism of Li Li-san . . . refers to the "Left" opportunist line which existed in the Party for about four months beginning from June 1930. . . . It violated the policy of the Party's Sixth National Congress; it denied that mass strength had to be built up for the revolution and denied that the development of the revolution was uneven; it regarded Comrade Mao Tse-tung's ideas that for a long time we should devote our attention mainly to creating rural base areas, use the rural areas to encircle the cities and use these bases to advance a high tide of country-wide revolution as "extremely erroneous . . . localism and conservatism characteristic of the peasant mentality"; and it held that preparations should be made for immediate insurrections in all parts of the country. . . .

[6] The "Resolution on Certain Questions in The History of Our Party" (see *Selected Works of Mao Tse-tung*, Eng. ed., FLP, Peking, 1965, Vol. III, pp. 177–225) adopted by the Seventh Plenary Session of the Sixth Central Committee in April 1945 made a detailed summing-up of the various aspects of this erroneous line.

[7] Chang Kuo-tao was a renegade from the Chinese revolution. . . . He joined the Chinese Communist Party in his youth, . . . made many mistakes, and ended by committing grave crimes. Most notoriously, in 1935 he opposed the Red Army's northward march, advocating a defeatist and liquidationist withdrawal by the Red Army to the minority-nationality areas on the Szechuan-Sikang border.

grew to such an extent that it undermined the discipline of the Party and of the Red Army and caused serious losses to part of the Red Army's main forces. But this error was also finally rectified, thanks to the correct leadership of the Central Committee and the political consciousness of Party members, commanders and fighters in the Red Army. Of course all these errors were harmful to our Party, to our revolution and the war, but in the end we overcame them, and in doing so our Party and our Red Army have steeled themselves and become still stronger.

The Chinese Communist Party has led and continues to lead stirring, magnificent and victorious revolutionary war. This war is not only the banner of China's liberation, but has international revolutionary significance as well. The eyes of the revolutionary people the world over are upon us. In the new stage, the stage of the anti-Japanese national revolutionary war, we shall lead the Chinese revolution to its completion and exert a profound influence on the revolution in the East and in the whole world. Our revolutionary war has proved that we need a correct Marxist military line as well as a correct Marxist political line. Fifteen years of revolution and war have hammered out such political and military lines. We believe that from now on, in the new stage of the war, these lines will be further developed, filled out and enriched in new circumstances, so that we can attain our aim of defeating the national enemy. History tells us that correct political and military lines do not emerge and develop spontaneously and tranquilly, but only in the course of struggle. These lines must combat "Left" opportunism on the one hand and "Right" opportunism on the other. Without combating and thoroughly overcoming these harmful tendencies which damage the revolution and the revolutionary war, it would be impossible to establish a correct line and win victory in this war. It is for this reason that I often refer to erroneous views in this pamphlet.

## CHAPTER III:  CHARACTERISTICS OF CHINA'S REVOLUTIONARY WAR

### 1. *The Importance of the Subject*

People who do not admit, do not know, or do not want to know that China's revolutionary war has its own characteristics have equated the war waged by the Red Army against the Kuomintang forces with war in general or with the civil war in the Soviet Union. The experience of the civil war in the Soviet Union directed by Lenin and Stalin has a world-wide significance. All Communist Parties, including the Chinese Communist Party, regard this experience and its theoretical summing-up by Lenin and Stalin as their guide. But this does not mean that we should apply it mechanically to our own conditions. In many of its aspects China's revolutionary war has characteristics distinguishing it from the civil war in the Soviet Union. Of course it is wrong to take no account of these characteristics or deny their existence. This point has been fully borne out in our ten years of war.

Our enemy has made similiar mistakes. He did not recognize that fighting against the Red Army required a different strategy and different tactics from those used in fighting other forces. Relying on his superiority in various respects, he took us lightly and stuck to his old methods of warfare. This was the case both before and during his fourth "encirclement and suppression" campaign in 1933, with the result that he suffered a series of defeats. In the Kuomintang army a new approach to the problem was suggested first by the reactionary Kuomintang general Liu Wei-yuan and then by Tai Yueh. Their idea was eventually accepted by Chiang Kai-shek. That was how Chiang Kai-shek's Officers' Training Corps at Lushan came into being and how the new reactionary military principles[8] applied in the fifth campaign of "encirclement and suppression" were evolved.

But when the enemy changed his military principles to suit operations against the Red Army, there appeared in our ranks a group of people who reverted to the "old ways." They urged a return to ways suited to the general run of things, refused to go into the specific circumstances of each case, rejected the experience gained in the Red Army's history of sanguinary battles, belittled the strength of imperialism and the Kuomintang as well as that of the Kuomintang army, and turned a blind eye to the new reactionary principles adopted by the enemy. As a result, all the revolutionary bases except the Shensi-Kansu border area were lost, the Red Army was reduced from 300,000 to a few tens of thousands, the membership of the Chinese Communist Party fell from 300,000 to a few tens of thousands, and the Party organizations in the Kuomintang areas were almost destroyed. In short, we paid a severe penalty, which was historic in its significance. This group of people called themselves Marxist-Leninists, but actually they had not learned an iota of Marxism-Leninism. Lenin said that the most essential thing in Marxism, the living soul of Marxism, is the

---

[8] These new military principles largely constituted the Chiang Kai-shek gang's policy of "blockhouse warfare" in accordance with which it advanced gradually and entrenched itself at every step.

concrete analysis of concrete conditions.[9] That was precisely the point these comrades of ours forgot.

Hence one can see that, without an understanding of the characteristics of China's revolutionary war, it is impossible to direct it and lead it to victory.

## 2. What Are the Characteristics of China's Revolutionary War?

What then are the characteristics of China's revolutionary war? I think there are four principal ones.

The first is that China is a vast, semi-colonial country which is unevenly developed politically and economically and which has gone through the revolution of 1924–27.

This characteristic indicates that it is possible for China's revolutionary war to develop and attain victory. We already pointed this out (at the First Party Congress of the Hunan-Kiangsi Border Area) when in late 1927 and early 1928, soon after guerrilla warfare was started in China, some comrades in the Chingkang Mountains in the Hunan-Kiangsi border area raised the question, "How long can we keep the Red Flag flying?" For this was a most fundamental question. Without answering this question of whether China's revolutionary base areas and the Chinese Red Army could survive and develop, we could not have advanced a single step. The Sixth National Congress of the Chinese Communist Party in 1928 again gave the answer to the question. Since then the Chinese revolutionary movement has had a correct theoretical basis.

Let us now analyse this characteristic.

China's political and economic development is uneven—a weak capitalist economy coexists with a preponderant semifeudal economy; a few modern industrial and commercial cities coexist with a vast stagnant countryside; several million workers coexist with several hundred millions of peasants and handicraftsmen labouring under the old system; big warlords controlling the central government coexist with small warlords controlling the provinces; two kinds of reactionary armies, the so-called Central Army under Chiang Kai-shek and "miscellaneous troops" under the warlords in the provinces, exist side by side; a few railways, steamship lines and motor roads exist side by side with a vast number of wheelbarrow paths and foot-paths many of which are difficult to negotiate even on foot.

China is a semi-colonial country—disunity among the imperialist powers makes for disunity among the ruling groups in China. There

[9] See V. I. Lenin, "Communism," (Collected Works, Russ., ed., Moscow, 1950, Vol. XXXI, p. 143).

is a difference between a semi-colonial country controlled by several countries and a colony controlled by a single country.

China is a vast country—"When it is dark in the east, it is light in the west; when things are dark in the south, there is still light in the north." Hence one need not worry about lack of room for manoeuvre.

China has gone through a great revolution—this has provided the seeds from which the Red Army has grown, provided the leader of the Red Army, namely, the Chinese Communist Party, and provided the masses with experience of participation in a revolution.

We say, therefore, that the first characteristic of China's revolutionary war is that it is waged in a vast semi-colonial country which is unevenly developed politically and economically and which has gone through a revolution. This characteristic basically determines our military strategy and tactics as well as our political strategy and tactics.

The second characteristic is that our enemy is big and powerful.

How do matters stand with the Kuomintang, the enemy of the Red Army? It is a party that has seized political power and has more or less stabilized its power. It has gained support of the world's principal imperialist states. It has remodelled its army, which has thus become different from any other army in Chinese history and on the whole similar to the armies of modern states; this army is much better supplied with weapons and *matériel* than the Red Army, and is larger than any army in Chinese history or for that matter than the standing army of any other country. There is a world of difference between the Kuomintang army and the Red Army. The Kuomintang controls the key positions of lifelines in the politics, economy, communications and culture of China; its political power is nation-wide.

The Chinese Red Army is thus confronted with a big and powerful enemy. This is the second characteristic of China's revolutionary war. It necessarily makes the military operations of the Red Army different in many ways from those of wars in general and from those of the civil war in the Soviet Union or of the Northern Expedition.

The third characteristic is that the Red Army is small and weak.

The Chinese Red Army, starting as guerrilla units, came into being after the defeat of the First Great Revolution. This occurred in a period of relative political and economic stability in the reactionary capitalist countries of the world as well as in a period of reaction in China.

Our political power exists in scattered and isolated mountainous or remote regions and receives no outside help whatsoever. Economic and cultural conditions in the revolutionary base areas are backward compared with those in the Kuomintang areas. The revolutionary base areas embrace only rural districts and small towns. These areas were extremely small in the beginning and have not grown much larger since. Moreover, they are fluid and not stationary, and the Red Army has no really consolidated bases.

The Red Army is numerically small, its arms are poor, and it has great difficulty in obtaining supplies such as food, bedding and clothing.

This characteristic presents a sharp contrast to the preceding one. From this sharp contrast have arisen the strategy and tactics of the Red Army.

The fourth characteristic is Communist Party leadership and the agrarian revolution.

This characteristic is the inevitable consequence of the first one. It has given rise to two features. On the one hand, despite the fact that China's revolutionary war is taking place in a period of reaction in China and throughout the capitalist world, victory is possible because it is under the leadership of the Communist Party and has the support of the peasantry. Thanks to this support, our base areas, small as they are, are politically very powerful and stand firmly opposed to the enormous Kuomintang regime, while militarily they place great difficulties in the way of the Kuomintang attacks. Small as it is, the Red Army has great fighting capacity, because its members, led by the Communist Party, are born of the agrarian revolution and are fighting for their own interests, and because its commanders and fighters are politically united.

The Kuomintang, on the other hand, presents a sharp contrast. It opposes the agrarian revolution and therefore has no support from the peasantry. Though it has a large army, the Kuomintang cannot make its soldiers and the many lower-ranking officers, who were originally small producers, risk their lives willingly for it. Its officers and men are politically divided, which reduces its fighting capacity.

3. *Our Strategy and Tactics Ensuing from These Characteristics*

Thus the four principal characteristics of China's revolutionary war are: a vast semi-colonial country which is unevenly developed politically and economically and which has gone through a great revolution; a big and powerful enemy; a small and weak Red Army; and the agrarian revolution. These characteristics determine the line for guiding China's revolutionary war as well as many of its strategic and tactical principles. It follows from the first and fourth characteristics that it is possible for the Chinese Red Army to grow and defeat its enemy. It follows from the second and third characteristics that is impossible for the Chinese Red Army to grow very rapidly or defeat its enemy quickly; in other words, the war will be protracted and may even be lost if it is mishandled.

These are the two aspects of China's revolutionary war. They exist simultaneously, that is, there are favourable factors and there are difficulties. This is the fundamental law of China's revolutionary war, from which many other laws ensue. The history of our ten years of war has proved the validity of this law. He who has eyes but fails to see this fundamental law cannot direct China's revolutionary war, cannot lead the Red Army to victories.

It is clear that we must correctly settle all the following matters of principle:

Determine our strategic orientation correctly, oppose adventurism when on the offensive, oppose conservatism when on the defensive and oppose flightism when shifting from one place to another.

Oppose guerrilla-ism in the Red Army, while recognizing the guerrilla character of its operations.

Oppose protracted campaigns and a strategy of quick decision, and uphold the strategy of protracted war and campaigns of quick decision.

Oppose fixed battle lines and positional warfare, and favour fluid battle lines and mobile warfare.

Oppose fighting merely to rout the enemy, and uphold fighting to annihilate the enemy.

Oppose the strategy of striking with two "fists" in two directions at the same time, and uphold the strategy of striking with one "fist" in one direction at one time.[10]

Oppose the principle of maintaining a large rear service organization, and uphold the principle of small ones.

Oppose an absolutely centralized command, and favour a relatively centralized command.

Oppose the purely military viewpoint and the ways of roving rebels,[11] and recognize that the Red Army is a propagandist and organizer of the Chinese revolution.

Oppose bandit ways,[12] and uphold strict political discipline.

Oppose warlord ways, and favour both democracy within proper limits and an authoritative discipline in the army.

---

[10] See *Selected Military Writings of Mao Tse-tung*, Eng. ed., FLP, Peking, 1966, pp. 134–35.

[11] *Ibid.*, Notes 4 and 5, pp. 63–64.

[12] "Bandit ways" refer to plundering and looting resulting from lack of discipline, organization and clear political direction.

Oppose an incorrect, sectarian policy on cadres, and uphold the correct policy on cadres.

Oppose the policy of isolation, and affirm the policy of winning over all possible allies.

Oppose keeping the Red Army at its old stage, and strive to develop it to a new stage.

Our present discussion of the problems of strategy is intended to elucidate these matters carefully in the light of the historical experience gained in China's ten years of bloody revolutionary war.

# 19

# The Contemporary French Doctrine of "La Guerre Révolutionnaire"

*George Armstrong Kelly*

⋘⋘⋘⋘⋘⋘⋘⋘⋘⋘⋘⋘⋘⋘⋘⋘⋘⋘⋘⋘⋘⋘⋘⋘⋘⋘⋘⋘⋘

## EDITORS' COMMENT

Charles de Gaulle, accused by many of holding doctrinaire and intransigent positions, is himself among the many who have charged the French Army with an ignorance of empirical reality in its grand strategy (*Au fil de l'épée*, Paris: Plon, 1932, p. 98). Although Napoleon was both a brilliant strategist and operator, creative innovation in the French army almost ceased until late in World War I. Again, in 1940, despite the warnings of a Colonel de Gaulle, the "Maginot psychology," the *a priori* dogmas founded on the "grandes leçons" of the previous war and an arrogant traditionalism contributed to military defeat. In the post-World War II period, the drug of doctrine was filled by a very different prescription, which the essay below seeks to analyze.

The connection between the concept of *la guerre révolutionnaire* and internal war is complex but important to grasp. Codified by military intellectuals who had been exposed to "the war in the social milieu" fought in Indochina, it was initially intended as a pondered re-

418

sponse to the problem of colonial insurgency. But because of its destined emphasis on the ideological, social, and propagandistic dimensions of modern warfare—especially as practiced by Communist "liberation movements"—it spilled over ineluctably into the political bloodstream of France, contributing to the decline and fall of the Fourth Republic and to some of the tense moments of the Fifth. It became, with a vengeance, a repatriated scheme of political violence.

The "dogmatism" of *la guerre révolutionnaire* is ambiguous. In the first place, given the French army's civilian-directed mission of winning and pacifying in Southeast Asia and, later, in North Africa, it was a creative response to these eventually insoluble problems. As such, many of its components (for example, the close and friendly contact with local populations, the administration of social services, and the productive occupancy of the vacuum of misunderstanding between Paris and the non-European peoples under the French flag) were implicit in the colonial policies of Marshal Lyautey and other heroes of the older overseas army. Their innovations had stood out boldly against the stagnation of doctrine in the métropole.

In the second place, however, *la guerre révolutionnaire,* with its adjunct "psychological action," fed on a rawly adapted Maoism and what frequently amounted to an intoxication with the "black arts" of population control and crowd psychology. In this sense, it was modernistic, quasi-technical, and totalitarian-inspired. But to leave it at that is to give a distorted picture of the phenomenon. Although it is true that *la guerre révolutionnaire* owed many of its recipes to a new intellectualism or, at least, to "new thinking" in a more democratized army than any that France had known since 1815, there were also connections with antecedent social and caste feelings and old wounds in the officer corps.

This is to say that there was no need for all the disaffected elements of the army to accept the thesis *en bloc.* Nor was the thesis articulated in a steadily consistent way. If for some it meant a viable theory of social war, for others it meant a doctrine of social harmony and order. If for some it meant turning the weapons of the enemy against himself, for others it implied the reassertion of "Christian, Mediterranean, and Western values"—at bottom, the values of French nationalism. When we recognize that French nationalism has persistently had both Jacobin and ultramontane strains and that each has left its mark on the military, the complexity will seem clearer if not simpler.

The disparate coalition of military malaise met most concordantly on three points: (1) a virulent anti-Communism, ranging from sheer reaction to "social nationalism"; (2) a hatred for the politicians and institutions of the Fourth Republic which, French officers felt, had sent them to fight and denied them the means of winning; and (3) a negative patriotism based on anguish over postwar French weakness and manifested in a refusal to relinquish the French Empire and in a conviction of the army's purifying mission as a force in national life. *La guerre révolutionnaire*, in a sense, was woven abstractly around these very concrete sentiments plus the whole experience of fighting, dying, and being frustrated in overseas but *French* wars.

A further explanation and chronology of the French army's problems and the genesis and consequences of this doctrine can be found in the book *Lost Soldiers*. Suffice it to say here that *la guerre révolutionnaire*, while incorporating notions specifically French and rooted very deeply in French military, colonial, and political history, can also be more widely understood as a possible response to the question of imposing military order on the inchoate social upheavals of the Third World. It is also illustrative of the extraordinary perils involved in such an operation for the intervenor's military organization and domestic political system.

# THE CONTEMPORARY FRENCH DOCTRINE OF "LA GUERRE RÉVOLUTIONNAIRE"

GEORGE A. KELLY

Few would claim that the dangers of nuclear war are sufficiently remote to be assuaged by faith in the rational conduct of states alone. But the obsession with utopian solutions to prevent nuclear apocalypse is equally fatuous. War exists, even if the nuclear recourse is not reached; and there remain political criteria that determine whether or not war will be the resort. If nuclear war cannot safely accommodate those goals to which nations are bound, then other doctrines of war have to be sought, unless, of course, war ceases to serve as an instrument for the pursuit of coherent aims and becomes nothing more than the killer instinct writ large.

The kind of war that would seem to be the logical result of these considerations has been recorded about twenty times (the catalogue will vary according to the prejudice of the analyst) in the past decade and a half.[1] The misleading treatment, particularly in America, of peripheral "revolutionary" conflicts as "brushfire wars" (implying their lack of importance),[2] the vast ambiguity of moral feeling surrounding colonial relationships, and the fact that the principal member of the Atlantic alliance had until recently to commit its own troops to a genuine "revolutionary" war were among the reasons for neglect

---

[1] The above was written in 1962.

[2] There had been occasional recognition, however, of the mode of revolutionary war. See, for example, James E. King, Jr., *Limited War in an Age of Nuclear Plenty*, L57–154, Industrial College of the Armed Forces, 1956–1957, p. 15: "In combatting guerrilla actions against us, our aim should be primarily at the population, and only secondarily at the guerrillas, as Magsaysay so brilliantly demonstrated in the Philippines."

SOURCE. George Armstrong Kelly, "The Contemporary French Doctrine of *La Guerre Révolutionnaire*," from *Lost Soldiers: The French Army and Empire in Crisis, 1947–1962* (Cambridge, Mass.: The MIT Press, 1965), pp. 107–125, excerpted. Reprinted with permission of the publishers. Copyright 1965 by the MIT Press.

of this type of conflict. Great Britain, while fighting "revolutionary" wars to successful conclusions in Kenya and Malaya and an unsuccessful one in Cyprus, and often innovating cleverly in the field of tactics, scarcely improved on the United States in doctrinal assessment of *la guerre révolutionnaire*. Her island defense remained paramount, and it belonged to another spectrum, another category of war.

The French, whose armies in the field knew no repose from the end of World War II on, were led to some very different conclusions. The consecutive rigor of ideological battle, combined with an unstable search for political values at home, made the concept of *la guerre révolutionnaire* vivid and potent. For it was the cardinal fact of the French military experience after 1945.

Deeply imbedded in French thought, and with a history whose major manifestations are well known to all students of politics and sociology, is the penchant for creating self-enclosed universes of ideas, for translating insights into mystiques, for acting under the banner of theory. However, when we return to the particular and the time-bound, it is difficult to anatomize *la guerre révolutionnaire* as an abstract intellectual idea, if only because it was closely implicated in the institutional pains of the French services and the political crises of the regime. Discontent with liberal democratic formulas pervaded the thinking of many officers returning from Indochina. Political judgments were undisguisedly voiced in the official and semiofficial publications of the French services. The enemy mobilizes his resources totally for the pursuit of *la guerre révolutionnaire*, the argument ran; how much less a mobilization can we afford? By the beginning of 1958 a field-grade officer was able to write in one of the service journals:

> To obtain these means [of combat] and adapt the present institutions for subversive war, a vast effort of national retrenchment is needed. The Nation must not tolerate the fact that the generosity and liberalism of its laws permit subversiveness to exploit its antinational activities.[3]

The proximity of this remark to McCarthyism is striking. Let us remember, however, that the French political picture has been much more complicated than the American, the atmosphere of institutional crisis infinitely more intense, the scars much deeper. Not least of all, the idea of Communist conspiracy underlying the premises of *la guerre révolutionnaire* was much more sophisticated than the disordered jargon of the American reactionaries of the early fifties.

The cause-effect relationship between the formulation of *la guerre*

[3] Commandant Mairal-Bernard, "Cinquièmes bureaux et septième arme," *Revue des Forces terrestres*, January 1958, p. 78.

*révolutionnaire* and the Army's re-entry to politics was ambivalent. On the one hand, there was the internalization of the experiences of combat; on the other, the notion of the inseparability of politics and war. The doctrine as a whole spurred the Army toward its political vocation, because it implied that the regime did not understand the ideological facts of the twentieth century. But the doctrine was more than a mere rationalization of discontent; it was an elaborate essay in creative history.

The context of *la guerre révlutionnaire* was the unlimited aspiration of the Marxist ideology, its inexorable designs on the entire world. By attributing not only tenacity but undeviating skill to the strategy of international communism and by virtually eliminating the independent seriousness of the anticolonial struggles of Africa and Asia, the theorists of *la guerre révolutionnaire* arrived at a unitary doctrine of subversion with little local variation. Thus the strength of the doctrine—its simplicity—was also its greatest logical fallacy. *La guerre révolutionnaire* was essentially a combination of two ingredients: (1) a large and evergrowing catalogue of guerrilla and other tactics combed from past and contemporary experiences and going at least as far back in time as the Peninsular War of 1808–1814.; and (2) the universal revolutionary ideology. Without the latter there could be no revolutionary war, only a series of isolated skirmishes such as those that have embellished classical warfare in other times.

In *la guerre révolutionnaire* the ex-colonial nations or those dependencies presently striving for national existence were either agents of communism or dupes. If they had not sold body and soul to the Kremlin before the launching of their struggle, they would infallibly do so during the course of it. Believing occasionally that they were acting independently, they would actually be at the mercy of their Soviet and Chinese manipulators. Communism recognized that direct intervention was not necessary in most cases; the action of the nationalists themselves would be enough to weaken the West. However, Moscow and Peking would maintain close liaison with these movements, bring them gradually to heel through financing, arms supply, and infiltration, and turn them in a Marxist direction at the right moment. It made little difference whether the revolutionaries were purely nationalist at the outset or at what speed they were being transformed into an advance guard of the Communist movement:

> The enemy is in the last analysis always the same. The Marxist-Leninist doctrine of revolutionary war has, in the past few years, shown itself to be sufficiently effective to impel subversive movements of all types, whatever their mystique, to borrow it henceforth. Per-

suaded that they are ultimately working for its own ends, the party of the Cominform aids and advises them with the best of good will.[4]

There has been general agreement among the analysts of *la guerre révolutionnaire* that the Marxist ideology strengthens the moral fiber of the revolutionary combatant and is thereby a much more potent force, both materially and psychologically, than mere nationalism alone. Autocriticism, "parallel hierarchies," and all the rest of the revolutionary machinery are at the base of this inculcation. Colonel Lacheroy quotes the story of a dying Viet Minh soldier (from the book *Journal d'un combattant vietminh*) in which a priest asks the young man if he is a Communist. "No, Father, not yet," replies the hero. "Because I am not yet worthy to be one."[5] In effect, it is believed that Marxism has shown an uncanny ability to substitute itself for traditional religion. Therefore, the type of war which *la guerre révolutionnaire* is held to appproximate most closely is the "holy war," or jihad, and, according to Claude Delmas, "one can say that revolutionary war is a secularization of the wars of religion."[6]

The reasons for this similitude have, of course, been carefully analyzed—and not by military experts alone. The earthly eschatology of the Communist society, achieving perfection in "future generations" (*les lendemains qui chantent*), is compared with the Christian revelation of immortality in paradise. Whatever hastens the day of the establishment of the Communist order is axiomatically good; it is the only Good. Conveniently, there is no appeal from this dictum, because it can never be tested in advance but only interpreted by the omniscient prophets of the movement. *La guerre révolutionnaire,* constantly magnetized toward simplicity, demands a universal and total commitment from the janissaries of communism. As Commandant Hogard writes:

> Impossible to ruse with communism. One can be its accomplice; but either one becomes a Communist through "engagement in action" or else he is sooner or later cast off, condemned, "physically liquidated." There is no "peaceful coexistence" possible. . . . Communism pursues the destruction of all that is not itself. . . . If it were otherwise, it would no longer be communism.[7]

Dominated by a resourceful ideology, one powerful enough to suppress and master its internal contradictions, the Communist nations

[4] Jacques Hogard, "Guerre révolutionnaire et pacification," *Revue militaire d'Information,* January 1957, p. 7.

[5] Charles Lacheroy, "La guerre révolutionnaire," *La défense nationale* (Paris, 1958), p. 319.

[6] Claude Delmas, *La Guerre révolutionnaire* (Paris, 1960), p. 31.

[7] Jacques Hogard, "La Tentation du Communisme," *Revue des Forces terrestres,* January 1959, p. 26.

are understood as a single entity which is threatening to storm the ramparts of the West. Traditional measures will, in this instance, be unavailing. *La guerre révolutionnaire* demands an antithesis that will in many respects resemble rather than differ from it, a *guerre contre-révolutionnaire*. It can be found only in the intensive study and critique of revolutionary tactics, and in the fastidious preparation of proper counter-measures, *la parade* and *la riposte* (that is, the "parry" and the "thrust").

Without the universal appeal of the Marxist ideology there could be no revolutionary war. Whether fought in the jungles of Malaya or the hills of Macedonia, revolutionary war exhibits certain essentials that can be modified by local factors but never dispensed with. Great flexibility in the realm of tactics is balanced against supreme rigidity of purpose and over-all strategy. *La guerre révolutionnaire* requires that every "nationalist" conflict be analyzed from the perspective of international ideological struggle. The case of a "half-revolutionary war" has never been posed; the doctrine is pure, or it is nothing.

In the global scheme the true base of *la guerre révolutionnaire* can never be attacked; all eruptions must be combated piecemeal. So-viet Russia could not be obliterated by the SAC, even if the United States were able and willing, simply because fifteen throat-cutters had terrorized a village in the Algerian Constantinois. This is a matter of political realism and also a function of the "balance of terror." The French have theorized that the incidence of *la guerre révolution-naire* will be in some kind of proportion to the minatory power of the deterrent, the vaunted but uncertain "pouvoir de dissuasion." This principle is necessarily somewhat modified by factors of opportunity. If the tactics of *la parade* are niggardly in the germinating period of a revolutionary war, this will obviously encourage the universal enemy to take advantage of the deficiency. But the paradox of modern war remains and can be thus stated: as military power approaches the conceivable limits of destructiveness, there is correspondingly less chance that the weapons threatening this cataclysm will ever be un-leashed. Wars of the future will be, therefore, "revolutionary." They will be no less *total* than general war in the sense that they will require the constant application of all relevant economic, social, and political levers, but they will reject as inappropriate the resort to weapons of mass destruction.

Another consequence of revolutionary war is that the conflict will almost inevitably be much more total from the point of view of the revolution than from that of the defenders. While Ho Chi Minh strained every resource to put his whole population on a war footing, the fleshpots of Saigon went uncurtailed, not to mention those of Paris or New York. This imbalance of commitment, if not disastrous to the posture of the "forces of order" in the field, will nevertheless give the revolution a keen psychological advantage in the spheres of morale, propaganda, and unity of political design. The rebel agents of the Communist bloc will be self-sacrificing, objectively admirable; but fifty miles away from the fighting the "forces of order" will seem, on the contrary, soft and decadent.

If revolutionary war is one and indivisible, it is potentially capable of breaking out anywhere, so long as the conditions are ripe. If its timing is occasionally haphazard and if it has, in fact, been prepared for decades by a local evolution that is a side issue of communism, it will sooner or later be adjusted to the Marxist global timetable. The possibilities of success interest the manipulators most; premature action that ends in defeat and the disruption of the revolutionary network is roundly condemned as "leftist opportunism." When the Markos rebellion in Greece (1945–1949) gave all signs of aborting, Moscow quietly and brutally dropped the case and failed to assure the resupply of the guerrilla army.[8] A revolutionary must know how to wait, like Lenin, for decades if necessary, and then seize his chance.

Recognizing its most favorable terrain, *la guerre révolutionnaire* will be generally restricted to the underdeveloped, and particularly the colonial, world. In this sense, it contradicts the premises of orthodox Marxism. Here the situation is organic and promising: the traditional West is in retreat, embarrassed, beset by a conflicting conscience; nationalist movements of quite long standing are already in place or are being born through diffusion and example. Therefore the scenario of *la guerre révolutionnaire* will customarily concern a hypothetical country of this character. But the techniques will still relate to those aimed at the seizure of power in a more modern state such as Greece or Czechoslovakia.

If there is, properly speaking, no revolutionary war without the Marxist-Leninist ideology, there is no revolutionary strategy that does not derive from the same source. Communism is the catalyst for both the military and political disciplines of revolutionary struggle; it combines them in a single instrument, a single reflection of the same goal: the seizure of power. Consequently—ignoring the fact that Russian national engagement in partisan or subversive war, especially during World War II, was not always an efficient or characteristic model

---

[8] The Titoist schism likewise had a profound influence on the ill fortunes of the Greek Communists.

of Leninist theory[9]—those who paint the canvas of *la guerre révolution-naire* usually credit its primary inspiration to the Soviets and cite their pioneer work of indoctrination among the peasantry in the Civil War of 1917–1921. The masters of revolutionary war are not, however, uniquely on the Communist side. Clausewitz is recognized as the spiritual father. And together with Lenin, Trotsky, Frunze, Tukhachevsky, Mao, and General Giap, one finds the illustrious Western names of T. E. Lawrence and Basil Liddell Hart. These men had the merit of recognizing the limitations of "classical" war.

To Mao Tse-tung the theorists of *la guerre révolutionnaire* have owed the recognition that control of the masses is the rational aim of the conflict. This is not just a matter of economy; it is one of necessity. If the criterion of a base of popular support could not be met in a country such as Algeria, the numerical balance of the regular fighting forces, although in some measure contingent on the tactics employed and the terrain of combat, would be of little relevance, particularly if the spirit of the revolutionary forces remained undaunted. This point can be illustrated by noting that in Indochina, a war that the French lost after seven years, the ratio of fighting effectives was, at its height, 6:4, in favor of the "forces of order." This meant, however, many instances of local superiority for the Viet Minh. In Greece, where the "forces of order" were victorious, they enjoyed an advantage over the rebels of approximately 8:1. In Algeria, on the other hand, where the estimated ratio was 16:1, the elusive pacification continued to escape the French.[10] The balance of the armies is a subsidiary feature of *la guerre révolutionnaire*, although local initiative and enterprises of attrition may count very heavily in the military operations. What we have here, whether in a rural or urban situation, is, as Colonel Nemo aptly expresses it, "a war in the crowd," "a war in the social milieu."

Leon Trotsky provided the skeleton of operational theory to the French strategists of revolutionary war through his description of the procedure by which small, well-drilled revolutionary cadres, the "vanguard of the proletariat," capturing the allegiance of the masses, could achieve the seizure of power.[11] In contemporary times, however, it

[9] See N. Galay, "Partisan Warfare," in Basil Liddell Hart (ed.), *The Red Army* (New York, 1955), pp. 153–171.

[10] See the chart of force totals presented to the United States Senate Armed Services Committee on January 22, 1959, by Secretary of the Army Wilber M. Brucker, quoted in Ivo D. Ducháček and Kenneth W. Thompson, *Conflict and Co-operation Among Nations* (New York, 1960), p. 451.

[11] Leon Trotsky, *The History of the Russian Revolution*, translated by Max Eastman (New York, 1932), esp. Vol. III, pp. 167–192.

has been widely conceded, following Mao, that the primary impetus will come through action among the rural masses, since these represent the constant numerical element of strength in most countries ripe for the revolution.

Below, we paraphrase two of the most characteristic descriptions of revolutionary tactics. The first is a "scenario-type" of revolutionary war, proposed by Colonel Lacheroy in 1956,[12] which places particularly detailed emphasis on the methodology of the five stages (the "sacred pentad"); the second is by Commandant Hogard, more precise and framed more in terms of the combat itself.[13] Both writers, despite certain differences of approach, insist on the desirability of squelching the revolutionary threat in its early stages; otherwise the task assumes immense proportions.

Colonel Lacheroy begins his exposé by sketching the conditions of the modern world which, in his opinion, make both the classical military *riposte* and the traditional conduct of *pacification* operations insufficient in a revolutionary situation. He forsees that the vigor of the Revolution may easily lead the civil authorities in a "spoiled" (*pourri*) territory to demand that the military forces assume their functions. Therefore he recommends that the military command devote serious study to this likely phase of its mission. Finally, he rejects Indochina as a model example of revolutionary war for reasons that are not spelled out but may be surmised: the peculiarities of the terrain, the inescapable link with the unsettled conditions left in the wake of World War II, the effective numerical strength of the enemy, the desire not to suggest a lost war as the prototype of future engagement.

Lacheroy then proceeds to describe the five stages. *Surprise* will be the typical element of the first stage. The revolutionary storm will at first be heralded by signs so vague and oblique that only specialists can be expected to discover their true meaning. Then, suddenly, aimless terror will burst forth "in a spectacular fashion." Bombs will go off, assassinations will be attempted, slogans will be spread. The objects of attack will not be especially notable or distinguished persons, but will rather be chosen with the end of creating an air of randomization, bewilderment, and suspense. A climate of insecurity will reign; the public press will react with huge black headlines, and international opinion will begin to take notice. This is described as the publicizing phase of *la guerre révolutionnaire*.

[12] Charles Lacheroy, "Scenario-type de guerre révolutionnaire," *Revue des Forces terrestres*, October 1956, pp. 25–29.

[13] Hogard, "Guerre révolutionnaire et pacification," *op. cit.*, 11–13.

The second phase will be more discreetly demonstrative. Besieged by the consequences of the terror, the public "forces of order" will be led to react with unpopular measures such as police control and curfews to ensure a proper degree of security. These measures, combined with the incipient fear created by the terror, will promote a psychological state of discontent in the population. Exemplary reprisals will now be carried out by the rebels, always with emphasis on the slogan: "Here is the destiny reserved for traitors." The victims again will be chosen not for their prestige but for their attachment and loyalty to France. Disturbed and terrorized, the bulk of the population will now enter the "complicity of silence," refusing the least collaboration with the "forces of order," suppressing all testimony they might give against the terrorists.

The scene is prepared for the third phase, in which political and military activities will begin to be distinguished. It is at this point that the first elements of the rebel armed forces will appear. However, they will still operate according to the formulas of guerrilla warfare, in small groups and usually at night, by day disguising themselves among the civilian population. At the same time, careful indoctrination will commence among the active elements of the civilian mass. The mission of these first cadres will be to "transform the passive complicity of silence into an active complicity, the spectators into actors, the neutrals into sympathizers, then into fanatics." This will be achieved both through the authority of threats and through blackmail.

The fourth phase is qualified as being one of transition. Semiregular forces are now differentiated from the guerrilla fighters. The quality and extent of the infiltration are constantly improved, and the formation of hierarchies commences. Some agents of the revolution specialize in agrarian questions, others in justice, still others in youth organizations, and so forth.

Finally, in the fifth and final phase, a regular army emerges. A unity of command over the entire rebellion will have been achieved through the ruthless elimination of all but the most reliable elements. An independent territory—snatched from the jurisdiction of the "forces of order"—is created, either in isolation or contiguous to some friendly state, whose resources or control of supply can support the campaign. "Parallel hierarchies" now envelop the entire territory and permit indoctrination to proceed under the most favorable conditions. The legal authorities, as well, are progressively duplicated by the organs of rebel government in all communities, so that from the point of view of the population the distinctions of administrative command are thoroughly nebulous.

"In practice," concludes Colonel Lacheroy, "legality and force have both changed camps."

Commandant Hogard, in his probably more "classical" interpretation of the five phases of revolutionary war, sees a similar procedure of expansion, but one that is distinctly attached to the creation and organic multiplication of bases of support. At the same time he recognizes the psychological factor, and insists on the parallel development of the "intoxication and demoralization" of the enemy, the famous *pourrissement* experienced in the Indochina War.

Hogard does not speak of terror or overt acts in his first phase but rather of the "constitution of clandestine nuclei of agitation and propaganda . . . which diffuse the chosen ideology" and take advantage of the internal contradictions that are present in any society. He removes the initiation of acts of revolutionary violence to the second phase, including among them strikes, sabotage, demonstrations, riots—a more traditional, and incidentally more Communist, interpretation than that of Colonel Lacheroy. At the same time, the primitive "kernels" (*noyaux*) are expanded steadily into intelligence networks.

In the third phase, in accord with Lacheroy, the revolutionary enemy passes to the offensive with guerrilla operations, while propaganda and psychological action achieve a greater density. The fourth phase anticipates Lacheroy's "creation of a liberated zone," as well as the formation of a revolutionary provisional government or government-in-exile (such as the Algerian Provisional Government, the GPRA). At this juncture it is presumed that the People's Democracies will extend diplomatic recognition. Finally, in the closing phase, the battle is massively joined between the two forces through a skillful mixture of "neoclassic" and revolutionary operations.

Hogard concludes his definition by describing what he sees as the peculiar features of *la guerre révolutionnaire* as contrasted with ordinary conflict.

> Revolutionary war . . . is very different from classical war: beginning "in dispersion" it little by little draws its strength and resources from the enemy, does not seek the conquest of military or geographical objectives, but of the population, in order to conclude, when the situation has ripened and if there is still need, with a single great battle where it concentrates all its means. This final battle is generally already won before being fought, for the enemy, intoxicated, demoralized, and subverted, is morally ready for defeat.

All commentators agree that, under ordinary circumstances, direct military defeat of the revolutionary forces will not suffice to stifle them. If their activity has progressed as far as Hogard's fifth phase, they will only have to fall back on the tactics of the preceding one while regrouping their forces.

Still another author (actually a group of officers writing collectively under the name of "Ximenès")[14] provides a summary of the "constructive" and "destructive" techniques of the revolution as they exist without direct reference to the five phases of operations. The "destructive" category includes: (1) dislocation of the former body social through riots, terrorist acts, and so on; (2) intimidation of populations, or what Lacheroy has called the "complicity of silence"; (3) demoralization of the adversary and intoxication of the neutrals through propaganda that places in doubt the good faith of the existing order; and (4) elimination through execution and reprisal of those whom it is impossible to convince or intimidate. The "constructive" techniques as listed by "Ximenès" are five: (1) selection and training of a base of activists; (2) propagation of bases and infiltration activities; (3) psychological indoctrination; (4) *encadrement* through the Party organization, "parallel hierarchies," and vertical and horizontal organizations; and (5) "edification" of the struggle through creation of a "liberated territory" and a "national government."

Finally, "Ximenès" insists on the necessity of three categories of "process crucial to the successful waging of revolutionary war." The first of these is "crystallization," which implies the ability to rally mass support and to manipulate it through periods of changing political tactics. Secondly, there is "organization," which is principally fulfilled through the construction of "parallel hierarchies." Thirdly, there is "militarization," which means simply that the whole apparatus is put on a total war footing, and that the actual fighting forces are properly and clearly distinguished as local forces, territorial guerrillas, or "units of intervention" capable of fighting a major battle.

Schematically, we might summarize all these descriptions by noting the following points about *la guerre révolutionnaire:* (1) Its conduct is distinguished from that of classical war by the fact that even though there may be units fitted to fight more-or-less classical battles, the bulk of the war effort is thrown back on smaller groups operating according to the tactics of guerrilla warfare. (2) It is ideologically motivated, ultimately by the Marxist doctrine. (3) It is a war, not for the control of territory or military objectives, nor even so much for the destruction of the opposing force, but for the conquest of the population. (4) It is a war waged with all relevant means within

---

[14] "Ximenès," "Essai sur la guerre révolutionnaire," *Revue militaire d'Information*, February–March 1957, pp. 11–14. This is the famous "special number" on Revolutionary War.

a restricted space. In this context the pursuit of the classical *ripostes* of *repression*, pacification by administrative reform, traditional *surface warfare*, or *war of total annihilation* will be generally inappropriate and self-defeating.

The question then becomes one of approaching a new methodology of "counter-revolutionary" war replying directly to the analysis of the weaknesses inherent in the procedures of the enemy. Experts of *la guerre révolutionnaire* generally summarize these strategies under the classical headings of *la parade* and *la riposte*, which may in some senses be said to correspond to the "constructive" and "destructive" techniques of the revolutionaries. It is worth while recalling Colonel Trinquier's article "Contre-guérilla" in this regard, where he urges measures to deprive the enemy of his food and arms supply through destruction of his local security. Commandant Hogard provides us in the same connection with a very instructive series of "do's" and "don't's" of this type of conflict, under the title "The Ten Rules of Anti-revolutionary Tactics."[15] His catalogue is as follows:

1. Negotiations on equal terms with a revolutionary enterprise could not be more dangerous; this will facilitate its success.
2. All rebel territory should, as quickly as possible, be isolated from the exterior, materially and morally.
3. Revolutionary war must be checked in its early stages.
4. Both strategy and tactics of counter-revolutionary war depend on the close linkage of all civil, military, social, cultural, and economic resources, with the view of holding or recapturing popular support and attacking the enemy apparatus from all angles.
5. Final victory over revolutionary forces can be achieved only through the destruction of the apparatus.
6. The conquest of popular support must be the main objective of the legitimate authority. This depends on the promotion of a vigorous *action psychologique* among the people that will stress the universal values of the "forces of order" and reveal the duplicity and contradictions of the enemy. At the same time, the hopes of the people must be fulfilled by continuous progress toward a better social order. The population itself must be trained in self-defense.
7. The destruction of the forces of the revolution should be regarded not as an end but as a means of securing popular support.
8. The irregular forces of the revolution need not be defeated in battle but can be suffocated if deprived of material and moral support in the previously friendly zones.
9. The single way of reducing the guerrillas is to wear them down morally and physically by tracking them with units suited to the purpose, operating always in familiar zones.

[15] Jacques Hogard, "Stratégie et tactique dans la guerre révolutionnaire," *Revue militaire d'Information*, June 1958.

10. The safety of arteries and vital points depends, not on static defense, but on the ability to create conditions of constant insecurity for the guerrilla forces operating in these areas.

All of Hogard's injunctions, properly speaking, belong to the phase called *la riposte* or are at least prohibitions of false *riposte*, because it is this side of tactics that pertains once the insurrection has broken out. In the eyes of Captain André Souyris, a close student of revolutionary organizations in both Indochina and Tunisia, an effective *parade* (the term given to preinsurrectional measures) is no less vital.[16] *La parade* is perhaps the more difficult phase of the counter-revolutionary operation, for its technicians must read and interpret the frequently ambiguous signs of which Colonel Lacheroy has spoken in his "scenario-type." Two other factors contribute to the problem of *la parade*, in the opinion of Captain Souyris. In the first place, the military command, which most fully understands the techniques of revolutionary war, will not normally be in place in the pre-insurrectional period, nor qualified to undertake the activation of *la parade*. Secondly, during the germinal period of revolutionary struggle the task is often made easier for the subversive forces owing to the tendency of the legal authority to interpret the disturbance in the "classical" manner and act accordingly. These defects are apt either to stifle the inception of proper measures of *parade* or raise contradictions that will limit its effectiveness.

A resourceful *parade* in the face of mounting revolutionary activity will depend on the avoidance of these "errors of appreciation" and on the utilization of qualified area specialists and a well-developed intelligence service. The legal authorities should be always abreast of the situation they are facing and will be strongly advised to cultivate numerous and fruitful contacts with the population.

Once this situation has been achieved, the technique of *la parade* is twofold. It will depend in the first place on the existence of a forceful, progressive, and humane administration of the territory. Social reforms cannot be allowed to fall behind the needs of the time or the legitimate demands of the people. Reforms must work not only toward the satisfaction of popular aspirations but also with the view of suppressing those "internal contradictions" of the society which would otherwise give fuel to the propaganda of the revolutionary forces. Administrative contact with the population must avoid the impersonal and the austere.

Secondly, a vigorous *action psychologique* must be waged among the masses, designed both to promenade the virtue of Western values

[16] André Souyris, "Les conditions de la parade et de la riposte," *Revue militaire d'Information*, February–March, 1957, pp. 91–111.

and to protect the subject from the revolutionary indoctrination. Souyris suggests that there is a conflict here between the end and the means, and concedes that the traditional democratic methods are not entirely compatible with this type of campaign. Therefore, citing the psychologist Serge Tchakhotine,[17] he dismisses the question of the means for the desirability of the end: "The author of the *Viol des foules* specifies . . . that a fundamental doctrine (i.e., democracy) can be independent of the methods of action." This, in effect, was the traditional justification  employed by the "African school" of psychological action for techniques that others have thought excessive—when indeed a justification seemed necessary to them. But it was a suspicious procedure for making perfect democrats, "individuals safeguarded against the snares of the State."

Between *la parade* and *la riposte* there is, in Souyris's analysis, an intermediary phase, the pre-insurrectional preparation for the *riposte*. Its specifications resemble those of *la parade*, with the exception that they are oriented toward the establishment of favorable conditions for the real *riposte*, once the revolution has broken out in earnest; it is recognized that a perfect *parade* could stifle revolutionary activity and thus obviate the need for more direct measures. The preparation of the *riposte* then, demands effective intelligence and civic indoctrination as well as the prior establishment of a counter-revolutionary military infrastructure, of which a part, under optimum conditions, will be clandestine. In any case, the forces must be properly located, dispersed, and mobilized so as best to combat the expected revolutionary activity, the type anticipated by the Lacheroy and Hogard models.

Once the revolution bursts forth and assumes a military character, the resort is to the *riposte* proper. If its preparations have been sufficient and skillful, it will go into immediate operation. As opposed to the "classical" *riposte* or surface warfare, the counter-revolutionary *riposte* will be swiftly and totally directed toward the surrounding population. Since *la guerre révolutionnaire* is essentially a "war in the crowd" and "a war for the crowd," the object of the *riposte* will be to mobilize the crowd for military and patriotic actions in defense of the legal order. The people will be immediately organized into groups for self-defense, and their leaders will be given indoctrination in village and local warfare. The aim will be to isolate the bases of rebel support and reduce them systematically without giving the contagion a chance to spread. "Moral mobilization" through an effective

[17] See Serge Tchakhotine, *Le viol des foules par la propagande politique* (Paris, 1939).

program of *action psychologique* will accompany this effort. Where the re-education of populations becomes necessary after they have been recovered from the grip of the enemy, camps for "disindoctrination" will be set up to facilitate the conversion by "persuasive and humane" means.

The technical conclusion that Captain Souyris reaches as a result of his examination of the conditions of *la parade* and *la riposte* in revolutionary war is that the Army must assume responsibility for the mobilization and organization of populations living in the danger zone. The implication is clearly that the administrative civil services of a modern democracy are ill equipped to perform this task with appropriate comprehensiveness, timing, and results. *La guerre révolutionnaire* is singular. It goes on in the Chamber of Deputies as well as in the combat zone. Consequently, the role of the Army that Souyris proposes, although seemingly confined to battle areas, is, in fact, indefinitely expansible. Again we have verged on politics in a way that is perhaps unavoidable. Doctrines, however, live on permissive license, the promise not to push their premises too far. By no means the greater part of the Army command was favorable to direct political involvement according to these premises. Nevertheless, latitude in defining the enemy and the limits of the battlefield became, and would continue to be, a useful tool.

The more extreme propositions of *la guerre révolutionnaire* invited skepticism and distaste. When, for example, Commandant Hogard assailed a book such as Duverger's *Les Partis Politiques* as a subversive Marxist tract,[18] one could only react with astonishment. Since the prophets of revolutionary war showed their political bias so often, one may ask why this theory, which other nations have been reluctant to endorse, took such a firm hold in French military circles. For its popularity was not restricted to that portion of the officer corps that believed in a "political mission," but extended to many loyalists. There were a number of reasons for the vogue.

In the first place, *la guerre révolutionnaire* was the French Army's answer, its defensive *riposte*, to the nuclear preoccupation of its Anglo-Saxon allies. Where military commentators did not go to the extremes of Colonel Lacheroy in proclaiming the inviolability of the "balance of terror" and the unlikelihood of limited nuclear war, they forged a dichotomy of "nuclear" and "revolutionary" war, making them both aspects of a new "total" war doctrine. The intellectual impulse was strong to insist on the importance of subversive as opposed to classical

---

[18] Jacques Hogard, "Stratégie et tactique du Communisme," *Revue des Forces terrestres*, October 1959, p. 53.

conflict, both for reasons of considered judgment and for requirements of national prestige.

Secondly, there was the matter of experience. A nuclear war has never been waged, except in *Kriegspiel*, whereas conflicts answering to the major characteristics of *la guerre révolutionnaire* are costing lives at this very moment. This fact, which is without real political significance to many, was nevertheless powerful persuasion to the French Army.

The third factor counseling the acceptance of the doctrine of *la guerre révolutionnaire* was of an unquestionably higher order: the intellectual satisfaction provided by a monistic interpretation of the world crisis. If a Colonel Trinquier could stake his conviction on the basis of combat experience and a rudimentary glimpse of the social forces at play in the world,[19] others had broader perspectives. They felt that history, in its grand outlines, would infallibly connect the surge of communism with the displacement of Western influence in the former colonial territories. According to their view, a "third way" was impossible. The underdeveloped countries were intellectually and economically incapable of supporting a real independence in the ideological competition and, sooner or later, would have to succumb to the persuasions of the stronger camp.

Once accepted as a cosmic theory, *la guerre révolutionnaire* drew its lines harshly. Gray was scarcely admitted to its bicolored palette. *Le Bien* and *le Mal* confronted each other, not simply across national boundaries, but throughout all nature; if the white had been dirtied through shabby upkeep, it must be purged and purified. Since the enemy played incessantly on the ambiguity of Western pluralism, manipulating the contradictions of the richer civilization, some of this richness would have to be curtailed in the interests of solidarity and survival.

If there was Good and Evil, and Evil possessed an effective operating doctrine, then Good had to be no less well equipped. It was not enough for Good to be the absence of Evil; no negative definition could secure anyone's faith or enthusiasm. As Claude Delmas wrote: "It is easier to rally crowds in the name of a false idea, as long as it seems seductive, than in the name of multiple ideas, true but prosaic."[20] The "counter-revolution" therefore attacked pluralism with might and main, for in pluralism there was no truth—only, at best, many competing half truths. Consensus, when achieved, was philosophically impure and simply a type of tactical compromise. "The apparent

---

[19] See Roger Trinquier, *La guerre moderne* (Paris, 1961).

[20] Delmas, *op. cit.*, p. 108.

weakness of the West is its inability to provide a total Truth in the face of an ideology which itself claims sufficient means to be the incarnation of such a Truth." But the formation of a synthetic "counter-ideology" would prove to be a particularly trying problem. Different cliques were to put forth the ideas of corporatism, Church-State fusion, "national socialism," and even "national communism," without discovering either the intellectual cause or the enthusiasm needed for a Western "single solution." Beside some of these formulas the regal personalism of Charles de Gaulle seemed centuries more modern.

To see the earth with one sweep of the naked eye was to miss the particularity of its atoms. The atoms were, to be sure, joined to a nucleus but only inferentially to each other. The rabid nationalism of the theorists themselves fitted rather badly with their interpretation of a Manichaean world. There was a fundamental illogic in feeling France so intestinally, while denying that Arab or Maghrebian nationalism was anything more than a kind of Communist measles.

Many proponents of *la guerre révolutionnaire* felt these reservations very keenly. As Delmas writes: "Is it possible to elaborate recipes of counter-revolutionary war with which to oppose revolutionary war, to build 'parallel hierarchies' to combat identical 'parallel hierarchies,' to 'organize' populations to disorganize the opponent's systems? These recipes will always remain conjectural, and it is not with counter-terrorism that one can lastingly oppose terrorism."[21] But, as the same author reminds us, "the Revolution fascinates."

Some were later to carry this fascination to the pitch of "intoxication." But these actions should not blind us to the things that were of real merit in the pioneer analysis of revolutionary war, tactical truths that Western military forces needed to learn. As for the "intoxicated" officers, their later acts could not be excused by the bitter circumstances that engendered their protest. Still, the profuse and often deep thinking that went into the elaboration of the doctrine of *la guerre révolutionnaire* established a rationale for what would follow. It suggested an antagonism that was more than peevish, a malaise more than transitory.

[21] *Ibid.*, p. 122.

# 20

# Castroism: The Long March of Latin America

*Régis Debray*

## EDITORS' COMMENT

Despite the abhorrence of rightist critics and the sectarian scandal waged by analysts on the revolutionary Left, Debray's writings on the political sociology of insurgency in Latin America have attracted far greater comment throughout the world than those of any competitor.

There is no need to introduce Régis Debray. He is a Marxist Leninist-revolutionist-idealist, a scion of a wealthy Parisian family (his mother has been a prominent rightist politician), a pupil of the famous Louis Althusser at the Ecole Normale Supérieure, a friend of the late Che Guevara, and an occasional correspondent of the French press amid the ill-fated guerrilla *foco* in Bolivia. Seized by the Bolivian military police, he is at present serving a thirty-year sentence for political crimes. In spite of the clamor for his release by many intellectuals throughout the world, he remains a captive and hostage (although not a completely silent one) against the impending revolutionary ferment

438

in Latin America. His more extended work *Revolution in the Revolution?* has been translated and widely read in English-speaking countries. In a certain sense, although Debray modestly and correctly disbars himself from the role of theoretician, he has become the leading codifier of revolutionary strategy in the depressed parts of the Western hemisphere.

The present essay was written prior to Debray's major book and appeared first in Jean-Paul Sartre's *Les Temps Modernes* in January 1964. It is an on-the-spot, practical attempt to weave together the threads of the Latin American revolutionary thrust and, as such, is much more an inductive enterprise than a Marxist theoretical classic. Debray has always had a horror of being considered as a builder of rigid models, and it is in deference to his own view that we present this essay, slightly shortened from its original form, as "a political tract containing extreme abbreviations and intentionally abrupt shortcuts . . . imposed by its practical context." Despite this lack of theoretical rigor and practical contemporaneity, we think that the essay covers the general revolutionary situation in Latin America more ably than any other writing in the field.

The most casual encounter with Debray's writings will show why he became a marked man for the "forces of order" in the Americas. His notion of social revolution, tied conclusively but not dogmatically to the experience of Fidelist Cuba, has threatened to break the logjam of militant social unrest in the nations to the south of us by superseding both communist bureaucracy and romantic adventurism. Consistent with the Latin temperament that he appears to share with the rebellious forces of South America, Debray seems to be at times more of a romantic—more a Garibaldi—than a *bona fide* Marxist. He seems like a Leninist without Lenin's patience—without his sense of the appropriate conjugation of forces. Nevertheless, in a recent smuggled letter (see *Monthly Review*, February 1969, p. 22), Debray has described this article as a mere literary study—"rough sketches intended for European readers," and not as a "body of theses." We can take this disclaimer at its face value. Debray did not set his sights to be a theorist, but only to be a publicist. Since we live in a cosmopolitan world, whether according to the Marxist definition or not, it becomes important to communicate the revolutionary experience of a hidden continent to others who are gasping to receive the good news. The fair observer will judge that Debray has been more than a good journalist, if less than an imperishable theorist.

Yet, from the beginning, Debray's writings have been highly designed to implicate theory in the welter of Marxist-Leninist chapels set adrift by "polycentrism," the Sino-Soviet rift and, above all, the experience of a socialist revolution pragmatically conceived and made by non-Marxists in Cuba. Since Debray in his writings has appeared to argue for the primacy of the Cuban model in "third-world" revolutionary change, his essays have immediately engaged the attention and the polemic of the doctrinaire Left. Especially called into question has been Debray's exaltation of the military over the political leadership (explicit in the "theory of the *foco*" presented in *Revolution in the Revolution?* and more subterranean in this essay). Yet who is to say, adhering to a strictly Marxist analysis, that the militant guerrillas of the Latin American countryside are not better interpreters of the prevailing mode of production than the radical politicians who conceal themselves in the cities?

To be sure, Debray's running criticisms and analyses of the various centers of disturbance in Latin America have expressed a preference for the rural mode of revolution, given the balance of forces in the situation. It is also true that, in the passages where analysis gives way to adulation, a kind of voluntaristic radical militarism appears. And, finally, it is true that this would appear to be a form of Maoism plus *machismo*, lethal to the Soviet perspective of the 1960's. Debray has never made any bones about consigning the majority of reigning Communist parties in Latin America to less-than-polite oblivion. Thus it is small wonder (his dangerous sequestration included) that he has emerged as a hero of the "New Left."

The other main charge lodged against Debray is that he has idealized and misrepresented the Cuban revolution. No doubt, urbanized Cuba is unique in the galaxy of Latin American states. As Debray himself concedes, "it is a ridiculous and aberrant idea to make Cuba into a 'model' or basic type to be brought out in several editions either by reproduction or exact copying." The reader will discover that the present essay is much less involved with the Cuban revolutionary model than with the mystique and prestige of Cuba as a revolutionary state wedged into the capitalist solidarity of the Western hemisphere. As for the *foco* theory, its relevance would seem to pertain to all states that feature fluctuating and uncertain middle class-agrarian relationships, revolutionary urban potential, and capable insurrectionary leadership. The charge that the *foco* theory is a mere exotic export from Cuba is, at least, a half-lie. But the acknowledgment that Latin America will require its own variegated procedures is no doubt quite true.

From a wider vantage point, Debray (given his concessions about practice and writing about practice as a highway for theory not yet capable of being formulated) can appear as a stalwart Leninist whose motto, quoted by Debray, was "the superior dignity of immediate reality." Debray has attempted to come to grips with that reality in a partisan but empirical manner. Even to the complacent Marxist, it should be evident by now that each socialist revolution passes on to the next one more enthusiasm and morale than education (for a comment on this, see Mao Tse-tung's essay, Selection 18 in this volume). If communist theory continually tempers itself with practice, as is often said these days, then there may be no theoretical, only an organizational worry over the orthodoxy of Debray. One suspects that his challenge to both the communist and capitalist worlds, whatever its theoretical heresies and empirical shortcomings, may have gone deeper than ordinary dogmatic affront.

# CASTROISM: THE LONG MARCH IN LATIN AMERICA[1]

## Régis Debray

### THE TRADITION OF MILITARY COUP

In semi-colonial countries, even more than in developed capitalist countries, the State poses the decisive political problem. For it is in these countries that the exploited classes are least able to influence, control or—*a fortiori*—conquer state power; and where—since the State concentrates all the elements of power in its apparatus—the question of State power becomes most intractable. The usual way of resolving the problem in South America is the *coup d'état*, by means of which almost all transfers or overthrows of established power take place, even when they are carried out in the name of the popular classes and against the oligarchy. Fidelism defines itself first of all by its refusal of the *coup d'état*.

This refusal, which may seem elementary, is in fact crucially important in a continent where the importance of power, and the absence of any power other than that of the State, have produced since the dawn of independence the classically Latin American ritual of the *golpe* or putsch. Both Peron and Vargas won power by a putsch, even if each expressed a general crisis—Vargas the 1929 crisis and the ruin of the Sao Paulo coffee economy, and Peron the crisis which

[1] North American propaganda hoped to discredit the term "Castroism" by using it in a pejorative sense. In many places, however, and particularly in France and Algeria, it has been consecrated in the political language of the Left, notably under the influence of Sartre. In all of these countries "Castroism" means the revolutionary movement in Latin America today. We should not forget that, in the same way, the European bourgeoisie, in its time, tried to discredit Marxism and Leninism with the same ironical and deprecatory intention.

SOURCE. Régis Debray, "Castroism: The Long March in Latin America," from *New Left Review*, No. 33 (September-October 1965), pp. 17–58, excerpted and slightly revised by the translator. Reprinted with permission of the publishers of Debray's *Strategy for Revolution*, Monthly Review Press, New York.

followed the Second World War and the rapid industrialization of Argentina in boom conditions. But whatever the forces which initially support it, a government brought to power by a putsch—that is, a lightning action at the top, in which the Army generally plays the principal role as protagonist or as arbiter—necessarily tends to the right. Compelled to obtain immediate successes in order to win the support of the expectant masses, it has to base itself on the institutions which already exist—established economic interests, the bureaucracy, the majority of the army. Since the masses lack political consciousness or organization—things which can only be acquired in a long and difficult revolutionary experience—on whom can the government base itself? How can it ask for the sacrifices which a real policy of national independence would demand, if the peasantry and above all the working-class are not convinced of the need for them?

These populist régimes—the late Vargas and the early Peron[2]—therefore bring in social reforms which seem revolutionary to their beneficiaries at the time, but are in fact merely demagogic, since they are not based on any solid economic foundation. Carried to power by the army or thanks to its neutrality, both régimes fell as soon as the armed forces—or their most reactionary sector, the navy—turned against them. Organized violence belongs to the dominant class, the *coup d' état* which manipulates that violence is fated to bear the mark of it. In his Manifesto of May 1930 Prestes refused to support Vargas—who was backed by almost all of the *tenentes*[3] who had emerged from the left insurrections of 1920, 1922, 1924 and from the Prestes Column itself: the method used by Vargas and his gauchos to take power was a sufficient indication of the reactionary character of the future Estado Novo. Five years later, the same Prestes returned from Moscow, and organized a localized military insurrection, independent of any mass movement, but in connivance with certain high personalities in the established power-structure—such as the Prefect of the Federal District of Rio. The putsch ended in disaster: Prestes went to prison, his wife Olga to a German concentration camp, and the Communist Party was driven underground for ten years. That is how strong the temptation of the coup or military insurrection is,

[2] In Brazil, Vargas held the Presidency twice (1930–45 and 1951–54). He committed suicide before the end of his second mandate. In Argentina, Peron's government (1945–55) seemed to be reconciled at the end with the United States and with the national oligarchy.

[3] *Tenente* is a lieutenant. Numerous left-nationalists formed the cadres of the first revolutionary insurrections. Prestes, the leader of the Brazilian Communist Party, was a career soldier.

even for the revolutionary left. In Brazil, in Argentina, in Venezuela, and until recently in Peru, the Army in fact recruits its junior officers from the lower middle classes. This has resulted in a theory of the army as a social microcosm, which reflects the contradictions of the national macrocosm. Numerous local military insurrections which have taken place in Latin America, from Rio de Janeiro in 1922 (the famous episode of the 18 heroes of the Copacabana fort) to Puerto Cabello in Venezuela in June 1962, might appear to confirm this view. But in reality, while one must not underestimate the revolutionary or nationalist politicization of some sectors of the army and the aid which they can give to the revolutionary movement, it is an absolute rule that one cannot base a strategy, or even a tactical episode of the struggle, upon the decision of a regiment or a garrison. In Venezuela, the revolts at Carupano and Puerto Cabello[4] accelerated the convergence of left nationalists in the army and civilian militants, which produced the FALN, but it achieved no more than that. The precondition for achieving even this is that there be already in existence a civilian organization with its own objectives and resources, into which men leaving the army can be integrated: in Venezuela, a guerrilla force already existed in Falcon and Lara, before the rising of the marines at Carupano. The inverse process is very revealing of the value of civilians who participate in a military coup. In October 1945, Betancourt, Leoni and Barrios, and all the main leaders of *Accion Democratica*,[5] took part in the putsch fomented by Perez Jimenez and the army against President Medina. Three years later, Jimenez, by means of a new coup, rid himself of Gallegos, the elected President of the Republic and leader of *Accion Democratica*. The revolutionary tradition of APRA[6] in Peru was based on the insurrections at Trujillo (birthplace and fief of Haya de la Torre) in 1930, and Callao in 1948. The lessons

---

[4] Venezuelan naval harbours where two important military risings took place in 1962.

[5] *Accion Democratica* is a Venezuelan party, which was founded in 1941, became the government party in 1958, and is now totally won over to imperialism. Betancourt and Leoni followed each other as Presidents of the Republic. Gonzalo Barrios is in charge of trade union affairs.

[6] APRA is the Popular Revolutionary Alliance of America. It was set up in 1924 as a kind of Latin American Kuomintang, a united front of anti-imperialist groups and parties with a section in each country. It was transformed into a party by Haya de la Torre in 1929. It was APRA which channelled the revolutionary upsurge of the Peruvian masses at the time of the fall of Leguia in 1930; it was able to maintain control of them until recent years. A seed-bed for the petit-bourgeois left movements of Latin America (Betancourt is a disciple of Haya de la Torre), APRA today provides the same spectacle of complete betrayal as did Chiang Kai Shek's Kuomintang in its time.

were the same. The devotion and sacrifice involved could not alter the fact that it is impossible to destroy the semi-colonial state in a day, with the State's own instruments—whatever their courage and worth. Putschism was also a latent tendency of Peronism, which paid as early as June 9th, 1956 for the unsuccessful rising of the Peronist general Valle, as a result of which 4,000 noncommissioned officers were cashiered. The most recent experience of this kind, in Brazil, is instructive: the sergeants' movement—25,000 as compared with 15,000 commissioned officers in the entire army—had favourable conditions at its disposal to oppose the reactionary putsch of April 1964 in a decisive fashion (acquiescence of the President of the Republic,[7] support of public opinion, relatively high degree of freedom). But it was incapable of breaking the army's vertical discipline and of taking the initiative. Its failure was the consequence of the absence of any central organization, or political homogeneity among the sergeants, and the lack of any organic link with trade union forces.

Thus Fidelism has truly transformed the traditional conceptions of revolutionary action in Latin America, by rejecting the *coup d'état* or the military rising—even when they are linked with a civilian organization—as a method of action. For everything seems to favour such methods: the normal political passivity of the masses and the struggle of bourgeois factions for control of the State, with its formidable means of repression. The strength of historical tradition is such that even the best and most resolute of militants do not always perceive the essentially different character of a revolutionary seizure of power—which is the installation for the first time of popular power, based on the awakened majority of the nation.

## THE MYTHS OF MASS ACTION

At the opposite extreme from "revolutionary putschism" (as distinct from Blanquism, which was the isolated action of a civilian rather than a military minority), there are the advocates of "pure mass action." Obviously, revolution requires the conscious entry of the masses into the struggle, and hence their ideological awakening and preparation. This is the cautious truism which many communist leaderships[8] now proffer, without saying *how* to awaken the masses in régimes

---

[7] However, by September 1963 Goulart had suppressed the sergeants' revolt in Brasilia, after which numerous units were deprived of their arms; they no longer had access as in the past to arms stores, and were subjected to the persecutions of the commissioned officers.

[8] We refer to the pro-Soviet Communist Parties.

whose repressive character makes legal, trade union, or political activity very difficult, normally confining it to the narrow stratum of the urban intelligentsia. In the Bolivian *altiplano* for example, a revolutionary agitator working among the Indian communities who was hostile to the MNR (the Revolutionary Nationalist Movement in power) had every chance of being physically liquidated by government mercenaries within a month. In the Brazilian North-East, the private police force of the latifundists, the *capanga*, forced Juliao to use wandering guitarists and minstrels, reciting popular ballads full of allusions and double meanings, to penetrate the most remote and dangerous estates. Thus when Codovilla and the Argentinian Communist Party at its 12th Congress brandished the slogan "Towards the conquest of power through the action of the masses," this hardly provided a serious counter-weight to the latent putschism of revolutionary Peronism. Without even stopping to consider what type of mass action the ACP is capable of today—within the CGT (General Workers Confederation) it controls the union of journalists, *gastronomicos* of Buenos Aires, chemists and musicians through the intermediary of the MUCS (Movement for Syndical Unity and Co-ordination)—it needs to be said that a mass action as such has never achieved power anywhere. The two general strikes called by the United Workers Confederation in Chile since 1952, and the crushing of the trade unions by the marine corps during the overthrow of Peron in Argentina in 1955—to take the only two countries in Latin America where one can speak of an organized and concentrated urban working-class—proved that any general strike which does not pave the way for some kind of insurrectionary strike tends to be blunted or broken by violence. But an insurrectionary strike presupposes arms and an organization of militia and of leadership which are not going to rise up from the mass action by a miracle of spontaneity. There is no better example than contemporary Argentina if one wishes to prove yet again that workers *if left to themselves*, that is to say under the direction of the bourgeoisie, will only reach *reformist* politics. In Argentina today, where the CGT (the Trade Union Federation) exercises political control over Peronism, the trade union leaders, substitutes for an absent political leadership, find themselves the logical allies of the industrial bourgeoisie; both sides are equally interested in economic expansion, hence in the increase of wages and in the demand for labour. The masses as such do not fight in the streets, nor do they fix on a plan of action, nor are they able to thwart the seven or eight political police forces which Argentina boasts, all tasks which Lenin recommended to apprentice revolutionaries in 1902. In discussion or propaganda, the term "masses" is bandied about by reformist communist parties like an inverted Sorelian myth, as a cover for inaction. A leader of the Argentinian Communist Party offered the following formulation of the party's policy to me: "With the masses, everything. Without the masses, nothing."[9] Questioned as to what would happen in the case of a military coup—an old Argentinian tradition—he was only able to express his fear of agents provocateurs, and to admit that if the masses did not come out on to the streets, the Party would not be able to organize resistance alone. This reasoning explains why, in Brazil, the streets of Rio de Janeiro and Sao Paulo remained deserted on April 1st and 2nd, 1964, when thousands of men and women were ready to demonstrate, even to fight. But with whom? Behind whom? Under what flag? It is the role of a revolutionary organization to confront such circumstances (in the most appropriate manner which is doubtless not by means of demonstrations or even battles in the streets of urban centres paralyzed by military repression), so that the masses can later enter into action, protected and led by it—even if months may go by before they regain confidence in themselves and see the military power in its true perspective. There is no reason why a docker or a railway worker (the two unions which put up the most resistance in Rio) should risk death on his own in the street, unarmed, and above all without leadership, without out any definite objective, while his political representatives have disappeared into the countryside or are negotiating with the government.

To sum up: the entire apparatus of organized violence belongs to the enemy. The violence with which the people can strike back, "mass action," is easily dismantled by the enemy's organized violence. A military coup can overnight pulverize democratic parties, trade unions, the combativity of the masses and their hope: the Brazilian example is valid for the whole continent. What, then, is to be done?

## THE THEORY OF THE FOCO

To Lenin's question, Fidelism replies in terms which are similar to those of Lenin in 1902 (precisely in *What is to be done?*). Under an autocratic régime, only a minority organization of professional revolutionaries, theoretically conscious and practically trained in all the

---

[9] This phrase was used as the title of an article by Jorge del Prado (former General Secretary of the Peruvian Communist Party, now leader of the pro-Soviet fraction) which appeared in the *Nouvelle Revue Internationale*, May 1964. In it will be found an interesting systematisation of reformism and a thinly veiled attack on Castroism, confused with Blanquism, together with all the quotations from Lenin (and, alas, Khrushchev) which this type of article requires.

skills of their profession, can prepare a successful outcome for the revolutionary struggle of the masses. In Fidelist terms, this is the theory of the *foco* of the insurrectionary centre, whose pre-conditions Che Guevara set out in his *Guerrilla Warfare*. "We consider," he wrote in the preface, "that the Cuban Revolution has made three fundamental contributions to revolutionary strategy in Latin America: 1. The popular forces can win *a war* against the army; 2. It is not always necessary to wait until all the conditions for revolution are fulfilled—the insurrectionary centre can create them; 3. In under-developed America the terrain of armed struggle must basically be the countryside." In 1964, after five years of experience of guerrilla war in almost all the countries of Latin America—five years worth a century—what is left of *foquismo?* Has it been invalidated by experience, or has it on the contrary been tempered and fortified under trial?

## THE FAILURES OF THE LAST FIVE YEARS

A first survey establishes almost total failure everywhere since 1959—the year in which Latin America entered an intensive phase of guerrilla wars—with the single exception of Venezuela. Leaving aside the thousand-and-one abortive movements, and those which never had any real importance, the following were the main experiences of insurrectionary centres in the countryside:[10]

### 1. *Argentina, December 1959*

Insurrectionary *foco* of the Uturunko ("tiger-men" in Quechua). Launched in the north-west of Tucuman by a group of revolutionary Peronists, influenced by John William Cooke, Peron's lieutenant during his last years in power, and a consistent partisan of armed struggle. The Uturunko, after some tactical successes, disappeared from sight.

### 2. *Paraguay, November 1959*

The tragic failure of the May 14th movement made up of young militants from the *Juventud Febrerista* and from the Liberal Party. On November 20th, a column of 80 guerilleros penetrated by way of the forest into North Paraguay. A few days later, there only remained some 10 survivors, who escaped by a miracle to Argentina.

---

[10] Before recounting these experiences, we should point out that the list is incomplete, as it was drawn up during 1965. Central America, Mexico, and the Caribbean islands are excluded from the list. We deeply regret that we are not able to make known here the rich experience of the Guatemalan revolutionaries, who are now in the vanguard of armed popular struggle on the continent.

### 3. *Santo Domingo, Summer 1960*

Failure of the landing carried out by the July 14th movement under the command of Enrique Jimenez Moya. No survivors.

### 4. *Paraguay, early 1962*

Failure of the guerrillas of the FULNA (United Front of National Liberation, which included the Febrerist youth and the Communist Party) installed in the regions of San Pedro, General Aquino and Rosario. This defeat can be attributed both to military difficulties and to a change of leadership in the Communist Party, which abandoned the line of armed struggle for that of a United Front with the national bourgeoisie and the Liberal Party.

### 5. *Colombia, 1961*

Failure of MOEC (Movement of Workers, Students and Peasants). In the State of Cauca, not far from Marquetalia, the leaders of MOEC, a Fidelista organization of the far left which grouped together numerous dissidents from the CP (Antonio Larotta, Federico Arango and others), were killed—some by *bandoleros* (bandits often linked to the army), others, after surrendering, by the army itself. They were attempting to start a political guerrilla movement, basing themselves on the old Liberal guerrilleros of the civil war, who had degenerated into bandits.

### 6. *Ecuador, March 1962*

Failure of the guerrilla of the URJE (Revolutionary Union of Ecuador Youth). Near Santo Domingo de los Colorados, an intermediary zone between the tropical coast and the high Andean plateau, some 40 young revolutionaries were encircled and captured by parachutists. They had only held the mountain for 48 hours.

### 7. *Venezuela, March 1962*

It is not unfair to include the failure of the first badly organized guerrilla centres in the State of Merida in the Andes and in the Charal region of Yaracuy State. These local failures were amply made up for later.

### 8. *Peru*

At Puerto Maldonado, on the Bolivian frontier, the vanguard of a sizeable column was cut to pieces. The guerilleros did not even have the time to move into action.

## 9. *Brazil*

One cannot really speak of insurrectionary centres. In the course of 1962 there were installed in certain States of the interior centres of military training, linked to Juliao's movement, which finally foundered for the lack of the support and leadership promised by Francisco Juliao; this failure was to set off a series of scissions in the Peasant Leagues, which died as a national political movement at the end of 1962.

## 10. *Peru*

The movement started by Hugo Blanco in 1961, in the Convencion valley, should logically have debouched on to an insurrectionary *foco*. But without political support, without a well-defined strategy, without cadres or equipment, Blanco could not pass over to armed struggle, and it was the peasants who paid the price under the terrible military repression unleashed in October 1962 against the unionized peasantry of Cuzco. Blanco was captured in May 1963, isolated and ill, after a four-month search.

## 11. *Argentina, February-March 1964*

Failure of the EGP (*Ejercito Guerillero del Pueblo*). Given the capabilities and size of the organization, this was doubtless one of the most serious failures of a guerrilla centre. For more than six months the EGP prepared itself for action in the provinces of Salta and Jujuy, in the north, where the police discovered sizeable training camps and several underground stores of provisions. Young dissidents from the Communist Party and other leftists made up the EGP. The official figures were: a dozen arrested, six dead—some of hunger, others shot. The guerrillas had not yet gone into action.

To set against these failures, the following freed territories and zones of combat at present exist with a solid base in South America:

## THE GAINS

### 1. *Venezuela*

The States of Falcon and Lara have for two years constituted what Douglas Bravo (commander of the guerrilla) in October 1963 called "stabilized zones," where despite the adoption of guerrilla warfare in depth—that is establishment of a liberated political and social régime—military engagements have not ceased. Besides these two zones, a new front was created in July 1964 in Bachiller, in the east, and another in the Andes to the West.

## 2. Colombia

The zones of peasant self-defence, often called "independent republics"—Marquetalia, Rio Chiquito, Sumapaz, El Pato–whose creation goes back to the Civil War (1948–58). They were born of a local armed struggle waged by the peasants, who, when the war was brought to an end by the reconciliation of the Conservatives and the Liberals, did not lay down their arms but organized themselves autonomously under peasant leaders (endowed with an exceptional military formation), who were members of the central committee of the Colombian Communist Party. After the elections of March 1964, the region of Marquetalia was the object of a massive and carefully prepared attack by the army and air force, trained and led by American officers. The commander of the region, Marulandia, refused to engage in a war of position which would have been disastrous, and abandoned control of the inhabited area to the army: this was a town of small importance, in which the army found itself effectively trapped–Marulandia and his peasants subjecting the soldiers to relentless guerrilla harassment.

## 3. Bolivia

Despite the ambiguity of the struggle, the tropical Bolivian North-East, on the Brazilian frontier, can be included. It is occupied by considerable guerrilla forces, who went over to the offensive after August 1964, under the control of the Falangist party. This party, the traditional representative of the latifundists of the East and of reaction by Whites (*kampas*) against Indians (*kollas* of the altiplano), adopted an anti-American and nationalist position after the failure of the Falangist insurrections of 1953 and above all of 1959, in which the founder of the Party, Unzaga de la Vega, was killed. This guerrilla is characterized by strong regionalist—in some cases almost separatist—demands; these are the result of the rivalry between the economic interests of Santa Cruz and those of the Indian capital, La Paz. Nevertheless, certain guerrilla chiefs (Valverde, etc.) are known to be authenic revolutionaries.

## 4. Bolivia

The Bolivian mines—the entire zone surrounding Oruro, including San José, Huanuni, Siglo Veinte, Catavi—constitute, by virtue of their economic importance (tin is the Bolivian mono-product), social importance (the 26,000 miners enrolled in the FSTMB[11] form the concentrated base of national production and of the national proletariat) and political importance (level of consciousness and of organization), the most important and solid liberated territory in the Continent. Since the 1952 revolution—the first in Latin America—of which they were the artisans and the true victors, the miners have been organized in each mine into militia; they are badly equipped in conventional arms, but highly trained in the use of dynamite, which they have made into a terrible weapon. The great mines are from 20 to 50 kilometres apart, but the Indian peasants of the intermediary zones are also armed and allied with the unions.

Since the first great massacres of miners in 1942, ordered by Patino, the miners have paid with their lives for every strike, and for each basic demand (such as the eight-hour day). Since their rupture with the MNR and Paz Estenssoro (1960) armed struggle has become the daily reality of the mine and is always on the point of debouching on to a strategic offensive: the march on La Paz. Bolivia is the country where the subjective and objective conditions are best combined. It is the only country in South America where a socialist revolution is on the agenda, despite the reconstitution of an army which was totally destroyed in 1952. It is also the only country where the revolution might take the classical Bolshevik form—witness the proletarian insurrection of 1952, on the basis of "soviets," which "exploded" the state apparatus by means of a short and decisive armed struggle.[12]

The theory of the *foco* is thus in Bolivia, for reasons of historical formation which are *unique* in America, if not inadequate, at any rate secondary. If one excepts Colombia, more industrialized and less colonial than Venezuela and where civil war has given the rural guerrilla its "Vietnamese" character (the peasants are at the same time

---

[11] The FSTMB is the Trade Union Federation of the Bolivian Miners. Its president is Juan Lechin, former second-in-command of the MNR, who broke with Paz Estenssoro in 1962 after the latter's complete capitulation to the United States.

[12] This text was written before the Bolivian uprising of October/November 1965, at the end of which the Falangist guerrillas marched upon La Paz. Once again the miners were in the forefront of the struggle, followed by the students and workers of La Paz and Oruro. The military junta carried into power by the departure of Paz Estenssoro was even less able to avoid the confrontation which the miners sought. The Communist Party, divided, prisoner of its own reformist timidity, could provide no concrete alternative to the constitution of the military junta. In the opinion of all the militants, the presence of a proper political vanguard would have transformed the outcome of the uprising. It is to be feared that the repression of the workers and other democratic forces will now be pursued with renewed vigour.

cultivators of their land and guerilleros), only Venezuela at present provides an example of the *foco* as Guevara conceives it. Contrasted with the impressive list of failures, this is very little. In fact, a rapid analysis of the reasons for these failures shows that they were due to a too hasty imitation of the Cuban model, and did not combine all the necessary conditions for success. This historical experience enables one to set out these conditions much more fully than was possible five years ago. Just as Leninism matured theoretically after the ordeal of 1905, so Fidelism has been strengthened and defined more closely after the ordeal of that immense, scattered "1905" which Latin America has undergone since the victory of the Cuban Revolution.

## CASTROISM AND BLANQUISM

The most serious mistake would be to see in the *foco* a revival of Blanquism. Although it starts as a tiny group—from 10 to 30 individuals, professional revolutionaries entirely dedicated to the cause and aiming to win power—the *foco* does not by any means attempt to seize power on its own, by one audacious stroke. Nor even does it aim to conquer power by means of war or through a military defeat of the enemy: it only aspires to enable the masses themselves to overthrow the established power. It is a minority, certainly, but one which, unlike the Blanquist minority of activists, aims to win over the masses before and not after the seizure of power, and which makes this the essential condition of the final conquest of power. This minority establishes itself at the most vulnerable zone of the national territory, and then slowly spreads like an oilpatch, propagating itself in concentric ripples through the peasant masses, to the smaller towns, and finally to the capital. The process is of course two-way, since from the towns themselves there comes a movement of mass strikes, demonstrations in defence of public liberties, fund-raising campaigns, and an underground resistance movement galvanized by the exploits of the rural guerrilla. This growth of an isolated minority into a minority which is the nucleus of a popular movement, which in turn gathers force in a final tidal wave, is not mechanical, in that the influence of the guerrilla centre accelerates by leaps. The first contact with the peasantry in the mountain where the guerrilla force must be based for reasons of security and natural cover, is the most difficult to establish and confirm. These isolated peasants, who cultivate small, barren clearings (the *conuqueros* of Falcon in Venezuela, or the share-cropping Indians of Northern Argentina), are also the most closed to any political consciousness, and the most difficult to orient and organize—because of their dispersion, their illiteracy, their initial mistrust towards strangers who only seem to presage bombardment, pillage and repression. But later, when the peasants have been won over and the *foco* has gained provisions, information and recruits, the guerrilla centre will encounter the agricultural workers of the plains: the cane workers of Northern Argentina, often migrants from neighbouring Bolivia; the unemployed from the market towns of Falcon; the wage-labourers from the coast of the Brazilian North-East. These form a social stratum which is far more receptive and better prepared for the struggle, because of its concentration, its chronic unemployment, its subordination to the fluctuations of the capitalist market. Finally, in the neighbouring towns, there will be a convergence with the small groups of politicized workers which already exist in the local transformer industries, without any need for the slow preliminary work which is indispensable in the mountains.

The second characteristic of the *foco* which distinguishes it radically from Blanquism, is that it does not in any way aim at a lightning victory, or even for a rapid outcome of the revolutionary war. The *foco* aspires to conquer power with and through the masses, that is to say with the poor and medium peasants, and with the workers. But these social classes, which have always been isolated from political life, require a long practical experience in order to gain consciousness of their exploited condition, and to organize and move into action. Besides, the chosen terrain of Blanquism was the working-class aristocracy of the 19th-century craft industries, with its high cultural level. This hardly has any equivalent in contemporary Latin America, apart from the anarcho-syndicalist sectors of Buenos Aires and above all of Montevideo (where there exists an important anarchist trade union federation)—products of the first wave of Italian and Spanish immigration: their importance cannot be decisive. . . .

The theory of the *foco* can be best situated among current political concepts, by relating it to the Leninist theory of the weakest link, which it merely re-interprets in different conditions. The *centre* is installed as a *detonator* at the least guarded position, and *at the moment* most favourable to the explosion. In itself, the *foco* will not overthrow a given social situation nor even, through its own struggles, reverse a given political situation. It can have no active function unless it finds a point of insertion within maturing contradictions. Geographically, this must be where class contradictions are at their most violent—though the least manifest on the political plane, the most fitful or repressed, i.e. in the zones of agrarian feudalism outside the framework of the repressive machinery concentrated in the towns—e.g., Cuzco in Peru,

Salta in Argentina, Falcon and Lara in Venezuela, the Sierra Maestra in Cuba. Chronologically the problem is more difficult. It is clear that a guerrilla centre cannot be born in the trough of the wave, but must be the culmination of a political crisis. "Insurrection must rely upon that *turning point* in the history of the growing revolution when the activity of the advanced ranks of the people is at its height, and when the *vacillations* in the ranks of the enemy and *in the ranks of the weak, half-hearted, and irresolute friends of the people* are strongest."[13] Such is the third point which distinguishes, in Lenin's eyes, Marxism from Blanquism on the question of insurrection, the first being that the insurrection must be based on the vanguard class, the second that it must be supported by a popular revolutionary upsurge. It is equally clear that one cannot just wait for "the moment" before taking to the hills, since a *foco* is not improvised in the space of a month. For the prairie to catch fire, it is necessary that the spark should be there, present, waiting. The very lengthy work of building up a *foco* can only be done on the spot, and only a centre that is politically rooted in an agrarian zone can seize the offensive at the appropriate moment. . . .

While "the terrain of armed struggle in under-developed America must be primarily the countryside" (Che Guevara), this does not exclude the development of secondary centres in the towns: the universities. These can act as nuclei of theoretical discussion, forums of political agitation or as reserve armies. It would take too long to analyze here why the students are in the vanguard of the revolution in Latin America and why they are always the first to bear the brunt of repression, as recent events in Venezuela, Panama, Santo Domingo and elsewhere have shown. One may simply mention the rupture between the generations, the demographic pressure,[14] the special importance of the factor of "consciousness" in under-developed countries lacking an organized mass working class, and the university reforms of Cordoba (1918). These last were applied to practically the whole of the Continent, conferring autonomy on all the major universities, and thus sheltering them constitutionally in the name of bourgeois liberalism from state intervention (though this legal protection is somewhat theoretical, of course, in the light of the military attacks on the University of Caracas and its recent occupation). In any case, the facts are

---

[13] V. I. Lenin, "Marxism and Insurrection," *Collected Works*, Vol. 26, pp. 22–23 (English Edition).

[14] South America has a population growth of almost 3 per cent per annum, higher than that of Asia and Africa. Brazil, for instance, will double its population in 20 years: 1960, 60 million; 1980, 120 million.

inescapable. Caracas, Bogota, Quito, San Marcos at Lima, the philosophy faculty at Buenos Aires, the University of Montevideo (where 300 students who demonstrated against the breaking of relations with Cuba in September 1964 withstood a siege by the police), Sao Paulo, the philosophy faculty at Rio (scene of the only shots fired during the April *coup d'état* in Brazil) are all key points for registering the latent political temperature of the country—not its present average temperature, certainly—but that of the crisis to come. A university election (where fraud cannot intervene), which is essentially political, is not only an advance report on which political tendencies predominate within the Revolution but also on the inner evolution of the political life of the country itself. When the Marxist left captured control of the university of San Marcos at Lima from APRA in 1959, this marked the end of a historical phase in Peru and indeed in the Continent. It indicated the irreversible decline not only of APRA but of the whole bourgeois ex-progressive ideology, and the irreversible advance of a new generation of men and of ideas definitely linked to Marxism-Leninism and to the Cuban revolution.

If the university *foco* is a political rather than military centre, it still runs the risks of the *foco*. First, the concentration of political agitation in the University, this precinct reserved for liberty, can also prove a trap: the abscess is fixed where everybody expects it and is insulated from the 'healthy' social body. The *foco* turns in on itself and simmers in isolation. This seems further proof that the countryside is the terrain for an effective struggle, for in the capital the autonomous university constitutes the only free or potentially free area; which in an already advanced phase of struggle is rather a Pyrrhic victory. In Caracas, for example, the vanguard role of the Central University— the only place where it is possible to post up bills, to hold a public meeting, to demonstrate, to publicly distribute revolutionary literature—has perhaps proved a snare at certain moments: however, the simultaneous presence of an active rural front and of an urban guerrilla in the working-class quarters has prevented this trap from being fully sprung. But, above all, like the insurrectional *foco* in its early stages, it is necessary at a certain point for the student vanguard to withdraw itself from the masses: separation both in the tempo and in the level of the forms of struggle . . . .

## THE LESSONS OF THE LONG MARCH

All the *focos* we have mentioned have had to be dissolved: it is already clear that armed struggle is not in itself a panacea. What were the reasons? Without going into details, one can sum up: almost all were destroyed by means of informers or the infiltration of police spies into the organization. And here it is worthwhile recalling the degree to which the war of infiltration and espionage has expanded since 1959, thanks to the North Americans: the "publicity coup" of Fidel's sister is only one example of the talents or the financial resources at the disposal of the CIA. While this aspect should certainly not be underestimated, it does not explain everything. The guerrilla group is always initially as small as possible precisely to minimize the risks in case of failure, for a single infiltration can easily jeopardize the whole organization. But there are deeper political conditions which explain why infiltration can occur in the first place and why it can each time shatter the whole movement. First, the absence of deficiency of political education of members of the organization. Again, there is the lack of adequate political preparation on the actual terrain where the guerrilla group operates: in this case, a void at once forms around the revolutionary centre, which will then be starved of information and foodstuffs and will lack even a rudimentary knowledge of the geography of the combat zone . . . .

All these negative experiences have been studied by the Latin American revolutionaries who appear to have drawn the following conclusions from them:

1. *The Recruitment, Military Training and Political Education of the First Group of Combatants Must Be Much Stricter than in the Past.*

The homogeneity of the group is the highest importance, all the more so since its limited size (from 10 to 60 members at most) allows for rigorous selection, thus eliminating the No. 1 danger, infiltration. This is not the place to discuss the technical aspects of preparation. One may merely note in passing the prime importance of keeping military secrets, and of simple physical as well as specifically military training. Guerrilla warfare is above all an endurance test of forced marches in difficult terrain rather than a series of military engagements, which in fact should be avoided rather than sought. In this perspective, romanticism is swiftly dissolved. A student from the lower middle class, accustomed to the minimum comforts of the town, could not survive the routine of guerrilla war for more than a week unless gifted with quite exceptional physical stamina. Instead of leaving matters to the workings of natural selection, it would be better to apply a deliberate selection before the launching of guerrilla operations: in Venezuela, for instance, there were very few students who, after volunteering with enthusiasm in the early stages, did not have to be sent down into the valley again after a few weeks, diseased and exhausted. The majority of the combatants in Falcon are now made up primarily of peasants and workers, and only lastly to make up the numbers, a few intellectuals of petit-bourgeois origin (doctors, students, etc) who have proved exceptionally tough, both morally and physically. Finally, closer contacts between the organizations of different countries seem necessary now, so that their various experiences can be pooled and so that organizational errors need not be repeated. At the very least, and failing anything more ambitious, the lack of a sort of continental information bureau grouping all anti-imperialist organizations and not merely the communist parties is having deleterious effects on the day-to-day conduct of the struggle.

*2. But Armed Struggle Understood as an Art—in the Dual Sense of Technique and Invention—Is Meaningless Except in the Framework of a Politics Understood as a Science.*

The solidity and seriousness of a military preparation and the organization of a *foco* is essentially a political question: it is determined by an overall strategy and by an understanding of the interests of the exploited. Only a reformist party without any theoretical foundation would regard the creation of an armed force as a separate problem, something secondary and local; as a simple internal police measure. The development of armed struggle in Venezuela, for example, has forced the communist party to articulate an overall strategy, based on a theoretical analysis of "double power" (formal and real) within a semicolonial state and of the dominant and secondary class contradictions existing within a society suddenly and grotesquely transformed by the exploitation of petrol since 1920. It was not a matter of justifying a given practice after the event, for this strategy and theoretical analysis had been laid down at the Third Party Congress held in 1961 before the opening of the rural fronts, but rather of providing an objective and a specific context for the struggle. Today, the Colombian communist party faces the same alternative: whether to regard the guerrilla *foco* in Marquetalia, initiated and led by the peasant Marulandia, as strictly regional and "accidental"—that is, to deny it any future, to refuse it any place or meaning within a general strategy of revolution, and thus in effect to kill it politically and physically; or to revise its dogmatic theses on the peaceful transition, the alliance with the MBL (Liberal Revolutionary Movement, the left section of the Liberal party, topped by a bourgeois leadership), the defense of democratic liberties, etc., and to re-interpret the whole strategy of the Colombian revolution.

Armed struggle absolutely cannot be brandished in Latin America as a categorical imperative or a remedy in itself: armed struggle conducted by whom, one may ask, when, where, with what programme, what alliances? These are concrete problems which no one in the world can resolve abstractly—only the national vanguards which alone carry the weight of these political responsibilities. In other words, the *foco* cannot constitute a strategy in itself without condemning itself to failure: it is a moment of struggle whose place can only be defined within an overall integrating strategy.

The military activities of the *foco* continually involve political criteria: in the choice of local alliances—with or against rich peasants; in the objectives or basic principle of certain attacks—for example whether to ambush a column made up of conscripts or to melt away before it without forcing a combat so as not to alienate potential natural allies (in this situation the Venezuelan revolutionaries do not attack but make their presence felt through notices posted at the forks of the forest footpaths). But, more than this, the detonation of a *foco* involves a political precondition: selection of time and place presuppose reference to the totality of the given political situation, and to a dialectical analysis of its revolutionary possibilities. The place to be occupied by the rural front within the whole national revolutionary struggle will vary from country to country. The political importance and military tactics of a *foco* established in North Tucuman (Argentina), that is in a country with a highly developed industrial proletariat concentrated in the capital, cannot be the same as those of an Andean centre in Peru, where 70 percent of the population lives on the land.

In the recent past, Latin America has experienced two types of armed struggle which offered their own political strategy. The first, and most terrible, was the civil war in Colombia sparked off by the assassination of the Liberal leader, Jorge Eliecer Gaitan, whose contemporary legacy is the chronic violence and *bandolerismo* which has claimed 200,000 deaths in 10 years according to official estimates, and 300,000 according to the Liberal party—a more likely figure. What has emerged from this vast cataclysm which reached depths of cruelty unexperienced in any other war? A few stabilized zones of peasant self-defence, the only areas which managed to set up some sort of organization and political leadership (and hence proper military discipline) during the course of the war. With the exception of the areas of Galilea, El Pato, Sumapaz and the guerrilla front south of Tolima, where the communist party succeeded in establishing a unified command of the peasant militias and in creating an institutional order, the whole country has been prey to continual anarchic violence, with no meaning; each party simply matching the excesses of the adversary (whether Liberal or Conservative) with excesses of its own, without coherence or leadership. Neither the communists nor the advanced wing of the Liberals has yet posed the question of power. A national conference of guerrilla fighters held at Boyaca in 1952 achieved nothing, and the 13 commandos existing in the territory were never able to fuse or to co-ordinate their action. Yet if there was ever a truly "popular" violence, erupting from "below," from the countryside without any intervention by "petit bourgeois intellectuals" from the towns (without "artificial stimulation from outside the peasant milieu," to cite the phraseology current in describing the Venezuelan revolution), then it was without doubt the wave of desperate jacqueries experienced in Colombia up to 1958. The problem of political power was only confronted in 1964 by the peasant guerrilla of Marquetalia, which articulated a serious organization, objectives, and a phased programme, in short a meaning for itself. This critique of spontaneity has been achieved only at the cost of many lives; but even so it is certain that if the peasant combatants of Marquetalia, who lack a national political leadership, fail to combine with a mass movement in other regions, they will be unable to bear the whole weight of repression alone.

Another recent form of mass violence—and one which proves that terrorism is not just the "spontaneity of the intellectual"—was the terrorist wave which rocked Argentina in 1959 and at the beginning of 1960. This terrorist outbreak erupted from the base, from the Peronist unions and youth organization, to protest against Frondizi's betrayals, against the signing of the petrol agreements, to obtain the return of the CGT to the workers (the CGT had been taken over by the military in 1955 and subsequently dissolved altogether) and for the return of Peron, etc.

Between 1958 and 1960 there were at least 5,000 terrorist incidents. The movement was of considerable importance, but it was only the work of isolated groups or even individual terrorists, without any common programme or leadership.

The movement first appeared in the form of support for strike actions, at the time illegal. Militants would plant a bomb against an industrial establishment (for instance, in a bakers' strike the flour-mill or the bakery itself would be sabotaged, and similarly such state enterprises as the telephone or electricity services were also targets) to force it to close down or as a reprisal. This spread rapidly and became almost a daily occurrence, without any very clear point: bombs in the road, underneath vehicles, against the front of buildings, more or less anywhere. Towards the end, some groups of young workers managed to introduce some direction into this wave of spontaneous protests, and bombs were placed at the various agencies representing imperialist interests, the British Council and the usis, for example. But the police had little difficulty in picking up the terrorists, who had no underground organization. A trade union group captured the cgt which had been reconstituted in 1961; and the movement was broken by the adoption of the "Conintes Plan" (a sort of siege launched by Frondizi); the terrorists were arrested and sentenced by emergency trials. Such terrorism obviously has nothing in common with the Venezuelan "terrorism," systematically directed against the imperialist economic infrastructure (pipe-lines, oil-wells, large warehouses, banks, the American military mission and so on). This confirms once again the justice of Lenin's theses on the subject of terrorism: that it can never be employed as a permanent and regular form of political action, but only at the moment of the "final assault;" that in conditions of illegality or repression it is not in itself contradictory to mass struggle but that it may easily become so unless it is firmly and fully subordinated by political factors (for there is no terrorist or armed action exempt from injustices and errors which can only be corrected in the practice). In Argentina, terrorism led to a decline after 1960 in working-class militancy and a marked falling off in revolutionary combativity.

This negative historical record in no way contradicts the necessity of armed struggle understood as the highest form of political struggle. Quite the contrary, for it confirms anew:

(1) that the appearance of a rural guerrilla centre is to be subordinated to a rigorous political analysis of the situation: the selection of the moment at which to launch the action and of the right place for it presumes a searching analysis of national contraditcions, understood in class terms;
(2) that the *foco* does not by definition exclude the conducting of other peaceful forms of mass action through the trade unions, in the national assembly, in the press, and so on, even though the Venezuelan experience demonstrates that peaceful means of struggle, essentially precarious, may not last long after the inception of an armed struggle.

In other words, more advanced forms of popular struggle, far from dispensing with the need for "normal" political organization and action, must precisely be accompanied by an improvement in political consciousness and organization. The frank hostility to armed struggle revealed by the leaderships of several Latin American communist parties (Peru, Colombia, Argentina, Chile, Brazil) may well derive not so much from any lack of courage or from deficiencies in material preparation as from a low degree of theoretical and political consciousness. These leaders are well aware that if a "people's war" (as the Cubans call a guerrilla war) were to break out, they would have to yield to a new generation of leaders formed in and by the struggle, as has happened today in Venezuela.

3. *The Presence of a Vanguard Party Is Not, However an Indispensable Precondition for the Launching of an Armed Struggle.*

Here the Cuban Revolution has established that *in the insurrectional phase of the revolution,* while it is indispensable to have some sort of organization and a firm political leadership (July 26th movement), it is possible to do without a vanguard Marxist-Leninist party of the working class. It should be emphasized that this applies only to the preparatory stage of the seizure of power, for the creation of such a party becomes indispensable in the construction of a socialist society. An anti-imperialist national liberation struggle in a colonial or semicolonial territory cannot be conducted under the banner of Marxism-Leninism or the leadership of the working class for obvious reasons: *de facto* "aristocratization" of the relatively small working class, the nationalist character of the anti-imperialist struggle. As for the party, this will be formed and its cadres will be selected through the natural processes of the liberation struggle, as happened in Cuba. In other words, the idea of a vanguard party counterposed to that of the *foco*—a party whose creation must precede any guerrilla or military initiatives—does not seem to correspond to the facts. This is evident in Argentina where all the organizations, little groups and parties of the revolutionary left (with the exception of the Portantiero group) aspire to transform themselves into the vanguard party of the working class at present "mesmerized" by Peronist ideology and overwhelmingly hostile to the Communist party on account of the latter's sectarian anti-Peronism (which on more than one occasion led it to ally with reactionary forces against Peronism and even to mobilize the unions alongside the military after the "Revolucion Libertadora" of 1955 in which Peron was deposed). But ideology without the masses and masses without ideology do not constitute a dialectical opposition; and the Argentinian left withheld even moral support from the EGP because it was devoting itself entirely to the evangelical work of penetrating the factories by distributing Marxist pamphlets at the gates.

*4. Politico—Military Organization Cannot Be Postponed. The Work of Setting It up Cannot Be left Merely to the Momentum of the Struggle Itself.*

Post-Cuban conditions—for guerrilla fighters are now less able to count on surprise effect, and the enemy is better prepared politically and militarily—do not allow the same degree of empiricism as was possible for Cuba. As a general rule, a guerrilla centre cannot survive without an organized means of liaison between town and countryside. This is not merely to assure political contacts but also to guarantee a supply of arms, funds, fresh recruits drawn from the capital or other regions of the country, foodstuffs (for the idea that the guerrilla centre is completely self-sufficient is a myth, especially in the early phases of its action) and so on. The centre additionally must have a local organization, however primitive, established among the thin and dispersed mountain population and in the zones of contact with the exterior, the "lowlands" which are crucial for the lines of supply and information. And at the apex of the pyramid: the kernel of the future people's army—a handful of hunted men, always on the move so as to multiply contacts with the population and so as not to be located by the enemy or even by the peasants of nearby villages who might, through indiscretions, give them away. This mobility also has the advantage of making them appear more numerous than they really are. Certainly this pyramid will not appear in *advance* of the installation of the *foco*, or one would wait two thousand years to begin the revolution. The pyramidal formation is created from its two extremities, the base and the summit, and will never by anything other than the dialectical process of its destruction and reconstruction on a wider base. The network of contacts between mountain and town, town and mountain (relay houses, vehicles to carry volunteers and equipment along roads or highways which are closely patrolled, radio transmitters, etc.) is clearly the most vulnerable sector because it is compelled to work "in enemy territory," in provincial towns and villages which are not densely inhabited and are hence easily controlled. This was where the greatest risks were taken and where in Cuba as in Venezuela repression took its greatest toll. This is just one more reason for the greatest care in preparing and setting up the pyramidal structure. Operations should only commence and the combatants should move up into the mountains only when the organization has been properly initiated. In this way the risks of hasty improvization will at least be minimized if not, of course, entirely eliminated: the room available for manoeuvre, improvisation or recovery during the active process of establishment has been considerably lessened since Cuba.

5. *In Under-developed and Predominantly Rural Latin America, a Revolutionary Ideology Can Be Permanently Propagated among the Masses Only on the Basis of an Insurrectionary "foco."*

The idea that peasant masses must first be politically educated, before anything else is done, is often opposed to that of guerrilla tactics. It is never said how this is to be done, only that it must be done as the *pre-condition of armed action*. In reality, it seems that the two tasks condition each other and can only be undertaken together: there can be no *foco* which does not have as its immediate objective the political formation of the surrounding peasantry, no organized oppositional peasant movements which are not supported by armed struggle if they are to avoid being wiped out by the forces of repression.

This was borne out in Peru, where Hugo Blanco did more in a few years' work by forming unions of "arrendires" (farmers who hold the *usufruct* of land which belongs to the latifundist who is paid his rent in labour) in the Valle de la Convencion than all the left-wing parties together in the last 30 years. In two years, 30,000 Indian peasants were enrolled for the first time in their lives in defence unions at the instigation of Blanco and a handful of cadres. But when, during the summer of 1961, the agrarian proletariat and farmers decided not to pay rent to the latifundists, the latter immediately secured state intervention, in the form of the army, and troops were dispatched to Cuzco. The neighbouring areas were prepared to join in action against the latifundists, as long as the peasants of Convencion could hold out. But the latter had no means of resistance; a few anarchic actions on their part gave the army the pretext for carrying out massive reprisals on the peasants themselves. Hugo Blanco, alone and without a fixed abode in the area, escaped. The peasants felt themselves betrayed; nobody could defend them against the army. Between staying alive and the union they chose the former: rent was again paid to the latifundists. Blanco was left to his fate by his own union members who felt abandoned by him. He was unable to pass to the stage of insurrection through lack of arms, money, cadres, and especially the support of national political organizations, all of which dropped him. In May, 1963, alone and ill, Blanco was captured by the army in a mountain hut. In a cell in Arequipa he awaits a trial which the government has postponed for fear of renewed publicity about the "Blanco affair." For all that, the work of unionizing the Cuzco area was not swept away by the repression. New unions were formed, this time with the full support of the revolutionary parties, unworked land was taken over, and the peasants again refused to pay rent for land they had occupied to owners who never dreamt of working it. But it is quite clear from the Blanco experience that every political and union struggle carried out in an area of agrarian feudalism, in the present conditions of brutal physical repression, brings with it a regression of the struggle at least temporarily. It discourages the peasants and, in their eyes, compromises the idea of liberation and social emancipation, for they are left to face the consequences of the struggle which the instigators do not face with and for them.

Much the same phenomenon was apparent in North-East Brazil where, from their creation by Francisco Juliao in 1954,[15] the peasant leagues carried on an irreplaceable work of agitation. This led to important improvements, such as the stoppage of rent payments in certain places, and the extension of union laws to sugar-cane workers along the coast, who won an obligatory minimum salary (35,000 cruzieros a month)—although this increase was also due to the increase in sugar prices on the international market after the blockade of Cuban exports. Juliao, in fact, was never much concerned about agricultural wages. But after the military coup, what happened in the North-East? The latifundists returned in force, league members were thrown off the land or out of the owner's sugar mill, and prohibited from working any land at all; the league organizers were assassinated and tortured. The minimum salary of sugar cane workers has not been reduced, but it appears that this is only a question of time. In other words, white terror. Without any means of defence, the peasants are again being oppressed. After the great wave of hope, the extent of their discouragement can be imagined.

At worst, it is an irresponsible and criminal act to lead a mass of peasants—dispersed, illiterate, fixed to their land, without the possibility of flight (whereas the political agitator from outside can flee)— into a social or political struggle which will certainly lead to repression. Only a *foco*, trained and prepared, can resist such repression. In the face of troops, guerrillas will certainly also have to retreat, but they

[15] Francisco Juliao's peasant leagues, although they were turned into profitable myths for export, never had the political importance which was attributed to them in Europe. Absence of organization and discipline, Juliao's inability to provide a coherent strategy, and over-estimation of the peasant's revolutionary role, all prevented the leagues from becoming a properly political movement. Towards the end, in 1961, Juliao attempted to form such a movement—which was a failure. Juliao seems to have understood his limitations better than his colleagues, from whom he could not always defend himself. "The only title I wish for myself," he wrote at the end, "is—if I deserve it—that of a simple social agitator."

can always keep account of the crimes committed on the peasant population, avenge these by lightning raids, and liquidate officers judged responsible by peasant tribunals. Even the distant presence of guerrillas gives hope to peasants and makes them feel themselves defended, "covered."

Illiterate peasants, without newspapers and radios, suffocated by centuries of "social peace" under a feudal régime, assasinated by the latifundists' private police at the first sign of revolt, cannot be awakened or acquire political consciousness by a process of thought, reflection and reading. They will reach this stage only by daily contact with men who share their work their living conditions, and who solve their material problems. Thrown into a revolutionary war, they acquire practical experience of resistance to repression and also of a limited agrarian reform in a liberated zone: the conquest from the enemy of a small area of fertile land belonging to the latifundist is better propaganda for agrarian reform than a hundred illustrated pamphlets on Ukrainian *sovkhoses*. The objective conditions of life of the peasant masses in the majority of Latin American countries allows only one type of propaganda and political formation: propaganda by deeds, by the practical experience of the peasants themselves.

This is even truer of the Indian communities, shut in on themselves since colonization, and periodically persecuted by the whites. From the south of Colombia to the north of the Argentine, the Indian peasants bear the chief brunt of feudal exploitation. The majority of the population in Ecuador, Peru and Bolivia is Indian; in general it does not speak Spanish but Aymara or Quechua. What contact can there be between the political elite of Lima or Guayaquil, where the political cadres of the country are grouped, and the communities of the high plateau, totally dominated by a feudal priest (who in certain regions of Ecuador still enjoys the *droit de seigneur* on the first night of an Indian woman's marriage)? Any person who comes to cause trouble in the community is killed by the rural police (or sometimes by fanatic Indians themselves) with the blessing of the priest who is also the political boss. Access to the Indian communities must be won from the repressive forces which traditionally control them: "peasant leaders" representing the government party and central power; detachments of police and army; ecclesiastical authorities; bailiffs or latifundists themselves. The whole forms a solid, thick crust which, moreover, is reinforced by the difference of language.

It is worth noting that the Bolivian miners were successful in penetrating the Indian populations which surround the mines of Potosi, and the government was no longer able to trick them for a loaf of bread or a bottle of "chicha." They were armed, elected their own village leaders, and taught themselves with the aid of broadcasts in Quechua from the miners' radio stations. The Miners' Federation had 13 such stations, administered by a local union commission, in each of the largest mines. This exceptional possibility of work on a mass scale within the Indian peasantry was only possible because the balance of power favoured the miners. Nonetheless, they had to pay with their lives, in constant armed struggle against the government mercenaries for the right to have the radio stations, which were heard all over Bolivia. On April 28th, 1964, five miners were killed defending the radio station of Huanuni, near Oruro, against a massive attack led by government forces. The attack was repulsed only after a night counter-offensive with dynamite and rifles by all the fit men of Huanuni.

6. *The Necessary Subordination of Armed Struggle to Central Political Leadership Must Not Be the Cause of a Division Between the Political and Military Movement.*

This abstract conclusion can be drawn from the many experiences of divisions which have arisen between internal resistance and a political leadership in exile, or in that place of asylum and exile which the political capital of a country can be. The concrete conditions of the struggle have often seemed to make a division of labour between leaders and executants necessary. The leader or *caudillo* sends a group of followers devoted to his cause into the mountains and directs them from a distance—it this way he can disavow them in case of failure and so save his legality. This is a traditional attitude in Latin America—with which Fidelism has completely broken. Betancourt, head of *Accion Democratica*, remained in exile in Puerto Rico while the leaders of the internal resistance, Luis Pineda and Alberto Carnevali, were assassinated by Perez Jimenez after the failure of the planned insurrection in 1951. By contrast, all Fidelist leaders, following Castro's example, have personally led guerrilla operations.

The Venezuelan experience is revealing, as long as its particular characteristics are taken into account.[16] The FALN was the result of the fusion into a single Front of parties that were already constituted: the Communist Party and the MIR (Revolutionary Left Movement) as well as independents or people who came from other organizations, including the military from the Carupano and Puerto Cabello risings. This, combined with the dispersal of the struggle in different points

[16] Unfortunately, there is no analysis here of the unexpected events after 1965 and the measures of reorganization recently adopted by Venezuelan revolutionaries.

of the country, explains why there could not be a national leader, a "Venezuelan Castro." The leaders of the Venezuelan Communist Party, Gustavo Machado, Jesus Farias, and Pompeyo Marquez, are exceptional in that they enjoy a popular prestige which is not accorded to other communist leaders in neighbouring countries. Not only have they had long experience, but they are also so closely in touch with national reality that they have sometimes been suspected of "nationalism." During Perez Jimenez's 10 years of police dictatorship, Pompeyo Marquez continued without break as party secretary inside the country, where he personally organized resistance. The political leadership, in this case, bears little resemblance to that in other countries. . . .

In the course of the Venezuelan revolution and alongside the main front of urban struggle, the rural *focos* were silently growing stronger. Leaders and fighters rapidly gained political and military experience. Then came the first surprise. The periodic dismantling of the contact organizations between Caracas and the guerrilla front, such as the arrest of couriers, the prevention of radio contact and of the supply of arms, did not at all cause the collapse of the *focos* whose capability, support and recruitment were reinforced on the spot among the peasants. This showed that the bridges between the FLN and the rural detachments of the FALN[17] could be cut without the latter ceasing to grow and become self-sufficient. The guerrilla leaders who, according to the press, had been killed a hundred times over, remained uncaptured and kept reappearing—which tended to turn them into figures of popular myth, which in turn served to mobilize the towns. Finally, the rural guerrilla movement appeared as the sole permanent and solid apparatus which was continually growing and out of range of repressive action. . . .

Meanwhile, the urban guerrilla needed to play only a secondary, tactical role with hold-ups and harassing actions. In its place, political action, campaigning for the freeing of prisoners, and the creation of new organizations on the left, can try to develop.

*7. The Political Framework of the Armed Action Can Only Be Created in the Countryside. An Urban Guerrilla Movement Cannot Be a Permanent Form.*

Here again, the Venezuelan experience is indicative. Guevara's irrefutable arguments on this subject are well known: a guerrilla centre must attack the weakest links and must therefore keep away from urban zones—the strongest links—where the State's administrative and repressive forces are concentrated. Social contradictions are also not

---

[17] Respectively, the political and military structures.

as explosive in the cities because even the least favoured strata are integrated into modern society. For all that, the rural exodus does create explosive social contradictions in the city, contradictions which increase yearly and are less capable of being solved by the ruling class. In Caracas, the *ranchos* are overflowing with unemployed migrants from the country; in Lima, 600,000 inhabitants live in the *barriadas*, earth huts built on the banks of the Rimac; in Buenos Aires there are the *villas miseria*. The *ranchos* of Caracas house a third of the city's population—350,000 people piled into a belt of interconnecting narrow streets, squares, alleyways on hills around the city; ordinarily the police, let alone the bourgeois, hesitate even to venture into this maze. Each year 70,000 Venezuelans migrate to Caracas and a good half of these come to live in the *ranchos*. It is this socio-economic fact which explains why for the first time in Latin America, an extraordinary form of guerrilla warfare could develop in Venezuela: the urban guerrilla movement. The *rancho* was its base of operations and its source of recruitment. Doubtless, too much was made abroad of the spectacular raids by tactical combat units—the capture of enemy soldiers, the seizure of money, arms and documents, and the sabotage of imperialist installations. Precisely because such operations required very few participants, using their arms as little as possible, these actions were usually staged in daylight. The composition of these commandos was primarily student and petit-bourgeois (the Cuban July 26th movement had the same social make-up, and it would be ridiculous to attach the implicit European value judgement to the term 'petit-bourgeois'). But there was another aspect of the urban guerrilla which was more important in terms of the number of people involved in the war in the *ranchos*. The recruitment was different: workers, unemployed, young men without jobs, sons of large and poor families—all these make up the politico-military organization of the guerrilla in each neighbourhood. Relations with the underworld were often tense, but this did not lead to warfare, and there are often local understandings, non-aggression pacts and even collaboration and regeneration of criminals such as happened in the Algiers Casbah during the war of independence. In the spring and summer of 1963, during the fiercest phase of the urban struggle, not a day went by without simultaneous armed engagements in different *ranchos*. At nightfall the shooting began, to die away only with the dawn. The operations included harassing the forces of repression, ambushes, full-scale battles against the army, and even complete occupation of a neighbourhood which became for a few hours a liberated territory until the concentration of armed groups in a small area became untenable and they evaporated. The aim was to pin down the military in Caracas, to wear them out, to divide them in order to hasten demoralization and desertion—of which there were numerous cases in the police. Another aim was often to create diversions for other operations, such as individual or collective escapes from detention centres. But, a few months later, silence returned to the *ranchos* and this form of urban guerrilla movement had disappeared. It should not be thought that the armed groups in the *ranchos* had all been liquidated and military conquered; if needed, this type of action could have continued a long time. It was rather a decision of the FALN which put an end to these operations. Why?

Operating in a fixed and naturally limited area, the urban guerrilla movement is easily pinned down. In effect, it has neither the choice of time nor of place. The guerrilla is forced to operate at night (the *ranchos* have very weak street lighting), to ensure the safety of the combattants by allowing them to escape identification—although this can be met by switching the groups of neighbouring areas in order to avoid the threat of informers; and to ensure the safety of the inhabitants. Streets deliberately deserted cause fewer innocent victims, although there are always some, since bullets pierce the cardboard or wood walls of the houses. Darkness allows the popular forces to make the most of their advantages such as knowledge of the terrain, mobility, and the enemy's difficulty in using heavy weapons. On the other hand, daylight allows houses to be searched, and cordons to be thrown around whole areas and massive reprisals to be staged. As far as choice of terrain is concerned, it is almost impossible for armed groups to move in the city, where the large avenues are closely controlled, in order to take a garrison or military detachment by surprise. Such an operation entails too many risks, because the lines of retreat are too easily cut off. The guerrilla has therefore to make the forces of repression fight in the hills outside their natural terrain. After a certain time the latter understand the trap and refuse to move, prefering to abandon the *ranchos* to the control of the guerrillas by night rather than lose a dozen men for each raid. All sorts of strategems may be used to try to attract detachments of police and army into the *ranchos*, among them false alarms: a large bomb explodes right at the top of the *rancho* where there had been apparent calm; when the column of soldiers arrives to investigate they are caught in an ambush. But the essential factor is that the guerrilla is pinned down in the *ranchos*, and the government's tactic is obvious: to station the army and police in such large numbers in the *ranchos* that it is not worthwhile attacking them. It is true that in the first stage of the struggle all police posts had to be evacuated from the working-class

quarters—the enormous apartment blocks of Urdaneta, Simon Rodri-
guez and January 23rd—as well as the *ranchos*. But the army and
national guard soon established nests of heavy machine guns at key-
points on roofs, crossroads and on high ground, and this practically
put an end to urban fighting. The life of a militant is too precious
to waste in useless sacrifice, and happily the revolutionaries have no
false sense of honour: the Venezuelans did not attack.

On the military level, an urban guerrilla movement cannot be
transformed into a flexible operation and even less into a war of fixed
positions. It remains limited to harassment and sabotage in which it
has to spend forces disproportionate to the objectives achieved. "Strike
and flee," the rural guerrilla's motto, is impossible for the urban armed
group which has no fixed base and thus no sure position to which
to withdraw. It is always exposed to the threat of annihilation by
encirclement, informing or imprudence. Just as important, the absence
of a fixed base also means the lack of a solid social and economic
base: unless power is won at one blow by a general rising, there are
no partial reforms that can be carried out in liberated territory. What
can a "social reforming" guerrilla achieve in a city? What benefits
can be brought which can convert an ever growing mass of people?
The small groups in which an urban guerrilla must be organized—
usually four to six people—can never therefore succeed in becoming
a *permanent* core which is localized, *concentrated, disciplined*, with
fire-power at its command and trained in conventional war and the
use of heavy arms. In short, an urban guerrilla capable of harassing
actions can never become a guerrilla army, and even less a regular
popular army, capable of finally confronting the repressive army—the
ultimate aim of every *foco*. . . .

It is the distinguishing characteristic of a rural guerrilla movement
to have constantly to create and to recreate its conditions of existence.
In the first and longest stage of the struggle, its essential activity is
not the military conflict—which, on the contrary, it should avoid—but
sowing, hunting, picking, harvesting, in short *surviving* . . . which in
the American jungle is an exhausting and heroic task in itself. The
*foco*, at the beginning, can only survive to the extent to which it obtains
the support of the peasantry: the centre is welded to the milieu, congen-
itally. For the Columbian *bandoleros* of Tolima, the problem does not
arise: as they do not reproduce their material conditions of existence,
the support of the population is irrelevant, and pillage, theft and forced
taxes are sufficient. The rural centre however is in direct and unmedi-
ated contact both with the inhabitants of the zone of operations and
with the material conditions of existence: by clearing a corner of the

forest so as to be able to grow crops, by the collective working of the soil, by hunting, etc. These material conditions force the guerrilla *to proletarize itself* morally and to proletarize its ideology. Whether its members are peasants or petit-bourgeois, the *foco* can only become an army of proletarians. It is in this way that guerrilla warfare always produces a profound transformation of men and of their ideology (the latter evidently not aware of itself as such). It explains why, for example, there was in Cuba such a great political disparity between the leaders of the rebel army on the one hand and the leaders of the urban organizations—like Faure Chaumon for the Directorate of "March 13th" or even the leaders of the Popular Socialist Party—on the other hand, who could not imagine the revolution moving so rapidly towards socialism. And at the beginning, however, the social and political experience of the urban leaders of the "March 13th" and of the "July 26th movement" was identical: "petit-bourgeois revolutionary intellectuals." Similarly in Venezuela, anyone who passes from the urban struggle to the rural struggle feels a change of human atmosphere, of quality of organization and even of political analysis: in the mountain, short-term analysis does not count. All the guerrilla fighters know *that the war will be long and must be long,* given the present relations of forces, because "we are not trying to seize power, by a suicidal attack, only to lose it after 24 hours. We will not be precipitate, but neither will we compromise on our objectives."

The rapid proletarianization of the rural centre thus gives to the guerrillas both confidence and modesty. Paradoxically, it is almost impossible that a *foco,* the embryo of a popular army, should develop a militarist tendency; the tendency to believe that everything can be reduced to *echar balas,* to "firing off," and that only military success is important. Similarly, romanticism too finds a hostile milieu. The rural fighter is educated and educates himself day and night by his contact with the external world. The fighter of the urban guerrilla, by contrast, tends to live in *an abstract milieu, since he must abstract himself from his natural milieu* (the town, regular work, friends, women, etc.) for his own security and that of the organization. . . .

In short, the material conditions of action of an urban guerrilla (isolation of militants meeting 24 hours before an operation of whose nature they may be unaware until the last moment; use of pseudonyms even inside the UTC; impossibility of developing relations of friendship; obligatory reciprocal ignorance; anonymity even of the leader who gives the orders, etc.) contribute to form a certain kind of conduct and morale which can lead to voluntarism and subjectivism. The technical and material conditions of an urban guerrilla cannot be separated from the political content of its action, but will have direct repercussions on it. . . .

These remarks in no way describe a general statistical condition of urban guerrilla warfare; they describe a tendency inherent in its immediate situation, which explains why the urban guerrilla cannot move to a higher and more permanent level of action. But in Venezuela there has been a genuine urban *guerrilla*, that is to say, military operations which correspond to an objective state of war created by imperialism and the semi-colonial State, and which are linked to an organization and a political programme expressing popular aspirations. There has never been any individual attack on the life of a political enemy, even of Betancourt, though such an attack would not have posed any insurmountable problems. The principal target has been the army and the imperialist economic potential. If by terrorism is meant individual action unrelated to the development and objectives of a revolutionary movement, indifferent to the historical and subjective aspirations of the masses, then nothing was less terrorist than the urban action of the FALN and nothing was more terrorist than the governmental repression.

8. *The Present Controversy over the Revolutionary Programme— Bourgeois-Democratic Revolution or Socialist Revolution—Poses a False Problem and in Fact Inhibits Engagement in the Concrete Struggle of a United Anti-Imperialist Front.*

One of the major controversies dividing revolutionary organizations in Latin America concerns the nature of the revolution. To the sectarian thesis—influenced by Trotskyism—of the immediate socialist revolution without preliminary stages is counterposed the traditional thesis of certain communist parties, of the anti-feudal agrarian revolution carried out with the national bourgeoisie (and in reality under their direction). Between these two poles, many militants think that the revolution is an indefinite process, without "separable phases," which if it cannot start from socialist demands, inevitably leads to them: this seemed to be the lesson of the Cuban Revolution. But the Cuban experience also suggests that *the nub of the problem lies not in the initial programme of the revolution but in its ability to resolve in practice the problem of State power before the bourgeois-democratic stage, and not after.* Cuba could only become a socialist State because at the moment of realizing its democratic national reforms, political power was already in the hands of the people. Even a cursory analysis of Latin-American capitalism reveals that it is organically bound to feudal relations in the countryside. To take countries which have a national capital sector: in Colombia, industrial profits tend to be reinvested in land, and the industrial families are also the great agrarian families; in Brazil, the sugar industry of the North-East and the coffee-trade of Sao Paulo are linked to agrarian latifundism. This is why, of course, no national bourgeoisie has been able to put through a real agrarian reform—even though this should be in its interests, since it would greatly expand the internal market. In short, it seems evident that *in South America the bourgeois-democratic stage presupposes the destruction of the bourgeois State apparatus:* if this is not done the habitual succession of military putsches is destined to repeat itself indefinitely, just as the revolutionary surge of the masses will repeat itself, without any firm base, in a constitutional agitation for democratic reforms (agrarian reform, vote for the illiterates, diplomatic and commercial relations with all countries, trade union laws, etc.). This is what happened in Brazil after Kubitschek, in Bolivia after 1952, in the Dominican Republic with Bosch. In effect, the present polemics over the nature of the revolution serve only to divide the revolutionary movement and to conceal the problem which conditions all others, the conquest of power and the elimination of the Army—that sword of Damocles which will always attempt to break any movement of the masses.

If it is much more difficult, *after Cuba,* to integrate any sizeable fraction of the national bourgeoisie in an anti-imperialist front, this latter can and must still be the prime objective. But such a front cannot be constituted except in the practice of a revolutionary struggle, and, far from contradicting the existence of a *foco* armed and resolved to advance, it requires an active *avant-garde* which can in no circumstances wait for the front to be fully constituted between the various leaders before launching its action. This is perhaps the greatest paradox of Fidelism: it is by nature both radical (aimed at the capture of power) and anti-sectarian (no party and no man can pretend to monopolize the Revolution). Of course, this ceases to be a paradox once revolutionary practice is taken as the criterion and referent of "truth." There is, in fact, a long-established connection in Latin America between the reformism of certain Communist Parties and their isolation: constantly calling for the creation of a national front, they are incapable of undertaking a real alliance since they lack a political line and a strong organization of their own. A speech by Castro to Latin-American visitors in 1961 suggested that two ideas determine his conception of the Liberation Front: that of the "beginning"—of a realistic initiative modifying the level of political struggle and launching military struggle (in Cuba, the Moncada attack); and that of the "selective practice" of alliances and of compromises necessary as the struggle develops. In other words, the revolution can give itself from the beginning a minimum anti-imperialist programme, based on concrete demands related to peasant, worker or petit-bourgeois conditions, analogous to the Moncada programme which was the banner of July 26th. When all the possibilities of legal struggle have been exhausted, the revolutionary war should be inaugurated on the largest possible base "where the sincere Catholic must occupy the same place as the old Marxist militant." The very practice of the struggle, which can never be determined in advance but only in action (consequently, no endless theoretical discussions on the modalities of the future agrarian reform, discussions which serve only to divide and to delay the arrival of the concrete conditions for the application of any agrarian reform, etc.), can be relied on to transform the system of social and political alliances, rupturing some and creating others. In other words, the concrete questions posed to revolutionaries by practical necessity will produce new responses on their part: each phase of the struggle has its own system of questions and answers, born of the way in which the questions of the preceding phase have been resolved, and it is useless to try to overtake the practice of a united front by dividing it on questions which perhaps will not be relevant when the time comes. No gesture, no heightening of the struggle for power or the struggle after the seizure of power (that is to say, no heightening of the objectives of government action)—none of these can be effective if they do not fulfil a historical requirement, a lack consciously felt by the masses. It is self-evident that this entire conception would become opportunist if it did not have as its foundation the existence of a united vanguard, honest, intransigent, unsectarian, without any preconceived model, ready to take the most unconventional paths to arrive at its ends, selected and steeled by the struggle: a vanguard which only the practice of the *foco* guarantees.


## NATIONALISM AND SOCIALISM

This confidence placed in the radical value of the practice of the *foco*, which creates the leaders and the cadres of the future Party and its own theoretical field, can be seen as the unconscious homage of Fidelism to its own history, transcended but never denied; Castro's self-criticism perhaps serves only to ratify once again the creative and unfinished character of every revolutionary practice. Historically, Fidelism is an empirical and consequent revolutionary action which encountered Marxism on its way as its own truth. The inverse is also true: for an honest Fidelista (a revolutionary who was with Castro in the Sierra Maestra, or fought in the urban underground) Marxism is a theory of history justified and verified by his own experience. This encounter is not new. Thirty-five years ago, in 1930, another great American revolutionary hero, Luis Carlos Prestes, carried to the pinnacle of fame by the long march of the Prestes Column (30,000 km. covered in three years in the Brazilian interior, by a thousand men who overcame all the armies of repression sent against them), also met scientific socialism as his truth. Prestes, with something like the same impact as that of Castro, lent his legend as the "Knight of Hope" to Marxism—but, in the way he did so, he destroyed all dialectical value in the legend. His 1930 Manifesto, issued to the Brazilian people from his exile in Buenos Aires, denied his past, his friends, his myth and his nationalism, and proposed the immediate installation of workers' soviets in Sao Paulo. Prestes' adoption of Marxism, at a time when socialism had not yet won its self-confidence in the world, also marked the divorce of Prestes and of the Brazilian Communist Party from Brazilian reality (a divorce which has perhaps still not been surmounted, despite the Communist Party's great postwar electoral victories). At the same moment, Prestes left for Moscow and was absorbed into the administrative machinery of the International. Such a contact with Marxism is an electrocution, not a transcendence. The great strength of the Cuban Revolution is the absence of any divorce between that which it is, socialism, and that which it was, nationalism. The same is true of Fidelism: its contact with its historic American roots ensures its place within Marxism and beside Leninism. Fidel Castro has never denied his origins, nor his past actions: he has reinterpreted his past career as a non-Marxist revolutionary by prolonging and transforming it from within. That July 26th remains the festival of the Cuban Revolution suggests the distinguishing mark of Fidelism. On that day, visitors who disembark at Havana to celebrate the victory of socialism are, in fact, commemorating an "adventurist" surprise attack, the assault on Moncada by a handful of activists, which made all the good Marxists in the Continent shudder with indignation.[18] Each year the Cuban Revolution pays homage, as if to its abso-

---

[18] Let us remind ourselves what "Moncada" means: on 26 July 1953, in Santiago de Cuba, 150 poorly armed men, under the command of Fidel and Raúl Castro, attacked the military garrison of Moncada. The attack failed: the best-armed group of fifty men arrived too late at the appointed meeting place, and got lost in the streets of Santiago. The resulting repression killed off nearly all those who had participated in the attack. Fidel, who had escaped death by chance, was arrested shortly after, and made his appeal before the court into an act of accusation which is known as *History will absolve me. . . .*

lute beginning, as if to the summit of its socialist genealogy, to that theoretical and historical scandal—the assault on Moncada.

It is this which makes the history of the Cuban Revolution and its continuous development so instructive. Refusing to let itself be divided into two distinct epochs of "national-democracy" and "socialism," the Cuban Revolution helps in return to clarify and encourage throughout Latin America "bourgeois-democratic" nationalist demands, and forms of action which are "impure" from a sectarian point of view. Fidelism, far from condemning these as "provocations" or scorning them as "petit-bourgeois," gives them all its support; for if their protagonists are sincere and determined they will end by confronting American imperialism, and by developing into socialism. The lesson of Fidelism is that a genuine nationalism in Latin America implies the final overthrow of the semi-colonial State, the destruction of its Army, and the installation of socialism.

There is a further reason why Fidelism lays a greater stress on revolutionary practice, when it is honest and sincere, than on ideological labels: this is the belief that, in the special conditions of South America, the dynamism of nationalist struggles brings them to a conscious adoption of Marxism. Unlike the anti-colonialist wars in Asia and Africa, the American national liberation struggles have been preceded by a certain experience of political independence. The struggle against imperialism thus does not take the form of a front against foreign forces of occupation, but proceeds by means of a revolutionary civil war: the social base is therefore narrower, and the ideology consequently better defined and less mixed with bourgeois influence—at least, that is the historical tendency. While in Africa and in Asia, the class struggle and national struggle may be blurred by the tactical implications of the national Front, or delayed until after liberation, in South America class struggle and national struggle must, in the final analysis, go together. The path of independence passes by way of the military and political destruction of the dominant class, organically linked to the United States by a co-management of its interests. Therefore, it is clearly impossible to classify the American wars of national liberation under the same rubric as those of Asia and Africa. The ancestral possession of political power by an indigenous group means that nationalist demands must be much more advanced. . . .

Flag, army, school, national language, street names—everything suggests that the nation exists, and the vague feeling of frustration or of humiliation, generated by the fact that this "nation" really belongs only to an infinitesimal minority, finds no immediate target: there is no foreign occupation. It is difficult to locate the oppression:

it is more "natural." The birth of the armed struggle will therefore be less "natural," less spontaneous than in Asia or in Africa. It will require a more advanced level of class consciousness. The armed struggle, or *foco*, will thus tend to go from the town to the country, the peasants being even more mesmerized by the natural social order. In the countryside these characteristics of semi-colonial countries are reinforced by the natural hypnosis of the feudal world. The class enemy becomes a part of nature, exists like the stones of the field, since it has all the appearances of fixity—while political discontent is displaced by religious protest on to nature. It is nature which attracts the attention and the wrath of the peasant, not the latifundist. . . .

The revolutionary nationalism, or Fidelism, of the new organizations or fronts of action created in Latin America since Cuba cannot constitute a special ideology, nor pretend to do so. It is this that distinguishes Fidelism from the mystifying nationalisms which preceded it. The exposure of the class realities which underlie nationalist aspirations and which are revealed during the process of the liberation war puts an end to "nationalism" as the sole object of speeches and as a political myth. What in fact is the relationship of Fidelism with the ideological nationalisms? One can start by taking the case of bourgeois nationalism, which demands industrial development and the construction of the national State by means of heavy industry and commercial protectionism—the classical programme of "nationalist" bourgeois spokesmen like Frigerio in Argentina, Jaguaribe in Brazil, Zavaleta in Bolivia. What is its relationship to Fidelism? The same as that between capitalism and socialism, even though Cuba is admired by these ideologues as the only country which has succeeded in liquidating feudalism—which they too dream of being able to attack. Revolutionary nationalism also distinguishes itself from the "nationalist and democratic government" demanded by most of the Communist Party programmes: for it is organically linked to a socialist programme and it aims at the transformation of State power by means of its conquest and the destruction of its bourgeois form. Fidelist nationalism, unlike that normally put forward by the Communist Parties, is not defensive but radical. It thus considers as illusory and ineffectual the partial demands, the transactions or the conciliations of an eventual "national government" which works for a revolution which would advance in such small steps that "nobody will see it coming." Fidelist methods of action will therefore be different; they will not be confined to electoral propaganda, the posting of notices, and summit meetings with the existing political parties, but will also prepare the conditions for a direct armed offensive of the masses. What is the relationship of Communist to Fidelist strategy? The same, more or less, as between the Second and the Third Internationals, *mutatis mutandis*. Fidelism, initially a minority tendency, is now winning over the most active sections of these Communist Parties—above all the youth, the most valuable element for the future.

There is a far closer relationship between Fidelism and the two most historically important forms of South American nationalism, which can today be called Bonapartist nationalism: Peronism in Argentina and the populism of Vargas in Brazil. These two ideologies have by now definitely entered into decline, leaving a vacuum which Fidelism is little by little, occupying. Here too Fidelism is mounting from the youth organizations upwards. These two movements became fully majoritarian in their countries, trying—for a moment successfully—to ally the proletariat and the bourgeoisie under the leadership of the latter. The anti-Yankeeism (tinged with fascist sympathies) of Vargas and of Peron did not prevent them from trying to conciliate the United States and from finally capitulating to it. This is an attitude symmetrical but contrary, to that of Fidelism, which also attempts to unite the proletariat and the national bourgeoisie but this time under the direction of the former, and which will therefore not be in a position to come to an "understanding" with us imperialism. Bonapartist nationalism, on the other hand, pretends to realize structural reforms from above, with an unchanged State power, without involving a conscious movement of the masses. Nevertheless, in its time, just after the Second World War this Bonapartism was understood and felt to be revolutionary by the Argentinian and Brazilian workers who made it their own: thus these two régimes created irreversible subjective conditions from which history must progress.

Bonapartist nationalism has delayed the advent of a revolutionary nationalism of the Fidelist type by mystifying the proletariat, but has not made it impossible. For, once the bourgeois-proletarian united Front is divided, the proletariat begins to radicalize its ideologies and its demands, slowly abandoning the political and union leaderships inherited from the past and which today are bankrupt. Peron saved himself as a political myth unifying the masses, thanks to his abandonment of power in 1955, for he would otherwise have been forced to choose between a truly proletarian régime and the public betrayal of his promises, an option which could no longer be evaded at the moment of his overthrow by the Army. The class definition of Peronism has in consequence been delayed, but has nonetheless finally emerged despite Peron. For the industrial bourgeoisie wants to see no more of him, while the Argentinian proletariat continues to hope for his return.

But because of the default of the union bureaucracy of the CGT, the principal operational force of Peronism, the idea of insurrection carries more and more weight at the base, in the unions and particularly among the Peronist working youth, which has lived through its own political experience without Peron after 1955, with Cuba as a point of reference and comparison. It is evident that revolutionary nationalism has slowly taken the place of traditional Peronism, while preserving the name and the traditional ambience of Peron's movement. It already has its leaders, Cooke, Villalon and Valotta, and above all hundreds of young middle cadres formed in the union struggle. It now has its own physiognomy—that of an essentially urban working-class movement in which the images of Lenin, of Evita Peron and of Fidel mingle in a still unstable synthesis. . . .

A separate study would be necessary to establish the specific ways in which each Latin American nation can transcend its old forms of nationalism and revolutionary action. In each case, it must examine its class structure and the possibilities of revolutionary solidarity both with its neighbours and with the socialist world. Each national variant of Fidelism will draw a revolutionary inspiration from its own tradition of national independence struggles: this can be a strength but may also be a weakness if unmodified by later thought and experience. Fidel read Marti before reading Lenin; a Venezuelan revolutionary nationalist will have read the correspondence of Bolivar before *The State and Revolution*, a Colombian the constitutional projects of Nariño, an Ecuadorian Montalvo, and a Peruvian will have read Mariategui and reflected upon Tupac-Amaru. We should not overlook the debt of revolutionary nationalism to the action and propaganda of Communist Parties, which were the pioneers of reasoned anti-imperialism after 1920 and whose general failure, apparent since the end of the Second World War, is doubtless to be explained by their inability to assimilate these national traditions, to find concrete historical roots, to situate themselves in a continental continuity. A summary dialectic would thus make of Fidelism an *a posteriori* synthesis of two currents, national and international, nationalist and communist. But such an interpretation risks giving Fidelism the consistency of a distinct ideology, which it does not have and does not want. Because it is not an ideology, Fidelism is not a special qualification, a constituted vanguard, a party of a band of conspirators linked to Cuba. Fidelism is only the concrete process of the regeneration of Marxism and Leninism in Latin American conditions and according to the historic traditions of each country. It will never be the same from one country to the next; it can only conquer through originality. Let us hope that even the word disappears. For Fidelism, Leninism rediscovered and integrated with the historical conditions of a continent of which Lenin was ignorant, is proving itself in the reality of revolutionary struggle.

Though the mode of its appearance may vary in each Latin American country, it has nonetheless irreversibly achieved a certain organic link between armed struggle and mass struggle, expressed by the *foco* theory. This achievement leads to others: when state power is conquered by those who are today the exploited and the oppressed in Latin America, and that will not be tomorrow, the new societies which will then be built will also have the elan inseparable from Fidelism. Indeed they will have something beyond that elan: that alliance of the Promethean lyricism of revolutionary action (never to be confused with the false enthusiasm of the apologist) and a pitiless lucidity with respect to its own efforts, an alliance which is symbolized with such mythic perfection in the encounter of two men: the Cuban Fidel Castro and the Argentinian Che Guevara.

# 21

# The French Student Revolt: Three Interpretations

(A) THE FRENCH PSYCHODRAMA:
DE GAULLE'S ANTI-COMMUNIST COUP

*Stanley Hoffmann*

(B) THE PSYCHOLOGY OF A
REBELLION—MAY-JUNE 1968

*Jacques Ellul*

(C) AN IMPOSSIBLE REVOLUTION
(Translated by George Armstrong Kelly)

*Maurice Duverger*

≪≪≪≪≪≪≪≪≪≪≪≪≪≪≪≪≪≪≪≪≪≪≪≪≪≪≪≪≪≪≪≪≪≪≪≪≪≪≪≪

## EDITORS' COMMENT

In the French student revolt (rebellion? revolution?) of May-June 1968, two lines of historical force were powerfully met: (1) the French revolutionary tradition with all its resonances and overtones, (2) and a mounting condition of turbulence and activism among the youth on a cosmopolitan scale in the 1960's. Obviously, the range and depth of both phenomena deserve careful study, apart and in conjunction. We can regard it as ironic, if not significant, that the political culture which gave birth to the very notion of cosmopolitan revolution experienced the heaviest shock waves of a new force whose universality is as difficult to deny as it is elusive to describe. No doubt one of the reasons for this is the receptivity of the French tradition, implanted from early childhood on the expanding student mind. But it is possible also that a deeper explanation exists in the nature of French authority relations, first brilliantly suggested by Alexis de Tocqueville and recently explored systematically by the sociologist Michel Crozier. At least, it is the contention of the essay by Stanley Hoffmann printed here that the typical French concoction of centralism and individualism was responsible for both the scope and the futility of the student uprising.

If Hoffmann stresses the peculiarly French style of the event, Jacques Ellul examines some of the reasons why a rebellion of young bourgeois, however serious its proportion, is limited by psychological, class, and more narrowly political motives. He also corroborates the "centralism" thesis with his comments on the French educational and bureaucratic structure and the role of the media as positive factors in the unfolding of the revolt. To be sure, other analysts, basing their evidence on group phenomena and even traffic patterns of demonstration going back to 1848, would insist that the student challenge to the political and social Establishment was quite as serious as it seemed at the time and that the Gaullist regime came within an ace of falling. Their question is: To whom? In the last analysis it does not seem that any of the traditional opposition of the Left or the Extreme Left was prepared or willing to seize power under these circumstances, and one can only speculate on what the role of the armed forces might have been.

Maurice Duverger comments on the events of May from the point of view that would be called in America "Old Leftist." Although he tempers his criticism of student theories of revolution with a certain admiration, he concludes that the efforts of the young *enragés* may be politically counterproductive, disturbing enough to the average Frenchman to push him grudgingly to the side of reaction. The subsequent parliamentary elections seem to have provided some tangible confirmation for this judgment although, as Hoffmann indicates, they also demonstrated the Gaullist skill in salvaging yet another irretrievable situation. A second point made forcefully by Duverger is that the student aspiration to substitute revolutionary youth groups for the nineteenth century proletariat in the Marxist scheme may disclose a fatuous understanding of the realities of twentieth-century political life.

Since these studies were written, General de Gaulle has abandoned power in a well-known set of circumstances. This remarkable event does not particularly alter any theories expressed here, except to add some confirmation to the suspicion that the original Gaullist regime was out of touch with the younger elements of the political community. With Georges Pompidou, one is perhaps in the "liberal empire"—or already beyond it.

The studies presented below make no pretense of being detailed or profound scholarly explorations of a complex event. From among the occasional writings on the French May crisis (which are legion) and from the analyses of the worldwide revolt of the young, spearheaded by the students (which are numberless), they seem to the present editors to be gifted examples of the kind of thinking and theories that must be brought to bear on the ongoing problem of modern internal violence. Because of the wide-ranging character of this volume of essays, an arbitrary decision was made to limit our coverage of student revolt to the single case study that most vividly illustrates its possible dimensions. This should not convey to the reader the impression that we are unaware of the critical implication of transnational forces. On a worldwide scale, one observer (J. Jousselin, *Les Révoltes des Jeunes*, Paris: Editions Ouvrières, 1968, p. 15) has counted 1688 violent incidents against authority on the part of students for the period of 1 April to 30 June 1968 alone. When one sees that the United States contributed only 21 of these incidents, the scope of the disturbance is clear. In fact, a careful scholar has recently stated that "the unprecedented number of young people in the world today can be isolated as one of the crucial reality factors conditioning political and cultural developments" [Herbert Moller, "Youth as a Force in the Modern World," *Comparative Studies in Society and History*, X (3), April 1968, p. 237].

That statement may seem banal in itself; and yet current political explanations often avoid the plain truth of the matter. What is even more interesting for our purposes is to observe that rebellious youth is no new thing: Christ was crucified at 33; Luther published his Ninety-five Theses at the age of 34; the tensions (at least, personal ones) leading to the French Revolution were to a large degree those of unsatisfied young intellectuals; Mazzini allowed no one to join his revolutionary organization, Young Italy, above the age of 40; both the Kuomintang and the Communist Party in China have owed their periods of vitality to the young, and so on. Thus what we are studying below is a historical and sociological question of prime importance—and one which, if the determinism of age is positively correlated with the tendency to rebellion, has scarcely reached its zenith, much less run its course.

## (A) THE FRENCH PSYCHODRAMA: DE GAULLE'S ANTI-COMMUNIST COUP

STANLEY HOFFMANN

The most interesting aspect of France's great crisis of May-June 1968 is neither its suddenness, nor its scope, nor its spectacular (if perhaps temporary) ending. It is its ambiguity. What remains at stake is nothing less than a nation's capacity to change, not its skin (France has done it often) but its soul.

Lightning revealed, in a flash, the strength of the aspiration to a change in the citizens' perennial attitudes toward authority, in the relation of each individual Frenchman to larger groups within France, in the traditional French conception of freedom. But the crisis also showed the resilience, even within the rebels, of those same old beliefs and patterns of behavior, which they themselves displayed in the midst of their challenge, whose origins had been analyzed over a century ago in Alexis de Tocqueville's study of the *Old Regime*, and whose characteristics have been examined in depth in Michel Crozier's recent *Bureaucratic Phenomenon*. Since the rebels could not overcome, in themselves and in the nation, the features they were rising against, can change now be worked out by the very forces they were denouncing? Was their fiasco a paradoxical prelude to the mutation they sought, or a conclusive demonstration of its impossibility?

The crisis of 1968 was largely due to the impact of widespread transformations: in an educational system hit by mass democratization, in an economy hit by the imperatives of growth and competition, in a regime insufficiently responsive to pressures from below. New tensions triggered a demand for total renovation. But they also triggered old reflexes—those which had shaped France's school system, brand of industrialization, and peculiar political regimes, and which will limit the scope and meaning of any reform as long as they themselves have not changed.

SOURCE. Stanley Hoffmann, "The French Psychodrama," from *The New Republic*, August 31, 1968, pp. 15–19. Reprinted with permission of the publishers. Copyright by Harrison-Blaine of New Jersey.

486

The object of the contest, and the key to its fate, is the French style of authority and of change. In a nation riddled by conflicts, the citizens have traditionally preferred, in every group from the family to the state, to entrust the solution of conflicts to higher authority. But authoritarianism has always been tempered by French individualism: by the citizen's determination to be protected from arbitrariness through a network of bureaucratic rules limiting the scope and intensity of Authority. Hence a permanent series of polar opposites: a rigid, often stifling set of regulations, but also the preservation of the individual's capacity to protest: tight hierarchies controlled by a handful of Important Ones, but also the perpetuation of the Small Ones' escape from involvement and responsibility; centralization coexisting with fragmentation into small groups of castes. Two aspects of this system are especially important: the brittleness of voluntary associations (parties, unions, etc.) which are merely defensive bodies protecting their members against arbitrariness from above, yet expect higher authority to settle their differences and problems; and, of course, the absence of participation and compromise. Liberty is freedom *from*, not freedom *to*; it is defined as resistance and non-dependence; compromise is a pejorative word. The two values served by this style are, first, what Crozier has called the flight from face-to-face relations, i.e. the desire for individual apartheid, and, secondly, the desire of every group to preserve its status in society so that the overall equilibrium (a key notion) would, despite all changes, remain essentially intact.

The highest authority, the ultimate source of regulations, is the state. In quiet periods, when the fear of authority dominates, the French prefer a weak parliamentary system, in which the executive does little more than supervise the bureaucracy, and the legislature supervises both. In troubled periods, the need for authority prevails, and the French turn to a savior, who will last only if he does not violate the citizens' opposition to arbitrary rule. Both types of regimes are supposed to preserve the two basic values. In such a system, the pattern of change is quite unique: the way of change is cataclysmic, not gradual, but the scope of change is usually limited, especially as it leaves intact and perpetuates the fundamental style of authority. On the other hand, except in times of turmoil, higher authority, hemmed in as it is, is rarely dynamic. Almost inevitably, in a nation where the bulk of education and a huge fraction of the economy are public services, where elected local authorities have little power and no resources, any large-scale demand for change will sooner or later be aimed at the state, either because it failed to protect the citizens from an upset in the equilibrium, or because its own actions had caused such an upset. Moreover, the non-participating citizens, when dissatisfied, behave as rebels rather than as reformers: their whole way of being, fed by a school system that leaves little initiative to its subjects, prepares them for wild utopianism, intransigence and self-righteousness. In other words, in the absence of "participatory" channels of moderate change, the demand for change will be radical. But on the other hand, rebels are not revolutionaries either: they are too negative, too much in love with protest and criticism, too much concerned with preserving the two basic values. Therefore, traditionally, the rebellion disappeared when central authority, aware of the rebels' clumsiness and inaptitude to build something together, granted some concessions at the right moment. Thus the most indispensable changes were made possible, while harmony was restored, and the pattern reaffirmed, as I wrote several years ago, "by flexibility on top and acquiescence at the bottom . . . . By an intriguing paradox, protest succeeds to the extent to which it contained a kernel of specific grievance but fails to the extent to which it was a broader challenge of the decision-makers."

At first, the crisis of 1968 was not a reenactment of the French style of authority, but a revolt against it. Students challenged their professors, denounced the centralized controls of the Ministry of Education over the school and university systems, demanded the two basic new rights of autonomy for every academic unit, and co-management within. In most of the professions, from architecture to medicine, the younger members challenged their less dynamic but all-powerful elders, and proclaimed self-rule. The personnel of the state-run radio and television struck on behalf of objectivity and exerted their own right of self-expression. In the factories, the younger workers challenged the authority of the *patrons* and occupied the plants as a prelude to the exercise of "worker power." Not only was it a rebellion against all establishments and their rules. It was also a moving orgy of face-to-face relations, a sudden, joyous, noisy release from silence and isolation, a delirium of stream-of-consciousness discussions, debates, dialogues. It was no longer the State that was sovereign, it was the word. In a society of highly formal, contractual human relations, there was a surge of spontaneity. In a society of separate individuals, suspicious groups and poor communications among them (symbolized by the retarded telephone system), there was a rush toward community. The students wanted to join hands with the workers, and open the University to all. Even the beneficiaries of the hierarchy: the established professors, the *agrégés* of the University, often took the lead in calling for the end of their own privileges.

This last point showed, however, that there was less novelty here than the young revolutionaries believed. It was not the first time those who had long blocked reform by their obstinate attachment to their privileges were trying to get ahead of a revolution once it had begun: the first to try to do so had been the nobles who, on the night of August 4, 1789, abolished their own special rights. The longing for a thoroughly decentralized nation, with little or no power on top, and power in the hands of "those who work where they work" is as old as French Socialism: overshadowed by Marxism, the dream of Fourier, Proudhon, Sorel had never died in the labor movement, despite the Paris Commune's debacle in 1871. Nor was there anything new in the hyperbolic attacks on industrial society. It had been a constant target, both for an intelligentsia that despises mercantile values and applied sciences, and for a working class half attracted by material comfort, but half repelled by the injustice of business authoritarianism or government deafness, in a fragile and not very dynamic economy easily derailed by high wages or high social benefits.

More striking was the inability of the rebels really to step outside the style of authority they were attacking. Centralization was out, but fragmentation was not: the reforms worked out by the students tended to make of every school or University a sovereign unit undisturbed by outside forces of nationwide concerns. Higher authority was defined, but there was no revolution in the attitude toward conflicts. On the one hand, there grew a mystical hope that self-management would abolish them magically; on the other hand, there was a significant shift from the reasonable and positive claim for "participation" to the romantic, negative and absurd assertion of a right to permanent challenge (*contestation*). Groups and men unprepared for responsibility prided themselves on behaving irresponsibly. As one young teacher put it, approvingly, "The revolutionaries are men without a program"; as one inscription on the walls of the Paris Law School said, "Let us push together but let us not think together." Instead of motion, movement became an end in itself, and motions became their own rewards. Instead of a program, the non-stop assemblies and committees all too often fell for the grand utopian sloganeering typical of French protest, and indicative of a deep nostalgia for the days when France was the world's pathfinder, of a desire to take the torch of revolution away from the Cubans or the Chinese: "Let us change man, let us build a new civilization, let us replace the fallacious tyranny of production and consumption with true socialism," etc. Or else, these meetings ended in discord, with each fragment insisting on the exclusive correctness of its own analysis. Or else inevitably, they were exploited by less naive if equally utopian small factions of ideologues, the *group-uscules* of Trotskyites, pro-Chinese or pro-Cuban Communists etc., whose skillful nihilism merged with, and manipulated, the spontaneous, inexperienced rebellion of unorganized students and young workers. The whole thing had a progressive thrust but little positive content, a good direction but no road map. Once again, it was easier to see what was being opposed than what was being proposed. Auguste Comte's old warning: one can destroy only what one can replace, was pathetically answered by another statement on a wall: "I have something to say, but I don't know what." Starting as a scream for innovation, the crisis became one more example of the ritual of French protest.

Moreover, not only did the tidal wave of face-to-face relations soak and sweep those who had generously thrown themselves into it, but the only basic value—the fear of a change in the overall equilibrium of groups, professions and statuses—remained unchallenged by the onslaught of *contestation*. Indeed, it inspired this onslaught. For although the occasion of the crisis in education was an extravagant, if familiar, concatenation of government passivity followed by belated brutality, the real cause was a new and drastic social imbalance. There had been a huge increase in the number of University students, in a system in which access to higher education is open to all the graduates of secondary schools. Young men and women who, fifteen or twenty years ago, would not have gone beyond high school, now invaded the University; most of them came from the more prosperous middle and lower middle classes. But there just weren't enough opportunities available to them, either in a University unprepared for such a flood, or in society—especially as so many students, guided by France's traditional scheme of values, were flocking to the humanities and social sciences, where the outlets were smallest. Tens of thousands of students who had gone through the grueling maze of French exams rightly feared that they would find no jobs appropriate to their knowledge, their labors and their degrees. Hence, paradoxically, a reinforced dislike for "industrial society" which condemned them to being misfits. Their revolt was largely based on their determination to preserve their status—on their own terms: without any *numerus clausus* restricting access to the University, without any forcible shift toward technical education, with adequate jobs for all, and with due legal and administrative protection for their rights and ranks!

As for the industrial crisis, it too had an occasion and a cause. The workers, quite spontaneously, seized the moment when Mr. Pompidou gave in to the students, in order to press for their own demands. But the real reason for those was also a new imbalance over the fears of Gaullist rule; planning and the concern for a more productive economy had resulted in strengthening business and its associations, whereas the workers' rate of material advance had slowed down and the unions remained divided and weak. Moreover, the mild recession of 1967 had led to considerable unemployment and to cuts in social services. Once again, a movement for change sprang from a desire for protection, from a fear of social retro-gradation.

None of this means that the drive toward more dignity—through a less authoritarian, bureaucratic and brutalizing school system, through a more equalitarian and humane industrial system—was not genuine. Nor does it mean that those aspirations must remain thwarted. But it means that the drive itself could not carry its masses to victory: the push carried the seeds of its fiasco. However, the crisis was of such a magnitude that the fiasco would have come much later and much more violently, if it had not been for two sets of political factors: France's Communist Party, and de Gaulle's regime.

As in the past, one of the reasons for the crisis had been the divorce between a troubled society and a political system that was both clumsy and complacent. There had been some educational reform, but it had failed to remodel the University, to free it from bureaucratic strangulation, to give it the freedom and resources to experiment, to integrate teaching and research, to create departments, to make teamwork prevail over formal lecture courses, to curb professorial absolutism. Yet it had been just extensive enough to multiply friction between fussy innovations and an old structure, and to antagonize students submitted to perpetual experimentation without fundamental change. Moreover, the last Minister of Education, intellectually lucid but politically too prudent, had stopped innovating—except for the highly unpopular decision, reluctantly taken by him under pressure from de Gaulle, to restrict in the future the hitherto free access of students to the University.

As for the economy, de Gaulle had to water down, and practically give up, his old plan for some kind of association between capital and labor in the factories, given the opposition of labor unions (afraid of being "integrated into the system"), of businessmen (fearful about a loss of authority), and of his own Cabinet: so that the only effective measures taken by the cabinet had been the unpopular ones that I have described here; moreover the political procedures for redress just weren't working. Academic reformers and workers were mainly on the Left— which almost assured that they would not be listened to carefully, given the Left's fierce hostility to the Gaullist regime. In the National Assembly elected in March 1967, the Gaullists had no majority, and the coalition of Gaullists with Giscard d'Estaing's group was too sluggish to be reform-minded. Also, in the Fifth Republic, it is anyhow not Parliament that provides the fuel for change. With docile Parliaments since 1962, and surface tranquility in the country, the civil service had become increasingly disdainful of criticism, and oppressively self-confident. When the explosion came, two of de Gaulle's most cherished beliefs were blasted away. He who had created a powerful Presidency capable of ruling France, even if the French Parliament should again be splintered, now explained that the timidity of the Executive in recent months was due to the absence of a strong majority in the National Assembly (a half-truth concerning the past, but one that could all too easily become a full truth in the post-de Gaulle future). And de Gaulle, who had so often celebrated the "stability, security, solidity" of his constitutional system, discovered that France's troubles had not all been due to weak parliamentary systems, and were not curable by a "strong state"—not only because a strong state breeds problems of its own, but also because constitutional reform does not by itself solve the deepest of France's difficulties, those that lie in the nature of French society.

And yet, the very divorce between society and politics which contributed to the drama squashed it. The rebels, in order to succeed, had to topple the regime. But they had no political experience. They were deeply suspicious of the non-Communist Left, whose inefficiency, fragmentation and social conformism had been amply demonstrated. As a relay toward power, they needed the support of the one true, coherent opposition force: the Communist Party. But the Party turned against them—and twice provided a regime that seemed on the verge of collapse with the help it desperately needed. In mid-May, the Communists prevented the liaison between students and young strikers and decided to generalize the strike so as to regain control of it. Shamelessly, they oriented it exclusively toward material issues (wage increases, social security) instead of "co-management," and toward negotiations with Pompidou. In the decisive days of May 28-29, when the agreement thus negotiated mainly between him and the Communists had been rejected by the workers, the rattled Party—still in order to regain control—finally gave a political content to the strike, but chose to call for a "popular government," or popular front. This meant that it had opted for legal, political action within the constitutional framework. But it also meant that it expected Gaullism to collapse, so that there would be a new government and new elections after de Gaulle's fall. This proved to be a fatal mistake. For although de Gaulle's first speech on May 24 had been a flop—which probably encouraged the Party to count him out—the Communists' call provided him with the opportunity to denounce as the real troublemakers, not the students and workers with whom so many sympathized, but the "totalitarian party" which so many disliked and which had imprudently, if legally, laid its claim to power.

After the crisis, and its defeat at the polls on June 23 and 30, the Communist Party's Secretary-General explained that the situation had not been truly revolutionary, that the Party behaved correctly in refusing to fall into a trap laid by adventurers and *agents provocateurs*, that there would otherwise have been bloodshed and far bigger losses of votes. Perhaps—yet this way of looking at things (with eyes fixed on free elections) contributed decisively to taking the revolution out of the situation. Why did the Party refuse to take any risk other than that of defusing the bomb built by the students and the young workers, for the greatest benefit of a shaken regime which the Communists had denounced for so long? We do not know whether Moscow had a large role in the French Party's bizarre strategy. (Is the unprecedented failure of the Party to support Moscow in the Czech crisis evidence of its autonomy, or of resentment against its servitude?) But there are at least three reasons that bring us back to the flow of French history.

Thus, given its Marxist origins, its Leninist model, and its Jacobin conception of seizing power where it is—at the center—the Party had always disdained and distrusted the anarchist or federalist strains in French Socialism: "worker power" in the factory would have weakened the hold of the Communist-led union, the CGT, on the workers. It would have transferred control not merely from the *patrons* to the workers, but also the CGT's representatives to either a majority of the workers (and in many industries, while the CGT was the biggest union, most of the workers were not members of any union) or to other more dynamic minorities. The Communist party had been molded by the French style of authority. The *groupuscules* of students who had started the revolution were hostile to the Party, precisely because its own rigid centralization, bureaucracy and orthodoxy appeared to them as the twins of the Gaullist regime's. Second, those very features of the Party, and the fact that it had been pretty much on the political defensive for over twenty years (despite recent changes of tactics), made it inordinately and clumsily hostile toward initiatives taken by groups that were either claiming to be to its left, or under no political control at all. Instead of joining such groups so as to dominate them, the Communists' defensive reflex was to oppose them.

Third, and most important, this action reflected the dilemmas and the fate of all anti-regime opposition movements—of the extreme left or of the far right—in France. They proclaim revolutionary goals, but on the other hand, in a country that remains wedded to stability with a sizable peasant population that often roars but never rises, and middle classes fiercely attached to their possessions and rights, the situation is almost never ripe for a violent seizure of power. On the other hand, if such movements try to reach their goals through parliamentary maneuvers and electoral politics, they get gradually and grudgingly absorbed into the system. This had happened to the Socialists even before 1914; it happened to de Gaulle's RPF in the early 1950's; it was happening to the Communist Party, which had decided some years ago that its best chances of success lay in a reassuring alliance with the non-Communist Federation headed by Mitterrand and led by Guy Mollet. When the crisis came, the Party's instinct was to denounce and try to drown a movement that conflicted with such tactics, and to reaffirm its course, in the hope that the voters would be grateful to the Communists both for having helped improve the workers' material lot, and for having saved France from civil war and illegality. The calculated misfired.

Gaullism, having been caught by surprise as much as, but of course far more graciously than, the political opposition (Communists included), first looked as if it would not recover from the shock. When de Gaulle returned from Romania on May 18, his life's work seemed in ruins. The man who had wanted to unify the French had apparently half of the French in revolt against him. The celebrator of the strong state presided over a paralyzed administration. The hero who had twice saved the French from disasters provoked by the impotence of their regime now faced a crisis aimed at him. His first reaction, on May 24, was ritualistic and totally inadequate. He announced a referendum—a personal vote of confidence in his own capacity to reform France, a plea to the citizens to delegate to *him* the power to organize *their* participation—just as the revolt, which was still spreading, not only seemed to demonstrate that such confidence was gone, but challenged the whole pattern of leaving public affairs to the sovereign wisdom of the highest authority. Had he stuck to his proposal, in a nation which says *no* more easily than *yes* in times of anger and in the absence of a savior, all the oppositions could have combined and ousted him.

At this point, two miracles happened. First, de Gaulle, despite his age, his well-known obstinacy, his obvious distress, and his exhaustion, realized immediately that he had blundered and, pragmatic as ever, looked for a new course. Second, the new stand of the Communists provided him exactly with what he needed. Instead of being the toppling target of discontent, pleading with his subjects for their trust, he could again become the nation's savior, leading the citizens in the fight against subversion and chaos.

Up to May 30, he had been on the defensive. Now he seized the offensive, as in 1940 and 1958, and made of the obliging Communists the focus of discontent of all those who, by now, felt annoyed or threatened by growing anarchy. It was a sensational coup.

By shelving the referendum and dissolving the Assembly he not only disarmed the Communists, who had themselves proposed the electoral arena as a battlefield, he also obliged the French to choose, not between yes and no, but between Gaullist candidates representing both order and reform, and various squabbling kinds of anti-Gaullists, who seemed to stand either for chaos, or for totalitarianism, or for nothing at all. . . .

## (B) THE PSYCHOLOGY OF A REBELLION—MAY-JUNE, 1968

### JACQUES ELLUL

Before proceeding to an analysis of France's student troubles of last spring (see the chronology thereof), certain characteristics of these disturbances should perhaps be mentioned.

First of all is the remarkable fact that in 45 days of disturbances, just about everywhere in France, there was only one death that unquestionably resulted from the fighting (a police superintendent in Lyons). In Paris, only about 2,000 people were hurt—half policemen, half demonstrators; remarkably few, considering the huge numbers of "combatants" involved.

A second trait was the unrepresentative character of the groups involved. The most important ones were the UNEF (*Union nationale d'étudiants français*, or National Union of French Students) and the SNE (sup.) (*Syndicat national de l'enseignement supérieur*, or National Union of Higher Education); in April, the first included perhaps seven or eight per cent of French students, and the second between 20 and 25 per cent of the professors. . . .

A third characteristic was the inflation of vocabulary. From the very start of the disturbances the newspapers enthusiastically encouraged the notion that the nation was experiencing a "revolution." Hundreds of articles opened with the words "From now on, nothing will be the same again, after what has just happened. . . ."

A fourth point: at the height of the fighting no more than a small minority of the students was ever involved. In Paris there were, at the very most, 40,000 demonstrators—out of 160,000 Paris-based students. Now, among the combatants there were young workers (not many, in my opinion) and a good many *blousons noirs*, hooligans, and so on. . . . Let us say that in the whole of France there were only 60,000 students actively mixed up in the events out of a total of 600,000.

SOURCE. Jacques Ellul, "The Psychology of a Rebellion, May–June 1968," from *Interplay*, December 1968, pp. 23–27, excerpted. Reprinted with permission of the publishers. Copyright 1968 by *Interplay* magazine.

Finally, there is a last characteristic to note: contrary to what the leaders maintained and what certain newspapers spread about, there was no getting-together of workers and students. When the students sought to support the workers by going into the factories, the workers more often than not threw them out. On only two or three occasions did the students manage to get their point across locally. . . .

All in all, as I see it, what happened was in no sense a revolution. There were some disturbances, no more serious than the ones France underwent in 1934, 1936, 1944, and 1947. Contrary to what was proclaimed, the government was never for a moment in danger, and there was no "vacancy of power." But the events should nevertheless not be taken lightly, for they were indications of a profound malaise.

Inevitably, then, the question arises, how did the local revolt of students (a few hundred in March) mushroom into a sort of national crisis, strike terror into a segment of the population, give evidence to the reality of a revolution and suspend life in France for two months, while not a single leader of the masses and not a single revolutionary party sought to seize power?

## The Role of Over-Centralization

All this can partially be explained by the passion the French brought to this "sensational" event, and by the considerable influence of the press and radio, which partly "fabricated" events, amplifying the whole thing, multiplying false reports of tragedy, putting fresh heart into the "revolutionaries" with bulletins transmitted direct to the very center of a crowd and relayed on to other crowds. There was a phenomenon of "resonance," or reverberation, in the multitude. The radio stations on France's periphery (Europe No. 1, Radio Luxembourg) played a significant role in provoking and directing the disturbances, putting their equipment at the service of leaders who, in the thick of combat, were able to address their troops all over Paris.

But there was a second element explaining the events: France's extreme degree of centralization. Everything depends on the state and on Paris. When something happens in Paris, all of France is involved. When something seems to attack the state, all of French society disperses: the social fabric seems to disintegrate because the state is threatened. Conversely, every serious problem can only be solved at the center, by the governmental apparatus. . . .

We should now briefly recall certain circumstances which favored the movement, playing the role of proximate causes without being the basic cause:

1. The very rapid growth of the number of students (from 150,000 in 1958 to 600,000 in 1968) and the very much slower growth of opportunities of employment for them (these probably doubled in the same period); hence, a shortage of openings for graduates, and an intense fear of unemployment.

2. The outmoded character of the university (teaching methods, hierarchy, etc.), its extreme centralization (the most insignificant matters must be referred to the Minister, and the deans have no power), its growth (especially in the number of professors), very much slower than that of the number of students (in one faculty the number of professors tripled while the number of students increased tenfold).

3. Finally, the development of "campuses" to which French students are hostile (in general, they consist of fine buildings, but are without a single club, a single movie theater; it adds up to the complete isolation of the students, without any means of distraction, in a "ghetto"). French students like to live in the city and mix with the people. . . .

Let us first enumerate a certain number of the variations. Successively, disturbances were launched in order to:

\* Obtain the right for men and girls to visit one another at night in their room in the Cité Universitaire;

\* Force the dismissal of certain professors from their teaching posts;

\* Force the reopening of the school at Nanterre, which had been shut down;

\* Stop classes at the Sorbonne;

\* Secure the acquittal of students called before the disciplinary council;

\* Protest against the police entering the Sorbonne;

\* Liberate the students who had been arrested;

\* Get the order for the expulsion of Cohn-Bendit annulled;

\* Prevent the examinations from being held;

\* Avenge the drowned student (asserting that the police had killed him).

One watchword succeeded another as soon as the previous one had served its purpose, with a view to stirring up the agitation again when it had slackened.

As for the programs, they were vague and contradictory. There were corporate demands for:

\* A pedagogical reform—of examinations, courses, seminars;

\* A curriculum better adapted to our society, to allow students to enter practical life, and find jobs, as soon as they leave the university;

\* Autonomy of the universities with respect to the government, and a system of joint management between professors and students to run each department.

This leads us to a second type of demand. Directly political, it consisted of launching a political revolution against the Gaullist regime (a significant slogan: "Ten years is enough").

## Challenging Society through the University

The third current is the most important: it was the total challenge of the university in order totally to challenge society. But here, too, there were great divergences. For some students, the university was in the service of capitalist society, supplying it with the engineers, sociologists and psychologists it needed: all the students were conditioned to become the cadres of capitalism, the "exploiters" of the rest. One rejects capitalism, therefore one should reject this university, which ought to become something else—"a place where knowledge is no longer the property of the exploiting elite but the means of transforming social relations, of abolishing the distinction between manual and intellectual work, of realizing the cultural revolution that is inseparable from the economic revolution." What is demanded, then, is a "critical" university, but in the sense of a "Marxist" university (Chinese type). The university would no longer have the function of providing intellectual and scientific education, but only political education.

For other students, what is called into question is not capitalist society but the consumer society—the "great society," the society of mass entertainment, in which "the medium is the message." These critics go much deeper than the others. The university must be critical, but in another sense—developing the student's critical spirit to enable him to rediscover imagination and an active participation, to criticize the society in which he finds himself and be truly independent of it.

We shall come back later to this position-taking. But in both cases the university is attacked in order to overthrow it, destroy it, and transform it into a weapon of war capable of attacking the entire social order. The first step, then, is the establishment of "student power" within the university, with the elimination of the authority of the professors, the obligation of self-criticism, etc. Raymond Aron can well say of this student power that "it is the power of those who are taught over those who earn their living teaching, and that consecrates the authority of those who do not know." Thus the purpose of the university is no longer to teach and learn, but to be the place politicized to the maximum in order to overthrow society.

It is easy to see how contradictory these objectives are. Often, it is the selfsame students who demand a more technical education so that they can be assured of a career in society and who refuse to take a place in that society; who demand the democratization of society (everyone having the right to take graduate courses) and the suppression of examinations, but at the time would like the diploma to guarantee them a job; who want to destroy the present state power and at the same time are asking it to allocate more money to the university, and so on. All this attests to the lack of unity among the groups and the incoherence of their motivations.

We should now listen to a certain number of arguments which have frequently been advanced to explain the events. I shall call three of them to mind.

First of all, the French university is accused of every fault— authoritarianism, dogmatism, mandarinism, etc. Now, all this is inexact: to be sure, the university is an old institution which should be brought up to date, but the mandarinate is a legend, as is the dogmatism. As for the sclerosis of the instruction, everything depended on the instructor; it is the human quality and not the institution that was in question. The university's greatest defect was centralization and submission to the government; but that alone could not have motivated these tremendous disturbances.

A second explanation advanced is the action of the *groupuscules* (mini-groups). It is true that innumerable little groups—Trotskyites, anarchists, Castroites, Guevarists, Maoists, *situationnistes*, and so on, all devoted to their respective cause and all able propagandists and tacticians—were remarkably adept at manipulating the mass of students and at coining slogans calculated to set them marching. But it is obvious that these few hundred agitators would not have been able to do anything if there had not been a predisposition to action among the mass of students, a situation of tension and unrest which these propagandists exploited. To postulate the activity of these mini-groups of the extreme left (the Communist party being out of it altogether) as the explanation of the disturbances is convenient for the government and practical for the police, but it is to consider a secondary cause a primary one, and to condemn oneself to not understanding the problem at all.

Finally, a third reason is sometimes invoked: the politico-economic situation created by the Gaullist regime was, it is said, disastrous, with unemployment, the suppression of democracy, a very slow rise in living standards and authoritarianism (sometimes compared to fascism!). In this view, it was discontent arising from the political system and the economic recession that caused the disturbances. Here, too, it is necessary to set this explanation aside. One might cite the sociologist E. Morin (favorable to the student movement and anti-Gaullist) who recognized, with honesty, that France had never enjoyed such a satisfactory state of things for a very long time. There had been the technical modernization, the social reforms, the economic recovery (while in 1958 the French economy had been in total recession), the establishment of a currency as solid as gold, a more rapid rise in the standards of living than ever before, the success of decolonization in Africa, the liquidation of the Algerian war and its after-effects, and the collapse of the opposition.

### "Marxization" after the Fact

The slight increase of unemployment could not really put the regime in danger and provoke the enormous student upheaval. No, it was neither the social and economic situation nor the political regime that was the cause of the disturbances. But once the student movement exploded it was used politically by enemies of the regime, without success by the political parties; but in any case it was very strongly "Marxized," to the extent of demanding the politicization of the university. Altogether, these diverse causes that are so often cited seem not to have been operative. But then, why those disturbances?

Unquestionably, E. Morin points out, there was "the conjunction of two contradictory factors: too little accommodation between the burgeoning production of university graduates and the scarcity of jobs, but also too much accommodation of the humane sciences to a society in which they are becoming auxiliaries of power." If, indeed, we leave aside everything in the general realm of the difficulties of youth—its lack of judgment, its quest for "something else"—in which the student movement shares (to the point that for some people it is simply an aspect of this crisis of youth and of the struggle between the generations), there are plenty of characteristics peculiar to this explosion.

Our first remark has to do with the fact that not all the students, by any means, participated, and that the cleavage did not occur between "those who understood, who became involved," and those who were passive, the "sheep," but rather between categories of students. These categories were of two kinds, the first being between students from relatively well-off backgrounds and poor students. Those who demonstrated violently were of the former category. I was able to determine this fact personally, and it was confirmed by all my impartial colleagues: scholarship students, sons of workers, young Africans, students earning their living—hardly any of these took part in the disturbances. The disturbances were conducted by the sons of bankers, doctors, lawyers, university professors and high officials (even of government ministers).

## The "Weekdays Only" Revolution

In Paris, "those of the 16th arrondissement" participated in great numbers, which explains some curious facts: some details (there was never any trouble during the weekends, because the students were taking it easy in the country or at the seaside) and also, perhaps, certain basic decisions (the workers' rejection of an alliance with the students). The revolution was, for them, a luxury, an escape from boredom and an affirmation of their being "grownups."

But there was another cleavage, too: only a tiny minority of the students of science and medicine demonstrated, as was the case among students of geography and languages. The demonstrators among the students of law, economics and political science were only slightly more numerous. The students who were the *provocateurs*, the driving force behind the disturbances, were those in philosophy, sociology and psychology. In these disciplines, almost all the students were involved.

Now, I believe—and this may seem like a rather dubious interpretation—that this fact has no connection with these students' greater degree of political consciousness or deeper understanding of current problems, but with their unconscious sense of being useless in our society. Scientists and doctors are "in phase" with our society, but philosophers (in France, at least), sociologists and psychologists are the "fifth wheel of the cart"; they are not really of any use, their knowledge is a false science, they have no hold over society and they feel useless. It is therefore not exactly the problem of the shortage of outlets, positions, jobs, but the feeling of uselessness, of the "vanity" of their work, even when they earn a living, thanks to sociology. They are not made for the technical society.

And this brings us to what I believe to be the principal cause: the discordance between the students' global judgment of our society and the instruction they receive. On the first point they share the unease of youth, the hippy orientation. On the one hand, it is the revolt against a society that is rationalized, technicized, efficient, productivist, dedicated to the production and consumption of material goods and having neither values nor meaning. It is a society which does not provide reasons for living, but which is, on the other hand, very demanding, and which seems "dehumanizing" or "alienating." Young people, whether they understand it or not, whether they know it clearly or not, are ill at ease in this society, not spontaneously adjusted to it, *afraid of entering it*.

Now, the students of philosophy, sociology and psychology are the ones who know this aspect of society best and who most often pass judgment on it. But at the same time the instruction provided in the university schools has no other purpose than to prepare the student to enter this society, to become a participant in and an active element of it. There is thus a cruel opposition between their feelings about this society and the studies they pursue—the more so as the philosopher clearly sees that he will change nothing by his studies, that, on the contrary, he is called upon to justify that society intellectually, while the sociologist is preparing to make the wheels of that society turn more smoothly and the psychologists to help men adjust to that society, which they themselves reject. They consequently accuse the university of being in the service of a society of which they disapprove.

This attitude is not shared to the same degree by chemists and geologists, because they are preparing for precise material functions which do not seem to them to reinforce that society particularly. Besides, their studies do not make them aware of what that society really is.

The student revolt is, then, a profound dispute provoked by a serious malaise: the students do not want to become the trained personnel, the leaders, the bearers of authority and responsibility of this society that they fear and of which they disapprove. When they speak of capitalist society, or of imperialism, they are mistaken in their analysis and in their name-calling. But they come close to exactness when they attack the consumer society and the hierarchical, state-dominated society, whether capitalist or socialist. We are in the presence of the reaction of the human being against a universe that seems to him inhuman.

Finally, the last fundamental aspect of the problem seems to me to be the contradiction between the students' intellectual development and their spiritual emptiness. They share this with all young people. The relativization of morals, the disappearance of traditional values, the absence of Christian faith, the difficulty of conducting genuine human relations with adults (parents), the acceleration of all changes, the invasion of minds by a negative irrationality, the eroticization of all relationships—all young people have suffered the consequences of these developments. But the effect is more serious with the students. What is only felt and/or experienced on the unconscious emotional level by all young people is lived on the conscious, relatively clear level by the students.

The latter are completely lucid as to the lack of morals, as to the impossibility of having clear references and a meaning to life in our society. They have intellectually accepted all the attacks on the Christian faith. They are aware that they are living in a secularized world. But in the face of this their education is more and more heavily intellectual. They attain an ever higher level of knowledge, of technical competence, of specialization. They are, then, in possession of a more developed intellectual instrument, while their existential "being" is more fragile. They are committed to a more rational, more exact and more precise intellectual path, in the grip of an apparent rationality of the world, society and organization, just when, to them, their life seems absurd, the world empty and society quite without purpose. In other words, they plunge into a "more irrational way of life" just when they are educated to a "more rational thought."

## The Keys: Anguish and Insecurity

I believe that this contradiction, a function of the students' situation, is the key to the revolt of the students, which expresses their anguish and insecurity. In this case, in order to respond to it, they hope to free themselves from the iron framework of rationality, and from alienation, by way of "action for action's sake" (one of the slogans of the disturbances was, "it is through action that we will discover what we must do"), or by way of eroticism. They do not realize that these orientations simply constitute an acceptance of the very things that plunged them into the catastrophe. It is obvious that the Eros of Marcuse is no answer to the situation. On the contrary! But it is this that gave the disturbances of May not so much a revolutionary character as a festive one (in the sociologists' sense), of a village fair, of a carnival, with the compensatory delirium that that implies and the simplicity of relationships it creates, all taboos being abruptly transgressed. And it is certainly this which explains, moreover, the contradictory and incoherent character of the demands, as we have shown they were. Certain demands concern the intellectual preparation and others the spiritual emptiness.

It is, finally, this situation that explains the lack of result of these disturbances. For there was no revolution, neither political, nor economic, nor social. Contrary to what certain people have written, nothing has changed. The problem posed is at the very heart of the relationship between man and modern society; it cannot be solved by mob activity and by demands. The students will certainly be able to continue to keep the university from functioning and the students in an uproar; they will accomplish nothing by this, and will not reach the root of the evil they sense without having fully analyzed.

## CHRONOLOGY

November 1967. Revolt of students at the University of Nanterre for the right of men and girls to visit each other freely at night in their quarters.

December 1967. Strike of 10,000 students for improved working conditions.

February 1968. Strike of Nanterre students against the Vietnam war.

February. Demonstration of solidarity with students threatened with expulsion; boycotting of classes by a small minority; abrogation of "home rule" in the students' quarters.

March. Nanterre students boycott examinations; violent demonstrations; arrest of "anti-imperialist" students; protest meeting and invasion of professors' premises; foundation of the "March 22 Movement."

April. Occupation by about 1,000 students of some Nanterre buildings; convocation of student extremists before the university's disciplinary council; a great many professors find it impossible to conduct classes.

May 2:.Closing of the *Faculté des lettres* (Liberal Arts School) of Nanterre.

May 3. Student meeting at the Sorbonne to protest against this last measure; the Sorbonne is occupied by the "March 22 Movement," driven out of Nanterre; the dean of the Sorbonne summons the police, who evacuate the school; mass meeting in the Latin Quarter.

May 6. Arrest and conviction of students; first big demonstration (10,000 participants).

May 7–9. Appeal of the students to the workers; the Communist party condemns the student movement (on the ground that it is "leftist"); Nanterre is reopened, but the Sorbonne remains closed.

May 10. Breakdown of negotiations between the Minister of Education and the students; a rising in the Latin Quarter to liberate the arrested students; barricades and fighting in the streets.

May 11. The unions announce a 24-hour general strike; the prime minister returns from a trip and announces concessions.

May 13. General strike; parade of 300,000 people (one million, according to the organizers); occupation of the Sorbonne.

May 15. First of the occupations of factories; occupation of the National Theatre of the Odéon.

May 18. The President of the Republic returns from Romania; strikes of the SNCF (national railway), PTT (Post Office, including telephone and telegraph systems), etc.

May 20. The parliamentary Left calls for the resignation of the government and for general elections; the CGT (*Confédération générale de travail,*

France's largest bloc of trade unions, Communist-dominated) states that it does not want an insurrection; Cohn-Bendit (the leader of the March 22 Movement) is banned from French territory.

MAY 22. Demonstrations for Cohn-Bendit's return; the CGT rejects the bid for solidarity of the UNEF (*Union nationale d'étudiants français,* the principal students' union).

MAY 23. First student-worker demonstrations.

MAY 24. Speech by the President of the Republic announcing a referendum; demonstrations, meetings, barricadings, street fights continue.

MAY 26. Agreement (known as the Agreement of Grenelle) between the union men and the government (salary hikes, etc.)

MAY 27. Second week of strikes: ten million strikers: the Agreement of Grenelle is rejected by the rank-and-file union men; important meeting between the UNEF and the CFDT.

MAY 28. M. (François) Mitterrand a candidate for the presidency of the Republic; Cohn-Bendit returns clandestinely; failure of a meeting of "revolutionary" leaders convened to regroup the multiple movements.

MAY 29. The president goes to Germany to assure himself of the loyalty of the French soldiers stationed there.

MAY 30. The president's speech: dissolution of the National Assembly, announcement of elections; demonstration in support of the president (on the Champs Elysées; between 500,000 and one million people).

MAY 31. The unions begin to accept the Agreement of Grenelle; a fire in the Sorbonne; Gaullist demonstrations in the provinces.

JUNE 1. Beginnings of the resumption of work.

JUNE 3. Resumption of work widespread.

JUNE 7. The students attempt to provoke the workers to fight (at a Renault plant).

JUNE 10. A student in a UNEF demonstration accidentally drowns; the students call it a police murder; enormous demonstrations in the Latin Quarter—battles, barricades.

JUNE 11. The Communist party again condemns the revolutionary student groups; another night of rioting.

JUNE 13. The Communist party and the CGT regain control of the workers; the government bans the revolutionary students' associations.

JUNE 15. A general resumption of work; one by one, the university buildings are abandoned by the students who had occupied them.

JUNE 17–20. The hardcore Sorbonne groups (known as *les Katangais,* the Katangans) of the Odéon and the *Faculté Censier* of Paris leave these buildings, under duress or of their own volition.

JUNE 20–30. Attempts to recommence the disturbances, which fail; the population hostile to the students; the election gives the Gaullist party a majority.

## (C) AN IMPOSSIBLE REVOLUTION
(Translated by George Armstrong Kelly)

MAURICE DUVERGER

Before May 1968 revolution was thought impossible in very industrialized countries. It was said that the general elevation of the standard of living had given the workers bourgeois traits and had mitigated the violence of class struggle. It was thought that if you brutally upset a very complicated and fragile system of production and exchange, it would remain disorganized for a long time and incur a deep economic recession. It was further thought that the masses of people had become more or less aware of this and would thus refuse to sacrifice their present welfare, even a mediocre one, to the fleeting glimpse of future improvement won at the price of a long period of troubles and restrictions.

These arguments were not only the property of the West. People's China's second-in-command, Marshal Lin Piao, implicitly agreed. He thought that from now on world revolution would be waged by underdeveloped countries, and that these rural areas of the world would progressively encroach on the industrial nations, just as Chinese communism, first widespread in the countryside, had later conquered the cities. Soviet and East European revisionism were a kind of illustration of the revolutionary incapacity of overdeveloped societies. The prestige of Mao, Castro, and "Che" Guevara in extreme leftist circles of the West resulted from this general analysis.

Today some see things in a different light. Based on the French experience of May 1968, they are building a new theory of the revolutionary conquest of power in industrial societies. According to this theory, the initial impulse is provided by the youth, less integrated in the existing order than their elders, even those of the working class. In their midst the students play the role of an avant-garde. Their

SOURCE. Maurice Duverger, "An Impossible Revolution," from *Le Monde*, July 12, 1968. Reprinted with permission of the publishers. Copyright 1968 by *Le Monde-Opera Mundi*. All rights reserved. Translated by George Armstrong Kelly.

numerical increase and their geographical concentration at certain points, analogous to the evolution of the proletariat in the nineteenth century, gives them a power of intervention whose scope was demonstrated by the barricades in Paris and the fighting at Flins. Moreover, their intellectual training gives them a heightened political consciousness.

In a second phase, the detonating charge of the student revolt will trigger the mass of workers. By means of a general strike, they will then paralyze the whole activity of the bourgeois state and reduce it to powerlessness. At the same time they will begin to introduce a socialist state in its place, themselves providing for the direction of businesses and services after they have been gotten started again: this amounts to the third phase. Thus the previous power structure will become progressively unreal and accidental, while a new power structure is replacing it. Finally, the former will collapse and the latter will have total charge of society.

The events of May are held to correspond to the first two phases of the process. The third phase failed only because the great workers' organizations (CGT and Communist Party) put a brake on the development instead of speeding it up. If they had not diverted the workers' strike toward salary raises and work reductions, toward "quantitative demands," if instead they had moved in a socialist perspective toward the seizure of the factories and administrative organs, Gaullist power would have fallen, as it came close to doing on May 29.

This new revolutionary theory neglects first of all the repressive capacity of the modern state. So long as the students were destroying the power of the professors, capitalism reacted sluggishly because it was not directly threatened. But if the power of the business community had really been touched, there might have been quite a different reaction.

The new revolutionary theory especially misconstrues the fact that the working masses have really no taste for revolution. The general strike cannot be the absolute weapon, as Georges Sorel believed, capable of blocking police and military repression, unless the strikers are really determined to go all the way and overturn the social order. And most of them didn't dream of that in May 1968.

The May crisis showed only that certain small groups within industrial societies—notably the students—were putting up a stronger resistance than people thought against social integration and that this resistance could provoke serious disorders. Already the German example had shown that universities could become centers of violent agitation. One had seen in the United States that such agitation could produce a national awareness of certain basic problems, notably Vietnam. We have just learned in France that it can also trigger the explosion of accumulated grievances.

But these grievances must not be confused with a will to revolution. The lack of that will among the vast majority of workers last May, with the exception of the younger ones, was not the result of CGT and Communist reformism. On the contrary, their reformism was the reflection of that lack of will, which itself is to be explained by the nature of industrial societies. The masses of people—including the proletariat—are sufficiently integrated to the established order so that they harbor no wish to shatter it with violence. That could one day change; but in the foreseeable future revolution in the overdeveloped countries still looks improbable.

.    .    .    .    .

Yet if the masses of citizens in industrial nations are not revolutionary and do not seem about to become so, the opposite is true of certain minority groups that are sometimes situated in strategic positions: this is the case of the students. Many of them think more about courses and examinations than about politics, and want to come to terms with society rather than overthrowing it. But they are pulled along by their more dynamic peers. The examples of the United States and Germany show that the universities can thus acquire great powers of confrontation (*contestation*) and agitation, even in countries with conformist traditions. In France, where tradition is nonconformist and the revolution is a part of the national mythology, those powers can be still greater.

Thus a dangerous situation may develop. The student movements cannot upset the existing order on their own head of steam. But they can threaten it enough—or at least give that impression—to maintain and increase a sense of insecurity throughout society which might push it toward the acceptance of authoritarian regimes once it saw no other way of escaping from anarchy. Thus Dutschke assists the rise of the NPD in West Germany. And in France Cohn-Bendit has contributed to the defeat of the Left at the polls.

Many responsible students are alert to the danger. They calculate the real relations of social forces, the integration of the masses (including the working class) in the existing order, the ineffectiveness and political risk of disturbances in the streets and the classrooms. If the university buildings were so easily cleared out by the police, this is because most of their former occupants sensed the uselessness and even the counter-productiveness of a prolonged holdout.

The new revolutionary theories are supported, if one may say so, by a few traditional extremists who have been swimming for years in the currents of the extreme Left, rather than by the leaders of the student movements. The latter try today to define a long-term strategy for transforming society: their goals remain revolutionary, but their means are better adapted to the conditions of overdeveloped countries.

The transformation of university education holds a central place here, because it shapes the technicians, scientists, administrators, and top managers who play an essential role in the industrial nations, where they constitute one of the primary productive forces. From this angle, the "Critical University" might furnish this leadership class— outside of its technical training—with the means of judging and creatively opposing the society it inspires, and thus the means of changing it instead of conforming to it more or less passively, as is the case today. In fact, this function was already partly fulfilled by French higher education. That education has never been the instrument of perfect social integration that is being talked about today. But through it Keynesianism, planning, and a certain kind of socialism have penetrated administration and business.

It can't be ruled out that university training might bring about a more radical questioning of the bases and objectives of the existing order. The majority of professors are conservative only in the professional spheres, and would not be too reluctant to take this step. And if we assume that capitalist society would be fiercely opposed from motives of self-defense, we are forgetting that the main object of business leaders is to hire technically competent managers, with little concern for theories and with much scepticism about the revolutionary virtue of education. Naturally, they would prefer conformist universities. But they will tolerate critical universities if these are not too obviously provocative and continue to dispatch competent engineers and administrators.

As for the effectiveness of a critical training, all will finally depend on the entire social evolution. Even if the choice recruits provided by the university are determined proponents of radical change, they will not be able to accomplish much without mass acceptance. Here lies the importance of the political education of the workers. The students are aware of this, without yet succeeding in defining realistic solutions of the problem. Opening the university buildings to the people recalls the utopias of the beginning of the century. And should the students themselves become factory workers—like Simone Weil and the worker-priests—it would have only a morally admirable, testimonial value. It seems that only a sustained contact between the university students and the large trade union organizations could furnish the answer. But we are far from it now.

Despite this evolution, there is always a risk that the student movements will slide once again toward revolutionary doctrine, with all its inevitable results. A handful of their leaders support a more radical conception of the "Critical University": the schools would become bastions of permanent agitation and places of sanctuary where the fuse would be kept to set off the mass powder keg in favorable circumstances. Such circumstances might shortly return, with economic troubles and the perspective of inflation and unemployment. A new explosion like that of May 1968 is possible, and many are expecting it.

But it would be an error to think that it would produce the advent of Socialism. It is generally ignored that General de Gaulle's victory of 1968 means pretty much the same thing as his victory of 1958. In both cases he was borne to power by a rightist tidal wave—churned up by the opposition to the Algerian rebellion ten years ago, and by the opposition to the student revolt last month. Similarly, in both cases he prevented this tidal wave from completely submerging the nation and destroying democracy. If tomorrow he should be overthrown by new barricades, new occupations of the universities and factories, and new street demonstrations, he would very likely not be replaced by the Left. It is much more likely that a Pattakos-style regime would be the successor of the Gaullist one. And then the revolutionary students would have been nothing but the pathbreakers of fascism.